Kathy Cooks...Naturally

Kathy Cooks...Naturally

by
Kathy Hoshijo

Published in Honolulu by

THE SELF-SUFFICIENCY ASSOCIATION

Distributed by The Self-Sufficiency Association,
2525 South King Street, Honolulu, Hawaii, 96826
P.O Box 1122, Glendale, California 91209

Paperback: ISBN 0-936602-24-4
Hardbound: ISBN 0-936602-23-6

For information contact The Self-Sufficiency Association,
2525 South King Street, Honolulu, Hawaii, 96826
or:
P.O. Box 1122, Glendale, California 91209

Jacket/Cover Design: Sammy Capulong
Designer: Kya Pond
Compositor: Cynthia Morris
Cover, Text Printer and Binder: George Banta Co.

Acknowledgment

This book is the result of at least five years' work. It has been a real labor of love on the part of many people who probably aren't even expecting a thank-you! To be able to put this book together for you has been reward enough! Still, as chairperson of the Self-Sufficiency Association and author of this book, which is one of the Self-Sufficiency Association's projects, I would like to thank all those who actually made this book possible.

There are special thanks to: Kia Pond, who did all the artwork and layout; Alan Compton, the photographer, who put in so much time and energy to add all the photos that give this book a special touch (except pp. 119, 408 and 409 provided by Sammie Capulong and pp. 52, 90, 96, 186, 194, 257, 336, 348, 472, 481, 484 and 485 by Tom McCarthy); and to Cynthia Morris, who typeset and patiently retypeset all the changes as this book came to be.

Also special thanks to the many tasters who helped as we formulated the recipes in this book, and the proofreaders who, I hope, have caught every mistake.

Preface

Dear Friends,

I'm hoping you'll read this, even though I know I rarely read the preface and introductions of the cookbooks I have at home. After all, a cookbook is simply a book of practical, everyday use. It would be like sitting around reading the yellow pages.

But this cookbook is a little different, and you will find it to be a valuable resource if you understand why.

Kathy Cooks — Naturally was written to provide not only recipes, but also information that I'm hoping will inspire and enable you to choose a healthy, economical and ecologically sound diet that can increase self-sufficiency in food needs for you as an individual, as well as in communities and entire countries.

You will likely notice that the introductions to many chapters sound as though they have been written for the people of Hawaii. Actually, our book began as a project of the **Hawaii Self-Sufficiency Association** in an effort to encourage people in the use of locally grown produce (both commercial and individual) and to prepare these foods in a healthful way. Preventive medicine practiced through proper care of the body is also an important aspect of self-sufficiency.

While this cookbook and other projects and research were being developed, we came to realize that self-sufficiency was an important issue not only for the state of Hawaii, but also for all communities both nationally and internationally.

For this reason, we dropped the "Hawaii" from the organization's title, changing it to the **Self-Sufficiency Association**, and have expanded the contents of this book to encompass the plant foods of climates elsewhere. Now it can be used everywhere by anyone.

Even if you do not embrace the concept of self-sufficiency and have no objection to buying imported produce, etc., you will find this book offers nutritiously and deliciously healthful recipes to use . . . and maybe it will plant a few thoughts about self-sufficiency along the way.

Aloha,

Kathy Hoshijo

Introduction

Like everything else in life, eating is a matter of consciously making wise choices. It is something everyone must do to keep the body healthy and alive — which is the practical purpose for eating — and it helps if the food eaten for that purpose is delicious as well!

Unfortunately for many, the purpose of eating has become centered around satisfying the tastes the tongue has become addicted to. Allowing the tongue's addiction for the taste of flesh and blood, refined sugar and grains, salt, etc., to dictate what nourishment the body gets, has resulted in what a U.S. Senate report called ". . . a wave of malnutrition" sweeping the country. This is a fact most Americans are aware of. In 1978, a Harris survey showed only 14% of those polled thought Americans ate a proper diet.

Awareness of this problem can motivate us to live more consciously and thus turn a negative into a positive. Rather than live as consumer zombies ultimately controlled by advertising campaigns (being dragged here and there as slaves to our tongues and other senses), we should take our lives into our own hands, beginning at home with the basics.

A natural starting point is to choose not to continue as blind food faddists eating newly developed non-foods that are chemically flavored and preserved, or that contain empty-calorie, refined flour and sugar products, or that are laden with saturated fat and cholesterol. Most of these foods have become popular in a relatively short period of time. Instead, choose the kinds of healthful, wholesome foods our ancestors thrived on (like whole grains, legumes, nuts and seeds, dairy products and fresh produce), which a major portion of the planet still thrives on. Such apparently small, insignificant choices as these benefit not only each individual, but all of society as well.

Though the concern for making new food choices may begin as a limiting, self-centered interest for personal health and well-being, it easily leads to an expanding consciousness and regard for others and the world around us when we understand that thoughtfully choosing the foods we eat actually renders decisions filled with moral and political ramifications about our use of the earth's precious resources.

For example, we know that the excessive meat consumption in the United States has been scientifically linked to the increase in heart disease and cancer of the colon. In addition to that, it has been scientifically and medically established that protein obtained from plant foods is not inferior to the protein obtained from flesh foods, but rather it is a superior source of protein because it is cholesterol and saturated fat free. While recognizing the fact that consumption of meat cannot be justified on a nutritional basis, we must not neglect the fact that in America, 14 to 20 pounds of nutritious legumes and whole grains are fed to livestock to obtain one pound of meat in return. This process of turning plant protein (in whole grains and legumes) to animal protein results in a 90% protein loss. The 179 million tons[1] of grain reported to have been consumed by livestock in 1971 could have provided the protein needs of 419 million people for an entire year. With this information available, the consumption of meat is proven to be unhealthy, unnecessary, and in a world where millions suffer from starvation or malnutrition every year, totally unjustifiable.

Unfortunately, the revaluation of the purpose of food and its fair distribution probably won't come from the people who are presently making an "unhealthy" profit on taste addictions. They justify their non-food hawking as simply supplying a demand, even though this demand was created by their multimillion-dollar advertising campaigns.

This sort of reasoning places the responsibility squarely on the people who have the most to gain from being supplied more healthful products — that is you and me! The fact is, in the marketplace of supply and

---

[1] U.S. Department of Agriculture, "Feed Statistics" (1971 Supplement, Statistical Bulletin #410).

demand, as long as a product is bought, that guarantees it will continue to be manufactured and marketed. But this also means that we have a choice — to say yes or no. We can say no by refraining from buying non-nutritious, non-quality "plastic" fad foods, and say yes by buying wholesome, natural foods. In a sense, every time you buy or don't buy a product, you are registering a vote in the marketplace of supply and demand.

It may seem to you that this may have about as much effect on the world's hunger situation as your voting for the president has on the world situation; but the fact is, individuals making such apparently insignificant choices do make a difference when there are enough of them. Consider the health food aisles that have appeared in supermarkets all over the country within the last few years.

It would be totally naive and misleading for me to say or even imply that your cutting out the meat and junk food consumption from your diet will solve the world's hunger problem and create a utopia on earth, because it won't. The philosophy, politics and economics that affect world food distribution are far more complicated than that.[2]

Making the change in the way we live our personal lives can be the beginning of a real commitment to work on another level to help solve the world hunger problem, beyond just spouting slogans or intellectually nodding our approval while living as hypo-crites whose real lives contradict the ideals being held forth. History speaks for itself in showing the difference a few committed individuals can make.

Besides making wise choices about the basic activity of eating, we can also make choices in so many other little ways in our daily lives: growing more of our own food, hanging clothes on the line instead of using the dryer, walking places when driving isn't necessary, recycling what we can, refraining from buying things we don't need, etc. Such choices will not only make our lives happier and healthier, but will insure the health and well-being of future generations as well.

This book was compiled in the hope that it will give the information, the reasons and the how-to's that will inspire and enable individuals to make an economical, healthful and ecologically sound diet part of their life.

On a practical level, to make it easy to use the recipes in this book, we have put a little symbol next to the title of each recipe.

A ☐ by the recipe means no cooking is required and it can be made in a matter of minutes. They are cholesterol and saturated fat free.

A ○ by the recipe means that cooking is required and it will take a while to prepare. These are good day-to-day meals that are cholesterol and/or saturated fat free.

A ☆ by the recipe indicates that this recipe contains cholesterol and/or saturated fat and shouldn't be used every day. Many of the ☆ recipes are gourmet dishes which can be served on special occasions.

[2] See "Food First" by Lappe and Collins, and "Food for People — Not for Profit" by Lerzat Jacobson.

CONTENTS

Contents

NUTRITION

Pure and Simple

Nutrition Pure and Simple

If you're like me—not a dietician or a nutritionist—the textbooks and jargon associated with the business of feeding our bodies a nutritious diet may alienate or even confuse you. It certainly did that to me when I first started trying to make sense of it all! And what a shame, because to be able to understand how to maintain a healthy body and a healthy mind is so basic and important to each one of us!

In this technological age, we probably use more logic and care in maintaining our cars than we do in caring for our bodies. We all know that unless we care for our cars and fuel them properly, that they'll break down on us. The mechanics of a car is simpler than the mechanics of our bodies, but the same principle applies.

Our bodies are like cars in the sense that they are vehicles we are passengers in for a while, and they require fuel or energy and proper care to keep them going. Eating is meant to provide proper fuel and energy for our bodies.

But feeding our bodies a nutritious diet has become an "energy problem" similar to and intertwined with the energy problem that modern man has become so preoccupied with lately. Our bodies are powered by solar energy, which we consume directly in the form of foods which have collected and stored energy from the sun, or indirectly by eating the bodies or by-products of living beings who ate foods which had stored solar energy. And, our highly industrialized society has come to be powered by the same solar energy stored in the bodies of past generations of plants and animals, which has been transformed into fossil fuels through time. Our dependence on fossil fuels as an energy source, how we get energy into our bodies, what it does there and what we do with it, are all inseparably linked together. Thus, it is hard to just talk about nutrition without taking a good, hard look at our personal lifestyles and the whole scheme of things.

The system which has developed over the years to raise and move food from farms and/or laboratories to our homes has become an insanely energy-intensive endeavor that manages to separate the links between agriculture, food, and nutrition. The total chain of events — from fertilizing, spraying, harvesting, transporting, processing and storing — adds up to an average of ten calories (units for measuring energy) of fossil fuels being used for every one calorie of energy in the form of food consumed in the United States (see **Progress as if Survival Mattered**, Friends of the Earth, 1977, pp. 111 - 112).

How has this inefficient use of energy come to be? First of all, agriculture has become a very centralized "industry," with 3% of the population in the United States growing the food for the rest of the population. This, of course, means large amounts of energy are spent just to transport harvested foodstuffs to different parts of the country, while nutrients are lost along the way. And large-scale intensive agribusiness has totally changed the face of farming from a more appropriate-technology business in touch with the laws of nature, to an industry dependent on fossil fuels that, as with other such large industries, plays its part in ravishing nature.

Large machines are replacing farm workers; thus, energy from fossil fuels is being used in the place of energy which people get from foods. Large-scale agribusiness has also led to an increase in the use of petrochemicals as fertilizers and sprays, which slowly deplete and pollute the soil and add harmful and unwanted pesticides to foods.

But the increase in fossil fuel consumption doesn't stop on the sprawling agribusiness "farms." Next come the processes which transform food into a technicolored product on the supermarket shelf. It's a fair generality to say that the more a food is processed, the more fossil fuels will have been burned to provide a food with less nutrients.

All this leads to the fact that it would be more energy-efficient to consume unrefined foods and foods that are locally grown — especially those grown in backyard or apartment gardens — to provide our bodies with energy. Of course, energy obtained from eating must be burned off, as an excess of energy consumed and stored in the body causes obesity and disease. In this highly industrialized society, which utilizes energy from fossil fuels to do the work, we have created "leisure activities" (physical work which doesn't produce anything) such as jogging, exercise spas and gymnasiums, etc., to burn unused energy. Since we must use the energy we consume, one alternative source we should seriously consider and not look down upon is people power, aided by appropriate and people-oriented technology.

Many of today's problems stem from underutilization and misdirection of people's energy and an overdependence on stored energy from past generations of living entities. Unemployment, pollution, inflation (overconsumption and underproduction), and bad health are a few obvious results of a system which is not in harmony with the arrangements of God and nature.

In short, the story of food is a story of energy, whether we're looking at the process by which solar energy provides nutrients for the body, or how that energy, in the form of fossil fuels, is used to bring energy in the form of food to our tables.

Here we'll concern ourselves with the nutritional aspect, bearing in mind that our patterns of consumption will not only affect our health, but also have much deeper and far-reaching ramifications.

Through the process of photosynthesis, plants convert the energy of the sun, carbon dioxide from the air, and minerals and water from the earth into atomic bonds that are solid enough for teeth to sink into. We can then consume these forms of energy directly, by eating plant foods, or indirectly, by eating animals who have eaten these plant foods. The process by which food gets broken down in the body, and by which the energy is released from the atomic bonds, is called digestion. Eating the right combinations and amounts of foods to provide energy and make it possible for that energy to be released in the body is what nutrition is all about. I have tried to include nutritional information here in a form which is easily understandable.

"The technology of production by the masses, making use of the best of modern knowledge and experience is conducive to decentralization and compatible with the laws of ecology, gentle in its use of scarce resources and designed to serve the human person instead of making him the servant of machines."
— E. F. Schumacher

The information is gathered from different "scientific" sources and studies. I had to put the word "scientific" between quotes because science means knowledge, and in the relatively new field of nutrition (as well as other fields) the so-called experts don't absolutely know.

In the field of nutrition there are still new vitamins being "discovered," average daily requirements changed, dietary rules changed, etc., so that none of the nutritional information that follows is the absolute last word. There are to this day some 50-plus labels or names that scientists have given to different nutritional elements they have become aware of, but there are probably many that haven't been identified. Yet, some elements have only been labeled or named in recent years and the exact role they play or amount needed for good, sound nutrition is not certain.

I am admittedly not neurotic about measuring milligrams of this and that in feeding my family, nor do we take any kind of pill supplements. There is such a perfect balance in nature, that using a great variety of fruits and vegetables — as fresh as they can be gotten — and unrefined, unprocessed whole grains, legumes, nuts and seeds, will easily and naturally provide all the necessary nutrients. (Refined and enriched foods never include all the known nutrients that were taken out. And, there is the very high probability that nutritional elements which haven't been identified yet are also removed. Of course, these can't be replaced if we don't know about them.)

I just try to feed my family a delicious variety of fresh produce and whole foods, which isn't difficult, as can be seen by the diversity of recipes found in this book! I find tables like those in the different chapters helpful in choosing nutritional variety for the day. Hopefully the following information will help make those tables more meaningful to you.

"MACRO" and "MICRO" NUTRIENTS

Good nutrition calls for a balanced diet, which means the right proportions of the right things. In discussing what the right proportions are, or the recommended daily allowance of the different nutrients, we hear the terms "grams," "milligrams," "International Units," etc. The three nutrients that are required in larger quantities by the body and which make up the bulk of our nutritional intake, as well as providing the body with burnable energy, are: carbohydrate, protein, and fat. The recommended daily allowances of carbohydrate, protein, and fat are measured in grams (1 gram = .035 of an ounce), whereas the recommended daily allowance of minerals and vitamins are measured in milligrams (1 milligram = 1 thousandth of 1 gram, which is pretty "micro" scopic).

Carbohydrate, protein, and fat are called "macro" or major nutrients because they comprise the major part of our diet as far as **quantity** is concerned. They are not called major because they are more important. Vitamins and minerals are referred to as micronutrients because they're required in such small amounts, not because they are microscopic in the role they play in our bodies.

As we will see in the following information, the presence of the proper portions of nutrients needed in both grams and milligrams is essential for energy to be properly released in the body.

At this point, since we're talking about right proportions, I thought it might be interesting to you to compare some recommended daily allowance tables.

RECOMMENDED DAILY ALLOWANCES

(From Code of Federal Regulations,
U.S. Food and Drug Administration)

Nutrient	U.S. RDA*	Nutrient	U.S. RDA*
Protein	65 gm.	Vitamin A	5000 I.U.
Vitamin C	60 mg.	Thiamine	1.5 mg.
Riboflavin	1.7 mg.	Niacin	20 mg.
Calcium	1 gm.	Iron	18 mg.
Vitamin D	400 I.U.	Vitamin E	30 I.U.
Vitamin B_6	2 mg.	Folic acid	.04 mg.
Vitamin B_{12}	6 mcg.	Phosphorus	1 gm.
Iodine	150 mcg.	Magnesium	400 mg.
Zinc	15 mg.	Copper	2 mg.
Pantothenic acid	10 mg.		

* U.S. Recommended Daily Allowance
for adults and children four or more years of age.

(From a Working Paper on Protein Requirements prepared by T. R. Davis and
J. Mayer, Nutrition Department, Harvard School of Public Health, on behalf of FAO.)

Age group	Author	Year	Optimal Protein g./day	Per cent Calories
0 - 1 years	Wang	1928	32	16
Mean weight: 8 kg.	Stearns	1939	27	13
Calorie allowance: 800	Holt	1940	32	16
	Levine	1945	32	16
1 - 3 years	Molchanova	1936	48	16
Mean weight: 12 kg.	Roubstein	1936	42	14
Calorie allowance: 1200	Leitch/Duckworth	1937	48	16
	Clements	1946	50	17
3 - 4 years	Daniels	1935	51	14
Mean weight: 16 kg.	Leitch/Duckworth	1937	60	17
Calorie allowance: 1400	Hawks	1938	64	18
4 - 5 years	Daniels	1935	54	14
Mean weight: 17 kg.	Leitch/Duckworth	1937	60	15
Calorie allowance: 1580	Maroney	1937	60	15
	Hawks	1938	68	17
	Farr	1938	53	14
5 - 6 years	Leitch/Duckworth	1937	64	16
Mean weight: 20 kg.	Maroney	1937	62	15
Calorie allowance: 1640	Hawks	1938	80	20
6 - 7 years	Holt	1921	60	13
Mean weight: 23 kg.	Leitch/Duckworth	1937	69	15
Calorie allowance: 1800	Maroney	1937	67	15
	Eppright	1954	53	12
7 - 8 years	Leitch/Duckworth	1937	68	14
Mean weight: 25 kg.	Maroney	1937	70	15
Calorie allowance: 1900	Eppright	1954	58	12
8 - 9 years	Wait	1933	56	11
Mean weight: 28 kg.	Molchanova	1936	78	15
Calorie allowance: 2100	Leitch/Duckworth	1937	70	13
	Maroney	1937	78	15
	Eppright	1954	64	12
9 - 10 years	Wait	1933	65	12
Mean weight: 31 kg.	Bjeloussoff	1935	93	17
Calorie allowance: 2200	Leitch/Duckworth	1937	78	14
	Maroney	1937	84	15
	Eppright	1954	65	12
10 - 11 years	Hasse	1882	73	12
Mean weight: 33 kg.	Herbst	1898	46	8
Calorie allowance: 2350	Sundstrom	1911	63	11
	Muller	1914	76	13
	Tigerstedt	1916	79	14
	Holt	1921	76	13
	Wait	1933	66	11
	Leitch/Duckworth	1937	83	14
	Maroney	1937	92	15
	Eppright	1954	69	12

(From a Working Paper on Protein Requirements, prepared by T. R. Davis and
J. Mayer, Nutrition Department, Harvard School of Public Health, on behalf of FAO.)

Age group	Author	Year	Optimal Protein g./day	Percent Calories
11 - 12 years	Hasse	1882	79	12
Mean weight: 36 kg.	Muller	1914	79	12
Calorie allowance: 2600	Tigerstedt	1916	50	8
	Holt	1921	83	13
	Sherman	1920	97	15
	Richet	1928	54	8
	Wait	1933	72	11
	Leitch/Duckworth	1937	90	14
	Maroney	1937	101	15
	Eppright	1954	79	12
12 - 13 years	Herbst	1898	60	8
Mean weight: 40 kg.	Muller	1914	80	11
Calorie allowance: 2840	Tigerstedt	1916	108	15
	Holt	1921	76	11
	Sherman	1920	84	12
	Wait	1933	64	9
	Leitch/Duckworth	1937	100	14
	Maroney	1937	104	15
	Eppright	1954	84	12
13 - 14 years	Sundstrom	1911	99	13
Mean weight: 45 kg.	Muller	1914	81	10
Calorie allowance: 3100	Tigerstedt	1916	99	13
	Holt	1921	77	10
	Sherman	1920	90	12
	Letich/Duckworth	1937	117	15
	Maroney	1937	117	15
	Eppright	1954	104	13
14 - 15 years	Herbst	1898	70	8
Mean weight: 50 kg.	Tigerstedt	1916	100	12
Calorie allowance: 3300	Holt	1921	70	8
	Wait	1933	65	8
	Leitch/Duckworth	1937	130	16
	Maroney	1937	125	15
	Eppright	1954	100	12
15 - 16 years	Sundstrom	1911	103	12
Mean weight: 57 kg.	Tigerstedt	1916	114	13
Calorie allowance: 3500	Holt	1921	120	14
	Wait	1933	86	10
	Leitch/Duckworth	1937	148	17
	Eppright	1954	103	12
16 - 17 years	Sundstrom	1911	108	12
Mean weight: 60 kg.	Tigerstedt	1916	102	12
Calorie allowance: 3550	Wait	1933	66	8
	Leitch/Duckworth	1937	150	17
	Eppright	1954	102	12
17 - 18 years	Tigerstedt	1916	93	10
Mean weight: 62 kg.	Holt	1921	124	14
Calorie allowance: 3600	Wait	1933	93	10
	Leitch/Duckworth	1937	124	14
	Eppright	1954	105	12

(From a Working Paper on Protein Requirements, prepared by T. R. Davis and
J. Mayer, Nutrition Department, Harvard School of Public Health, on behalf of FAO.)

Age group	Author	Year	Optimal Protein g./day	Percent Calories
18 - 19 years Mean weight: 64 kg. Calorie allowance: 3600	Leitch/Duckworth Eppright	1937 1954	96 102	11 12
19 - 20 years Mean weight: 65 kg. Calorie allowance: 3600	Eppright	1954	98	11
20 - 30 years Mean weight: 65 kg. Calorie allowance: 3200	Sherman	1920	44	5.6
	Leitch/Duckworth	1937	50	6.4
	Hegsted, Stare, et al.	1946	50	6.4
	Stare	1945	25	3.2
	Harte	1947	25	3.2
	Rose	1949	25	3.2
	Bricker	1949	40	5.4
	NRC	1953	65	8.8
	Leverton	1954	20	2.4
	Hegsted	1955	25	3.2

(From The World Almanac and Book of Facts 1945)*

Age and Sex	Calories	Protein (gm.)	Calcium (gm.)	Iron (mg.)	Vitamin A (I.U.)	Vitamin B$_1$ (mg.)	Vitamin B$_2$ (mg.)	Vitamin B$_3$ (mg.)	Vitamin C (mg.)	Vitamin D (I.U.)
Man (70 kg.)										
Sedentary	2500	...	...	...	...	1.5	2.2	15	...	...
Mod. active	3000	70	0.8	12	5000	1.8	2.7	18	75	**
Very active	4500	...	...	...	...	2.3	3.3	23	...	...
Woman (56 kg.)										
Sedentary	2100	...	...	...	...	1.2	1.8	12	...	...
Mod. active	2500	60	0.8	12	5000	1.5	2.2	15	70	**
Very active	3000	...	...	...	...	1.8	2.7	18	...	...
Pregnancy (later half)	2500	85	1.5	15	6000	1.8	2.5	18	100	400 - 800
Lactation	3000	100	2.0	15	8000	2.3	3.0	23	150	400 - 800
Children										
Under 1 yr.	100/kg.	3 - 4/kg.	1.0	6	1500	0.4	0.6	4	30	400 - 800
1 - 3 yrs.	1200	40	1.0	7	2000	0.6	0.9	6	35	**
4 - 6 yrs.	1600	50	1.0	8	2500	0.8	1.2	8	50	...
7 - 9 yrs.	2000	60	1.0	10	3500	1.0	1.5	10	60	...
10 - 12 yrs.	2500	70	1.2	12	4500	1.2	1.8	12	75	...
Girls										
13 - 15 yrs.	2800	80	1.3	15	5000	1.4	2.0	14	80	**
16 - 20 yrs.	2400	75	1.0	15	5000	1.2	1.8	12	80	...
Boys										
13 - 15 yrs.	3200	85	1.4	15	5000	1.6	2.4	16	90	**
16 - 20 yrs.	3800	100	1.4	15	6000	2.0	3.0	20	100	...

* Source: Food and Nutrition Board, National Research Council.
** Vitamin D is undoubtedly necessary for older children and adults. When not available from sunshine, it should be provided probably up to the minimum amounts recommended for infants.

Age and Sex	Body Weight (kg.)	Energy (calories)	Protein (gm.)	Vitamin A (mcg.)	Vitamin D (mcg.)	Thiamine (mg.)	Riboflavin (mg.)
Children							
1 yr.	7.3	820	14	300	10.0	0.3	0.5
1 - 3 yrs.	13.4	1360	16	250	10.0	0.5	0.8
4 - 6 yrs.	20.2	1830	20	300	10.0	0.7	1.1
7 - 9 yrs.	28.1	2190	25	400	2.5	0.9	1.3
Male adolescents							
10 - 12 yrs.	36.9	2600	30	575	2.5	1.0	1.6
13 - 15 yrs.	51.3	2900	37	725	2.5	1.2	1.7
16 - 19 yrs.	62.9	3070	38	750	2.5	1.2	1.8
Female adolescents							
10 - 12 yrs.	38.0	2350	29	575	2.5	0.9	1.4
13 - 15 yrs.	49.9	2490	31	725	2.5	1.0	1.5
16 - 19 yrs.	54.4	2310	30	750	2.5	0.9	1.4
Adult man (moderately active)	65.0	3000	37	750	2.5	1.2	1.8
Adult woman (moderately active)	55.0	2200	29	750	2.5	0.9	1.3
Pregnancy (later half)		+350	38	750	10.0	+0.1	+0.2
Lactation (first 6 months)		+550	46	1200	10.0	+0.2	+0.4

Age and Sex	Body Weight (kg.)	Niacin (mg.)	Folic acid (mcg.)	Vitamin B_{12} (mcg.)	Vitamin C (mg.)	Calcium (gm.)	Iron (mg.)
Children							
1 yr.	7.3	5.4	60	0.3	20	0.5 - 0.6	5 - 10
1 - 3 yrs.	13.4	9.0	100	0.9	20	0.4 - 0.5	5 - 10
4 - 6 yrs.	20.2	12.1	100	1.5	20	0.4 - 0.5	5 - 10
7 - 9 yrs.	28.1	14.5	100	1.5	20	0.4 - 0.5	5 - 10
Male adolescents							
10 - 12 yrs.	36.9	17.2	100	2.0	20	0.6 - 0.7	5 - 10
13 - 15 yrs.	51.3	19.1	200	2.0	30	0.6 - 0.7	9 - 18
16 - 19 yrs.	62.9	20.3	200	2.0	30	0.5 - 0.6	5 - 9
Female adolescents							
10 - 12 yrs.	38.0	15.5	100	2.0	20	0.6 - 0.7	5 - 10
13 - 15 yrs.	49.9	16.4	200	2.0	30	0.6 - 0.7	12 - 24
16 - 19 yrs.	54.4	15.2	200	2.0	30	0.5 - 0.6	14 - 28
Adult man (moderately active)	65.0	19.8	200	2.0	30	0.4 - 0.5	5 - 9
Adult woman (moderately active)	55.0	14.5	200	2.0	30	0.4 - 0.5	14 - 28
Pregnancy (later half)		+2.3	400	3.0	30	1.0 - 1.2	(9)
Lactation (first 6 months)		+3.7	300	2.5	30	1.0 - 1.2	(9)

	Age (years)	Weight (lbs.)	Protein (gm.)	Vit. A (I.U.)	Vit. D (I.U.)	Vit. E (I.U.)	Vit. C (mg.)	Vit. B_1 (mg.)	Vit. B_2 (mg.)	Vit. B_3 (mg.)	Vit. B_6 (mg.)
Infants	0 - ½	13	kg. x 2.2	420	10	3	35	0.3	0.4	6	0.3
	½ - 1	20	kg. x 2.0	400	10	4	35	0.5	0.6	8	0.6
Children	1 - 3	29	23	400	10	5	45	0.7	0.8	9	0.9
	4 - 6	44	30	500	10	6	45	0.9	1.0	11	1.3
	7 - 10	62	34	700	10	7	45	1.2	1.4	16	1.6
Males	11 - 14	99	45	1000	10	8	50	1.4	1.6	16	1.8
	15 - 18	145	56	1000	10	10	60	1.4	1.7	18	2.0
	19 - 22	154	56	1000	7.5	10	60	1.5	1.7	19	2.2
	23 - 50	154	56	1000	5	10	60	1.4	1.6	18	2.2
	51+	154	56	1000	5	10	60	1.2	1.4	16	2.2
Females	11 - 14	101	46	800	10	8	50	1.1	1.3	15	1.8
	15 - 18	120	46	800	10	8	60	1.1	1.3	14	2.0
	19 - 22	120	44	800	7.5	8	60	1.1	1.3	14	2.0
	23 - 50	120	44	800	5	8	60	1.0	1.2	13	2.0
	51+	120	44	800	5	8	60	1.0	1.2	13	2.0
Pregnant			+30	+200	+5	+2	+20	+0.4	+0.3	+2	+0.6
Lactating			+20	+400	+5	+3	+40	+0.5	+0.5	+5	+0.5

	Age (years)	Weight (lbs.)	Folacin (mcg.)	Vit. B_{12} (mcg.)	Calcium (mg.)	Phosphorus (mg.)	Magnesium (mg.)	Iron (mg.)	Zinc (mg.)	Iodine (mcg.)
Infants	0 - ½	13	30	0.5	360	240	50	10	3	40
	½ - 1	20	45	1.5	540	360	70	15	5	50
Children	1 - 3	29	100	2.0	800	800	150	15	10	70
	4 - 6	44	200	2.5	800	800	200	10	10	90
	7 - 10	62	300	3.0	800	800	250	10	10	120
Males	11 - 14	99	400	3.0	1200	1200	350	18	15	150
	15 - 18	145	400	3.0	1200	1200	400	18	15	150
	19 - 22	154	400	3.0	800	800	350	10	15	150
	23 - 50	154	400	3.0	800	800	350	10	15	150
	51+	154	400	3.0	800	800	350	10	15	150
Females	11 - 14	101	400	3.0	1200	1200	300	18	15	150
	15 - 18	120	400	3.0	1200	1200	300	18	15	150
	19 - 22	120	400	3.0	800	800	300	18	15	150
	23 - 50	120	400	3.0	800	800	300	18	15	150
	51+	120	400	3.0	800	800	300	10	15	150
Pregnant			+400	+1.0	+400	+400	+150	**	+5	+25
Lactating			+100	+1.0	+400	+400	+150	**	+10	+50

* Source: Food and Nutrition Board, National Academy of Sciences — National Research Council (Revised 1980)
** The use of 30 - 60 milligrams of supplemental iron is recommended.

As can be seen from these tables, the proportions of recommended daily allowances varies a great deal comparing tables from the past and those in use today; and even tables in use today vary a good bit (for example, compare the FAO table with the FDA table).

"MACRO" NUTRIENTS

The three macronutrients — carbohydrate, protein, and fat — are the foods that give our body energy to burn, much the same as fuel, wood and paper give a fire energy to burn. It's important to include all three in a well-balanced diet; and, in fact, if a diet of whole, natural foods is eaten, all three are naturally provided.

Just a word about calories. The nutrients which make up the bulk of our diets — the "major" or "macro" nutrients — are sources of calories in our diet. Probably because about 60% of Americans are overweight, the word calorie has come to take on a negative connotation. Calories are simply a measurement for energy, not really a dirty word or something harmful to our health. The amount of fuel or energy in a food is measured in terms of calories, which simply tell us how much energy may be released as heat when the food is metabolized.

We eat to put energy into our bodies, which is precisely what carbohydrates, protein, and fat do. The problem begins when the amount of calories, or energy, consumed is more than the amount which is burned up or utilized. This is what has led to so much calorie-consciousness in the United States, which, in general, is a place with a very sedentary lifestyle.

If too much energy is consumed and there is not enough activity to burn it off, that energy becomes stored in the body in the form of fat and can cause disease. So it's not that calories are undesirable; it's just that it's undesirable to consume more calories than are burned.

To keep calorie consumption in a healthy perspective, two things are important. One is, as mentioned above, to consume the right proportion of calories to the amount burned off in daily activities. In the United States — where calorie consumption is high and the lifestyle is sedentary due to a dependence on fossil fuels for energy to do most of the work — energy has to be burned off somehow or it will turn into obesity. To burn off excess energy we see everyone jogging or participating in other "leisure activities" (which amounts to physical work that doesn't produce anything). The right amount of calories needed to balance how much are burned has to be determined by each individual by an analysis of daily activities.

The body burns a certain amount of energy just to keep the heart beating, lungs breathing, etc. These automatic body functions, without any other activity, burn about 60 calories an hour. This amount of energy burned when sleeping or vegetating is called basal metabolism. Different activities besides the basic body functions burn different amounts of energy. The table below gives some idea of how much energy is burned for certain activities.

From "Ho-ping, Food for Everyone"
by Medard Gabel

ENERGY REQUIREMENTS FOR VARIOUS ACTIVITIES
(kilocalories/hour)

Light Work

Sitting	.19	Writing	20
Standing relaxed	.20	Typing	.16–40
Sewing	.30–90	Typing quickly	55
Dressing/undressing	.33	Drawing	.40–50
Lithography	.40–50	Violin playing	.40–50
Tailoring	.50–85	Washing dishes	60
Ironing	.60	Bookbinding	.45–90

Moderate Work

Shoemaking	.80–115	Sweeping	.85–110
Dusting	.110	Washing	125–215
Metalworking	120–140	Walking	130–240
House painting	145–160	Carpentering	150–180

Hard work

Polishing	.175	Joiner work	195
Blacksmithing	.275–350	Riveting	275
Marching	.280–400	Cycling	180–600
Rowing	120–600	Swimming	200–700

Very Hard Work

Stonemasonry	.350	Sawing wood	420
Coal mining (average for shift)	.320	Running	800–1000
Walking quickly	.570	Climbing	400–900
Running quickly	1240	Rowing quickly	1240
Walking upstairs	1000	Skiing	500–950
		Wrestling	1000

The second important thing to do is to be sure to get all the necessary nutrients (such as vitamins, minerals, enzymes, etc.) contained in the calories consumed. Different calorie sources contain different vitamins, minerals, etc. In this connection it's important to steer clear of "empty-calorie" foods (foods which supply calories but contain no vitamins, minerals, protein, etc.) like refined white flour and sugar, and to use a variety of the major nutrient foods which include other necessary nutrients.

CARBOHYDRATES. An easily burnable form of energy comes to us in the form of sugars or starch. Carbohydrates have a very bad public image in that they're generally thought of as fattening. This is because most of the carbohydrate consumed in this country has been processed or refined, leaving an empty calorie.

In their whole, natural, unadulterated state, all carbohydrates come packaged with the vitamins and minerals which make the energy in the carbohydrate digestible by the body. When an empty calorie, refined food product is eaten it does two things to rob the body of nutrients. First of all, certain vitamins must be present for the body to metabolize the energy that is present (see section on vitamins). If the energy food is eaten without the vitamins and minerals present which help the body make use of the energy, then vitamins and minerals must be drained from the body. In this way, eating empty calories literally robs nutrients from the body. Indirectly the body is robbed of nutrients also, because refined carbohydrates make the body feel full, so a person may fill up on them and leave out foods that would actually offer good nutrition. Then, because refined carbohydrates get burned rapidly, the body gets hungry shortly and usually ends up snacking on another refined carbohydrate. Since refined white sugar and white flour, as well as alcohol, are carbohydrate foods eaten in America in large quantities, it's no wonder that carbohydrates have the reputation that they do!

Yet, when stopping to think, in countries on this planet where people's diets are made up mostly of carbohydrates and where they are too poor to afford refined products, it can be observed that the people aren't fat at all. Of course, a lot of this has to do with the great amount of physical labor they engage in, but some of it has to do with the fact that carbohydrates eaten in their whole, natural state are a nutritional score.

Our family's diet is centered around complex carbohydrates like whole grains and legumes. They offer B vitamins in proper proportion to enable the body to burn the energy in the starches present. Also, the protein, fat, and fiber which are naturally part of the neat little grain and/or legume package slows the digestive process down and stretches out the assimilation of the carbohydrate into the bloodstream over a long period of time. Thus, the carbohydrate in its whole, natural state doesn't rob the body of nutrients in order to burn the energy present, and it also gives a fuller feeling for a longer period of time, keeping the blood sugar levels steady. This means less eating yet more nutrition each time you do eat, especially if grains and legumes are mixed to get a complete protein (see "Protein" heading in this section).

We also get carbohydrates, along with loads of vitamins and minerals, in fruits (natural fruit sugar) and starchy vegetables. And occasionally — but only occasionally — we get our carbohydrate through an out and out sweet treat, but always using honey as the sugar source. Honey contains at least some vitamins and minerals (but the amount depends a great deal on how the honey was processed). You will find lots of recipes in this book containing honey for those special occasions that call for a sweet. But the best thing is to use carbohydrates like whole grains and legumes for day-to-day meal planning. They can be used in such a great variety of dishes. It won't be boring to do so either!

PROTEIN. Since over half of the human body (not including the water) is protein, we definitely need a steady supply in our diet to be able to maintain the body protein. Proteins are needed for cell and tissue maintenance, as every cell wall contains protein. It acts as the framework for keratin in hair, skin, nails, muscle, and other connective tissues, blood cells, etc. Besides maintenance, it's also needed for cell growth and repair. Protein is also an intrinsic part of the DNA and RNA makeup, as well as the functions of enzymes, hormones, and antibodies.

For all these reasons, protein is one nutrient that most everyone is familiar with and concerned about getting enough of. In fact, in America it could almost be said that we have been overly obsessed with concern about getting enough protein, but not in balance with a concern over getting other essential nutrients at the same time.

Usually when someone considers leaving flesh foods out of the diet, the number one worry that pops up is, "Will I get enough protein?" This question raises many points to be considered.

The first is, what is "enough protein?" From the tables of Recommended Daily Allowances (this section, pp. 6 - 12), it can be seen that the answer to this question is not a definite one. The amount of protein thought to be required by the human body has changed from time to time and even varies presently depending on the source of information. Up to the time around World War II, it was actually thought among nutritionists that the human body required 100 or more grams of protein a day. Since then it has been concluded that not only does the body not need that much protein, but also that too much protein can be bad for health. Today there are differences in opinion as to what the recommended allowance should be. Some sources say about 65 grams per day (USFDA), some say about 45 grams (FAO/WHO), and some say even as low as 20 grams are needed by the body for proper maintenance. As with all the other major nutrient foods which have the primary function of supplying energy for the body, the amount required by the body varies a great deal according to how much energy is actually burned by the person; whether or not the body is in a rapid state of growth; the individual rate of metabolism, etc. The recommended daily requirements made by the different sources are a safe, general average.

The other thing to be considered is whether or not all the protein consumed is digestible or usable by the body. It's actually possible for someone to consume large amounts of protein and literally have the body "starve" even with so much available protein in its midst due to a deficiency in certain vitamins and/or certain essential amino acids.

Proteins are made up of complex combinations of amino acids. Of all the many amino acids, there are eight which can't be synthesized by the body and must be obtained through the diet. These are called the eight essential amino acids, as they are essential for the body's ability to use protein that is consumed. If one or more of the eight essential amino acids is short or lacking, the amount of protein which can be utilized by the body is cut back to the degree that the amino acid is lacking.

For this reason, certain foods have come to be considered good protein sources. Actually all foods contain protein, because, as mentioned earlier, protein is present in all cell walls. Since this is so, a food must contain a large percentage of protein, and that protein must be digestible by the body to be considered a good protein source. Whether or not a food is to be considered a good protein source is measured by what percentage of the total weight of the food is protein and what the Net Protein Utilization (NPU) is; in other words, what amount of the protein consumed is actually usable by the body.

PERCENTAGE PROTEIN BY WEIGHT
(From "Diet for a Small Planet"
by Frances Moore Lappe)

Soy flour, defatted	.51%	Cheeses	.30%
Soy flour, natural	.40%	Fish	.22%
Soybeans, dry	.35%	Chicken	.21%
Whole wheat flour	.13%	Beefsteak	.20%
Brown rice, uncooked	.6%	Hamburger	.13%
Cottage cheese	.20%	Eggs	.13%
Milk, whole	.3%	Tofu	.11%

NET PROTEIN UTILIZATION

Brown rice	.70%	Soybeans	61%
Cottage cheese	.75%	Soy flour	61%
Wheat germ	.67%	Lentils	30%
Beef/hamburger	.67%	Peanuts	43%
Chicken	.65%	Oatmeal	66%
Fish	.80%	Tofu	65%
Eggs	.94%	Cheeses	70%

There are certain foods in which a good percentage of the total weight is protein, and because all eight essential amino acids are present, the protein can be readily utilized by the body. These foods are all flesh foods (the bodies of four-legged animals, birds, reptiles, and fish), dairy products, and eggs. All of these foods are generally thought of when the word "protein" is mentioned. Unfortunately, these foods also come packed with cholesterol and/or saturated fats, which are undesirable in a healthy diet (see information under "Fats" in this section).

There are other sources of available protein which have been largely ignored on this part of the planet but are used by 70% of the world's population presently and in the past. These sources are: legumes, nuts, seeds, and grains. In Western nutrition, these foods haven't really been counted as good protein sources because they all lack one or more of the eight essential amino acids. In nature's balance, however, it can be found that where a legume is short or lacking a particular amino acid, a grain will have that amino acid in abundance. Simply by combining the two at a meal, a whole protein is obtained which is nondifferent in quality to the protein provided by the high-protein foods mentioned in the previous paragraph. In truth, it could be said to be a superior protein since none of the legumes, seeds, nuts or grains contain cholesterol or saturated fat; and all come naturally packed with vitamins (which help with protein metabolism in the body), as well as essential fiber, polyunsaturated fat and carbohydrates.

There is a whole book which deals with the science of mixing these foods to balance amino acids, so there is no need for me to duplicate this information. I simply refer you to **Diet for a Small Planet** by Frances Moore Lappe. As for myself, I think it's enough to consciously mix "complementary proteins" in day-to-day meals (legumes with nuts and seeds and/or grains; grains with nuts and seeds and/or legumes; nuts and seeds with grains and/or legumes) so the balance gets taken care of. I think it's very interesting that a study of eating habits of past and some present cultures on this planet shows that the balancing of amino acids was naturally done without having any of the laboratory information now available. In the Far East, primarily soybeans, adzuki, and mung beans were used with rice or millet; in the Middle East, primarily garbanzo and fava beans with rice and wheat; in South America, corn and beans, etc.

Actually, I've found that the more I learn about protein and other nutrients, along with the nutritional content of whole foods, the less anxiety and effort is involved in serving my family nourishing meals which are economical and easy to prepare. I hope that the information and recipes included throughout the book will help make it easier for you.

FATS. Fats are another of the calorie or food-energy sources which have received a bad reputation in the public's eyes in recent years. Actually, the human body needs fat in the diet, as there are certain functions in the body that no other substance besides fat can carry out. As an energy food, fat gives at least twice as much energy as an equal weight of the other energy foods — protein and carbohydrates. And because fat is not water soluble, it also acts as an energy-storing facility. Because of the quality fat has of not mixing with water, the fatty tissues also store and transport the fat-soluble vitamins A, D, E and K, which cannot be carried in the bloodstream since it is water-based. Fatty layers surround, protect and hold vital organs in place (like the heart, kidneys, liver, etc.), as well as insulate the body from environmental temperature changes and preserve body heat.

For these important functions, fat in the diet is essential. The problem with fat really is caused by how much, and what kind, is consumed. Our bodies need one nutrient in fats which can't be provided by any other food substance or be synthesized by the body from other foodstuffs. That is the fatty acid called linoleic acid. The body can synthesize all other fatty acids except linoleic acid. To prevent a deficiency of linoleic acid, only between 1% and 2% of our total caloric intake needs to be linoleic acid, which could be considered the bare minimum of fat required by the body. Today in America, fat makes up 42% of the total caloric intake, which obviously is way out of proportion with the amount of fat actually needed as a nutrient. The U.S. Senate report "Dietary Goals" made a recommendation that Americans try to reduce their consumption of fat to make up only 30% of their total caloric intake.

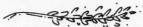

This particular Senate report was a landmark in that it was the first time that a branch of the government ever came out and connected America's dietary habits with America's health problems. However, the report must be read with a grain of salt, bearing in mind the fact that members of the Senate committee were under very heavy pressure from lobbyists representing large food manufacturers, etc., who profit by people eating the kinds of foods that the Senate committee was recommending be reduced in consumption. Obviously even 30% of the total caloric intake is a generous "recommendation," even for someone who burns a lot of energy in their day-to-day life.

It's also important what kind of fat makes up the 30% or less. There are three kinds of fat: saturated, monounsaturated, and polyunsaturated. These are differentiated by their molecular structure. A saturated fat is one which is totally saturated with hydrogen atoms connected to each carbon atom; a monounsaturated fat is two hydrogen atoms short of being a saturated fat; a polyunsaturated fat is one which is four or more hydrogen atoms short of saturation.

To be able to tell one kind of fat from another by these descriptions could only be done under laboratory conditions. But there are simpler ways to tell. Saturated fats are solid at a cool room temperature, whereas polyunsaturated fats always remain as a clear liquid. The other general rule is that saturated fats exist only in animal foods and animal by-products (lard in flesh foods, butter, milk, etc.) with the exception of coconut oil, which is a saturated fat; monounsaturated and polyunsaturated fats are found in the plant food kingdom.

The kind of fat used in a diet is especially important to serum-cholesterol levels (the level of cholesterol in the bloodstream) in connection with cardiovascular diseases. Cardiovascular diseases have reached epidemic proportions in the United States and are the number one cause of death. They cause more deaths than all othere causes of death in the U.S. combined. Although there is still a controversy over what the risk factors are that cause cardiovascular diseases, it is agreed that cholesterol is a constant factor, among other factors, which results in heart attack or stroke.

Cholesterol — that fatlike substance which is present in every cell of the body and is therefore present and essential in the bloodstream — becomes a danger to health when it reaches a certain level. In countries with very low cardiovascular disease rates, the average serum-cholesterol count is 150 milligrams of cholesterol per 100 milliliters of blood serum. In America, with its high rate of cardiovascular disease-caused deaths, the average serum-cholesterol count is 250 milligrams of cholesterol per 100 milliliters of blood serum. When the cholesterol count gets this high in the bloodstream, fat deposits form in the lining of arteries, which leads to arteriosclerosis (hardening of the arteries) and cutting off of vital blood circulation, which leads to strokes and heart attacks.

There are many factors which contribute to raising the serum-cholesterol level that are not totally understood yet. Eating foods high in cholesterol will raise the serum-cholesterol level. (Cholesterol is naturally present in the body, and though it's essential for keeping the body running, there is no need to eat any cholesterol because the body synthesizes all the cholesterol it needs on its own.) And in case you're wondering how all this talk about cholesterol fits in with fats, consumption of saturated fats raises serum-cholesterol levels; monounsaturated fats have no effect on serum-cholesterol counts; and polyunsaturated fats actually will lower the serum-cholesterol level over a period of time. All fats have the same calorie value but differ in the effect they have on serum-cholesterol levels.

Interestingly enough, all the foods which contain cholesterol also contain saturated fat, and the foods which are cholesterol-free contain polyunsaturated fats. Only foods in the animal kingdom contain cholesterol, which is not present in any of the plant kingdom foods. By refraining from eating foods in the animal kingdom (especially all flesh foods and eggs), consumption of cholesterol and saturated fat is automatically eliminated.

In my own personal cooking, I use sunflower, safflower or corn oil because they are light tasting, pleasant oils which are the highest in linoleic acid content and are the most unsaturated of all vegetable oils.

Of course, in cooking with whole foods, addition of extra oils isn't necessary for getting the required minimum. Whole foods, which are staple energy sources, contain a balance of fats, carbohydrates and protein. All whole grains, legumes, nuts and seeds provide a healthy supply of polyunsaturated fats naturally.

Some of the recipes in this book include dairy products which, even in a vegetarian diet, are a source of cholesterol and saturated fats. Often when people leave behind flesh eating, they rely heavily on dairy products for protein. If this is the case, a vegetarian's diet can actually be as high in cholesterol and saturated fats as a meateater's. The best word again, as in reference to a healthful natural foods diet, is variety and moderation. You will find recipes containing dairy products included in this book; those high in cholesterol and fat content are marked with a star. These are recipes which are better served on occasion rather than as regular, everyday meals. You will notice that many of the recipes with the star call for "butter or magarine." In essence, any margarine made with hydrogenated vegetable oil does the same thing in the body as saturated fat. This is because when an unsaturated oil is hydrogenated (pumped full with hydrogen), its structure and function in the body is the same as saturated fat. In getting a margarine, it is only more beneficial than butter if it contains no chemical additives and lists liquid vegetable oil rather than hydrogenated vegetable oil.

Generally, cooking oils add to texture and distribution of flavor, and because they digest more slowly, they make the body feel full sooner and longer. Most of the recipes here make use of polyunsaturated oils, and most in small quantities. I think you'll find that cooking with such small quantities of oil and using whole, natural foods is anything but a dry affair!

VITAMINS

Vitamins are essential for the body to be able to put the nutrients in food to use. Because vitamins aren't produced by the body, we have to get them through the food we eat also! You may notice from the tables that there is quite a small amount of vitamins present in each food. That is no mistake I'm sure!

Our bodies only need a certain amount of vitamins, which can be provided by eating reasonable amounts of foodstuffs that contain those vitamins. This certainly makes more sense to me than eating all kinds of refined, vitamin-depleted foods and then guzzling vitamin supplement pills to make up for it.

The amounts of vitamins found in foods in their fresh, natural state are enough to supply our bodies nicely, provided we're not eating foods which, in the digestion process, deplete vitamins from our bodies (e.g., empty-calorie foods such as white sugar—see **U.S. Senate Dietary Goals Report**, December 1977, p. 32), or living in environments which deplete our bodies of vitamins (see **How to Get Well** by Paavo Airola, Health Plus, Phoenix, 1974). Under these circumstances, vitamin supplements may be necessary. For example, whenever I have to go to a smog-laden city like Los Angeles, I always take along vitamin supplements to keep up the supply of vitamins that smog is known to deplete. And, of course, if there is a bad vitamin deficiency from prolonged depletion, vitamins may also be necessary. But that is vitamin therapy, and the information provided here and in the tables are an attempt to introduce you to vitamins as nutrients and not meant to be taken as medical advice. You should go to an expert in the field for that!

Vitamins are like vital links in the chain of biochemical actions and reactions taking place in the process of digestion, which make nutrients available from the food we eat for the body's growth, regeneration, repair, and energy. There are an innumerable number of these chains of biochemical reactions throughout the body: some for using fat, others for using carbohydrates, others for protein digestion, etc. If a link or many links of the chain (vitamins) are missing, the bringing together of one element with another for the desired reaction doesn't happen, and thus cells can literally starve to death in the presence of plentiful nutrients— all for lack of a vitamin.

There are certain vitamins which need to be replaced on a more regular basis than others because they are water-soluble, whereas the others are fat-soluble. Most vitamins (C and the B's) are soluble in water and are carried through the bloodstream, which is primarily made of water. As the vitamins pass through the body via the bloodstream, they only get absorbed by cells wherever they're needed, and the unneeded vitamins are flushed out in urine. Because these water-soluble vitamins don't get stored in the body, they need to be supplied on a regular basis.

There are other vitamins which are fat-soluble and collect in the fatty tissues of the body. These vitamins become soluble and are carried throughout the system in any fats or oils contained in the food which is eaten. Because they don't pass out of the body like the water-soluble vitamins, but are stored in fatty tissues in the body, there is a possibility of building up toxic levels of fat-soluble vitamins in the body. (This is why vitamins A, D, E and K — all fat-soluble — are recommended to be taken under an expert's guidance.)

A vitamin deficiency shows itself relatively quickly through quite a wide range of physical malfunctions. Because vitamins often work with other vitamins, it may sometimes be hard to determine what is a vitamin deficiency and which vitamin is deficient without the help of a physician. It would be simpler to be sure to include varying foods in your diet which contain the different vitamins and avoid a shortage in the first place! One hint in preparing your good foods high in vitamins: avoid overcooking them, as this will destroy a lot of vitamins.

The vitamins listed below are listed alphabetically and not according to their importance.

VITAMIN A
(Carotene, provitamin A, retinol)
Fat-soluble

Necessary for: Health of the tissues which make up a protective covering on outside and inside of the body, meaning the skin and the mucous membranes which line the digestive, respiratory and eliminating systems. It is therefore essential for healthy skin and healthy organs that are protected by the mucous membranes, which act to prevent infection of these organs. Also essential in giving eyes the ability to adapt to bright and dim light. For growing children, vitamin A is needed for proper formation of tooth enamel, bones, and other growth processes.

Good sources: In a lacto-vegetarian diet, animal sources of dairy products as well as any and all green, leafy vegetables and yellow-orange fruits and vegetables (like winter squashes, yams, sweet potatoes, mangoes, papayas, cantaloupe, apricots, nectarines, carrots, kale, turnip greens, spinach, broccoli, etc.). The darker the green or yellow-orange the better, since the darker color marks the presence of more vitamin A.

Deficiency symptoms: Night blindness and in further gone cases, drying up of mucous membranes (eyes are usually the first to be affected, which results in permanent blindness), which leaves organs usually protected by the mucous membranes wide open to infection. Also worth a mention here is the other end of the spectrum: too much vitamin A. This is a danger to be watched for by those taking vitamin A supplements. Because vitamin A stores in fat cells and excesses don't just pass through the urinary tract, taking supplements can easily lead to a toxic buildup which is indicated by headaches, blurry vision, loss of appetite, nausea, diarrhea, loss of hair and/or loss of menstrual period.

VITAMIN B₁
(Thiamine)
Water-soluble

Necessary for: Releasing energy from carbohydrates (sugars and starches), proteins, and fats. Keeps brain and nervous system functioning normally. Helps maintain stamina and endurance (of body and mind). Helps to keep digestive tract functioning and also to maintain a healthy appetite.

Good sources: Nutritional yeast (read the label for the best one), all unrefined whole grains, sunflower and sesame seeds, legumes (especially soybeans), oranges, avocados.

Deficiency symptoms: Fatigue, depression, inability to concentrate. If unattended, will increase to muscle cramps, loss of appetite, loss of weight; and extreme deficiency develops into beriberi.

VITAMIN B₂
(Riboflavin)
Water-soluble

Necessary for: Utilization of food energy, protein, and fats (along with other B vitamins). Carries hydrogen through the system and helps the body use oxygen to get energy from food. Important for healthy skin tissue and eyes.

Good sources: Milk and milk products, nutritional yeast, collard greens and other green leafies, broccoli, millet, wheat germ.

Deficiency symptoms: Soreness and cracking at the corners of the mouth, or a scaly, oily rash on the face; swollen membranes in the mouth with a purplish tint on the tongue. Eyes may appear bloodshot, water constantly and feel irritated all the time.

VITAMIN B₃
(Niacin)
Water-soluble

Necessary for: Utilization of carbohydrates, protein, and fat (along with other B vitamins). Keeps nervous tissues, skin tissues, and digestive tract healthy.

Good sources: Soybeans and tofu, collard greens, rice polish, dry legumes, nutritional yeast.

Deficiency symptoms: Insomnia, headaches, irritability, digestive disturbances, and a reddish, sore, swollen tongue. Extreme deficiency results in pellagra.

VITAMIN B₆
(Pyridoxine)
Water-soluble

Necessary for: Metabolism of proteins, so the amount of B₆ required by the body depends a lot on the amount of protein consumed. Vitamin B₆ is also needed for the absorption of amino acids and the transportation of them to different parts of the body. Plays an important role in releasing energy to cells in the body; therefore has a direct and important role in the production of red blood cells and the proper functioning of nervous tissue.

Good sources: Whole grains, wheat germ, peanuts, corn, soybeans and other legumes, blackstrap molasses, nutritional yeast, sunflower seeds, raisins, avocados, bananas, spinach, kale and other green vegetables.

Deficiency symptoms: Convulsive seizures, greasy rash around the eyes, cracks at the corners of the mouth, irritation of sweat glands, nervous disorders, sore and rough tongue. Prolonged deficiency could lead to dizziness, nausea, vomiting, anemia and kidney stones. Oral steroid contraceptives and alcoholism are two practices that drain so much B_6 from the body that it is impossible to try replacing the vitamin through diet.

VITAMIN B$_{12}$
(Cobalamin)
Water-soluble

Necessary for: Formation and functioning of all body cells, because it's needed for the metabolism of all the major nutrients, proteins, fats, and carbohydrates, and also for the metabolism of nucleic acids. Especially important for red blood cell formation and prevention of pernicious anemia.

Good sources: Cottage cheese, yogurt, whey, buttermilk, most dairy products, and some types of nutritional yeast. Because it is not found in any plant foods (except possibly in comfrey and some sprouts such as alfalfa), B_{12} is a vitamin that vegetarians may lack. That's why my family and I include nutritional yeast as a part of every meal. Check the labels on different types of yeast, as there are some which do contain this important vitamin. Miso and other naturally fermented foods also contain vitamin B_{12}.

Deficiency symptoms: Sore tongue, back pain, indigestion, weakness, constipation or diarrhea, loss of weight, and prickly sensation in the arms and legs are early warning symptoms that damage to the central nervous system is beginning. Prolonged deficiency results in mental defects, damage to the central nervous system, delusions, psychosis, and eventual death.

VITAMIN C
(Ascorbic acid)
Water-soluble

Necessary for: Formation of collagen in connective tissues, which cements body cells together and helps in the repair and healing processes; metabolism of proteins and many amino acids; proper functioning of adrenal glands; important for absorption of iron from the intestine and storage of it in the liver. Also helpful in combatting infections since vitamin C in the tissues is depleted when infections occur. Research is still continuing as to what role vitamin C plays in infectious illness.

Good sources: Citrus fruits, strawberries, tomatoes, cantaloupe, sprouts, broccoli, cabbage, green and sweet red peppers, leafy greens, brussel sprouts, other fresh fruits and vegetables.

Deficiency symptoms: Bleeding gums, delayed healing of burns and wounds, joint pains, lack of energy and endurance, and in prolonged deficiency, hemorrhaging of small blood vessels underneath the skin causing many small red spots to appear on the skin.

VITAMIN D
Fat-soluble

Necessary for: Enabling the intestines to absorb calcium and phosphorus into the system; therefore vitamin D is connected with good bone and cartilage formation. Because young children's bones are growing so quickly, vitamin D is especially necessary in preventing rickets, a disease in which the bones become soft due to their inability to absorb the calcium and phosphorus.

Good sources: Sunshine on the skin, alfalfa sprouts, milk and butter. Vitamin D is called the "sunshine vitamin" because it is naturally formed by sunlight on the oily substance in the skin. The skin has a controlling mechanism which prevents too much of the vitamin from being formed; and in colder climates where there is little sunshine, the capacity of the skin to form vitamin D is high.

Deficiency symptoms: Rickets in children, characterized by bowed legs due to the soft bones bending under the weight of the body; beadlike protrusions on the ribs. Osteomalacia in adults (loss of calcium from the bones), symptomized by pain and tenderness in the bones and pressure in the pelvis and lower back and legs; slow healing of fractures.

VITAMIN E
(Alpha-, beta-, gamma-, delta-tocopherol)
Fat-soluble

Necessary for: Preventing oxidation and consequent destruction of vitamin A and red blood cell membranes, and keeps the polyunsaturated fats in the body from going rancid and decomposing. Much research and speculation has gone on about vitamin E but its function in the body is still not clear, although the vitamin has had much PR and false claims given to it.

Good sources: Oils and germs of grains (such as wheat germ oil and wheat germ); sunflower, walnut, safflower and other oils; green leafy vegetables, some sprouts such as alfalfa; legumes, nuts (especially almonds, walnuts, filberts and sunflower seeds), wild blackberries.

Deficiency symptoms: The minimum daily requirement has not yet been established, as there is still research being carried out about vitamin E. So far the only deficiency symptoms connected with a lack of vitamin E in humans is anemia caused by the rupture of red blood cell membranes. In animals a lack of vitamin E has been observed to cause paralysis, muscle degeneration, degeneration of sexual organs, and sterility. Vitamin E is a fat-soluble vitamin which will store in fatty tissues of the body.

VITAMIN K
Fat-soluble

Necessary for: Normal clotting of blood.

Good sources: Leafy green vegetables, soybeans and soybean oil, some sprouts such as alfalfa.

Deficiency symptoms: Because this vitamin

is partly synthesized by the body, deficiencies are said to be rare except occasionally in newborn infants or people with abnormal medical problems. In these cases, blood clotting is slowed or may not form, endangering a person's life.

The following four vitamins are part of the B vitamin group:

BIOTIN
Water-soluble

Necessary for: Work involved in the metabolism of fat and protein; also required for releasing energy from glucose sugar and for the synthesis of certain amino and other acids.

Good sources: Nutritional yeast, cauliflower, nuts, legumes. Also made by bacteria in the intestine and absorbed by the body.

Deficiency symptoms: Eczema of face and body, hair loss, and paralysis. Because biotin is made in the body, deficiencies are said to be rare. The only possibility of deficiency comes if someone eats raw egg whites, which contain a substance that prevents biotin from getting into the bloodstream.

CHOLINE
Water-soluble

Necessary for: Transport and metabolism of fats in the body.

Good sources: Lecithin, yeast, whole grains, legumes, wheat germ, milk, vegetables.

Deficiency symptoms: Very little is known about this vitamin, but deficiency is said to be unlikely because the body is able to make it with the help of two other B vitamins and an amino acid.

FOLACIN
(Folic acid)
Water-soluble

Necessary for: Blood cell formation; the metabolism of proteins and nucleic acids (substances formed by each cell for transfer of hereditary characteristics from one generation of cells to another as the body grows).

Good sources: Leafy green vegetables and other vegetables such as sweet potatoes, beets, brussel sprouts, cabbage and broccoli; legumes, whole grains, nutritional yeast, and fruits (especially oranges, cantaloupe, avocados, strawberries, and bananas).

Deficiency symptoms: Smooth red tongue, gastrointestinal disturbances, diarrhea, reduction in the number and enlargement of the red blood cells (known as macrocytic anemia).

PANTOTHENIC ACID
Water-soluble

Necessary for: Metabolism of carbohydrates, as well as fats and proteins; involved in the synthesis of cholesterol, steroid hormones and hemoglobin (iron-containing substance in red blood cells). Found in every cell of living tissues.

Good sources: Nutritional yeast, peanuts, whole grains, potatoes, tomatoes, peas, broccoli, milk, soybeans and other legumes, brussel sprouts, sweet potatoes, yellow corn.

Deficiency symptoms: Unobserved in humans and said to be unlikely to occur except possibly in connection with other nutritional deficiencies. Bacteria in the intestines make an unknown quantity, so nutrition scientists have been unable to determine how much our bodies need.

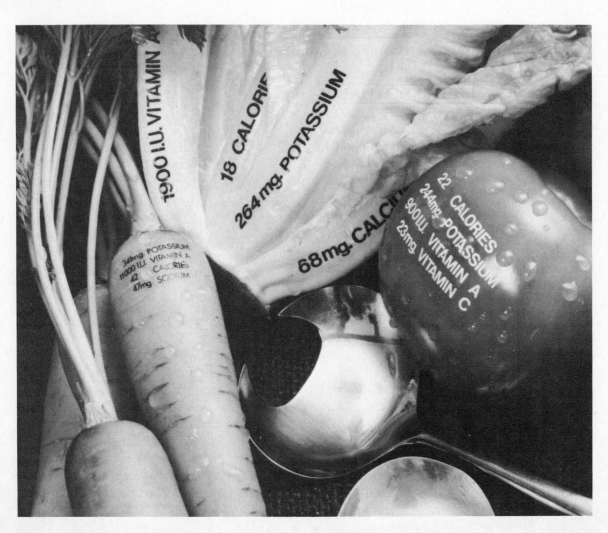

MINERALS

Like vitamins, minerals are micronutrients which our bodies require in small but steady supplies. As micronutrients, the importance of minerals in our diet is far greater than the required amount indicates.

Our material bodies are made up of more than 100 elements which have been identified. Of these, four elements make up 96% of our bodies: carbon, hydrogen, nitrogen, and oxygen. The elements which make up the remaining 4% are referred to as minerals. The bulk of these minerals are stored in the bones, mostly in the form of calcium and phosphorus, with the soft tissue and bloodstream carrying a great variety of minerals in very microscopic proportions.

A body weighing 160 pounds contains about five pounds of minerals distributed in the following proportions: 2 pounds of calcium, 1 pound of phosphorus, 4 ounces of potassium, 2 ounces of sodium and chlorine, ½ ounce magnesium, 1/10 ounce iron, and 14 other minerals which have been proven to be needed by the body but are present in such small amounts that they are called trace minerals. There are also minerals in our bodies which have not been shown to be needed by our body, such as gold, silver, etc. There are also minerals which are present in our bodies that can actually be dangerous in just a little larger quantity, such as lead and mercury. Unfortunately, these are becoming well-known as pollution of the environment makes its way into the food chain.

Since minerals are obtained from the earth, water, and air, maintaining the natural balance of our environment and the environment our food is raised in is important. The mineral content of foods varies a great deal depending on the mineral content of the soil they were grown in, which is a strong reason for growing your own vegetables in soil that you are personally replenishing with organic materials. In the following information about the good food sources of minerals, just bear in mind that the list is a general one which will vary depending on the mineral content of the soil and water the plants feed on.

CALCIUM

Necessary for: Formation of bones and teeth; also works with vitamin K in blood clotting; helps keep muscle tone healthy and nerves functioning properly; required in a delicate balance with several other minerals so muscles like the heart can contract and relax.

Good sources: Leafy green vegetables, water, almonds, legumes, dairy products, tofu, blackstrap molasses, alfalfa sprouts.

Deficiency symptoms: Stunted growth of bones and teeth if the deficiency is in early life. Therefore it is especially important for pregnant women to get enough calcium in their diet since the fetus gets its supply from the mother's blood and bone. It is also very important that infants and growing children get an adequate supply. Deficiency may cause stunted growth, deformed or poor quality bones and teeth, or irregular development of teeth and jaws. Soft bones in children (rickets) and brittle bones in adults (osteomalacia) may result if there is either a calcium deficiency or a lack of vitamin D in the diet to enable the calcium to be absorbed by the body.

SODIUM and POTASSIUM

Necessary for: Maintaining a balance inside and outside body cells so that nerves and muscles can function properly; maintaining a balance between acids and bases in body fluids. Sodium is also needed for the body to be able to absorb various nutrients; potassium is needed for releasing energy from proteins, fats and carbohydrates.

Good sources of sodium: Soy sauce, water, dairy products, miso, olives. *Vegetables*

Good sources of potassium: Leafy green vegetables, tomatoes, potatoes, dates, cantaloupe, bananas, apricots, citrus fruits, peas, bamboo shoots, prunes, butternut squash, legumes, papaya, avocado, brussel sprouts, beet greens, blackstrap molasses, alfalfa sprouts.

Deficiency symptoms: Sodium is another mineral which is found to be in excess rather than deficient in modern diets because of salt being added to commercially-prepared foods such as bread, butter, cheese and processed food products, as well as due to the popularity of salty snack foods and the habit most people have of adding salt to foods at the dinner table. Excessive salt intake may result in high blood pressure, hypertension, and strokes. However, in fever or excessive sweating, sodium and body fluids may be depleted which causes muscle cramping. Potassium deficiency is symptomized by muscular weakness, heart muscle irregularities, and respiratory and kidney failures. Use of medicinal diuretics may cause abnormal loss of potassium.

MAGNESIUM

Necessary for: Bones and teeth; release of energy from carbohydrates; synthesis of proteins; regulation of body temperature; proper contraction of nerves and muscles; neutralizing acid in the stomach; flushing out intestines.

Good sources: Whole grains, legumes, nuts, leafy vegetables; also found in fresh fruits and vegetables, alfalfa sprouts, dates, figs, dairy products and nutritional yeast.

Deficiency symptoms: Muscle weakness, irregular heartbeat, irritability of nerves and muscles, spasms and convulsions. Most deficiencies are due to highly refined and processed food diets or use of diuretics for long periods.

PHOSPHORUS

Necessary for: Metabolism and release of energy from carbohydrates; formation of protein and transfer of hereditary characteristics from one generation of cells to another. Works in connection with calcium in bone formation and teeth structure.

Good sources: Legumes, whole grains, dairy products, nuts, tofu, nutritional yeast, wheat germ, bran, lima beans, peas, pumpkin seeds, blackstrap molasses, sesame seed and almond meal.

Deficiency symptoms: Possible softness or brittleness of the bones, since too much or too little phosphorus in relationship to the amount of calcium in the body results in an inability to use the calcium efficiently. Because phosphorus is plentiful in a variety of foods, it is more likely that phosphorus intake may be too high rather than too low, especially in meat-eaters' diets and in the diets of people who eat processed foods in which phosphates are used.

IODINE

Necessary for: Formation of a thyroid hormone which regulates various body functions, especially the "basal metabolic rate" (the minimum amount of energy the body needs just to exist without moving).

Good sources: Seaweed, water, vegetables grown close to the seashore.

Deficiency symptoms: Enlargement of the thyroid gland, called goitre; weight gain, extremely dry skin and development of a husky voice, feeling cold even in warm weather. Iodine deficiency in pregnancy will cause the baby to become a dwarf and be mentally retarded. Due to iodine being used in many store-bought, commercially prepared foods and overuse of iodized table salt, excessive consumption of iodine is more likely to take place than a deficiency. The results of too much iodine in the diet are the same as if there is a deficiency, since it interferes with the action of the thyroid gland in producing enough hormone to burn a normal amount of energy.

IRON

Necessary for: Carrying oxygen to the muscles to release the energy that they need to work.

Good sources: Leafy green vegetables, dried apricots, prunes, peaches, raisins, dates, legumes, nuts, whole grains, blackstrap molasses, tofu, sesame meal, alfalfa sprouts, peas, pumpkin seeds; also wheat germ, bran, soybean milk and nutritional yeast.

Deficiency symptoms: Weakened, tired, "washed-out" feeling; lowered resistance to infection. Teenagers and women are especially prone to iron-deficiency anemia, which results in reduced size of the red blood cells and less oxygen being able to reach the body and muscle cells.

ZINC

Necessary for: Formation of many hormones, including insulin, which regulates carbohydrate metabolism; formation of many enzymes, such as those involved in transporting carbon dioxide in the blood; growth and repair of tissues; synthesis of proteins and nucleic acids.

Good sources: Wheat germ, legumes, whole grains, nutritional yeast, milk products.

Deficiency symptoms: Subject of recent nutrition research. Case reports have included dwarfism, anemia, slow healing of wounds.

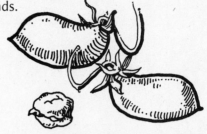

TRACE MINERALS

There is so much investigation going on in laboratories but there isn't anything conclusive except that there are many trace minerals which are thought to be essential in human nutrition and which can be supplied by eating a variety of whole, natural foods. It hasn't been established how much of the trace minerals are present in different foods, or even how much the body needs, although it has been observed that animals who are deprived of one or more of these trace minerals don't grow normally and have deformed offspring.

Some trace minerals include chromium, copper, chlorine, fluorine, manganese, and sulphur, which are contained in water, whole grains, legumes, nuts, milk, cheese, and leafy green vegetables. Fresh and dried fruits and both raw and cooked vegetables also supply some trace minerals needed by the body.

Deficiencies or imbalances may occur from such modern practices as refining grain, which removes some iron, manganese, chromium, zinc, and other essential minerals from the food supply. Since plants absorb minerals from the soil, modern agricultural methods which do not take into account possible unbalancing of soil minerals, may also affect the supply of such trace minerals as iodine, copper, zinc, chromium and selenium in produce. The environment also plays an important part, with heavy concentrations of lead coming from car fumes and industrial waste, as well as water supplies which often show major trace mineral imbalances.

"If a vegetarian became ill and a doctor prescribed beef tea, then I would not call him a vegetarian. A vegetarian is made of sterner stuff. Why? Because it is for the building of the spirit and not of the body. Man is more than meat. It is the spirit in us for which we are concerned."
— Mahatma Ghandi

BASICS

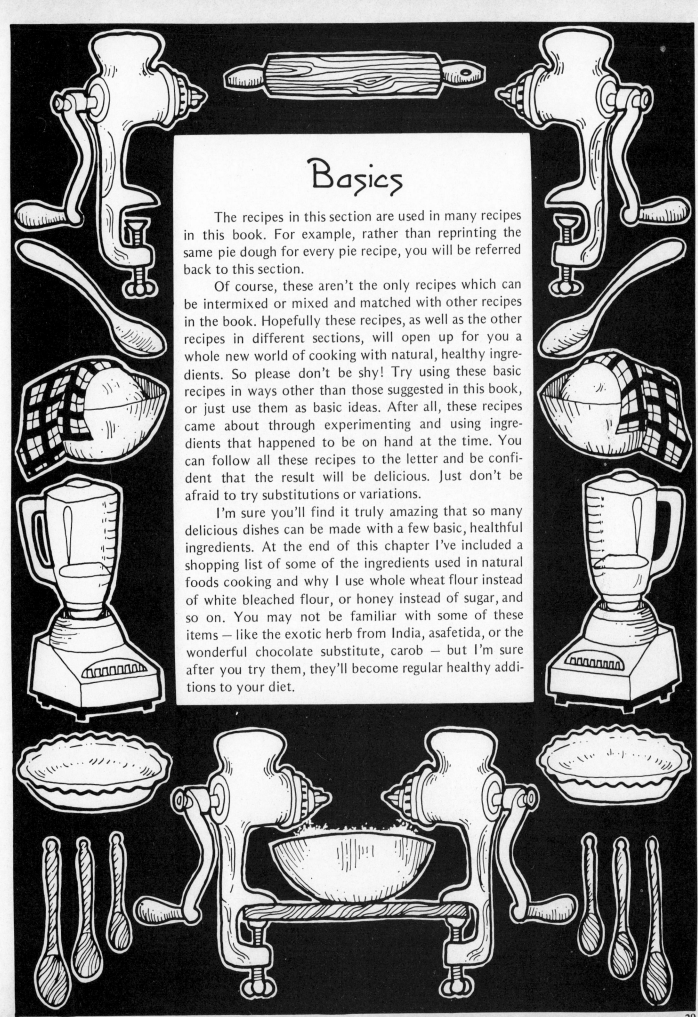

Basics

The recipes in this section are used in many recipes in this book. For example, rather than reprinting the same pie dough for every pie recipe, you will be referred back to this section.

Of course, these aren't the only recipes which can be intermixed or mixed and matched with other recipes in the book. Hopefully these recipes, as well as the other recipes in different sections, will open up for you a whole new world of cooking with natural, healthy ingredients. So please don't be shy! Try using these basic recipes in ways other than those suggested in this book, or just use them as basic ideas. After all, these recipes came about through experimenting and using ingredients that happened to be on hand at the time. You can follow all these recipes to the letter and be confident that the result will be delicious. Just don't be afraid to try substitutions or variations.

I'm sure you'll find it truly amazing that so many delicious dishes can be made with a few basic, healthful ingredients. At the end of this chapter I've included a shopping list of some of the ingredients used in natural foods cooking and why I use whole wheat flour instead of white bleached flour, or honey instead of sugar, and so on. You may not be familiar with some of these items — like the exotic herb from India, asafetida, or the wonderful chocolate substitute, carob — but I'm sure after you try them, they'll become regular healthy additions to your diet.

Raw Sunflower Seed Pie Shell, p. 32   Candy No-bake Pie Shell, p. 32   Raw Carob-Nut Crust, p. 32

BASIC BREAD DOUGH ○

1 Tbsp. bulk dry yeast
or 1 envelope Fleischmann's, etc.
1¼ cups warm water

1 Tbsp. oil
¼ cup honey
1/3 tsp. salt

3 cups whole wheat flour
½ tsp. baking powder

Put yeast in warm water and let sit a few minutes until it dissolves. Add next 3 ingredients. Sift in dry ingredients and mix well. Turn dough onto floured counter and knead until it forms a soft, firm ball. Shape dough into desired shapes, put on oiled baking sheet or bread pan and set in oven on warm or pilot light for 10 minutes. Leaving bread in oven, turn up to 400° and bake for 20 to 25 minutes. Test to see if it's done by tapping with fingernail, listening for a hollow sound. This dough is very versatile and makes good bread, buns, cinnamon rolls, manapua, etc.

BASIC BROTH ○

4 stalks celery
4 beets, grated
4 small potatoes, cubed
¼ cup olive oil
¼ cup soy sauce or miso

½ cup fresh basil leaves, chopped
6 cups water

Lightly sauté first 5 ingredients until vegetables are covered with oil and soy sauce. Add last 2 ingredients and simmer at least 20 minutes. Strain through a strainer. Use this broth as a base for soups, gravies, etc.

HOMEMADE YOGURT ○

Yogurt is a tangy, semisolid, cultured milk that is low in fat and calories. One cup plain yogurt made from part skimmed milk contains 125 calories and 4 grams of fat. It is high in nutritional value, very easily digested, assists the digestive system to assimilate other foods and helps to maintain a healthy intestinal system. It is a good source of protein (1 cup containing 8 grams), calcium and other minerals, and it can be prepared easily and inexpensively at home.

Recipe:
4 cups water
1 cup noninstant dry milk
(nonfat or whole)
2 oz. yogurt

Set out yogurt culture (to reach room temperature). Blend up milk powder and medium-hot tap water until smooth. Pour into large enough saucepan (holds at least 1 quart) and let cool to 110° — not too hot or it will destroy the yogurt culture. Blend up 1 cup of milk with yogurt until smooth and add to remaining milk. Pour into a 1-quart jar and either place in oven with pilot light on (wrapped in a towel) or wrap in a towel and set in sun for 4 to 6 hours. Milk must be maintained at 110° to 115° to turn to yogurt. After it has set, place in refrigerator to chill (will thicken more as it cools). For tangier yogurt, leave it heated for an extra hour or so.

Variation: Yogurt may also be made with milk from a carton. Bring to a boil, let it cool to 110° and follow instructions as above.

HEALTHY SODA ▢

1 part unsweetened fruit juice
(apple, orange, grape, etc.)
1 part fizzy mineral water

Pour the two chilled ingredients together and serve immediately.

RAW PIE CRUST ☐

1 cup toasted, grated coconut
½ cup bran
½ cup wheat germ
½ cup mashed, pitted dates
4 Tbsp. honey
1 tsp. lemon juice

Combine ingredients and mix well. Press evenly into an oiled 9'' pie plate. Pour in filling, chill and serve.

RAW SUNFLOWER SEED PIE SHELL ☐

1 cup sunflower seeds
1/3 cup honey

Run sunflower seeds through a food grinder or a blender to get sunflower seed meal. Add honey and press into an oiled pie tin. Use any pudding or kanten recipe as a filling.

RAW COCONUT PIE CRUST ☐

1½ cups toasted, grated coconut
¼ cup peanut butter
¼ cup honey
½ cup currants or raisins

Combine ingredients and press into pie tin.

CANDY NO-BAKE PIE SHELL ☆

4 Tbsp. butter or margarine
½ cup maple syrup

Puffed rice or millet
Assortment of chopped nuts or seeds
¼ cup raisins

Cook first 2 ingredients to a soft-ball candy consistency (test by dropping a tiny drop into some cold water — should form a soft ball). Remove from heat and add enough of the remaining ingredients so they are nicely coated with syrup. Pour into a buttered pie pan and press down with a buttered spoon. Good with any raw filling or pudding, etc. One good filling for this is 1 cup of Soy Whipped Cream (see Basic Recipes Section, p. 34) with fruit of the season folded in.

OILLESS CRACKER CRUST ☐

1 cup ground, oilless
whole-grain cracker crumbs

1 Tbsp. liquid lecithin
¼ cup honey
1 Tbsp. water

Blend crackers in blender until almost like a flour. Combine with rest of ingredients and press into a pie pan. If the mix sticks to your hands, dip hands into water to prevent sticking.

SPROUTED WHEATBERRY PIE CRUST ○

2 cups sprouted wheatberries

¼ cup chopped dates
½ cup chopped sunflower seeds

Put wheatberries through a food grinder. Mix in other ingredients and press into oiled pie tin. Place in direct sun all day long to "bake." Fill with filling that doesn't require baking.

RAW CAROB-NUT CRUST ☐

1 cup nuts or seeds or a combination
½ cup carob powder
2 Tbsp. nut butter
½ cup dates, chopped or
put through a food grinder
1 tsp. grated orange rind
Enough water to make moldable

Put nuts or seeds through a food grinder or a blender to get nut or seed meal. Combine with all other ingredients and press into a pie tin. Fill with any pudding or raw pie filling.

FLAKY PIE CRUST ☆

2 cups whole wheat flour
2 Tbsp. wheat germ or bran
1 tsp. salt

¾ cup butter or margarine (softened)

4 to 5 Tbsp. ice water

Preheat oven to 450°. Combine first 3 ingredients. Add butter and mix with a fork until mixture is like cornmeal. May need to rub it together with your hands. Sprinkle in ice water, a little at a time, and mix with fork until pastry is just moist enough to hold together. Roll into a ball and cut in half. Roll into two balls. Place one between two sheets of wax paper and roll out to an 11" circle. Remove top sheet of paper and turn the piece with pastry over the pie tin; remove paper and mold into place. Crimp edges and pierce generously with a fork. Bake at 450° for 10 minutes. Makes two 9" pie shells.

PLAIN PASTRY (for fruit pies) ☆

2 cups whole wheat pastry flour
1 tsp. salt

½ cup butter (softened) or margarine

¼ cup cold milk

Sift first 2 ingredients. Work in butter with a fork or pastry cutter. Gradually pour in milk. Mix well — lightly and quickly. Place between two 12" pieces of wax paper and roll out in a circle until it reaches the edge. Peel off top paper. Turn the piece with pastry over a 9" pie tin. Remove paper and mold into place. Pierce with a fork. Roll out the top crust in the same way. Place over filled pie and tuck edges under bottom crust. Crimp edges or press with a fork to seal. Snip four slits in center of pie or pierce with fork. Bake at temperature indicated in specific recipe being used.

GRAHAM CRACKER CRUST ☆

2 cups finely crushed graham crackers
½ cup butter or margarine, melted
4 Tbsp. honey

Crush crackers with a rolling pin between two pieces of wax paper or in a plastic bag. Mix with butter and honey. Should be moist enough to hold together; if necessary, add a little water. Press into a 9" pie plate and set in freezer to chill. Pour in filling.

CRUMBLY CRUST ☆

Crust:
1 stick butter or margarine (softened)
2 Tbsp. honey
1 cup whole wheat flour
¾ cup rolled oats
½ cup sesame seeds

Combine crust ingredients. Mix well with a fork or fingers. Add a little water if necessary. Press and mold into pie plate. Put in pie filling.

Topping:
1 stick butter or margarine (softened)
¾ cup whole wheat flour
½ cup rolled oats
½ cup sesame seeds
Honey

Prepare topping by combining first 4 ingredients. Mix until nice and crumbly. Sprinkle evenly over filled pie. Drizzle generously with honey and follow baking directions in recipe. Usually 375° for 20 minutes until browning on top.

DIRECTIONS FOR MIXING SOY MILK POWDER □

For 1 quart:
4 cups water
1 cup soy milk powder

For 1 cup:
1 cup water
¼ cup soy milk powder

Combine and blend in blender or shake or stir with a whisk. For a better tasting soy milk, mix water and soy powder as above and let stand at room temperature for about two hours, stirring occasionally. Cook in double boiler over boiling water for 20 minutes. Allow to cool. Strain through cheesecloth and refrigerate. Very good with a pinch of salt, drop of vanilla and ½ tsp. of honey per cup.

SOY WHIPPED CREAM □

1 cup soy milk
1 tsp. vanilla
1 - 2 Tbsp. honey

1½ cups oil (safflower is good)

1 Tbsp. lemon juice

Combine first 3 ingredients and mix in blender until blended. Blending on the lowest speed, gradually add oil. Mixture will thicken and become a bit fluffy. Scoop from blender into a bowl. Add lemon juice, mixing with a fork or whisk until it whips up. Set in refrigerator and chill. Use wherever whipped cream is called for.

DIRECTIONS FOR MIXING NONINSTANT DRY MILK □

1 cup water
1/3 cup noninstant dry milk powder
(nonfat, whole or buttermilk)
or ¼ cup milk powder

When using non-instant dry milk, it is necessary to liquify it either in a blender or with a whisk. Combine ingredients and blend until smooth and free from lumps. If you prefer thinner milk, use ¼ cup powder. Refrigerate until cold, then serve.

EGGLESS SOY MAYONNAISE □

1 cup rich soy milk
4 tsp. honey

1 - 1½ cups safflower oil

4 tsp. apple cider vinegar

1 tsp. salt
¼ tsp. black pepper

Blend first 2 ingredients on a low speed, gradually adding oil until it whips up and no longer agitates. Scoop into a bowl and whip in (with a fork or whisk) the next 2 ingredients, adding gradually. Mixture will stiffen. Add last 2 ingredients. Mix well and chill. Serve just like mayonnaise.

BASIC FRUIT SAUCE ○

½ cup honey
½ cup water or fruit juice
1 Tbsp. arrowroot powder
1 Tbsp. lemon juice

2 cups sliced fruit

Combine first 4 ingredients and mix until arrowroot dissolves. Put on heat, stirring to prevent lumping. Simmer, add fruit, and cook on low heat for 10 minutes until thick.

FRUIT LEATHER ○

4 cups fruit
Honey to taste

Puree fruit (if it is berries, work through a fine sieve to remove seeds). Thoroughly blend desired amount of honey into fruit puree. Pour fruit on lightly oiled cookie sheets, 1/8" to 1/4" thickness, or else onto wax paper that has been secured to cookie sheet with tape. (This helps to prevent curling.) May place in warm oven (under 200°, leaving door slightly ajar during drying) or outside in the sun (a solar food dryer is ideal). Dry for 24 hours or until moisture-free and firm like leather. Peel off while warm and roll up, paper and all. Store in tight container to keep pliable. May freeze also and take out to thaw 10 minutes before eating.

MILK POWDER FROSTING ☆

½ cup butter or margarine
¾ cup honey
1 tsp. vanilla

1 cup milk powder
3 - 4 Tbsp. water

Cream together first 3 ingredients. Gradually mix in milk powder until smooth. Add water until desired consistency is reached. Frost cooled cake. Can make variations by adding different flavor extracts, carob powder, etc.

FRUCTOSE FROSTING ☆

2/3 cup butter or margarine
2 cups fructose
¼ cup milk or water
1 tsp. vanilla
5 Tbsp. carob powder
1 tsp. Pero (coffee substitute)
in 3 Tbsp. hot water

Cream all ingredients together. Any frosting using powdered sugar can be made by substituting fructose.

BASIC WHITE ICING ☆

½ cup butter or margarine
½ cup honey
1 tsp. vanilla

½ cup non-fat milk powder
½ cup buttermilk powder
¼ - ½ cup water

Cream together first 3 ingredients. Gradually mix in milk powder and then water.

Variations:
1) Use ½ tsp. lemon rind and lemon juice instead of water.
2) Use 2 tsp. orange rind and orange juice instead of water.
3) Leave out water and use ½ cup or so of mashed fruit (strawberries, blueberries, etc.).

PAKORA BATTER
(Indian Spicy Tempuras) ☆

1 cup whole wheat or garbanzo flour
1 tsp. ground cumin
1 tsp. turmeric
1½ tsp. ground coriander
¼ tsp. crushed chilies or 1/8 tsp. cayenne
1/8 tsp. clove powder
1/8 tsp. asafetida

2 Tbsp. yogurt
1 cup water

Mix together first 7 ingredients. Add last 2 ingredients and stir until it makes a smooth batter. Dip vegetables of your choice into the batter and deep fry following directions for Tempura Batter #1. These are delicious served with Tomato Chutney (see Garden Vegetables Section, p. 263).

TEMPURA BATTER #1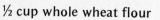

½ cup whole wheat flour
½ cup brown rice flour
½ cup egg replacer
½ tsp. asafetida or onion/garlic powder
1 Tbsp. soy sauce
2 cups water

Oil for deep frying

Heat oil to about 345°. In the meantime, mix ingredients together to form a thick batter. Dip vegetables (most cut to ½" thickness), tofu, etc., one at a time into the batter to coat them evenly and drop into medium-hot oil. Test oil before putting a whole tempura in to cook by dropping a few drips of the batter into the oil. If the oil is the right temperature, the batter should bubble rapidly and float to the top of the oil within 10 to 15 seconds. Put as many pieces of tempura in as the pot can hold. Fry on both sides until batter is golden brown and crisp to the touch of the slotted spoon used to remove them. Remove the tempura with a slotted spoon, allowing excess oil to drip back into the pan. Place the tempura on paper toweling to absorb excess oil. If you are cooking a great deal of tempuras and want to keep them crisp and warm, just have the oven preheated to 200° and place some paper toweling on a cookie sheet and wire cake coolers or any other wire rack on top of the paper toweling. Place already cooked tempuras on top of the wire rack. Serve the tempuras with an Oriental dipping sauce (see Tofu Section, p. 373) or a favorite but not exactly traditional ketchup or tomato sauce.

TEMPURA BATTER #2 ☆

½ cup arrowroot
½ cup whole wheat flour
½ cup brown rice flour
1 Tbsp. soy sauce
1 Tbsp. oil
1 tsp. baking soda
1 tsp. baking powder
2 cups water

This batter can be made if you don't have egg replacer. Follow procedure as for Tempura Batter #1.

TEMPURA BATTER #3

¼ cup soy flour
¼ cup arrowroot
¼ cup whole wheat flour
¼ cup brown rice flour
2 Tbsp. corn flour

1 Tbsp. soy sauce
1 cup fizzy water (bubbly spring water)

Combine first 5 ingredients and mix well. Heat oil and prepare vegetables. As soon as everything is ready, at the very last moment add last 2 ingredients to the first 5. Mix thoroughly. Quickly dip vegetables and cook as described in Tempura Batter #1.

WHEAT-FREE THIN TEMPURA BATTER

½ cup arrowroot
¼ cup brown rice flour
½ tsp. baking powder
1 tsp. turmeric
2 tsp. soy sauce
½ cup water

Follow procedure as for Tempura Batter #1 (see recipe this page).

A DIFFERENT DEEP-FRYING OIL

2 cups peanut oil
1 cup safflower or sunflower oil
1 cup toasted sesame oil

Mix together and heat for deep frying as recipe calls for. This mix of oils makes a delicious oil for deep frying. It adds a different taste to your deep-fried foods.

You'll probably notice that many of the recipes use a great deal of herbs and spices for flavoring. Buying herbs and spices in places where you can weigh out your own turns out to be cheaper (many health food or natural food stores offer this option). Buying the herbs and spices in a whole or semiwhole form and grinding them yourself makes for fresher spices in your cooking. Of course, a real luxury is a fresh herb garden in your own yard where you can pick herbs fresh or dry them yourself. All the recipes I've given below for some of the most commonly used spice and herb blends call for the spice in its ground or powdered form. You can buy them in their whole form and grind them in the blender or in a special hand grinding mill which you can purchase specifically for grinding spices.

CURRY POWDER

5 Tbsp. turmeric
1/3 cup coriander
1 Tbsp. + 2 tsp. fenugreek seeds
1 Tbsp. white pepper
1½ tsp. mustard powder
1 tsp. cayenne
2 tsp. allspice or cinnamon
1 tsp. ginger
1 tsp. cloves
1 tsp. asafetida or garlic powder

Grind spices if they're not already in their powdered form. Measure and mix together thoroughly. Keep in a covered jar out of the reach of sunlight.

SRI LANKA CURRY POWDER

¾ cup coriander
1 cinnamon stick (2 inches)
6 black peppercorns

1/3 cup cumin seeds
1/3 cup fennel seeds
2 Tbsp. fenugreek seeds
5 cloves
4 cardamom pods (seeds only)
2 heaping Tbsp. raw rice

1 tsp. black mustard seeds

In a dry skillet, roast first 3 ingredients until coriander seeds are light brown. Remove from the skillet. In the same skillet, roast next 6 ingredients. When the spices are crisp, add the black mustard seeds and continue to roast for 2 or 3 minutes more. Mix both batches of roasted spices and grind to a fine powder in a blender or with mortar and pestle.

FRESH GROUND CURRY POWDER

¼ cup turmeric
¼ cup cumin seeds
3 Tbsp. coriander seeds
1 Tbsp. ginger powder
1 Tbsp. black peppercorns
1 Tbsp. cardamom pods
2 tsp. whole cloves
1 tsp. fennel seeds
1 tsp. cayenne pepper
1 tsp. black mustard seeds
1 tsp. fenugreek seeds
1 tsp. nutmeg
1 tsp. cinnamon
1 tsp. asafetida

Grind herbs in food mill or blender until all are like a fine powder. You will be especially surprised and pleased at how much fresher and nicer your curries taste using fresh ground spices!

PUMPKIN PIE SPICING

7 Tbsp. cinnamon
3 Tbsp. + 1 tsp. ginger
3 Tbsp. + 1 tsp. nutmeg
1 Tbsp. + 2 tsp. allspice
1 Tbsp. + 2 tsp. cloves

Grind spices if they are not already in the powdered form. Measure and mix together thoroughly. Store in a covered jar out of the reach of sunlight.

GOMASIO (Sesame Salt) ○

5 parts sesame
1 part salt

Toast sesame seeds and grind. Add salt to ground seeds. Use in place of salt on top of vegetables, rice, etc.

CHILI POWDER ☐

5 Tbsp. cayenne pepper
4 Tbsp. cumin
4 Tbsp. oregano
2 Tbsp. marjoram
2 Tbsp. coriander
2 tsp. asafetida
1 tsp. allspice
½ tsp. cloves

Grind spices if they are not already in the powdered form. Measure and mix together thoroughly. Store in a covered jar out of the reach of sunlight.

POULTRY SEASONING SPICE ☐

¼ cup white pepper
3 Tbsp. sage
2 Tbsp. thyme
2 Tbsp. marjoram
2 Tbsp. savory
1 Tbsp. + 2 tsp. ginger
2½ tsp. allspice
2½ tsp. nutmeg

Grind spices if they are not already in the powdered form. Measure and mix together thoroughly. Store in a covered jar out of the reach of sunlight.

BASIC FRUIT JELL ○

3¾ cups fruit juice
¼ cup honey
1 stick agar-agar (½ cup flakes)

Mix ingredients together and let soak until agar-agar softens. Then bring to a boil, stirring often until agar is melted. Remove from heat, pour into a mold and refrigerate until set. The amount of juice and honey may vary according to the kind of juice being used. The main idea is to use 4 cups of liquid to 1 stick of agar. Chopped fresh fruit may be added to this. If the fruit is a juicy kind, decrease the amount of juice accordingly. It is best to add the fruit after mixture has been cooked, removed from heat and allowed to cool down a bit. This prevents fruit from getting cooked and losing vitamins.

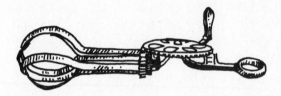

JELLY ROLL DOUGH ☆

1 cup sifted whole wheat flour
1 tsp. baking soda
¼ tsp. salt

3 tsp. egg replacer
6 Tbsp. water

½ cup honey
¼ cup soft butter or margarine
¼ cup yogurt
1 tsp. vanilla

Fructose

Preheat oven to 375° F. Grease a 15"x 10" x 1" pan, line with wax paper and grease the paper. Sift first 3 ingredients together. Beat egg substitute and water in bowl until fluffy. Cream next 4 ingredients and mix in. Fold in dry ingredients and spread batter evenly in pan. Bake at 375° for about 12 minutes (until center of cake springs back when touched lightly with finger). Immediately turn cake onto a clean towel that has been sprinkled with fructose. Peel off wax paper. Fill with desired fillings, or use Pineapple Jelly Roll Filling (see recipe in Pineapple Section, p. 215). Use the towel to support the spongy cake while rolling up. This will help to prevent the jelly roll from sticking and cracking.

CREPES

Crepes are an economical, yet gourmet way to serve an entree, a dessert, or dress up leftovers. Here are a few basic recipes for making crepes which can then be filled and covered with many of the recipes in the other sections of this book. Just use your imagination!

BASIC CREPE RECIPE #1   O

1 cup whole wheat flour
2 cups milk (soy or other)
3 Tbsp. butter, margarine or oil
1 Tbsp. arrowroot

Blend ingredients together in blender. Let sit 10 to 15 minutes. It will be thin as milk, but don't worry. In small 8" or 10" T-fal skillet, pour 1/4 to 1/3 cup batter with one hand, turning skillet at the same time with the other hand so batter spreads evenly on the bottom of the skillet. Cook on medium-high flame until golden brown on one side. Slide spatula under and gently flip. Let cook about 30 seconds on opposite side. Fill with your favorite garden vegetable or entree (good way to use up leftovers) and top with your favorite sauce or dressing.

BASIC CREPE RECIPE #2   O

1 cup brown rice flour
1½ cups milk (soy or other)
1 Tbsp. vegetable oil

Follow directions for Basic Crepe Recipe #1 except let sit one hour at room temperature or all day/overnight in the refrigerator after blending ingredients together.

HOW TO MAKE A CREPE ROLL:

1. Place crepe with best-looking side down on working surface. Spread filling over entire surface of crepe, leaving a little of the edge bare.

2. Just start at one end of the crepe and start rolling as you would for a jelly roll.

3. Place with loose end tucked underneath.

This shape is recommended for thicker, firmer fillings, not runny ones. This is a good shape for hors d'oeuvres because the roll can be cut into finger-food sizes.

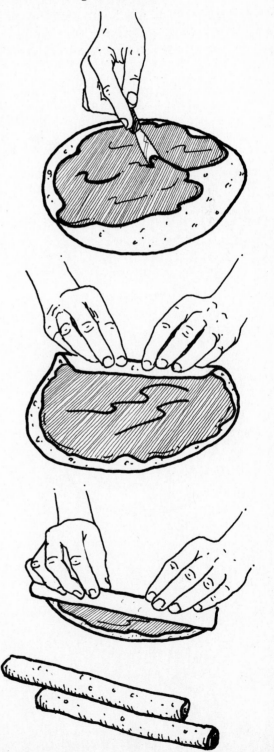

HOW TO FOLD CREPE SUZETTES:

1. Place crepe with best-looking side down on working surface. Place filling in center and fold in half. This is a good way to fold crepes to use for making sandwiches.

2. Fold in half again to get a triangle shape.

These are good filled with a creamy filling, then cooked and served in hot syrups or sauces. They can also be served plain as hors d'oeuvres.

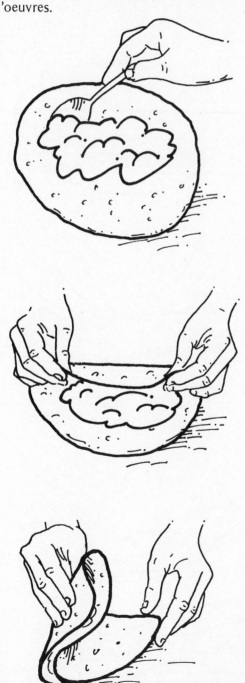

HOW TO MAKE THE TRADITIONAL CREPE FOLD-OVER:

1. Place crepe with the best-looking side down on working surface. Spread filling in a 1" to 2" strip right down the center of the crepe.

2. Fold one edge of the crepe over filling.

3. Fold the other side over so it overlaps the first fold. The filling should be peeking out on both ends.

This is a good way to serve and show off entrees and desserts. Usually serve topped with a sauce or syrup.

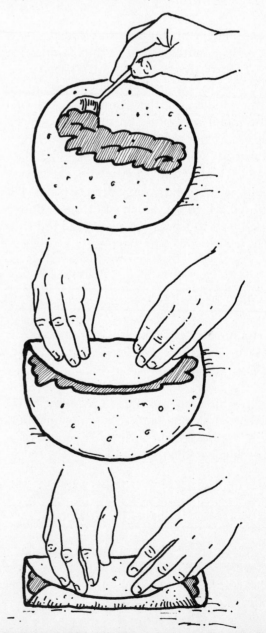

HOW TO STACK A GATEAU:

1. Place crepe with best side up. Spread filling over entire surface of crepe, leaving about ½" around edges bare.

2. Spread as many crepes as you desire and just stack them one on top of another to the desired height. A spatula will be a big help in doing this.

This is a good way to make an entree or dessert. Top with sauces or Soy Whipped Cream (see Basic Recipes Section, p. 34).

3. Then fold two edges to the right and left of the already-folded edge over each other.

4. Fold the remaining edge over all the already-folded edges. Place with folded side down on working surface.

This is similar to a burrito. You can also roll crepes like you would roll a burrito. This way of folding keeps the filling inside so it's not leaking out everywhere! It's ideal for hors d'oeuvres and if you want to deep fry the blintzes. (For deep frying, keep the darker side of the crepe on the inside.)

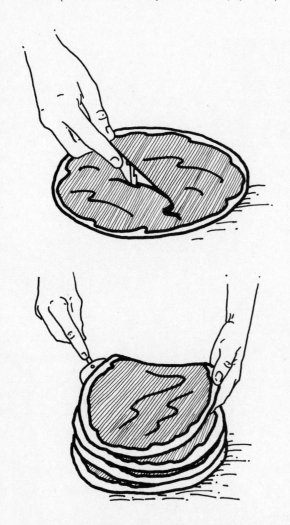

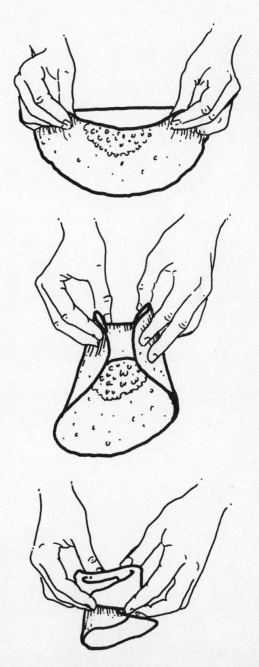

HOW TO FOLD A BLINTZ:

1. Place crepe with the best-looking side down on working surface. Spoon the filling into the center.

2. Fold bottom edge of crepe over so it covers at least half the filling.

GHEE (Clarified Butter)

Ghee is butter that has had all the water, salt and impurities cooked off, turning it into a very light, delicate, sweet oil of the finest quality. Ghee once made will keep indefinitely without refrigeration. It will stay on the shelf sweet, golden and semiliquid, ready for use whenever needed. It takes 10 pounds of butter to make 1 gallon of ghee.

Recipe:

Place butter in a heavy pot, filling the pot ½ to ¾ of the way when melted. Let the butter melt on a medium flame until it begins to foam up. With a large spoon, skim off the foam into a large bowl, being careful not to take any liquid with it. Lower the heat and keep cooking. The butter will clarify gradually and solids will keep rising to the top. The solids will begin to be crusty instead of foamy. Be careful not to burn the ghee. Keep skimming every 10 minutes or so until it is an amber color and no more solids rise to the top (1½ to 2½ hours). The few impurities which remain at the bottom can be strained by pouring the ghee into a container through a piece of muslin cloth, etc. Cover with lid and store until needed.

1) MELTING   2) CLARIFYING   3) SKIMMING   4) STRAINING

SHOPPING LIST

Changing over to a more nutritionally sound, healthy diet is not really that much of an endeavor. It just seems that way because of having to use ingredients that are totally new, not knowing what they are or what to do with them. Walking into a natural food store or down the health food aisle of your local supermarket can be a confusing experience in this case.

I know from personal experience that you can end up spending a lot of money on unnecessary and overpriced ingredients. After many years, we have gotten shopping for family meals down to a science. Out of a few basic, inexpensive ingredients, we make a whole spectrum of preparations.

For a family of five, we spend anywhere from $150 to $200 a month on food. Besides the ingredients I buy in bulk — fresh fruit, sunflower seeds, brown rice and legumes — there are relatively few items that regularly appear on my shopping list. I have made up a list of these ingredients, and, as you can see, the list is not that long. In preparing the recipes in this book, these are the few items that may be new to you and your shopping list. There are not that many ingredients listed, and I think you will find that rather than complicate your life, cooking natural foods will actually help to simplify it.

AGAR-AGAR and/or OTHER SEAWEEDS.

As more and more foods commonly used in the East for centuries are becoming recognized for their healthful properties, seaweed is becoming more familiar. In fact, these foods are now available in the Oriental aisle of most supermarkets, natural and health food stores, whereas they used to be available only in Oriental food stores a few years ago.

This increased availability should logically lead to an increased use of seaweed, especially if we can get over the mental block that exists in a lot of people's minds concerning sea vegetables. I hope the recipes in the Seaweed Section will help with that and make the different seaweeds a healthful addition to your diet.

(From U.S.D.A. Agriculture Handbook #8)
AGAR-AGAR and GELATIN
100 gm. edible portion

	Agar-Agar	Gelatin, dry
Water	16.3%	13.0%
Food energy	–	335 calories
Protein	–	85.6 gm.
Fat	.3 gm.	.1 gm.
Carbohydrate	– (Total)	0 gm. (Total)
	.7 gm. (Fiber)	0 gm. (Fiber)
Ash	3.7 gm.	1.3 gm.
Calcium	567 mg.	–
Phosphorus	22 mg.	–
Iron	6.3 mg.	–
Sodium	–	–
Potassium	–	–
Vitamin A	–	–
Thiamine	–	–
Riboflavin	–	–
Niacin	–	–
Vitamin C	–	–

(From U.S.D.A. Agriculture Handbook #8)
ARROWROOT and CORNSTARCH
100 gm. edible portion

	Cornstarch	Arrowroot
Water	12.0%	13.9%
Food energy	362 calories	344 calories
Protein	.3 gm.	1.4 gm.
Fat	Trace	0
Carbohydrate	87.6 gm. (Total)	84.4 gm. (Total)
	.1 gm. (Fiber)	
Ash	.1 gm.	.3 gm.
Calcium	(0)	19 mg.
Phosphorus	(0)	54 mg.
Iron	(0)	3.4 mg.
Sodium	Trace	
Potassium	Trace	
Vitamin A	(0)	
Thiamine	(0)	
Riboflavin	(0)	
Niacin	(0)	
Vitamin C	(0)	

ARROWROOT. I use arrowroot in my recipes in place of cornstarch. Cornstarch is a refined, empty-calorie food. (Just as a note: This doesn't mean cornstarch is worthless. I have found cornstarch to be a superb baby powder and good for making paste for papier-mâché and other arts and crafts materials.) I prefer arrowroot because it's an easily digestible, unrefined product which contains enough vitamins and minerals (such as 58 mg. calcium per 100 gm.) to make the substitution worthwhile.

If you check prices, you'll note that

arrowroot is definitely more costly than cornstarch, but I always see it as what is saved on a food bill will end up being spent on a doctor bill if the so-called savings buys a less nutritious product. If you are looking for arrowroot, you'll probably have to go to a natural foods store, although a few supermarkets carry it in their health food aisles.

ASAFETIDA. Learning the art of using herbs for flavoring can really cut back on use of butter and salt in your diet. Most of the herbs and spices used in this cookbook are probably familiar to you except asafetida.

Asafetida is an herb made from the resin of the asafetida tree and used medicinally in the Far East as a stomach calmative and blood cleanser. It used to also be worn around people's necks in pouches "down South" in this country where it was believed to ward off disease. Most likely what happened was the pouch of asafetida smelled so bad that no one was able to get close enough to the wearer to pass any germs on! Asafetida definitely does have a strong smell!

It smells a lot like onions and garlic, and that's what I use in my cooking in place of onions or garlic. Asafetida doesn't leave any odor on the breath or come out through the pores (as garlic and onions do). Asafetida also doesn't cause belching or burping like onions or garlic do in some people.

Unfortunately, asafetida isn't easy to find. It can sometimes be found in Indian or Middle Eastern import food stores (sometimes known as "hing" in these stores), and sometimes in natural food stores. Just a little bit of asafetida goes a long way. A pinch adds the flavor equivalent to a clove of garlic or about a quarter of an onion, which you may have to use in these recipes if you can't find asafetida. There is also a liquid form of asafetida, which is even stronger than the powdered form. If you use this, decrease the amount of asafetida called for in a recipe to just a drop (the recipe measurements are given for powdered asafetida).

CAROB. This is another item you may be unfamiliar with. I use it in my cooking as a chocolate substitute, because not only does it taste better than chocolate, but it's better for the body as well.

Carob is more than just a flavor — it's actually a food. Another name for carob is "St. John's Bread" because St. John the Baptist is said to have lived on carob while he was in the desert. And no wonder! Gram for gram, carob has three times the amount of calcium that milk has; as much thiamine as asparagus, strawberries and dandelion greens; as much niacin as dates or lima beans; as much riboflavin as brown rice; as much vitamin A as beets; as well as being a fairly good source of minerals like phosphorus, iron and magnesium. All this good nutrition while getting the pleasing chocolatelike flavor and at the same time getting no caffeine and much less fat (23.7% in cocoa compared to 1.4% in carob!).

(From U.S.D.A. Agriculture Handbook #8)
CAROB and COCOA
100 gm. edible portion

	CAROB, powder	COCOA, powder (High-fat, plain)
Water	11.2%	3.0%
Food Energy	180 calories	299 calories
Protein	4.5 gm.	16.8 gm.
Fat	1.4 gm.	23.7 gm.
Carbohydrate	80.7 gm. (Total)	48.3 gm. (Total)
	7.7 gm. (Fiber)	4.3 gm. (Fiber)
Ash	2.2 gm.	5.0 gm.
Calcium	352 mg.	133 mg.
Phosphorus	81 mg.	648 mg.
Iron	–	10.7 mg.
Sodium	* 10.5 mg.	6 mg.
Potassium	* 787.5 mg.	1,522 mg.
Vitamin A	–	30 I.U.
Thiamine	–	.11 mg.
Riboflavin	–	.46 mg.
Niacin	–	2.4 mg.
Vitamin C	–	0

* Figures from University of Arizona College of Agriculture (Dashes denote lack of reliable data for a constituent believed to be present in measurable amount.)

You'll probably be amazed and pleased with how much carob powder resembles cocoa in appearance and taste! And it is becoming more available to you. It used to be that carob and candies made with it were only available in health food stores, but they are becoming more and more available in supermarkets as well. Carob can be bought either raw or roasted. The roasted kind has more of a chocolate flavor. The raw powder is very mild and sweet (carob is 46% natural sugar), which can cut down on the need to add sweetener to your preparation. And the cost? Carob is cheaper! Carob is $1.25 a pound compared to $1.97 for a half pound of cocoa powder and $2.17 for a half pound of unsweetened chocolate squares.

DATE SUGAR. Date sugar, as a healthy sweetener, certainly deserves a mention here; although, as can be seen in my recipes, I personally don't use it much.

It can't be used, as honey can, as a white sugar alternative because it's not as sweet and is too granular. When cooked in a sweet sauce, it doesn't dissolve but instead turns to the mushy consistency of dates, and when sprinkled on things to be baked will burn quickly. The best use I've found for date sugar is sprinkling it on top of already baked desserts, on top of frostings, or to top off a special fruit salad.

Date sugar definitely adds a special finishing touch, which could be seen by some as rather expensive and unnecessary. But if you want to add this touch, you can find date sugar in any health food or natural food store.

EGG REPLACER. Because I don't use eggs in my cooking, obviously they also aren't included in any of my recipes. In baking I usually replace eggs with yogurt, and you'll notice there are a few entrees where tofu actually replaces eggs nutritionally and in texture and taste. There are some recipes which call for egg replacer, and this means neither yogurt nor tofu. Rather, it means a commercially made egg replacer manufactured by "Jolly Joan." There may be other egg replacers on the market, but since this is an item I don't use often or shop around for, I'm not aware of any others. This egg replacer is used in my recipes strictly for duplicating the texture of eggs and not for the nutritional value. It is available through natural food stores and sometimes in the health food aisle of supermarkets. If you use this item as rarely as I do, it may be a good idea to buy the small packet size or store the flourlike mix in a glass jar with a lid.

HONEY. Throughout history, honey has played an important role as a food and a medicine, and, for the reasons it has played such an important role in the past, honey is the key sweetener used in my kitchen today.

The ancient Egyptians used honey as a dressing for wounds and burns and in many medicines to be taken internally. This isn't surprising, as honey is a natural antiseptic and antibiotic (bees manufacture a few different kinds of antibiotics which they inject into the honey, honeycomb and beeswax). These antiseptic and antibiotic properties explain why ancient Egyptian tombs have been opened up and jugs of honey found in them still perfectly intact.

Mohammed wrote, "Honey is a remedy for every illness of the body, and the Koran is a remedy for every illness of the mind. Therefore I recommend to you both remedies, honey and the Koran."

In our home, if and when the family gets a little cold or something, I do use honey as a medicine in a home remedy, but mostly it is in our kitchen as a food and sweetener. I use honey in place of white sugar, which is just an empty-calorie food.

(From U.S.D.A. Agriculture Handbook #8) HONEY and SUGAR 100 gm. edible portion		
	HONEY	SUGAR (granulated)
Water	17.2%	.5%
Food energy	304 calories	385 calories
Protein	.3 gm.	0
Fat	0	0
Carbohydrate	82.3 gm. (Total)	99.5 gm. (Total)
	—	0
Ash	.2 gm.	Trace
Calcium	5 mg.	0
Phosphorus	6 mg.	0
Iron	.5 mg.	.1 mg.
Sodium	5 mg.	1 mg.
Potassium	51 mg.	3 mg.
Vitamin A	0	0
Thiamine	Trace	0
Riboflavin	.04 mg.	0
Niacin	.3 mg.	0
Vitamin C	1 mg.	0

Not only does white sugar not add any nutrition to the body, it actually may deplete the body of B vitamins. Honey, on the other hand, is a food that adds nutrients along with the carbohydrates or sugars.

The exact nutritional value of honey depends on many variables, such as the kind of flowers the bees collected nectar from, the weather, etc. But no matter what kind of honey it is, honey contains vitamins B_1, B_2, B_3, B_6, pantothenic acid, folic acid, biotin, iron, copper, sodium, potassium, manganese, magnesium, phosphorus, calcium and enzymes. A general rule is the darker the honey, the more vitamins and minerals there are in it.

There are some things that are done to honey that will reduce its nutritional value. Very efficient filtering can remove some vitamins, and heating the honey will destroy vitamins also. When shopping for honey, it's important to look for words such as "raw," "unheated" and "unfiltered."

You'll probably find that you'll have a personal preference for a certain kind of honey, because each type of honey adds its own unique flavor to a preparation.

All of these wonderful aspects of using honey in your cooking may seem too expensive if you compare prices with white sugar. In actuality, honey is about twice as sweet as sugar so only half as much is needed, which makes the price about the same as white sugar. Honey is available in all supermarkets, natural food stores, etc. But if you are fortunate enough to be living by a beekeeper and can find out how he raises the bees (whether or not he supplements feeding the bees with white sugar water) and how he processes the honey from the hive, this is the best place to shop for your honey!

LECITHIN. Lecithin is a substance that is manufactured in our bodies in the liver and is contained in all cells. Lecithin is needed by our bodies to maintain a healthy lecithin-cholesterol balance. It acts as an emulsifier which keeps cholesterol in an emulsified state and flowing through the blood veins, preventing large, fatty deposits from building up on artery walls. (A buildup of such deposits leads to arteriosclerosis and heart disease.) It also regulates fat deposits in the liver.

Recent research has shown lecithin can actually lower blood cholesterol levels and break up fatty deposits already formed in the body. Considering all this, it's no wonder that there has been a rush of interest in lecithin. A reasonable question came to my mind when I began learning about lecithin. If it's so commonly and naturally occurring in foods we eat, is it really necessary to buy lecithin as a food supplement? On doing a little research, I found that the liver's production of lecithin can be affected by prolonged dietary insufficiencies, stress and/or overexertion. As far as the lecithin that is naturally contained in many foods, I found out that it is easily destroyed by food processing and heat. Thus the necessity for lecithin as a food supplement depends largely on dietary habits and lifestyle.

I add some to our family menu every day nonetheless, as there is no danger of getting too much lecithin and it is not a "trauma" to take.

Lecithin supplements come in many forms: liquid, tablets, powders, granules, etc. I personally use the granules and the liquid, and they are even in a lot of the recipes! Most of the lecithin on the market is made from soybeans, and that is the kind I'm always sure to get. (Eggs are a source of lecithin, but there is a great deal of controversy over whether the lecithin in eggs may be too saturated to do the body any good. Liver is also sometimes listed as a lecithin source, but the fact that eating the organ of an animal which has become a storehouse of

toxins because of its function of filtering poisons out of the bloodstream, combined with the fact that much of the lecithin is destroyed in cooking, make it an obvious source to avoid.) Lecithin is tasteless and adds a lot to texture in certain recipes as well.

If you've decided to add this healthy food to your diet, you will be able to find it in any natural food store and in many health food aisles in supermarkets.

MISO. There's a whole section on miso in the back of the book next to tofu because they're both by-products of the soybean. Miso is available in some supermarkets in the Oriental food aisle, but it would be better to get the miso found in the health food aisle or a health food or natural food store. This is because, as with soy sauce, miso has an impostor that is synthetically and chemically put together. Once again, reading the label is crucial. Look for information on how long it has been aged (natural miso will be anywhere from one-half to three years) to check whether it is a naturally fermented miso. Avoid miso that has been pasteurized or has the words "temperature controlled" on the container, as this indicates a synthetically made miso.

NONINSTANT POWDERED MILK. Nonfat, noninstant milk powder is a bit of a pain to work with, but I feel it's definitely worth the extra effort. It makes thick, rich yogurt, candies and frostings. And you'll find if you try using instant powdered milk in its place for the recipes in this book, that they probably won't even turn out.

I first started using this nonfat, noninstant powdered milk when I started making my own yogurt. It made a good quality, inexpensive yogurt as opposed to very watery yogurts made from instant powders. Since then I have used it in place of instant powdered milk in most recipes. The only places the instant powdered milk may be preferable are when used in frostings and candies because the texture is much fluffier and lighter. If you are going to try finding noninstant milk powder for the first time, you'll probably have to try health food or natural food stores, as these are the only places I've been able to find this kind of milk powder.

NUTRITIONAL YEAST. Nutritional yeast is something altogether different from active baker's yeast (the kind for making bread and rolls), so don't run out and buy those little envelopes of active baking yeast! Although nutritional yeast is a cultivated yeast as is baking yeast, the similarity ends there. Nutritional yeast may also be familiar to you as brewer's yeast or food yeast.

Anyone who's ever heard of brewer's yeast or nutritional yeast knows how good it is for the body! Although the amount varies from brand to brand (again, this calls for label reading), it's safe to say that all nutritional yeasts are a good source of B vitamins, including vitamin B$_{12}$, protein and iron.

Many years ago, after reading about the nutritional value of brewer's or nutritional yeast, I decided to add it to the family's diet. After gagging our way through yeast in our fruit and smoothies (some people do like it this way), we discovered that nutritional yeast was absolutely delicious on vegetables, grains, or entree-type food. It seems to add a rich, cheesy flavor. It has replaced the salt and pepper shakers on our table and made its way into many a recipe, as you'll see in the following pages.

My children like nutritional yeast so much, and on everything, that I sometimes have to hide it so we won't run out too quickly! After all, it is fairly expensive at an average of $3 per pound at this writing. I told someone that the other day and they didn't think that was very expensive at all (in comparison to meats, poultry, fish, cheese, etc.), but I guess it's all pretty relative. Yeast is certainly one of the most expensive food items I buy for our family.

Yeast can be purchased in any natural food store and some supermarkets with health food sections in them. You may want to do a little experimenting when choosing a yeast, as they all have a different taste. There are some I like and some that I don't, although my children like any kind! There are some cheesy flavored ones, some with a sweet flavor, smoked flavored kinds, and some very yeasty tasting—quite a wide range to choose from to find one to your liking!

OILS. All the recipes in this book that call for oil or vegetable oil leave you with a large selection to choose from. I use vegetable oils because they are polyunsaturated; and specifically when I shop, I'm sure to get cold-pressed safflower or sunflower oil because they are the most unsaturated oils of all and stand #1 and #2 in linoleic acid content.

In our everyday home cooking, I rarely heat oil and therefore go out of my way to get cold-pressed oils, which are available in all natural food stores.

RED BEAN CURD. This is not an item you'll need to make a majority of the recipes given in this book. But if you happen to be in or by Chinatown or an Oriental food store, it might be something you may want to pick up for the time you do need it in a recipe. It comes canned and will last indefinitely on a shelf until the can is opened. I thought I would just make a quick mention of this so you would know where you can get it.

RICE, NATURAL BROWN. Although refined, white rice is more familiar to us in the United States and is even a status symbol in some countries (because the brown, unrefined rice is the kind the peasants eat), you'll notice that, as with other grains, I use the whole, unrefined grain in my recipes.

Unrefined, brown rice contains all the nutrients put there by nature, whereas polished or white rice usually retains only 53% of the minerals, 84% of the protein and 38% of the vitamins. In the refining process, the naturally nutrition-packed grains go through so much. Processors rub them, polish them (removing the polish which is high in vitamins A, B_1, niacin, calcium and phosphorus) and sometimes bleach and then cover them with talc and glucose!

So, not only is it unnecessary to go to the expense of refining grains, but it is also unhealthy! The result of this modern, "progressive" refining method is that it not only decreases the nutrients, but at the same time removes the natural fiber — what grandma refers to as "roughage." Do you ever remember having your grandmother tell you to be sure to eat your "roughage foods" because they're good for you? Of course, this is something which has been proven in recent medical findings. We now know that fiber is essential to the diet and plays a large role in preventing constipation, hemorrhoids and cancer of the colon, etc.

What is ironic is that the discarded bran or rice polish, after being refined off of the whole grain, is then sold as is in health food stores or in the form of vitamin B pills (which might not be needed if foods were left in their natural state in the first place) at a cost greater than the original cost of the unpolished grain. This is also done with whole wheat.

The total lack of logic of this situation reminds me of a remark the British economist E. F. Schumacher made in his book, **Small Is Beautiful:**

"If human vices such as greed and envy are systematically cultivated, the inevitable result is nothing less than a collapse of intelligence. A man driven by greed or envy loses the power of seeing things as they really are, of seeing things in their roundness and wholeness, and his very successes become failures. If whole societies become infected by these vices, they may indeed achieve astonishing things but they become increasingly incapable of solving the most elementary problems of everyday existence."

He was, of course, addressing the subject of economics with this remark. But our economic system and even our very attitude towards life, as addressed in the quote also, has everything to do with the most basic parts of our living — like what our eating habits are, what our consumption patterns are, what goods are readily available to us, and even why unrefined grains cost more than refined grains in the market.

It used to be that brown rice could only be found in health food stores. But, because demand for it has grown — along with a growing awareness on the part of people in America about how diet and health are in-

(From U.S.D.A. Agriculture Handbook #8)
RICE
100 gm. edible portion

	Brown, cooked	White enriched, cooked	White unenriched, cooked
Water	70.3%	72.6%	72.6%
Food energy	119 calories	109 calories	109 calories
Protein	2.5 gm.	2.0 gm.	2.0 gm.
Fat	.6 gm.	.1 gm.	.1 gm.
Carbohydrate	25.5 gm. (Total)	24.2 gm. (Total)	24.2 gm. (Total)
	.3 gm. (Fiber)	.1 gm. (Fiber)	.1 gm. (Fiber)
Ash	1.1 gm.	1.1 gm.	1.1 gm.
Calcium	12 mg.	19 mg.	10 mg.
Phosphorus	73 mg.	28 mg.	28 mg.
Iron	.5 mg.	.9 mg.	.2 mg.
Sodium	282 mg.	374 mg.	374 mg.
Potassium	70 mg.	28 mg.	28 mg.
Vitamin A	(0)	(0)	(0)
Thiamine	.09 mg.	.11 mg.	.02 mg.
Riboflavin	.02 mg.	.01 mg.	.01 mg.
Niacin	1.4 mg.	1.0 mg.	.4 mg.
Vitamin C	(0)	(0)	(0)

separably linked — brown rice can now be found in supermarkets. The question of why unrefined, brown rice should cost the same as or more than refined, white rice (which undergoes more refining, thereby taking up more energy, labor, etc.) is still unanswered.

I'd like to make mention here of an alternative to brown rice, which is usually more palatable to those who've developed a taste for white rice and prefer its texture. Basmati rice is just as nutritious as brown rice and has the same taste and light texture that white rice has. I am mentioning it here because it is hard to find (usually only in gourmet or Mid-Eastern food stores) and is quite expensive (at about $.85 a pound).

SOY SAUCE.

In most of the recipes, as well as in my home cooking, I use soy sauce rather than salt. This is for a number of reasons. Soy sauce adds a unique flavor to food and at the same time adds a salty flavor. For all its salty flavor, you may be surprised to find out that there's usually an average of only 14% to 18% salt in most soy sauces. (For those of you on a low sodium diet, Kikkoman makes an equally delicious soy sauce that contains only 8.8% salt — "Kikkoman Milder Soy Sauce.") Soy sauce also contains about 7% protein and, because it is naturally brewed and fermented, it's full

(From U.S.D.A. Agriculture Handbook #8)
SOY SAUCE and SALT
100 gm. edible portion

	SOY SAUCE	SALT, table
Water	62.8%	.2%
Food energy	68 calories	0
Protein	5.6 gm.	0
Fat	1.3 gm.	0
Carbohydrate	9.5 gm. (Total)	0
	0	0
Ash	20.8 gm.	99.8 gm.
Calcium	82 mg.	253 mg.
Phosphorus	104 mg.	—
Iron	4.8 mg.	.1 mg.
Sodium	7,325 mg.	38,758 mg.
Potassium	366 mg.	4 mg.
Vitamin A	0	0
Thiamine	.02 mg.	0
Riboflavin	.25 mg.	0
Niacin	.4 mg.	0
Vitamin C	0	0

of enzymes and lactobacillus (the same kind of friendly bacteria whose presence benefits the stomach and intestines and aids digestion). With the popularity of Eastern cooking spreading, soy sauce is now available in just about any supermarket (although, as you'll see in these recipes, soy sauce isn't to be limited to only Eastern cooking). In shopping for soy sauce, you'll need to exercise a little care and read labels, as there are many synthetic or chemically made, so-called soy sauces that will neither give you the delectable flavor nor the healthy benefits of naturally brewed soy sauces. These synthetic soy sauces are characterized by listing such ingredients as hydrolyzed soy protein, corn syrup and caramel coloring on the label, which are put in to add color and flavor — but they don't measure up or come close to the taste of the real thing. Look for the words "naturally brewed."

SPIKE OR VEGIE-SALT. As I mentioned in the asafetida description, using herbs as a flavoring can cut way down on your salt and/or butter intake. Spike and Vegie-salt are two brands of dried herb and vegetable blends which are available in natural food stores and some supermarket health food aisles. Of course, both are more expensive than salt because of all the good dried vegetables and herbs in them, but they are so tasty that you only use a tiny bit at a time. The unique flavor of these herb and vegetable mixes often make a recipe, and if you try to substitute something else, the flavor just won't be the same.

TOASTED SESAME OIL. Sesame oil is called for in a few recipes and adds such a nice flavor to dishes that it's certainly worth trying. As its name implies, this oil is made from toasted sesame seeds, which make it distinctive in appearance and taste. The oil is a dark golden-brown color and smells and tastes like toasted sesame seeds. It lends a nice, toasted, sesame seed flavor to whatever dish it is used in. The taste is rather strong, so I sometimes dilute it half and half with a more tasteless, cold-pressed oil.

This is an oil that has been used for centuries in the Far East and so, logically, can be found in Oriental food stores and/or the Oriental food aisle in most grocery stores. A few health food distributors have started distributing this oil, marked with their own trade name, so it should be available in natural food stores as well.

TOFU. There is a whole section in the back of the book reserved for tofu, as it is one of our family's main sources of cholesterol-free protein! I do need to make mention of it here, though, in case it is a new ingredient you might be adding to your shopping list. It's being found in more and more supermarkets around the country, usually in the produce department or sometimes in the dairy or meat section. I think no one knows exactly how to categorize it! It's also known as bean curd, soybean curd or dofu in Chinese markets (where you can look if your local supermarket doesn't have tofu). Japanese markets are also a place you're guaranteed to find tofu. You will find that tofu comes in different sized blocks, but for the recipes in this book, 1 block of tofu is equal to 2 cups.

WHOLE WHEAT FLOUR. Of all the grains used in the United States, wheat and rice are the two most common. All the reasons for using whole wheat flour instead of refined white flour are essentially the same as those given in this shopping list for using brown rice rather than refined white rice.

Good reasons! And because of them, the demand for whole wheat flour has increased to the point that supermarkets regularly stock whole wheat flour now. This hasn't always been the case. I can remember well over a dozen years ago, when I first started to become aware of such things, that the only place to find whole wheat flour was in very high-priced health food stores. The supermarkets help to bring the cost of whole wheat flour down to a reasonable price.

YUBA. Yuba is another soybean by-product which has its own little section in the Soybean Chapter of this book. It will be more difficult to find than tofu, but once found will probably be a desired addition to your shopping list. Unlike tofu, yuba can't commonly be found in grocery stores or even natural food stores. The best place to look for yuba (also called "jai" or "dried bean curd") is in Chinatown or an Oriental foods specialty shop.

(From U.S.D.A. Agriculture Handbook #8)
WHEAT FLOUR
100 gm. edible portion

	Whole wheat	White enriched	White unenriched
Water	12.0%	12.0%	12.0%
Food energy	333 calories	364 calories	364 calories
Protein	13.3 gm.	10.5 gm.	10.5 gm.
Fat	2.0 gm.	1.0 gm.	1.0 gm.
Carbohydrate	71.0 gm. (Total)	76.1 gm. (Total)	76.1 gm. (Total)
	2.3 gm. (Fiber)	.3 gm. (Fiber)	.3 gm. (Fiber)
Ash	1.7 gm.	.43 gm.	.43 gm.
Calcium	41 mg.	16 mg.	16 mg.
Phosphorus	372 mg.	87 mg.	87 mg.
Iron	3.3 mg.	2.9 mg.	.8 mg.
Sodium	3 mg.	2 mg.	2 mg.
Potassium	370 mg.	95 mg.	95 mg.
Vitamin A	(0)	(0)	(0)
Thiamine	.55 mg.	.44 mg.	.06 mg.
Riboflavin	.12 mg.	.26 mg.	.05 mg.
Niacin	4.3 mg.	3.5 mg.	.9 mg.
Vitamin C	(0)	(0)	(0)

(From U.S.D.A. Agriculture Handbook #8)
BREAD
(made with 1% - 2% nonfat dry milk)
100 gm. edible portion

	Whole wheat	White enriched	White unenriched
Water	36.4%	35.8%	35.8%
Food energy	243 calories	269 calories	269 calories
Protein	10.5 gm.	8.7 gm.	8.7 gm.
Fat	3.0 gm.	3.2 gm.	3.2 gm.
Carbohydrate	47.7 gm. (Total)	50.4 gm. (Total)	50.4 gm. (Total)
	1.6 gm. (Fiber)	.2 gm. (Fiber)	.2 gm. (Fiber)
Ash	2.4 gm.	1.9 gm.	1.9 gm.
Calcium	99 mg.	70 mg.	70 mg.
Phosphorus	228 mg.	87 mg.	87 mg.
Iron	2.3 mg.	2.4 mg.	.7 mg.
Sodium	527 mg.	507 mg.	507 mg.
Potassium	273 mg.	85 mg.	85 mg.
Vitamin A	Trace	Trace	Trace
Thiamine	.26 mg.	.25 mg.	.09 mg.
Riboflavin	.12 mg.	.17 mg.	.08 mg.
Niacin	2.8 mg.	2.3 mg.	1.2 mg.
Vitamin C	Trace	Trace	Trace

(Numbers in parentheses denote values imputed — usually from another form of the food or from a similar food. Zero in parentheses indicates that the amount of a constituent probably is none or is too small to measure. Dashes denote lack of reliable data for a constituent believed to be present in measurable amount. Calculated values, as those based on a recipe, are not in parentheses.)

"It is only by softening and disguising dead flesh by culinary preparation that it is rendered susceptible of mastication or digestion, and that the sight of its bloody juices and raw horrors does not excite loathing and disgust."
— Shelley

APPLES

Apple

In my mind, the apple tree on the continental U.S.A. is comparable to the coconut tree in Hawaii, though they are certainly not comparable in taste or nutrition, as can be seen by the table on the next page.

The similarity that occurs to me exists because of stories I heard as a child about Johnny Appleseed. He planted apple trees all around without any desire to be the enjoyer of the fruits. This is similar to the fact that native Hawaiians used to plant a coconut tree for every child that was born to ensure an adequate food supply. In either case, the fact is that a future food supply was being planted by someone who really had no plan to be the harvester of the fruit. Yet this simple, unselfish activity benefited so many others for generations to come.

Working in harmony with the laws of God and nature for the benefit of others, as well as doing the work as an offering to God, is also known as **karma yoga**. This spirit is an essential part of working towards self-sufficiency, both for individuals and society in general.

If you're planning to plant a vegetable garden and/or fruit trees in the spirit of self-sufficiency, apples are a good crop to consider. You must, however, live in a place that gets frosts and is cold enough to allow the tree a dormant period.

You don't have to live on acres of land to plant apple trees. As a matter of fact, I know a few people whose chief complaint about their small apple orchards is that they produce more fruit than they and their friends can use. This is understandable, since an average, healthy apple tree in peak production will produce over a dozen bushels of apples easily. This is an important factor to bear in mind when trying to plan the best way to utilize land available to you for planting.

Also keep in mind that if you are planning to plant apple trees, you'll have to plant at least two or three varieties that bloom at the same time so they can pollinate each other. This shouldn't be hard, since there are so many varieties of apples from which to choose. There are so many, I won't list them all here! But you can look them up in any good gardening book.

In deciding which trees to plant, remember to choose ones that bloom at the same time. And, of course, check for nutritional value because nutritional value in apples varies as greatly as the number of varieties of apples.

As with almost all fruits, you can grow apples from seed, but they do not produce fruit identical to the parent plant. The recommended way to plant apple trees for the correct variety is to plant grafted stock.

I really have to tell you, the truth of the situation is that I have never personally grown apple trees because I have lived in Hawaii all my life. For really expert planting advice, you'll want to consult a gardening book written for places where there is a change of seasons. I also have rarely cooked with apples, as I try to use fruits that grow locally as much as possible. Even so, I have managed to collect a few tried-and-true recipes from the times we've used apples. I hope you like them.

(From "Encyclopedia of Organic Gardening")
APPLES
Milligrams per 100 grams

Variety	Vitamin C
Calville Blance	35 - 40 mg.
Sturmer Pippin	.29 mg.
Yellow Newton	.16 mg.
Northern Spy	15 - 20 mg.
Baldwin	15 - 20 mg.
Winesap	.10 mg.
York Imperial	8 mg.
MacIntosh	4 mg.

(From U.S.D.A. Agriculture Handbook #8)
APPLES
(Commercial varieties, raw)
100 gm. edible portion

	FRESHLY HARVESTED:		STORED:	
	Not Pared	Pared	Not Pared	Pared
Water	84.8%	85.3%	83.9%	84.8%
Food energy	56 calories	53 calories	60 calories	55 calories
Protein	.2 gm.	.2 gm.	.2 gm.	.2 gm.
Fat	.6 gm.	.3 gm.	.7 gm.	.3 gm.
Carbohydrate	14.1 gm. (Total)	13.9 gm. (Total)	14.8 gm. (Total)	14.4 gm. (Total)
	1.0 gm. (Fiber)	.6 gm. (Fiber)	1.0 gm. (Fiber)	.6 gm. (Fiber)
Ash	.3 gm.	.3 gm.	.4 gm.	.3 gm.
Calcium	7 mg.	6 mg.	7 mg.	6 mg.
Phosphorus	10 mg.	10 mg.	10 mg.	10 mg.
Iron	.3 mg.	.3 mg.	.3 mg.	.3 mg.
Sodium	1 mg.	1 mg.	1 mg.	1 mg.
Potassium	110 mg.	110 mg.	110 mg.	110 mg.
Vitamin A	90 I.U.	40 I.U.	90 I.U.	40 I.U.
Thiamine	.03 mg.	.03 mg.	.03 mg.	.03 mg.
Riboflavin	.02 mg.	.02 mg.	.02 mg.	.02 mg.
Niacin	.1 mg.	.1 mg.	.1 mg.	.1 mg.
Vitamin C	7 mg.	4 mg.	3 mg.	2 mg.

Dips (l to r):   Fig Dip, Peanut Butter Dip, Cream Cheese Dip, p. 58   Apple Pancakes, p. 62   Caramel Apples, p. 61

FRESH APPLE SLICES WITH DIPS ☐

Simply prepare any of the following dips and use them to dip fresh apple slices in. Especially good if the apples are chilled before slicing.

CREAM CHEESE DIP ☆

½ cup cream cheese
(softened at room temperature)
2 Tbsp. honey
2 Tbsp. water (or a little more)
½ tsp. vanilla

Combine ingredients and mix until creamy and smooth.

PEANUT BUTTER DIP ☐

½ cup peanut butter
2 Tbsp. honey
4 Tbsp. water
¼ tsp. cinnamon

Combine ingredients and mix until creamy and smooth.

FIG DIP ☐

¼ cup black mission figs, chopped
2 Tbsp. honey
½ cup water
1 Tbsp. lemon juice

Combine ingredients in blender and blend until smooth.

CASHEW DIP ☐

1 cup raw cashews (pre-soaked)
¾ cup apple juice
2 Tbsp. honey
1 Tbsp. lemon juice

Combine ingredients in blender and blend until smooth.

DATE DIP ☐

½ cup soft dates, chopped
¾ cup water
2 Tbsp. lemon juice

Combine ingredients in blender and blend until smooth.

RAW APPLE PIE ☐

Raw pie crust
(see Basic Recipes Section, p. 32)

Filling:
4 - 5 apples, peeled and grated
(2 cups firmly packed)
¼ cup natural peanut butter
2 Tbsp. honey
1 Tbsp. liquid lecithin
½ tsp. cinnamon
¼ tsp. nutmeg
1/8 tsp. salt (if using unsalted peanut butter)
2 - 4 Tbsp. currants (to sprinkle on top)

Prepare your favorite raw pie crust and press into 8" pie plate. Pyrex is the best. Peel, core and grate apples. Combine with remaining ingredients, except currants, and mix well. Spread evenly in pie shell, sprinkle on currants and chill at least one hour before serving.

RAW MINCE PIE ☐

3 cups grated, raw apples

½ cup raisins
½ cup dates
1 cup figs
1 cup sunflower seeds or walnuts

2 Tbsp. lemon juice
1 tsp. cinnamon
½ tsp. nutmeg

Grate apples. Grind next 4 ingredients in food grinder. Combine apples, ground ingredients and last 3 ingredients and mix well. Pour into a raw pie crust (see Basic Recipes Section, p. 32) and refrigerate beofre serving.

FROZEN APPLE DATE NUT LOAF □

½ cup raw almonds
½ cup raw cashews
½ cup pitted dates
1 cup grated apple (firmly packed)
2 Tbsp. lemon juice (or a little more)
2 Tbsp. honey (or a little more)

Combine nuts and dates and run through a food grinder. Combine with apple, lemon and honey and mix well. Press into a small loaf pan, cover with foil and set in freezer to firm and freeze. If frozen very solid, let sit at room temperature just long enough to make slicing a little easier. Slice loaf and serve. A rich and delicious dessert. Almost like an ice cream loaf.

HEARTY BREAKFAST DRINK □

2 cups apple juice
1 large banana
1 cup sunflower seeds
1 tsp. cinnamon

Blend in blender until smooth. Or, for variation, blend just enough so that you will have a chunky drink that will need to be chewed.

APPLE CARROT SLAW □

2 cups packed, grated apple
(about 4 medium apples)
2 cups grated carrots (about 2 medium)
½ cup sunflower seeds
1 cup Eggless Soy Mayonnaise
(see Basic Recipes Section, p. 34)
½ tsp. cinnamon
1 tsp. honey

Peel and grate apple. Combine with remaining ingredients and mix well. Chill salad and serve on top of lettuce leaves or alfalfa sprouts. Also good served with cottage cheese. An optional but delicious addition to the salad would be to mix in ½ cup currants or to top each serving with a good sprinkling of them.

APPLE SALAD □

4 apples, diced
1 cup diced celery
1 cup Eggless Soy Mayonnaise
(see Basic Recipes Section, p. 34)
¾ cup walnuts, chopped

Peel, core and dice apples. Combine with remaining ingredients and mix well. Serve immediately on top of some crisp lettuce leaves. Salad will discolor if left to sit.

APPLE PSYLLIUM TREAT □

2 cups apple juice
¼ cup dates
3 Tbsp. psyllium seed powder
1 tsp. chia seeds
¼ tsp. cinnamon

1 large apple, grated or finely diced

Blend first 5 ingredients in blender until dates are chopped. Pour into a bowl and top with diced or grated apples. Chill and serve.

APPLE YOGURT COOLER □

1 cup apple juice, unsweetened
1 cup low-fat yogurt
¼ cup crushed ice
2 tsp. honey (or more)

Combine ingredients and blend well. Serve immediately. A few fresh mint leaves can be blended in for a refreshing addition.

APPLE WALNUT JELL ○

2 cups apple juice
1½ sticks agar-agar (¾ cup flakes)

1 Tbsp. lemon juice
2 Tbsp. honey
2 apples, grated
¼ cup finely chopped walnuts

Pour apple juice into saucepan. Tear agar-agar and let soak in apple juice for 1 hour. Bring juice to a boil and then let simmer until all the agar-agar has dissolved. Add remaining ingredients, mix well and pour into gelatin mold, bowls or a small, square pan (8" or less). Set in refrigerator and chill until firm. This is a very cool and refreshing summer treat.

APPLESAUCE SPICE CAKE ○

¼ cup butter or margarine
½ cup honey
½ tsp. cinnamon
1/8 tsp. cloves
1/8 tsp. nutmeg

1½ cups whole wheat flour
1 tsp. baking soda
1 tsp. baking powder

1 cup applesauce

½ cup chopped walnuts (opt.)
½ cup raisins (opt.)

Cream together first 5 ingredients. Sift in the next 3 ingredients and add applesauce. Now mix everything together vigorously for about 3 minutes. You can now mix in the optionals if you like. Spread out evenly in greased and floured 8" cake pan and bake at 350° for 30 to 35 minutes.

WARM & SPICY APPLE DRINK ○

2 cups water
2 Tbsp. dried, edible hibiscus herb

4 cups apple juice
½ tsp. finely grated ginger
½ tsp. cinnamon

¼ tsp. nutmeg
1 Tbsp. honey

Bring water to boil with lid on. Remove from heat. Add dried herb, cover and simmer for 5 minutes. Strain. Add apple juice to strained tea along with spices and honey. Cover and simmer 5 to 10 minutes. Mix well. Strain and serve.

APPLE CHUTNEY ○

5 lbs. apples
½ cup water
¼ cup butter or margarine
½ tsp. crushed chili pepper
1 tsp. nutmeg
½ tsp. allspice
1 tsp. ginger
1 - 2 tsp. cinnamon
2 cups honey

Peel, core and chop apples into quarters. Steam apples in water until tender. When done, remove lid and cook off excess water. Be careful not to burn. In deep skillet or wok, heat butter and toast spices in it. Add apples and cook away excess liquid on high heat, stirring often. Add honey and cook on medium-high heat until jamlike, stirring frequently to prevent sticking and burning. Remove from heat, allow to cool, then refrigerate. Can be served warm, but is better chilled.

STEAMED APPLE PUDDING ☆

Dough:
2 cups whole wheat flour
½ cup butter, margarine or oil
¼ cup honey
2 tsp. baking powder
2 Tbsp. cold water

Filling:
4 medium apples, sliced thin or grated
¾ cup natural maple syrup
¼ cup yogurt
½ tsp. cinnamon
1/8 tsp. nutmeg
1 Tbsp. arrowroot powder

Combine dough ingredients and mix together well. Cut dough in half and roll out between wax paper to line the bottom of an 8" round Pyrex, Corningware or casserole dish with lid. Combine the filling ingredients and mix well. Put in filling and cover with other rolled out piece of dough. Cover dish with its Pyrex lid or with aluminum foil and place on a steamer rack. Steam for 1½ to 2 hours. Serve warm topped with milk or yogurt, or serve cold.

APPLE YAM CASSEROLE ○

¼ cup melted butter or margarine
¼ cup apple juice or cider
¼ cup maple syrup
¼ tsp. asafetida

4 cups thinly sliced yams or sweet potatoes
4 cups thinly sliced apples

1 cup grated cheddar cheese
1 cup crushed sesame crackers

Combine together first 4 ingredients to make sauce. Grease an 8" square casserole or baking dish and alternate with layers of apples, potatoes, cheese and crumbs, and a bit of sauce. Then repeat, saving most of the sauce for the top. Bake at 350° for 1 hour. Serve warm.

APPLE PIE ○

Simply use the Plain Pastry recipe (see Basic Recipes Section, p. 33) and follow recipe for Mango Pie (see recipe in Mango Section, p. 148), replacing mangoes with sliced apples.

CARAMEL APPLES ☆

1 cup honey
½ cup evaporated milk

2 Tbsp. butter or margarine
½ cup non-instant milk powder
6 apples
Raw, blanched peanuts

Combine first 2 ingredients in a saucepan. Bring slowly to a boil, stirring constantly. If milk begins to curdle, lower the heat. Continue cooking, stirring often, to the soft ball stage (230° on a candy thermometer). Pour into a mixing bowl, add butter, mix and let semicool 10 to 15 minutes. Beat in milk powder with a fork until the warm sauce will pour very slowly. Insert sticks in apples and coat each apple by turning it in the caramel sauce until well coated. If caramel begins to harden or cool too much, set pot of caramel in another bowl or pot of **hot** water until it softens again. Roll dipped apple in peanuts which have been chopped a bit. Set on oiled cookie sheet; refrigerate until caramel sets.

BAKED APPLES

Simply take one whole apple and cut out the core through the top, being careful not to go through the bottom. Then fill the center with any of the following fillings and wrap in aluminum foil. Place on a baking sheet or shallow pan and bake at 350° for 15 to 20 minutes. Remove the foil and serve with a knife and fork. Delicious! You can multiply each filling according to how many apples you want to bake. To make fillings, simply combine ingredients and mix well.

Peanut Butter Filling:
2 Tbsp. peanut butter
1 Tbsp. currants
2 tsp. honey

Tahini Filling:
1 Tbsp. tahini
1 Tbsp. mashed banana
1 Tbsp. molasses (or less)

Cream Cheese Filling:
2 Tbsp. cream cheese
1 Tbsp. chopped dates
1 tsp. honey

Cheese-Almond Filling:
2 Tbsp. grated cheddar cheese
1 tsp. finely chopped almonds

APPLE PANCAKES

1 cup whole wheat flour
1/3 cup nonfat, noninstant milk powder
½ tsp. salt
2 tsp. baking powder

1 cup grated apple
1 cup water or apple juice

Sift the first 4 ingredients together into a mixing bowl. Add last 2 ingredients and mix. Ladle onto hot, greased griddle and turn when bubbling as with regular pancakes. Serve with maple syrup and yogurt.

APPLE CRISP

3 cups sliced apples
½ cup honey

¾ cup wheat germ
¾ cup crushed sesame crackers
½ tsp. cinnamon
¼ cup melted butter or margarine

Preheat oven to 350° F. Butter a casserole or 8" Pyrex baking dish. Arrange apple slices and evenly drizzle on the honey. Combine the next 4 ingredients and mix well. Sprinkle evenly over the top and bake at 350° for 1 hour. Serve warm or cold.

APPLE-DATE BARS

½ cup butter or margarine
½ cup honey
1 tsp. vanilla

1½ cups whole wheat flour
1 tsp. baking powder
¼ tsp. salt
1 tsp. cinnamon

2 cups finely chopped or grated apples
1 cup chopped dates

Preheat oven to 350° F. Cream together first 3 ingredients. Sift in the next 4 ingredients. Add last 2 ingredients and mix everything together well. Spread in a greased 7" x 11" baking pan and bake at 350° for 30 to 35 minutes. Cool and cut into squares or bars.

AVOCADO

Avocado

This is one fruit that I couldn't bear when I was little and eating meat. I don't think it had anything to do with being little, as my children love avocados. But I have noticed that my tastes have changed a lot since I've stopped eating meat.

I have come to really like avocados. The taste varies from nutty to buttery or sometimes watery, according to the species and location grown. There are many species of avocados. The more common ones here in the Islands are:

1. **Seyde or Summer** avocados, which have purple, smooth skins and are oval-shaped.
2. **MacDonald** avocados, which are round with thick, green, bumpy skins.
3. **Kaguah** avocados, which are oval with green, smooth skins.
4. **Beardslee**, which are in between oval and round with green, smooth skin.

The Beardslee trees are recommended for your yard because they are quick-growing trees that often bear fruit when only four years old. Also, their fruit-yielding season starts in the fall and stretches through the winter.

Avocado lovers should be delighted to know that avocados are available almost all year long, especially if you plant one winter-pear tree (fall-winter bearing season) and one summer-pear tree (spring-summer bearing season) in your yard. Avocado trees should be grafted because they tend to be unlike the parent when planted from seed. Avocado trees must have good drainage. If you plant an avocado tree in soil that has too much clay or does not drain well, the tree may grow for three to four years and then die back.

Except for olives, avocados are the richest fruit in fat. They contain about 7% to 26% fat, because the amount of fat varies from one variety to another. The amount of water varies in the same way. The amount of calories varies according to the amount of water and fat, so it is difficult to say how many calories avocados have because there are so many different varieties. Depending on the variety, one-fourth to one-half of an avocado contains about 100 calories. One thing is certain, calorie-wise, avocados have more nutritious value in terms of food energy pound-per-pound than beef.

(From U.S.D.A. Agriculture Handbook #8) AVOCADOS (raw) 100 gm. edible portion			
Water	74.0%	Iron	.6 mg.
Food energy	167 calories	Sodium	4 mg.
Protein	2.1 gm.	Potassium	604 mg.
Fat	16.4 gm.	Vitamin A	290 I.U.
Carbohydrate	6.3 gm. (Total)	Thiamine	.11 mg.
	1.6 gm. (Fiber)	Riboflavin	.20 mg.
Ash	1.2 gm.	Niacin	1.6 mg.
Calcium	10 mg.	Vitamin C	14 mg.
Phosphorus	42 mg.		

In comparison with other fruits, avocados are a good source of vitamins B_2 and B_3, a fair source of vitamins A and B_1, but a poor source of vitamin C.

As far as minerals go, in comparison to other fruits, avocados are a fair source of phosphorus and iron and a poor source of calcium.

So now that you are ready to add avocados to your menu, here are some recipes for you to try. You may notice that there aren't any recipes calling for cooked avocados. This is because they turn bitter for some reason when cooked. However, they can be added successfully to hot foods if they're put in just before serving.

Here are some new recipes for all avocado lovers! If you don't like avocados, try

recipes like the Avocado Cream Pie or the Avocado Cake. You probably won't be able to tell there are any avocados in the dish at all!

AVOCADO GUACAMOLE ☐

1 medium avocado
2 medium tomatoes

1 Tbsp. lemon juice
2 tsp. soy sauce
¼ tsp. salt
1/8 tsp. cayenne
1/8 tsp. chili powder
1/8 tsp. ground cumin

Peel first 2 ingredients and mash together. Add remaining ingredients, mix well and chill. Serve with chips or crackers, carrot, celery or cucumber sticks. This can also be used as a sandwich spread. Makes about 4 servings.

Variation #1: Add sour cream or yogurt and serve as a dressing over fresh, green salad.

Variation #2: Omit the soy sauce. Add some fresh grated ginger, honey and pre-soaked raisins and you have avocado chutney.

One thing that a very dear friend of mine taught me has saved many a guacamole from spoiling! My friend visited Mexico, where they have a lot of avocados but rarely any refrigerators. How do they keep avocados from spoiling? They simply put the pit back into the guacamole and this keeps the avocado from spoiling so quickly! You can do this with an avocado that's been cut in half and only half used. Just leave the pit intact and refrigerate. You'll find that it lasts longer than if the pit had been taken out.

These natural ways of doing things are always so simple, yet they never fail to amaze me!

TOSTADAS

6 corn tortillas
3 cups refried beans
2 cups grated cheese
4 large tomatoes, chopped
Lettuce and sprouts, tossed together
7 oz. can olives, chopped (opt.)
6 cups Avocado Guacamole
(see recipe this section, p. 66)

Fry tortillas in hot oil until golden brown. Have beans ready and all vegetables cut and set out. Top each tortilla with about ½ cup of beans; then sprinkle with cheese, then tomatoes, lettuce, sprouts and olives. Top with guacamole and serve. Makes 6 servings.

GUACAMOLE CHALUPAS ☆

4 cups Masa Harina
2-2/3 cups water
2/3 cup butter or margarine
2 tsp. salt

Combine ingredients and mix well. Pat about 2 Tbsp. of dough into round cake. Cook in ungreased frying pan on medium heat, turning occasionally until masa begins to lose its doughy look. Remove from heat and let cool slightly, then pinch edges to make a rim. Deep-fry in about ½" hot oil until lightly browned. Do not turn; ladle hot oil onto cake to cook the top. Drain and cool. Fill with Avocado Guacamole (see p. 66).

Variations: Add some diced green pepper, celery and/or cucumber to guacamole and top each chalupa with a little grated cheese.

AVOCADO AND COTTAGE CHEESE □

1 avocado, mashed
1 cup cottage cheese
1 Tbsp. soy sauce

Mix ingredients together and use as a dip, over a salad or as the main protein dish. Makes about 2 servings.

AVOCADO GAZPACHO □

3 medium avocados
1 cup chopped cucumber
1 cup chopped bell pepper
2 tomatoes, chopped
¼ tsp. asafetida
2 Tbsp. chopped parsley
Pinch cayenne
1 Tbsp. soy sauce
1/8 tsp. black pepper
2 Tbsp. lemon juice
1 quart tomato juice
1/8 tsp. cumin
1 tsp. basil
½ tsp. oregano

Peel and cube avocados. In a large bowl, combine all ingredients. Stir to blend; chill. Makes about 2 quarts (8 servings).

PLAIN FROZEN AVOCADO □

Cut avocado the long way around. Scoop out avocado and mash until smooth. Add 1 Tbsp. of lemon juice per avocado to keep from turning brown. Fill container with mashed avocado or refill avocado shells and freeze.

If the avocados are falling off of the trees faster than you can eat them or give them away, they can be successfully frozen for some day when they're not so plentiful. They can be blended into a sweet sauce (like Avocado Fruit Salad Dressing) and frozen to be served as an ice cream or frozen in the form of ice cubes to be added to blended fruit drinks.

COOL AVOCADO SOUP WITH NUTS □

2 ripe avocados
1½ Tbsp. lemon juice
½ cup buttermilk powder
2½ cups water

1 cup toasted cashews
½ cup raw cashews
3 pinches asafetida
(Continued next page)

1 Morga bouillon cube (salted)

Blend all ingredients until smooth and creamy. Pour into a bowl (with an avocado pit to keep it green and fresh) and chill in the refrigerator. When cool, pour into soup bowls and serve. This can also be used as a sauce over brown rice or vegetables. Yields 6 servings.

AVOCADO VEGETABLE SOUP □

2 cups water
2 cups tomato juice
1 medium carrot, chopped
2 stalks celery, chopped
2 tomatoes, chopped
2 tsp. Spike
1 tsp. basil
1 Tbsp. marjoram
1/8 - 1/4 tsp. asafetida

1 cup mashed avocado

Combine first 9 ingredients in blender and blend until smooth. Add mashed avocado and blend. Heat on stove just to warm (about 120°) and serve. Delicious!

OPEN-FACE AVOCADO SANDWICH WITH CRUNCHY TOFU CRISPS ○

2 - 3 Tbsp. sour cream or yogurt
3 - 4 Tbsp. Eggless Soy Mayonnaise
(see Basic Recipes Section, p. 34)
1 tsp. mustard powder
3 pinches asafetida
1 pinch black pepper
2 pinches salt
1 cup diced Crunchy Tofu Crisps
(see recipe in Tofu Section, p. 384)

4 slices whole wheat bread, toasted
1 ripe avocado, sliced
4 slices cheese
Alfalfa sprouts

Mix together first 7 ingredients and spread on toast. Top with avocado slices and then cheese. Put under broiler until cheese melts. Top with alfalfa sprouts. Makes about 2 to 4 servings.

MULTIUSE AVOCADO CURRY

4 Tbsp. oil
¼ tsp. asafetida

¼ cup whole wheat flour

1½ cups water
1 Morga bouillon cube
2 tsp. curry powder
½ tsp. vegetable salt
½ tsp. black pepper

2 firm, ripe avocados, diced
1 Tbsp. fresh lemon juice
½ cup sour cream or yogurt

Sauté first 2 ingredients. Add flour and stir until toasted. Gradually add next 5 ingredients, stirring constantly over medium heat. When heated, add last 3 ingredients just before serving. Makes a delicious sauce for rice, vegetables or pasta. Also makes a tasty soup. Makes 4 to 6 servings.

OLE SALAD

½ head of lettuce
2 medium tomatoes

7 oz. can green chilies
2 cups cooked kidney beans
7 oz. can diced olives
1 cup grated cheese
1 avocado, diced

Dressing:
½ cup sour cream or yogurt
1 tsp. chili sauce
2 Tbsp. Italian dressing
¾ tsp. chili powder

9 oz. bag corn chips

Chop lettuce and tomatoes. Mix together with next 5 ingredients. Add dressing and corn chips right before serving. Serve on bed of sprouts.

AVOCADO AND BEAN SALAD ◯

1 avocado, cubed (mashed if very ripe)
1½ cups green beans, cut
1½ cups cooked kidney beans
1½ cups cooked garbanzo beans
1 cup cubed cheddar cheese
½ cup chopped green pepper
¼ cup chopped pimiento

2/3 cup olive oil
2/3 cup lemon juice
2 - 3 Tbsp. honey
½ tsp. basil
¼ tsp. dill
¼ tsp. fresh parsley
½ tsp. salt
¼ tsp. black pepper
1 - 2 tsp. asafetida

Toss first 7 ingredients. Combine next 9, mix well and pour over bean mixture. Mix well and refrigerate. Serve over alfalfa sprouts or lettuce. Makes about 8 salad servings.

AVOCADO MOLDED SALAD ◯

4 cups hot water
2 sticks agar-agar (1 cup flakes)

1 avocado, mashed
¼ cup cucumber, chopped
¼ cup bell pepper, chopped
¼ cup celery, chopped
¼ cup apple, chopped
¼ cup raisins
¼ cup nuts, chopped
3 Tbsp. honey
½ tsp. salt
½ cup sour cream
1 tsp. lemon juice

Soak first 2 ingredients for at least 15 minutes. Bring to a boil, stirring until thickened. Partially cool (until warm, but don't allow to set). Stir in remaining ingredients and pour into a mold or flat pan and refrigerate until set. Can be served on top of a lettuce leaf plain, or with cottage cheese or whipped cream. Makes about 4 servings.

HAWAIIAN AVOCADO AND MACARONI SALAD ◯

1 cup whole wheat elbow macaroni

1 Tbsp. olive oil
1 Tbsp. apple cider vinegar

2 firm, ripe avocados, diced
2 tsp. lemon juice
½ tsp. mustard powder
½ tsp. basil
½ tsp. fresh parsley, chopped
½ tsp. fresh dill, chopped, or ¼ tsp. dried dill
½ cup prepared chili sauce

Lettuce leaves
Alfalfa sprouts
Sunflower seeds

Cook macaroni until tender. Rinse with cold water and drain. In a salad bowl, combine noodles with next 2 ingredients and mix well. Add next 7 ingredients and mix well. Refrigerate until serving time. Place each serving on top of fresh lettuce leaves. Top with sprouts, sprinkle with sunflower seeds and serve. Makes about 4 servings.

AVOCADO SALAD DRESSING ☆

1 large avocado
2 Tbsp. lemon juice
4 Tbsp. sour cream or yogurt
1 good pinch asafetida
½ tsp. salt or 1 tsp. kelp
1/8 tsp. crushed dill

¼ cup chopped bell pepper

Combine first 6 ingredients. Blend in blender or mash and mix well. Add bell pepper. Mix and serve on your favorite, fresh, green salad. Good on alfalfa sprouts. Makes 2 to 4 servings.

AVOCADO FRUIT SALAD DRESSING ☐

1 avocado
2 Tbsp. yogurt
¼ cup orange juice
1 Tbsp. lemon juice
¼ tsp. salt
2 Tbsp. honey or more

Put all ingredients in blender and blend until smooth. Serve over your favorite fruit salad, or else this can be placed in the freezer and served later on as a frozen dessert. Makes about 1 cup of dressing.

AVOCADO-PINEAPPLE SALAD ☐

1/3 cup avocado, mashed
½ cup yogurt
2 Tbsp. lemon or lime juice
2 Tbsp. honey

3 cups fresh pineapple juice
2 cups avocado slices

Mix first 4 ingredients well. Add the next 2 ingredients and fold in gently so as not to break any pieces of fruit. Garnish with fresh mint leaves if you have any. This will make about 6 servings.

AVOCADO-ORANGE SALAD ☐

1 avocado
1 orange

¼ cup grated coconut
1 Tbsp. honey (or more)

2 fresh pineapple rings

Cube the first 2 ingredients. Toss with next 2 ingredients. Scoop onto fresh pineapple rings and serve for breakfast or a light dinner. Makes 2 servings.

AVOCADO-BANANA SALAD ☐

1 avocado, cubed
2 bananas, sliced

2 Tbsp. honey
2 Tbsp. lemon juice

Prepare fruit. Drizzle or toss last 2 ingredients over the fruit.

AVOCADO-ORANGE JELL ○

3 cups coconut cream
1 cup honey
3 sticks agar-agar (1½ cups flakes)

2 cups blended avocado
1½ cups fresh orange, diced
1 tsp. vanilla

Soak first 3 ingredients for about 30 minutes. Bring to boil and cook until agar-agar dissolves. Cool. Stir in last 3 ingredients and pour into flat baking sheets or gelatin molds and refrigerate.

AVOCADO-PAPAYA-COCONUT CREAM KANTEN ○

4 cups coconut cream
3 sticks agar-agar (1½ cups flakes)
1 cup honey

1 cup ripe papaya, blended
1 cup avocado, blended

Soak first 3 ingredients for about half an hour. Cook until agar-agar (kanten) dissolves. Allow to semicool. Add last 2 ingredients to coconut cream and mix well. Pour into flat cake pan or molds and refrigerate until set. Cut into squares and serve. Makes enough for a dozen people to snack on.

AVO SHAKE ☐

1 cup cold milk or nut milk
2 Tbsp. honey or more
1 tsp. lemon or lime juice
½ cup avocado, mashed
½ banana

Combine all ingredients in a blender and blend until thoroughly smooth. Be sure to put the lid on before blending to avoid getting the ingredients all over the wall. Pour into glasses and sprinkle with a dash of nutmeg if you like. This makes about 2 servings.

AVOCADO MOCHA MINT COOLER ☐

1 ripe avocado
2 cups milk (soy or dairy)
4 Tbsp. honey
2 tsp. Pero (cereal coffee substitute)
½ tsp. nutmeg
20 fresh mint leaves

1 cup crushed ice

Blend first 6 ingredients in blender until smooth and creamy. Mix in crushed ice and serve. This drink is at its best if served very cold. Can chill in freezer a bit before serving. Makes 3 servings.

GREEN NECTAR ☐

3 cups cold milk (nut, soy or dairy)
2 - 3 fresh comfrey leaves
1 ripe avocado
¼ cup raisins
¼ cup pitted dates
3 bananas
1/8 tsp. cayenne

Blend ingredients until smooth. Serve cold.

AVOCADO-CITRUS SMOOTHIE ☐

1 avocado
1 cup crushed pineapple
2 cups orange juice
½ cup pitted dates, chopped
1 Tbsp. honey
1 Tbsp. non-instant milk powder

1 cup crushed ice

Combine first 6 ingredients and blend in a blender until dates are well blended. Add crushed ice, mix and serve. This is also very good if set in the freezer for a while and served for dessert like a sherbet. Makes about 4 servings.

AVOCADO CREAM PIE

Crust:
Use Graham Cracker Crust
(see Basic Recipes Section, p. 33)

Filling:
2 cups mashed avocado
1 Tbsp. lemon juice
8 oz. cream cheese or 8 oz. thick yogurt plus ¼ cup powdered milk
½ to 2/3 cup mild honey

Topping:
1 large banana, sliced
Juice of 1 lemon

1 cup coconut, grated and toasted
(see recipe in Coconut Section, p. 124)

Combine ingredients in blender and blend until smooth. Scoop into pie shell. For topping, soak bananas in lemon juice to add flavor and to prevent darkening. Arrange slices on top of avocado filling, sprinkle with coconut and chill at least 4 hours before serving. It may also be frozen. Makes 1 pie. (This pie is delicious made with cream cheese and passable made with yogurt. I've just included the yogurt choice in case you are a dieter and do not want to use the cream cheese.)

AVOCADO FRUIT CAKE ☆

1 cup honey
¾ cup butter or margarine

1 cup date sugar
1½ cups avocado, mashed

3 cups whole wheat flour
½ tsp. salt
¾ tsp. cinnamon
½ tsp. allspice

¾ cup sour milk or yogurt
2 tsp. baking soda

¾ cup chopped nuts
¾ cup chopped dates
¾ cup raisins

Preheat oven to 350° F. Cream first 2 ingredients. Add next 2 and mix well. Sift next 4 and mix. Add next 2 ingredients. Fold in last 3 ingredients. Mix well and pour into a greased and floured oblong cake pan. Bake at 350° for 1 hour. It's one of the moistest and most flavorful fruit cakes yet. Makes 1 average-sized cake.

AVOCADO ICE CREAM ☐

Pulp from 2 avocados
3 bananas
½ papaya (or equivalent of fresh apricots, peaches or nectarines)
¼ cup lecithin granules
2 Tbsp. sesame tahini
1 tsp. vanilla

2 - 3 cups orange juice or lemonade

Blend first 6 ingredients until smooth. Pour into ice cube tray and freeze. When completely frozen, blend the cubes in 2 to 3 cups orange juice, dropping a few cubes in at a time. Add cubes until mixture in blender is a soft, frothy ice cream texture.

HAWAIIAN FRUIT SHERBET ☐

1½ cups avocado, mashed
½ cup pineapple juice
½ cup orange juice
2 Tbsp. lemon juice
1 cup coconut milk

Put ingredients in a blender and blend until smooth. Pour into a stainless steel bowl and put in freezer. Every 20 minutes, take the bowl out and mix with an electric mixer, or if you don't have one, a wire whisk will do. Do this about three times before allowing to freeze completely. The mixing keeps it from crystallizing and becoming hard as a rock. Just before serving, mix quickly again. Delicious! Makes 2 to 4 servings.

AVOCADO TOFU WHIP ☐

½ avocado
1 cup tofu
4 Tbsp. honey
Juice of 1 lime
Pinch of cinnamon

Blend ingredients in a blender until smooth. Put in freezer or refrigerator to chill. Makes about 2 servings.

AVO-ICE CREAM SANDWICHES ☆

Pkg. of Midel Honey Graham Crackers

Avocado Cream Pie filling
(see recipe this section, p. 72)

Make Avocado Cream Pie filling. Lay Midel Honey Grahams in a single layer on bottom of a cookie sheet. (Lay whole sheet of crackers down; don't break apart.) Top cracker with Avocado Cream Pie filling about ¾" to 1" thick. Top with another cracker and freeze. When the filling is frozen hard, cut into smaller sandwiches by cutting along perforations on the crackers. Store many at a time. These are delicious served with a topping of carob syrup.

"Who is to say birds are irrational because they cannot speak? Birds communicate with a language we cannot understand, nor can we understand the tongue of a foreigner — but do we pluck out his hair? A man who eats a harmless diet will be less inclined to slaughter another man's flesh since the idea would be unthinkable."
— Porphyry

BANANA

Banana

Everyone in Hawaii knows what a banana is! What has always puzzled me is that we import bananas when they grow so beautifully right in our backyards.

Particularly hard to understand is the fact that locally grown bananas are either equal in price or even more expensive than bananas shipped in from Mexico, South America and the West Indies (Dole and Chiquita) — all the way across the Pacific Ocean!

I guess the problem is that we continue to treat our precious agricultural land as a commodity and not as the unrenewable natural resource that it is. Thus the land is open to speculation. We keep covering our land with more and more concrete and buildings, driving land prices up so high that farmers can't make a decent living without being forced to charge very high prices for their produce. Part of the problem, too, is that the large corporations* which control so much of what goes on in this state make more money by paying cheap labor overseas. They produce food to be transported on their shipping lines back to Hawaii, thus allowing them to grow hotels and big businesses rather than food here.

* For practical examples of what I mean, see: Charles Kepner's **Social Aspects of Banana Industry and Banana Empire**, Charles Wilson's **Empire in Green and Gold** and Thomas McCaan's **An American Company**.

Banana trees can be found growing wild (not on Oahu so much anymore) in well-rained-upon valleys where the Hawaiians first planted them. The few commercial banana farmers also choose similar surroundings in which to grow their bananas. Knowing the reasons for this may help you select the best spot in your yard to plant your banana tree(s).

Because banana trees have a shallow root system, they require a lot of water close to the surface of the soil. Also because of the shallow root system, banana trees are very easily toppled over by strong winds and require some shelter. This is why they are usually grown in valleys or gullies. If you live in a windy area, you can still harvest bananas by planting the trees on the side of the house that is sheltered from the wind. Or you could get around the wind problem by planting Chinese banana trees which are so short that the wind hardly ever bothers them.

Banana trees require full sun, so you have to plant them far enough apart so they aren't shading each other too much. After the mother plant is chopped down, it's wise to leave only two "keikis," or baby plants, to grow each time. (Don't throw the other ones away, though! There's life there and potential fruit! So why not give the extra ones to a friend or go for a hike in the mountains and plant them?) Thus, every year you will have two more banana trees than the previous year. After many years of increasing in this way, you'll find the clump of banana trees sitting somewhat on top of the soil. At this point, a hole needs to be dug and the trees replanted.

If you're thinking of planting some

banana trees in your yard, you have quite a few varieties from which to choose.

The most common eating bananas:

Bluefields are the largest and most common. They have a smooth, yellow skin and creamy, white flesh. This and the apple banana are the eating bananas that are recommended for cooking. When the others are cooked, they get rubbery or weird.

Brazilian or Apple are small to medium in size. The skins are yellow. The sides are squarish between the ridges with a blunt tip. This is my favorite kind of banana, as the taste is a little tart and the banana stays firm even after it gets very ripe. This kind can also be cooked.

Chinese are small to medium in size with deep-yellow skins. The flesh of these is yellowish and tender.

Ice Cream are small and stubby with light-yellow skins that are tender and crack easily. The flesh is white, tender and sweet.

Cuban are medium to large in size. The skin is yellow-orange with some red. The flesh is anywhere from creamy white to pink, slippery and tender, with a strong smell and a nice taste.

Hamakua are medium to large in size. The skins are light-green or light-yellow even when ripe. The only way to tell if this kind is ripe is to check and see if the banana is soft, as the flesh is very tender when ripe.

The two common cooking varieties:

Miamaoli are large, long and round and full at both ends. The skin is yellow. The flesh is tender and pink when raw, yellow and translucent when cooked. Taste is tart.

Popoulu are small, very thick, short with round ends. Skin is yellow. The flesh is pink when raw and yellow and translucent when cooked with a tart taste.

So, planting a few banana trees in your backyard is not only rewarding economically and as a personal experience (watching the tree grow and bear fruit), but it is also a declaration of independence. As a matter of fact, since it takes a banana tree less than a year to produce fruit, if you started planting one banana tree every month for a year, you would soon have bananas to pick all year round.

You may find yourself with a stalk of bananas that ripens all at once — I've noticed bananas have a tendency to do that! If this happens, you are faced with a number of alternatives.

1. Give some away to friends, neighbors, enemies, anyone!

2. Dry the bananas. We sell dried bananas in our store, shipped in from Taiwan via New York, no less! They're very good. I had a friend in Kihei who made large, wooden frames and covered them with screen. He would then put the bananas inside and put the frames on the roof. He always had dried bananas on hand for snacks. You could also dry the bananas in the form of fruit leather (see recipe in Mango Section, p. 144).

3. Bananas freeze well. When I was little I used to buy frozen bananas on a stick, which were almost like ice cream bars but healthier. You can freeze them plain or you can make "chocolate"-coated bananas by just melting down some carob candies in a double boiler and dipping the bananas in the carob. If you want nuts on top, just roll the banana in nuts after dipping. If the bananas are real mushy, just peel them and

drop into a plastic bag. You can chip chunks off as needed to add to smoothies, and anyone who has a juicer can make a wonderful ice cream by running the frozen bananas through.

The nutritional value of bananas varies as much as there are varieties of bananas. Here, they are divided into two general groups: cooking bananas, which are very starchy and therefore require cooking; and eating bananas.

(From U.S.D.A. Agriculture Handbook #8) BANANAS (raw, common) 100 gm. edible portion			
Water	75.7%	Iron	.7 mg.
Food energy	85 calories	Sodium	1 mg.
Protein	1.1 gm.	Potassium	370 mg.
Fat	.2 gm.	Vitamin A	190 I.U.
Carbohydrate	22.2 gm. (Total)	Thiamine	.05 mg.
	.5 gm. (Fiber)	Riboflavin	.06 mg.
Ash	.8 gm.	Niacin	.7 mg.
Calcium	8 mg.	Vitamin C	10 mg.
Phosphorus	26 mg.		

PLANTAIN (Cooking Bananas) 100 gm. edible portion			
Water	66.4%	Sodium	5 mg.
Food energy	119 calories	Potassium	385 mg.
Protein	1.1 gm.	Vitamin A	Ranges
Fat	.4 gm.	from 10 I.U. (white	
Carbohydrate	31.2 gm. (Total)	flesh) to 1200 I.U.	
	.4 gm. (Fiber)	(deep-yellow flesh)	
Ash	.9 gm.	Thiamine	.06 mg.
Calcium	7 mg.	Riboflavin	.04 mg.
Phosphorus	30 mg.	Niacin	.6 mg.
Iron	.7 mg.	Vitamin C	14 mg.

Compared to other fruits, all bananas are a fair source of vitamin A, B_2 and B_3 and are poor sources of vitamin B_1 and calcium. While eating bananas are a poor source of phosphorus and iron, cooking bananas have been found to be a fair source of phosphorus and a good source of iron. The two most popular bananas locally, namely the Bluefields and Chinese, are poor sources of vitamin C, but some others, like Brazilian, Ice Cream and all cooking bananas are fair sources.

The stage of ripeness of a banana makes a great deal of difference in the nutritive value. When bananas are green, they are full of starch and therefore should be cooked and served like a potato. Most people eat bananas when they are only half-ripe. They mistakenly think the banana is ripe if its peel is a picture-perfect, bright yellow. However, the half-ripe banana is still one-third to one-half carbohydrate in the form of starch and is difficult to digest for some people. When completely ripe the peel gets brown spots on it, and some varieties turn completely brown. Unfortunately, most markets throw bananas away at this stage of ripeness. And many people, being conditioned to the picture-perfect bananas in the store, often think their bananas are rotten when they get brown dots and throw them away also. This is most unfortunate, because at this stage almost all the starch turns to sugar and the carbohydrates are very easily digested.

Not only is the banana a wonderful food in that it can be served as a potatolike vegetable when green or a sweet fruit when ripe, but the whole tree is a wonder. The purple blossom or flower of the tree can be cut after bananas have developed and cooked into a vegetable or a chutney (see recipes). Dried, green bananas can be ground into a flour. The banana leaves can be used as plates, woven into cloth or chopped up fine and cooked into rice. The banana peel contains antibiotic properties. The native Hawaiians used to cover wounds with the pulp of pounded, ripe banana peels to prevent infection.

Banana trees only bear fruit once, so they must be cut down after harvesting the bunch of bananas. This is not the end of the tree, however. The Supreme Person, who controls the whole universe perfectly, down to even the banana tree, has arranged it so that when the tree is cut down, three or four "keikis," or baby banana trees, sprout from its root. There is no waste if we learn to live in harmony with nature. Not only does chopping down the tree create new life, but within the center of the chopped-down tree trunk there is a round, cylinderlike, white tube with a smooth, shiny covering. This is the banana heart. It can be cooked (see recipe, p. 89). It is somewhat like celery and has a taste and texture similar to bamboo shoots.

The easiest way to get to the heart of the banana tree is to chop the trunk into 12- to 18-inch sections and peel off the layers of fibrous bark. But don't throw these away, either. They make perfect disposable plates (that can be composted later), or your children might have fun cutting out shapes and hanging them for decoration.

There are probably many more things one can do with the banana tree. I can only share with you these few things that I have learned since I began realizing that fruits don't grow on supermarket shelves.

Here are some new ways to prepare bananas and parts of the banana tree. I hope you will try some of these and try experimenting and making some up. After all, this is how these recipes came into being in the first place!

BANANA WALDORF ☐

2 cups diced banana
1½ cups diced apple
1 cup diced celery
½ cup chopped walnuts
½ cup raisins (opt.)
½ cup yogurt
1 Tbsp. lemon juice

Use well-chilled fruit. Prepare it and combine all ingredients. Mix well and serve immediately on top of lettuce leaf or some alfalfa sprouts. Yields 6 small servings.

GINGERED BANANA ☐

8 bananas, sliced
Juice of 4 lemons
4 tsp. grated ginger

Toss ingredients together. Makes 4 servings.

BANANA COCO-PEANUT SALAD ☐

3 large bananas, diced
¼ cup grated coconut
¼ cup chopped peanuts
2 Tbsp. lemon juice

½ cup yogurt
1 Tbsp. honey or more

Combine first 4 ingredients. Combine next 2 and place about 2 Tbsp. on top of each serving. Yields 4 small servings.

BANANA SALAD ☐

6 bananas
2 Tbsp. sesame tahini
2 Tbsp. honey
2 Tbsp. protein powder
Raisins, seeds, nuts, etc.

Mix tahini, honey and protein powder together and chop bananas into it. Mix bananas and desired seeds, etc., into sauce.

CAROB BANANA ☐

2 cups blended bananas
½ cup sunflower seeds (soaked overnight)
¼ cup carob powder
¼ cup pitted dates
1 tsp. vanilla or mint extract

Blend ingredients together until smooth. Serve as pudding or use as a raw pie filling. Makes about 4 servings.

BANANA BUTTER SALAD ☐

8 bananas, sliced
3 Tbsp. sesame tahini or nut butter
3 Tbsp. honey
2 Tbsp. carob or soy powder
½ cup raisins or currants

Mix all ingredients together and serve as a salad. Makes 4 servings.

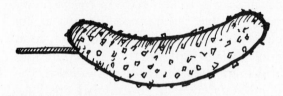

CAROB-COATED FROZEN BANANAS ☐

Icing:
1 cup honey
1 tsp. vanilla
1 Tbsp. butter or nut butter

½ cup carob powder
½ cup water

Noninstant milk powder
Firm-ripe bananas, peeled and whole
Chopped sunflower seeds or grated coconut

Cream first 3 ingredients. Blend next 2 ingredients, combine with first 3 and mix well. Gradually add milk powder until it reaches desired consistency. Dip and roll bananas in carob until evenly coated. Roll in seeds or coconut. Place on cookie sheet covered with wax paper and set in freezer. A popsicle stick or chopstick can also be inserted into the center of each banana for a frozen banana pop.

BANANA PUDDING ☐

½ lb. cashew nuts	½ tsp. cinnamon
2 Tbsp. sesame tahini	Dash of nutmeg
4 bananas	2 tsp. honey (opt.)

Blend all ingredients and pour into bowls. Garnish with toasted coconut, sliced bananas, etc. Makes 4 servings.

BANANA SUNDAE

8 bananas

Soy Whipped Cream
(see Basic Recipes Section, p. 34)

Carob syrup (see No-bake Banana
Cheesecake Filling recipe, p. 85)

1 cup chopped cashews

Slice bananas in half lengthwise. Lay ingredients in layers one on top of another until you run out. Makes about 6 servings.

HOT BANANA MILK ○

4 cups milk
Pinch ground cinnamon
Pinch ground nutmeg
Pinch ground coriander

1 large, ripe banana, mashed
2 Tbsp. honey
2 Tbsp. butter or margarine

Bring first 4 ingredients to a boil. Add next 3 ingredients. Mix well with a fork or whisk and serve hot. Good on cool mornings or for a late evening drink. Yields 4 servings.

BANANA-CAROB SMOOTHIE

1 cup cold milk
1 large, very ripe banana
1 tsp. honey
½ tsp. vanilla
1 Tbsp. dry milk powder
1 Tbsp. carob powder

Combine ingredients. Blend in blender until smooth. Chill thoroughly and whiz in blender again before serving. Yields 1 serving. Good served over ice (crushed or cubes). This may also be set in freezer 'til solid and served as a frozen dessert like ice milk.

BANANA-DATE SMOOTHIE □

1 cup coconut milk
2 bananas
¼ cup pitted dates
Drop of vanilla extract

Blend ingredients together. Makes 2 servings.

MINIATURE BANANA-COCONUT PANCAKES

1 cup whole wheat flour
1 cup unbleached white flour
2 tsp. baking powder (heaping)

2 large cans evaporated milk
or 4 cups fresh milk or buttermilk

½ cup mashed ripe banana
½ cup fresh grated coconut (lightly toasted)
2 Tbsp. melted butter or margarine

Sift first 3 ingredients into a mixing bowl. Slowly add milk, mixing well (whisk works well). Fold in next 3 ingredients. Mix well, lightly and quickly. Add some water if batter is too thick. Ladle small spoonfuls onto lightly oiled skillet at medium heat. Turn when bubbly. Very good served with real maple syrup, mango sauce, mango butter or guava butter, etc.

BANANA JELL ○

6 Tbsp. lemon juice
2 cups water
2 Tbsp. honey
1 stick agar-agar (½ cup flakes)
¼ cup raisins

5 bananas

Soak first 5 ingredients for about 30 minutes. Cook until agar-agar dissolves. Set aside to cool. Blend bananas and pour into other ingredients when cooled to room temperature. Pour into baking tray or gelatin mold. Makes enough dessert for about 8 people.

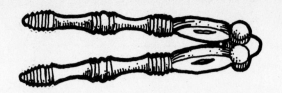

BANANA CHUTNEY　O

1-inch piece tamarind (or more)

1 tsp. ghee or oil
¼ tsp. ground cumin
¼ tsp. ground red pepper (or less)
¼ tsp. ginger powder
¼ tsp. nutmeg
¼ tsp. cinnamon

12 bananas, mashed
½ cup honey

Soak tamarind in small amount of water overnight. Press through a strainer into a large bowl. Lightly cook the next 6 ingredients. Add the next 2 ingredients and mix well over the flame. Remove from heat and cool. Mix with tamarind and serve cold.

BANANAS 'N BATTER　☆

1 cup whole wheat flour
2 tsp. baking powder
1 tsp. salt

¼ cup honey
2/3 cup milk
2 Tbsp. ghee or melted butter

3 firm bananas

Sift first 3 ingredients into a bowl. Add next 3 and mix well. This should be a thick batter. Cut bananas into 3 or 4 pieces each, dip in batter (make sure they are well covered) and deep fry in hot oil or ghee for about 6 minutes or until browned. Turn frequently. These will stay crisp for 10 to 15 minutes and are good served as a side dish or as a dessert with your favorite fruit sauce such as Mango Sauce or Coconut Cream (pp. 146, 122). This also works well using pieces of firm, ripe avocado. Yields 2 to 4 servings.

BANANA-NUT OATMEAL COOKIES　☆

1 cup butter or oil
¾ cup honey

1 cup diced (firm-ripe) bananas
1¼ cups rolled oats (quick-cook)
1 cup chopped walnuts

1½ cups whole wheat flour
¼ tsp. salt
¼ tsp. nutmeg
1 tsp. cinnamon
½ tsp. baking powder

Preheat oven to 375° F. Cream first 2 ingredients. Add the next 3 and mix well. Sift in the next 5, mix well and drop by teaspoons onto an oiled cookie sheet about 1½" apart. Bake at 375° for 13 to 15 minutes. Cool and serve. Makes about 2 dozen.

BANANA BREAD　☆

¾ cup honey
½ cup butter or oil
1 Tbsp. yogurt

3 cups whole wheat flour
1 tsp. baking powder
½ tsp. salt
1 tsp. cinnamon

1½ cups mashed banana
½ tsp. baking soda

1 cup chopped nuts (opt.)

Preheat oven to 350° F. Cream first 3 ingredients. Sift next 4 ingredients into honey mixture and mix well. Combine next 2 ingredients and add with nuts to the others. Mix well, quickly and lightly. Spoon into greased and floured loaf pan and bake at 350° for 1 hour.

NO-BAKE BANANA CHEESECAKE FILLING

5 bananas

8 oz. cream cheese
½ cup yogurt
1 tsp. vanilla
2 Tbsp. lemon juice

Carob syrup:
2 Tbsp. sesame tahini
1 Tbsp. carob powder
2 Tbsp. honey
1 Tbsp. water

Slice 4 bananas and line a no-bake pie crust with them (see Basic Recipes Section, p. 32), or use the No-bake Banana Pie Crust recipe on this page. Blend next 4 ingredients and pour over bananas. Refrigerate for at least 4 hours. Slice remaining banana and dip in a little lemon juice to keep from browning. Top the pie with the banana slices, drizzle carob syrup over the whole thing and serve.

NO-BAKE BANANA SOY WHIPPED CREAM PIE

Crust:
Use Candy No-bake Pie Shell
(see Basic Recipes Section, p. 32)

Filling:
Soy Whipped Cream
(see Basic Recipes Section, p. 34)

3 - 4 lbs. chopped bananas, ripe but firm
1 cup raisins

Make no-bake pie crust and press into pan. Make Soy Whipped Cream. Fold fruit into the Soy Whipped Cream very gently. Spread in pie crust. Chill in refrigerator a few hours before serving. This will work with any fruit that isn't too juicy. Juicy fruits make the Soy Whipped Cream runny.

NO-BAKE BANANA PIE CRUST

½ cup toasted coconut
¼ cup bran
¼ cup wheat germ
¼ cup chopped dates or date sugar
1 banana, mashed
Few drops of lemon juice

Combine ingredients and press into a pie tin. Fill with assortment of fresh fruit and top with yogurt or Soy Whipped Cream (see Basic Recipes Section, p. 34).

BANANA-COCONUT CREAM PIE
(or use filling as a pudding)

Filling:
4 cups whole milk
½ cup honey
1 cup fresh grated coconut
¼ tsp. salt
1 tsp. vanilla
7 Tbsp. arrowroot powder

1 cup mashed banana
(sprinkled with lemon juice)

Crust:
Use Flaky Pie Crust or Raw Pie Crust
(see Basic Recipes Section, pp. 32, 33)

Combine first 6 ingredients in blender until very smooth. Pour into saucepan and stir constantly over medium heat until thick (about 20 minutes). Remove from heat and add mashed banana. Mix well and pour into a baked pie shell. Top pie with banana slices that have soaked in lemon juice and with fresh, grated coconut (raw or toasted). Chill 1 hour. This amount makes two 9" pies.

Variation: Lemon-soaked banana slices may be lined in the pie shell and layered alternately with the pie filling. For carob flavor, add ¼ cup carob powder with blender mixture before cooking.

BAKED BANANA CREAM PIE ☆

Crust and Topping:
Use Crumbly Crust recipe
(see Basic Recipes Section, p. 33)

Filling:
1½ cups unbleached white flour
2 cups whole milk

½ stick butter or margarine
1 cup honey

2 cups mashed banana
1 tsp. vanilla
3 tsp. pure maple syrup
1 tsp. cinnamon
¼ tsp. nutmeg

Preheat oven to 375° F. Prepare filling by placing milk in saucepan and gradually adding flour, mixing with a whisk and stirring out the lumps. Add next 2 ingredients and continue cooking and stirring over medium heat. When thick, turn off heat and add the next 5 ingredients. Pour into an unbaked pie shell. Sprinkle topping evenly over filled pie shell and drizzle honey generously over the top. Bake at 375° for 20 minutes until brown on top. Serve warm or cooled.

FRIED BANANAS ☆

4 large ripe bananas (cooking or eating)
2 Tbsp. ghee or oil

2 Tbsp. orange juice plus
2 Tbsp. date sugar
    or
2 Tbsp. lemon juice plus
2 Tbsp. honey

Fry lengthwise-cut banana halves until lightly browned. Add either set of the next 2 ingredients, cover and simmer until soft. Yields 4 servings.

BOILED BANANAS ○

Cook washed, firm-ripe cooking bananas in boiling water about 15 to 20 minutes or until skin is easily pierced. Drain. Slit open the long way and serve hot with butter, salt and black pepper.

BAKED BANANA ○

Place washed, firm-ripe cooking bananas in a pan with water just covering the bottom. Bake at 350° for about 20 to 30 minutes or until easily pierced with a fork. Slit open the long way and serve hot as a vegetable with butter, salt and black pepper.

BANANA FRITTERS ☆

1 tsp. baking soda
1 cup whole wheat pastry flour
¼ tsp. salt
2 tsp. baking powder
½ tsp. cinnamon

2 diced bananas (firm-ripe)
1 mashed banana
¼ cup milk

Ghee or oil for deep frying

8 oz. yogurt

Sift first 5 ingredients into a mixing bowl. Add next 3 ingredients and mix well. Drop by teaspoons into hot ghee or light oil and deep fry until golden. Drain on paper towel and serve with yogurt. Makes about 4 to 5 servings.

BANANA DUMPLINGS ○

1 cup whole wheat flour
2 tsp. baking powder
½ tsp. salt

1 heaping Tbsp. butter or margarine

1/3 cup cold water

1 large (minced) banana
1 tsp. butter or margarine
1 tsp. honey
½ tsp. lemon juice

Sauce:
¼ cup boiling water
4 Tbsp. honey
2 Tbsp. butter or margarine
Pinch of cinnamon
Pinch of salt

Preheat oven to 350° F. Sift first 3 ingredients into bowl. Add softened butter and rub together. Gradually add water, mixing lightly with a spoon. Divide into 4 balls and roll out lightly and quickly on a well-floured surface to the size of large saucers. May have to pat with hands rather than roll; dough is very moist and delicate. Combine last 4 ingredients, divide into fours and put some in the middle of each pastry. Wet edges of pastry, bring to the top and press closed. Pierce tops with a fork to allow steam to escape. Bake on a greased and floured cookie sheet at 350° for 25 minutes. Combine sauce ingredients, heat and pour over hot dumplings. Let soak for a few minutes and serve warm. Makes 4 large dumplings.

RICH AND CREAMY BANANA BAKE ☆

8 bananas, cut in half lengthwise
Butter or margarine

8 oz. cream cheese
4 Tbsp. honey
½ tsp. cinnamon (or more)

Yogurt

Preheat oven to 375° F. Brown banana halves in butter. Place 8 halves on the bottom of an 8" or 9" pie plate. Cream the next 3 ingredients and spread half of it on top of the bananas. Place next 8 bananas on top, spread with rest of cheese mixture, top with yogurt and bake at 375° for 20 minutes. This may be served warm or cold. One-half cup of raisins may also be added to the cream cheese mixture.

BANANA CAKE ☆

2 cups mashed banana
½ cup butter, margarine or oil
1½ cups honey

3 cups whole wheat flour
2 tsp. baking soda
2 tsp. baking powder
1 tsp. cinnamon
1 tsp. cloves

½ - 1 cup chopped nuts (opt.)

Preheat oven to 350° F. Cream first 3 ingredients. (May use an electric mixer.) Sift in next 5 ingredients and stir. Add nuts. Mix well and pour into a greased and floured cake pan — one large, oblong (13" x 22") or two small, square pans. Bake at 350° for 25 to 30 minutes. Light and delicious!

PLANTAIN, EGGPLANT AND TOMATO ☆

5 medium-sized round eggplants, cubed

4 ripe yellow cooking bananas, sliced
Ghee for deep frying

½ cup ghee or oil
1 tsp. cumin seed
½ tsp. anise seed
½ tsp. coriander seed
½ tsp. crushed red pepper

1 tsp. coriander powder
¼ tsp. clove powder
½ tsp. asafetida
2 tsp. turmeric
½ tsp. thyme
½ tsp. finely chopped fresh ginger
½ tsp. mango powder (opt.)

8 oz. tomato purée
Salt to taste

Steam eggplant and drain. Deep fry bananas in ghee until golden. Set aside to drain. Combine next 5 ingredients in skillet and cook until brown. Add next 7 ingredients and cook a few minutes. Add tomato purée, salt and cooked eggplant. Simmer together for 15 minutes. Remove from heat. Add bananas, mix and serve.

Note: Mango powder is available in Japanese sections of most grocery stores.

BANANA FLOWER VEGETABLE ○

2 cups banana flowers
Salt water (for squeezing)

4 Tbsp. butter or oil
1 cup cubed tofu

2 cups water
2 red or green peppers (cut in strips)
2 - 3 tsp. salt
3 Tbsp. lemon juice
2 tsp. coriander

2 chilies, minced
Squeezed banana flower

Remove rough covering of blossom, slice thin and squeeze with salt water several times. Rinse. Fry tofu in butter, add next 5 ingredients. Cook a few minutes, then add last 2 ingredients and cook until tender.

BANANA FLOWERS IN COCONUT MILK ○

2 cups banana flowers
Salt water

4 cups thick coconut milk
1 tsp. salt or 2 tsp. kelp
2 tsp. finely chopped fresh ginger
¼ tsp. black pepper

Cut blossoms in thick slices crosswise. Squeeze with salt water and drain. Combine with last 4 ingredients and cook until tender.

SPICY BANANA HEART ◯

2 cups finely chopped banana heart
2 cups coconut milk
¼ cup diced green pepper
¼ cup grated carrot
½ tsp. cinnamon
½ tsp. salt or 1 tsp. kelp
½ tsp. turmeric
¼ tsp. black pepper
1 tsp. coriander

½ tsp. mustard powder
½ tsp. cumin powder
2 Tbsp. whole wheat flour

Combine first 9 ingredients and cook in skillet on medium heat until banana heart is tender. Stir often to prevent milk from curdling. Combine last 3 ingredients with just enough water to form a paste. Gradually add to the vegetable mixture, stirring well. Simmer for about 10 minutes and serve. This is very nice served with fluffy, steamed brown rice. Yields 4 to 6 servings.

FRIED GREEN BANANA CHIPS ☆

Preferably cooking bananas, but any kind of green banana will do. Peel them (may have to cut skins off when in this stage) and cut lengthwise in thin slices. Deep fry in ghee or light oil. When crispy, remove and drain on paper towels or place in a paper bag. Sprinkle well with salt and lightly with cayenne pepper.

Note: The bananas should be green but they can be showing some slight signs of yellow. Ten average-sized bananas should yield 5 servings.

BANANA SOUP ◯

1 Tbsp. butter, margarine or oil
1 Tbsp. whole wheat flour

1 cup milk

¾ cup mashed and strained Chinese banana
¼ tsp. salt
1/8 tsp. black pepper

Toast first 2 ingredients, mixing well. Slowly add milk, stirring constantly. When it boils, add last 3 ingredients. Mix well, cook for a few minutes. Stir and serve hot with crackers. Yields 1 serving.

SWEET BANANA FLOWER ◯

1 average banana flower
Hot, salty water

1 cup water

1 cup coconut milk

1 Tbsp. butter or margarine
1 - 2 cups honey

Slice off top and bottom ends of the blossom. Remove first few outer layers. Slice and chop the remaining layers and interior of the flower. Place in a pan and cover with hot, salty water. Let set and when cool enough, squeeze with hands and rinse. Repeat several times; this helps to remove any bitter taste. After squeezing with salt water several times, rinse well and return to pan with 1 cup fresh water and boil until water cooks off. Rinse and drain, return to pan and add coconut milk prepared with meat of 1 coconut and 1 cup hot water (see Coconut Section, p. 120, for directions). Add butter and honey and cook for about 1 hour, stirring occasionally. This cooks down fairly thick, is similar to a chutney and is quite sweet. It is very good served as any chutney might be served.

"I have from an early age abjured the use of meat, and the time will come when men such as I will look upon the murder of animals as they now look upon the murder of men."
— Leonardo da Vinci

BERRIES
and
CHERRIES

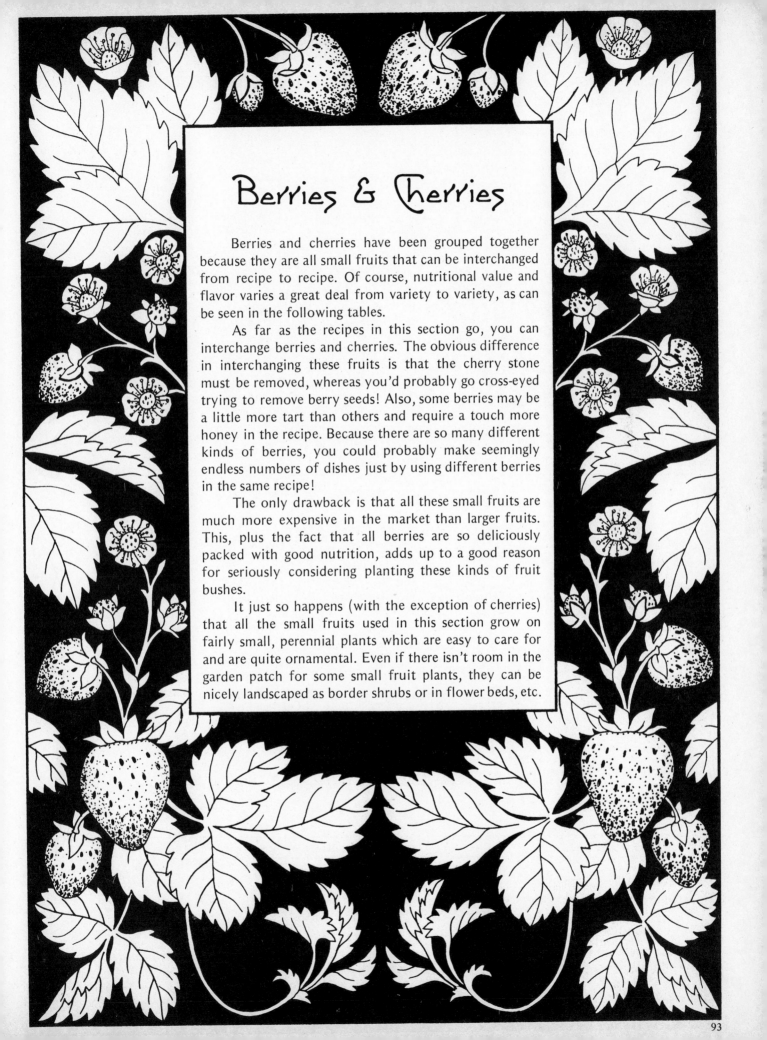

Berries & Cherries

Berries and cherries have been grouped together because they are all small fruits that can be interchanged from recipe to recipe. Of course, nutritional value and flavor varies a great deal from variety to variety, as can be seen in the following tables.

As far as the recipes in this section go, you can interchange berries and cherries. The obvious difference in interchanging these fruits is that the cherry stone must be removed, whereas you'd probably go cross-eyed trying to remove berry seeds! Also, some berries may be a little more tart than others and require a touch more honey in the recipe. Because there are so many different kinds of berries, you could probably make seemingly endless numbers of dishes just by using different berries in the same recipe!

The only drawback is that all these small fruits are much more expensive in the market than larger fruits. This, plus the fact that all berries are so deliciously packed with good nutrition, adds up to a good reason for seriously considering planting these kinds of fruit bushes.

It just so happens (with the exception of cherries) that all the small fruits used in this section grow on fairly small, perennial plants which are easy to care for and are quite ornamental. Even if there isn't room in the garden patch for some small fruit plants, they can be nicely landscaped as border shrubs or in flower beds, etc.

It certainly makes sense to make the most efficient use of space available in a yard or landscape by cultivating plants which are attractive, yet produce edible fruit.

Perhaps the deliciousness of one or a few of these recipes along with the high prices of berries in stores, plus the fact that most of these small fruit plants are easy to care for, will encourage you to plant a few of your favorites!

(From U.S.D.A. Agriculture Handbook #8)
CHERRIES (Raw)
100 gm. edible portion

	Sour, red	Sweet
Water	83.7%	80.4%
Food energy	58 calories	70 calories
Protein	1.2 gm.	1.3 gm.
Fat	.3 gm.	.3 gm.
Carbohydrate	14.3 gm. (Total)	17.4 gm. (Total)
	.2 gm. (Fiber)	.4 gm. (Fiber)
Ash	.5 gm.	.6 gm.
Calcium	22 mg.	22 mg.
Phosphorus	19 mg.	19 mg.
Iron	.4 mg.	.4 mg.
Sodium	2 mg.	2 mg.
Potassium	191 mg.	191 mg.
Vitamin A	1,000 I.U.	110 I.U.
Thiamine	.05 mg.	.05 mg.
Riboflavin	.06 mg.	.06 mg.
Niacin	.4 mg.	.4 mg.
Vitamin C	10 mg.	10 mg.

(From U.S.D.A. Agriculture Handbook #8)
BERRIES (Raw)
100 gm. edible portion

	Raspberries (Black)	Raspberries (Red)	Strawberries	Blueberries	Blackberries Boysenberries
Water	80.8%	84.2%	89.9%	83.2%	84.5%
Food energy	73 calories	57 calories	37 calories	62 calories	58 calories
Protein	1.5 gm.	1.2 gm.	.7 gm.	.7 gm.	1.2 gm.
Fat	1.4 gm.	.5 gm.	.5 gm.	.5 gm.	.9 gm.
Carbohydrate	15.7 gm. (Total)	13.6 gm. (Total)	8.4 gm. (Total)	15.3 gm. (Total)	12.9 gm. (Total)
	5.1 gm. (Fiber)	3.0 gm. (Fiber)	1.3 gm. (Fiber)	1.5 gm. (Fiber)	4.1 gm. (Fiber)
Ash	.6 gm.	.5 gm.	.5 gm.	.3 gm.	.5 gm.
Calcium	30 mg.	22 mg.	21 mg.	15 mg.	32 mg.
Phosphorus	22 mg.	22 mg.	21 mg.	13 mg.	19 mg.
Iron	.9 mg.	.9 mg.	1.0 mg.	1.0 mg.	.9 mg.
Sodium	1 mg.	1 mg.	1 mg.	1 mg.	1 mg.
Potassium	199 mg.	168 mg.	164 mg.	81 mg.	170 mg.
Vitamin A	Trace	130 I.U.	60 I.U.	100 I.U.	200 I.U.
Thiamine	(.03 mg.)	.03 mg.	.03 mg.	(.03 mg.)	.03 mg.
Riboflavin	(.09 mg.)	.09 mg.	.07 mg.	(.06 mg.)	.04 mg.
Niacin	(.9 mg.)	.9 mg.	.6 mg.	(.5 mg.)	.4 mg.
Vitamin C	18 mg.	25 mg.	59 mg.	14 mg.	21 mg.

(Numbers in parentheses denote values imputed — usually from another form of the food or from a similar food.)

A VERY PURPLE JUICE ☐

1¼ cups seedless grapes
¾ cup blueberries and strawberries
1 tsp. lecithin
1 tsp. vanilla

Blend together and serve.

FRESH FRUIT MALT ☐

2 cups pineapple
¾ cup strawberries
1 tsp. lecithin

Blend ingredients in blender until smooth.

A BERRY DELIGHTFUL EXPERIENCE ☐

1 lb. blueberries
¼ lb. raspberries
¼ lb. strawberries

Dressing:
½ avocado
½ cup yogurt or kefir
2 tsp. honey
2 tsp. lemon juice
1 tsp. vanilla
1/8 tsp. cardamom

Mix berries gently in a bowl. Blend dressing ingredients in blender and pour over berries. Toss and serve.

PINK DELIGHT ☐

2 cups fresh strawberries

3 Tbsp. honey
2 cups plain yogurt

Clean strawberries and purée them in a blender. Mix with last 2 ingredients. Pour in chilled glasses. Makes four 8-ounce servings.

CRANBERRY FRESH-UP ☐

2 cups chilled cranberry juice
4 Tbsp. honey
2 cups chilled, plain yogurt

2 cups chilled, fizzy water
(Perrier, Calistoga, etc.)

Combine first 3 ingredients in blender. Then add the fizzy water. Mix well and serve. Makes 4 to 6 servings.

A FRUIT 'N BERRY FIZZ ☐

1½ cups blueberries
1 cup orange juice
1 cup pineapple juice
1 Tbsp. honey
1 Tbsp. lemon juice

1 cup fizzy water (Perrier, Calistoga, etc.)

Put first 5 ingredients in blender and whiz. Then stir in natural fizzy water. Makes 2 to 3 servings.

Cherry Parfait, p. 98   Strawberry Shortcake, p. 99

FRUIT SHERBET

1 cup yogurt or kefir
¼ cup honey
1 cup berries

Combine ingredients and freeze until mushy. Then take out and whip with a whisk. Return to freezer until solid. Serves 4.

AMBROSIA TROPICANA

3 medium oranges, peeled
8 slices pineapple
3 medium bananas, peeled & sliced
3 cups sliced strawberries

3 Tbsp. lemon juice
¼ cup honey

1 cup plain yogurt
3½ oz. flaked coconut

Cut fruit into a bowl. Combine next 2 ingredients and spoon over the fruit. Toss lightly. Chill. When ready to serve, add last 2 ingredients and toss together. Serves 6 to 8.

RAW CHERRY PIE

Raw pie crust
(see Basic Recipes Section, p. 32)

½ cup lemon juice
¼ cup maple syrup
1 - 2 tsp. arrowroot

4 cups cherries, pitted

Mix first 3 filling ingredients together until arrowroot dissolves. Cook over heat until mixture thickens (stir to prevent lumping). Pour over raw cherries in a raw pie crust and refrigerate.

RAW FRUIT PIE

Raw Coconut Pie Crust
(see Basic Recipes Section, p. 32)

4 peaches
4 bananas
Strawberries

Sauce:
½ cup lemon juice
1 - 2 tsp. arrowroot

¼ cup honey

Topping:
1 cup plain yogurt
2 tsp. honey
¼ tsp. vanilla

¼ cup chopped pecans

Layer fruit in pie shell by placing thin slices of bananas, followed with a layer of thinly sliced peaches, covered with halved berries. Set aside. Make sauce by mixing first 2 ingredients until arrowroot dissolves. Heat to boil, stirring until thick. Add honey. Cool a bit; then pour over fruit before it sets up. Refrigerate to set. Mix first 3 topping ingredients and spread on top of cooled, set pie. Soy Whipped Cream may be used instead of the yogurt topping if desired (see recipe in Basic Recipes Section, p. 34). Sprinkle with chopped pecans.

BERRY OF THE SEASON SOUP

2 tsp. grated fresh ginger root
2 cups sliced bananas
4 cups peaches, apricots,
nectarines or mangoes
2 Tbsp. lemon juice

2 cups berries in season, sliced or whole

Fresh mint leaves (opt.)

Blend together first 4 ingredients. Mix in berries. Garnish with mint leaves.

STUFFED CHERRY ALMOND SALAD ☆

Big black cherries

Cream cheese
Toasted chopped almonds
3 drops almond extract

Salad greens
French dressing

Soften cream cheese. Add equal parts cream cheese and toasted chopped almonds. Add almond extract and mix well. Stuff the cherries with this cream cheese mixture and toss with crisp salad greens. Dress the salad with French dressing.

CREAM OF BERRY SOUP □

3 cups berries in season
2 cups coconut or other nut milk
¼ cup honey (or to taste)
2 tsp. grated fresh ginger root

Blend all ingredients together until smooth and serve.

CHERRY PARFAIT □

1 cup thick yogurt
¼ cup honey
½ tsp. nutmeg
¼ tsp. ginger

1 cup cottage cheese

2 cups cherry pie filling
(see Raw Cherry Pie recipe, p. 97)

¼ cup Midel honey graham crackers, crushed

Combine first 4 ingredients and whip. Fold in cottage cheese. Alternate layers of mixture, cherry pie filling and honey graham cracker crumbs in parfait glasses. Top with crumbs and refrigerate.

CHERRY ASPIC ○

1 cup orange juice (unsweetened)
3 sticks agar-agar (1½ cups flakes)
½ cup water

1 cup cherries
2 Tbsp. honey
1/8 tsp. cloves
½ tsp. almond extract

Almonds

Soak first 3 ingredients together for 10 minutes. Bring to boil until agar is melted. Add next 4 ingredients and mix well. Pour one-fourth of the mixture into a mold and let set. Repeat until mixture is gone. This will distribute cherries. When ready to serve, unmold and sprinkle with almonds.

FRESH FRUIT FILLING ○

Raw pie crust
(see Basic Recipes Section, p. 32)

1 cup fresh or frozen strawberries, sliced
(or other berry in season)
2 cups mashed banana
¼ cup tahini or cashew butter

1 stick agar-agar (½ cup flakes)
¼ cup hot water

Combine first 3 ingredients in a bowl. Break agar into small pieces. Soak in hot water for 15 minutes (may need a bit more water). Bring to boil and cook until agar dissolves. Gradually add to fruit mixture, stirring well. Pour into raw pie shell and chill 2 hours. Good served with Soy Whipped Cream (see Basic Recipes Section, p. 34).

STRAWBERRY WHIP PIE □

Raw Coconut Pie Crust
(see Basic Recipes Section, p. 32)

Filling:
1 stick agar-agar (½ cup flakes)
1 cup cold water

2½ cups strawberries
1 tsp. lemon juice
1 Tbsp. honey

Topping (opt.):
1 cup yogurt
2 tsp. honey
¼ tsp. vanilla

Break up agar-agar stick and combine first 2 filling ingredients. Set aside to soak until agar-agar softens. When softened, boil until agar-agar is melted. Blend next 3 ingredients and put in saucepan with agar-agar mixture. When mixture starts to thicken, pour into pie shell. Keep in refrigerator until it sets. Top with last 3 ingredients blended together, or use Soy Whipped Cream as a topping (see Basic Recipes Section, p. 34).

FRUIT AND NUT JELL ○

3 sticks agar-agar (1½ cups flakes)
1 cup water
1½ cups applesauce

1 cup Cranberry Sauce (see recipe, p. 102)
2 oranges, chopped
1 cup nuts, chopped
½ cup raisins
½ cup figs, chopped
1½ cups honey

Mix first 3 ingredients and soak until agar-agar softens. Bring to a boil until agar melts. Remove from heat. Add next 6 ingredients and cool slightly. Pour into a mold or flat Pyrex dish. Set in refrigerator to cool and jell.

* Just as a quick note: As mentioned in the basic products shopping list, agar-agar is sold in different forms. 1 stick agar-agar = ½ cup flakes = 2 Tbsp. powdered agar-agar.

STRAWBERRY SHORTCAKE ☆

Shortcake
(see recipe in Mango Section, p. 147)

Strawberries
Honey

Use Mango Shortcake recipe to make the shortcake. Mash berries with honey to taste. Put together in the same way as Mango Shortcake.

BLUEBERRY MUFFINS ○

3 Tbsp. butter or margarine
¼ cup honey
2 Tbsp. yogurt

¾ cup milk
1½ cups fresh blueberries
(or other berries in season)

2 cups whole wheat flour
3 tsp. baking powder

Cream first 3 ingredients. Gently mix in next 2 ingredients. Sift in last 2 ingredients and mix gently. Fill oiled muffin tins halfway and bake at 400° for 25 minutes.

STEAMED BERRY PUDDING   ○

1 cup berries in season
(blueberries, cranberries, etc.)
¼ cup chopped pitted dates
¼ cup chopped dried pineapple
¼ cup chopped dried papaya or banana
¼ cup shredded coconut
¾ cup whole wheat flour
Pinch salt
¼ tsp. nutmeg
½ tsp. vanilla

¼ cup barbados molasses
3 Tbsp. boiling water
1 tsp. baking soda

Combine first 9 ingredients in a bowl. (You can use any variation of dried fruit that you like. Raisins, currants, apricots, pears, etc., all work well.) Combine last 3 ingredients together in a separate bowl. Mix well and add to dry ingredients. Stir until mixed well. Pour into a baking dish and steam for about 1½ hours, following steaming directions for Plum Pudding (see Plum Section, p. 225).

CHERRY SURPRISE SOUP   ○

3 small beets

1 quart water
4 whole cloves

2 Tbsp. honey
2 cups pitted cherries
Juice of 1 lemon

Yogurt

Scrub beets well and remove stems. Add next 2 ingredients and boil until beets are tender. Save water; discard cloves. Skin beets and purée in a blender with some of the water. Add next 3 ingredients. Serve hot or cold topped with yogurt.

SOUTH AMERICAN FRUIT SOUP   □

½ cup strawberries
½ cup mango
½ cup papaya
½ cup pineapple
1 Tbsp. citrus juice
2 Tbsp. avocado

Blend ingredients until smooth. Garnish with orange slice and mint leaf.

CRANBERRY CREAM PIE   ☆

Graham Cracker Crust
(see Basic Recipes Section, p. 33)

Cream Filling:
8 oz. cream cheese, softened
½ cup yogurt
½ tsp. vanilla
4 Tbsp. honey (lehua is good)

Cranberry Topping:
½ lb. fresh cranberries
½ cup water

½ cup honey

2 Tbsp. arrowroot powder
2 Tbsp. water

Combine filling ingredients and mix well. May use electric mixer. Spread evenly in pie shell. Then prepare topping by washing cranberries and placing in a pan with water. Bring to boil with lid on, then lower to simmer. Simmer until berries are popping and getting soft, about 20 minutes. Add honey and mix well. Make a paste with arrowroot and water. Add to berries and honey and mix well. Continue mixing and cooking 3 to 5 minutes until thick. Remove from heat and allow to cool. Top evenly with cooled cranberry sauce and set in refrigerator to chill at least 4 hours before serving.

SPECIAL CHERRY PIE ☆

Unbaked Flaky Pie Crust
(see Basic Recipes Section, p. 33)

4 cups fresh, pitted cherries

½ cup cherry juice
4 Tbsp. whole wheat pastry flour
½ cup pure maple syrup
1½ Tbsp. lemon juice
2 Tbsp. arrowroot powder

Soy Whipped Cream
(see Basic Recipes Section, p. 34)

Put cherries in mixing bowl. Combine next 5 ingredients and bring to boil. Add cherries and pour into pie shell. Bake at 375° F for 45 minutes. Top with Soy Whipped Cream. Delicious!

CHERRY PIE WITH CRUMB TOPPING ☆

Unbaked pie crust
(see Basic Recipes Section, p. 33)

3 cups pitted cherries
½ cup honey
2 Tbsp. whole wheat pastry flour
2 Tbsp. butter or margarine

1 cup flour
½ cup honey
2/3 cup butter or margarine
¾ cup raw, rolled oats
1 tsp. cinnamon

Mix together first 4 ingredients and pour into pie shell. Combine last 5 ingredients and sprinkle on top of pie. Bake at 350° for 40 minutes.

MAPLE BLUEBERRY PIE ☆

Unbaked Flaky Pie Crust
(see Basic Recipes Section, p. 33)

3½ cups blueberries

Cinnamon
2 tsp. whole wheat pastry flour

1 Tbsp. butter or margarine
1 cup maple syrup

Line pie pan with pastry and fill with berries. Sprinkle with next 2 ingredients. Dot berries with butter or margarine and evenly pour maple syrup over mixture. Place top crust, seal and flute edges. Slit top and bake at 450° for 20 minutes. Turn down to 400° and bake for 20 minutes more. Turn down to 350° and bake for 20 minutes or until golden. Cool.

BLACKBERRY ROLL-UP ☆

Filling:
4 cups berries
¼ cup honey
½ tsp. lemon juice

Dough:
1¾ cups whole wheat pastry flour
1 tsp. baking powder
½ tsp. cinnamon

¼ cup butter or margarine
¼ cup milk

Preheat oven to 425° F. Combine filling ingredients in a pan and cook down until syrupy. Set aside. Mix together first 3 dough ingredients and cut in the butter or margarine. Add milk and mix well until dough is soft. Roll dough on floured board to 3/8" thickness in a rectangular shape. Brush with melted butter and sprinkle with cinnamon. Spread blackberry mixture down center of dough going lengthwise. Roll up and shape in a ring on well-greased 14" x 10" pan. Bake at 425° for 25 to 30 minutes, or until brown.

CRANBERRY SAUCE ◯

2 cups water
1 cup honey

1 lb. cranberries

Combine first 2 ingredients in saucepan. Stir until well mixed. Add cranberries and bring to a boil. Cook 10 to 15 minutes or until skins pop.

SPICED CRANBERRY SAUCE ☆

2 cups cranberries
2/3 cup water
1/8 tsp. asafetida

4 Tbsp. vinegar
1 tsp. soy sauce
¼ tsp. cloves
¼ tsp. allspice
¼ tsp. mace
¼ tsp. paprika

Combine first 3 ingredients. Bring to boil and cook over moderate heat until cranberries burst. Put mixture in blender and blend, adding remaining ingredients. Then bring to a boil, reduce heat and simmer slowly until it becomes thick. Pour into hot, sterilized jars. Seal and store.

CHERRY COMPOTÉ ◯

1 lb. black cherries

¼ cup maple syrup
½ cup orange juice

Yogurt

Put cherries into a bowl. Drain any juice that may have collected into a pot. Combine juice and next 2 ingredients. Bring to a boil and cook until thick. Pour over cherries and let cool. Serve in individual dishes topped with yogurt and garnished with mint leaves.

CHERRY SAUCE ◯

½ cup honey
½ cup water
1 Tbsp. arrowroot powder
1 Tbsp. lemon juice

2 cups pitted cherries

Combine first 4 ingredients and mix until arrowroot dissolves. Put on heat, stirring to prevent lumping. Simmer, add cherries, and cook on low heat for 10 minutes until thick.

SPICED CHERRY SAUCE ☆

12 oz. red cherries, pitted

1 cup honey
3 Tbsp. lemon juice
¼ tsp. allspice
¼ tsp. cloves
¼ tsp. cinnamon

Drain cherries. Save juice. Combine juice with remaining ingredients and cook over medium flame. Remove from heat. Stir in cherries and cook for 10 minutes more. Serve over ice cream, yogurt, crepes, pancakes, etc.

SPICY BLUEBERRY RELISH ☆

3 cups blueberries
½ cup honey
2 Tbsp. vinegar
½ tsp. cinnamon
1/8 tsp. cloves
1/8 tsp. allspice

2 tsp. arrowroot

Place first 6 ingredients in pan and bring mixture to boil. Simmer for 5 to 8 minutes, until berries are tender. Then take ½ cup liquid out and mix in arrowroot. Pour back in and mix rapidly. Ladle into sterilized jars, leaving ½" head space. Adjust lids and store in refrigerator.

BREADFRUIT

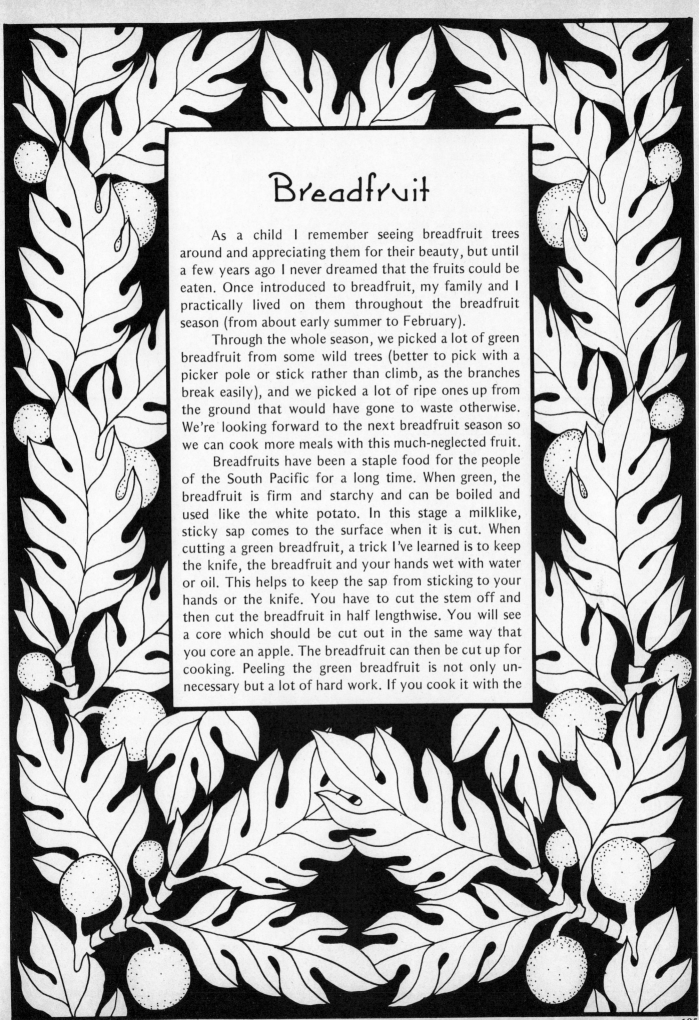

Breadfruit

As a child I remember seeing breadfruit trees around and appreciating them for their beauty, but until a few years ago I never dreamed that the fruits could be eaten. Once introduced to breadfruit, my family and I practically lived on them throughout the breadfruit season (from about early summer to February).

Through the whole season, we picked a lot of green breadfruit from some wild trees (better to pick with a picker pole or stick rather than climb, as the branches break easily), and we picked a lot of ripe ones up from the ground that would have gone to waste otherwise. We're looking forward to the next breadfruit season so we can cook more meals with this much-neglected fruit.

Breadfruits have been a staple food for the people of the South Pacific for a long time. When green, the breadfruit is firm and starchy and can be boiled and used like the white potato. In this stage a milklike, sticky sap comes to the surface when it is cut. When cutting a green breadfruit, a trick I've learned is to keep the knife, the breadfruit and your hands wet with water or oil. This helps to keep the sap from sticking to your hands or the knife. You have to cut the stem off and then cut the breadfruit in half lengthwise. You will see a core which should be cut out in the same way that you core an apple. The breadfruit can then be cut up for cooking. Peeling the green breadfruit is not only unnecessary but a lot of hard work. If you cook it with the peel on, the peel gets so soft in cooking it's as if it's not there at all.

When the breadfruit begins to ripen, the skin turns from green to yellow or even a crusty brown and the flesh becomes very soft and sweet, as the starches all turn to sugars. A ripe breadfruit must be peeled, but that's no sweat, as the skin usually separates from the pulp very easily if you just take a knife and pull the peel away from the pulp. After the peel is all pulled off, the soft pulp can be pulled off of the core very easily and cooked.

As can be seen in the table below, there is a bit of difference in nutritional value between green and ripe breadfruit. And if you try the recipes, you'll see there is a world of difference in taste between the two stages.

(From Food Composition Table for Use in East Asia) BREADFRUIT 100 gm. edible portion		
	Mature, boiled	Green, raw
Water	65.2%	69.3%
Food energy	121 calories	108 calories
Protein	1.4 gm.	1.3 gm.
Fat	0.3 gm.	0.3 gm.
Carbohydrate	31.7 gm. (Total)	28.2 gm. (Total)
	– (Fiber)	– (Fiber)
Ash	1.4 gm.	0.9 gm.
Calcium	24 mg.	21 mg.
Phosphorus	67 mg.	59 mg.
Iron	0.4 mg.	0.4 mg.
Sodium	–	–
Potassium	–	–
Vitamin A	41.6 I.U.	16.6 I.U.
Thiamine	.11 mg.	.12 mg.
Riboflavin	.06 mg.	.06 mg.
Niacin	1.3 mg.	0.9 mg.
Vitamin C	10 mg.	17 mg.

(Dashes denote lack of reliable data for a constituent believed to be present in measurable amount.)

Most of the breadfruits that grow here in Hawaii are seedless, but you may luck out and find one of the varieties that have seeds as large as pecans or hazelnuts. Don't throw the seeds away — they're edible! Not only that, but they're ono and good for you, too! The seeds contain about 8% protein and 5% fat (most nuts contain around 40% to 60% fat) and taste to me like artichoke hearts.

When you're looking for them, it's surprising how many breadfruit trees there are around. And it's even more surprising

how few people use them! In our search for breadfruits, we met so many nice people who gave us breadfruits from their yards. We also had a few adventures and misadventures picking the wild ones. If you're too embarrassed to knock on someone's door and ask them for a breadfruit, or if you're not into spending money on the gas to drive around looking for a wild tree and you'd rather just plant a tree in your yard, there are a few things you need to know before you start digging that hole.

One thing I should not forget to mention is the fact that breadfruit trees can't be grown from cuttings or graftings. Since avocado trees and so many other trees can be grown from cuttings or graftings, I assumed that breadfruit could be grown in the same

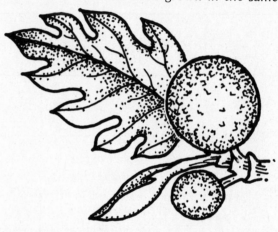

way. After many months of impatient waiting and waiting, I finally found out through a phone call to the Department of Agriculture that breadfruit branches will not root and that the way to start them is by getting a baby plant from a nursery or friend.

The trees send shoots up from the root system. When the shoot gets to be three to four feet tall, it can be dug up and planted. There is one catch to where you're going to plant it. The breadfruit tree has a very extensive root system. Most trees' root systems stretch out only as far as the branches, but the breadfruit tree's root system reaches out about twice as far as its branches. Since breadfruit trees grow anywhere from 30 to 60 feet tall and the branch span is about the same, this should give you some idea of how far away from everything you'll want to plant the tree. You won't want to plant it too close to your house or sewer system (breadfruit trees' roots have been known to break pipes).

If you plant a breadfruit tree now, it may be years before it bears fruit. But if we follow the tradition of the native Hawaiians of planting for future generations, it would be a wise thing to do. The early Hawaiians would cook the breadfruit in an underground oven known as an **imu**, which is a pit filled with stones that are heated to become hot coals. The whole breadfruit is placed on the coals and covered with leaves of taro, breadfruit and banana or sometimes boiled in a pot over the hot coals.

Here are some breadfruit recipes that can be prepared easily in your kitchen. Next breadfruit season, give some of these recipes a try. I think that once you do, you'll probably not let another breadfruit season slip uneventfully by.

BREADFRUIT LEATHER O

1 ripe breadfruit

Peel and take seed out of one very ripe, sweet breadfruit. Boil in a little water until real soft — 8 or 10 minutes. Add enough water so it will blend easily (like a thick smoothie) and blend or mash breadfruit until smooth. Oil cookie sheet and spread breadfruit to 1/8" thin. Then bake in oven for several hours at your lowest temperature, 150° or 200°, or put out in direct sun until it's leatherlike in texture. Eat like a dried fruit roll.

BREADFRUIT & COCONUT PUDDING O

3 cups fresh, grated coconut
1 cup boiling water

3 cups soft, ripe breadfruit (mashed)
½ cup honey

Prepare coconut milk to measure 1 cup rich coconut milk using proportions listed (see Coconut Section, p. 120, for directions). Combine with next 2 ingredients and mix well with an electric mixer or in blender until creamy and smooth. Pour into an oiled baking dish and bake at 350° F for 1 hour. Serve warm or cooled topped with cinnamon and/or Coconut Cream (p. 122). Ono! A very rich and sweet dessert. Can be frozen and sliced to serve after thawed. After freezing, the texture is more like cake.

BREADFRUIT CAKE

1 cup honey
½ cup butter, margarine or oil

¾ cup mashed, ripe breadfruit
½ cup date sugar
2 tsp. vanilla

2 cups whole wheat flour
1 tsp. baking powder
1¼ tsp. baking soda
¼ tsp. salt

½ cup sour milk or yogurt

Cream first 2 ingredients. Add next 3 and mix well. Sift in next 4 alternately with the sour milk. Mix well and spoon into a greased and floured cake pan. Spread evenly and bake at 350° for 1 hour.

Variation: ½ cup chopped macadamia or cashew nuts and ½ cup chopped raisins or dates can be added.

CAROB-BREADFRUIT CHEWS

1 cup ripe, uncooked breadfruit
1 cup honey

1 Tbsp. butter or margarine

1 tsp. grated orange rind
¼ cup carob powder
½ cup chopped nuts and/or dried fruit
1 tsp. vanilla

Bring first 2 ingredients to a boil over medium-high heat for 10 minutes, stirring often. Add butter and stir constantly for about another 10 minutes. Breadfruit should have a taffylike appearance and be sticking together in a ball. Add remaining ingredients and beat about 2 minutes. Drop by spoonfuls onto a platter and let cool.

MINIATURE FRUIT CAKES

½ cup mashed, ripe, uncooked breadfruit
½ cup softened butter or oil
¼ cup honey
2 Tbsp. date sugar
Egg replacer equal to 1 egg or 2 Tbsp. yogurt
1 tsp. vanilla

1 cup whole wheat flour
½ tsp. baking soda
1/8 tsp. salt
½ tsp. cinnamon

¼ cup chopped walnuts
¼ cup chopped raisins
¼ cup chopped dried pineapple
¼ cup chopped dates

Shredded coconut (not too finely grated)

Combine first 6 ingredients and mix with an electric mixer until smooth and fluffy. Sift in next 4 ingredients and mix. Add last 4 ingredients. Drop by teaspoons into shredded coconut and roll into balls. Place on cookie sheet and flatten with the palm of your hand. Bake at 325° for 20 to 25 minutes.

BREADFRUIT FRY CAKES

2 Tbsp. butter or margarine
1 Tbsp. honey
½ tsp. vanilla

1 cup mashed, ripe breadfruit

1 cup whole wheat flour
3 tsp. baking powder
½ tsp. salt
½ tsp. cinnamon
¼ tsp. nutmeg

Ghee or light oil for deep frying

Cream first 3 ingredients; add breadfruit and mix well. Sift in remaining ingredients and mix. Drop by tablespoons into hot ghee (or light oil) and deep fry until golden. Yields about 20.

NOT PORTUGUESE SWEET BREAD ○

1½ cups ripe, uncooked breadfruit
½ cup hot water
¼ cup honey

2 packages yeast

½ cup warm milk
1 cup honey
4 Tbsp. butter, margarine or oil
¼ cup yogurt
2 tsp. vanilla

6 cups whole wheat flour
1 tsp. salt

Preheat oven to 325° F. Combine first 3 ingredients; when lukewarm, add yeast and stir. Cover bowl and let rise in warm place until doubled in bulk. Punch down and add next 5 ingredients. Add last 2 ingredients and knead until dough gets rubbery. Oil a bowl and ball of dough. Put dough in bowl and cover with a damp towel. Put in warm place and let rise until double in bulk. Punch down, knead and shape and put into bread pans. Cover again with damp towels and let rise until double in bulk again. Bake at 325° for about 45 minutes.

BOILED, MASHED BREADFRUIT ○
(with or without gravy)

Follow cooking instructions (this page) for Boiled Breadfruit. When water has cooked off, mash well, add seasonings and about ½ cup fresh cow's milk, coconut milk, or evaporated milk. Add more milk if necessary.

Variation: Serve with Mock Chicken Gravy (recipe in Tofu Section, p. 376). Delicious!

BREADFRUIT JAM ○

1 cup ripe, uncooked breadfruit
1 cup crushed pineapple
1 cup honey

Boil over medium-high heat, stirring occasionally and often towards the end, for about 25 minutes. Use in a jelly roll!

BAKED RIPE BREADFRUIT ○

Preheat oven to 350° F. Place a ripe and washed breadfruit in a pan with a little water to prevent sticking. Bake at 350° for 1 hour. Pull out the stem and core, cut in half and serve with butter, salt and black pepper.

Variation: For sweeter baked breadfruit, remove the stem and core before baking. In the middle, place 1 Tbsp. butter, 1 Tbsp. honey and a pinch of cinnamon. Cover with the stem and bake. When done, cut in half and serve topped with coconut cream.

BOILED BREADFRUIT ○

4 cups diced green, firm breadfruit
3 cups water

1 Tbsp. butter or oil
¾ to 1 tsp. salt or 2 tsp. kelp
1 tsp. curry powder (opt.)
Black pepper to taste

Cook breadfruit in water for about 1 hour until tender. Remove lid and let extra water evaporate. Toast next 4 ingredients for a few minutes. Then toss with breadfruit. Mix well and serve like potatoes. Yields 4 to 6 servings.

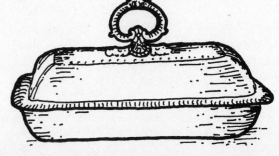

FRIED BREADFRUIT ○

1 breadfruit (just ripe but not too soft)
Whole wheat flour
Soy sauce
Light oil

Boil the breadfruit for about 1 hour. Drain, let cool, cut in half and take out the core. Peel (opt.) and cut into pieces about ¾" thick. Dip them in soy sauce and then dredge in flour. Deep fry in hot oil. Drain. Salt lightly and serve. Yields 2 servings.

Variation: Some ground sesame seeds or sesame meal may be added to the flour for extra flavor.

BREADFRUIT CHIPS ☆

Wash, peel and core a green breadfruit. Slice with a sharp knife into thin chips. Soak them in ice water for about half an hour. Dry them on a cloth and deep fry in hot ghee (or light oil). Drain well and salt. Much like potato chips, but these are said to be better!

BREADFRUIT FRITTERS ☆

1 green breadfruit, grated
2/3 cup milk

1-1/3 cups whole wheat flour
1 tsp. salt or 2 tsp. kelp
2 tsp. baking powder

Combine first 2 ingredients. Sift in next 3 and mix well. Drop balls into hot ghee (or light oil) and fry until golden. Remove and drain. Yields about 2 dozen.

Variation: Leave out a little flour and replace it with sesame meal and/or bran flakes.

BREADFRUIT-CAULIFLOWER PATTIES WITH SAUCE ☆

1 medium head cauliflower
1 medium, green breadfruit

Batter:
2 cups chickpea flour (garbanzo)
2 tsp. ground cumin
2 tsp. turmeric
1½ tsp. ground coriander
¼ tsp. cinnamon
¼ tsp. allspice
1½ tsp. salt or 3 tsp. kelp
1/8 tsp. ground red pepper
2 tsp. curry powder

2 Tbsp. soy sauce
1 cup warm water

Sauce:
8 cups tomato puree

1 tsp. salt or 2 tsp. kelp
½ tsp. black pepper
2 tsp. sweet basil
2 tsp. oregano powder
½ tsp. oregano leaves
¼ tsp. chili powder
¼ cup soy sauce
3 Tbsp. ghee or oil
1 cup grated cheese (opt.)

Grate first 2 ingredients and set aside. Combine next 9 ingredients and gradually add next 2, mixing out any lumps. Toss in grated vegetable and mix thoroughly. Drop by spoonfuls into hot ghee (or light oil) and fry 20 minutes until golden brown and crispy. Remove and drain. Place blended tomatoes in a skillet on high flame, stirring occasionally. When thick, add remaining ingredients and stir. Serve over fried patties. They may be soaked in the sauce for a while before serving. Delicious! Tastes like spaghetti and meatballs.

and fill with breadfruit. Top with cheese and bake at 350° for 10 to 15 minutes.

Variation: Some grated carrot and sesame or sunflower seeds can be combined with the filling for added flavor and texture.

BREADFRUIT CHOWDER O

2 Tbsp. butter or margarine
1 tsp. curry powder
½ cup diced carrot
½ cup chopped celery
2 cups diced, green breadfruit

2½ cups boiling water
1 - 1½ tsp. salt or 3 tsp. kelp
Black pepper to taste

4 cups milk

Combine first 5 ingredients. Toss and cook for about 10 minutes. Combine with next 3 and simmer for about 1 hour until tender. Add milk, mix well and serve. (Do not cook the milk.) Delicious! Tastes almost like clam chowder. Yields 6 servings.

STUFFED PEPPERS WITH BREADFRUIT AND CHEESE ☆

1 large, green breadfruit

1 cup milk, canned or creamy
2 Tbsp. butter or margarine
1 tsp. salt or 2 tsp. kelp
½ tsp. black pepper

8 medium, green peppers (cut in half)

Grated cheese

Preheat oven to 350° F. Cut and core breadfruit. Cut into wedges and steam until tender. Drain and mash with the next 4 ingredients. Slightly steam pepper halves

BREADFRUIT SALAD #1

4 cups diced, green breadfruit

1 cup sour cream
1 tsp. turmeric
1 tsp. salt or 2 tsp. kelp
¼ tsp. cumin powder
¼ tsp. black pepper
Pinch of celery seed
Pinch of dill seed
Pinch of dry mustard

3 sticks celery, chopped
2 bell peppers, chopped
1 cucumber, diced
4 tomatoes (small), firm-ripe

Steam breadfruit until tender (not mushy) and cool. Combine next 8 ingredients. Mix well and toss with cool breadfruit. Toss in last 4 ingredients and mix well. Chill and serve cold.

Variation: Yogurt or an eggless mayonnaise may be used instead of sour cream.

BREADFRUIT SALAD #2 ☆

1 green breadfruit, peeled and cored

1 cup finely chopped, steamed kale
or 1 cup chopped celery
½ cup grated carrot
¼ cup grated beet, raw
½ cup chopped olives, green or ripe
¼ cup chopped, crisp Chinese peas

3 - 4 Tbsp. oil
½ tsp. asafetida
¼ tsp. cumin powder
¼ tsp. turmeric

½ cup canned milk
1 cup yogurt
2 tsp. lemon juice
½ tsp. dill
1 - 2 tsp. salt or 3 tsp. kelp
1 tsp. black pepper
1 - 2 Tbsp. honey

Steam breadfruit until tender. Cool slightly and mix with next 5 ingredients. Toast next 4 ingredients in a skillet, mix well with next 7 ingredients. Add to vegetables. Mix well and refrigerate to chill. Serve sprinkled with a little sesame and sunflower seeds.

BREADFRUIT SEEDS O

Obtain seeds from a ripe breadfruit. Wash well and steam about 20 to 30 minutes. Slice and serve with lemon juice. Tastes somewhat like artichoke hearts. (Only certain kinds of breadfruits have these large seeds.)

Here's a breadfruit dessert to top off the breadfruit section. It's one of those kamaaina specials. The Hawaiian word "kamaaina" means someone who's lived in Hawaii a long time. Anyone living in Hawaii a long time has a life comprised of a mixture of East and West. Here is a traditional Western (French) dish combined with a strictly tropical food (breadfruit)!

BREADFRUIT CREPE SURPRISE O

Basic Crepe Recipe
(see Basic Recipes Section, p. 39)

1 cup coconut milk or nut milk
Pulp of 1 ripe breadfruit

2 bananas

¼ cup chopped, dried fruit

Simmer first 2 ingredients together until breadfruit looks translucent (stir often to prevent burning). Allow breadfruit to cool, then blend with bananas. Mix in chopped, dried fruit. Fill crepes with this or stack gateau-style. Top with carob syrup or melted carob chips, Soy Whipped Cream (see recipe in Basic Recipes Section, p. 34) and slivered almonds. This can also be used as a filling for a jelly roll.

COCONUT

Coconut

The Hawaiians used to plant one coconut tree for each newborn baby. The idea was that since the coconut tree lives about the same amount of years as a human being, the child would be guaranteed food for his lifetime. If we could learn to live in harmony with nature, and most important with the One who has made nature and us, we would probably be inclined to make this practice a common one.

I don't pretend to be an expert on Hawaiiana or anything, but from what little I know about the virtues of the coconut tree, I know that the planting of coconut trees followed by practical knowledge of how to make the best use of them would assure us of lifetimes of not only food but many of our basic necessities.

From the nut can be made puddings, candies, chips, milk or cream, butter, oil and soap. From the shell can be made bowls, spoons, buttons, tools, etc. And baskets, hats, mats, shelter, brooms, etc., can be made from the fronds. In India, the shells are burned to make charcoal for fuel and medicines, and are also powdered and sold as a dentifrice. How economical!

As the late British economist E. F. Schumacher pointed out while discussing "Buddhist economics" in his book **Small Is Beautiful**, "Just as the modern economist would admit that a high rate of consumption of transport services between a man's home and his place of work signifies misfortune and not a high standard of life, so the Buddhist economist would hold that to satisfy human wants from far away sources rather than from sources nearby signifies failure rather than success . . . production from local resources for local needs is the most rational way of economic life, while dependence on imports from afar and the consequent need to produce for export to unknown and distant peoples is highly uneconomical and justifiable only in exceptional cases and on a small scale."

When I went looking for coconuts a couple of years ago, this was really brought home to me as the situation that Hawaii is in. From the top of a hill looking down on Waialae-Kahala, there were coconut trees as far as the eye could see. Wanting to find some nice, ripe coconuts to make some candy to hand out at our store's grand opening (Down to Earth Natural Foods), I hopped into the car and drove down there. I drove around for about three hours and found three trees with green coconuts on them! Trees are trimmed now before the coconuts have a chance to develop. And what happens to this precious fruit? They end up at the dump!

Of course on the outer Islands, being less mainlandized, coconuts are a little easier to find. But I urge you (especially if you have a coconut tree in your yard) to let the coconuts grow. If you have your trees trimmed, then use the coconuts or put them out by the sidewalk for someone to take and use.

Let's follow a coconut through its different stages of development and examine its nutritive value; then we can really understand why it's such a shame to waste this valuable fruit.

The blossom of the tree is developed with a covering that looks like a large ear of green corn. The blossom grows and breaks out of the covering to produce a cluster of about 10 to 20 coconuts. In six months they should be full-sized drinking nuts, and fully mature in less than one year. **The coconut tree has no season, so nuts of all stages can be found on the same tree at one time all year-round.**

The edible part of the coconut is inside the husk and surrounded by a shell. The sweet husks of some varieties can be eaten when very young.

To begin development, the coconut is fertilized by a neighboring staminate flower and the shell fills with sweet water (coconut water). The development is at first soft and jellylike (spoon "meat"), forming inside the walls of the shell, then gradually absorbing the water and becoming firm, with a thickness of ¼ to ½ inch (coconut "meat").

(From U.S.D.A. Agriculture Handbook #8)
COCONUT
100 gm. edible portion

	Coconut cream	Fresh coconut	Dried coconut	Coconut milk	Coconut water
Water	54.1%	50.9%	3.5%	65.7%	94.2%
Food energy	334 calories	346 calories	662 calories	252 calories	22 calories
Protein	4.4 gm.	3.5 gm.	7.2 gm.	3.2 gm.	.3 gm.
Fat	32.2 gm.	35.3 gm.	64.9 gm.	24.9 gm.	.2 gm.
Carbohydrate	8.3 gm. (Total)	9.4 gm. (Total)	23.0 gm. (Total)	5.2 gm. (Total)	4.7 gm. (Total)
	— (Fiber)	4.0 gm. (Fiber)	3.9 gm. (Fiber)	—	Trace
Ash	1.0 gm.	.9 gm.	1.4 gm.	1.0 gm.	.6 gm.
Calcium	15 mg.	13 mg.	26 mg.	16 mg.	20 mg.
Phosphorus	126 mg.	95 mg.	187 mg.	100 mg.	13 mg.
Iron	1.8 mg.	1.7 mg.	3.3 mg.	1.6 mg.	.3 mg.
Sodium	4 mg.	23 mg.	—	—	25 mg.
Potassium	324 mg.	256 mg.	588 mg.	—	147 mg.
Vitamin A	0	0	0	0	0
Thiamine	.02 mg.	.05 mg.	.06 mg.	.03 mg.	Trace
Riboflavin	.01 mg.	.02 mg.	.04 mg.	Trace	Trace
Niacin	.5 mg.	.5 mg.	.6 mg.	.8 mg.	.1 mg.
Vitamin C	1 mg.	3 mg.	0 mg.	2 mg.	2 mg.

(Dashes denote lack of reliable data for a constituent believed to be present in measurable amount.)

The perfect drinking nut is full-sized, but immature and dark-green, without a trace of yellow color which means the nut is ripening. In the prime drinking stage, coconuts hardly ever fall to the ground and must be picked. The best device is a small, curved, pruning hook mounted on the end of a bamboo pole. A first-class drinking nut will contain nearly one quart of cool coconut water and will be so full that you can't hear any water sloshing around when you shake it. It also may have a bit of a fizz to it which adds to its refreshing effect, just like a natural soda. Don't bother to husk it; just slice off a bit of the husk on the bottom (not into the cavity) to make a flat-bottom surface, and whack off the top and serve with a straw. After it is empty, split it open to find the spoon meat.

The coconut is mature when yellow, or when the green husk begins to turn brown and the white meat is thick and firm. It then drops to the ground. In this stage there is still some water in the cavity which can be used when making coconut milk. As the coconut matures, the water goes into the meat and the meat becomes thicker and harder. The meat goes from the spoon meat stage to a rubbery stage until it gets to be about ½-inch thick and very hard with only a little water left sloshing around inside. The coconut will keep developing through these stages even if it's not connected to the tree.

After a coconut ripens, two things can happen to it as it matures, depending on whether or not the seed (that is what the coconut is — the seed of the coconut tree) is fertilized or not. If the seed is not fertile, after all the water is absorbed into the meat, it then begins turning into oil. The coconut at this stage is called copra. A copra coconut will not make any sound at all when shaken, and will be very light to the touch when picked up. Copra is very sweet and makes good candy, and it is also excellent when grated and used in baked goods. Because of the high oil content, it may be hard to

digest for those of you with sensitive digestive systems. If you do have a sensitive digestive system and you've chopped into a copra coconut, it doesn't have to go to waste. Copra coconuts are used to make coconut oil and soap.

If the coconut is fertilized, after all the water is absorbed into the meat, it will sprout! You've probably tried alfalfa sprouts, mung bean sprouts, soy bean sprouts . . . now try coconut sprouts! As the sprout begins to grow, a crisp, spongy ball begins to form inside the cavity of the coconut. This is the food the sprout will live on until its root system is established. Sometimes you may chop open a ripe coconut and find a little ½-inch or 1-inch ball at the top of the coconut. This means that the coconut was beginning to sprout. When leaves are visible on the outside of the coconut, the spongy material inside is filling the whole cavity and you have a choice to make: you can either chop open this sprouted coconut and use the spongy material for food (best plain as is, or chopped up in a salad), or you can place the coconut in a spot where a coconut tree would be appreciated, cover with a little dirt and watch a coconut tree grow.

The coconut heart is, of course, in the center of the tree. Each time a heart is gathered, the coconut tree dies. So, rather than killing the tree just for the heart, one may find trees which have already been knocked down, clearing the way for lots, roads, etc. Unfortunately, this is a sight that's becoming more common in Hawaii.

The palm heart keeps fresh inside the fallen tree for about two weeks. It is located just below the crown of leaves and can be as long as your leg. You'll need an ax or machete to cut the trunk in two just below the crown; then remove the leaves and outside layers of the palm until you find the center. It is white, tender and crisp with a sweet coconut milk flavor. It can be sliced into small pieces, covered with dressing and served as a salad, or steamed and served with

butter and your favorite seasonings. It can also be served as a very nice cooked vegetable by lightly sautéing in peanut oil.

Whatever stage of development you find the coconut in, it is full of nutritional value.

Immature coconuts are very important in supplying an ever-available source of safe drinking water. The amount of nutrition in the water is small. It can contain as much calcium as some fruits and vegetables. The iron content is low and the phosphorus content is less than that of the flesh (which is a good source of iron and phosphorus). Both the liquid and the flesh have a slight acid reaction in the body. It contains little, if any, vitamin C. When the spoon meat is eaten along with the drinking water, one can obtain 150 calories from one nut.

As the **coconut meat** develops, the water content decreases, the fat and total ash increase, and the protein and sugar stay pretty much the same. The meat contains a large amount of crude fiber, about 40% fat (which is high) and about 15% carbohydrate. The **mature nut** is a poor source of thiamine and riboflavin and a fair source of niacin. It has little or no vitamin C or provitamin A. Coconut contains natural iodine and vitamin D, which is rarely found in foods. The milk and meat are full of enzymes, and coconut is supposed to be a natural remedy for worms and sore throat.

Coconut milk is high in fat and low in protein. Neither the water nor milk are comparable to cow's milk in organic nutrients or calcium and phosphorus content. It is not a satisfactory substitute for mother's milk but could be used in an emergency for a day or two. After that, it would be necessary to have a good protein that would supply riboflavin and vitamin A, and also some calcium, phosphorus and iron. This could be obtained by mixing coconut milk with cashew or almond milk. Almonds are a good source of riboflavin (B_2) and protein; also thiamine (B_1), niacin, iron, calcium, phosphorus and potassium. Cashews are a good source of vitamin D, iron, thiamine, protein and fat.

The preparation of coconut milk or cream from mature coconuts is a simple way to obtain the most important nutrients without the fiber. The milk or cream is about as good a source of protein, phosphorus, iron, niacin, thiamine and ascorbic acid as the mature coconut, but has less fat, carbohydrates and riboflavin.

Coconut buttermilk is the whey left over after coco cream has been churned to butter. It supplies a complete protein, furnishing all the amino acids essential to growth and health. All its fats, sugars and proteins are highly digestible. The fat content is greatly reduced during the churning. It contains sufficient amounts of calcium, iron, phosphorus, potassium and some vitamin C. Among the B vitamins, it contains thiamine, riboflavin and niacin, but it is not rich enough in these nutrients to furnish all our daily requirements and should therefore be supplemented with other foods. It is not sour like regular buttermilk, but has a sweet and light taste.

Following are some recipes using different stages of the coconut. I have included recipes for different stages because it's sometimes hard to tell by looking at the outside of a coconut what it's going to be like inside. So, if you chop open a coconut with a plan to make something for dinner and find it at the wrong stage of maturity, there's a recipe provided for you to be able to change your menu and make use of that coconut anyway.

COCONUT MILK   ☐

Grate meat of one coconut (3 cups), or cut into ½-inch cubes and put in a blender. Pour 1½ to 2 cups boiling water and the coconut water over coconut. The amount of water used varies in some recipes. Let it set for about 10 minutes. Mash and knead it or run through blender. Squeeze through double thickness of cheesecloth or a fine sieve. (Save pulp for other recipes.) Coconut milk can be used in any recipe in place of milk for a delicate, sweet taste. Yields 1½ cups coconut milk. Coconut milk blended with some almonds and then strained is supposed to be closer to human mother's milk in nutritional content than any other milk.

COCONUT CREAM

Simply pour coconut milk in a container and let sit in a cool place for 6 to 8 hours. The thick cream will separate and rise. Carefully skim off with a spoon and use wherever cream is called for.

COCONUT WHIPPED CREAM

Use thick coconut cream that has been set in freezer to chill thoroughly; must be ice cold. Whip with an electric mixer or in a blender until fluffy. May be sweetened and used wherever whipped cream is called for.

COCONUT BUTTER ☆

Use tepid coconut cream (65° to 70°) and churn with a mixer. The butter should separate in thick lumps. Gather up the lumps and knead in a chilled bowl until creamy and smooth. Pour off any liquid that has separated. Mold into shape and refrigerate. You should have a very digestible, sweet, white butter.

COCONUT BUTTERMILK ☆

This is the whey left over after the cream has been churned for butter. Originally, buttermilk from cow's milk was what was left after removing the butter. Now it is mostly cultured, coagulated and sour in taste. Coconut buttermilk is not sour or coagulated. It resembles sweet cow's milk in appearance and can be used as a drink or in cooking.

COCONUT OIL (Clarified Coconut Butter)☆

Cook butter over a low heat until it stops bubbling. The oil will separate. Strain through double cheesecloth, muslin or flannel and store in glass jars. This oil can be used for cooking, frying, baking or for skin and hair. **Commerical** coconut oil is expressed from dried coconut (called copra) with petroleum solvents and is distilled in petroleum. Therefore the **commercial** kind is unfit to eat. It can be used for making soap and for skin and hair. Homemade coconut oil extracted from the copra can be eaten.

YOUNG COCONUT PUDDING ☐

Serve spoon meat right from the shell or scoop it out and serve in a dish. A puree can be made with spoon meat, a little water and a little honey, heated almost to the boiling point. This has long been used in the Islands for feeding young babies and sick adults.

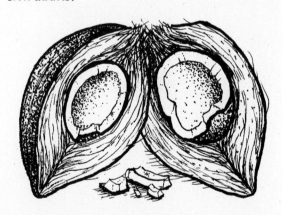

SPOON MEAT PUDDING ☐

1 spoon meat coconut
1 mango
2 Tbsp. lemon juice
4 Tbsp. honey
¾ cup non-instant dry milk
Dash of cinnamon

Combine ingredients and blend in blender until smooth. Refrigerate a few hours and serve as a pudding for breakfast or dessert. Also good frozen! Yields about 4 servings.

NO SWEAT SPOON MEAT "PUDDING" □

1 spoon meat coconut
3 Tbsp. malt powder
(available in health food stores)

If you have chopped open a spoon meat coconut, a quick dessert to fix is as follows. Just rinse the coconut off. Leaving spoon meat in the shell, put about 1½ Tbsp. malt powder in each half and serve. Good combination!

SPOON MEAT "CHICKEN"   ○

4 spoon meat coconuts
(firm enough to be scooped out)

Bowl of soy sauce

1/3 cup nutritional yeast
2 Tbsp. whole wheat flour
2 Tbsp. bran

Dip pieces of spoon meat in soy sauce and then dredge them in dry mixture (last 3 ingredients) until evenly coated. Fry in a hot, buttered skillet until crispy. Serve with Mock Turkey Gravy (see recipe in Tofu Section, p. 379). Delicious!

COCONUT STRIPS   ○

1 coconut in rubbery stage
2 tsp. oil
1 Tbsp. grated fresh ginger

2 Tbsp. soy sauce
2 Tbsp. honey

Sauté first 3 ingredients. Add soy sauce and brown. Add honey, mix well and cook until caramelized. This is also very good without the honey, using firm, mature coconut cut into strips. Coconut strips cooked in ginger, honey and soy sauce syrup are very good served alongside any vegetable and/or rice dish.

VEGETABLE TERIYAKI WITH COCONUT STRIPS   ○

½ tsp. grated fresh ginger
1 tsp. oil
¼ tsp. asafetida

¼ cup soy sauce
¼ cup honey

Meat of 1 coconut (in rubbery stage), cut in strips

½ cup chopped cauliflower
½ cup thinly sliced celery
½ cup thinly sliced carrots

½ cup sliced zucchini
¼ lb. whole sugar peas (Chinese)

Brown ginger and asafetida in oil. Add next 2 ingredients and cook to syrup consistency. Add coconut strips and cook in syrup for a few minutes. Lightly steam first 3 vegetables, adding last 2 at the end. When almost tender, remove from heat. Be careful not to overcook! Drain well and mix with coconut strips and sauce until vegetables are well-coated. Serve alongside fluffy, buttered brown rice. Yields 2 servings.

Variation: Vegetables can also be added to the syrup with coconut strips and cooked in the sauce rather than steaming.

VEGETABLE COCONUT SUKIYAKI ⃝

2 Tbsp. oil
1 cup thinly sliced eggplant (1" long)
1 cup coconut slices (rubbery stage)

½ cup soy sauce
1 Tbsp. grated fresh ginger
½ tsp. asafetida
¼ cup honey

1 cup celery (cut diagonally)
2 large tomatoes (cut in eighths)
4 cups greens: sweet potato leaves,
spinach, swiss chard, watercress, etc.
(use any or all of them)

1 Tbsp. whole wheat flour
1/3 cup water

1 cup bean sprouts

Use wok or large skillet. Fry first 3 ingredients. Add next 4 and stir. Cook a few minutes, then add next 3. Mix flour and water in a bowl, add to vegetables, stir well and cook until celery is almost tender. Turn off heat and mix in bean sprouts. Yields about 4 servings.

COCONUT CHIPS ⃝

1 mature coconut
2 tsp. soy sauce (or more)
1 tsp. nutritional yeast (or more)

Place whole husked coconut in oven at 500° for 15 minutes. Meat will separate from shell. Crack in half and remove coconut. Slice in strips 2" long and 1/8" to 1/4" thick. Toast strips in oven at 250° for 2 hours, stirring occasionally until golden and crisp (will snap when broken). Place chips in a skillet with soy sauce and stir-fry to distribute evenly. Sprinkle with yeast. Stir and serve. Store extra in an airtight container.

GRATED TOASTED COCONUT ⃝

Husk coconut, cut in fours with a machete and pick meat out with a round-nosed knife or butter knife. Wash and dry the meat, grate on a fine grater. Spread evenly in a baking pan or cookie sheet and bake at 225° to 250° F. for about 1 hour, stirring occasionally until dry and lightly toasted. Delicious whenever toasted coconut is called for. Or if the coconut is husked and left whole, some people like to place the coconut in the oven at 300° for about an hour. It is supposed to crack and come out of the shell more easily when this is done. Tap it with a hammer, pick out the meat and prepare as directed above.

DOWN TO EARTH COCONUT CANDIES
(Served at the Grand Opening of ⃝
Down to Earth Natural Foods)

4 cups fresh grated coconut

¾ cup honey
½ cup butter or margarine

Toast coconut and set aside. Combine honey and butter and cook to candy consistency (soft ball stage to 235° on candy thermometer; when dropped in cold water it will form little soft balls). Toss in coconut, mix well and as soon as it's cool enough to touch, roll into balls or press onto a cookie sheet and cut into squares. Simple but surprisingly delicious!

Note: If a finely grated store-bought coconut is used, use less (about 3 to 3½ cups).

COCONUT BURFI MELTAWAYS ☆

¾ cup butter or margarine
1 cup honey
1 cup canned milk
3 to 3½ cups noninstant dry milk
1 cup chopped walnuts or almonds
1 cup grated coconut

Melt butter and honey. Add milk and stir until boiling. Lower heat and **gradually** add milk powder, stirring **constantly**. Keep stirring and add coconut and nuts. Pour into a buttered, flat pan or rimmed cookie sheet. Refrigerate. When cool and set, cut into squares and serve.

COCONUT COOKIES ◯

3 cups grated or shredded fresh coconut
¾ cup honey
1 tsp. lemon juice

½ cup whole wheat flour

Preheat oven to 350° F. Mix first 3 ingredients. Sift in flour and stir and knead well. Roll into balls and bake on a buttered cookie sheet at 350° F for 25 to 30 minutes. Yields 12 to 16 cookies.

COCONUT BREADS ☆

½ cup whole wheat flour (sifted)
1 tsp. salt
1/8 tsp. coriander or cinnamon
1 cup grated coconut

3 Tbsp. honey
Water

Combine first 4 ingredients. Add honey and enough water to make a soft dough (not too soft). Pat into palm-sized patties and deep fry in ghee or light oil until crisp and light brown. Serve plain or soaked in sweetened, flavored yogurt. Makes about a dozen breads.

COCONUT HALAVAH #1 ◯

1½ cups finely grated coconut
1½ cups milk

½ cup honey
1 tsp. crushed cardamom

Combine first 2 ingredients and bring to a boil, then simmer slowly for half an hour, stirring often. Add next 2 ingredients, mix well and stir constantly for about 10 minutes or until thick. Pour into a medium-sized, buttered dish and chill. Cut into pieces and serve.

COCONUT HALAVAH #2 ☆

½ cup honey
¼ cup butter or margarine

2 hard, dry coconuts, ground
¼ cup sesame seeds
¼ cup sunflower seeds
¼ cup raisins

Cook honey and butter until it threads (candy consistency). Toss in next 4 ingredients and mix well. Cool and serve. Very sweet like candy. Yields 6 or more servings.

COCONUT HALAVAH #3 ◯

¼ cup honey
¼ cup water

3 cups grated fresh, young coconut

2 Tbsp. butter or margarine
1 cup chopped banana
½ cup chopped walnuts (opt.)

Melt first 2 ingredients in saucepan. Add coconut, stirring constantly for 10 to 15 minutes. Add next 3 ingredients and cook for 5 minutes more. Serve warm or cold.

COCONUT TURNOVERS ☆

2 cups whole wheat flour
½ tsp. salt

2/3 cup soft butter or margarine
¼ cup ice water

½ cup soft butter or margarine, creamed
¾ cup honey
3 cups grated coconut
½ tsp. vanilla

Preheat oven to 350° F. Sift flour and salt into a bowl. Add butter and mix. Rub together with hands if necessary. Add cold water gradually to make a stiff dough. Roll out on a floured surface into a 4" circle, ¼" thick. Combine next 4 ingredients and mix well. Place 2 tsp. in the center of each pastry and gently fold in half. Wet the edges and secure, then gently crimp with fingers. Pierce with a fork a few times and bake at 350° F for 30 to 35 minutes.

Variation: Some finely chopped walnuts and raisins may be added to the filling.

COCONUT AND CARROT SALAD WITH YOGURT DRESSING ☐

1 coconut, shredded (3 cups)
3 cups shredded carrot

1 cup yogurt
¼ cup honey
Pinch cayenne

Finely grate carrot and coconut and mix. Combine next 3 ingredients, mix well and toss with first 2. Serve on individual lettuce leaves and sprinkle with some finely grated, fresh beet.

SPICY COCONUT AND STRING BEANS ○

2 - 3 Tbsp. oil
1 tsp. turmeric
¼ tsp. cayenne (or less)
1 tsp. salt or 2 tsp. kelp

2 lbs. fresh, tender string beans

¼ cup grated fresh coconut
1 tsp. coriander

In a pan, heat the first 4 ingredients. Add (washed) lengthwise-cut beans and stir until coated. Cook covered for 5 minutes. Add last 2 ingredients, cover and cook 5 minutes more. There should be no need to add water, especially when using oil. If it seems too heavy in oil, leave most of it in the pan. Yields 6 servings.

SPICY COCONUT WITH YOGURT AND OKRA ○

1 Tbsp. oil
½ lb. okra (halved the long way)

½ tsp. salt or 1 tsp. kelp
½ tsp. turmeric
½ tsp. grated fresh ginger

½ cup yogurt
¼ cup toasted coconut
½ tsp. coriander
¼ tsp. cayenne or less
1 tsp. lemon juice

Heat oil and stir-fry okra for 5 minutes. Add next 3 ingredients; fry until done (toasted). Combine last 5 ingredients, mix well with okra and serve.

COCONUT MUNG BEAN SOUP ○

3 cups hot water
1 coconut

3 cups water
1 cup raw mung beans (soaked overnight)

1 cup finely chopped sweet
potato or spinach leaves
½ - 1 red pepper, minced
1 tsp. grated fresh ginger
Salt or kelp to taste

Prepare thin coconut milk (using 3 cups water). Pour milk through a sieve into a bowl and save pulp. Cover the pulp with **hot** water and steep for 15 minutes. Blend and strain. Set this second extraction of milk in another bowl. Bring next 2 ingredients to a boil and boil for 5 minutes. Add second extraction of coconut milk and boil until soft. Add first extraction of coconut milk and last 4 ingredients. Cover and cook for 5 to 10 minutes more. Yields 6 to 8 servings.

RED BEANS WITH COCONUT MILK ○

2 cups thick coconut milk

2 Tbsp. butter or margarine
1 cup chopped tomato
½ tsp. ground coriander

2½ cups cooked, drained red beans

1 tsp. salt or kelp
1 cup spinach or sweet potato leaves

Prepare coconut milk from two nuts using 1 cup hot water per coconut. Cook next 3 ingredients thoroughly. Add beans and coconut milk and let boil. Add salt and leaves and cook for 5 minutes. Yields 2 to 4 servings.

COCONUT SWEET RICE ○

6 cups grated coconut
3½ cups water (makes 1 quart coconut milk)

¼ cup mochi rice (washed)
½ cup honey

Prepare coconut milk to measure 4 cups. Bring to boil, stirring occasionally to prevent sticking (if it sticks, pour it into a clean pot). Add next 2 ingredients, stir and let boil a few minutes. Lower flame and cook partially covered for about one hour, until rice is soft and milk has thickened. This is best served in cups and drunk like nectar, or in a bowl with a spoon. Yields 4 servings.

HAUPIA (Coconut Pudding) ○

9 cups grated coconut (3 nuts)
3½ cups coconut and boiling water

¾ cup arrowroot *
½ cup honey
A little water

Prepare coconut milk. There should be 4¼ cups of milk expressed. If not, add more water. Mix next 3 ingredients to make a smooth paste. Heat coconut milk to boiling point and **gradually** add paste, stirring **constantly**. Continue until mixture thickens. Pour into a pan, allow to cool and refrigerate until set. Cut into squares and serve. Yields 16 two-inch squares.

* **Note:** Arrowroot has long been used for making Haupia. The early Hawaiians called the arrowroot made into a paste with a little coconut milk "pia." Polynesian arrowroot grew wild and was also cultivated along the edges of wet taro patches. Arrowroot is a nutritious food with a high calcium content (58 grams per 100 grams).

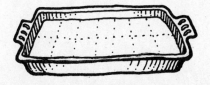

COCONUT CREAM PIE   ○

Crust:
Use Graham Cracker Crust or Raw Pie Crust
(see Basic Recipes Section, pp. 32 and 33)

Filling:
3 fresh coconuts
1 cup water
2 cups hot milk
¾ cup arrowroot
½ cup honey

½ cup grated coconut (opt.)
1 banana, sliced, or other fruit (opt.)

½ cup grated coconut

Prepare crust. While crust is chilling, prepare filling by making coconut milk and following the instructions given for Haupia (recipe, p. 127). The only difference is that you use 2 cups hot milk and 1 cup hot water. This makes a creamier pie filling. If coconut water is used, do not heat it with the cow's milk; heat separately and then combine and prepare extracted coconut milk. When filling is done, pour into chilled pie shell. If you want, you can mix coconut and bananas into filling before pouring into pie crust. Top with fresh, toasted, grated coconut. Refrigerate until cool and set. Makes 1 pie.

COCONUT PUDDING   ○

3¾ cups coconut milk
1 cup cornmeal
1/3 cup honey
3 Tbsp. molasses
1 tsp. vanilla
½ tsp. cinnamon
¼ tsp. nutmeg
1 Tbsp. butter or margarine

Mix ingredients together. Pour the batter into an oiled 9" square baking pan. Bake at 350° for about 1¼ hours or until a knife inserted in the middle comes out clean. Cool and cut into squares. Serve topped with favorite sweet sauce or fruit sauce.

AND FOR THOSE OF YOU WITH A PIONEERING SPIRIT:

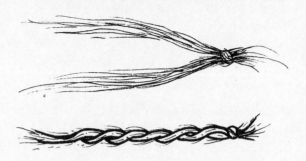

ROPE FROM COCONUT HUSK

Remove smooth outer fibers from coconut husk (about ¼" of this part cannot be used). Remove small strips of the longest fibers from husk. Clean the fibers of any soft or spongy matter with a scraper (fingernails work) until the fibers are separated and smooth. Take approximately 10 to 15 fibers in a bunch and tie a knot at one end. Divide this bunch into two equal parts. Twist one part tightly and hold twisted between thumb and finger. Twist the other part together in the opposite direction of the twists. Let it go and the two parts will coil neatly together. You can also braid for variety.

BROOM

Cut midribs from fronds. Tie them together onto a bamboo handle in an equal length bunch, and you have a broom.

GUAVA

Guava

Here's another one of those fruits growing abundantly here in the Islands that we're blind to. I have at least one friend who isn't, though. He makes canned guava juice on Maui and his juices have become well liked not only locally, but nationwide. My friend told me that most of the guavas used in his juice are brought in by people who go out and gather them from wild trees to make a little extra money. A person could earn enough to sustain himself if he really worked at it and brought in enough poundage.

My friend is encouraging people with land to cultivate it and grow fruit, including guavas, on a commercial level to help develop this local industry which is unique in Hawaii. He just takes the pulp of the guava and mixes it with the perfect amount of water and honey and has a real seller. Such a simple idea, that it would take someone with a pioneering spirit to think of it!

I get excited every time I talk about this juice company, not only because I like the juices, but because I think it's a very good example of the kind of appropriate industry that should be encouraged here in Hawaii to help make us self-sufficient. Personally, I can't afford to buy bottled or canned juices; but who needs to go get an extra job to make the money to go to the store and by the cans, when the guava is found growing wild practically everywhere?

Once, in Haiku, Maui, I tasted a beautiful, pear-shaped guava. I was really surprised at how good and sweet it was even though it looked green and unripe. It actually tasted like a compromise between a pear and a good guava. When I asked someone at the Board of Agriculture why this variety wasn't grown commercially, I was told that the trees don't yield enough fruit to make it worthwhile. Well, money isn't everything. I figure it'd be worthwhile to have one of these or another kind of guava tree in every yard, as they're so simple to grow and you can make so many good, healthy things with the guavas to share with your family and friends. The University of Hawaii already has developed an orchard guava tree which bears large, juicy fruits on short, easy-to-pick trees.

To get the fastest, best results in your yard, the guava is best grown from cuttings or air layering, rather than seed. All that you have to do is slice off a branch of any size at about a 45° angle and place it in some soil and just keep it watered until it has roots. Instant guava tree! It will only take two to five years to bear fruit. The trees can grow to be anywhere from just a few feet high (shrub size), to about 30 feet tall. Guavas are most abundant from April to October but can be found growing all year round. They are just about the most abundant and easily obtainable fruits here in the Islands.

The common guava varies in taste from sweet to sour, but there's always that unique guava flavor. When a guava has reached the perfect stage, it is a bit tender to the touch, but not mushy, and should be used rather soon as they become overripe very quickly.

All guavas are an excellent source of vitamin C. The rind contains more vitamin C than both the pulp and seeds because there is usually more rind per pound of fruit than pulp. The guava shells or rinds have a nice taste and are similar to a pear in texture. Compared with other fruits, the common guava is a poor to fair source of niacin, provitamin A, thiamine and riboflavin.

When I was little, we had a guava tree growing along the borderline of the land that we lived on, and I remember my mother making all kinds of delicious guava preparations for the family and friends. Guavas are excellent fruits for making jellies, jams and guava butter (see recipes) because they contain so much natural pectin. They also make good juice, desserts and other things you'll find recipes for on the following pages. Oh, just in case you're curious, that wonderful, wild guava tree that produced many a guava jam, jelly, juice, etc., no longer stands. It was replaced by a stone wall — "progress!"

(From U.S.D.A. Agriculture Handbook #8) GUAVA (Common raw) 100 gm. edible portion			
Water	83.0%	Iron	.9 mg.
Food energy	62 calories	Sodium	4 mg.
Protein	.8 gm.	Potassium	289 mg.
Fat	.6 gm.	Vitamin A	280 I.U.
Carbohydrate	15 gm. (Total)	Thiamine	.05 mg.
	5.6 gm. (Fiber)	Riboflavin	.05 mg.
Ash	.6 gm.	Niacin	1.2 mg.
Calcium	23 mg.	Vitamin C	242 mg.
Phosphorus	42 mg.		

RAW GUAVA JUICE ☐

Put whole, lightly pared guavas in blender with some water. Blend and strain. Return to blender and add honey and lemon juice (if desired). This may be diluted and sweetened to suit your liking. Delicious and nutritious — high in vitamin C. Guava juice can serve as an excellent substitute for orange or tomato juice.

GUAVA SHAKE ☐

1 cup cold milk
2 Tbsp. guava pulp (purée)
2 tsp. honey

Whiz ingredients in blender until fluffy. Tastes almost like a strawberry milk shake. Delicious! Yields 1 glass.

GUAVA-BANANA CHILL WITH YOGURT ☐

8 large (unbruised), ripe guavas
2/3 - 3/4 cup honey
2 large bananas
1 cup grated coconut
½ - 1 cup yogurt (sweetened)

Pare guavas lightly. Cut and scoop out pulp and press through a sieve. Add honey to strained pulp and mix well. Slice guava shells and bananas ¼" thick. Place half of the guava shells in a dish. Top with half of the bananas, half of the guava pulp, then half of the coconut and repeat. Cover and chill for about 3 hours. Top with yogurt and serve. Yields 6 servings.

GUAVA-COCONUT-LIME DRINK ☐

2 cups coconut milk
½ cup fresh lime juice
6 cups guava juice
1 cup honey

Combine ingredients. Mix well. Chill and serve.

STRAWBERRY GUAVA DRINK ☐

2 cups orange juice
½ cup lemon juice
3 cups strawberry guava juice
(or 2 cups pulp + 1 cup water)
¾ - 1 cup honey

Combine ingredients. Blend in two batches and chill. Stir before serving. Yields about six 8-ounce servings.

CELESTIAL GUAVAS ☆

6 guavas

¾ cup cream cheese, softened
2 Tbsp. honey

1 Tbsp. toasted coconut

Cut guavas in half. Scoop pulp and press through a sieve to separate seeds. Combine pulp with next 2 ingredients and whip until fluffy. Fill each guava shell, sprinkle with coconut and chill before serving. Yields 6 servings. Delicious!

GUAVA PURÉE ☐

Scoop out pulp and seeds from guava and press with a spoon through a fine sieve. This purée can be used in a variety of ways and may be kept fresh or frozen for later use. Can also be made by first blending pulp in blender and then pressing through a sieve.

WHIPPED GUAVA □

2 cups guava pulp
½ cup honey
Juice of half lemon

½ cup heavy cream, whipped, or
Soy Whipped Cream (see recipe
in Basic Recipes Section, p. 34)

Mix first 3 ingredients well. Set in freezer.
When half-frozen, remove and whip in the
whipped cream. Freeze until set.

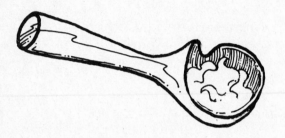

RICH AND CREAMY, FROSTY GUAVA ☆

1 cup guava pulp + 2 Tbsp.
½ cup honey

1 cup guava pulp + 2 Tbsp.
2 Tbsp. lemon juice

1 cup water
2/3 cup whole or nonfat milk powder

Combine first 2 ingredients and boil for 2 to
3 minutes. Cool and add next 2 ingredients.
Mix well and set in an ice tray and freeze.
Combine next 2 ingredients and whip in
blender or mix with whisk until smooth. Put
frozen guava into a mixing bowl; combine
with thick milk and whip with an electric
mixer. Return to freezer until frozen and
serve.

GUAVA JAM ○

2 cups guava pulp
½ cup honey
2 tsp. lemon juice (opt.)

Cook until thick.

GUAVA-GINGER MARMALADE ○

12 guavas

1 cup honey
½ cup water

1 cup grated pineapple
½ tsp. finely grated lemon rind
½ tsp. finely grated ginger root

Cut guavas in half. Scoop out pulp and
save (use to make juice, etc.). Cut shells
into thin strips. Put in bowl with next 2
ingredients and soak overnight. Combine
with last 3 ingredients and cook, stirring
often, until thick. Pour into a hot, sterilized
jar; cool and seal. Makes about 3 cups. Delicious over ice cream or as a spread on whole
wheat bread.

GUAVA BUTTER ○

4 cups guava pulp
½ tsp. allspice
½ tsp. cinnamon
3 cups honey
1½ Tbsp. grated fresh ginger
3 Tbsp. lemon juice

Combine ingredients. Cook slowly until
thick, about 45 minutes. Stir frequently to
prevent burning. If you will be storing this,
pour it into hot, sterilized jars, cool, and seal
with paraffin. This is a very good spread for
bread, a topping for ice cream, etc. This
should make about 1 quart.

GUAVA TAPIOCA ○

¾ cup water
¾ cup honey
1/8 tsp. salt
¼ cup minute tapioca

1 cup fresh (unsweetened) guava juice
1 Tbsp. lemon juice (opt.)
½ cup sliced guava shells

Grated coconut

Combine first 4 ingredients. Cook slowly until tapioca is clear (about 5 minutes). Stir in last 3 ingredients; cook for a few minutes and remove from heat. Pour into dishes. Top with grated coconut. Chill. This should make 4 servings.

GUAVA-COCONUT PUDDING TARTS ○

Filling:
Haupia (see Coconut Section, p. 127)

Guava Topping:
1 cup guava pulp
2 Tbsp. honey
1 Tbsp. arrowroot
1 Tbsp. water

Crust:
8 baked tart shells
(see Basic Recipes Section, p. 33)

Finely grated, toasted coconut

Prepare Haupia as directed in Coconut Section. Use half of a Flaky Pie Crust recipe for tarts. Roll out dough and cut with a 1-cup measuring cup into circles. Press dough into muffin tins. Pierce with a fork and bake at 375° for 10 to 12 minutes. Cool and fill three-fourths of the way with Haupia. Prepare guava topping by combining first 2 ingredients. Bring them to a boil. Combine last 2 ingredients; pour into hot guava, stirring constantly until thick. Cool slightly and pour over tarts. Sprinkle with finely grated, toasted coconut and refrigerate.

GUAVA BREAD ○

2 cups whole wheat flour
1 tsp. salt
2 tsp. baking powder
1 tsp. baking soda
½ cup butter or oil
¾ cup honey
½ cup guava pulp
¼ cup milk or less

Preheat oven to 350° F. Cream butter and honey (use electric mixer if possible). Add sifted, dry ingredients alternately with milk, mixing well with a spoon. Pour into greased and floured loaf pan and bake at 350° for 45 minutes. When done, a knife or toothpick will come out clean.

GUAVA CHEESE ○

8 guavas
1 quart milk
8 Tbsp. honey
Juice of one lemon

Press guava pulp through sieve. Bring milk to a boil. Add lemon juice and guava pulp and stir. Remove from heat and stir again. The whey of the milk will separate from the curd and guava. Pour off whey through double thickness of cheesecloth (or flannel cloth) into a container and save to use in baking or to serve as a sweetened ice drink (add about ½ cup honey, chill and serve over ice). Let curd hang in cloth until excess liquid has dripped off. Serve immediately or refrigerate. It is very good served on toasted whole wheat bread and topped with honey or on pineapple slices served on a lettuce leaf.

GUAVA PUDDING ○

Whey from Guava Cheese
(see recipe this section, p. 135)
8 Tbsp. honey
6 Tbsp. arrowroot
Sliced and diced guava shells
(from 4 guavas or more)

Make a paste with arrowroot and some cool guava whey. Sweeten whey with honey and bring to a boil. Gradually add arrowroot paste, stirring constantly. Quickly stir in guava shells. Chill. Makes about 8 servings.

COOKED GUAVA JUICE ○

5 lbs. guavas
Water to cover fruit

Slice firm, ripe guavas and place in a large pot with just enough water to cover. (Use only stainless steel or enamel pots without chips because others will destroy the vitamins.) Boil, stirring occasionally, until fruit is mushy (20 to 30 minutes). Pour into a jelly bag (a thin flannel cloth may be used) and hang to drip. For clear juice, don't squeeze the bag. This may also be poured through a fine strainer. Use this juice for making jelly or for punch. Yields about 6 cups.

If you will be storing the juice, it should either be put in dark bottles or stored away from light. There is always a slow loss of vitamin C, so preserves and such should be used within one year. Cooked juice will stay fresh and nutritious in a refrigerator no longer than one week. Once opened, it loses vitamins more quickly. The flavor and color of the juice will stay, but it will lose over half of its vitamin C content in two weeks and almost all will be gone in a month's time.

HOT AND SPICY GUAVA DRINK ○

1 cup water
1 cup guava juice
1 tsp. lemon juice
¼ tsp. grated fresh ginger
¼ tsp. cinnamon
5 cloves
Honey

Combine spices with water. Cover and boil 10 minutes. Strain. Combine with other ingredients. Heat and stir. Serve hot. Delicious!

GUAVA-BANANA BAKE ○

½ cup guava pulp
2 Tbsp. honey
¼ cup orange juice
2 Tbsp. butter or margarine (softened)

8 firm (just barely ripe) bananas,
sliced in half lengthwise

2 Tbsp. date sugar
2 Tbsp. finely grated coconut

Combine first 4 ingredients and mix well with an electric mixer or whisk. Place banana halves in a shallow baking dish and pour guava mixture evenly over them. Sprinkle on last 2 ingredients and bake at 350° for 45 minutes. Remove and serve warm or cooled.

DELICIOUS GUAVA CAKE ☆

1 cup butter or margarine (softened)
1½ cups honey
4 Tbsp. yogurt

3 cups whole wheat flour
2 tsp. baking soda
2 tsp. baking powder
1 tsp. ground cinnamon
¼ tsp. ground cloves
¼ tsp. ground ginger
¼ tsp. ground nutmeg

1½ cups guava pulp (pureé)

Preheat oven to 350° F. Cream first 3 ingredients with a whisk or an electric mixer on high speed. Sift in next 7 ingredients and mix well. Pour in guava and mix thoroughly with an electric mixer. Pour into a buttered and floured, oblong cake pan or two 8" round or square pans. Spread evenly and bake at 350° for 30 minutes. Cool. Very moist and delicious! Yields 8 to 12 servings.

GUAVA FROSTING ☆

¼ cup butter or margarine (softened)
½ cup honey

1 cup milk powder
4 Tbsp. guava pulp

Cream first 2 ingredients. Add last 2 and mix until smooth and creamy. Spread on cooled guava cake and let set a while before cutting. Delicious!

GUAVA MUNCHIES (Fruit Chewies)

2½ cups guava shells
6 oz. natural fruit juice
1 cup honey

¾ cup noninstant milk powder
¾ cup ground sesame seeds
6 Tbsp. bran

Finely grated coconut

Blend first 3 ingredients in blender until smooth. Place in a skillet (teflon, if possible) and cook slowly on a low heat, stirring often, until thick. Cool slightly and mix in last 3 ingredients. Mix well, roll into balls and roll in finely grated coconut. If mixture doesn't stay in balls, cook it a little longer.

EXTRA FANCY PUDDING ☆

A finished jelly roll (preferably homemade with guava jam — see recipe for Jelly Roll Dough in Basic Recipes Section, p. 38, and Guava Jam recipe this section, p. 134)

2 cups Guava Puree (see recipe, p. 133)
¼ cup arrowroot powder

Half of Custard Pie Filling recipe (see Dairy Section, p. 465)

Cut the jelly roll into slices ½" to ¾" thick and arrange to cover the sides and bottom of a quart-sized baking or serving dish. Mix the next 2 ingredients together until lumps of arrowroot are dissolved. Then bring to a boil, stirring constantly until thickened. Pour over sliced jelly rolls. Make half of the Custard Pie filling recipe and pour over the guava filling. Refrigerate at least 6 hours or overnight. To serve, cut pieces and top each piece with a dollop of whipped cream or Soy Whipped Cream (see Basic Recipes Section, p. 34) and a sprinkling of chopped nuts.

"This is dreadful! Not (only) the suffering and death of the animals, but that man suppresses in himself, unnecessarily, the highest spiritual capacity—that of sympathy and pity towards living creatures like himself—and by violating his own feelings becomes cruel."
— Leo Tolstoy
(from his essay, "The First Step")

Strawberry Guavas

MANGO

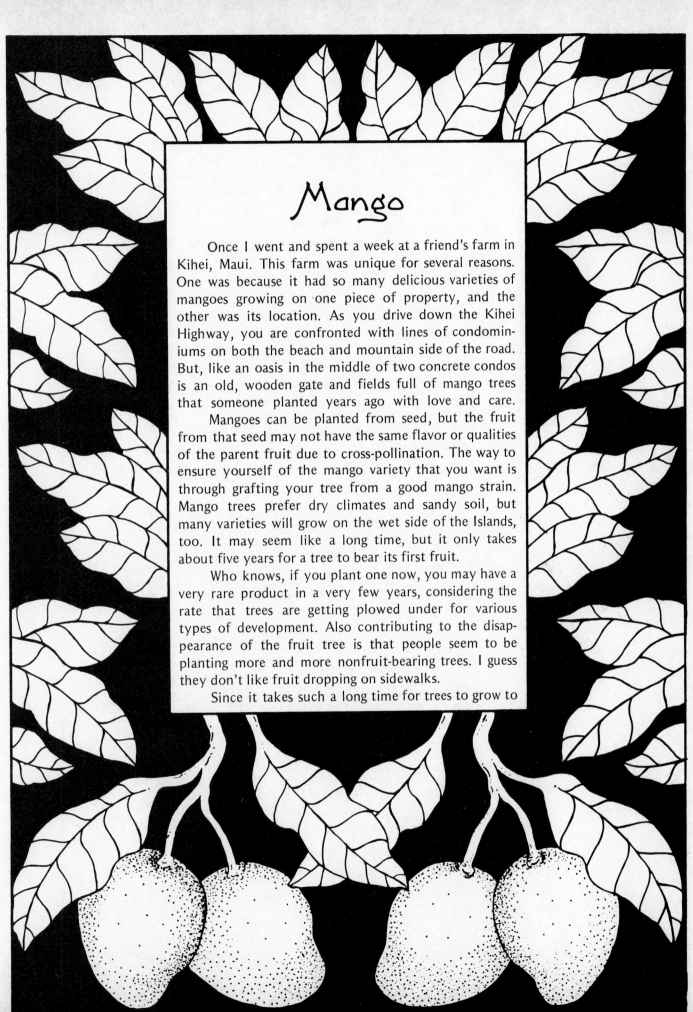

Mango

Once I went and spent a week at a friend's farm in Kihei, Maui. This farm was unique for several reasons. One was because it had so many delicious varieties of mangoes growing on one piece of property, and the other was its location. As you drive down the Kihei Highway, you are confronted with lines of condominiums on both the beach and mountain side of the road. But, like an oasis in the middle of two concrete condos is an old, wooden gate and fields full of mango trees that someone planted years ago with love and care.

Mangoes can be planted from seed, but the fruit from that seed may not have the same flavor or qualities of the parent fruit due to cross-pollination. The way to ensure yourself of the mango variety that you want is through grafting your tree from a good mango strain. Mango trees prefer dry climates and sandy soil, but many varieties will grow on the wet side of the Islands, too. It may seem like a long time, but it only takes about five years for a tree to bear its first fruit.

Who knows, if you plant one now, you may have a very rare product in a very few years, considering the rate that trees are getting plowed under for various types of development. Also contributing to the disappearance of the fruit tree is that people seem to be planting more and more nonfruit-bearing trees. I guess they don't like fruit dropping on sidewalks.

Since it takes such a long time for trees to grow to

the point where we can reap their fruits, most people are turning their land over for speculation to reap the "fruit" of quicker profits. I become saddened when I remember that peaceful mango orchard. I think of how, many years ago, the Chinese family who owned the property took that dry, barren land and worked it, thinking that in the future the trees would bear the fruits for the family's maintenance and for others to eat, too. Although the owner thought he was doing the right thing for the future, little did he know that someday the taxes on his land would be so high because of zoning, that he'd have to sell the property and give up his trees to the bulldozers. No more will little children be able to run out in the morning and climb the trees to pick the hanging gifts from God. We can't eat concrete, but we can certainly eat mangoes!

Mangoes usually begin ripening in April and remain available in abundance until the beginning of October. The season varies with the conditions of climate from one year to the next. Common mangoes can usually be found on the dry sides of the Islands from April through June, and when these are pau (finished), they can usually be found ripening on the wet sides until about the beginning of October.

The most widely grown mango in the Islands is the **Hayden** mango, which is originally from Florida. Next is the **Pirie** from India, and then some Hawaiian seedlings (**Common** mangoes). Mango trees grow and flourish best at low elevations, up to 1,000 feet above sea level, but some may be found at 3,000 feet. These trees can grow as high as 70 feet tall and are covered with dark-green, heavy, collective leaves.

Mangoes are high in natural sugars. Half of a mango (about three ounces) has 66 calories in comparison with half of a papaya which has 34 calories. In comparison with other fruits, they are a good to excellent source of vitamin A, and some types are very high in vitamin C. The ascorbic acid content varies greatly from one mango to the next.

The Pirie and Hayden are fair sources of vitamin C. All varieties contain more vitamin C in the green stage than the half-ripe stage, and more in the half-ripe than ripe stage. They are a fair to poor source of thiamine, riboflavin and niacin, and poor in calcium, phosphorus and iron. All this can be gathered from the nutrition tables below. As you can see, the nutrition table for raw mangoes is a general average, as nutritional value varies a great deal from variety to variety.

(From U.S.D.A. Agriculture Handbook #8)
MANGO (raw)
100 gms. edible portion

Water	81.7%	Iron	.4 mg.
Food energy	66 calories	Sodium	7 mg.
Protein	.7 gm.	Potassium	189 mg.
Fat	.4 gm.	Vitamin A	4800 I.U.
Carbohydrate	16.8 gm. (Total)	Thiamine	.05 mg.
	.9 gm. (Fiber)	Riboflavin	.05 mg.
Ash	.4 gm.	Niacin	1.1 mg.
Calcium	10 mg.	Vitamin C	35 mg.
Phosphorus	13 mg.		

(From "Fruits of Hawaii," Miller, Bazore and Barton)
MANGO – 100 gms.

	COMMON	HAYDEN	PIRIE
Vitamin A	1600 I.U.	2500 I.U.	3000 I.U.
Thiamine	.04 mg.	.04 mg.	.05 mg.
Riboflavin	.06 mg.	.05 mg.	.04 mg.
Niacin	.5 mg.	.3 mg.	.3 mg.
Vitamin C	114 mg.	10 mg.	14 mg.

When I was little, my favorite way of eating green mangoes was to mix some soy sauce, black pepper, Tabasco sauce and sugar. Then my friends and I would slice the green mangoes thin and dip them in the mixture and sit around and dare each other to eat. Then we'd try to blink back the tears and pretend it wasn't hot. My mother always told me I'd get a stomachache, and I must admit just thinking about eating green mangoes that way gives me a bellyache now! Since then, I've learned a few more palatable ways to fix green mangoes. These recipes are included.

Next mango season, try some of these recipes. They're really great, new, exciting ways to use the bumper crop of mangoes instead of letting them rot on the ground! Gather them up, use them in a new recipe,

give them to your friends, neighbors, enemies, strangers—rather than let them rot. And if you are one of the unfortunate ones (like me) who doesn't have a mango tree dropping your next breakfast in your lap, don't be afraid to ask if you see fruit lying on the ground in abundance. The owner will probably be more than glad to share them with you. A common sight in some of the towns on the outer Islands (maybe because they have more fruits and maybe because they have more aloha) during mango season, is to see a boxfull or a pile of mangoes near the curb that's been placed there for someone who needs or wants them from someone who has and wants to give. The land of aloha—lucky you live Hawaii! Let's do our part to keep Hawaii, Hawaii.

In case you have too many mangoes and you've run out of people to give them to (which isn't likely!):

Mangoes can be canned like any other fruit, but I don't like to do that for a number of reasons. Number one, I like to put as little energy into kitchen work as possible so I can put my energies elsewhere! Canning takes so much energy in the form of time and fuel.

I prefer to just peel my ripe (or a little overripe) mangoes and squeeze the pulp off the seed into a plastic bag. Then I just put a twist-tie on the bag and put it in the freezer. This saves on time, fuel that would be used for cooking, and also saves vitamins. Chunks of mango can be broken off to be added to smoothies, or melted down to be put in cakes, etc.

My friend in Kihei (as I mentioned in the Banana Section) used to also dry mangoes. I only had a dried mango once, but I'll never forget it! All I can do is urge you to try drying some at home.

P.S. Just a last note. A friend of mine asked me to be sure to mention the fact that mangoes contain the same substance as poison ivy in their peels, leaves and sap, and that some people are very allergic to them. Allergic reactions vary from skin rashes to swelling of the throat causing inability to breathe.

MANGO "LEATHER" ○

4 cups mango

Mango leather needs no honey, as the mango is full of natural sugars. Blend mango. Pour onto buttered cookie sheets 1/8" thick. Lay cookie sheets out in the sun and cover with a screen. This must be done on a hot, dry day or the fruit won't get a chance to dry out and may mold. If you live in a place where weather doesn't permit you to do this, you can dry the fruit by placing it in an electric oven on lowest heat overnight, or in a gas oven with a pilot light overnight. When fruit is dried out (hard like leather), you can peel it off of the cookie sheet and either roll it up or let your kids cut it into shapes for healthy, natural candy. Any fruit can be used for this.

MANGO NECTAR □

½ cup orange juice
¼ cup lemon juice
¾ cup ripe mango purée
1 cup water
½ cup yogurt
2 Tbsp. honey

Combine ingredients. Mix well in blender and chill. Whiz in blender again before serving. This is a cool, refreshing and delicious summer drink. Yields 3 cups.

WHIPPED MANGO □

1 cup whipping cream or Soy Whipped Cream (see Basic Recipes Section, p. 34)

1 Tbsp. lemon juice
2 Tbsp. honey

2 cups frozen mango

Whip cream in a blender or make Soy Whipped Cream. Add other ingredients gradually in order listed. Drop cubes of frozen mango in, one or two at a time until completely blended. Serve as a whipped dessert or freeze and serve as sherbet.

SUMMER SOUP □

4 cups mango
1 cup yogurt *
1 orange

½ cup chopped figs
2 bananas, sliced
1 apple, diced

Fresh mint leaves
2 cups coconut, grated and toasted

Blend first 3 ingredients. Chill. Add chopped fruit. Garnish with fresh mint leaves and grated, toasted coconut.

*Recommend Altadena brand vanilla yogurt.

HEALTHFUL MANGO ICE CREAM SODA □

4 cups mango
4 scoops honey ice cream
2 cups cold milk

1 cup mineral water, chilled *

8 scoops honey ice cream

Blend first 3 ingredients. Pour in mineral water. Fill cups ¾ full of blended mixture and plop in 2 scoops of ice cream in each cup. Serve immediately.

* Perrier, Health Valley, etc.

VITAMIN A & C SALAD ☐

2 cups ripe mango, diced
1 cup green mango, grated

3 bananas, blended
1 Tbsp. lemon juice

Combine ingredients. Refrigerate and serve.

HUA LANI — FRUIT OF HEAVEN ☐

4 cups mango, sliced thin
4 Tbsp. lemon juice
2 tsp. honey

1 cup yogurt
2 tsp. orange rind, grated
3 drops almond extract *

Combine first 3 ingredients well. Mix in remaining ingredients and refrigerate a few hours before serving. This allows tastes to mingle.

* Don't put in more than this, as almond extract is very strong!

GREEN MANGO CHUTNEY OR RELISH ☐

2 cups green mango, grated
2 Tbsp. red chili pepper, minced
2 bunches or 2 handfuls Chinese parsley, chopped fine
½ tsp. salt (or less)
2 tsp. honey
1 tsp. lemon juice

Combine all ingredients. Mix well and marinate (or chill) for at least 1 hour before serving. Yields 4 to 6 servings.

MANGO FROSTING ☆

1 cup mango, peeled and squeezed from seed
4 heaping Tbsp. noninstant, powdered milk
2 Tbsp. butter or margarine
2 Tbsp. honey
2 Tbsp. cream cheese

Blend ingredients. Let sit out 10 to 15 minutes. Frost cake when it cools off.

MANGOES 'N CREAM ☆

¼ cup butter or margarine
¼ cup honey
1 cup whole wheat flour
½ cup chopped nuts

2 cups mango
½ cup honey
1 Tbsp. lemon juice
4 cups whipped cream or Soy Whipped Cream (see Basic Recipes Section, p. 34)

Preheat oven to 400° F. Combine first 4 ingredients. Spread thin on a cookie sheet and bake at 400° for about 12 minutes. Let cool. If you don't have the time to do this, granola will work fine. Fold mango, lemon juice and honey into whipped cream. In a large bowl or bread pan, layer crumbs, whipped cream, crumbs, whipped cream, etc. Freeze 3 to 4 hours, until semifrozen.

MANGO HAUPIA ○

1 Tbsp. lemon juice
2 cups mango, squeezed from peel
6 Tbsp. arrowroot powder

1 cup coconut milk
¼ cup honey
6 Tbsp. arrowroot powder

Boil together first 3 ingredients until they thicken, stirring constantly. Mix next 3 ingredients together in a separate bowl. Pour into thickened mango, stir constantly until thickened. Pour into a shallow, buttered pan. Refrigerate. Cut into squares to serve.

SWEET & SPICY MANGO CHUTNEY ○

½ cup oil
¼ tsp. cumin seed
¼ tsp. crushed red pepper

8 cups chopped mango

1 cup honey
1 tsp. ground cinnamon
1 tsp. ground nutmeg
½ tsp. ground ginger
¼ tsp. ground cloves

Combine first 3 ingredients and cook 'til brown. Toss in mango. Cook to liquid consistency. Add next 5 ingredients and bring to boil. Simmer for 2 hours, stirring occasionally until mushy and thick.

MANGO TOPPING ○

2 mangoes, diced
1 Tbsp. honey
2 Tbsp. lemon juice

1 stick agar-agar (½ cup flakes)
½ cup cold water
1/8 tsp. almond extract *

½ cup water
1 cup milk powder
1 Tbsp. lemon juice

Combine first 3 ingredients. In saucepan, combine next 3 ingredients and cook until agar-agar dissolves fully. Cool until it begins to thicken. Blend together last 3 ingredients until whipped, then blend in thickened agar-agar. Fold in mangoes and refrigerate. Good served with granola for breakfast, over cookies, pies, cakes, sliced bananas, etc.

* Careful — almond extract is very strong!

MANGO SAUCE #1 ○

1 - 1½ cups water
6 cups half-ripe mango slices
¾ - 1½ cups honey

Cook mango in water until soft. Add honey and cook 10 minutes longer. May be used wherever a sauce is desired.

MANGO SAUCE #2 ○

Cut up ripe mango. Blend in blender until smooth and cook over low flame until thick. Six cups mango cooks down to 4 cups sauce. Use for fillings and in cake recipe (p. 148).

MANGO BUTTER ○

6 cups half-ripe mango slices
1 cup water

3 cups honey
½ tsp. ground cinnamon
½ tsp. ground nutmeg
¼ tsp. ground cloves
¼ tsp. ground allspice

Combine first 2 ingredients. Cook until very soft. If stringy, press with a spoon through sieve. Add next 5 ingredients and cook slowly until thick (15 minutes or more). Stir frequently to prevent burning. For storing, put in hot, sterilized jars and seal. Yields 1 quart.

MANGO SPREAD ○

2 cups mango, squeezed from seed
¼ cup honey
2 Tbsp. butter or margarine

Combine in a frying pan (teflon or tefal work best, as it won't stick and burn). On medium-high flame, bring to boil. Stir constantly until juice cooks out. Mango will turn translucent and stick together in a lump. Serve warm or cold by itself, or in crepes sprinkled with dextrose sugar; use as jam or as a filling in Orange Coconut Cookies (see Orange Section, p. 159).

MANGO MOUSSE

½ cup honey
Grated rind of 1 lemon
2 Tbsp. lemon juice
2 cups lilikoi juice (or other fruit juice)
1 Tbsp. butter or margarine

2 Tbsp. arrowroot powder

Combine all ingredients in a saucepan. In a little cup, put some of the juice with the arrowroot and stir until arrowroot dissolves. Now pour this into the saucepan. Bring to boil, constantly stirring until mixture thickens. Remove from heat and chill. When cool, layer in cups about 1 inch of mango, an inch of sauce, inch of mango, etc. Then top with mango and whipped cream, if you like.

MANGO BETTY

4 cups mango
½ cup raisins
¾ cup walnuts
2 Tbsp. lemon juice
¼ cup honey

2 cups crushed graham crackers
(preferably Midel, as they have no sugar)

Preheat oven to 350° F. Mix together first 5 ingredients. Stir in graham crackers at last minute. Bake at 350° for about 45 minutes or until set.

MANGO CRISP ☆

Fresh, just ripe mangoes

½ cup butter or margarine
2 cups date sugar
2/3 cup whole wheat flour
1 cup rolled oats
½ cup grated coconut

Preheat oven to 350° F. Cube mangoes and fill baking pan halfway. Combine last 5 ingredients, mix well and sprinkle over mangoes. Bake at 350° for 30 minutes until golden and crisp.

MANGO JELL

4 cups mango, diced and squeezed from seed

2 cups juice (juice poured off of mango and fill the rest of the way with orange juice)
2 Tbsp. honey
2 sticks agar-agar (1 cup flakes)

Pour juice out of mangoes and fill in with orange juice. Add next 2 ingredients. Bring to boil and cook until agar-agar is melted. Pour into mango. Mix in and refrigerate.

MANGO SHORTCAKE

½ tsp. salt
1¾ cups whole wheat flour
1 Tbsp. baking powder

2 Tbsp. honey
½ cup butter or margarine

¾ cup milk

Sliced, ripe mangoes

Whipped cream or Soy Whipped Cream
(see Basic Recipes Section, p. 34)

Preheat oven to 425° F. Combine first 3 ingredients well. With tips of fingers, cut next 2 ingredients into dry ingredients until it is the texture of cornmeal. Make a crater in the middle and pour in milk all at once. Stir 20 to 30 times with fingertips (don't overmix or you'll wear out the baking powder and the cake won't rise). Turn onto well-floured surface and knead with fingertips 15 times. Divide in half and fill two cake pans with batter. Pat to ¼" thick. Brush tops with melted butter and milk. Bake at 425° for about 12 minutes. Split cake in half and cover with a layer of mango slices; then top with whipped cream or Soy Whipped Cream. Put other half of cake on top and repeat.

MANGO CAKE

½ cup butter or oil
1½ cups honey

3 cups whole wheat flour
2 tsp. baking soda
2 tsp. baking powder
1 tsp. cinnamon (opt.)
1 tsp. cloves (opt.)

2 cups cooled Mango Sauce #2 (see recipe, p. 146), or thick, raw mango purée
1 cup chopped walnuts (opt.)

Preheat oven to 350° F. Cream first 2 ingredients. Sift in next 5 ingredients and mix well. Add last 2 ingredients. Mix well and pour into a greased and floured, large, oblong cake pan or two small, square (or round) pans. Bake at 350° F for 25 to 30 minutes.

MANGO CHEESECAKE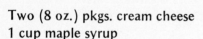

Two (8 oz.) pkgs. cream cheese
1 cup maple syrup

2 cups ground walnuts (1 lb.)
¼ cup maple syrup

4 mangoes, sliced
            or
2 cups Mango Sauce #2
(see recipe this section, p. 146)

Preheat oven to 350° F. Mix first 2 ingredients with an electric mixer or in blender until creamy and smooth. Combine next 2 ingredients and press into an 8" (buttered) pie tin and fill with first 2 ingredients. Bake at 350° for 15 to 20 minutes until set and firm. Cool. Top with Mango Sauce #2 or fresh mango slices. Sprinkle with walnut meal and refrigerate at least 1 hour before serving.

MANGO PIE #1

Crust:
Use Plain Pastry recipe for fruit pies (see Basic Recipes Section, p. 33)

Filling:
½ - ¾ cup honey
½ tsp. cinnamon
¼ tsp. nutmeg
3 Tbsp. whole wheat flour

3½ cups half-ripe mango, sliced
1 Tbsp. lemon juice

Preheat oven to 425° F. Combine first 4 ingredients and mix well. Line pie pan with pastry and put in one layer of mango slices. Top with honey mixture and repeat layers until all is used. Sprinkle on the lemon juice and cover with pastry. Crimp edges, poke top with a fork (to release steam) and bake at 425° for 10 minutes, then at 350° for 45 minutes. Serves 6.

MANGO PIE #2 ○

Crust:
Use Plain Pastry recipe for fruit pies (see Basic Recipes Section, p. 33)

Filling:
4 cups fresh mango, squeezed from seed
½ cup honey
¼ tsp. salt
2 Tbsp. lemon juice
¼ cup pineapple, diced
¼ cup tapioca pearls

Preheat oven to 450° F. Combine all ingredients and let sit in bowl about 15 minutes so tapioca pearls can soak and soften. Pour into pie shell. Cover with more pie dough or lattice. Bake at 450° for 10 minutes. Turn down to 350° and bake for 30 minutes.

SAUTÉD GREEN MANGOES ○

1 Tbsp. melted butter or oil
1 tsp. fresh ginger, grated

½ tsp. cumin seed
½ tsp. anise seed
2 pinches crushed chilies

2 pinches asafetida
2 pinches ground cloves
2 pinches black pepper
½ - 1 tsp. soy sauce
1½ cups green mango, grated

Sauté ginger a little in melted butter or oil. Add next 3 spices and let fry until toasted and you can smell the aroma in the air. Add pinches of spices and let sauté for a few seconds. Add soy sauce and mango; sauté until tender.

BROILED MANGO ○

1 Tbsp. butter or margarine
2 Tbsp. honey
¼ tsp. cinnamon

4 ripe mango halves, peeled

Whipped cream
Sunflower seeds
Date sugar

Combine first 3 ingredients and rub on top of mango halves. Broil 3 inches from heat until browned. Serve warm topped with whipped cream and sprinkled with sunflower seeds and date sugar.

MY MOM'S GREEN MANGO CHUTNEY ○

6 cups green mangoes, peeled and sliced
4 Tbsp. salt

1½ tsp. asafetida
3 cups honey
1½ cups vinegar
¼ cup fresh ginger, grated
1½ fresh red peppers
1 lb. raisins
1½ cups slivered almonds

Mix first 2 ingredients and let sit overnight to draw out excess water. Rinse and drain. Simmer all ingredients together until thickened. Bottle in prepared canning jars or seal with wax.

My mom told me about a way she just discovered to serve chutney. Take your favorite cracker and put a dab of chutney on top; top that with a slice of cheese and broil until cheese is melted.

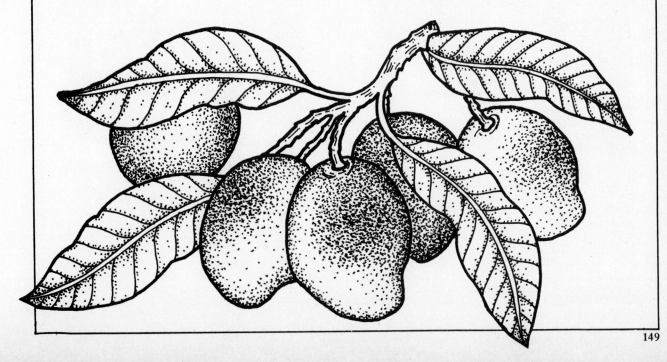

149

"Great cultures of the past have become only a matter of interest to the archaeologists. They have fallen when they became too materialistic, acquiring all manner of material things but neglecting the spirit. Not that matter doesn't matter. But spirit must be given priority. Vegetarianism helps people to think of these things."
— Shri Morarji Desai
(Prime Minister of the
Republic of India — 1977)

ORANGES

Oranges

I'll be one of the first to admit to being brainwashed and conditioned about oranges. Having been brought up on oranges shipped in from the mainland, it took me a while to even give local oranges a second thought. I mean, after all, they don't even look like a "real" orange, all full of artificial food coloring and stamped "Sunkist" on the peel. Instead, local oranges (though they're about the right size) have a yellow-green peel that often is covered with brown or black spots.

We also seem to be brainwashed into thinking that if something comes from somewhere else, then it must be better, tastewise and economywise. I began wondering about the truth of this myth when I was in California for a while. I noticed that although oranges were being grown throughout California, the supermarkets mostly sold and advertised (as if they were something special) Florida oranges. Where were all the California oranges? Being sold in Florida supermarkets! This is the kind of "economics" that makes me shake my head and think we've lost our intelligence.

Being driven by greed for the almighty dollar, we've lost our ability to see things as they really are, the way that they were made in perfect, natural order by the Supreme Lord. Therefore, we're creating a society that's all crazy and backwards, upside down, kapakahi — a society that has nothing to do with the laws of nature.

As the late British economist, E. F. Schumacher,

(From U.S.D.A. Agriculture Handbook #8)
ORANGES (raw)
100 gm. edible portion

		CALIFORNIA:			FLORIDA:
	All commercial varieties	Navel	Valencia	Fruit, incl. peel	All commercial varieties
Water	86.0%	85.4%	85.6%	82.3%	86.4%
Food energy	49 calories	51 calories	51 calories	40 calories	47 calories
Protein	1.0 gm.	1.3 gm.	1.2 gm.	1.3 gm.	.7 gm.
Fat	.2 gm.	.1 gm.	.3 gm.	.3 gm.	.2 gm.
Carbohydrate	12.2 gm. (Total)	12.7 gm. (Total)	12.4 gm. (Total)	15.5 gm. (Total)	12.0 gm. (Total)
	.5 gm. (Fiber)	.5 gm. (Fiber)	.5 gm. (Fiber)	—	.5 gm. (Fiber)
Ash	.6 gm.	.5 gm.	.5 gm.	.6 gm.	.7 gm.
Calcium	41 mg.	40 mg.	40 mg.	70 mg.	43 mg.
Phosphorus	20 mg.	22 mg.	22 mg.	22 mg.	17 mg.
Iron	.4 mg.	.4 mg.	.8 mg.	.8 mg.	.2 mg.
Sodium	1 mg.	1 mg.	1 mg.	2 mg.	1 mg.
Potassium	200 mg.	194 mg.	190 mg.	196 mg.	206 mg.
Vitamin A	200 I.U.	200 I.U.	200 I.U.	250 I.U.	200 I.U.
Thiamine	.10 mg.	.10 mg.	.10 mg.	.10 mg.	.10 mg.
Riboflavin	.04 mg.	.04 mg.	.04 mg.	.05 mg.	.04 mg.
Niacin	.4 mg.	.4 mg.	.4 gm.	.5 mg.	.4 mg.
Vitamin C	50 mg.	61 mg.	49 mg.	71 mg.	45 mg.

points out in his book, **Small Is Beautiful,** "If whole societies become infested by these vices (greed, envy), they may achieve astonishing things (like complicated, money-making shipping systems) but they become increasingly incapable of solving the most elementary problems of everyday existence (like what are we going to eat if the ships can't get here)."

Some little things we can do to begin getting back to solving the most elementary problems would be retaining our agricultural land in Hawaii and opening other lands for agriculture; training people how to live with and on the land as an honorable, productive way of making a living; and, growing and using foodstuffs locally. Plant your own orange tree(s) and eat local oranges. If you just close your eyes and open your mouth, you'll be delighted to find they have a very juicy, mild and sometimes even spicy flavor that varies from tart to sweet. In short, they're ono! They're good for you, too.

As can be seen in the nutritional tables, oranges are an excellent source of vitamin C. Compared to other fruits, they are a good source of vitamin A, thiamine and calcium, and are equal or better sources of phosphorus and iron. With the membrane left on, the calcium and vitamin C content are almost doubled.

Unfortunately, local orange trees only grow in certain areas, and your yard must be in one of them if you want to grow oranges in it. Local oranges are grown commercially in Kona on the Big Island, but wild trees can be found growing in valleys throughout the Islands. In areas that are always wet, oranges don't flower very well because they need a definite dry season to allow time for the buds to form. In very dry areas, orange trees need irrigation in intervals (one-week to two-week spans) rather than constant watering which keeps them too wet to allow for good bud formation.

Local oranges are usually in seasonal abundance during October, November and December of each year. The buds form during the prolonged dry season and normally bloom each year at the beginning of the rainy season. Orange trees are almost always grafted when grown for commercial use.

They are usually grafted onto lemon or lime trees which were planted from seed. This grafting can be done when the tree is only pencil high. The most desirable variety here in Hawaii has a good local name — Washington Navel! It is a seedless, very sweet orange grown commercially in Puna on the Big Island and takes about three to five years to bear fruit.

Local oranges can be used in the same way mainland oranges are used, so here are some recipes in which you can use either orange. But I hope next time you see a local orange in the store, you won't pass it up for a mainland orange.

TROPICAL ORANGE NECTAR ☐

1 cup fresh orange juice
1 cup yogurt
2 - 4 Tbsp. honey

Obtain 4 local oranges. Squeeze and strain to measure 1 cup juice. Combine with last 2 ingredients and whiz in blender. Chill and serve. The amount of honey needed varies with the sweetness of the orange juice. This is a cool, refreshing, delicious drink which yields 2 servings.

ORANGE QUENCHER ☐

1½ cups orange juice
1 cup water
6 Tbsp. noninstant dry milk
(whole or skim)
2 Tbsp. honey
½ tsp. vanilla

Combine ingredients and whiz in blender until smooth. Add ice and blend again. Yields 2 servings.

SPICED ORANGES □

6 oranges, peeled, seeded and diced
4 Tbsp. honey
Pinch of cinnamon
Pinch of cardamom
Pinch of cloves

Combine ingredients. Mix well and chill. Serve with a topping of sour cream or yogurt. Yields 6 servings.

ISLAND COCONUT ORANGE □

6 oranges
½ cup fresh, grated, toasted coconut
Honey
Whipped cream

Peel oranges. Cut crosswise in fairly thin slices (remove seeds). Place a layer of oranges in a casserole dish, top with layer of toasted coconut, drizzle with honey and repeat until all ingredients are used. Chill. Top with whipped cream before serving. Yields 6 servings.

ORANGE LOTUS □

6 oranges
6 Tbsp. honey
6 pinches cardamom powder

Slice top off orange crosswise, about 1 inch from top. Pierce each section with a knife and slowly and carefully pour 1 Tbsp. of honey and cardamom on each orange and rub in gently. You won't be able to rub the honey in all the way, and there will be a little well of honey on top of each orange. Place oranges in a tray with cut sides facing up and refrigerate overnight with tops off. Honey and cardamom will soak down into the orange. Serve the next day by cutting orange down across the top, almost to bottom, first in half, then quarters, then eighths, so pieces are still connected and resemble a lotus flower.

ORANGE JUICE BANANA SMOOTHIE □

1 cup orange juice
1 banana, frozen
1 Tbsp. cream cheese
1 tsp. honey

Combine ingredients. Whiz in blender until smooth. Yields 1 serving.

MARINATED ORANGES

6 oranges

½ cup grape juice
½ cup honey

1 (8 oz.) pkg. cream cheese
1 Tbsp. caraway seeds

Peel oranges and cut in ¼" slices crosswise. Soak in juice and honey overnight in refrigerator. Pour excess juice into a blender and blend in last 2 ingredients. Pour this over oranges.

DICED ORANGE CUPS

1 Tbsp. grated, fresh ginger
1 Tbsp. honey

3 oz. cream cheese
1 Tbsp. honey
Dash of salt
2 tsp. fresh lemon juice

2 oranges

Cook first 2 ingredients over low flame so honey soaks into ginger. Do not let honey heat into candy. Mix with next set of ingredients. Cut oranges in half, cut out insides from the shells and dice. Mix diced pieces with mixture and pour back into orange halves. Chill and serve.

ORANGE SLAW　□

3 oranges, peeled and diced
1 apple, diced
2 Tbsp. raisins
½ cup fresh, finely grated coconut
1/8 tsp. ground coriander
½ tsp. salt
½ - 1 tsp. honey
3 Tbsp. Eggless Soy Mayonnaise
(see Basic Recipes Section, p. 34)

Combine ingredients, mix well and chill several hours. Place a lettuce leaf on individual serving dishes. Top with a serving of cottage cheese and place Orange Slaw on top of that. Yields 6 servings.

ORANGE RELISH　□

1 lb. raw cranberries
2 whole oranges with skins
(seeds removed)
1 cup honey

Run ingredients through a food grinder or blend together in a blender. Chill and serve.

ORANGE DRESSING
(for vegetable salads)　□

½ cup orange juice
2 tsp. grated orange peel
1 tsp. grated, fresh ginger
¼ tsp. salt
¼ tsp. black pepper
2 Tbsp. soy sauce

2 Tbsp. olive oil
¼ tsp. asafetida (or more)

Combine first 6 ingredients. Mix well and let set awhile. Toast asafetida in oil. Pour in orange juice mixture and mix well. This is a nice dressing served on vegetable salad. Especially good when served with finely chopped, fresh ong choy leaves. Combine dressing and leaves and set in refrigerator to marinate for about 20 to 30 minutes before serving.

FROZEN ORANGES　□

This was one of my favorites when I was little. Cut an orange into eighths and freeze.

ORANGE FROZEN YOGURT JELL　○

3 cups orange juice
½ cup honey
1 stick agar-agar (½ cup flakes)

6 oz. frozen vanilla yogurt
or ice cream or sherbet

2 bananas, sliced thin
1 orange, diced

Combine first 3 ingredients and bring to rapid boil until agar-agar dissolves. Cool to room temperature. Mix half of this mixture with frozen yogurt. The cold yogurt will cause the fruit juice to jell, so stir quickly and place into the mold. Top this with the next 2 ingredients and then pour on remaining fruit juice with agar. Set in refrigerator to cool and jell. Unmold and garnish with orange slices and/or whipped cream.

ORANGE SNOW　☆

1 cup blended, frozen oranges
4 cups vanilla ice cream

Peel and seed oranges. Freeze, then blend in blender or put through juicer. Add ice cream and blend until smooth but not melted.

ORANGE CRANBERRY NUT JELL

1 cup raw cranberries
3 cups water

3 sticks agar-agar (1½ cups flakes)
1 cup water
1 cup orange juice

2 cups honey
3 oranges, finely chopped
½ cup chopped walnuts
½ cup chopped black mission figs
½ cup raisins

4 oz. cream cheese, cut in cubes (opt.)

Simmer first 2 ingredients until cranberries are tender and begin to dissolve. Combine next 3 ingredients and soak for 30 minutes. Add to boiling cranberries with remaining ingredients and mix until thoroughly blended. Pour into a mold or flat Pyrex dish and set in refrigerator to cool and jell.

Variation: Little cubes of cream cheese can be pushed into jell while it is cooling, before it is set.

ORANGE SCENT BALL

3 oranges
1 lb. whole cloves
String

This is not a recipe to eat, but is very nice for scenting a room or drawer, or to give away as a present! Poke cloves into the entire surface of the orange. Tie a string around the orange and hang in a cool, shady, windy part of the house so the orange can gradually dry out. As it dries, the orange will shrink, so the cloves must be pushed in every day. When the orange is completely dried out, it will be hard as a rock and about the size of a golf ball. It can then be put into drawers, closets, etc.

ORANGE NUT LOAF ○

1/3 cup butter or oil
½ cup honey

4 Tbsp. grated orange rind
Egg replacer equal to 2 eggs

2¼ cups whole wheat flour
3 tsp. baking powder
1 tsp. baking soda

1 cup chopped cashews
1 cup chopped dates

¾ cup fresh squeezed orange juice
4 Tbsp. yogurt

2 Tbsp. orange juice
2 Tbsp. honey

Preheat oven to 350° F. Cream together first 2 ingredients. Add next 2 and mix. Sift in next 3 ingredients, then add chopped dates and cashews and mix well. Add next 2 ingredients, mixing quickly and thoroughly. Scoop into a buttered and floured loaf pan and bake at 350° for 1 hour. In the last 30 minutes of baking, baste the top every 5 minutes with orange juice and honey mixture. When cool, remove from pan. Wrap in wax paper and then in a plastic bag. Set in refrigerator for one day before serving. Yields about 12 slices.

ORANGE DATE MUFFINS ◯

1 cup whole wheat flour
½ tsp. salt
3 tsp. baking powder

Egg replacer equal to 2 eggs
½ cup orange juice
2 Tbsp. oil, melted butter or margarine
2 Tbsp. honey
2 Tbsp. grated orange rind

½ cup chopped walnuts
½ cup chopped, pitted dates
¼ cup toasted coconut

Preheat oven to 350° F. Sift first 3 ingredients into a mixing bowl. Combine next 5 ingredients and beat quickly and thoroughly with a spoon. Add to flour mixture and mix. Add last 3 ingredients. Mix well and drop into buttered muffin tins, filling them three-fourths of the way full. Bake at 350° F for 15 to 20 minutes.

FRESH ORANGE PANCAKES ☆

1/3 cup oil, melted butter or margarine
2 Tbsp. honey
4 tsp. grated orange rind
Egg replacer equal to 2 eggs
¾ cup fresh orange juice
½ cup milk

1½ cups whole wheat flour
¼ tsp. salt
1 tsp. baking powder
½ tsp. baking soda

Combine first 6 ingredients in a mixing bowl and mix with an electric mixer or with a whisk. Sift in next 4 ingredients and mix thoroughly, quickly and lightly with a fork. Fry in an oiled skillet and serve with fresh orange-coconut syrup. Makes about 12 medium-sized pancakes.

FRESH ORANGE-COCONUT SYRUP ◯

1 cup honey
1 cup fresh orange juice
(with some of the orange pulp)
4 - 6 Tbsp. finely grated coconut

Combine ingredients and cook to syrup consistency, about 10 minutes. (It will thicken more as it cools.) Serve over pancakes and waffles. Delicious!

ORANGE COCONUT COOKIES ☆

1 cup butter or margarine
½ cup honey
4 Tbsp. grated orange rind
1 tsp. grated lemon rind
1 tsp. salt

2½ cups whole wheat flour

½ cup bran
1 cup grated coconut

Filling:
2 oranges, peeled and seeded
½ cup honey

Preheat oven to 375° F. Cream first 5 ingredients. Sift in flour. Add next 2 ingredients and mix well. Roll into balls and place on a buttered cookie sheet. Flatten just slightly and press an indentation in the center with your finger. Bake at 375° for 10 to 15 minutes. Blend oranges and honey in blender. Cook on medium flame until thick and jelly-like. When cookies are done, fill the indentations with orange jelly. Cool and serve. Makes about 4 dozen.

NUTTY ORANGE-CARROT SOUP

1 qt. milk (nut, soy or dairy)
2 cups sunflower seeds

¾ cup frozen orange juice concentrate
¾ cup honey
2 cups finely grated carrots
1 tsp. vanilla extract

Blend first 2 ingredients together until smooth. Add to next 4 ingredients and mix well. Bring to a boil over low heat. Serve warm.

Variation: To make a pudding, add:

    3 Tbsp. milk
    1½ Tbsp. arrowroot

Mix above 2 ingredients together and add to the above 6 ingredients before starting to heat. Stirring constantly, bring to a boil and cook until thick. Refrigerate until cold.

ORANGE PECAN PIE

Crust:
Use Flaky Pie Crust
(see Basic Recipes Section, p. 33)

Filling:
1 cup orange juice
1 tsp. vanilla
2 Tbsp. butter or margarine
½ cup honey
¼ tsp. salt
½ orange rind, grated fine
¼ cup whole wheat flour
Egg replacer equal to 1 egg
4 Tbsp. powdered milk
1 cup chopped pecans

Pecan halves

Combine filling ingredients together and cook until thickened, then cool. Pour into baked pie crust when cooled. Top with pecan halves; refrigerate until cold and set.

ORANGE CREAM PIE ☆

Graham Cracker Crust
(see Basic Recipes Section, p. 33)

¼ cup water
2 tsp. egg replacer

1 tsp. finely grated orange peel
½ stick agar-agar (¼ cup flakes)
¾ cup honey
½ cup fresh squeezed orange juice
or 2 Tbsp. frozen orange juice and enough water to make ½ cup

2 Tbsp. honey
¼ cup frozen orange juice concentrate
½ tsp. baking powder
1 tsp. finely grated orange peel
¼ tsp. vanilla extract
2 tsp. egg replacer
¼ cup water

2 cups whipping cream

¼ cup honey
½ tsp. vanilla extract

1 whole orange

Mix first 2 ingredients together. Put in a saucepan along with next 4 ingredients. Bring to a boil over medium-low heat; cook until agar dissolves. Refrigerate. Stir occasionally until ingredients start to thicken. Put next 7 ingredients in blender and whip for 15 seconds. Pour into thickened ingredients and mix together well. Put whipping cream in blender and whip until thick. Add next 2 ingredients and whip again until thick. Fold 1 cup of whipped cream into other ingredients. Pour into a graham cracker crust. Top with all but ½ cup of whipped cream. Drop a tablespoon of whipped cream in eight places about 1" in from the edge of pan. Peel and section an orange and place a section in the middle of each tablespoon of whipped cream. Sprinkle finely grated orange peel over top of pie if desired.

PAPAYA

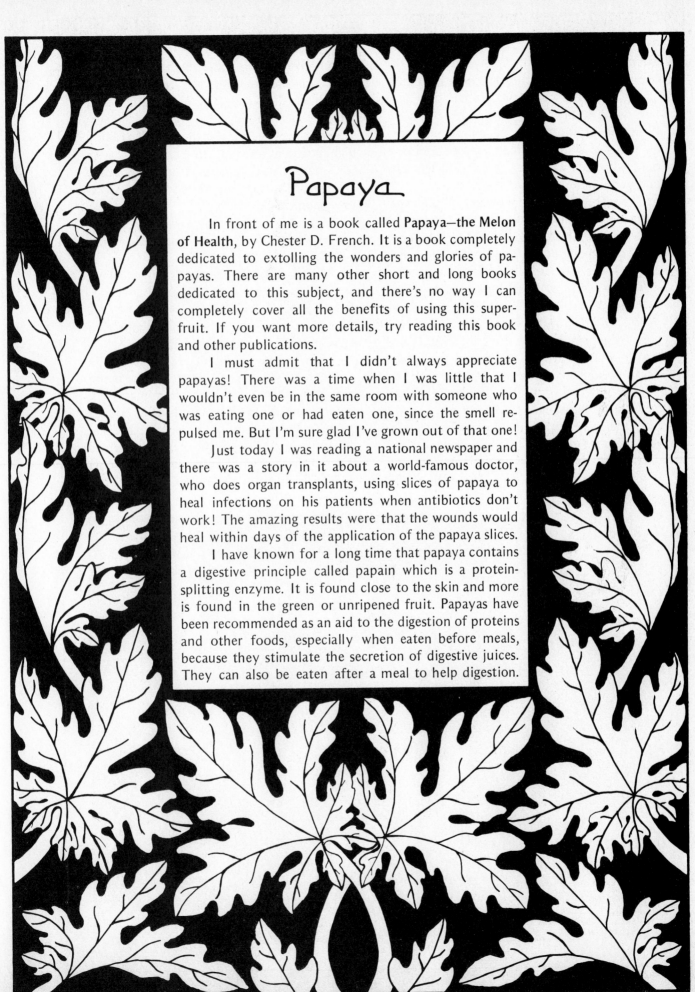

Papaya

In front of me is a book called **Papaya—the Melon of Health**, by Chester D. French. It is a book completely dedicated to extolling the wonders and glories of papayas. There are many other short and long books dedicated to this subject, and there's no way I can completely cover all the benefits of using this super-fruit. If you want more details, try reading this book and other publications.

I must admit that I didn't always appreciate papayas! There was a time when I was little that I wouldn't even be in the same room with someone who was eating one or had eaten one, since the smell repulsed me. But I'm sure glad I've grown out of that one!

Just today I was reading a national newspaper and there was a story in it about a world-famous doctor, who does organ transplants, using slices of papaya to heal infections on his patients when antibiotics don't work! The amazing results were that the wounds would heal within days of the application of the papaya slices.

I have known for a long time that papaya contains a digestive principle called papain which is a protein-splitting enzyme. It is found close to the skin and more is found in the green or unripened fruit. Papayas have been recommended as an aid to the digestion of proteins and other foods, especially when eaten before meals, because they stimulate the secretion of digestive juices. They can also be eaten after a meal to help digestion.

Some people I know take the papaya skins after they've eaten the fruit and rub their faces with the peels. They let this sticky substance near the peel dry on their skin and later rinse it off. They tell me it helps sunburn and promotes a good complexion for all types of skin. I used to rub peels on my baby's bottom whenever he got a diaper rash and it would heal within half a day.

There are many varieties of papayas with their distinctive flavors and qualities. For planting, just keep the seeds from the type of papayas that you eat and like the most. The seeds must be dried, but not in direct sunlight, as this seems to kill them. For myself, I like the strawberry or watermelon varieties, but I wanted to make sure I could grow a papaya tree suitable for the area in which I lived. It was not far from the ocean (about six houses down) and there were very strong winds. So, I found a papaya tree called Waimanalo Low-bearing. It is a type that gives fruit but the tree stays very short. Sometimes the first papayas will start only three feet off the ground. As long as you keep it in rich soil, it will stay very short

and develop a thick trunk for quite some time before getting taller. Papaya trees grow very fast and you can get your first fruit somewhere between 10 months and a year after your seedling has begun. Papayas grown in wet sections of the Islands at fairly high altitudes are apt to be watery, with little taste. But papayas from dry, sandy areas are flavorful and very sweet — sometimes almost too sweet.

Whether sweet or watery tasting, papayas are wondrously good for your body!

Economically, papaya is an excellent source of vitamins A and C, and in comparison to other fruits it is a fair source of riboflavin and calcium. It is a poor source of phosphorus, iron, thiamine and niacin.

Stewing or baking papaya destroys 7% to 12% of the vitamin C content. The use of lemon or lime juice with it increases the acidity and retains the vitamin C in cooked papaya. The vitamin C content increases as the fruit ripens. When the skin is dark-green and the flesh is light-yellow, it contains only 60% to 70% as much vitamin C as when ripe,

although the papaya at this stage has more protein-splitting enzymes than it will when it gets ripe. So, the nutritive advantage which you are looking for in your papaya will determine whether you'll want it green or ripe.

The leaves of the papaya tree can also be used. The new, young leaves that grow from the center of the top of the tree can be clipped (with no bad effects on the tree's growth) and steamed or cooked as any leafy

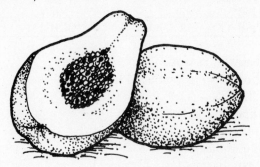

vegetable. And don't throw away or pass off as useless the brown leaves that are all dry and hanging down. They make an excellent tasting tea (sold at most health food stores for high prices) that aids digestion and can act as an appetizer.

Papayas (as all fruits) can be dried and frozen. To freeze, just scoop out the fruit part (no seeds and peels, please!) into a plastic bag.

Dried papayas are another dried fruit item that we ship in from Taiwan. It certainly seems that if such a small island with so many people can produce fruit to export, then we could do the same! We probably have a lot to learn from people in other parts of the world about how to use our agricultural land most efficiently! At any rate, I know of a few people here in Hawaii who are now drying papayas, on a small scale, for commercial purposes. All you have to do is peel and de-seed an unbruised papaya, cut it into quarters or strips (whatever you like) and dry. The methods and alternatives for drying are so varied that that is another book. There are books available in case you're interested.

Seeing as how this fruit is so beneficial, how can you pass up making your whole family a good, healthful dish featuring papayas?

(From U.S.D.A. Agriculture Handbook #8)
PAPAYA (raw)
100 gms. edible portion

Water	88.7%	Iron	.3 mg.
Food energy	39 calories	Sodium	3 mg.
Protein	.6 gm.	Potassium	234 mg.
Fat	.1 gm.	Vitamin A	1,750 I.U.
Carbohydrate	10 gm. (Total)	Thiamine	.04 mg.
	.9 gm. (Fiber)	Riboflavin	.04 mg.
Ash	.6 gm.	Niacin	.3 mg.
Calcium	20 mg.	Vitamin C	56 mg.
Phosphorus	16 mg.		

STUFFED RAW PAPAYA

2 papayas, cut in halves lengthwise and de-seeded

¾ cup cottage cheese
¼ cup crushed pineapple
3½ oz. cream cheese
2 Tbsp. lemon juice
½ cup pitted dates, chopped
¼ cup honey
Dash of salt

Combine last 7 ingredients and spoon into papaya halves just before serving. This is important, as dairy products make papayas turn bitter if they sit together for a long period of time.

BREAKFAST PAPAYA

1. Papaya halves served with lemon or lime juice.
2. Papaya halves filled with yogurt and drizzled with honey.
3. Papaya halves sprinkled with fresh, grated coconut (raw or toasted).

PAPAYA SMOOTHIE

2 cups ripe papaya, mashed
1 cup yogurt
2 Tbsp. honey or more
½ tsp. cinnamon

Combine ingredients. Blend in blender until smooth. Good served for breakfast. Very easy on the stomach. Yields 2 servings.

PAPAYA-CASHEW BLEND ☐

¾ cup raw cashews
1 whole papaya
1 tsp. vanilla (opt.)
¼ cup shredded coconut
2 Tbsp. honey

Blend together all ingredients and taste a creamy, healthful pudding.

PAPAYA-BANANA-ORANGE DRINK ☐

1 cup mashed papaya
½ cup mashed banana
1 cup orange juice
1 cup water
¼ cup honey
2 Tbsp. lemon juice

Combine ingredients. Blend in blender until smooth. Chill and whiz in blender again before serving. Yields 4 servings.

PAPAYA SHAKE ☐

1½ cups cold milk
1 cup ripe, mashed papaya, chilled
¼ cup honey
2 Tbsp. lemon juice
2 Tbsp. dry milk powder
Cinnamon or nutmeg to taste
½ cup ice

Combine ingredients. Whiz in blender until smooth and serve immediately. Yields 2 to 3 servings.

PAPAYA COCONUT MILK DRINK ☐

2 ripe papayas
1 cup coconut milk
3 oz. cream cheese
2 - 4 Tbsp. honey
1 cup grated coconut (opt.)

Scoop out papaya. Combine with next 4 ingredients and blend until smooth.

BEAUTY SECRET

The enzymes and vitamin A in papaya are beneficial to your skin when taken internally or externally. Next time you eat or scoop out a papaya, rub the fruit side of the peel over your face and allow fruit to dry on your face. The enzymes in papaya are more concentrated near the peel. Then just rinse the papaya off your face.

PAPAYA-COCONUT-DATE DELIGHT ☐

1 cup thick coconut cream, chilled
2 - 4 Tbsp. crystallized honey

½ cup shredded coconut
(may use pulp from coconut milk)
½ cup diced dates
2 tsp. orange juice (or more)
1½ cups firm, ripe papaya (cut in cubes)

Whip first 2 ingredients. Quickly and gently mix with next 4 ingredients. Chill well and serve. Yields 2 to 3 servings.

PAPAYA ICE CREAM ☐

1½ cups ripe papaya
½ cup orange juice
3 Tbsp. lemon juice
1½ cups whipping cream
½ cup honey

Press the papaya through a sieve and combine with the fruit juice. Dissolve the honey in the cream. Add the fruit mixture gradually and mix thoroughly. Freeze in ice trays, stirring several times during the freezing process.

PAPAYA PEANUT BUTTER SPREAD □

1 tsp. peanut butter
1/8 cup shredded coconut
½ cup cashews
½ ripe papaya
Dash of cinnamon
½ tsp. vanilla

Blend together all ingredients and place on buttered toast for a treat kids and adults will love.

PAPAYA RELISH □

1 papaya, cubed
1 avocado, cubed

½ cup pineapple juice
½ tsp. olive oil
2 Tbsp. chili sauce
1 Tbsp. lemon juice
2 pinches powdered clove
3 pinches asafetida

Combine first 2 ingredients in a bowl. Combine last 6 ingredients and mix in with avocado and papaya. Sprinkle with baco-bits or Crunchy Tofu Crisps, if desired (see Tofu Section, p. 384).

PAPAYA-CAROB PUDDING □

2 cups papaya pulp
1 tsp. lemon juice
2 Tbsp. honey
¼ cup grated coconut
6 - 8 Tbsp. carob powder

Blend ingredients until smooth. Use as pudding or pour into raw pie crust (see Basic Recipes Section, p. 32) and refrigerate overnight or at least 2 hours.

PAPAYA-COCONUT PUDDING (Haupia) ○

3 cups fresh coconut, grated (1 coconut yields 1-1/3 cups extracted coconut milk)
1 cup boiling water

1-1/3 cups thick papaya pulp
½ cup honey
½ cup arrowroot

Drain the coconut and grate the coconut meat. Pour boiling water over the coconut and allow it to remain 15 to 30 minutes. Strain the liquid through several thicknesses of cheesecloth, squeezing out as much liquid as possible. Press the papaya pulp through a sieve, then measure it. Mix the arrowroot and honey together. Stir this mixture into the papaya. Cook over a low flame, stirring constantly until it thickens. Add the coconut milk and cook for 5 to 10 minutes, or until the mixture is thick. Pour into pan and chill.

PAPAYA-GUAVA HAUPIA ○

2 cups mashed papaya
2 cups guava pulp
1 cup honey

8 Tbsp. arrowroot powder
A little water to make a paste

Diced guava shells

Combine first 3 ingredients and bring to a boil. Gradually add arrowroot paste and stir continuously about 5 minutes or until mixture thickens. Quickly blend in last ingredient and pour into greased, fancy molds or rimmed cookie sheets or cake pans. Let cool and refrigerate. Yields 4 to 6 servings.

PAPAYA CHUTNEY ○

1 Tbsp. ghee or oil
1 - 2 tsp. fresh ginger, grated

1 papaya
1/8 tsp. fennel seed
1/8 tsp. anise seed

2 Tbsp. honey

Brown ginger in ghee or oil. Add next 3 ingredients and cook until water begins to evaporate. Add honey and cook down until it is a nice, thick consistency.

PAPAYA-GINGER MARMALADE ○

2 lemons, sliced thin
2 cups water

1 tsp. chopped ginger root
3 cups honey
2 cups water

8 cups firm, ripe papaya, sliced

Cook thinly sliced lemons in water for 30 minutes until transparent. Boil together next 3 ingredients until syrupy. Combine lemon and syrup with firm, ripe papaya. Cook slowly for 30 minutes or until thickened. Pour into hot, sterilized jars and seal with paraffin.

PAPAYA TOPPING ○

1½ Tbsp. arrowroot powder
1 cup orange juice
1½ tsp. lemon juice
½ cup honey
1½ tsp. orange rind

2 peeled, seeded and cubed papayas

Cook first 5 ingredients until thickened and then cool in refrigerator. Add papaya cubes. Serve over ice cream or frozen yogurt.

PAPAYA COBBLER ☆

1½ cups whole wheat flour
½ tsp. baking soda

½ cup melted butter or oil
1 cup rolled oats

1½ - 2 cups mashed papaya
½ cup honey
¼ tsp. nutmeg
½ tsp. cinnamon

Preheat oven to 350° F. Sift first 2 ingredients into a bowl. Add the next 2 and mix well. Place a very thin layer of mixture on the bottom of a square cake pan. Combine next 4 ingredients and pour them over the thin layer in the pan. Top it with remaining oat mixture and bake at 350° for 25 to 30 minutes, until top crust is golden. Very good served warm. This may also be filled with guava or mango purée. Yields 8 to 12 servings.

PAPAYA CAKE ○

1 cup papaya
1 cup grated coconut
1 tsp. vanilla
1 cube butter or margarine
1 cup honey

3 cups whole wheat pastry flour
3 Tbsp. baking powder
1 tsp. cinnamon
1 tsp. nutmeg
1 tsp. cloves

Mix wet ingredients, mix dry ingredients; then mix wet with dry. Pour into oiled pans. Bake at 350° for 30 to 40 minutes or until a knife or toothpick inserted in the middle comes out clean.

PAPAYA PIE

Crust:
Use Plain Pastry recipe
(see Basic Recipes Section, p. 33)

Filling:
½ - ¾ cup honey
½ tsp. cinnamon
¼ tsp. nutmeg
3 Tbsp. whole wheat flour

Papaya slices
Lemon juice

Preheat oven to 425° F. Combine first 4 ingredients and mix well. Line pie pan with pastry and put in one layer of papaya slices. Top with honey mixture and repeat layers until all is used. Sprinkle with lemon juice and cover with pastry. Crimp edges, poke with fork, and bake at 425° for 10 minutes; then turn down to 350° and bake for 45 minutes more. Serves 6.

PAPAYA MARBLE PIE ☆

Crust:
Use any baked or raw food pie crust
(see Basic Recipes Section, pp. 32, 33)

Filling:
½ tsp. Postum (coffee substitute)
4 Tbsp. carob powder
½ stick agar-agar (¼ cup flakes)
½ tsp. vanilla
1½ cups papaya juice
¼ cup honey

½ blended papaya
2 oz. cream cheese
½ papaya, cut in chunks
2 bananas

Blend together first group of filling ingredients and cook on stove to boiling point. Then refrigerate until cooled and **partially** jelled. At that time, stir in remaining ingredients to make a marbled effect. Pour very carefully into baked or raw food pie crust of your choice. Chill and serve.

PAPAYA CRUMB PIE ☆

1 stick butter or margarine
2 Tbsp. honey
1 cup whole wheat flour
1 cup rolled oats
½ cup bran
½ cup sesame seeds

Filling:
3 average-sized, ripe papayas
1 Tbsp. lemon juice
½ cup honey
1 tsp. vanilla
1 tsp. maple syrup or flavoring
1 tsp. cinnamon
½ tsp. cardamom or allspice

½ cup chopped dates and raisins

½ stick butter or margarine
1 cup whole wheat flour
½ cup rolled oats
½ cup sesame seeds
¼ cup honey

Preheat oven to 375° F. Combine first 6 ingredients. Mix with fork. Add a little water if needed. Press with hands into a pie plate. Combine next 7 ingredients and blend 'til smooth. Add dates and raisins, mix, and pour into unbaked pie shell. Melt butter in skillet and mix in remaining 4 ingredients. Sprinkle on top of pie; dot with butter and drizzle with honey. Bake at 375° for 15 to 20 minutes or until toasty on top.

PAPAYA FRUIT CHEWIES   ○

Peels from 1 papaya
½ cup honey
½ cup natural fruit juice

Blend all ingredients and cook down to a candylike texture by stirring constantly over a medium-high heat until thick and gooey, or put on low heat and stir occasionally during the day (it will take hours on low) and just watch more carefully when thickened. A good idea is to use a nonstick pan like teflon or tefal. When thick, cool and roll into balls or serve in squares. For an attractive touch, roll in finely shredded coconut or fruit sugar.

SESAME FRUIT CHEWS   ○

Add the following ingredients to
Papaya Fruit Chewies (previous recipe):
¼ cup sesame meal
¼ cup powdered milk
2 tsp. bran

A nice variation is a sesame fruit chewy which can be made by adding sesame meal (ground up sesame seeds), bran and milk powder to taste, with a squeeze of orange or lemon to keep it pliable.

STEWED PAPAYA   ○

2 cups diced papaya
¼ cup water
½ cup raisins
Juice of 2 lemons

½ cup honey
Cinnamon to taste

Combine first 4 ingredients and cook until hot. Add last 2 ingredients. Mix well and serve as a dessert or as a warm breakfast fruit. Yields 2 - 3 servings.

BAKED PAPAYA   ○

2 firm, ripe papayas

2 Tbsp. lemon juice
2 Tbsp. butter or margarine
½ tsp. salt

Preheat oven to 350° F. Sprinkle and dot papaya halves with last 3 ingredients and bake at 350° for 30 to 35 minutes in a pan with a little water on the bottom to prevent sticking. Serve warm as a vegetable. These are also good served with some honey instead of salt and sprinkled with nutmeg. Yields 4 servings.

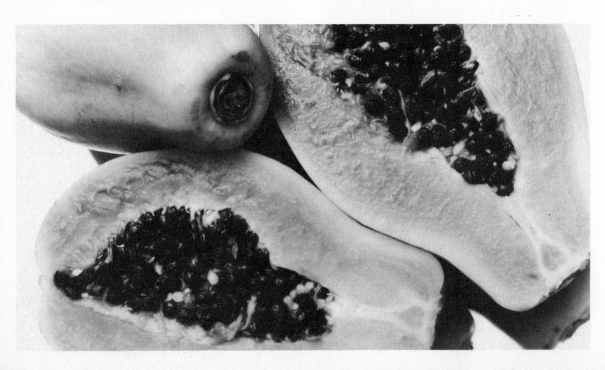

GOLDEN BAKED PAPAYA ☆

1 medium-large, firm, ripe papaya

½ cup cream cheese, softened
½ cup cottage cheese
4 tsp. mango chutney
¼ tsp. curry powder
1 Tbsp. date sugar
¼ cup cashews, chopped fine
2 Tbsp. raisins

1½ Tbsp. butter or margarine
1½ Tbsp. date sugar
¼ tsp. cinnamon

Preheat oven to 400° F. Cut papaya in half and scoop out seeds. Combine next 7 ingredients in a bowl and mix until well blended. Scoop the mixture into the papaya halves. Combine last 3 ingredients and cook until melted and combined. Place filled papayas in a baking dish. Top each with melted mixture and bake at 400° for 15 to 20 minutes. This is an unusual and delicious preparation; good for breakfast or dessert. Serve hot, since it turns bitter when cool.

STEWED GREEN PAPAYA ○

1 green papaya, peeled and diced
Boiling water
Salt

Black pepper
Butter or margarine

Combine first 3 ingredients and cook until soft. Drain and serve like squash with butter, black pepper and more salt if desired. Yields 1 to 2 servings.

BAKED SPICY PAPAYA ○

½ firm, ripe papaya

1 tsp. honey
½ tsp. butter or margarine
Sprinkle of cinnamon
Sprinkle of nutmeg
Sprinkle of allspice
A few raisins
A few chopped dates
Grated coconut
½ tsp. date sugar

Preheat oven to 400° F. Combine last 9 ingredients and fill papaya halfway with them. Bake at 400° for 10 minutes. Serve immediately, since the papaya will turn bitter as it cools.

PAPAYA CHOWDER ○

2 Tbsp. oil
1 tsp. curry powder
2 cups green papaya, peeled and diced
½ cup diced carrots
½ cup chopped celery

2½ cups boiling water
1 - 1½ tsp. salt or kelp

1-1/3 cups milk

Combine first 5 ingredients and cook lightly. Add next 2 ingredients; cook until tender (about 1 hour). Add milk at the very end, stir well and serve hot. Yields 6 servings.

GREEN PAPAYA WITH COCONUT MILK ○

1 medium-sized, green papaya
3 cups coconut milk
½ - 1 tsp. fresh ginger, grated
Salt or kelp and black pepper to taste

Peel, wash and dice papaya. Combine with next ingredients; cook until papaya is tender. Serve as a vegetable. Yields 2 servings.

PASSION FRUIT

Passion Fruit

Passion fruit is not only a good, strong-tasting fruit that can be used for juice and flavoring, but also the vine and flower are very decorative. I prefer vine-covered fences, so I figured that it would be doubly nice to have our fence "bear some fruit."

I took the seeds from my favorite lilikoi types, like the big, yellow one and the purple type, and dried them in the sun. Boy, there were a lot of seeds from just one or two lilikois! I then buried a row of them about an inch deep along the fence line, and in no time I had the beginnings of vines. Now, a year later, the vines have covered the fence and are reaching out to anything they can find —such as nearby trees and porches. I'm anxious to see the yellow and purple bulbs of fruit hanging down the numerous vines.

If you don't want vine-covered fences or passion fruit everywhere, just try one plant near a wooden, trellised patio covering or porch, for they make a decorative, shady covering. We discovered this from watching how they grow in the wild. Old, established passion fruit will cover trees and bushes. In some places where we would gather them, like in Waiehu, Maui, it was like walking under great canopies. Near the beach there's a great place under tall bushes and kiawe trees where you can enter a forest and it's like a kid's paradise; a nature-made tent with dots of yellow fruit all over the ground.

My kids like to eat the fruit, but I try to make sure they don't eat too many because they tend to swallow all the black seeds, which are constipating. The process for getting the tasty juice out is so simple. I usually save it by freezing and taking it out when I need it. Then without thawing, you can just blend it with water and honey for juice.

The purple passion fruit grow better at a higher elevation than the yellow and are smaller with a slightly nicer flavor and aroma. The yellow grow well at low elevations — from sea level to 2,500 feet — and grow more vigorously, producing more fruit than the purple passion fruit. When they are perfectly ripe and sweet (as sweet as passion fruit will get), the shell becomes dry and wrinkled.

Flowers of the purple kind open at dawn and close before noon, while the yellow open at noon and close before midnight; therefore there is very little crossing between the two. There is also a third type called Grandilla or Watermelon. It is orange-colored, not very tasty, and seen only occasionally — mostly on the Big Island. Passion fruit season is during the summer and fall and sometimes as late as January.

(From U.S.D.A. Agriculture Handbook #8) PASSION FRUIT (raw) 100 gm. edible portion			
Water	75.1%	Iron	1.6 mg.
Food energy	90 calories	Sodium	28 mg.
Protein	2.2 gm.	Potassium	348 mg.
Fat	.7 gm.	Vitamin A	700 I.U.
Carbohydrate	21.2 gm. (Total)	Thiamine	Trace
	— (Fiber)	Riboflavin	.13 mg.
Ash	.8 gm.	Niacin	1.5 mg.
Calcium	13 mg.	Vitamin C	30 mg.
Phosphorus	64 mg.		

The U.S.D.A. Agriculture Handbook #8 only had a table for purple passion fruit. A less complete table in Fruits of Hawaii shows that yellow passion fruit is generally about the same in nutrients, except that it contains 2,400 I.U. of vitamin A and 20 mg. of vitamin C per 100 gm.

Yellow passion fruit contains a higher percentage of juice and acid than the purple kind and is an excellent source of vitamin A and niacin in comparison to other fruits. It is a good source of riboflavin, a fair source of ascorbic acid, and a poor source of thiamine.

The juice of the purple passion fruit is high in sugar content and a good source of vitamin A, riboflavin, niacin and ascorbic acid. It is low in calcium, phosphorus, iron, and a poor source of thiamine.

Here's some tart, tasty recipes.

LILIKOI JUICE (Passion Fruit)

Cut fruit in half. Scoop pulp and seeds into a fine sieve. Press through by mixing vigorously with a spoon. Add lemon juice and chill. Twelve lemon-sized lilikoi will yield about 1-1/3 cups.

LILI-ADE (Light Passion Juice)

½ cup passion fruit juice
4 cups water
¾ - 1 cup honey
2 Tbsp. lemon juice

Combine ingredients. Whiz in blender. Chill and serve. Yields about 5 cups.

PASSION PINEAPPLE DRINK

1½ cups passion fruit juice
1½ cups pineapple juice
1½ cups water
¾ - 1 cup honey
2 Tbsp. lemon juice

Combine ingredients. Whiz in blender. Chill and serve. Yields about 5 cups.

LILIKOI COCONUT JUICE

¾ cup coconut milk
¼ cup passion juice
2 tsp. honey (or more)

Blend ingredients. Serve over ice or chill and then serve. Yields 1 cup.

LILIKOI DAHI

1 cup yogurt
2 Tbsp. passion juice
2 Tbsp. honey
¼ cup ice water (if very thick yogurt) or ice cubes

Combine ingredients. Whiz in blender and serve. Yields 1 to 2 servings.

LILIKOI-PAPAYA ICE CREAM

1 cup fresh passion fruit juice
1 cup honey (crystallized lehua or kiawe)

3 cups ripe papaya pulp

3 cups cream or Soy Whipped Cream (see Basic Recipes Section, p. 34)
Dash of cardamom (opt.)

Combine first 2 ingredients. Add papaya and blend until smooth. (You can use a blender or electric mixer.) Gradually add cream, mixing slowly with a whisk or fork. Pour into two refrigerator ice trays and set in freezer. Stir every 15 minutes until it starts to set up hard. It is important to do this stirring to prevent it from getting icy. This makes a creamy, sweet, exotic dessert.

LILIKOI DRIED FRUIT COMPOTE □

4 Tbsp. passion juice
2 Tbsp. honey
¾ cup water

6 dried figs, chopped
12 dried apricots, chopped
1 Tbsp. raisins, chopped
4 dried pears, chopped
10 dates, chopped
2 Tbsp. shredded coconut

Combine first 3 ingredients until blended. Pour into a bowl and fill with remaining ingredients until they are covered three-fourths of the way with juice. Set in refrigerator to soak 6 to 8 hours. Serve over plain yogurt.

FROZEN HAWAIIAN FRUIT SALAD ○

8 oz. passion juice
2/3 cup honey
10 oz. Hoppings honey lemon soda

12 oz. fresh pineapple chunks
2 - 3 bananas, sliced thin

Combine first 3 ingredients and mix until blended. Mix in fruit. Pour into an 8- or 10-inch pan and set in freezer until solid. Yields 6 servings.

LILIKOI FLOATING DESSERT □

1 cup orange juice
½ stick agar-agar (¼ cup flakes)

½ cup passion fruit juice
½ cup honey
1 cup water

Combine first 2 ingredients. Soak for 5 minutes, then bring to a boil, stirring until dissolved. Pour into a pan and chill until firm. Combine last 3 ingredients. Mix well and chill. Cut orange kanten into small cubes; float them in juice and serve.

HOT & SPICY LILIKOI DRINK ☐

4 cups water
10 whole cloves
10 whole allspice
3 pcs. cinnamon sticks (2'' long)
1 lemon (cut peel into strips)

¾ cup passion juice
2 Tbsp. lemon juice
¾ - 1 cup honey

Combine first 5 ingredients. Boil 10 minutes. Strain. Mix in next 3 ingredients. Heat to simmer and serve hot. Yields 5 to 6 cups.

TANGY PASSION FRUIT CAKE ☆

1 cup butter or oil
1½ cups honey

3 cups whole wheat flour
2 tsp. baking powder
2 tsp. baking soda

1 cup passion fruit juice

Preheat oven to 350° F. Cream first 2 ingredients until smooth. Sift in next 3 ingredients and mix well. Add lilikoi juice while mixing until well blended. Pour into a buttered and floured, oblong cake pan (or two 8-inch square pans) and bake at 350° for 30 to 45 minutes. Cool and cover with Passion Fruit Glaze.

PASSION FRUIT GLAZE ☆

½ cup butter or margarine
½ cup honey
½ cup passion fruit juice

Combine ingredients in a saucepan and bring to a boil. Boil 4 to 5 minutes, stirring constantly, just until mixture leaves the side of the pan. Be careful not to overcook. Pour glaze evenly over cooled cake. When cool, cut and serve. Delicious!

LILIKOI JELL ◯

1½ sticks agar-agar (¾ cup flakes)
2½ cups water

1 cup honey
¼ tsp. salt

½ cup passion fruit juice

2 bananas, sliced

Whipped cream or Soy Whipped Cream (see Basic Recipes Section, p. 34)

Soak first 2 ingredients until soft. Combine with next 2 and cook until dissolved. Remove from heat and mix in juice. Pour into a pan and chill. When half set, insert banana slices and chill until firm. Cut into servings and top with whipped cream.

LILIKOI CREAM CHEESE PIE ☆

1½ cups ground walnuts
3 Tbsp. maple syrup

8 oz. cream cheese (soft)
3 Tbsp. passion fruit juice
4 Tbsp. honey
Egg replacer equal to 2 eggs

Crush walnuts with a rolling pin. Mix well with syrup and press into 8'' pie tin. Combine next 4 ingredients and whip with an electric mixer or whisk until smooth and fluffy. Pour into pie shell and bake at 350° for 15 to 20 minutes.

LILIKOI PIE ☆

Crust:
Use Flaky Pie Crust recipe
(see Basic Recipes Section, p. 33)

Filling:
½ cup passion fruit juice
½ cup honey
¾ cup water

1/3 cup arrowroot powder

2 Tbsp. finely grated lemon rind
1 Tbsp. butter or margarine

1 cup whipped cream or Soy Whipped
Cream (see Basic Recipes Section, p. 34)

Combine first 3 filling ingredients and mix
until blended. May use blender. Remove 1/3
cup and mix with arrowroot to make paste.
Heat the rest of the juice to boiling. Gradually add arrowroot mixture, stirring constantly
until thickened. Reduce heat and mix in
next 2 ingredients and cook slowly for a few
more minutes. Cool slightly and pour half
of the filling into a baked pie shell. Let cool
at room temperature. Chill the other half of
the filling and fold into chilled whipped
cream, just enough to get a marbled effect.
Spoon lightly on top of pie and set in
refrigerator for about 1 hour before serving.
Yields 6 servings.

Variation: The whipped cream can also be
mixed with all the chilled filling until evenly
blended and then placed in pie shell for Lilikoi Cream Cheese Pie (see recipe, p. 179).

LILIKOI COCONUT MILLET DESSERT ○

¼ cup millet
1¾ cups milk
½ cup shredded coconut

¼ cup honey
¼ cup passion fruit juice

¼ cup chopped almonds

Combine first 3 ingredients and simmer for
40 minutes. Remove lid; gradually stir in
next 2 ingredients. Raise heat a bit and cook
about 5 to 10 minutes longer, stirring occasionally until thickened. Mix in nuts; scoop
into a bowl. Chill before serving. Can also
be served warm. Yields 2 to 4 servings.

LILIKOI DATE BARS ☆

1 cup chopped dates
½ cup chopped walnuts
½ cup grated coconut
½ cup passion fruit juice
1 Tbsp. whole wheat flour

1½ cups whole wheat flour
1 tsp. baking soda

1½ cups rolled oats (quick-cook)
½ cup toasted sesame seeds
½ cup honey plus 2 Tbsp.
1 cup melted butter or oil

Preheat oven to 350° F. Combine first 5
ingredients and simmer for about 5 minutes
until thick. Remove from heat. Sift next 2
ingredients into a mixing bowl. Add next
4 ingredients and mix well. Press half of
this into a buttered 10" square pan. Pour in
and evenly spread filling. Top with remaining oat mixture. Lightly press until evenly
covered and bake at 350° for 25 to 30 minutes. Let cool and cut into bars. Delicious!

LILIKOI BISCUITS ☆

Filling:
½ cup passion fruit juice
¼ cup honey plus 2 Tbsp.
2 Tbsp. water

4 tsp. arrowroot
4 tsp. water

Pastry:
¼ cup butter or margarine plus 2 Tbsp.
3 oz. cream cheese

1 cup whole wheat flour

Preheat oven to 350° F. Combine first 3 ingredients and bring to a boil. Reduce heat. Make a paste with the next 2 ingredients and add to lilikoi, stirring constantly until thick. Set aside to cool. Cream next 2 ingredients. Sift in flour and mix well. Roll into a ball. Wrap in wax paper and chill 1 hour. Roll out dough and cut 12 circles with the rim of a 1-cup measuring cup. Place 1 tsp. filling in the center of each round. Wet edges with water, bring four sides together and pinch closed. Then bring the four corners together in the center to form a round, and seal. Place on a buttered cookie sheet. Pierce with a fork and bake at 350° for 15 to 20 minutes. Dust with dextrose. Cool and serve. Yields 6 servings (2 each).

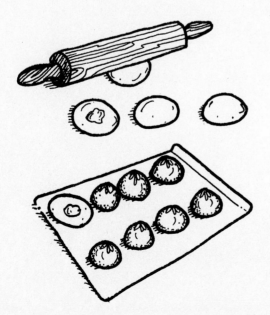

LILIKOI RAISIN NUT LOAF ☆

2¼ cups whole wheat flour
1½ tsp. baking powder
½ tsp. baking soda
½ tsp. salt

¾ cup passion fruit juice
½ cup honey
¼ cup melted butter or oil

½ cup chopped walnuts
½ cup seedless raisins

Preheat oven to 350° F. Sift first 4 ingredients. Combine next 3 and mix well. Add to sifted flour with nuts and raisins and mix until moist and blended but not completely smooth. Pour into a greased and floured 9" x 5" x 3" loaf pan. Bake at 350° for 45 minutes. Cover with aluminum foil after 30 minutes to prevent cracking. Cool. Slice thin and serve with butter. Good toasted, too.

LILIKOI COCONUT CANDIES ☐

2 Tbsp. butter or margarine
3 Tbsp. honey
3 Tbsp. passion juice

½ cup finely grated coconut

Combine first 3 ingredients and boil 4 to 5 minutes, just until it reaches soft ball stage. Test by dropping a little into a cup of cold water; if it beads up, it is ready. (Be careful not to overcook. It will get too hard.) Mix in coconut and stir over flame until coconut is well-coated. Remove from heat and set aside to cool just enough to handle. Shape into balls and roll in finely grated coconut. Let set until cold; serve. Makes 12 candies.

APRICOTS
PEACHES
and
NECTARINES

Apricots, Peaches and Nectarines

These three stone fruits are grouped together here because of their similarities in planting and care, and most importantly, in taste and texture. This similarity will make the fruit in the recipes interchangeable. In other words, you can replace apricots in a recipe with peaches or nectarines.

I never had many of these fruits in Hawaii, since they can't be grown well in a tropical climate. Any that are available in markets there have been picked green to survive the shipping. Therefore they never get as sweet and juicy as you can get them in a place where they are allowed to ripen a bit on the trees. And there is such a difference! I discovered this one summer in California when I tasted fresh, tree-ripened apricots, nectarines and peaches.

These fruits are very similar in flavor, texture and nutritional value to the mango, which grows in a tropical climate. As a matter of fact, you can use any of these fruits to replace mangoes in the Mango Section, or vice versa.

I am including both tropical fruits and fruits which grow in a place where there are seasonal changes. This is because a part of self-sufficiency is being able to use what grows locally — ideally what you yourself have grown. Imported mangoes are probably as expensive and "blah" tasting as imported apricots, peaches or nectarines.

(From U.S.D.A. Agriculture Handbook #8)
PEACHES, APRICOTS, NECTARINES (Raw)
100 gm. edible portion

	PEACHES	APRICOTS	NECTARINES
Water	89.1%	85.3%	81.8%
Food energy	38 calories	51 calories	64 calories
Protein	.6 gm.	1.0 gm.	.6 gm.
Fat	.1 gm.	.2 gm.	Trace
Carbohydrate	9.7 gm. (Total)	12.8 gm. (Total)	17.1 gm. (Total)
	.6 gm. (Fiber)	.6 gm. (Fiber)	.4 gm. (Fiber)
Ash	.5 gm.	.7 gm.	.5 gm.
Calcium	9 mg.	17 mg.	4 mg.
Phosphorus	19 mg.	23 mg.	24 mg.
Iron	.5 mg.	.5 mg.	.5 mg.
Sodium	1 mg.	1 mg.	6 mg.
Potassium	202 mg.	281 mg.	294 mg.
Vitamin A	1,330 I.U.	2,700 I.U.	1,650 I.U.
Thiamine	.02 mg.	.03 mg.	–
Riboflavin	.05 mg.	.04 mg.	–
Niacin	1.0 mg.	.6 mg.	–
Vitamin C	7 mg.	10 mg.	13 mg.

(Dashes denote lack of reliable data for a constituent believed to be present in measurable amount.)

By interchanging mangoes, apricots, nectarines and peaches according to what is available in your locale, you'll be able to make delicious meals that are a nutritional bonus as well.

As can be seen, these yellow-orange balls of nutrition are an especially good source of vitamin A.

I hope these recipes will give you a few ideas of the different ways these fruits can be used.

EASY PEACH FREEZE

4 cups peaches (ripe and peeled)
1 cup yogurt
2 Tbsp. honey

Blend peaches in a blender. Add honey and yogurt. Freeze.

APRICOT COOLER

1 cup yogurt
8 ripe apricots
½ tsp. vanilla
2 Tbsp. honey
1/8 tsp. cinnamon

Blend all 5 ingredients in a blender. Serve in ice-cold glasses and garnish with mint leaves.

TROPICAL PEACHES

Slice fresh peaches. Pour some peach nectar over peaches and sprinkle with coconut and finely chopped, candied ginger. Delicious!

STUFFED HALVES

Halves of apricots, peaches or nectarines

¼ cup peanut butter
¼ cup sesame tahini
1 Tbsp. + 1 tsp. honey
½ cup carob powder
Few drops vanilla (opt.)

1 lemon

Cut ripe fruit in half and lift out the pit. Mix next 5 ingredients together to form a ball (you can use different combinations and kinds of nut butters). Break off pieces of this nut butter ball which are a little bigger than the pit and flatten into fruit halves where the pit was. Arrange on a platter and squeeze lemon juice over all of them. (This is especially delicious with the carob stuffing, but any other nut butter, dried fruit or dairy confection can be used.) For a different dish, you can dilute the stuffing with water by adding the water a little at a time to make a thick sauce and pour over the fruit halves. (This can also be done with any of the other confections mentioned previously.)

FRUIT ICE CREAM

1 cup prune juice
2 Tbsp. raw nut butter or sesame tahini
2 tsp. carob

1 cup frozen apricot,
peach or nectarine slices
2 frozen bananas

In a blender, blend first 3 ingredients (any flavor fruit juice can be used; use a mild-tasting nut butter). Blend in next 2 ingredients until frozen fruit is blended smooth and mixture is an ice cream texture. You may want to make more than this, but you should probably only blend as much as the recipe calls for at a time so the blender motor doesn't burn out.

The Most Wonderful Apricot Cake, p. 191   Sunshine Pudding, p. 189   Easy Peach Freeze, p. 187

FRUIT CAROB BARS ☆

Filling:
1½ cups blended apricots,
peaches, nectarines
¼ cup honey
1½ tsp. arrowroot
¼ cup carob powder
¼ cup chopped dried apricots,
peaches, nectarines (presoaked)

Dough:
½ cup butter or margarine
1 cup honey
1 tsp. vanilla
1 Tbsp. yogurt

1¼ cups whole wheat flour
1½ cups rolled oats
½ cup chopped nuts or seeds
½ tsp. baking soda

Prepare filling by presoaking dried fruit overnight or in hot water for a couple of hours. Chop dried fruit and add to rest of filling ingredients in a pot and mix them together off the heat until arrowroot dissolves. Cook over heat, stirring constantly until thickened. Set aside to cool. Prepare dough by combining first 4 ingredients, then cutting in next 4 ingredients. Press half of this into an oiled cake pan, pour in cooled filling and crumble remaining dough on top. Bake at 350° for 25 to 30 minutes. Remove from oven and cool. Cut into bar shapes.

SUNSHINE PUDDING ◯

8 peaches or nectarines or 16 apricots

1 cup apple juice or water
¼ cup honey
1 tsp. vanilla
¼ tsp. almond extract

2 cups milk
¼ cup arrowroot

¼ cup carob powder

Chopped toasted almonds
or toasted coconut

Cut fruit in half and remove pits. Bring the next 4 ingredients to a boil. Poach fruit by cooking on both sides for about a minute on each side. Remove fruit from liquid with a slotted spoon. Slip peels off of fruit. Lay fruit pit side down in a pie plate. Add next 2 ingredients to the water fruit was stewed in and stir constantly over medium-high heat until it thickens. Pour half of this over the fruit in the middle of pie plate. Sift carob into remaining sauce in pot and stir over heat until thoroughly mixed in. Pour this along the edges of the pie plate. Sprinkle with toasted nuts and refrigerate to cool. This can also be arranged the same way but served in individual dessert bowls.

BROILED PEACHES ◯

Wash, peel, halve and pit fresh peaches. Brush round side with lemon juice and butter or margarine. Broil until browned a little on this side, then turn over with hollow side up and dab with ½ tsp. natural honey, jam or preserves (available in natural food stores). Broil for 3 to 5 minutes or until golden brown. Serve warm.

HOT PEACH SAUCE ◯

1 cup milk (nut or dairy)
1 Tbsp. arrowroot
1 Tbsp. honey
1 tsp. vanilla
½ tsp. almond extract

1 cup fresh peaches, sliced

Combine first 5 ingredients and cook over medium heat until thickened. Stir in fresh peaches, lower heat and cook until peaches are tender. Pour over banana bread, carrot cake, crepes, or as a topping for any favorite dessert.

PEACH MELBA

6 peach halves
2 cups yogurt

Slivered almonds

Red Raspberry Sauce:
10 oz. frozen raspberries, thawed
1/3 cup peach preserves
¼ cup honey
1 tsp. arrowroot
1/3 cup liquid (water or fruit juice)

Combine sauce ingredients in saucepan and cook over medium heat until thickened, stirring constantly to prevent lumping. Cool and refrigerate. Place peach with empty pit side up and fill with yogurt. Also good filled with honey ice cream or Soy Whipped Cream (see Basic Recipes Section, p. 34). Then pour raspberry sauce over the top and sprinkle with slivered almonds.

PEACH DELIGHT

1 cup water
1 Tbsp. agar-agar flakes

2 cups fresh peaches
1 cup pineapple
1 tsp. lemon juice
½ cup coconut shreds
2/3 cup honey
¼ cup oil
1/8 tsp. salt

Soak first 2 ingredients until agar softens. Bring to a boil until agar is dissolved. Set aside and let cool (but not jell). Blend the next 7 ingredients in a blender, add the first 2 ingredients and whip until smooth. Freeze and serve.

PEACHES 'N CREAM

1 stick agar-agar (½ cup flakes)
¾ cup water

1 lb. fresh peaches, chopped
2 Tbsp. lemon juice
¼ cup honey
¼ tsp. almond extract

2 cups Soy Whipped Cream
(see Basic Recipes Section, p. 34)

Soak first 2 ingredients in a pan until agar softens. Stir on medium heat until agar is dissolved and starts to thicken. Let cool for 1 minute. Add next 4 ingredients and chill until thick, but not set. Fold in whipped topping. Pour into 1-quart mold and chill until set.

APRICOTS 'N CREAM

1 lb. fresh apricots, pitted

Sauce:
4 cups unsweetened apricot juice
½ cup maple syrup
1 tsp. cinnamon
2 tsp. arrowroot

Topping:
2 cups milk (nut or dairy)
½ cup maple syrup
1 tsp. almond extract

Combine sauce ingredients in a saucepan. Stir and bring to a boil. Reduce heat and add apricots. Simmer until soft, about 5 minutes. Cool and chill. Then combine all topping ingredients in a small pan. Bring to a boil, stirring constantly over medium heat. Cool and then chill several hours. Serve over apricots. Also good using Soy Whipped Cream as a topping (see Basic Recipes Section, p. 34).

APRICOT-DATE SURPRISE

Apricot-Date Filling:
2 cups apricots, pitted and chopped
2 cups dates, pitted and chopped
2 Tbsp. honey
2 Tbsp. water
Pinch of cinnamon

Crumble Dough:
½ cup oil
½ cup honey
¼ tsp. almond flavoring
1½ cups whole wheat pastry flour

2 Tbsp. shredded coconut
¼ tsp. salt (opt.)
1½ cups rolled oats

Mix filling ingredients in saucepan and stir over low heat until thickened. Cool. Then mix first 4 dough ingredients together and stir in last 3 ingredients. Press half of the crumble dough into an oiled and floured 8"x 12" oblong pan. Spread with cooled filling and cover with remaining crumbs. Bake at 375° F for 30 minutes.

APRICOT CAKE ☆

½ cup butter or margarine
1½ cups honey
2 cups blended apricots,
peaches or nectarines

3 cups whole wheat flour
2 tsp. baking soda
2 tsp. baking powder
1 tsp. cinnamon
½ tsp. cloves

1 cup chopped dried peaches,
apricots or nectarines (presoaked)

Soak dried fruit overnight or a few hours in hot water. Cream first 3 ingredients together. Add next 5 ingredients and mix well. Fold in chopped dried fruit. Pour into oiled cake pans and bake at 350° for 45 minutes. Cool and frost or serve plain.

THE MOST WONDERFUL APRICOT CAKE ☆

Topping:
¼ cup butter or margarine
¼ cup honey
1 lb. fresh apricots, halved and pitted

Batter:
¼ cup butter or margarine
¼ cup honey

1 tsp. egg replacer
2 Tbsp. water
½ cup light molasses
½ cup milk (soy, dairy or nut)

1-2/3 cups whole wheat pastry flour
1 tsp. baking soda
½ tsp. salt
1 tsp. cinnamon
1 tsp. ginger

Soy Whipped Cream
(see Basic Recipes Section, p. 34)

Melt ¼ cup butter or margarine in 8" square cake pan. Pour honey evenly over bottom of pan. Arrange apricot halves, with round side down, in single layer. Cream next 2 ingredients together. Add next 4 ingredients and mix well. Sift last 5 ingredients and combine all together, stirring only enough to blend. Pour batter over apricots and bake 1 hour at 325° F. Remove from oven and loosen cake from sides of pan. Turn upside down on a serving plate and let stand a couple of minutes before removing. Serve warm with Soy Whipped Cream.

PAN-FRIED PEACHES ☆

Wash, peel, halve and pit 2 peaches. Then melt 3 Tbsp. butter or margarine in frying pan. Fry peaches over moderately low heat until tender (about 12 to 15 minutes), turning to brown evenly. Drizzle 1 Tbsp. of honey over peaches while warm and sprinkle with cinnamon to taste.

PRETTY PEACH TART

Unbaked Flaky Pie Crust
(see Basic Recipes Section, p. 33)

3 Tbsp. peach preserves
3 Tbsp. whole wheat pastry flour

6 fresh peaches, peeled and sliced

2 Tbsp. apricot preserves
1 tsp. hot water

2 Tbsp. peach preserves

Preheat oven to 350° F. Mix together first 2 ingredients in a small bowl. Spread on the bottom of prepared pastry tart in spring-form pan. Arrange peach slices in a circular pattern on peach mixture. Mix next 2 ingredients together and brush on peaches. Bake until peaches are tender and pastry is golden brown, about 30 to 40 minutes. Then melt last ingredient in a small saucepan and brush over baked tart. Cool tart on wire rack. Remove side of pan before serving.

PEACH BLUEBERRY PIE

Unbaked pie pastry
(see Basic Recipes Section, p. 33)

2 cups blueberries

¼ cup honey
3 Tbsp. whole wheat pastry flour
2 Tbsp. butter or margarine

2½ cups sliced peaches

Cover bottom of pastry-lined pan with blueberries. Combine next 3 ingredients and drizzle half the mixture over berries. Top with peaches and pour on remaining half of ingredients. Put on top crust and cut steam vents. Bake at 425° F for 35 to 40 minutes, or until juice starts to bubble in vents and crust is golden.

APRICOT OR PEACH PIE

Unbaked Flaky Pie Crust
(see Basic Recipes Section, p. 33)

2 cups apricots, pitted
  or 2½ cups sliced peaches
¼ cup honey
1 Tbsp. quick-cooking tapioca
¼ tsp. mace (for apricot pie)
  or 1/8 tsp. nutmeg (for peach pie)

1½ tsp. butter or margarine

Mix pie filling ingredients in a bowl. Pour into a pastry-lined 9'' pie pan. Dot with butter or margarine. Put on top crust, seal and flute edges. Cut steam vents. Bake at 425° for 45 minutes or until apricots or peachers are tender.

PEACH CREAM PIE

Raw Coconut Pie Crust
(see Basic Recipes Section, p. 32)

1 stick agar-agar (½ cup flakes)
½ cup cold water

2½ cups peaches, peeled and sliced
1 tsp. lemon juice
1 Tbsp. honey

1 cup yogurt
2 tsp. honey
¼ tsp. vanilla

Soak agar-agar in water until agar softens. Bring to a boil until agar is dissolved. Blend next 3 ingredients in blender until smooth and then combine with agar mixture. Pour into pie shell and keep in refrigerator until set. Then top with last 3 ingredients, mixed together, or with Soy Whipped Cream (see Basic Recipes Section, p. 34).

BAKED PEACHES ○

8 peach halves

1 cup boiling water
½ cup honey
8 tsp. lemon juice
2 tsp. cinnamon

Preheat oven to 400° F. Wash and peel peaches and remove the pits. Arrange with hollow side up in shallow baking dish. Combine remaining ingredients and pour over peaches; then evenly drizzle over 1 Tbsp. of honey. Bake uncovered for 15 minutes or until tender.

PEACH DUMPLINGS ☆

Pie crust (use pastry recipe from Basic Recipes Section, p. 33)

6 peaches, halved
3/8 cup honey
Cinnamon

Preheat oven to 425° F. Grease an 8"x8"x2" oblong pan. Make pastry dough and roll out on lightly floured surface into a 12"x18" rectangle. Cut into 6" squares. Drizzle honey over peach halves, sprinkle with cinnamon and place peach halves with hollow side down in the center of each pastry square. Bring corners together over peach, moisten and seal. Place in baking dish and bake at 425° for 40 minutes.

NATURAL PEACH OPEN-FACE COBBLER ○

2 Tbsp. butter or margarine
3/8 cup honey

½ cup milk
1½ cups sifted whole wheat flour
1 tsp. vanilla
4 tsp. baking powder

6 Tbsp. honey
1 cup water
1 Tbsp. butter or margarine
1 tsp. arrowroot

2 cups sliced peaches

Cream first 2 ingredients and mix in the next 4 ingredients. Pour mixture in a greased 8½" baking dish. Set aside. Mix together next 4 ingredients to dissolve arrowroot, then bring to a boil. When sauce starts to thicken, add peaches. Simmer for a few minutes, then pour over the raw batter. Bake at 375° F for 20 minutes, then lower to 325° F for 20 to 25 minutes more. Serves 4.

GOLDEN CURRY ○

1 tsp. butter or margarine
1 Tbsp. + 1 tsp. grated ginger root

4 cups apricots and/or peaches, nectarines, diced
¼ cup raisins
1 tsp. cinnamon
1/8 tsp. clove powder
2 tsp. curry powder
1 Tbsp. honey

1 tsp. lemon juice

Saute first 2 ingredients. Add next 6 ingredients and cook until heated through. Remove from heat and squeeze in lemon juice. Serve piping hot or warm. Delicious as a side dish or served over ice cream.

"Whenever I injure life of any sort, I must be quite clear whether it is necessary. Beyond the unavoidable I must never go, not even with what seems insignificant. The farmer who has mowed down a thousand flowers in his meadow as fodder for his cows must be careful on his way home not to strike off in wanton pastime the head of a single flower by the roadside, for he thereby commits a wrong against life without being under the pressure of necessity."

— Albert Schweitzer

PEARS

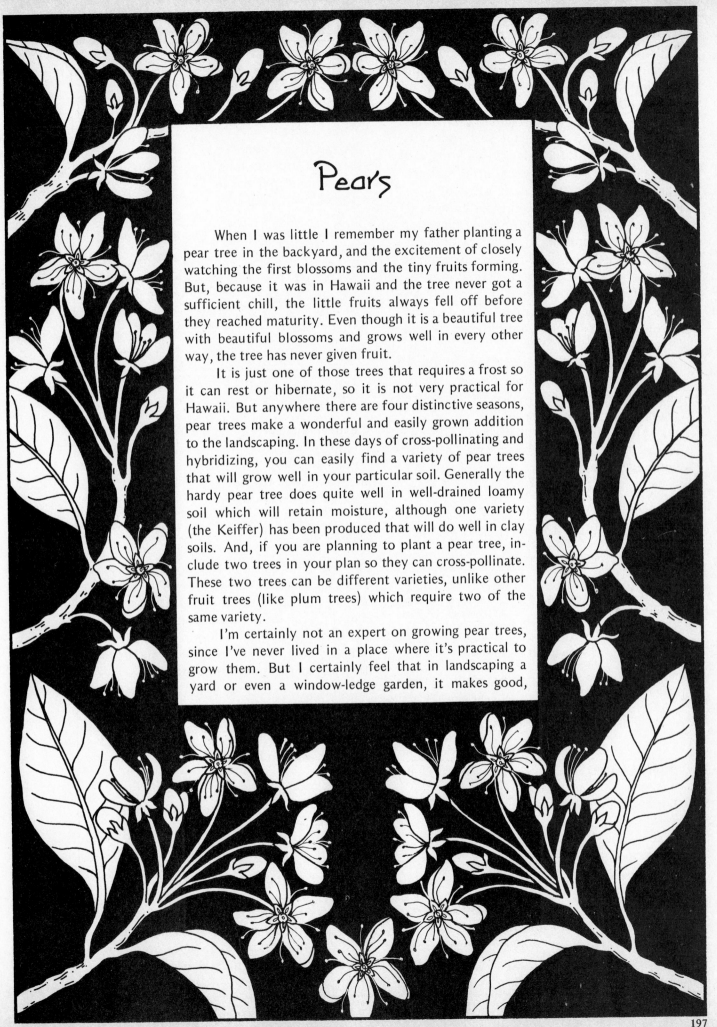

Pears

When I was little I remember my father planting a pear tree in the backyard, and the excitement of closely watching the first blossoms and the tiny fruits forming. But, because it was in Hawaii and the tree never got a sufficient chill, the little fruits always fell off before they reached maturity. Even though it is a beautiful tree with beautiful blossoms and grows well in every other way, the tree has never given fruit.

It is just one of those trees that requires a frost so it can rest or hibernate, so it is not very practical for Hawaii. But anywhere there are four distinctive seasons, pear trees make a wonderful and easily grown addition to the landscaping. In these days of cross-pollinating and hybridizing, you can easily find a variety of pear trees that will grow well in your particular soil. Generally the hardy pear tree does quite well in well-drained loamy soil which will retain moisture, although one variety (the Keiffer) has been produced that will do well in clay soils. And, if you are planning to plant a pear tree, include two trees in your plan so they can cross-pollinate. These two trees can be different varieties, unlike other fruit trees (like plum trees) which require two of the same variety.

I'm certainly not an expert on growing pear trees, since I've never lived in a place where it's practical to grow them. But I certainly feel that in landscaping a yard or even a window-ledge garden, it makes good, common sense to utilize the space, time and energy involved in growing something to grow plants that serve more than an ornamental purpose. Most assuredly all plants that are or that bear edible food are ornamental and beautiful to look at, as evidenced by the pear tree that grew in my parents' backyard. So in landscaping why not plant in such a way that two purposes are served: 1) the aesthetics, and 2) cutting down on food bills by growing as much as you can at home. If pear trees are practical to grow in your area and you happen to like pears as one of your favorite fruits, I'm sure you can find more exact information on varieties and growing from more authoritative sources than myself!

I hope this little bit of information and good variety of delicious recipes will encourage you to consider planting a fruit tree rather than another ornamental!

Just to add to the encouragement, please consider these nutritional benefits offered by pears:

(From U.S.D.A. Agriculture Handbook #8) PEARS (raw) 100 gm. edible portion			
Water	83.2%	Iron	.3 mg.
Food energy	61 calories	Sodium	2 mg.
Protein	.7 gm.	Potassium	130 mg.
Fat	.4 gm.	Vitamin A	20 I.U.
Carbohydrate	15.3 gm. (Total)	Thiamine	.02 mg.
	1.4 gm. (Fiber)	Riboflavin	.04 mg.
Ash	.4 gm.	Niacin	.1 mg.
Calcium	8 mg.	Vitamin C	4 mg.
Phosphorus	11 mg.		

PEAR COMPOTÉ

6 pears, cut into bite-sized chunks

½ cup orange juice
½ tsp. almond extract
½ cup maple syrup

Mix last 3 ingredients together and pour over pears. Chill. Serve in individual bowls topped with yogurt or Soy Whipped Cream (see Basic Recipes Section, p. 34).

PEAR DATE NECTAR

4 pears
8 dates, pitted
¾ cup sunflower seeds
3½ cups milk or nut milk
¼ tsp. almond extract
¼ tsp. cinnamon (opt.)

Combine all ingredients in blender and whiz until smooth. Serve.

PEARS IN THE SURF

4 cups pears, diced

¼ cup lemon juice
2 Tbsp. honey
2 tsp. grated fresh ginger root
or ½ tsp. ginger powder
1 tsp. grated lemon rind

Fizzy water

Cut and cube pears. Mix together next 4 ingredients and marinate pears in them, turning pears occasionally, for at least 30 minutes. Chill fruit if you won't be serving this right away. Right before serving, spoon fruit and sauce into individual cups and pour fizzy water over fruit to fill cups.

PEARADISE SALAD

3 pears, halved and cored

¼ cup cream cheese
¼ cup Plum Sauce or Cranberry Sauce (see Plum or Berry Sections, pp. 102, 221, 224)
1 Tbsp. finely chopped walnuts

Extra plum or cranberry sauce

Cut fresh whole pears in half and core. Mix next 3 ingredients together and heap empty cores with filling. Pour extra sauce over pear halves. Serve on a bed of lettuce leaves.

RAW PEAR PIE

Raw Pie Crust
(see Basic Recipes Section, p. 32)

1 cup fruit juice (strawberry, grape
or other stronger tasting juice)
1 stick agar-agar (½ cup flakes)

2 oranges, peeled and chopped
2 cups thinly sliced pears

3 cups pureed pears

½ cup yogurt
½ tsp. almond extract

½ cup orange juice
2 tsp. arrowroot
1 tsp. honey

Soak first 2 ingredients together until agar softens. Meanwhile, prepare a raw pie crust and line bottom of the crust with a layer of thinly sliced pears and the chopped orange. Bring fruit juice and agar to a boil, stirring until agar dissolves completely; then remove from heat. In a blender, blend enough fresh chopped pears to make 3 cups puréed pears, and pour this into the cooked fruit juice and melted agar and mix thoroughly. Pour this over the layers of sliced fresh fruit and chill until firm. Pour mixture of yogurt and almond extract over set pear puree to form a white background for the orange glaze. Make glaze by combining last 3 ingredients and mixing until arrowroot dissolves. Then cook over heat, stirring constantly until thickened. Allow orange glaze to cool, then pour over chilled pie to cover layer of yogurt. Chill, then serve.

EASY YOGURT PEAR PIE

Raw Pie Crust or Graham Cracker Crust
(see Basic Recipes Section, pp. 32, 33)

Filling:

1½ cups grape juice, strawberry juice,
or any of the more flavorful fruit juices
1 stick agar-agar (½ cup flakes)

2 cups plain yogurt (cold)
2 cups diced pears

Topping:

1 cup pineapple juice or lemonade
1 tsp. arrowroot

Kiwi fruit sliced crosswise, or
seedless grapes or pears sliced thin

Prepare raw pie crust. Soak agar and fruit juice until agar softens. Bring agar and fruit juice to a boil and cook until agar dissolves and juice thickens. Turn off heat and allow to sit at room temperature while you dice the fresh pears and prepare the arrowroot sauce topping. For the topping, just mix juice and arrowroot until arrowroot dissolves. Put on heat and stir constantly until mixture thickens. Remove from heat and set aside to cool. Take the cold yogurt and diced pears and mix in with the agar and fruit juice. The agar will begin to harden because the yogurt is cold, and it will make little lumps as you mix. Don't worry. Now pour this mixture into your blender and blend until smooth. Pour into raw pie crust. Finish topping by adding kiwi, grapes or thinly sliced pears to the now cooled arrowroot sauce, and toss lightly to glaze the fruit. Pour over and arrange attractively on top of the raw pie. Refrigerate.

DAIRYLESS PEARS & CREAM □

2 pears, sliced
4 - 6 pitted dates, sliced

Nut Cream:
2/3 cup nuts
1/3 cup water
2 tsp. honey
1 tsp. vanilla
¼ tsp. cinnamon (opt.)

Topping:
1 cup fruit (strawberries,
chopped pineapple, etc.)
1 tsp. arrowroot

Slice pears and pitted dates. Make nut cream by combining nuts and next 4 ingredients in a blender until smooth. Combine topping ingredients in a small saucepan. Mix well until arrowroot is dissolved. Then put on medium heat, stir until thickened and set aside to cool. In clear custard cups place layers of sliced pears, then dates, and top with nut cream. Layer again in same order and then top with the fruit sauce. Serve at room temperature or chill if you desire.

PEAR BON BONS □

2 Tbsp. carob powder
1 Tbsp. + 1 tsp. water
1 Tbsp. + 1 tsp. honey

¼ cup finely chopped granola or nuts

2 - 3 small pears sliced 1/8" thick (bite-size)

In a small dish, blend water into carob powder to make a paste. Stir in honey and mix until smooth. Dip pear in carob sauce using toothpick and spoon for easier handling. Then dip in chopped granola and place on wax paper. Freeze until firm and serve while still frozen.

PEAR PARFAIT ○

2 cups fruit-flavored kefir
¼ cup arrowroot
2 Tbsp. honey

3 cups diced fresh pears
2 tsp. honey
2 tsp. lemon juice or orange juice
1/8 tsp. cardamom

¾ cup cookie crumbs or granola
1 tsp. grated orange rind

Mix first 3 ingredients in a pot until arrowroot dissolves. Place on heat and bring to a boil, stirring constantly to prevent lumping or burning. Cook until thickened. Mix next 4 ingredients in a bowl. In a separate bowl, combine last 2 ingredients. In a gelatin mold or salad bowl lay in half of the pears on bottom. Cover this with a layer of half the kefir pudding (you can substitute your favorite custard or other pudding recipe). Cover entire surface of kefir pudding with crumb mixture. Make another layer of remaining pears and crumbs and top with remaining pudding. Refrigerate, then turn out of mold onto a platter to serve. This can also be done in individual parfait cups.

CAROB COVERED PEARS □

2 cups blended pears

2 Tbsp. carob
2 tsp. raw cashew, sesame or almond butter
1 tsp. lemon juice

4 pears, sliced
Chopped nuts or seeds

Blend pears to make 2 cups of smooth sauce. Add the next 3 ingredients and blend until well mixed. Pour this sauce over sliced pears in bowls and garnish with chopped nuts or seeds. A wintertime version of this can be accomplished by stir-frying sliced pears in a little butter until warm and pouring heated Carob Coating over them (see Dairy Section, p. 466).

CHAUNCED PEARS □

2 Tbsp. butter or ghee
1 tsp. cinnamon
1½ Tbsp. whole coriander seeds
½ tsp. nutmeg

2 Tbsp. honey
2 Tbsp. chopped pitted dates (packed)

3 pears

Melt butter in saucepan. When melted, add cinnamon, nutmeg and whole coriander seeds. When the coriander seeds begin to pop, remove from heat and add honey and dates. Mix with seeds until a soft paste. Wash and core pears and cut into small pieces. Mix in bowl with sauce.

GLAZED PEARS ○

5 pears, poached

½ cup + 2 Tbsp. lemon juice
¼ cup + 1 Tbsp. honey
2 cups finely chopped fresh fruit
(peaches, berries, etc.)
¼ cup raisins
2 Tbsp. arrowroot
1 tsp. cinnamon
1/8 tsp. clove powder

Poach pears by dropping the whole pear in boiling water for about half a minute. Remove from water and slip peels off. Combine next 7 ingredients in a saucepan off of the heat and mix until arrowroot dissolves. Place on heat, stirring constantly until mixture boils and thickens. Remove from heat. Pour hot (or refrigerate and allow to cool) over poached pears which have each been set in individual bowls on beds of grated coconut and sliced bananas. You can garnish this with grated coconut or a small amount of grated fresh ginger root. Pears can be served coated with your favorite chutney or Basic Fruit Sauce (Basic Recipes Section, p. 34).

GINGER PEAR CUSTARD ○

2 cups poached, cubed pears

2 cups milk
2 Tbsp. honey
2 tsp. vanilla
3 Tbsp. arrowroot

¼ cup molasses
2 tsp. ginger

Poach pears according to directions in recipe for Glazed Pears, this page. Lay pears on bottom of a pie pan and set aside. In a saucepan, mix the next 4 ingredients until smooth and arrowroot has dissolved. Place pan on medium heat and stir until it's a thick, custardlike consistency. Now pour half of this custard over the pears from the middle on out. To the other half of the custard remaining in the saucepan, add the next 2 ingredients and mix well until smooth. Pour the ginger custard along the border of the pie pan with the pears and first custard. Chill and serve. Sprinkle sliced almonds on top or sprinkle with nutmeg, if desired.

PICKLED PEARS ○

3/8 cup water
½ cup vinegar
¼ cup honey

Cinnamon sticks and
cloves tied in a bag

4 cups pickling pears

Bring first 3 ingredients to a boil for 10 minutes. Add spices tied in a muslin bag. When mixture is syrupy, add pears and simmer until done but not too soft.

PEAR KUCHEN

1¼ cups oil
3/8 cup honey

5 cups whole wheat pastry flour
½ tsp. baking powder
1¼ tsp. salt

5 cups fruit (pears, peaches, apples,
apricots, nectarines, pineapple, etc.)
¾ cup honey

2½ cups yogurt
¼ cup soy milk powder
Cinnamon and nutmeg to taste (opt.)

Mix first 2 ingredients together. In a separate bowl, mix together next 3 ingredients, sift into the oil and honey mixture and cut in with a fork. Press into two 9" round cake pans. Top with mixture made of fruit and honey. (If fruit is tart, may need more honey.) Bake for 30 minutes at 375° F. Then top with mixture of last 3 ingredients. Bake 40 minutes to 1 hour longer.

PEAR FRITTERS ☆

½ cup whole wheat flour
1 Tbsp. oil
2 Tbsp. egg replacer
2 Tbsp. water
1 tsp. honey
¼ tsp. lemon peel
1 Tbsp. almond extract
½ cup water
¼ tsp. cardamom

3 - 5 pears

Combine first 9 ingredients and beat until smooth. Let stand for 1 hour. While batter is standing, cut pears in ¼" thick bite-sized pieces and dip each piece into batter. Heat oil and deep fry until batter turns light golden. Drain and dribble honey over them or sprinkle with fructose or dextrose.

CRISPY PEAR DELIGHT

6 pears, sliced
½ cup honey
¼ tsp. ground cloves
1½ tsp. cinnamon
2 tsp. lemon juice

¾ cup whole wheat pastry flour
1/8 tsp. salt
6 Tbsp. butter or margarine
¼ cup walnuts, chopped

½ cup honey

Mix together first 5 ingredients and set aside. Combine next 4 ingredients. Place a layer of the pear mixture in lightly oiled 9" square baking pan and top with flour mixture. Then repeat — one layer of pear and one layer of flour mixture. Drizzle honey over the top and bake at 350° F for 25 to 30 minutes, until top is golden.

CURRIED FRUIT BAKE O

1 lb. pears, sliced
(or peaches, apricots, pineapple, etc.)

2½ Tbsp. butter or margarine

3/8 cup honey
2½ tsp. curry powder

Melt butter or margarine. Stir in last 2 ingredients. Spoon this mixture onto fruit in a baking pan. (Cook fruit with its natural juice.) Bake 1 hour at 325° F. Cool several hours, then reheat at 350° F for 45 minutes.

PEARS 'N SPICE CAKE

6 pears, sliced
¼ cup oil
1 cup honey
1 tsp. lemon juice
1 cup walnuts

2 cups whole wheat pastry flour
¾ tsp. baking soda
1/8 tsp. salt
1 tsp. cinnamon

Combine first 5 ingredients. Add last 4 ingredients and mix well. Fill 8"x 12" cake pan half full. Bake at 350° for 40 minutes or until toothpick inserted in middle comes out clean.

PEAR PIE

Unbaked pie crust
(see Basic Recipes Section, p. 33)

4 cups sliced pears

1½ Tbsp. quick tapioca
¼ tsp. mace
¼ tsp. ginger

3 Tbsp. orange juice
1 tsp. lemon juice
1/3 cup honey

1 Tbsp. butter or margarine

Line pie plate with pastry. Arrange pears in pie shell, heaping somewhat in center. Combine next 3 ingredients and sprinkle over pears. Add next 3 ingredients and dot with butter. Adjust top crust, seal and flute edges. Cut steam vents. Bake at 425° until pears are tender, about 45 minutes.

PEAR CRUMBLE PIE

Unbaked pie crust
(see Basic Recipes Section, p. 33)

1 Tbsp. honey
1½ Tbsp. arrowroot
Dash nutmeg
1 cup apple or pear juice (unsweetened)

½ tsp. grated lemon rind
2 tsp. lemon juice
1 Tbsp. butter or margarine

4 - 5 pears, halved

Crumble Topping:
¼ cup honey
½ cup chopped seeds or walnuts
¼ tsp. cinnamon

In a pot, combine first 4 ingredients and mix until arrowroot dissolves. Cook over heat, stirring constantly until thickened. Add next 3 ingredients. Arrange pear halves in pie shell and pour syrup mixture over them. In a bowl, combine crumble topping ingredients and sprinkle over pie filling. Bake at 425° for 20 to 25 minutes.

PEAR NECTAR PIE

Unbaked pie crust
(see Basic Recipes Section, p. 33)

3 cups sliced pears

½ cup honey
2 Tbsp. arrowroot
Pinch cinnamon
Pinch nutmeg
¼ cup yogurt
2½ tsp. maple syrup
1 Tbsp. orange juice or lemon juice
1 Tbsp. butter or margarine

Line pie plate with pastry. Fill with sliced pears. Combine next 8 ingredients in a bowl. Pour over pears. Dot with butter. Top with lattice pie topping. Bake 35 to 40 minutes at 450° F.

PEAR DUMPLINGS WITH PEAR SAUCE ☆

Pie Crust (use pastry recipe
from Basic Recipes Section, p. 33)

4 ripe pears

½ cup cream cheese (softened)
2 Tbsp. honey
2 tsp. lemon juice
1 Tbsp. raisins
1 Tbsp. sunflower seeds

Sauce:
½ cup milk
¼ cup cream cheese (softened)
1 cup honey
¼ cup butter or margarine
½ cup molasses

1 ripe pear (cored)

Wash and core 4 pears. Mix next 5 ingredients together and stuff the pears generously so the mixture is flowing over the top and bottom. Then make pie crust and roll dough out as instructed in crust recipe. Cut into four squares and roll into squares approximately 7"x 7". Place a pear on each square. Moisten corners of each pastry square, bring two opposite corners up over the pear and pinch together. Repeat with remaining corners; pinch all edges of pastry to seal. Place pear dumplings on an ungreased baking dish and bake at 350° for 40 minutes. Meanwhile, make the sauce by heating first 5 sauce ingredients together in saucepan until boiling (about 5 minutes) on low heat. Cut cored pear and put in blender on low speed to purée the pear. Add the boiled ingredients to the blender and blend together. Return sauce to pan and continue to cook over low heat for 20 minutes, stirring occasionally. Serve dumpling hot with cooled, thick sauce poured over it.

LIGHT AND EASY O

3 pears, halved and cored
1½ cups fruit juice
½ tsp. cinnamon
6 whole cloves

½ cup chopped pitted dates

½ - 1 cup yogurt

Halve and core fresh pears and trim a thin slice from the round side of each half so pears can lie flat in pot. Place the trimmed side down in pot with other 3 ingredients. Cover pot and bring to a boil, then lower heat and simmer until pears are tender. The time will vary with different kinds of pears. Be careful not to overcook them or they'll get mushy. Remove pears and clove sticks from the juice and put dates into pot. Lightly boil dates in juice until they begin to dissolve and thicken the juice to make a syrup. Fill warm pear halves with yogurt and pour hot date syrup over them. You can garnish with chopped seeds or nuts.

PEAR BANANA CAKE ☆

1 cup honey
½ cup butter or margarine
1 tsp. almond extract

2 bananas
1 ripe pear, peeled

1 large carrot, grated

1/3 cup milk
1 tsp. baking soda

2 cups whole wheat flour
½ tsp. salt

Cream together first 3 ingredients. Mix in next 2 ingredients, mashed together. Add grated carrot. In a small saucepan, boil milk and add baking soda. Combine with fruit and honey mixture. Mix in last 2 ingredients and pour into an oiled and floured 9" square baking pan. Bake at 350° F for 50 minutes.

"It is my view that the vegetarian manner of living, by its purely physical effect on the human temperament, would most beneficially influence the lot of mankind."
— Albert Einstein

PINEAPPLE

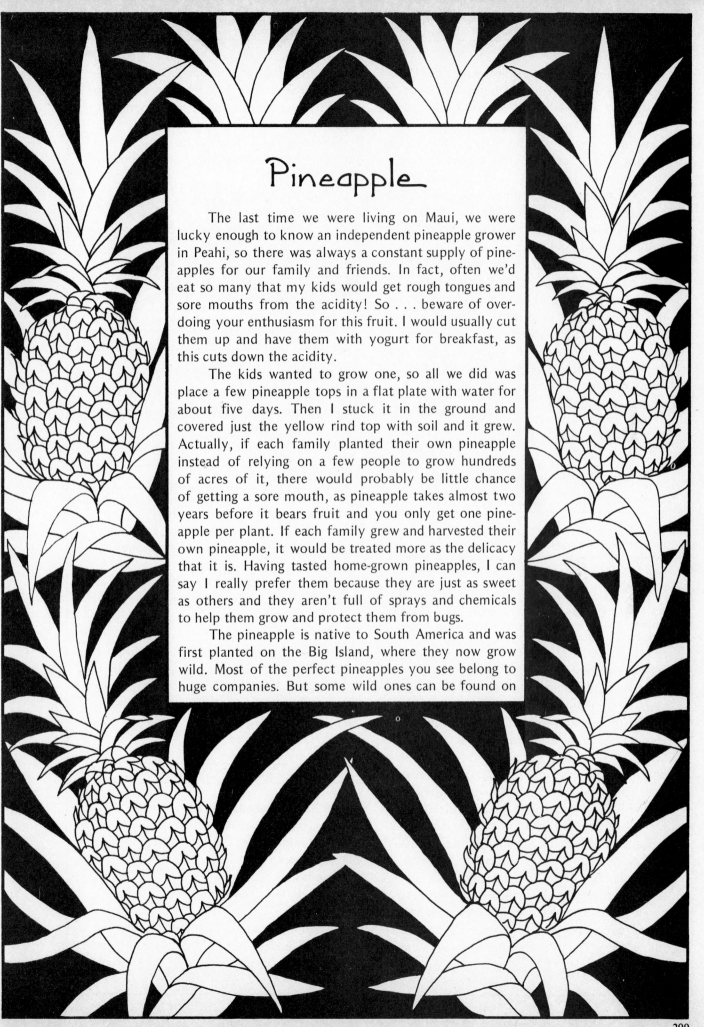

Pineapple

The last time we were living on Maui, we were lucky enough to know an independent pineapple grower in Peahi, so there was always a constant supply of pineapples for our family and friends. In fact, often we'd eat so many that my kids would get rough tongues and sore mouths from the acidity! So . . . beware of overdoing your enthusiasm for this fruit. I would usually cut them up and have them with yogurt for breakfast, as this cuts down the acidity.

The kids wanted to grow one, so all we did was place a few pineapple tops in a flat plate with water for about five days. Then I stuck it in the ground and covered just the yellow rind top with soil and it grew. Actually, if each family planted their own pineapple instead of relying on a few people to grow hundreds of acres of it, there would probably be little chance of getting a sore mouth, as pineapple takes almost two years before it bears fruit and you only get one pineapple per plant. If each family grew and harvested their own pineapple, it would be treated more as the delicacy that it is. Having tasted home-grown pineapples, I can say I really prefer them because they are just as sweet as others and they aren't full of sprays and chemicals to help them grow and protect them from bugs.

The pineapple is native to South America and was first planted on the Big Island, where they now grow wild. Most of the perfect pineapples you see belong to huge companies. But some wild ones can be found on

Molokai and Hawaii, and in some deserted fields. They are neither as big nor uniform as the commercially grown kind but are often sweeter and more fragrant. The fruit is most plentiful during June, July and August, but a second crop ripens during December and January.

In choosing a nice pineapple, color and size are not always dependable. If the crown is small and compact the fruit should be well-developed and first quality. The best test is to snap the side of the fruit with the thumb and forefinger. If you hear a hollow thud, the fruit is sour, not mature and dry. If you hear a dull, solid sound like the sound your finger makes when flicked against the palm of your hand, it is a well-ripened, sound and juicy pineapple. Use this fool-proof test to pick your next pineapple full of these nutrients!

(From U.S.D.A. Agriculture Handbook #8) PINEAPPLE (raw) 100 gm. edible portion			
Water	85.3%	Iron	.5 mg.
Food energy	52 calories	Sodium	1 mg.
Protein	.4 gm.	Potassium	146 mg.
Fat	.2 gm.	Vitamin A	70 I.U.
Carbohydrate	13.7 gm. (Total)	Thiamine	.09 mg.
	.4 gm. (Fiber)	Riboflavin	.03 mg.
Ash	.4 gm.	Niacin	.2 mg.
Calcium	17 mg.	Vitamin C	17 mg.
Phosphorus	8 mg.		

Fresh pineapple is a good source of sugar and thiamine and a fair source of calcium in comparison to other fruits. It is low in phosphorus and iron and a poor source of vitamin A, riboflavin, niacin and ascorbic acid. To my surprise, pineapple is not high in or even a good source of vitamin C. But it does contain about 87% citric acid, which is probably what gets your tongue so sore!

Most people throw out the cores of the pineapple, but that's my favorite part. As a matter of fact, when I worked in the pineapple cannery one summer many years ago, this was the part that most of the workers loved the best. I take pineapple cores and either refrigerate or freeze them to give to the baby when he's teething. He loves the cool sweetness.

Having lived on pineapples every morning for breakfast, I have had to come up with different ways to serve it. Plain, baked, chopped, blended, cooked, etc. — you name it, I've tried it. Following are some of the ones we liked the best. Hope you like them, too!

FRESH PINEAPPLE JUICE ☐

Cut a peeled, ripe pineapple into small cubes. Squeeze with hands through a double thickness of cheesecloth or run through a juicer. Chill well and serve.

PINEAPPLE WHIP ☐

1 medium-sized pineapple (chilled)
1 cup ice cold water
3 - 4 Tbsp. maple syrup or 2 Tbsp. honey

Remove core. Cut pineapple into small pieces. Combine with remaining ingredients and whiz in blender until fluffy.

Variation: This can also be strained through a fine sieve after blending. For a Pineapple Fluff, add 2 Tbsp. nonfat dry milk powder. Blend until fluffy and serve immediately. Yields 2 - 4 servings.

PINEAPPLE CITRUS PUNCH ☐

4 cups fresh pineapple juice
2/3 cup orange juice
1/3 cup lemon juice
2/3 cup water
2/3 cup honey
1 tsp. finely chopped mint leaves

Combine ingredients. Mix well. Chill and whiz in blender before serving. Cool and refreshing. Yields 6 servings.

HAWAIIAN FRUIT BOATS ☐

1 large pineapple, cubed
1 large papaya (firm, ripe), cubed
1 cup diced black mission figs
1 large banana, sliced
1 cup fresh, grated coconut

Dressing:
¼ cup yogurt
¼ cup honey
2 Tbsp. orange juice
2 tsp. orange rind

Cut pineapple into halves or fourths lengthwise. Carefully cut rind away from pineapple leaving the rind in whole pieces. Remove the core and cut the pineapple into cubes, then combine with next 4 ingredients. Mix well and fill each "boat" rind with fruit mixture. Combine dressing ingredients, mix well and pour some over each fruit boat. Garnish with fresh mint leaves. Chill and serve. Yields 4 servings.

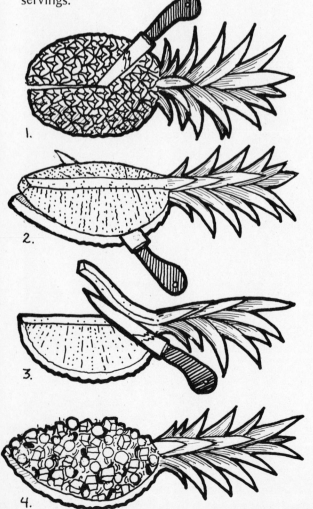

SUNSHINE SALAD ☐

1 cup chopped, dried apricots
4 cups chopped pineapple

1 cup sour cream
¼ cup honey

Mix first 2 ingredients a few hours ahead of time so apricots can absorb some pineapple juice and become softer. Add last 2 ingredients just before serving time so pineapple won't make sour cream curdle or get weird.

IMITATION CHOCOLATE SUNDAE ☐

½ cup sunflower seeds
1 Tbsp. liquid lecithin
2 Tbsp. honey

About 4 bananas, sliced thin

4 oz. cream cheese
2 cups crushed pineapple

Carob Sauce:
¼ cup carob powder
¼ cup milk powder
2 Tbsp. honey
1 Tbsp. liquid lecithin
¼ cup water

½ cup crushed pineapple
¼ cup raisins

Grind sunflower seeds in blender until it is sunflower meal. Mix with lecithin and honey and pat into a thin layer in bottom of a cake pan or any pan with sides 1½" or 2" high. Cover with a layer of sliced bananas, then layer with cream cheese and crushed pineapple. Pour carob sauce over for next layer and top with last 2 ingredients. Refrigerate a few hours before serving.

CANDIED PINEAPPLE   ○

12 pineapple cubes about 1½" - 2" big

1 cup honey
2 Tbsp. butter or margarine

1 tsp. vinegar

Bowls of ice cold water
1 bowl full of toasted, grated coconut

Put toothpicks in each pineapple chunk. Combine next 2 ingredients and bring to boil. Let simmer until honey forms a hard ball when dropped into cold water. Be sure to use a pot 4 times deeper than the honey, as it bubbles up quite a bit. Add vinegar immediately and pour into a warming bowl (bowl over a candle flame), or use **very quickly** before honey cools and hardens. Place bowl of cooked honey, bowl of coconut, and bowl of pineapple in center of table. Give each person a bowl of ice cold water. Let each person dip their pineapple in the coconut, then into the honey and immediately into the cold water. Eat immediately.

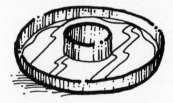

PINEAPPLE JELL   ○

1 stick agar-agar (½ cup flakes)
2 cups cold water

2 cups hot water

2 cups pineapple juice
4 Tbsp. lemon juice
1 cup raw honey
1 cup chopped pineapple
½ cup chopped walnuts

Combine first 2 ingredients and let set one minute. Add to hot water, boil 2 minutes and let cool. Add last 5 ingredients and mix well. Chill, undisturbed, in refrigerator. Should set in 2 hours. Other fresh fruits can be added to this jell.

PINEAPPLE CHUTNEY, SWEET & SPICY ○

½ stick butter or ¼ cup oil
¼ tsp. cumin seed
1/8 tsp. crushed red peppers

8 cups finely chopped, fresh pineapple

1 - 1½ cups honey
1 tsp. ground coriander
1 tsp. ground cinnamon
1 tsp. ground nutmeg
¼ tsp. ground cloves
½ tsp. turmeric
1 cup raisins

Combine first 3 ingredients. Cook until brown. Toss in pineapple and cook until liquidy. Add last 7 ingredients. Bring to boil, then simmer for 2 hours, stirring occasionally until it becomes mushy and thick. Yields 6 to 8 servings.

PINEAPPLE UPSIDE-DOWN CAKE

2 Tbsp. butter or margarine
¼ cup honey

¼ cup date sugar

4 - 6 pineapple rings, ¼" thick

2 tsp. vanilla
1 cup honey
¼ cup butter or margarine
1 cup water
2 Tbsp. yogurt

3 cups whole wheat pastry flour
4 tsp. baking powder
½ tsp. salt

Preheat oven to 350° F. Melt first 2 ingredients together in a 9" square baking pan. Add date sugar. Lay pineapple rings in syrup. Mix next 5 ingredients. Sift in dry ingredients and mix until lumps are out. Pour on top of pineapples; wet hand and pat flat and even. Bake 45 minutes at 350° F. Turn upside down and empty onto a plate as soon as it comes out of the oven.

GLAZED PINEAPPLE   ○

Preheat broiler. Place single layer of fresh pineapple slices in baking pan. Drizzle well with honey. Add a few dabs of butter. Broil for about 10 minutes and serve. Sprinkle with cinnamon powder, if desired.

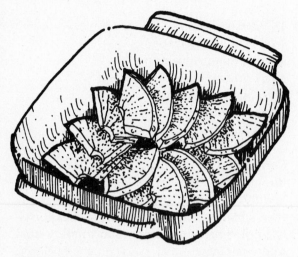

PINEAPPLE-COCONUT DATE LOGS   ☆

1 cup butter or margarine
1½ cups honey

4 tsp. egg replacer
6 Tbsp. water

1 cup crushed, drained pineapple
1 cup chopped, raw cashews
½ lb. dates, chopped
½ cup grated, toasted coconut

1½ cups whole wheat flour
½ tsp. salt
½ tsp. baking soda
½ tsp. baking powder

Preheat oven to 350° F. Cream first 2 ingredients. Combine next 2 ingredients and whip with a fork. Combine with butter and honey. Add next 4 ingredients and mix well. Sift last 4 ingredients several times. Combine with other ingredients and mix well. Pour into an 8" x 12" x 2" buttered pan lined with wax paper. Bake at 350° for 50 to 55 minutes. Let cool slightly — when still warm, cut into bars and press with fingers to form logs. Roll in toasted coconut and set aside to cool.

PINEAPPLE SWEET-SOUR SAUCE   ○

2 Tbsp. oil
1/8 tsp. asafetida
1 tsp. grated fresh ginger
1 cup pineapple pieces

1 Tbsp. soy sauce
1/3 cup honey
¼ cup apple cider vinegar
¼ cup catsup
1 cup unsweetened pineapple juice
1 green bell pepper, sliced

2 Tbsp. arrowroot powder

Stir-fry first 4 ingredients together for a few minutes. Add next 6 ingredients. Dissolve arrowroot in a little bit of water and pour into cooking sauce, stir in and continue to stir until thick.

PINEAPPLE SQUARES   ☆

Cake:
¾ cup honey
½ cup butter or margarine

1½ - 2 cups rolled oats

1½ cups whole wheat flour
½ tsp. baking soda
½ tsp. salt

Filling:
1½ cups cooked pineapple
¼ cup honey
2 tsp. arrowroot

Preheat oven to 350° F. Cream first 2 ingredients. Add oats and sift in next 3 ingredients. Mix well. Press 2/3 of mixture into an oiled pan. Combine last 3 ingredients and spread evenly over crust. Crumble remaining 1/3 of flour mixture on top of filling. Bake at 350° for 25 to 30 minutes. Cool and cut into squares.

PINEAPPLE-CHEESE REFRESHER

1 cup warm water
1 stick agar-agar (½ cup flakes)

3 cups crushed pineapple with juice

3 Tbsp. lemon juice
½ cup honey

1 cup heavy cream, whipped, or
   Soy Whipped Cream (see recipe
   in Basic Recipes Section, p. 34)
1 cup cheddar cheese, grated
½ cup chopped walnuts

Dissolve agar in water. Simmer pineapple with juice on stove. Add dissolved agar and next 2 ingredients and bring to a quick boil. Remove and cool to room temperature. As soon as it cools and before it jells, mix in next 3 ingredients (make sure it's not too hot so the whipped cream doesn't melt). Pour into a buttered mold and set in refrigerator until cool and set. Serve with whipped cream topping.

PINEAPPLE KEFIR PUDDING ○

1 quart pineapple kefir

½ cup honey
½ cup arrowroot powder
½ cup drained, small pineapple chunks

Grated coconut

Bring kefir to a boil. Make a paste with the honey and arrowroot. Gradually add to kefir, stirring constantly until thickened. Quickly fold in pineapple. Pour into an 8" square cake pan. Sprinkle with grated coconut and refrigerate 2 to 4 hours until set.

Serving Suggestion: This is very good served on top of Pineapple Cream Cheese Bake (see following recipe). Yields 6 servings.

PINEAPPLE CREAM CHEESE BAKE

2 cups pineapple chunks
8 oz. cream cheese (cut in cubes)

¾ cup orange juice
¼ cup honey
1/8 tsp. salt
2 Tbsp. whole wheat flour with
2 Tbsp. juice (to make paste)

1 cup whole wheat bread crumbs
¼ cup date sugar

2 Tbsp. butter or margarine

Preheat oven to 350° F. Layer first 2 ingredients in a buttered, 1-quart casserole dish. Combine next 5 ingredients. Heat and stir in a saucepan until well blended. Pour over first two. Combine next 2 ingredients and sprinkle evenly over pineapple mixture. Dab with butter and bake at 350° for 30 minutes. Yields 6 servings.

PINEAPPLE JELLY ROLL

Jelly Roll Dough
(see Basic Recipes Section, p. 38)

½ pineapple, blended
½ cup honey

Make the Jelly Roll Dough in the Basic Recipes Section. Cook down pineapple and honey in a skillet (preferably a nonstick type) until it thickens so much that it sticks together in a lump. Use as jelly roll filling. Also can be used as a jam, crepe filling, etc.

PINEAPPLE STRUDEL ☆

2 Tbsp. butter or margarine
1½ cups whole wheat flour

1 Tbsp. yogurt
1/3 cup water

2 Tbsp. butter or margarine
1 cup whole wheat bread crumbs
¼ cup melted butter or margarine

3 cups crushed, fresh pineapple
1 Tbsp. tapioca pearls
¼ cup raisins
¼ cup grated, toasted coconut
½ cup honey
½ tsp. cinnamon

Fructose sugar

Preheat oven to 400° F. Combine first 2 ingredients, breaking up butter with fingertips until the flour is the texture of cornmeal. Make a crater in the center and add wet ingredients. Knead for 10 minutes, cover with bowl and let sit 30 minutes. Flour a counter and roll out as thin as possible, lifting dough now and then to reflour to prevent dough from sticking to the counter. When rolled out almost paper thin, stretch dough as thin as possible with fingers. Dough should be so thin that if held up, light can be seen through it. When dough is as thin as possible without tearing, brush the entire surface with butter and sprinkle with bread crumbs that have been toasted in the 2 Tbsp. of butter. Pour fruit filling along 1 inch of dough, about 2 inches in from edge. Fold the 2 inches over the fruit and roll the dough over and over on itself until completely rolled up. Seal the two ends so filling won't ooze out. Place roll seam side down on a buttered baking pan and bake at 400° for 35 to 40 minutes. Brush top with butter and bake a few minutes longer. Allow pastry to cool. Sprinkle with fructose sugar.

PINEAPPLE CREAM CHEESE BALLS ☆

8 oz. cream cheese, softened
4 Tbsp. pineapple, crushed and well-drained
4 Tbsp. finely chopped cashews

Date sugar

Combine first 3 ingredients and mix well. Scoop a tablespoonful into hand and roll into balls. Roll in date sugar until completely coated. Set in freezer or refrigerator until firm and chilled. Serve cold. Yields about 10.

PINEAPPLE RAISIN BRAN MUFFINS ☆

2 Tbsp. butter or oil
4 Tbsp. honey

1¼ cups whole wheat flour
1½ tsp. baking powder
½ tsp. baking soda
½ tsp. salt

¾ cup crushed pineapple, well-drained
¼ cup pineapple juice
¼ cup chopped walnuts
¼ cup raisins
½ cup bran

Preheat oven to 350° F. Combine first 2 ingredients and mix well. Sift in next 4 and mix well. Add remaining ingredients and quickly mix until thoroughly blended. Fill buttered muffin tins three-fourths of the way full and bake at 350° for 30 to 35 minutes. Let cool a few minutes; loosen sides with knife and gently lift from muffin tins. Yields about 10 muffins.

PLUMS

Plums

Plum trees are another one of those stone fruit trees that really need a frost (or at least a good chill) to be able to bear fruit, so having grown up in Hawaii, I never saw a lot of them around. I saw a few growing successfully on the side of Haleakala Mountain in the area known as Kula, where the elevation makes for a mainland U.S.A. type climate right in the middle of tropical Hawaii!

I had never seen so many plums in my whole life until I visited California recently! There were purple-skinned ones, red-skinned ones, yellow-red-skinned ones, large ones, small ones, extra sweet ones, tart ones. I learned there are so many varieties that I couldn't possibly list them all here! To make it simple, the almost innumerable varieties of plums are divided into four general categories: American, Damson, European and Japanese.

Of course, if you're planning to plant plum trees at home, you'll want to check the different varieties of plums in each category and pick the one that suits your preference best. For example, in the European category some of the more widely grown varieties are the Stanley, Hall and Italian prune varieties, and the Washington, Imperial Epineuse and Reine Claude. Even among these few more common varieties in the European category we find such a great range of variegatedness—from very sweet to a little tart, from yellow to red fruit to dark purple. Of so many varieties it shouldn't be hard to find one to suit your taste!

Having once made your choice of what variety to plant, check to see if the kind of soil in your yard is right. (This is as varied as the number of varieties of plums — from heavy, loamy soil to light, sandy soil. The important thing is that the type of soil must match what the chosen variety requires, and remember that all plum trees must be in a well-drained situation.) Usually two-year-old trees are planted, and it is important that at least two trees of the same variety be planted for proper cross-pollination. They only need to be planted about 20 ft. apart, and since plums are one of the easiest stone fruits to grow — why not?

Not only do you get the beautiful vision of trees laden with delicate plum blossoms once a year, you also get a cropful of delicious and nutritious fruits. The U.S. Department of Agriculture's nutrition tables list the following plum varieties and their nutritive values.

(From U.S.D.A. Agriculture Handbook #8) PLUMS 100 gm. edible portion			
	Damson	Japanese	Prune
Water	81.1%	86.6%	78.7%
Food energy	66 calories	48 calories	75 calories
Protein	.5 gm.	.5 gm.	.8 gm.
Fat	Trace	.2 gm.	.2 gm.
Carbohydrate	17.8 (Total)	12.3 (Total)	19.7 (Total)
(gm.)	.4 (Fiber)	.6 (Fiber)	.4 (Fiber)
Ash	.6 gm.	.4 gm.	.6 gm.
Calcium	18 mg.	12 mg.	12 mg.
Phosphorus	17 mg.	18 mg.	18 mg.
Iron	.5 mg.	.5 mg.	.5 mg.
Sodium	2 mg.	1 mg.	1 mg.
Potassium	299 mg.	170 mg.	170 mg.
* Vitamin A	300 I.U.	250 I.U.	300 I.U.
Thiamine	.08 mg.	.03 mg.	.03 mg.
Riboflavin	.03 mg.	.03 mg.	.03 mg.
Niacin	.5 mg.	.5 mg.	.5 mg.
Vitamin C	–	6 mg.	4 mg.

* (Except Italian and Imperial prunes which average 1340 I.U. per 100 gm.)

Of course, these tables are figured on an average, and nutritive value may vary a great deal from variety to variety. But, in general it can be said that plums are a good

Plum Dessert Mold, pg. 226

source of vitamin A and potassium, and a fair source of phosphorus and iron.

Here are a few recipes that will help your body reap the nutritional benefits that plums have to offer. Since I'm not very familiar with plums and preparing them, I'm sure you'll be able to add to this list of recipes to make use of this fruit when it's in season!

RAW PLUM SAUCE

2 cups plum sauce

2 tsp. honey
1 Tbsp. psyllium powder

Blend washed, fresh, ripe plums in blender (remove pits first). Rub through strainer to get peels out. For every 2 cups of sauce, add the other ingredients. Let sit for a few minutes to thicken. This sauce is delicious eaten as applesauce or served poured over your favorite ice cream, yogurt or cut bananas. This is also delicious blended with other fruit for a blender drink.

PLUM NECTAR

3 cups raw plum sauce
2 bananas
½ cup apple (or other mild) juice

Blend ingredients together and let sit in refrigerator 15 to 25 minutes before serving.

PLUM SILLY

4 - 5 cups plums, cut up
1 tsp. grated lemon rind
1 tsp. grated fresh ginger root
¼ cup psyllium seed powder
2 Tbsp. honey

Mix ingredients together thoroughly and let sit in refrigerator 15 to 25 minutes before serving.

RICH PLUM SAUCE

1 cup raw plum sauce
4 oz. cream cheese

½ cup diced fresh plums

Mix plum sauce into cream cheese that has been softened at room temperature. This is best done by starting with the cream cheese in a bowl and adding a little plum sauce at a time, thoroughly creaming together. Add diced fresh plum pieces and chill. Delicious served poured over fresh pear halves or chopped apples, bananas or pineapple.

PLUMS & APRICOTS

12 plums, cut in quarters
12 apricots, cut in quarters

4 bananas
2 tsp. vanilla
1 cup fresh orange juice
2 tsp. lemon juice (opt.)

Pit and chop first 2 ingredients into bite-sized pieces. Blend next 4 ingredients in blender until smooth. Pour as a sauce over plums and apricots.

RAW PLUM PIE

Raw Pie Crust
(see Basic Recipes Section, p. 32)

1 cup apple juice
1 stick agar-agar (½ cup flakes)

2 cups plum purée

¼ cup chopped, pitted dates

Prepare Raw Pie Crust. Break agar-agar into pieces and soak agar and fruit juice until agar softens. Bring to a boil and cook until agar dissolves. Blend pitted fresh plums in blender until smooth. Pour in cooked agar fruit juice and blend to mix thoroughly. Mix in pitted dates and pour into raw pie shell. Refrigerate until it sets.

PLUM SALAD ☆

10 - 12 ripe plums
½ cup chopped, pitted dates
½ cup walnuts
½ cup green seedless grapes
¼ cup mandarin orange wedges

3 cups whipped cream or Soy Whipped Cream (see Basic Recipes Section, p. 34)
1 Tbsp. honey

Cut plums into bite-sized pieces and place in bowl with dates, nuts, grapes and oranges. Whip cream with the honey and combine with fruit.

PLUM SMOOTHIE

10 plums, cut up
2½ chopped bananas
1 Tbsp. honey
1 cup apple juice
1 tsp. vanilla
½ tsp. cinnamon

Place all ingredients in blender and blend until smooth. Chill if desired. Makes 4 cups.

PLUM SOUP

3 cups plums, chopped
1½ cups white grape juice
4 Tbsp. plum preserves

2 cups plain yogurt

Toasted coconut

Purée first 3 ingredients in blender. Transfer to large bowl and whisk in yogurt. Refrigerate covered until cold, about 1 hour. Ladle soup into chilled bowls and sprinkle with coconut. (To chill bowls, just place empty bowls in freezer.)

FRESH PLUM PUDDING

½ cup raisins
½ cup pitted dates

1 cup diced plums

1 cup sunflower seeds

Grind raisins and dates in food grinder. Mix in bowl and add chopped plums. Put sunflower seeds in blender and grind to meal. Add to other ingredients and mix well.

Plum Silly, p. 221   Plum Pinwheels, p. 224

CREAMY PLUM SALAD □

8 plums, sliced
¼ cup chopped sunflower seeds or walnuts
¼ cup finely diced celery

Dressing:
½ cup tahini
¼ cup apple juice
1½ Tbsp. honey
½ tsp. cardamom
½ tsp. cinnamon

Wash and slice plums in a bowl; add chopped nuts and celery. In separate bowl combine dressing ingredients until mixed well and smooth. Pour over plums and serve. Can also be served in individual cups. Serves 4.

PLUM ALMOND DELIGHT

½ cup buttermilk
¼ cup sour cream
1 Tbsp. honey
¼ tsp. almond extract

1 lb. plums (about 6 large)

¼ cup toasted sliced almonds

Whisk first 4 ingredients in small bowl until well blended. (You may substitute ¾ cup plain yogurt for the sour cream and buttermilk.) Slice or quarter plums into mixture and toss well. Chill at least 30 minutes. Serve in individual dessert dishes. Sprinkle with almonds. Makes 4 servings.

PLUM PINWHEELS   O

6 cups diced plums
½ cup chopped pitted dates
½ cup raisins
1/3 cup honey
1 Tbsp. whole wheat flour
¼ tsp. nutmeg

Pinwheels:

2 cups whole wheat flour
1 Tbsp. baking powder
1½ Tbsp. honey
1/3 cup butter or margarine

½ cup milk
2 Tbsp. yogurt

Pinwheel Spread:

3 Tbsp. butter or margarine
3 Tbsp. honey
1 tsp. cinnamon
¼ cup chopped nuts

Oil a large pie or cake pan. Mix first 6 ingredients together and pour into the bottom of the pan. Now make pinwheels by combining next 4 ingredients in a bowl and mix until flour is a sandy texture. Add the yogurt and milk to this and mix to form a dough. Pour the dough onto a well-floured counter; knead a dozen times so dough is a tender, soft ball. Roll the dough out on the floured counter to form a ½" thick rectangle. In a small bowl, mix last 4 ingredients together and spread over entire surface of the rectangle. Roll the rectangle up like a jelly roll and cut across the log shape about 1" apart. This should make 8 to 10 cinnamon-rolllike pinwheels. Place pinwheels so swirls show on top of plum mixture. Bake at 350° for 40 to 45 minutes. To serve, put warm pinwheels on individual plates and spoon extra plums over them. A scoop of ice cream or Soy Whipped Cream (see Basic Recipes Section, p. 34) to top this off makes it extra rich.

PLUM TORTE   ☆

Filling:
10 - 12 plums
1/3 cup honey
1 cup water
3 Tbsp. arrowroot

Cake:
½ cup butter or margarine
½ cup honey
1 tsp. vanilla extract
1 tsp. almond extract

1½ cups milk

2 cups whole wheat flour
2 tsp. (heaping) baking powder, sifted

Combine first 4 ingredients in a pot and mix off of heat until arrowroot dissolves. Place over medium-high heat and cook until thickened, stirring constantly. Cool and refrigerate. In bowl, cream first 4 cake ingredients. Then add milk and mix. Gradually add last 2 ingredients. Be sure not to beat batter too much — just enough to mix ingredients. Pour batter ½" deep in muffin tins or all of batter in 8" x 11" cake pan or two round cake pans. Bake at 350° for about 15 to 20 minutes or until golden brown. When partly cool, turn out of pan onto plate and continue to cool. When cooled, spread about half of the plum filling on top of one layer of cake (if you used a rectangular pan, cut cake in half). Top with other layer of cake and spread rest of plum filling on top and sides of this layer, but not on sides of bottom layer. Decorate with Soy Whipped Cream in Basic Recipes Section, p. 34, (or the real thing!) and finely chopped nuts.

PLUM SAUCE   O

3 cups plums, chopped or blended
1 cup honey
2 tsp. arrowroot

Mix ingredients in pot until arrowroot dissolves. Put on heat and bring to a boil, stir-
(Continued next page.)

ring constantly. Cook until sauce thickens.
Serve hot or cold over whatever you like —
pancakes, waffles, ice cream, fruit salads, etc.

PLUM PUDDING ☆

1 cup chopped plums
1 tsp. cinnamon
1 tsp. nutmeg
1 tsp. cloves
1 cup whole wheat flour
1-1/3 cups raisins
1 cup currants
½ cup chopped figs
½ cup milk
1/3 cup butter or margarine
½ cup molasses
½ cup honey
2 cups bread crumbs
1 tsp. baking soda, sifted

Mix all ingredients thoroughly and pour into
a 2-quart mold. Cut foil to cover top of
pudding allowing an inch overhang. Oil one
side of foil and place oiled side down on top
of pudding. Tie lid in place with a piece of
string to prevent any water from getting in
during steaming. Place a trivet in a pot large
enough to contain the pudding bowl or
mold. Add about 2 inches of water. (When
the pudding bowl or mold is set on trivet,
water should come about halfway up bowl
but not touch foil; otherwise the pudding
could become soggy.) Then heat over high
flame until water comes to a boil. Reduce
heat to low and simmer for 2 hours or until
a toothpick inserted in the pudding comes
out clean. Remove from steamer and cool
pudding on a wire rack for 5 minutes. Then
loosen pudding and invert onto a platter.

PLUM PUDDING-PUDDING ◯

1 cup dates
1 cup milk

2½ cups Plum Sauce (see recipe, p. 224)
½ tsp. almond extract (opt.)

Put first 2 ingredients in saucepan and place
on medium heat until the consistency of
peanut butter (about 10 minutes), stirring
constantly. Now fold in the next 2 ingredients until they're well mixed together and
a nice pudding consistency. Chill and serve
garnished with Soy Whipped Cream (see
Basic Recipes Section, p. 34) and almond
slices.

Variation: You can continue to cook down
the plum pudding until it's a peanut butter
consistency, stirring constantly. Refrigerate,
then roll into balls and roll in milk powder
or date sugar to coat the ball. Serve as a
special candy.

PLUM PIE ◯

Flaky Pie Crust
(see Basic Recipes Section, p. 33)

12 - 16 prune plums, pitted and quartered
1 cup honey
8 Tbsp. quick cooking tapioca
¼ tsp. nutmeg
¼ tsp. cloves

1½ tsp. lemon juice
1 Tbsp. butter or margarine

Line pie plate with pastry. Combine next 5
ingredients. Turn into pie shell and sprinkle
with lemon juice. Dot with butter. Adjust
top crust, seal and flute edges, cut steam
vents. Bake for 45 minutes at 350° F.

PLUM CHUTNEY

3 cups finely chopped ripe plums
¼ cup honey

1 Tbsp. ghee or vegetable oil
1 tsp. crushed chili pepper seeds
Pinch ground cloves

Cook first 2 ingredients together until they
reach a thick and jamlike consistency. Heat
ghee or oil and toast chili seeds in it. When
seeds have browned, add the pinch of clove
and toast a few seconds more. Pour this
(called a chaunce) into cooked plums and
mix well. Can be served hot or cold.

PLUM DESSERT MOLD   ○

First Layer:

1 cup water
1 stick agar-agar (½ cup flakes)

3 cups roughly blended
or finely chopped fresh plums

2 cups fresh orange juice
½ tsp. grated, fresh ginger root

Second Layer:

1 cup water
1 stick agar-agar (½ cup flakes)

2 cups prune juice
2 Tbsp. lemon juice
2 Tbsp. honey
½ tsp. grated orange rind
¼ cup finely chopped walnuts

1 cup flavored yogurt

Use an 8-cup gelatin mold. Place an assortment of whole pieces or large sliced pieces of fresh fruit in bottom of mold for decoration (like whole grapes, cherries, etc., or orange wedges, peach wedges, etc.). In a pot soak 1 agar-agar stick in 1 cup of water; also in a bowl soak the same amount of water and agar. When agar is softened, make the first layer by bringing the water in the pot to a boil, stirring often until agar dissolves. Turn off the heat and pour in the finely chopped fresh plums and stir for a minute. Then add next 2 ingredients and pour into the mold over the pieces of fruit. Immediately begin the second layer by pouring the agar soaking in the bowl into the pot and bringing it to a boil as with the agar for the first layer. When agar is dissolved, add the next 5 ingredients. When this starts to set, fold in the yogurt and pour onto first layer. Refrigerate until set. Right before serving, pour out of mold.

DELICIOUS PLUM BAKE   ○

3 Tbsp. honey
¾ cup tofu, mashed
¾ cup buttermilk, yogurt or sour soy milk
1 Tbsp. butter or margarine

1/3 cup finely chopped almonds
1/3 cup whole wheat flour
¾ tsp. baking powder

3 cups fresh plums, diced
3 Tbsp. honey
¾ tsp. almond extract

Blend first 4 ingredients in blender until smooth. Mix in next 3 ingredients and pour into an oiled pie or cake dish. Mix last 3 ingredients together and pour over the tofu mixture in baking pan. Bake at 350° for 50 minutes. Remove from oven and cool 10 to 15 minutes. Serve this puddinglike dish warm topped with Soy Whipped Cream (see Basic Recipes Section, p. 34) or a dollop of yogurt and chopped almonds.

PLUM DATE SQUARES   ☆

1 lb. butter or margarine
1½ cups honey

4 cups rolled oats
2 cups whole wheat flour

Filling:
6 fresh plums

1 cup pitted dates
1 Tbsp. honey

Cream together butter and honey. Add next 2 ingredients and mix well. Cut up plums, place in a saucepan and simmer for 5 minutes. Add last 2 ingredients and continue to cook until thickened. Spread half of the oat mixture in 8" x 11" baking pan. Spread filling on top and cover with other half of oat mixture. Bake at 350° for 30 minutes or until top is browned.

MELONS

Melons

Watermelons have got to be the most refreshing, thirst-quenching fruit that exists. I think the small, Hawaiian varieties grown here have the sweetest, best texture around and they've got those mainland mushies beat hands down. Of course, the mainland watermelons are probably good to begin with, but after the long voyage across the ocean, they lose something in the flavor and gain something in the price.

Watermelon is another item that in spite of being grown on the mainland and shipped here—with freight charges and all—is still cheaper than local watermelon! Seems pretty discouraging, but that's economics here in Hawaii. The market is flooded with big shipments from Mexico and the mainland that compete with the farmers here, who have to pay outrageous prices for their land, water and expenses. With this kind of economics we'd better hope nothing stops the ships—a war, depression, or even a fuel shortage—or we're going to get awfully hungry! If you don't mind the price, the sweetness and quality of these local fruits are superior by far.

At the mango farm I stayed at in Kihei, they grew watermelons between the trees. The dry, sandy soil was perfect. I guess the major problem would be the stinging of fruit flies. So, if you're not into spraying poison all around, you might have to bag the small fruits or cover them with a light covering of sawdust or soil to protect them. The finest melons are produced in rich, rather sandy soils. Hawaiian-grown watermelons average from 10 to 20 pounds, with thin rinds from 3/8" to 1/2" thick. For local melons, the season varies from year to year, but they are usually most abundant from May through September.

I usually pick out the good melons by the old sound test. When you flick the melon with your finger, if it's a good one you get a hollow sound and if it's not so good, mushy, or cracked, it has a thud, hard sound. Sometimes I've gotten those not-so-crisp ones and I prefer to blend them at a low speed in a blender and strain out the seeds and pulp for a fine juice. The juice is a great one to fast on for short periods to clean out your body of toxins and give your digestive organs a needed rest. Also, I have heard watermelon juice is very good for kidney ailments and flushing the kidneys out.

I've gone into a rave about watermelon — probably because they're about the only melon grown commercially in Hawaii. (Other melons would grow here as easily as watermelon but haven't really entered onto the local growers' lists.) The fact that other melons are shipped in from the mainland is what makes them unpalatable. Not that there is anything wrong with the mainland — but most fruit that is shipped to Hawaii

from there must be picked green. This, in the case of melons, makes for a watery, not very sweet and oddly textured fruit. If I were in a place where vine-ripened melons were available, I would definitely be as enthusiastic about them as I am about watermelon!

As can be seen from the table on melons, the nutritional values of melons vary as much as the kinds of melons available. This table just lists the more popular ones.

A fresh, chilled melon is perfect by itself in its natural state, but for those of you who want to experiment a bit, here are some simple recipes. You can use other melons in the recipes for watermelon. There are even some recipes for making use of watermelon rind. Many years ago, a friend of mine returned from a stay of a few years in India and was horrified to see me throwing away the watermelon rind. He scolded me and told me, "In India they don't waste anything." Since then I've learned to use the rind. The watermelon rind is a lot like a squash that the Japanese call **togan**, and can be substituted in recipes that call for it. After you're done making some of the watermelon recipes, try fixing the rind for dinner!

(From U.S.D.A. Agriculture Handbook #8)
MELON
100 gm. edible portion

	Cantaloupe	Casaba	Honeydew	Watermelon
Water	91.2%	91.5%	90.6%	92.6%
Food energy	30 calories	27 calories	33 calories	26 calories
Protein	.7 gm.	1.2 gm.	.8 gm.	.5 gm.
Fat	.1 gm.	Trace	.3 gm.	.2 gm.
Carbohydrate	7.5 gm. (Total)	6.5 gm. (Total)	7.7 gm. (Total)	6.4 gm. (Total)
	.3 gm. (Fiber)	.5 gm. (Fiber)	.6 gm. (Fiber)	.3 gm. (Fiber)
Ash	.5 gm.	.8 gm.	.6 gm.	.3 gm.
Calcium	14 mg.	14 mg.	14 mg.	7 mg.
Phosphorus	16 mg.	16 mg.	16 mg.	10 mg.
Iron	.4 mg.	.4 mg.	.4 mg.	.5 mg.
Sodium	12 mg.	12 mg.	12 mg.	1 mg.
Potassium	251 mg.	251 mg.	251 mg.	100 mg.
Vitamin A	3,400 I.U.	30 I.U.	40 I.U.	590 I.U.
Thiamine	.04 mg.	.04 mg.	.04 mg.	.03 mg.
Riboflavin	.03 mg.	.03 mg.	.03 mg.	.03 mg.
Niacin	.6 mg.	.6 mg.	.6 mg.	.2 mg.
Vitamin C	33 mg.	13 mg.	23 mg.	7 mg.

FRESH MELON

Cut watermelon into 5" x 5" x 1" squares. Pile cantaloupe or honeydew melon balls on top and garnish with a mint sprig. Or serve cantaloupe rings with grapes in the center, or use watermelon balls and serve on grape leaves.

WATERMELON JUICE — A Cooler

Scoop out the pulp of one medium-sized watermelon. Mash the pulp with a fork and strain through a fine sieve or jelly bag, or run through a juicer. Chill and serve. Yields approximately 2 quarts. Persons suffering from too much acidity in their stomachs will find this drink very soothing as well as healing!

MELON FRAPPÉ

½ ripe cantaloupe, diced
2 ripe bananas, diced
1 or more cups milk

Freeze melon and bananas overnight. Put milk in blender and add fruit slowly. Blend for 1 to 2 minutes. Makes a nice, creamy fruit whip. Honey can also be added; also dates or raisins.

WATERMELON COCKTAIL

2 Tbsp. honey
Pinch of salt
4 Tbsp. lemon juice
4 cups ripe watermelon cubes

Add salt and honey to lemon juice. Mix well and pour over melon cubes. Sprinkle with fresh mint (opt.) and chill one hour before serving. Yields 6 servings.

WATERMELON FRUIT FIZZ

10 oz. natural black cherry
soda (unsweetened)
¼ cup honey
¼ cup lemon juice
4 cups melon balls

Combine ingredients and mix well. Chill and serve. Yields 4 to 6 servings. (Soda is available at natural food stores.)

WATERMELON BOAT

Cut watermelon according to instructions given in recipe for Watermelon Basket (see p. 233). Scoop out melon, remove seeds, and either dice or scoop to form watermelon balls. Mix melon with scoops of cantaloupe, grapes, diced apple, chopped walnuts, raisins, etc., and refill the melon with this melon fruit salad. Chill and serve.

MELON BOWL FOR A PARTY

Watermelon	Honey
Honeydew melon	Chopped mint
Cantaloupe	Orange juice
Berries	

Cut watermelon in ½" slices and cut out different shapes — hearts, diamonds, spades and clubs, etc. — with small cookie cutters. Scoop out other melons into balls. Add 2 to 3 cups berries in season and garnish with chopped mint. Drizzle honey over all and then add orange juice.

WATERMELON BASKET

1 medium-sized watermelon
2 lbs. seedless grapes
1 honeydew melon
3 papayas
2 apples (cubed and peeled)

First cut top half of watermelon into the shape of a basket with a handle. I suggest drawing on the melon where you will cut out two almost quarter-sized pieces, leaving about two inches of rind in the middle as a basket handle. Once you have cut out the two pieces, take out the remaining watermelon with spoon and de-seed. Then make into watermelon balls and use your remaining watermelon for juice. Make honeydew melon balls and papaya balls and add these with the cubed apples and juice into the watermelon basket for a refreshing fruit combination. Serve chilled.

WATERMELON POPSICLES

2 cups watermelon juice
4 tsp. lemon concentrate

4 tsp. agar-agar flakes
½ cup water
4 tsp. lemon concentrate
4 tsp. honey

Soak last 4 ingredients in a pan for 10 minutes; then heat until mixture thickens. Add the first 2 ingredients and stir. Pour into popsicle holders and freeze.

COLD MELON SOUP

1 medium-sized, chilled honeydew melon
or 1 large cantaloupe

Juice of 1 lime
1 - 2 Tbsp. honey (depending
on the sweetness of the melon)
2 tsp. lemon juice
½ tsp. nutmeg

½ cup yogurt
1 Tbsp. honey
Mint leaves (opt.)

Scoop out 1/3 of the melon with small ball scooper and set aside. Blend the remaining melon to make purée. Add next 4 ingredients and blend again. Pour purée in bowl and add the melon balls. Serve topped with sweetened yogurt and mint leaves. Makes 2 to 3 servings.

CANTALOUPE AND BERRY BOWLS WITH ORANGE-YOGURT SAUCE

3 cantaloupe melons, halved and de-seeded
3 cups fresh berries

1 cup yogurt
2 Tbsp. honey
½ cup orange juice
½ cup chopped walnuts

Slice melon in half widthwise and remove seeds. Cut bottom of melon halves so they will stand. Scoop out pulp with ball scooper and mix with berries. Refill melon bowls with this mixture of fruit. Combine last 4 ingredients and pour over melons.

PINEAPPLE HONEY DRESSING

½ cup honey
¼ cup lemon juice
3 Tbsp. crushed pineapple

Mix and shake well.

MELON WITH YOGURT SAUCE ☐

Melon of your choice

1 cup yogurt
2 Tbsp. honey
¼ cup nuts, chopped fine
¼ cup dates, raisins, or figs

Seeds for garnish
(sunflower, pumpkin, etc.)

Cut melon into wedges. Mix together next 4 ingredients and pour over melon wedges. Top with seeds.

WATERMELON SALAD ☐

4 cups watermelon chunks
1 cup honey
4 Tbsp. lemon juice
1 tsp. cardamom powder

Combine ingredients. Mix well and set in refrigerator to chill and marinate. Yields 4 to 6 servings.

FRESH FRUIT SALAD ☐

Pink grapefruit   Fresh figs
Strawberries   Grapes (halved)
Watermelon (cubed)   Papaya

In a bowl, arrange a circle of pink grapefruit sections, then a circle of strawberries, alternating with watermelon cubes. Add 2 more circles of figs with centers of halved, purple grapes and crescent-shaped pieces of papaya.

HONEY FRUIT SALAD ☐

Salad greens
2 avocados, peeled and
cut in lengthwise strips
1 Tbsp. lemon juice

2 cups cantaloupe balls
1 cup fresh berries

Fruit Salad Dressing or Pineapple Honey Dressing (see recipes on pp. 236, 443, 233)

Arrange greens with avocado strips placed on top. Sprinkle with lemon juice. Combine melon and berries and mound on top of avocado. Serve with a fruit salad dressing.

PATCHWORK SALAD ☐

1 cup melon balls
2 large pineapples
1 orange, peeled and sectioned
1 grapefruit, peeled and sectioned
1 banana, peeled and sliced
1 peach, skinned and sliced
1 cup sweet cherries, pitted
1 cup blueberries

Fruit Salad Dressing or Pineapple Honey Dressing (see recipes on pp. 236, 443, 233)

Cut pineapples in half lengthwise. Scoop out fruit and cut in cubes. Mix all the fruit together and spoon into pineapple shells. Pour dressing over and serve.

MELON COMPOTE ☐

Cantaloupe, honeydew melon, watermelon, Cranshaw, etc.

Syrup:
Rind and juice of 1 lime or lemon
½ cup orange juice
¼ cup maple syrup

Scoop out melon into balls. Boil syrup 'til thick. Cool; then pour over melon. Chill before serving.

BUBBLY WATERMELON SURPRISE ☐

Cut a hole about 4 inches wide on the side of a watermelon in the middle. Slowly pour honey soda or carbonated juice (you can buy it in natural food stores or make your own by combining apple juice, grape juice, etc., with Calistoga, Perrier, or other fizzy mineral waters) into the hole that was cut out. As you pour, tilt the melon to one side and then to the other so the soda will be absorbed by all parts of the melon. Then replace the piece of watermelon which was cut out to make the hole and chill overnight. More soda can be poured in when the melon is chilling. Slice melon as usual. This is a nice treat for a picnic.

WATERMELON JELL ◯

½ cup water
1 stick agar-agar (½ cup flakes)

1½ cups watermelon juice (see p. 232)
1 Tbsp. honey
½ tsp. lemon juice
Pinch of salt

¼ cup watermelon balls
or honeydew melon balls
¼ cup cantaloupe or papaya balls

Soak first 2 ingredients for 5 minutes. Then cook until dissolved. Let cool a little and mix with next 4 ingredients. Pour into gelatin molds and chill until half set. Press in pieces of fruit and chill until set. Serve.

EASY YOGURT AND HONEY
SAUCE FOR MELONS ☐

2/3 cup yogurt
1/3 cup pineapple or orange juice (unsweetened)
2 Tbsp. honey

Combine ingredients. Makes about 1 cup. Good over cantaloupe or any type of melon.

MINTY WATERMELON A LA MODE ◯

2 Tbsp. dried peppermint or spearmint leaves (or 10 - 12 fresh, tender mint leaves)
2 cups water

½ cup honey
Juice of ½ lemon
1 Tbsp. grated fresh ginger

1 Tbsp. arrowroot powder
Enough water to make a paste

Watermelon balls
Honey vanilla ice cream

Let dried mint leaves steep in boiling hot water for 10 minutes (or boil fresh leaves for 10 minutes). Strain and add next 3 ingredients. Cook for 10 minutes; strain again. Make a paste with arrowroot and cold water. Gradually add to mixture while stirring. Cook until syrup begins to thicken and turns clear. Let cool. Pour over melon balls; top with ice cream and more syrup, if desired.

WATERMELON PUDDING ◯

4 - 5 lbs. watermelon

6 tsp. arrowroot
¾ cup honey
6 tsp. orange juice concentrate
1 tsp. vanilla

6 Tbsp. carob powder

Cinnamon
Yogurt
Honey to taste

Use pulp and make 4 cups melon juice. Put into saucepan. Add next 4 ingredients and mix together off heat until arrowroot dissolves. Put on heat and bring to boil. Stir until mixture thickens and coats the spoon. Add carob powder and stir into juice. When it is thoroughly mixed, remove from heat and cool. Pour into custard cups. Chill well and serve with sweetened yogurt and a sprinkling of cinnamon.

FRUIT SALAD DRESSING

1 cup pineapple juice
2 Tbsp. frozen orange juice
1 tsp. lemon juice
2 Tbsp. honey
1 tsp. egg replacer
1½ Tbsp. arrowroot

Combine all ingredients in a saucepan and boil until thick. Cool. Serve over bowl full of melon balls or any fruit salad.

MELON BALL COBBLER ☆

1½ cups melon balls

Batter:
3 Tbsp. butter or margarine
6 Tbsp. honey

¾ cup milk
2 tsp. vanilla

1½ cups whole wheat flour
3 tsp. baking powder

Cooking Sauce:
½ cup honey
3 Tbsp. butter or margarine
½ cup orange juice

Topping:
¾ cup orange juice
1 Tbsp. lemon juice
1 Tbsp. arrowroot
1 Tbsp. butter or margarine

Yogurt
Honey to taste

Cream together butter and honey and add next 2 ingredients. Then add remaining 2 batter ingredients and mix into a smooth consistency. Put melon balls into a greased 8" dish and cover with batter. Mix cooking sauce ingredients together and pour over batter and melon mixture. Bake for 20 minutes at 350°, then for 20 minutes more at 325°. Blend topping ingredients together and boil until mixture thickens. Cool, then add last 2 ingredients. Pour over melon cobbler.

WATERMELON LEMON JELL ○

2 sticks agar-agar (1 cup flakes)
4 cups lemon juice

Balls scooped from ½ medium watermelon

To make lemon juice, squeeze 7 or 8 lemons and add 7 or 8 Tbsp. honey to the juice. Add water up to the 4-cup level and then crumble in agar-agar. Let set in lemon juice for 5 minutes; then boil juice and place in refrigerator until partially cooled. Have the watermelon balls ready to drop into the jell and return to refrigerator until set.

MELON PIE

Flaky Pie Crust
(see Basic Recipes Section, p. 33)

2½ cups cubed cantaloupe
or honeydew melon
Grated rind of 1 lemon or lime
Juice of 1 lemon or lime
1/3 cup of honey
½ tsp. nutmeg
3 Tbsp. whole wheat flour
3 Tbsp. butter or margarine

Mix together last 7 ingredients. Pour into pie crust and dot with butter. Cover with lattice top and bake at 400° for 15 minutes; then turn oven down to 350°, cover and bake for 20 minutes more.

WATERMELON SEEDS ○

Preheat oven to 150° F. Just collect the seeds, wash them and spread on a cookie sheet. Allow to dry out and bake in the oven at a very low heat until crisp. Good snack!

SAUTÉD WATERMELON RIND #1 O

4 cups shredded watermelon rind

¼ tsp. asafetida
4 Tbsp. soy sauce

1 Tbsp. butter or margarine (opt.)
Salt and black pepper to taste

Trim green from the rind. Using a coarse shredder, prepare 4 cups of shredded rind. Sauté prepared rind with next 2 ingredients and cook for 15 to 20 minutes. Add butter, if desired, and season to taste with salt and black pepper. Good added to steamed vegetables, potatoes, squash or tofu, or garnished with baco-bits.

SAUTÉD WATERMELON RIND #2

2 cups watermelon rind, cut in thin strips
2 tsp. oil

3 - 4 tsp. soy sauce

Sauté first 2 ingredients. When turning golden and getting a bit crispy, add soy sauce and quickly stir-fry. Good served with fluffy, steamed brown rice.

Variation: Also very good with about 1 teaspoon nutritional yeast mixed in just before serving.

WATERMELON RIND IN MISO SOUP O

2 cups water
½ cup firm tofu cubes
¼ cup slivered green beans
½ cup thin-sliced rind

1 Tbsp. miso
¼ cup grated carrot
½ tsp. soy sauce (opt.)

Bring first 4 ingredients to a boil for about 5 minutes. Turn down to simmer, add next 3 ingredients and mix well. Simmer a few minutes and serve. Yields 2 servings.

WATERMELON RIND GLAZE O

8 cups watermelon rind
Cold water

2 cups honey
6 oz. water

2 lemons, thinly sliced and seeded
½ tsp. vanilla

Remove outer green skin from rind and the inner pink flesh, leaving only lightest part of the rind. Cut in ½" cubes and make about 8 cups. Cover cubes with cold water in a pan. Bring to boil, then pour off. Add more cold water and boil and drain again. Repeat once more; this time simmer for 20 minutes before draining rind into colander. Place rind in pan and cover with next 2 ingredients. Add last 2 ingredients and cook over medium heat, shaking frequently until all honey has melted. Simmer uncovered for approximately 1 to 2 hours, or until syrup temperature is 234° or reaches soft ball stage.

SPICY WATERMELON RIND O

2 cups watermelon rind, cut in thin strips
2 tsp. oil

1 tsp. oil
1 pinch asafetida
¼ tsp. turmeric
¼ tsp. cumin
1/8 tsp. ginger powder
1 pinch cayenne

Sauté first 2 ingredients. Toast next 6 ingredients. Mix with sautéd watermelon rind and serve alongside fluffy, steamed brown rice. Yields 1 to 2 servings.

"Until mankind can extend the circle of
his compassion to include all living things,
he will never, himself, know peace."
— Albert Schweitzer

DATES
and
DRIED FRUIT

Dates & Dried Fruit

All the different kinds of fruits featured in other sections can be dried. This can be done either by cutting fruit into pieces, or by blending and then making a fruit leather. In Hawaii (and probably other places where the sunshine is intense) we accomplish this by just setting the fruit outdoors in a screened box to keep bugs out. There are a great many drying units that have been developed, from solar fruit dryers to indoor electrical units. I can't really recommend any commercial products, since I've always just put things out in the sun and that has always been quite satisfactory.

Drying units certainly come in handy, considering the astronomical cost of store-bought dried fruit. Also, drying is a nutritious and compact way to preserve excess fruit (and vegetables as well), which can later be used once the harvest season is past. There is some nutritional loss but, as can be seen in the following table, it is not very great.

Of course, dried fruit is delicious by itself and makes a healthy snack for the children. However, here are a few recipes which will enable you to make everything from simple to elaborate preparations using different dried fruits. You can substitute certain fruits for others, depending on the cost and availability, and this will give a whole new taste, and a new recipe!

Date Bars, p. 250

FRUITED FROSTING ☆

½ cup cream cheese
½ cup plain yogurt
½ cup dried papaya, sliced very thin
½ cup dried pineapple, sliced very thin
½ cup honey
½ cup butter or margarine
1 cup Monukka raisins
1 cup chopped almonds
1 Tbsp. chopped dates
½ cup carob powder

Mix all ingredients together and use as a frosting on your favorite cake. To make a fudge, simply add ¼ cup carob powder to above ingredients and press into a cake or pie pan. Refrigerate to harden, then cut squares of fudge.

RAW NUT BREAD WITH SPREAD ☐

2 cups chopped black mission figs
2 cups raw nuts
4 Tbsp. raw wheat germ or bran

Spread:
½ cup pitted dates
2 Tbsp. nut butter
2 Tbsp. prune juice

Run first 2 ingredients through food grinder. Add wheat germ or bran and mix in. Mold into a loaf shape, wrap in wax paper and chill at least one hour. Slice thin and serve plain or with spread. Tastes almost like rye bread. For spread: Blend ingredients in blender. Store in refrigerator. Good on apple and banana slices.

WINTER FRUIT PUDDING ◯

8 oz. chopped, assorted dried fruit
3-1/3 cups fruit juice (any kind)
¼ cup honey
1/8 tsp. ground cardamom
1/8 tsp. cinnamon

Slices of soft, fresh whole grain bread

Combine first 5 ingredients in a bowl and let sit overnight, or else gently stew over low flame until dried fruit softens. In an 8" diameter baking dish or bowl, lay whole pieces of bread on bottom and sides of the dish. (You will have to cut bread into triangles, oblongs, etc., to fit pieces together like a puzzle so that all edges meet. This is very important. If edges don't meet, when you turn the pudding out of the bowl the bread may fall apart.) Set aside ¼ to ½ cup of the liquid that the fruit was soaked in. Pour the fruit filling and remaining liquid into the bread-lined dish and top with a single layer of bread. Again cut so edges will meet. Place platter on top of the pudding that will fit inside of the container which the pudding is in. On top of the platter, place a weight (such as a jar full of honey or dried beans) and refrigerate like this 6 to 8 hours. To serve, turn pudding out of bowl by inverting. It should come out easily like a molded pudding. Then pour and smooth liquid (reserved from soaking fruit) over top of pudding, especially if there are any dry places. Good served with yogurt or Soy Whipped Cream (see Basic Recipes Section, p. 34).

RAW FRUIT CAROB CANDIES ◯

2 cups pitted dates
1 cup raisins

½ cup finely chopped nuts
6 - 8 Tbsp. carob powder

Toasted sesame seeds

Run first 2 ingredients through a food grinder. Mix in next 2 ingredients and blend well. Roll into balls about 1 inch in diameter and roll in toasted sesame seeds. Chill and serve.

CAROB MINT BALLS ☐

2 cups pitted dates
1 cup raisins or currants
½ cup sunflower seeds

1/8 tsp. mint extract
½ cup carob powder

Put first 3 ingredients through a food grinder (hand ones will keep the children happily busy for quite a while) or food processor. Combine in mixing bowl with the last 2 ingredients. Roll into balls.

DRIED FRUIT YOGURT WHIP ☐

1 cup black mission figs, diced
¼ cup dried papaya, diced
½ cup dried apricots, diced
1 cup water
2 Tbsp. honey
1 Tbsp. lemon juice

2 cups yogurt
1 Tbsp. lemon juice
1 tsp. honey

Soak first 6 ingredients together for about 30 minutes to 1 hour. Blend in blender until smooth. Mix next 3 ingredients together and fold gently into the blended fruit. Refrigerate. Serve as a pudding or refreshing summer meal.

FRUIT OF THE SEASON SOUP ☐

4 cups fruit of the season
1 cup yogurt
1 orange

½ cup chopped figs
2 bananas, chopped
1 apple, diced

Fresh mint leaves
2 cups toasted, grated coconut

Blend together first 3 ingredients. Chill. Add chopped fruit. Garnish with fresh mint leaves and coconut.

PASHKA ☆

½ cup cream cheese
¼ cup butter or margarine
½ cup sour cream
½ cup grated organic orange rind
½ cup dried papaya, thinly sliced
plus a few extra slices
3 Tbsp. finely chopped Brazil nuts
½ cup finely chopped almonds
1 cup Monukka raisins
1 cup dried pineapple, chopped very fine
¼ cup chopped dates

About a dozen almonds, split in half
¼ cup slices of dried pineapple

Mix together first 10 ingredients and press into a glass, plastic or pottery pan 1" thick. Decorate with almonds and dried pineapple and refrigerate overnight. Cut into cubes and serve as dessert and hors d'oeuvres.

ORANGE-DATE COMPOTE ☐

2 cups pitted dates, diced
¼ cup dried pineapple, diced
¼ cup frozen orange juice concentrate
1 cup warm water
2 Tbsp. + 2 tsp. lemon juice

1 Tbsp. chopped almonds
1 Tbsp. chopped cashews

Soak first 5 ingredients overnight in the refrigerator. Put them in a blender and blend on high speed until smooth. Add next 2 ingredients and blend until smooth or until there are little chunks of nuts. Refrigerate. Serve when cool with Soy Whipped Cream (see Basic Recipes Section, p. 34) or yogurt on top.

PRUNE COOLER ☐

¼ cup dried apricots
2 cups prune juice

2 cups plain yogurt
1 Tbsp. lemon juice
1 Tbsp. honey
¼ tsp. nutmeg

Soak first 2 ingredients in refrigerator overnight. Blend them with rest of ingredients in a blender until smooth.

FRUIT SPUMONI ☐

8 medium-sized frozen bananas
1 cup yogurt

1½ Tbsp. dried apricots, chopped
¼ cup dried pineapple, chopped
½ cup chopped cashews or pistachios

Blend first 2 ingredients in blender. Only blend 2 bananas at a time with ¼ cup of yogurt so bananas can get blended thoroughly. (Overloading the blender prevents the bananas from blending properly.) Blend until it is the consistency of ice cream. Pour into a bowl, fold in next 3 ingredients and serve immediately.

FRUIT AND NUT DELIGHT ☐

½ cup raisins
½ cup dried peaches or apricots (presoak in hot water for 30 minutes if they are hard)

1 cup roasted cashews

2 Tbsp. frozen orange juice concentrate

Grind fruit in a blender or a food grinder. Chop ¼ cup of the cashews. Grind the rest so they are like a flour. Mix together the ground fruit, chopped nuts and orange concentrate. Roll into balls and then roll into nut flour.

CELESTIALS ☆

¼ cup butter or margarine
¼ cup honey
1 cup noninstant powdered milk
1 Tbsp. liquid lecithin

Filling:
¼ cup raisins
¼ cup dried pineapple, chopped
½ cup apple juice

½ cup almonds

½ cup walnut meal

Mix first 4 ingredients together well. Mash half of this in the bottom of an 8" square cake pan to 1/8" thickness. Pinch candy up along sides to make a ridge along the edges. Make filling by blending the 3 filling ingredients in a blender until smooth. Pour into a bowl. Put almonds into a blender and blend until they are chopped fine. Scrape this into the already blended dried fruit and mix well. Pour this on top of the candy lining the cake pan. Take other half of candy mixture and roll out to 1/8" thickness between wax paper, as you would pie dough. Peel off one side of wax paper, flip over with candy side on top of filling. Peel wax paper off other side and pinch edge seams together to seal filling in. Refrigerate a while (at least 15 minutes), slice into bite-sized squares or oblongs and roll these each in walnut meal so they'll be coated. Refrigerate until ready to serve. (Walnut meal can be made quickly by dropping about ¾ cup walnuts into blender and blending 'til almost a flour texture.)

BUGS BUNNY PUDDING ☐

1 cup fresh carrot juice
½ cup black mission figs, chopped
1 cup dates, chopped
1 Tbsp. liquid lecithin

Place all ingredients in blender and blend until smooth and puddinglike. Chill and serve.

FIG-DATE CHUTNEY

2 Tbsp. butter or margarine
1½ tsp. cumin seeds
¾ tsp. turmeric
½ tsp. chili seeds

½ cup dates, diced
½ cup figs, chopped
¼ - ½ cup water

¼ cup honey
2 Tbsp. lemon juice

Melt butter in quart-sized pan and toast next 3 ingredients until seeds turn blackish-brown and aroma of spices fills the air. Add next 3 ingredients, stirring well. Add enough water to cover dried fruit and simmer for 30 minutes or until water evaporates. When fruit is soft and water is cooked out, add last 2 ingredients and cook on medium-high flame, stirring constantly, until it is a puddinglike consistency. Take off heat and cool. Serve as a condiment.

DREAMY BURFY

½ cup grated coconut
½ cup honey
1/3 cup dried apricots, diced
1/3 cup water

¼ cup butter or margarine

1¾ cups powdered milk

1/3 cup pistachios or walnuts, chopped fine
1/3 cup dried apricots, chopped

Put first 4 ingredients in blender and blend until smooth. Pour ingredients into a saucepan along with butter. Bring to a boil over medium-low heat for 3 minutes, stirring constantly. Take off heat and slowly add powdered milk, ½ cup at a time, whipping the ingredients together. When all powdered milk is whipped in, add chopped apricots and nuts. Whip again. Refrigerate at least an hour or until able to cut with knife into bite-sized pieces.

EKADASI (GRAINLESS) PIE CRUST

2/3 cup water
2/3 cup dried apricots
½ cup honey

½ cup finely grated coconut
2 Tbsp. butter or margarine

1-2/3 cups noninstant powdered milk

Soak first 3 ingredients together in refrigerator overnight; then pour into blender and blend until smooth. Toast next 2 ingredients in a skillet over medium heat until coconut is a toasty golden color. Pour in blended fruit mixture and cook at slow boil over low heat, stirring occasionally, until a peanut-butterlike texture is reached. Remove from heat and mix in powdered milk. Press this into an oiled pie pan and bake at 350° for 15 minutes. Fill with your favorite raw fruit filling or the following Creamy Yogurt Fruit Filling.

CREAMY YOGURT FRUIT FILLING ☆

1 cup yogurt cheese (see recipe in Dairy Section, p. 453)
½ cup honey

¼ cup each of diced raisins, prunes, apricots and dates
¾ cup water

2 Tbsp. slivered almonds

Combine first 2 ingredients. Soak next 5 ingredients together for 15 minutes, then drain off excess water (reserve water for drinking, making teas, syrups, etc., later). Fold dried fruit into yogurt cheese mixture and pour into prebaked pie crust or a raw food pie crust (see recipes in Basic Recipes Section, pp. 32 and 33). Top with slivered almonds.

TROPICAL BANANA NUT ROLL □

1/3 cup dried banana
1/3 cup dried papaya
1/3 cup dried pineapple

1/3 cup walnuts
1/3 cup cashews
1/3 cup almonds
1/3 cup sesame seeds
1/3 cup unsweetened coconut

1 Tbsp. orange juice

Chop the first 3 ingredients and put through a food grinder or Champion juicer and set aside. Combine next 5 ingredients, place in blender and blend until ground up. Blend a little bit of the nut mixture at a time to avoid burning out blender motor. Mix all ingredients and knead into a dough, slowly adding the orange juice. Then roll into a log and chill. Slice into wafers and serve with yogurt and fresh fruit or top with apricot marmalade or other puréed dried fruit.

RAW FOODS FRUIT BAR ○

1-2/3 cups sesame or sunflower seed meal
1 cup granola
¼ cup chopped nuts

½ cup nut butter
2 Tbsp. honey

3 cups assorted dried fruit

2/3 cup fruit juice
1 tsp. lemon juice (opt.)

Combine first 3 ingredients. Reserve 1/3 cup of this mixture for sprinkling on top of bar filling. Add next 2 ingredients to the larger portion of dry ingredients. Mix well and pat this into the bottom of a 9'' square cake pan. For the filling, run dried fruit through a food grinder. Mix in the fruit juice and pour on top of crust already patted into the cake pan. Sprinkle remaining dry crumbs on top of entire layer of filling. Refrigerate or let set at room temperature a few hours. Cut and serve.

GINGER CREAMS ☆

1 Tbsp. minced fresh ginger
2 tsp. minced, dried papaya
2 chopped dates
1 dried calimyrna fig, minced
1 dried black mission fig, minced
1 Tbsp. minced Monukka raisins
¼ cup cream cheese

12 or so dried fruits for stuffing, sliced partially through (dates, figs, prunes, apricots, peaches)

Mix first 7 ingredients together. Stuff this mixture into dried fruits which have been split open. Let sit for at least an hour so flavors can blend.

DATE PUDDING ○

2 cups soft dates, pitted
2½ cups milk

Put both ingredients in a pot on the burner and cook over medium heat. In the beginning stir occasionally to prevent burning or sticking. When dates soften and begin to dissolve, stir constantly. Stir and mash with the back of the spoon until dates and milk cook to the consistency of mashed potatoes. Remove from heat and cool. Refrigerate. This makes a delicious pudding sprinkled with date sugar, chopped nuts and/or granola. It also makes a good filling for Manju (see recipe in Legume Section, p. 404) or little prebaked tart shells made from Flaky Pastry (see Basic Recipes Section, p. 33) or a filling for Danish Pastries (see recipe in Grain Section, p. 434).

CORNUCOPIA FRUIT CAKE ○

1 Tbsp. egg replacer
1/3 cup water

2/3 cup honey
¾ cup whole wheat flour
½ tsp. baking powder
1½ tsp. vanilla

1 cup whole dried apricots
1 cup pitted prunes
1 cup pitted dates
1 cup dried pineapple, cut in 1" pieces
1 cup dried papaya, cut in 1" pieces
1 cup whole brazil nuts
1 cup whole almonds
1 cup walnuts

Mix first 2 ingredients together in a large bowl. Then add the next 4 ingredients and cream together. Add the next 8 ingredients and mix thoroughly. Line two 7½"x 3½" bread pans with wax paper. Butter the wax paper and pour ingredients evenly into the pans. Bake at 300° for 1½ hours. Cover with wax paper and bake for 30 minutes longer. Refrigerate at least 1 hour. Slice very thin. Keep refrigerated.

DATE-NUT BARS ○

1 cup pitted dates, chopped
(or other soft dried fruit)
1 cup chopped nuts
¾ cup honey
½ cup flour
½ cup crushed graham cracker crumbs

Combine all ingredients, press into an oiled 8" cookie sheet and bake at 350° for 35 minutes. Cool and cut into bar shapes.

DATE CREAM PIE ☆

Crust:
1 pkg. honey graham crackers
(about 1½ cups of crumbs)

1/3 cup sunflower seed meal

1 cup bran
¼ cup butter or margarine
1/8 cup honey
3 Tbsp. water

Filling:
1/3 cup raisins
1/3 cup pitted dates, chopped
2/3 cup water

1/3 cup honey
1/8 cup molasses
3 cups yogurt
4 Tbsp. quick-cooking tapioca pearls
1 mashed ripe banana

Break up graham crackers and blend in blender until a fine flour is made. Grind sunflower seeds in blender in the same way. Put blender-ground ingredients in a bowl and mix in the next 4 ingredients. Press crust into pie dish. To make filling, either soak first 3 filling ingredients together overnight or boil on stove top until dates begin to dissolve. Blend softened dried fruit and water in blender until fruit is chopped fine. Mix with next 5 ingredients. Allow to sit 10 to 15 minutes so tapioca pearls can soften. Pour into pie dish lined with graham cracker crust and bake at 350° for 25 minutes. Top with some date paste or halves of pitted dates arranged nicely. Cool and refrigerate.

APRICOT MARMALADE ○

2 Tbsp. butter or margarine
½ cup dried apricots, chopped
¼ cup raisins

1 cup orange juice

1 Tbsp. honey

2 Tbsp. orange rind

Melt butter in pan and stir-fry with next 2 ingredients until they soften. Add orange juice and cook over medium heat, stirring occasionally. When the mixture starts to thicken, remove from heat and place in blender. Blend until smooth, pour back into pan, add honey and cook, stirring constantly on medium-high flame. Cook down 'til thick like jam (takes about 8 to 10 minutes), then add orange rind and cook another 3 minutes. Take off heat and cool. Use as marmalade on fresh whole-grain biscuits, buns, etc., or over ice cream, yogurt, etc.

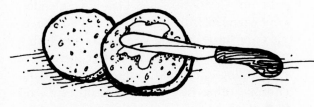

CHRISTMAS BALLS ☆

Syrup:
¾ cup maple syrup
2 Tbsp. butter or margarine
2/3 lb. pitted dates

Drippings:
1 cup garbanzo or whole wheat flour
Water
Ghee or light oil for deep frying

Filling:
½ cup raisins
½ cup walnuts, chopped
¼ cup roasted cashews, chopped
¼ cup toasted sesame seeds
¼ cup roasted sunflower seeds
¼ cup chopped figs or apricots
or other dried fruit

Place ingredients for syrup in saucepan and cook over medium flame until dates dissolve and mixture thickens. Stir often. For drippings, make a thin batter and drip into hot ghee or light oil by pouring through a collander. Fry until golden brown, remove from ghee with a slotted spoon and drain on a paper towel. Repeat until all batter is used. Combine last 6 filling ingredients with cooked drippings, add maple syrup paste and mix well. Oil or butter hands to prevent sticking and roll mixture into balls. Rich and expensive, but a wonderful gift or party offering.

FESTIVE HOLIDAY STUFFING ☆

¼ cup pumpkin seeds

¼ cup diced celery
½ tsp. asafetida
½ tsp. fresh thyme, diced
½ tsp. basil
1 tsp. Spike

1 cup cooked rice
½ cup butter or margarine
½ cup dried apricots, chopped
½ cup dried peaches, chopped
¼ cup chopped dates
¼ cup flaky nutritional yeast
4 cups crumbled bread crumbs
¼ tsp. Dr. Bronner's Seasoning
1½ tsp. chopped fresh parsley

Soak pumpkin seeds in water overnight or in hot water for 1 hour (keep soaking water for use in smoothies, gravies, etc.). Sauté next 5 ingredients together for 2 minutes. Add next 9 ingredients to sautéed ingredients and mix together thoroughly. Put ingredients in a covered casserole dish and bake at 350° for 40 minutes. Serve with Mock Turkey Gravy (see Tofu Section, p. 379) or other gravy.

FRUIT CAKE

1 tsp. orange rind
½ cup barbados molasses
¼ cup honey
5 Tbsp. butter or margarine
¼ cup yogurt
1 tsp. vanilla

2 cups whole wheat flour
1½ tsp. baking powder
½ tsp. baking soda
1 tsp. salt

1 cup shredded coconut
1 cup dried papaya
1 cup dried pineapple
1 cup dried currants
½ cup dried figs
½ cup fresh cranberries
¾ cup water

Glaze:
1½ cups butter or margarine
3 cups honey
1 tsp. vanilla

Cream together first 6 ingredients. Sift in next 4 ingredients. Then fold in last 7 ingredients (or use other variations of dried fruit and/or berries). Pour into two oiled 5½" round baking pans and bake at 350° for 1 hour. While still warm, mix glaze ingredients and brush over the tops of fruit cakes. Wrap in tin foil and allow to sit in cool place for a few days.

DATE BARS ☆

1 cup whole wheat flour
Pinch salt
1 tsp. vanilla
¾ cup honey

1 cup butter or margarine

½ cup bran
1½ cups rolled oats

Filling:
1 cup soft dates, pitted
1½ cups water or fruit juice

Mix first 4 ingredients together. Cut in butter. Stir in oats and bran. Spread half of the mixture in an 8" square baking pan. Make filling by soaking dates a few hours in water or juice. (You can use other dried fruit for variation.) Then blend in a blender. Pour blended fruit into a pot and cook over medium heat, stirring constantly until mixture thickens to mashed potato consistency. Pour filling onto mixture in baking pan and crumble other half of mixture on top. Add ½ cup chopped nuts or seeds if you like. Bake at 325° for 35 to 40 minutes. Cool and cut into bar shapes.

COMPARING FRESH AND DRIED FRUIT
(From U.S.D.A. Agriculture Handbook #8)
100 gm. edible portion

Food and description	Iron (mg.)	Sodium (mg.)	Potas-sium (mg.)	Vit. A (I.U.)	Thia-mine (mg.)	Ribo-flavin (mg.)	Niacin (mg.)	Vit. C (mg.)
GRAPES (raw)								
American type (slip skin) such as Concord, Delaware	.4	3	158	100	(.05)	(.03)	(.3)	4
European type (adherent skin) such as Thompson Seedless	.4	3	173	(100)	.05	.03	.3	4
RAISINS (natural, uncooked)	3.5	27	763	20	.11	.08	.5	1
PLUMS (raw)								
Damson	.5	2	299	(300)	.08	.03	.5	–
Japanese and hybrid	.5	1	170	250	.03	.03	.5	6
Prune-type	.5	1	170	300	.03	.03	.5	4
PRUNES (uncooked)								
Dehydrated, nugget-type	4.4	11	940	2,170	.12	.22	2.1	4
Dried, soft	3.9	8	694	1,600	.09	.17	1.6	3
APRICOTS								
Raw, fresh	.5	1	281	2,700	.03	.04	.6	10
Dehydrated, uncooked	5.3	33	1,260	14,100	Trace	.08	3.6	15
Dried, uncooked	5.5	26	979	10,900	.01	.16	3.3	12
PEACHES								
Raw, fresh	.5	1	202	1,330	.02	.05	1.0	7
Dehydrated, uncooked	3.5	(21)	(1,229)	(5,000)	Trace	.10	7.8	14
Dried, uncooked	6.0	16	950	3,900	.01	.19	5.3	18
PEARS								
Raw, fresh	.3	2	130	20	.02	.04	.1	4
Dried, uncooked	1.3	7	573	70	.01	.18	.6	7
APPLES								
Freshly harvested:								
Not pared	.3	1	110	90	.03	.02	.1	7
Pared	.3	1	110	40	.03	.02	.1	4
Stored:								
Not pared	.3	1	110	90	.03	.02	.1	3
Pared	.3	1	110	40	.03	.02	.1	2
Dehydrated, uncooked	2.0	7	730	–	Trace	.06	.6	10
Dried, uncooked	1.6	5	569	–	.06	.12	.5	10
FIGS								
Raw, fresh	.6	2	194	80	.06	.05	.4	2
Dried, uncooked	3.0	34	640	80	.10	.10	.7	(0)
BANANAS (raw)								
Common	.7	1	370	190	.05	.06	.7	10
Red	.8	1	370	400	.05	.04	.6	(10)
Dehydrated	2.8	4	1,477	760	.18	.24	2.8	7
DATES (domestic, natural)	3.0	1	648	50	.09	.10	2.2	0

Dashes denote lack of reliable data for a constituent believed to be present in measurable amount.
Calculated values, as those based on a recipe, are not in parentheses.

COMPARING FRESH AND DRIED FRUIT
(From U.S.D.A. Agriculture Handbook #8)
100 gm. edible portion

Food and description	Water (%)	Food Energy (calories)	Protein (gm.)	Fat (gm.)	Carbohydrate Total (gm.)	Carbohydrate Fiber (gm.)	Ash (gm.)	Calcium (mg.)	Phos-phorus (mg.)
GRAPES (raw)									
American type (slip skin)									
such as Concord, Delaware	81.6	69	1.3	1.0	15.7	.6	.4	16	12
European type (adherent skin)									
such as Thompson Seedless	81.4	67	.6	.3	17.3	.5	.4	12	20
RAISINS (natural, uncooked)	18.0	289	2.5	.2	77.4	.9	1.9	62	101
PLUMS (raw)									
Damson	81.1	66	.5	Trace	17.8	.4	.6	18	17
Japanese and hybrid	86.6	48	.5	.2	12.3	.6	.4	12	18
Prune-type	78.7	75	.8	.2	19.7	.4	.6	12	18
PRUNES (uncooked)									
Dehydrated, nugget-type	2.5	344	3.3	.5	91.3	(2.2)	2.4	90	107
Dried, soft	28.0	255	2.1	.6	67.4	1.6	1.9	51	79
APRICOTS									
Raw, fresh	85.3	51	1.0	.2	12.8	.6	.7	17	23
Dehydrated, uncooked	3.5	332	5.6	1.0	84.6	3.8	5.3	86	139
Dried, uncooked	25.0	260	5.0	.5	66.5	3.0	3.0	67	108
PEACHES									
Raw, fresh	89.1	38	.6	.1	9.7	.6	.5	9	19
Dehydrated, uncooked	3.0	340	4.8	(.9)	88.0	(4.0)	3.3	(62)	(151)
Dried, uncooked	25.0	262	3.1	.7	68.3	3.1	2.9	48	117
PEARS									
Raw, fresh	83.2	61	.7	.4	15.3	1.4	.4	8	11
Dried, uncooked	26.0	268	3.1	1.8	67.3	6.2	1.8	35	48
APPLES									
Freshly harvested:									
Not pared	84.8	56	.2	.6	14.1	1.0	.3	7	10
Pared	85.3	53	.2	.3	13.9	.6	.3	6	10
Stored:									
Not pared	83.9	60	.2	.7	14.8	1.0	.4	7	10
Pared	84.8	55	.2	.3	14.4	.6	.3	6	10
Dehydrated, uncooked	2.5	353	1.4	2.0	92.1	3.8	2.0	40	66
Dried, uncooked	24.0	275	1.0	1.6	71.8	3.1	1.6	31	52
FIGS									
Raw, fresh	77.5	80	1.2	.3	20.3	1.2	.7	35	22
Dried, uncooked	23.0	274	4.3	1.3	69.1	5.6	2.3	126	77
BANANAS (raw)									
Common	75.7	85	1.1	.2	22.2	.5	.8	8	26
Red	74.4	90	1.2	.2	23.4	.4	.8	10	18
Dehydrated	3.0	340	4.4	.8	88.6	2.0	3.2	32	104
DATES (domestic, natural)	22.5	274	2.2	.5	72.9	2.3	1.9	59	63

Numbers in parentheses denote values imputed — usually from another form of the food or from a similar food. Zero in parentheses indicates that the amount of a constituent probably is none or is too small to measure.

GARDEN VEGETABLES

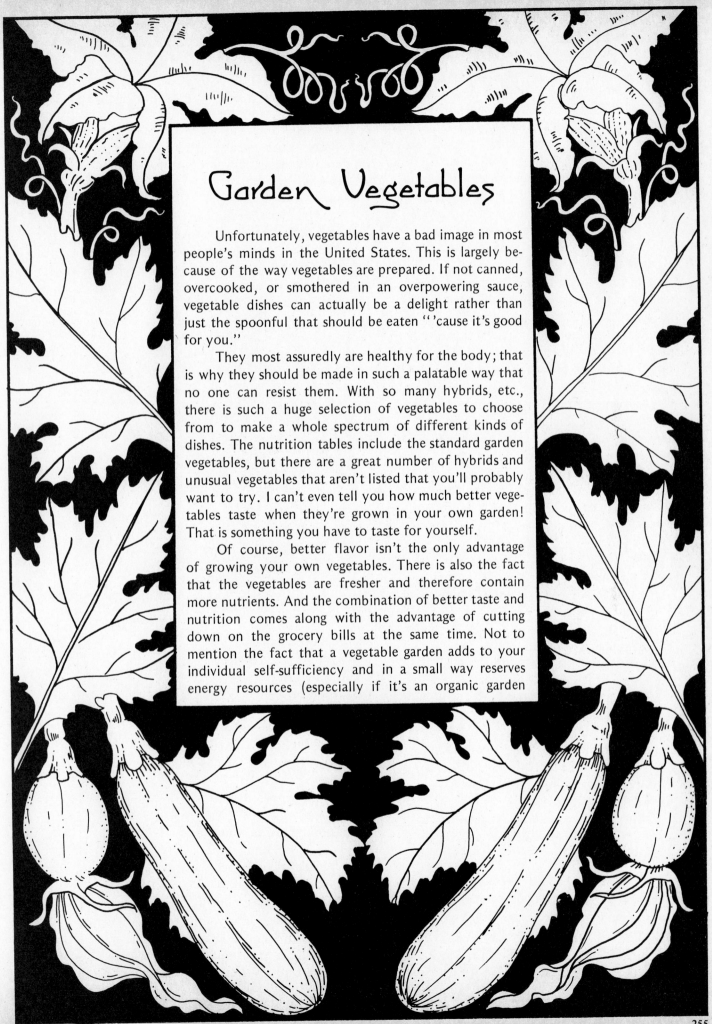

Garden Vegetables

Unfortunately, vegetables have a bad image in most people's minds in the United States. This is largely because of the way vegetables are prepared. If not canned, overcooked, or smothered in an overpowering sauce, vegetable dishes can actually be a delight rather than just the spoonful that should be eaten "'cause it's good for you."

They most assuredly are healthy for the body; that is why they should be made in such a palatable way that no one can resist them. With so many hybrids, etc., there is such a huge selection of vegetables to choose from to make a whole spectrum of different kinds of dishes. The nutrition tables include the standard garden vegetables, but there are a great number of hybrids and unusual vegetables that aren't listed that you'll probably want to try. I can't even tell you how much better vegetables taste when they're grown in your own garden! That is something you have to taste for yourself.

Of course, better flavor isn't the only advantage of growing your own vegetables. There is also the fact that the vegetables are fresher and therefore contain more nutrients. And the combination of better taste and nutrition comes along with the advantage of cutting down on the grocery bills at the same time. Not to mention the fact that a vegetable garden adds to your individual self-sufficiency and in a small way reserves energy resources (especially if it's an organic garden where petroleum-based sprays aren't used) in that you and/or your family would be one less consumer who would be dependent on produce which had to be transported by energy-consuming, refrigerated trucks, or as in Hawaii's case, ships. Individuals' self-sufficiency can lead to a more self-sufficient community.

There is another benefit from growing your own vegetable garden which isn't materially tangible as the benefits mentioned thus far. It is the simple satisfaction derived from being in touch with the earth, being more in tune with the laws of God and nature, and the greater appreciation and respect for life that grows as you watch a tender seedling sprout from the seed, gradually grow, become fruitful, be harvested, or dwindle and die.

Gardening has been a real learning experience for me on all levels, and to even share practical how-to's with you would be another whole book. So, rather than even make an attempt, I'd like to just list here some books that have been a great help in our attempts to become more self-sufficient in our food needs through a backyard garden.

1. **Encyclopedia of Organic Gardening** by the Staff of "Organic Gardening and Farming Magazine," Rodale Books.
2. **The Organic Gardening and Farming Magazine**, a monthly publication. Subscribe by writing to 33 East Minor St., Emmaus, Pennsylvania 18049.
3. **No-Work Garden Book** by Ruth Stout and Richard Clemence, Rodale Press, Inc.
4. **Companion Plants and How to Use Them** by Helen Philbrick and Richard Gregg, Devin-Adair Co., Old Greenwich, Connecticut.
5. **How to Grow More Vegetables** by John Jeavons, Ten Speed Press.

Of course, even with the help of these good books, our first gardens weren't as bountiful as they have become through the many years of experience and learning. The biggest suggestion I can make is to start small and reasonably and expand the garden

as your skills grow!

If a backyard garden is not possible, practical or desirable for you, there is a way that you can garden in your own kitchen: by sprouting, which is also described in this section. This is an easy, foolproof way anyone, anywhere, can grow cheap, organic, fresh vegetables.

Whether in your kitchen or in your garden, raising your own produce is certainly rewarding in more ways than one. Here are some recipes to try your garden vegetables in . . . and they do taste good even if you are using store-bought produce.

RAW VEGETABLE NUT LOAF

2 cups chopped celery
1 cup chopped bell pepper
½ cup grated carrot
1 tsp. oil (opt.)
4 Tbsp. parsley
2 tsp. summer savory
2 Tbsp. sweet basil
¼ tsp. sage powder
½ tsp. salt
¼ tsp. black pepper
1/8 tsp. asafetida
2 cups ground raw peanuts

Chop vegetables. Mix with spices and oil. Run through food grinder, combine with nuts that have been ground and run through grinder again. Place in oiled loaf pan. Mold into shape. Cover and chill at least one hour. Good served in slices plain, with tomato sauce or nut butter sauce.

STUFFED SUMMER SQUASH ☆

3 zucchini or yellow crookneck squash

Creamy Stuffing: ☆

½ cup cream cheese
¼ cup grated carrots
¼ cup chopped olives
2 tsp. soy sauce
1/8 tsp. asafetida
Pinch cayenne

Baco-bits or toasted nuts

Avocado Stuffing: □

½ cup mashed avocado
1 Tbsp. lemon juice
2 tsp. soy sauce
¼ cup nutritional yeast

Toasted sesame or sunflower seeds

Use fairly young squash (up to 5" long). Cut squash in half lengthwise and scoop out center, leaving at least ¼" of solid squash inside of the peel. Finely chop the scooped out squash and mix with ingredients for Creamy Stuffing or the Avocado Stuffing. Stuff squash until heaping full and sprinkle with toasted nuts or seeds, baco-bits, etc. Serve as hors d'oeuvres, or as a salad by putting stuffed half on a bed of lettuce and sprouts, putting tomato wedges around the squash and drizzling with your favorite dressing. You can also use your leftover sandwich spreads or paté as stuffing (be sure to mix in the scooped out squash).

SPROUT STUFFED TOMATOES □

3 large tomatoes

1 medium avocado
¼ tsp. asafetida
2 Tbsp. yogurt
1 Tbsp. lemon juice
1 Tbsp. vegetable oil
Dash of cayenne (opt.)
Pinch of vegetable salt

1½ cups alfalfa sprouts
Lettuce or spinach leaves

Wash, stem and cut tomatoes in half lengthwise. Scoop out the pulp and put in blender with next 6 or 7 ingredients. Blend quickly, pour into a bowl and fold in alfalfa sprouts. Arrange lettuce or spinach leaves on individual salad plates and place a tomato half on top of each one. Fill tomato halves with alfalfa mixture and garnish with a bit of alfalfa sprouts.

RAW CHOP SUEY □

½ cup Chinese peas, sliced
¼ cup each: green and red bell pepper
(slice lengthwise thinly, then in half)
½ cup celery, diced
½ cup carrots, slivered
2 cups Chinese cabbage, bite-sized pieces
1 cup bean sprouts, cut

1 Tbsp. sesame seeds
¼ cup almonds, slivered

1 tsp. toasted sesame oil
Sweet 'n Sour Ginger Dressing
(see recipe this section, p. 262)

Cut vegetables Chinese style—cutting diagonally across the vegetable—in the sizes suggested. Add seeds and nuts. Then toss with last 2 ingredients.

GAZPACHO □

2½ cups chopped tomatoes
Pinch asafetida
2 lemons, juiced
1 Tbsp. olive oil
¼ tsp. oregano
1½ tsp. kelp
¼ cup chopped celery
¼ cup chopped bell pepper
1 Tbsp. soy sauce

Blend ingredients together. Then add sliced scallions, chopped cucumber, grated zucchini, carrots and/or beets. Decorate with chopped parsley.

VEGETABLE ENTREE #1 ☐

2 cups grated carrots
2 cups grated parsnips

1 cup chopped walnuts
1 tsp. fennel seeds

1 tsp. horseradish sauce
or grated radish or daikon
1 - 2 tsp. Dr. Bronner's Balanced
Protein Seasoning

Combine vegetables. Blend next 2 ingredients until walnuts are like flour. Mix all ingredients together. Can serve rolled in lettuce or cabbage leaves.

VEGETABLE ENTREE #2 ☐

4 cups chopped cauliflower
2 cups chopped celery

¼ tsp. asafetida
1 tsp. sesame tahini
1 Morga or other vegetable bouillon cube
6 Tbsp. nut butter
½ tsp. poultry seasoning
2 Tbsp. nutritional yeast
½ tomato

Chop or grind vegetables very fine. Blend last 7 ingredients. Mix together and chill. Good rolled in lettuce or cabbage leaves or flat bread, served in avocado halves or on top of salads.

CARROT ICE CREAM FLOAT ☆

4 cups fresh carrot juice
1 small container honey ice cream

Make 1 quart fresh carrot juice in juicer. Pour 1 cup juice into cups and drop in a few scoops of ice cream into each cup.

CARROT-ALMOND PATÉ ☐

1½ cups almonds

2 cups grated carrots, chopped fine
2 Tbsp. soy sauce
1¼ - 1½ cups water/tomato juice/soup stock
3 Tbsp. Eggless Soy Mayonnaise (opt.)
(see Basic Recipes Section, p. 34)

Blend almonds into a nut meal (raw and roasted will give different tastes). Blend in remaining ingredients until smooth, adding water to desired thickness. Let sit in refrigerator about 30 minutes before serving. Can be used as a dip for, or served on top of, crackers and raw vegetable slices as a canape.

RICH STUFFING FOR FRUITLIKE VEGETABLES

¼ cup celery, diced
½ tsp. asafetida
¼ cup bell pepper, diced
1¼ cups sour cream or yogurt
¼ cup cream cheese
2 Tbsp. flaky nutritional yeast
1 tsp. Spike
2 tsp. honey
½ cup walnuts, chopped fine

Dressing:
1 Tbsp. lemon juice
1 Tbsp. olive oil
2 tsp. flaky nutritional yeast

This stuffing can be used for vegetables such as tomatoes, bell peppers or squash (raw summer or steamed winter). To prepare vegetable to be stuffed, either cut in half to form boats or cut about a quarter of the way down the vegetable from the stem so there will be a bottom and a little cap to top it off. Hollow out the center (if you're stuffing tomatoes, use the pulp in the stuffing and leave out the sour cream or yogurt; if you're stuffing winter squash, reserve the seeds to toast later to make pumpkin seed snacks). Fill the cavity with the stuffing. Serve with dressing on a bed of sprouts and/or greens.

RELISHABLE CAULIFLOWER

2½ cups finely chopped raw
or lightly steamed cauliflower
½ cup catsup
2 Tbsp. lemon juice
2 Tbsp. fresh parsley, chopped fine
2 Tbsp. finely grated radish
½ tsp. soy sauce
1/8 tsp. cayenne
1/8 tsp. asafetida
Few dashes black pepper

Mix all ingredients together and let stand
10 to 20 minutes for flavors to blend. Serve
as a relish or as a stuffing for lettuce or cabbage leaves or bell peppers, celery sticks, etc.

RAW RELISH

1 tomato
1 green bell pepper, diced very fine
1 red bell pepper, diced very fine
1 cucumber, diced very fine
2 average-sized zucchini, diced very fine
3 sticks celery, diced very fine
½ cup honey
½ cup vinegar
1 tsp. asafetida
1 tsp. lemon juice
½ tsp. Spike
1/8 tsp. black pepper

1 Tbsp. psyllium seed powder
or slippery elm powder

Cut and mix all ingredients together and
refrigerate all day or overnight so flavors can
blend. Mix in psyllium seed powder or slippery elm powder to thicken. Serve relish as
is or toss in following toasted spices:

    2 tsp. safflower oil
    1 tsp. dry basil
    ½ tsp. dry oregano
    ½ tsp. coriander powder
Heat oil, add spices and cook until spices
are toasted and aromatic. Pour into relish.

FLOWER & NUT TOSS

1 cup pecans
1 cup cauliflower (cut in small flowerettes)

1 cup yogurt
1 cup sour cream
4 tsp. horseradish
1 tsp. prepared mustard
½ tsp. asafetida
½ tsp. coriander
2 tsp. tahini
2 tsp. peanut butter
1 tsp. honey
1/8 tsp. cayenne
8 Tbsp. finely grated carrots

Mix sauce together well, then mix in cauliflower and pecans. Refrigerate for about
1 hour to let flavors blend. Serve by itself,
on top of salad greens or stuffed in other
raw vegetables.

CUCUMBER-ZUCCHINI-HERB SALAD

2 Tbsp. fresh parsley
2 Tbsp. fresh mint
1 Tbsp. cilantro (Chinese parsley)
4 Tbsp. chopped walnuts·
1 cup yogurt
1 ~~Tbsp. honey~~
2 pinches ~~asafetida~~ green onion/1 clove garlic

1 cucumber
1 zucchini

Wash and pick just the leaves from the herbs
and chop very fine. Mix first 7 ingredients
together in a salad bowl. Wash cucumber and
zucchini and run fork through the skins of
vegetables down the sides. Then slice very
thin across the width of the vegetables. This
should give you round slices with flower-
petallike edges from the fork. Mix all ingredients together. Refrigerate 2 hours to let
herbs blend with sauce.

ROOT-SLAW □

1 cup raw carrots, grated
½ cup raw beets, grated
½ cup raw radish or turnip, grated

½ cup Eggless Soy Mayonnaise
(see Basic Recipes Section, p. 34)

Chop all grated roots finer with a large knife. Mix in Eggless Soy Mayonnaise. Serve on a bed of greens.

HERB DRESSING □

¼ cup oil
3 - 4 Tbsp. lemon juice
½ - 1 tsp. vegetable salt
¼ tsp. thyme
¼ tsp. rosemary
¼ tsp. sage
1/8 tsp. asafetida
2 Tbsp. honey
4 Tbsp. parsley, finely chopped
4 Tbsp. water

Combine ingredients and whiz in blender until creamy and smooth. Serve over salad.

OIL DRESSING #1 □

¼ cup oil
3 Tbsp. lemon juice
1/8 tsp. asafetida
1 tsp. vegetable salt
2 Tbsp. honey
¼ tsp. thyme
¼ tsp. rosemary
¼ tsp. sage
¼ cup chopped parsley

Combine ingredients and blend in blender.

OIL DRESSING #2 □

6 Tbsp. olive oil
2 Tbsp. lemon juice
2 Tbsp. soy sauce
Dash of cayenne
1 Tbsp. nutritional yeast (opt.)

Combine ingredients and blend in blender.

OIL DRESSING #3 □

¼ cup lemon juice
¼ cup oil
¼ cup water
1/8 tsp. asafetida
1 tsp. each of fresh basil, oregano, sage, savory, marjoram, parsley and mint
Pinch salt
Pinch cayenne
2 cups yogurt

Combine ingredients and mix well.

SWEET 'N SOUR GINGER DRESSING ○

1 Tbsp. soy sauce
2 Tbsp. honey
3 Tbsp. water
1 Tbsp. grated fresh ginger
½ tsp. arrowroot

Mix ingredients for sauce in a small pot off of the heat until arrowroot dissolves. Cook over medium heat, stirring constantly until thickened like a gravy. Pour over salad and toss.

VEGIE-NUT CHEESE BALLS ☆

½ cup raw cauliflower, diced very fine
½ cup raw broccoli, diced very fine
½ cup raw bell peppers, diced very fine
½ cup cream cheese
1 tsp. Spike
½ tsp. dill
¼ tsp. asafetida

Mix all ingredients together. This can be refrigerated and rolled into balls as is, used as a stuffing, or served in sandwiches, etc. You can also roll them in the following:

    ½ cup roasted peanuts without skins
    ½ cup sunflower seeds

Blend nuts in the blender until ground fine. Divide nut meal in half and mix half the nuts with vegetable ingredients (listed above). Mix together very well. Roll this mixture into balls and roll the balls in the remaining nut meal so balls are coated. For cheese balls, roll in 2 oz. of grated cheese after rolling mixture in nuts. This recipe can be served as a dip for crackers or served on half of an avocado.

SALSA SAUCE ○

2 tomatoes (large and cored)
½ bell pepper
1 jalapeño pepper
1 yellow chili pepper
2 Tbsp. lemon juice
1 Tbsp. honey
2 Tbsp. olive oil
¼ tsp. asafetida
¼ tsp. cumin powder
1/8 tsp. coriander powder

2 Tbsp. diced bell pepper
2 Tbsp. diced carrot
2 Tbsp. finely chopped cilantro
(Chinese parsley)

Blend first 10 ingredients in blender until smooth. Add last 3 ingredients and refrigerate at least an hour so tastes can blend. Serve with tacos, enchiladas or any other Mexican-style food.

TOMATO CHUTNEY ○

2 lbs. tomatoes, cut
2 tsp. salt
1 tsp. coriander

2 Tbsp. ghee or oil
½ tsp. cumin seed

1 tsp. crushed chilies

2 Tbsp. honey

Combine first 3 ingredients and cook with cover until liquidy. In another skillet, combine next 2 ingredients. When brown, add chilies and toast lightly. Add to tomatoes, cook uncovered until thick. Stir in honey.

BASIC ITALIAN SAUCE ○

¼ cup vegetable oil
2 tsp. sweet basil
2 tsp. oregano leaves
2 tsp. marjoram
1 tsp. ground cumin
¼ tsp. asafetida
1/8 tsp. cinnamon or cloves

4 cups tomato sauce
1 Tbsp. honey
1 tsp. salt
8 cups chopped, assorted vegetables
(celery, bell pepper, zucchini, etc.)

¼ - ½ cup nutritional yeast (opt.)

Combine first 7 ingredients in large skillet or saucepan and lightly toast. Add last 4 ingredients, bring to boil, then lower to simmer and cook until vegetables are just cooked but not overdone — still a bit crispy. Turn off heat and add yeast. Use this sauce for spaghetti or pizza.

HOMEMADE TOMATO SAUCE ○

8 cups tomato purée

12 oz. tomato paste
2 Tbsp. oil
½ tsp. salt (opt.)
½ tsp. black pepper
3 tsp. oregano
2½ tsp. sweet basil
¼ tsp. chili powder
¼ tsp. ground coriander

2 Tbsp. soy sauce
1 Tbsp. honey

Wash, chop and blend tomatoes to measure 8 cups. Combine with next 8 ingredients and cook on medium-high heat, stirring occasionally, until thick. Add soy sauce and honey and mix well. This makes a delicious tomato sauce which can be used in a variety of recipes. Cheese can be added for spaghetti, etc. Another way to use it is to cut an assortment of mixed vegetables into bite-sized pieces — such as green beans, carrots, cauliflower, potatoes, etc. — to measure 4 heaping cups. Combine and steam until tender. Drain and serve topped with heated gravy and tofu balls. Ono! Makes 6 to 8 servings.

TABOULI SALAD ○

2 cups sprouted grain
or 1 cup dry cracked wheat
1-1/3 cups water

1 cup chopped watercress
1 cup finely chopped celery
2 cups chopped parsley
1 cup alfalfa sprouts, chopped fine
10 fresh mint leaves, chopped fine
2 tomatoes, diced
1 cup chopped cucumber (opt.)

Dressing:
6 Tbsp. olive oil
2 Tbsp. lemon juice
2 Tbsp. soy sauce
Dash of cayenne or asafetida (opt.)

Use fresh sprouted grain or cooked, cooled grain. To cook, combine water and cracked wheat and bring to a boil, then cover and lower heat to simmer until done. Cool completely. Combine the sprouted grain or cooked cracked wheat with the next 6 or 7 ingredients and toss well. Whiz dressing ingredients in blender and serve. Good served with crackers and cheese. Makes a complete meal.

POT PIE ○

Gravy for Filling:
2 Tbsp. oil
¼ cup whole grain or legume flour
¼ tsp. asafetida

½ cup nutritional yeast

1½ cups water
2 Tbsp. soy sauce
1/8 tsp. black pepper

3 cups tofu, cut in ½" - 1" cubes
3 cups chopped assorted garden vegetables
(such as celery, carrots, broccoli, etc.)

Toast first 3 ingredients together over medium heat, stirring constantly until flour toasts to golden brown. Mix in the nutritional yeast and stir over medium heat until yeast and flour are a sandy texture. Combine last ingredients in a cup and slowly add a little at a time to the toasting grain mixture, mixing constantly to prevent lumping. Bring to a boil and cook until gravy is thickened. Pour this gravy over the chopped tofu and vegetables in a casserole dish or other large, fairly deep baking pan. Now top this with any of the following toppings.

WHOLE WHEAT TOPPING/BISCUITS ○

1/3 cup oil
1¾ cups whole wheat flour
2½ tsp. baking powder

¾ cup milk
Dried herbs (opt.)

POTATO TOPPING/BISCUITS ○

½ cup butter or margarine
1½ cups mashed potatoes
1½ cups whole wheat flour
2 Tbsp. baking powder

try

¾ cup milk

For the above two toppings, just combine first 3 or 4 ingredients and mix together until a sandy texture. Add liquid and mix thoroughly. The dough will be a little wet and sticky. Turn dough out onto a well-floured counter and knead 10 times. With a rolling pin, roll dough out to ¼" to ½" thick in a sheet as large as the baking dish is. Trim to right size and just set sheet of dough on top of the ingredients already in the baking dish. Bake at 400° for 25 to 30 minutes. If there is any extra dough, it can be rolled out and cut into circles or other shapes and baked into delicious biscuits. To make a shepherd's pie, simply top the tofu, vegetable and gravy mix with mashed potatoes and bake until potatoes start turning golden brown. To serve, just cut with a knife through topping; spoon out topping and tofu-vegetable inside.

TOMATOES PROVENCALE ○

6 large tomatoes
Soy sauce and black pepper

¼ cup olive oil
¼ tsp. asafetida

1 cup whole-grain bread crumbs
1/3 cup fresh parsley, chopped fine

Cut tomatoes in half and season with soy sauce and pepper. Sauté tomato halves in next 2 ingredients on both sides. Lift tomatoes out and gently place in a shallow baking dish or cake pan. Add crumbs to remaining oil and sauté a few minutes. Sprinkle the crumbs and parsley over the top of tomatoes. Heat in 350° oven, but don't allow to become soft and mushy.

MARINATED STUFFED LEAVES O

½ cup chopped pecans
½ cup chopped cashews
(or other nut or seed)

½ cup finely diced celery
½ cup finely diced broccoli
½ cup finely diced zucchini or cauliflower
1 tsp. asafetida
2 tsp. Spike
1 Tbsp. nutritional yeast

1 small avocado, mashed
          or
1 large tomato, diced
and ½ cup nutritional yeast

Raw spinach or swiss chard leaves

Sauce:
2/3 cup olive oil
¼ cup lemon juice
¼ cup soy sauce

Soak first 2 ingredients in water overnight or in hot water for 1 hour. Drain, saving the soaking water for drinking or for use in smoothies, gravies, etc. Make sure nuts and/or seeds are chopped up fine. Mix with next 6 ingredients along with the avocado or tomato and yeast. Then stuff as you would grape leaves, removing ribbing from backs of the leaves if necessary. Place stuffing mixture at bottom end of leaf where the stem starts. Fold the stem end over the stuffing. Then fold side edges over the folded edge that is already covering the stuffing. Now just roll the stuffed pocket into the rest of the leaf. Place stuffed rolls with seam end down, side-by-side in a shallow tray or bowl. Marinate in the sauce a few hours in the refrigerator until leaves become softened, turning them over once to allow top side to marinate also. To serve, lift out of sauce and serve as an entree. You can keep marinating sauce in the refrigerator for repeated use or for use as a salad dressing another day.

GARDEN VEGETABLE BAKE O

4 cups chopped raw green garden vegetables
(use just one kind — like spinach,
broccoli, asparagus or peas — or
mix in a little bit of carrot, etc.)
2 cups milk
¼ cup grated cheese
2 Tbsp. nutritional yeast
1 Tbsp. egg replacer
¼ tsp. chili powder
¼ tsp. curry powder
1/8 tsp. asafetida

Blend all ingredients together in a blender until smooth. This can be poured into an unbaked pie shell (see Basic Recipes Section, p. 33) and baked quiche-style, or poured into an oiled baking pan and baked soufflé-style. Bake at 350° for 30 minutes.

COLD SOUR CREAM POTATO SALAD ☆

3 sticks celery
2 bell peppers
4 tomatoes
1 cucumber

4 potatoes

1 cup sour cream
1 tsp. turmeric
½ tsp. vegetable salt or 2 Tbsp. soy sauce
Pinch each of celery seed, dill weed,
cumin powder, cayenne, dry mustard

Dice first 4 ingredients. Cook potatoes with skins on. Cool and slice into thin rounds. Mix together remaining ingredients and combine with vegetables. Toss gently, refrigerate and serve cold.

Variation: Make potato salad by using the recipe for Breadfruit Salad #1 or #2 (see Breadfruit Section, pp. 111, 112), replacing breadfruit with potatoes.

VEGETABLE ENCHILADA CASSEROLE WITH SOUR CREAM

1 dozen corn tortillas
Light oil for frying

1 cup Homemade TVP (see p. 383)
or soaked Granburger (about ½ cup dry)
1 cup chopped vegetables (diced celery,
grated carrot, chopped cauliflower, etc.)

½ cup shredded cheese

Sauce:
2 Tbsp. salad oil or butter
3½ cups tomato purée
4 Tbsp. chili powder
1 tsp. asafetida
½ tsp. ground cumin
¼ tsp. dried oregano
1 tsp. salt
3 Tbsp. green chilies, chopped
1 yellow chili (pickled), chopped
Juice from pickled chilies

Topping:
Sour cream
Chopped olives

Heat sauce ingredients together. Lightly fry tortillas in oil just enough to soften. Coat tortillas in heated sauce. Place tortilla in ungreased casserole dish. Sprinkle over 1 or 2 Tbsp. Granburger or TVP, 2 Tbsp. vegetable filling (sautéd) and a little sauce. Add remaining tortillas, preparing each the same way. Pour remaining sauce on casserole and top with cheese. Bake uncovered at 350° for 15 minutes or until hot. Garnish with sour cream and olives. Cut in wedges and serve. Serves 4.

Variation: This can also be made like a regular enchilada by rolling filling in the tortillas and laying them side by side in a cake pan, pouring remaining sauce over rolled enchiladas and following rest of steps as for making the casserole.

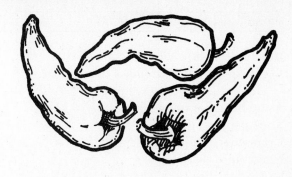

CHILI RELLENOS (Stuffed Peppers) O

6 - 8 fresh chili peppers (or one 7 oz. can)
Cheese or tofu filling
Oil for frying

Batter:
1 cup whole wheat flour
1 tsp. ground cumin
¾ tsp. salt
½ tsp. crushed chilies (opt.)
1 tsp. turmeric
¾ tsp. baking powder
Less than 1 cup water

Mix batter ingredients well until smooth. Stuff chilies with a slice of cheese (½" wide and ½" thick and 1" shorter than the chili). Coat with batter, deep fry until crisp and lay chili in salsa. Serve topped with salsa.

Salsa:
1 cup finely chopped celery
½ medium eggplant, thinly sliced
¼ cup butter or margarine
1 big bunch parsley, chopped fine

10 cut tomatoes

¼ tsp. crumbled oregano
¼ tsp. rosemary
¼ tsp. sweet basil
Pinch curry powder
Pinch asafetida

Sauté vegetables in butter or margarine until tender. Add tomatoes and last 5 ingredients and simmer for 25 to 30 minutes.

VEGETARIAN STROGANOFF ○

1 lb. boiled whole wheat, sesame, artichoke or spinach noodles

¼ cup butter or margarine
2 bell peppers, diced
5 tomatoes, cut into wedges
2 zucchinis, sliced
1 eggplant, diced
1 cup celery, diced
1 cup string beans, chopped

¼ tsp. black pepper
½ tsp. cumin powder
½ tsp. asafetida
1 tsp. chili powder
1 Tbsp. soy sauce
2 Tbsp. fresh parsley, chopped
1 cup Homemade TVP (see p. 383)
or soaked Granburger (about ½ cup dry)

3 cups sour cream
½ cup nutritional yeast

Boil the noodles. In the meantime, sauté the next 7 ingredients or use other assorted vegetables to make about 12 cups chopped vegetables. When vegetables are translucent, add next 7 ingredients and saute a few minutes longer. As soon as the eggplant is cooked, add the last 2 ingredients as well as noodles that have been boiled and drained. This makes a whole meal served with a crisp, fresh salad.

POTATO CREPES ○

3 cups milk (soy or dairy)
1 mashed potato (or sweet potato)
2/3 cup brown rice flour
2 Tbsp. oil
1/8 tsp. nutmeg
1/8 tsp. black pepper

Blend ingredients in blender until smooth. Let stand at room temperature for 1 hour (this is crucial). In a small 8" or 10" heated tefal skillet, pour 1/4 to 1/3 cup batter with one hand, turning skillet with other hand so batter spreads evenly on bottom of skillet. (This should be easy, as the batter should be almost as thin as thick cream.) Cook on medium-high flame until golden brown on one side. (You can see the gold through the top side.) Slide spatula under and gently flip. Let cook about 30 seconds on opposite side. These can be filled with your favorite garden vegetable or main entree and topped with your favorite sauce; or you can layer like tortillas in Enchilada Casserole (see recipe, p. 267).

STOVE-TOP CASSEROLE ITALIANO ☆

2 potatoes
½ eggplant, diced
2 zucchini, sliced
2 carrots, sliced
2 stalks of broccoli
½ head cauliflower
¼ cup olive oil

¼ tsp. asafetida
¼ tsp. vegetable salt
¼ cup water

2 cups Basic Italian Sauce
(see recipe this section, p. 263)
1 cup tofu, drained and crumbled
1 cup grated cheese

Sauté all vegies in wok with oil. Sprinkle in next 3 ingredients while sautéing. Cover and leave on medium flame for 5 minutes. Then pour the Basic Italian Sauce evenly over vegies, sprinkle with tofu and top with cheese. Cover and cook on low heat for 10 to 12 minutes or until potatoes are tender.

HOT DRESSINGS
FOR YOUR FAVORITE SALAD

Make about 6 to 8 cups of your favorite tossed salad and dress with one of the following.

SEEDS 'N THINGS

2 Tbsp. oil
¼ cup sunflower seeds

1 tsp. coriander seeds
1 Tbsp. sesame seeds
1/8 tsp. chili seeds

½ tsp. basil

¼ tsp. cumin powder
1/8 tsp. cloves
1/8 tsp. asafetida
1/8 tsp. black pepper

1 tsp. soy sauce

Premeasure seeds and spices, grouping separately as they are listed. Just before you're ready to serve the salad, toast oil and sunflower seeds until seeds just begin to get golden brown. Add next 3 ingredients and continue stirring and toasting until sesame seeds start to turn a light gold. Add basil and stir, toasting for 10 to 15 seconds. Add next 4 ingredients and stir until all seeds are golden brown and spices can be smelled in the air. Remove from heat, add soy sauce and immediately pour onto prepared salad. Toss well and serve.

MOCK BACON DRESSING

½ cup soaked, sliced strips of yuba
¼ cup soy sauce
¼ tsp. hickory smoke

¼ cup olive oil

3 tsp. vinegar

Refer to Mock Bacon for preparation (see Tofu Section, p. 363). Take soaked yuba and cut into strips about ¾" wide and 2" long. Toss in frying pan with olive oil and fry until crisp. Then pour over prepared salad or fresh spinach leaves. Pour vinegar in pan to deglaze and pour vinegar on salad. Then toss until well-coated and serve.

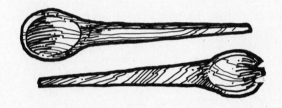

CURRIED POTATO, CAULIFLOWER
AND CREAM CHEESE ☆

1 lb. cauliflower
1 lb. potato

Sauce:
2 Tbsp. butter or margarine
2 tsp. curry powder
1 tsp. sage, ground
½ tsp. paprika
¼ tsp. asafetida

1 tsp. salt
¼ tsp. black pepper
4 oz. cream cheese
2 Tbsp. tomato paste
½ cup milk

Wash and cut vegetables. Place on a steamer rack or in a pot with a little water and steam about 20 minutes until tender. Then combine next 5 ingredients in a skillet and toast on medium-high heat. Add last 5 ingredients and mix until creamy and smooth. Drain cooked vegetables. Mix with sauce and serve.

EGGPLANT PARMIGIANA

Basic Italian Sauce
(see recipe this section, p. 263)

Filling:
Same as filling for Lasagne
(see recipe in Grain Section, p. 418)

Breading:
3 large eggplants

1 cup soy sauce

2 cups cornmeal
2 cups whole wheat flour
2 tsp. salt
2 tsp. black pepper
4 tsp. turmeric
2 tsp. curry powder
2 tsp. cumin powder

1 block tofu, mashed

1 cup grated cheese
or ½ cup nutritional yeast

Slice eggplants in half lengthwise, then slice each half into ¼" thick fillets. Dip in soy sauce, then into cornmeal, flour and spice mixture. Fry on both sides until golden and tender with enough butter or oil to prevent sticking. Continue process until all eggplant is used. Place a little sauce in the bottom of an oblong pan, then a layer of the fried eggplant. Cover with more sauce and sprinkle the tofu on top. Add another layer of fried eggplant and remaining sauce. Top with cheese or nutritional yeast. Bake at 350° for 15 minutes. Serve.

MAHABRINGAL O
(Eggplant, spinach & tomato)

4 tomatoes
1 large eggplant
2 bunches fresh spinach

2 Tbsp. butter or margarine
1 tsp. turmeric
1 tsp. cumin, ground
1/8 tsp. cayenne pepper

½ tsp. salt
½ tsp. honey

Wash and chop vegetables. Put in a pan on medium heat and cover. Allow to simmer until completely cooked. Stir occasionally to prevent sticking. Combine next 4 ingredients in a skillet and toast on medium-high heat. Add to cooked vegetables along with salt and honey. Mix well and serve.

ZESTY GREEN BEANS O

1 lb. fresh string beans

2 Tbsp. butter, margarine or olive oil
1 tsp. coriander, crushed
1 tsp. dill
½ - ¾ cup macadamia nuts
(in halves or quarters)

2 - 4 Tbsp. water

2 Tbsp. lemon juice
½ tsp. salt
¼ tsp. black pepper

Wash beans. Cut at an angle into bite-sized pieces. Place in skillet with next 4 ingredients and sauté for 5 to 10 minutes. Add water, cover and simmer until just tender, about 5 minutes. Remove cover to let any excess water evaporate. Add last 3 ingredients, mix well and serve.

VEGETABLE TURNOVERS ☆

Dough:
Use Puri dough (see Grain Section, p. 421)

Filling:
1 cauliflower
1 lb. peas

1 Tbsp. ghee or oil
½ tsp. cumin seeds
Dash of cayenne pepper
1/8 tsp. ginger powder
or 1 tsp. grated fresh ginger
¼ tsp. cinnamon
1/8 tsp. clove powder
1/8 tsp. nutmeg
1/8 tsp. allspice
1¼ tsp. turmeric
¾ tsp. black pepper
¼ cup soy sauce

Oil or ghee for deep frying

Steam cauliflower and peas until tender. Meanwhile make dough, knead a few minutes and set on counter covered with a bowl turned upside down. In a skillet toast all spices in oil (or dry pan if you prefer). First toast cumin seeds and cayenne pepper until brown. Immediately add steamed vegetables. Lower flame and mash vegetables as they cook. Add remaining ingredients; mix well. Cook 5 minutes, then remove from heat and cool. Pinch off bits of dough and roll out into circles on a smooth surface to about 1/8" thickness. Fill rolled dough with cooled vegetable mix and fold dough over as in making turnovers. Press edges together and crimp like pie dough, or press with edge of a fork along edge to seal well. Make all turnovers at once, placing on an oiled cookie sheet. When they are all rolled, stuffed and sealed, heat ghee (especially delicious when cooked in ghee) or a light oil (like safflower or sunflower) over medium-high heat. The oil or ghee should be hot enough that the turnover sits on the bottom of the pot for a while, mildly bubbling. But the oil should not be so hot that the turnovers, when dropped in, make a lot of bubbles and pop to the top of the oil immediately. The turnovers should come to the surface of the oil after a few minutes. They should cook for about 15 minutes until golden brown and they make a hollow sound when lightly tapped with a spoon. Remove from oil and place on paper towels. If cooked properly, the crust will be crispy, light and smooth. If the oil is too hot, the crust will have bubbles on the surface and be soft.

STUFFED LEAF ROLLS □

Lettuce or cabbage leaves

Filling:
1 cup tomato, diced
1 cup lettuce, sliced fine
1 cup grated carrot or turnip
½ cup avocado, diced in ¼" cubes
¼ cup celery, diced

¼ cup Eggless Soy Mayonnaise
(see Basic Recipes Section, p. 34)
2 Tbsp. tomato sauce
1 tsp. curry powder
1 tsp. soy sauce

Wash and drain fresh lettuce or cabbage leaves individually, breaking each individual leaf off. Combine next 5 ingredients together in a bowl. Mix next 4 ingredients together and add to grated and chopped vegetable mixture. Spread Nutty Protein Gravy (see Fresh Leaves Section, p. 311) on leaves that have been washed and drained. At one end of leaf, lay a strip of filling. Roll from filled end, jelly roll or strudel fashion. Fasten roll closed with toothpick. A good variation is Hoisin Sauce on the leaves (see recipe in Miso Section, p. 389) and a stir-fried Chinese vegetable dish for stuffing.

VEGETARIAN CHOP SUEY ○

3 cups celery, thinly sliced
2 cups bean sprouts
1 cup water chestnuts, thinly sliced
½ cup sweet peas (Chinese)

Sauce:
3 Tbsp. oil
¼ cup water
½ tsp. salt
¼ tsp. black pepper

¼ tsp. salt
1 tsp. soy sauce
1½ tsp. arrowroot mixed with
enough water to make a paste

Put sauce ingredients in a skillet. Then add vegies, except peas, and cook with lid on for about 10 to 15 minutes. Add peas last 5 minutes. Drain sauce from vegies to measure 1¼ cups (if not enough, add water). Add last 3 ingredients to sauce over heat and mix well until thickened. Add cooked vegies, mix well and serve with rice.

VEGETABLE CORN BREAD ○

1 cup whole wheat flour
1 cup yellow cornmeal
4 tsp. baking powder
½ tsp. chili powder
¼ tsp. salt
¼ cup milk powder
½ tsp. asafetida (opt.)

¼ cup honey
1 stick butter or margarine, melted
¾ cup milk
¼ cup diced bell pepper
¼ cup corn
¼ cup finely chopped string beans
or kale or comfrey, etc.

Mix dry ingredients. Add remaining ingredients and mix well. Put in an oiled 8-inch square pan and bake at 350° for 25 to 30 minutes.

VEGETABLE PATTIES WITH SAUCE ○

Batter:
2 cups chickpea flour (or whole wheat)
2 tsp. ground cumin
2 tsp. turmeric
1½ tsp. ground coriander
¼ tsp. cinnamon
¼ tsp. allspice
1½ tsp. salt
1/8 tsp. ground red pepper
2 tsp. curry powder
2 Tbsp. soy sauce
1 cup warm water

1 medium head cauliflower
1 medium potato or breadfruit

Ghee for frying

Sauce:
8 cups tomato purée

½ tsp. black pepper
2 tsp. sweet basil
2 tsp. oregano
¼ tsp. chili powder
¼ cup soy sauce
½ tsp. oregano leaves
3 Tbsp. ghee

Grate cauliflower and potato. Set aside. Place chickpea flour in bowl with spices. Add water gradually, mixing out any lumps. Combine the grated cauliflower and potato with the batter and mix thoroughly. Drop by spoonfuls into medium-hot ghee. Fry 20 minutes, until golden brown and crispy. Remove and drain. Then prepare sauce by placing blended tomatoes in a skillet on high flame. Add spices and simmer until thick. Serve over fried patties.

VEGETABLE ROAST   ○

3 medium potatoes
1 medium yam

1/3 cup oil
½ tsp. asafetida
½ tsp. basil
½ tsp. oregano

1 Tbsp. Spike
½ cup nutritional yeast

Wash potatoes and cut into bite-sized pieces. Add the next 4 ingredients and mix well. Bake at 350° for 45 minutes. Remove and add last 2 ingredients. Turn potatoes and bake 15 minutes more or until crisp. Remove from oven and serve as is or sprinkle with more yeast.

VEGETABLE STRUDEL   ☆

Filling:
1 Tbsp. butter or margarine
½ tsp. powdered cumin
¼ tsp. asafetida

4 cups finely chopped, assorted vegetables
1 tomato, chopped

2 Tbsp. nutritional yeast
¼ cup cheese or cream cheese

Toast first 3 ingredients together until spices brown and aroma fills the air. Add vegetables and stir-fry a short while, just until vegetables look translucent (they will cook further in baking). Turn off heat and add last 2 ingredients, stirring until cheese melts. Use as a filling in the Pineapple Strudel recipe (see Pineapple Section, p. 216) and follow assembly directions there.

GARDEN STEW   ○

4 large beets
3 carrots
5 potatoes
2 crookneck squash
2 cups chopped celery
Water

1 Tbsp. Spike
¼ cup olive oil

1 Tbsp. soy sauce
½ cup nutritional yeast

Chop first 5 ingredients together into 1" to 2" chunks. Put in a large pot and cover with water. Add next 2 ingredients. Mix together well. Cover and simmer over a low heat for 4 hours. The last 15 minutes add yeast and soy sauce. Stir well and serve.

CREAMED SQUASH AND VEGETABLE SOUP

3 cups mashed, cooked butternut squash (approximately 2 lbs. raw)

3 cups coconut milk

1 tsp. sweet basil
¼ tsp. asafetida
1 tsp. salt
½ tsp. black pepper

1 cup corn
1 cup peas
½ cup carrot, cut in cubes
½ cup thinly sliced celery

Cut squash and remove seeds. Place in baking pan with a little water face down and bake at 375° until soft (30 to 45 minutes). Remove and cool a bit. Scrape away from skin and mash. Combine with coconut milk and spices. Blend in batches in blender until smooth. Place in saucepan with prestrained vegetables. Simmer for about 15 minutes; then serve topped with a sprig of fresh parsley.

WONDERFUL POT

3 - 4 potatoes, diced
3 carrots, sliced
1 small stalk of celery, chopped
1 small head of cauliflower (flowerettes)
2 zucchini, sliced
6 - 8 medium-sized tomatoes, chopped
1 tsp. basil
1½ tsp. marjoram
2 - 3 bay leaves
½ cup butter or margarine
¼ cup soy sauce or 2 Tbsp. miso
4 - 6 cups water

Combine all ingredients in a 2-quart pan or large pot and cook covered on low heat for 1 hour or until vegetables are tender.

POTATO CELERY SOUP

4 cups water
4 medium-sized potatoes
1 medium stalk of celery, chopped
½ cup butter or margarine

¼ cup nutritional yeast
2 Tbsp. soy sauce or ¾ tsp. vegetable salt
2 Tbsp. nut or seed butter
(sesame, almond, etc.)

Combine first 4 ingredients in a saucepan, bring to a boil and simmer for 10 to 12 minutes or until tender. With slotted spoon, take out 2 cups of vegies. Then combine remaining vegies and soup stock in a blender with the last 3 ingredients and whiz until smooth. Combine with the vegetables and serve.

RATATOUILLE

2 zucchini, diced
1 celery stalk, diced in ½" cubes
1 large eggplant, diced
4 fresh tomatoes, diced
2 potatoes, diced
½ cup olive oil
1 Tbsp. oregano
2 - 3 bay leaves
1 tsp. vegetable salt
½ tsp. black pepper
10 capers

Mix all ingredients and place in casserole dish. Bake 1 hour at 350° F. Very rich. Serve hot or iced.

RICE SALAD

2 cups cooked brown rice
1 cup chopped celery
1 cup alfalfa sprouts
1 cup shredded carrot
1½ cups parsley
Pinch asafetida

Combine ingredients and toss in Oil Dressing #2 (see recipe this section, p. 262). Serve on a lettuce leaf.

BROCCOLI SOUP

1 big bunch of broccoli, chopped
4 Tbsp. butter or margarine
¼ cup soy sauce or 1 Tbsp. miso
2 tsp. basil
1 tsp. marjoram
3 cups water

Combine all ingredients in a 2-quart saucepan and bring to a boil. Cover and simmer for 12 to 15 minutes or until broccoli is tender. Take off heat and let cool for a few minutes. Then take half the soup and put in a blender; whiz until smooth. Repeat until all is blended and serve. Can top with sour cream or yogurt and garnish with a carrot curl or parsley.

SWEET SPICED ROOT VEGETABLES ○

2 potatoes, diced
2 carrots, diced
4 small, tender beets, diced

6 - 8 pitted dates, chopped
1½ tsp. ground coriander
4 Tbsp. butter or margarine

1/3 cup water

Dice all roots in about ½" cubes and set aside. In a wok, combine next 3 ingredients and saute dates until almost mushy. Add diced roots. Mix well until the vegies are partially covered with date-spice mixture. Add the water, cover and cook on medium heat for 10 minutes or until vegies are tender. Can top with a scoop of yogurt or Soy Whipped Cream (see Basic Recipes Section, p. 34) when serving. Serves 4.

STIR-FRY CHINESE STYLE ○

¼ cup oil
½ tsp. asafetida
¼ tsp. black pepper

8 cups mixed hard vegetables
(carrots, cauliflower, celery, etc.)

1 Tbsp. soy sauce
1 Tbsp. ginger
1 tsp. honey
4 tomatoes, chopped
2 cups quick cooking vegetables
(zucchini, Chinese peas, etc.)

Prepared gluten sliced in strips
(see recipes in Grain Section, pp. 418, 419)

Sauté first 3 ingredients. Add hard vegetables and stir-fry until vegetables become translucent. Add next 5 ingredients. Stir in, lower heat, cover and simmer until vegetables are tender (usually 5 to 10 minutes). Add Braised Gluten or Char Siu gluten strips as garnish, or use fried tofu pieces.

GARDEN VEGETABLE PIE ☆

Pie Crust:
1 cup whole wheat flour and
1 cup unbleached white flour
or 2 cups whole wheat pastry flour
½ - ¾ cup butter or margarine, soft
1/8 tsp. salt
1/8 tsp. thyme
1/8 tsp. sage

Water to moisten

Filling:
2 - 3 cups cooked and
mashed sweet potatoes

½ cup cauliflower
¼ cup carrots, diced
¼ cup slivered green beans or Chinese peas
¼ cup corn
¼ cup eggplant, diced
½ cup comfrey, chopped,
or ¼ cup comfrey and ¼ cup kale, chopped
¼ cup butter or margarine

1 Tbsp. grated ginger, sautéd in butter
1 - 2 tsp. salt
½ tsp. black pepper
2 - 3 tsp. soy sauce
¾ tsp. asafetida
2 Tbsp. honey

Mix 6 crust ingredients well. Add enough water to moisten and hold together. Cut in half and roll between two sheets of wax paper. Fit in pie pan. Crimp edges, pierce well with a fork and bake at 350° for 10 minutes. Combine mashed sweet potatoes and lightly steamed vegetables along with remaining ingredients. Mix well and spread in pie shell. Roll out another pie crust. Place on top, crimp edges, pierce with fork and bake at 375° for 15 to 25 minutes, until top is golden. Serve warm as a main course.

FRESH PUMPKIN & COCONUT PIE

Crust:
1 cup whole wheat pastry flour
1 cup toasted coconut
1 stick butter or margarine
¼ - ½ cup honey
Water, if necessary

Filling:
1 fresh small pumpkin (2 cups)
½ stick butter or margarine
½ cup thick coconut milk
½ cup honey
1 Tbsp. molasses
¼ tsp. cinnamon
1/8 tsp. nutmeg
1/8 tsp. ginger
1/8 tsp. cloves
1/8 tsp. allspice

Mix crust ingredients together and press into a 9" pie pan. Then cut pumpkin, remove seeds and steam until tender. Cool, remove skins and mash. Make the coconut milk by blending 1 cup grated coconut with ½ cup very hot water and then pressing through sieve to extract thick milk. Measure ½ cup. Add to mashed pumpkin with remaining ingredients and mix well. Pour into pie shell and bake at 400° for 15 to 20 minutes. Top with toasted coconut or coconut cream.

CANDIED BEETS ◯

2½ cups (approximately) diced beets
Water

1 Tbsp. butter or margarine
1 Tbsp. honey or maple syrup

Dice beets into ¼" to ½" cubes and cover about three-fourths of the way with water in a skillet. Put the lid on and bring to a boil, turn heat down and let simmer until beets are tender. Remove lid from skillet and let water cook out (watch carefully so it won't burn). Add last 2 ingredients and stir constantly until they thicken and coat the beets. Carrots are delicious prepared this way also.

CURRIED YAMS ◯

4 medium yams, cut into 1" cubes

4 Tbsp. oil
1 tsp. asafetida

1½ cups vegetable stock or water
2½ Tbsp. curry powder
2 Tbsp. lemon juice
1½ Tbsp. honey

Parboil yams 10 minutes or until soft. Drain, save the water and use later. Set aside yams. Heat oil and brown or toast asafetida. Add next 4 ingredients, mix well and bring to a boil. Add parboiled yams. Then reduce to a simmer and cook until all the liquid evaporates. You can cook other steamed vegetables in the same way.

CARROT HALVAH

10 - 12 lbs. carrots or beets

1 cup butter or margarine
2 cups honey

½ tsp. cardamom
½ tsp. cinnamon
Tiny pinch black pepper

Grate or chop carrots in a food grinder. Put half of the butter or margarine in a wok or large pot to melt. Add carrots and stir in with butter thoroughly. Cover and simmer until carrots are tender. Add rest of butter and honey. Cover and simmer 20 to 30 minutes, stirring occasionally to prevent sticking and burning. When carrots are soft and mashable, remove lid and turn up heat. Stand over wok or pot and stir constantly until carrots reach a jamlike consistency (like a dry, mashed potato). Add last 3 ingredients and any dried fruit or nuts, if you like. You can use either a bumper crop of carrots or beets or a combination of both. Good served hot or cold as a dessert.

GARDENING IN THE KITCHEN

And God said:
"Behold, I have given you every herb-bearing seed which is upon the face of all the earth, and every tree in which is the fruit of a tree-yielding seed. To you it shall be for meat."
Genesis 1:29

Self-sufficiency begins with the self, with each individual working for self-sufficiency in his own life. Some people have more facility than others to work towards self-sufficiency, but one thing everyone can do is grow sprouts. Whether we live in condominiums, suburban houses, or have our own homesteads, growing sprouts is one easy way to become more self-sufficient for our food needs.

Sprouting is a foolproof way of gardening. You don't have to worry about warding off garden pests with sprays, etc. The result is cheap, organic, vital, fresh vegetables at your fingertips. No more paying high prices in grocery stores for salad greens and food which has lost much nutritional value between the time of harvest and appearance on the supermarket shelf. And all of this accomplished with a minimal amount of labor.

I would like to share the how-to's of sprouting with you and the benefits you can experience in your own life. But the test of the pudding is in the eating!

Just about any whole seed, grain, nut or legume can be sprouted. One warning: when buying your seeds, be sure to get seeds that have not been treated with chemicals. Heat treated and/or broken seeds will not sprout. Hulled seeds will not always sprout because they may be broken or bruised. Pick out all broken or shriveled seeds, as they will not sprout and may rot and ruin the whole batch.

Certain nuts and seeds are better germinated (grown only until sprout emerges from seed—no longer than ½") than actually sprouted, as they tend to become bitter when they get long.

Nuts and seeds to be germinated only are as follows: Almonds, hazelnuts, peanuts,

hulled sunflower seeds, corn, pumpkin, squash and sesame seeds.

Germinating does so much for increasing nutritional value. For example, about 10% of nutritional value is digestible when nuts are eaten raw. Soaking overnight increases digestibility to 20%, and when made into nut or seed milk, up to 40% of the nutritional value becomes digestible.

All you need to do is soak your seeds or nuts overnight. The following morning, drain off the water. (This is full of nutrition, so don't throw it away. It can be used for making nut or seed milk or used in salad dressing, etc.) Then just follow directions for soilless sprouting method. The nutritional value of your nuts or seeds will double after sprouting for two days, rather than using them immediately after an overnight soaking.

In our home, we always start the day off by having a seed or nut milk along with our breakfast fruit (see Nuts and Seeds Section for Breakfast Drink and Nut Milk recipes, p. 441).

There are basically two methods of sprouting — soilless and with soil. The first step for both is the same: soak seeds in enough water to cover them overnight. You can save the water from soaking all seeds and nuts for use in nut milk smoothies and all the water from wheat for rejuvelac, a very healthful drink. But the water from the legumes must be cooked before using or put on house plants.

Soilless Method
(4 to 5 days sprouting time)

Step 1

You will need:
1. A wide-mouth jar
2. Plastic screen or thin cotton cloth
3. Strong rubber band
4. Any of the following seeds

Seeds that do especially well with this method are:
(amount per quart)

Radish. . . . . 1½ Tbsp.
Alfalfa. 1½ Tbsp.
Mung bean. . . . . .½ cup
Lentil . . . . .½ cup
Adzuki .½ cup
Wheatberries. . . . . 1½ cups
Cress . . . . 1½ Tbsp.
Mustard. . . . . 1½ Tbsp.
Fenugreek. . . . . 1½ Tbsp.
Soybeans. . . . . .½ cup
Garbanzo beans. . . . . .½ cup
Pintos, etc. . . . . .½ cup

Step 2

Drain soaking water from seeds through the screen. (Rubberband the screen securely to top of jar.) Keep water for drinking, for use in soups and gravies, or to water plants. Rinse seeds well.

Step 3

Turn jar upside down in dish drainer, wire stand or specially made sprout stand and put in a dark, warm place. It is important to invert jars to allow water to drain.

Step 4

Rinse seeds through screen 2 to 4 times a day. Keep jar upside down; gently shake bottle to evenly distribute seeds around walls of jar.

Step 5

After 4 to 5 days, or when sprouts are 1" or 2" long, put sprouts in sun for a couple of hours to develop bright green color (vitamin A and chlorophyll).

All large beans, like soybeans and garbanzos, etc., should only be germinated to no longer than ½" (don't allow leaves to form) and should be steamed or cooked for 10 to 15 minutes (unsprouted takes hours) before eating. Wheatberries grown this way should not be allowed to germinate over ¼" long.

With Soil Method
(1 week sprouting time)

Step 1

You will need:
1. 12" x 22" sprouting trays, which can be gotten at most garden nurseries.
2. Enough soil to fill each tray 2/3 of the way full of soil.
3. Any of the following seeds.

Seeds that do well in soil:
(amount per tray)

Buckwheat .2 cups
Wheatberries. . . . . .2 cups
Sunflower seeds (unhulled). . . . . . . .3 cups

Step 2

(The same as soilless sprouts.)

Step 3

(The same as soilless sprouts.)

Step 4

Fill trays 2/3 of the way full with soil and water to dampen. Spread sprouted seeds evenly on smoothed-out dirt which is damp but still crumbly. (Seeds should touch but not be on top of each other.) Spread all the way to the edges. Do not cover seeds with more soil.

Step 5

Water as you would a regular garden, just enough to keep soil moist. Don't overwater!

Seeds grown this way take about one week until they are ready for harvest. Wheat grass is ready to eat when it is 8" high. Cut with scissors just above ground. Let it grow up again, cut, eat and start procedure again.

Soil can be composted by putting in a special corner of your garden or in a trash can and left until all the roots die and compost, about three weeks. Soil is then ready to be used again. These trays can be grown on a balcony or lanai, a backyard, garage, or even inside your apartment. Sunflower and buckwheat only grow up once and are ready when hulls fall off. Cut with scissors and use in a salad. You can cut these over a week's time. After a week, extra sprouts can be put in airtight containers in the refrigerator. They will keep for a few days if properly covered.

In our highly technological society, there is one energy source often overlooked or looked down upon as the last resort. People's bodies are powered by solar energy. This is easily seen when eating sprouts you've just grown. People consume foods which have collected and stored energy from the sun either directly (vegetables, fruits, grains) or indirectly (dead bodies of animals which have fed upon plants). But in our industrialized society, instead of using solar energy obtained from eating vegetation to do work, we use solar energy stored in past generations of plants (coal, oil) to power machines to do the work.

Energy obtained from eating must be burned off, as too much energy consumed and stored in the body causes disease, obesity, etc. To expend this excess energy we have created "leisure activities" (physical work which doesn't produce anything) such as jogging, exercise clinics, etc. Since we must use the energy we consume, one alternative energy source that we should seriously consider is people power, aided by appropriate and people-oriented technology.

"The technology of production by the masses, making use of the best of modern knowledge and experience is conducive to decentralization, compatible with the laws of ecology, gentle in its use of scarce resources and designed to serve the human person instead of making him the servant of machines."
— E. F. Schumacher, Small Is Beautiful

Many of today's problems stem from the underutilization and misdirection of people's energy and overdependence on stored energy of past generations of living entities. Unemployment, pollution, inflation (overconsumption and underproduction) and bad health are a few obvious results of a system that is not in harmony with the arrangements of God and Nature.

ORANGE JULIUS ALFALFA

1 cup alfalfa sprouts
3 cups orange juice
6 ice cubes
1/3 cup powdered milk
¼ tsp. vanilla

Blend all ingredients in a blender until smooth. A refreshing drink!

SPROUTED WHEAT MILK

2 cups sprouted wheatberries
(about 2 days old)
1 quart water or rejuvelac
¼ cup pitted dates

Blend ingredients together until smooth. Strain through strainer. Use as a drink, for smoothies, baking, etc.

GREEN DRINK

1 cup alfalfa sprouts
¼ cup parsley
1½ cups pineapple juice
2 Tbsp. cress sprouts
¼ cup mint leaves
1 cup cold water
1 tsp. honey (opt.)
1 Tbsp. lemon juice

Blend ingredients 2-3 minutes until smooth. Strain and serve cold or over crushed ice.

SPROUTED WHEAT TREATS

1¼ cups sprouted wheat
2 cups pitted dates

1 cup chopped nuts
½ cup sesame seeds
¼ cup honey
2 Tbsp. nut butter or nut meal
2 Tbsp. grated orange or lemon rind

Pecan or walnut halves

Put first 2 ingredients through a food grinder. Work in the rest of the ingredients with hands. Form into balls with a pecan or walnut half in the center. Roll each ball in shredded coconut. Ready to eat or freeze.

SPECIAL SPROUT SPREAD

1 cup alfalfa, cabbage,
clover or radish sprouts
½ cup mung bean sprouts
½ cup sprouted wheatberries

try?

1/8 tsp. asafetida
3 Tbsp. vegetable oil
1 - 2 Tbsp. lemon juice
1/8 tsp. vegetable salt

Grind first 3 ingredients. Blend in the next 4 ingredients. Refrigerate until ready to serve. This is a good basic spread that can be made ahead and kept in the refrigerator up to a week. Add a little cream cheese or more oil and it can be used as a dip.

SWEET SPROUTED WHEAT BALLS

½ cup cream cheese
1 cup sprouted wheatberries
1 cup chopped nuts
1 cup raisins

Wheat germ or sesame seeds

Mix all ingredients until well-blended. Shape into bite-sized balls and roll in toasted wheat germ or sesame seeds. Refrigerate.

SPROUTED MUESLI

½ cup sesame seeds
½ cup sunflower seeds

½ cup chopped dates
½ cup chopped dried apples
½ cup raisins or currants
½ cup sprouted wheat, ground

Blend first 2 ingredients to a fine meal. Mix in a bowl with last 4 ingredients. To serve, moisten with apple juice.

HI-PROTEIN SALAD

3 cups alfalfa sprouts
1 cup germinated sunflower seeds
1 cup cubed tofu

1 Tbsp. soy sauce
1 Tbsp. nutritional yeast
1 Tbsp. olive oil
Juice of ½ lemon

Combine first 3 ingredients. Mix together last 4 ingredients and pour over sprouts and tofu for a power-packed salad.

RAW SPROUTED WHEAT MUSH

2 cups sprouted wheat
1 cup water
¼ cup dates, raisins or figs

Blend all ingredients in blender until smooth and creamy. Serve as is or topped with chopped nuts and/or fruit.

SPROUTED WHEAT MILK CREAM

3 cups sprouted wheatberries
2 cups water
¼ cup pitted dates

1 Tbsp. carob powder
2 bananas
Pinch cinnamon

Blend first 3 ingredients and strain as for Sprouted Wheat Milk (see recipe, p. 281). Pour liquid back into blender and blend in next 3 ingredients. Blend until smooth. This is delicious with 2 Tbsp. of peanut butter blended in at the end for variation.

NUTTY SPROUT SALAD

2 cups alfalfa sprouts
Salad greens
1/3 cup finely chopped hazelnuts
(or almonds, etc.)

Herb Dressing:
¼ cup apple cider vinegar
2 Tbsp. water
¼ tsp. marjoram
¼ tsp. basil
Pinch thyme
Pinch asafetida
1 tsp. vegetable salt
2/3 cup sesame oil

Combine salad ingredients. Then whiz dressing ingredients in blender until smooth and pour to taste over Nutty Sprout Salad. (Yields ¾ cup dressing.)

FRUIT & SPROUT BREAKFAST ☐

1 ripe banana
2 Tbsp. honey

3 apples, grated
3 Tbsp. lemon juice

1 cup germinated sunflower seeds
1 cup wheat sprouts
½ cup wheat germ

Chopped almonds

In a large bowl, mash and whip banana with honey. Add next 2 ingredients and mix well. Fold in next 3 ingredients. Serve in individual bowls and top with chopped almonds. May also fold in Soy Whipped Cream (see Basic Recipes Section, p. 34) just before serving, or add as a garnish. Makes 4 generous servings.

MARINATED RICE SPROUTS ◯

1 cup germinated brown rice
1 cup mung or soy sprouts
1/8 tsp. asafetida
¼ cup chopped pimento or tomato
¼ cup chopped green pepper
¼ cup diced celery

¼ cup salad oil
¼ cup apple cider vinegar
½ tsp. honey
½ tsp. vegetable salt
Pinch black pepper

Combine first 6 ingredients. In a small bowl, mix together last 5 ingredients for the dressing. Add dressing to sprout mixture and toss lightly. May be served chilled, but the flavor improves if marinated overnight.

SPROUTED WHEAT SURPRISE ☐

1¼ cups sprouted wheat
2 cups pitted dates

1 cup chopped nuts
½ cup sesame seeds
¼ cup honey
2 Tbsp. nut butter
2 Tbsp. grated orange or lemon rind

Put first 2 ingredients through food grinder. Work next 5 ingredients in with hands and form into balls. Roll in shredded coconut.

SWEET ESSENE BREAD (Sun Bread) ◯

Grind desired amount of sprouted wheatberries (2 to 3 days old) in food grinder. Shape into bread or biscuit shapes and bake as described in directions for variations that follow.

Variety #1:
2 cups ground, sprouted wheatberries
½ cup chopped nuts or seeds
½ cup chopped raisins
1 tsp. orange rind

Variety #2:
2 cups ground, sprouted wheatberries
½ cup raisins
¼ tsp. cinnamon
1/8 tsp. cardamom
Few drops vanilla

Variety #3:
2 cups ground, sprouted wheatberries
½ cup raisins
½ cup shredded coconut
1/3 cup carob powder

Combine ingredients and mix together well, kneading with hands if necessary. Form into one large, round loaf or several small ones. Place on a baking sheet covered with a thin screen (to keep bugs off) and set in the sun all day to bake. Or set in the oven (without a screen) at 200° to bake all day. Cool and serve. All varieties are good served just plain or with butter or cream cheese. Keeps best in the refrigerator.

RAW SPROUT BURGERS ⭕

2 cups ground wheatberries
2 Tbsp. ghee or oil
2 tsp. cumin seeds
2 tsp. turmeric
2 tsp. ground coriander
½ tsp. black pepper
½ tsp. cayenne
2 tsp. cinnamon
¼ tsp. asafetida
1 tsp. salt

Place wheatberries in wide-mouthed jar covered with screen and secured with a rubber band. Cover with water and soak in jar overnight. Drain through screen. Save water (rejuvelac) for drinking or watering plants. Place jar at angle (for drainage) in dark, warm place. Rinse 2 to 4 times per day. Ready in about 4 to 5 days — in 3 days for this recipe. Measure 2 cups and run through food grinder. Place next 9 ingredients in skillet and toast them. Add to ground wheatberries and mix well. Form into patties and either bake in full sunlight for 8 hours, turning them over at noon, or in oven at 200° for 4 hours. Serve on whole wheat bun with dressing, etc.

SPROUTED WHEATBERRY PATTIES ⭕

2 cups ground wheatberries
1 Tbsp. soy sauce
½ cup nutritional yeast

2 Tbsp. oil
2 tsp. cumin seeds
2 tsp. turmeric
2 tsp. ground coriander
½ tsp. black pepper
¼ tsp. asafetida
1/8 tsp. ground cloves

Combine first 3 ingredients. Toast spices and add to first ingredients. Make into patties and bake in sun all day or in oven at 200°, turning once.

SOUTHERN STYLE SOY SPROUTS ⭕

2 Tbsp. oil
1/8 tsp. asafetida
1/3 cup celery

2 cups tomatoes
¼ bay leaf
1 tsp. vegetable salt

2 cups soy sprouts

Heat oil and sauté with next 2 ingredients. Then add next 3 ingredients and simmer for 10 minutes. Remove bay leaf and add sprouts. Bring to boil, then lower to simmer for 15 - 20 minutes until sprouts are tender. You may also use any other large, starchy bean in place of soybeans, such as mung bean or lentil sprouts. Cook these only 8 to 10 minutes.

BUCKWHEAT SPROUTS

SIMPLE SPROUT SAUTÉ ○

2 Tbsp. sesame seeds

1 Tbsp. oil
1/8 tsp. asafetida

2 cups mung bean sprouts
Soy sauce to taste

Toast sesame seeds in dry frying pan until seeds begin to pop. Stir to prevent burning. Set aside. Heat oil in heavy wok or skillet and lightly toast asafetida. Add sesame seeds and last 2 ingredients. Stir-fry until sprouts become translucent. Yields 4 servings.

CREAMY FRESH VEGIE ASPIC ○

1 cup agar-agar flakes (2 sticks)
1¼ cups cold water

¼ cup lemon juice
½ tsp. grated lemon rind

1/8 tsp. asafetida
1 large cucumber, peeled and chopped
1 grated carrot
½ cup celery, diced
½ cup green pepper, diced
1½ cups Eggless Soy Mayonnaise
(see Basic Recipes Section, p. 34)
2 tsp. soy sauce
2 cups cubed tofu
1 cup chopped alfalfa, mung
or other mild-tasting sprout
¼ cup radish or fenugreek sprouts

Mix agar-agar flakes in water and let set 10 minutes. Then bring to a boil until dissolved. Remove from heat to cool. Add next 2 ingredients and refrigerate until it starts to set. Then mix and fold in last 10 ingredients. When firm, serve on lettuce leaves.

Fruit Variation: Omit vegetables and soy sauce. Add 2 cups chopped fruit in season, ½ cup grated coconut and sprouts.

MOCK EGG ROLL ○

2 Tbsp. butter or margarine
2 Tbsp. whole wheat flour
2/3 cup milk

1 tsp. soy sauce
2/3 cup grated cheese
¼ tsp. basil
¼ tsp. thyme
1/8 tsp. asafetida
¼ cup diced celery

1 tsp. egg replacer
2 Tbsp. water
2 cups barely sprouted
wheatberries (ground)

1 cup whole-grain bread crumbs
2/3 cup wheat germ

Melt butter or margarine in small pan. Add flour and mix well. (Toast for a while for a nutty-tasting gravy. For a plainer gravy, add milk immediately.) Add milk, stirring until smooth. Add next 6 ingredients, mixing until gravylike. Remove from heat. Add next 3 ingredients and let cool somewhat. Mix in last 2 ingredients and form into croquettes or balls. Dip into bowl of wheat germ and coat on both sides. Flatten slightly and fry on low heat until browned. Serve with mustard or sweet-sour sauce for Oriental touch.

BEAN SPROUT SAUTÉ ○

2 Tbsp. butter or margarine
½ tsp. ground coriander
¼ tsp. asafetida
½ tsp. celery seed
½ tsp. grated fresh ginger

6 cups mung bean sprouts
½ cup finely chopped green pepper

¾ tsp. vegetable salt

Sauté first 5 ingredients for 2 minutes, then add next 2 ingredients and saute for 5 to 7 minutes or until sprouts look a little translucent. Add vegetable salt, stir and serve.

(From U.S.D.A. Agriculture Handbook #8)
GARDEN VEGETABLES
100 gm. edible portion

Food and description	Water (%)	Food Energy (calories)	Protein (gm.)	Fat (gm.)	Carbohydrate Total (gm.)	Fiber (gm.)	Ash (gm.)	Calcium (mg.)	Phosphorus (mg.)	Iron (mg.)	Sodium (mg.)	Potassium (mg.)	Vit. A (I.U.)	Thiamine (mg.)	Riboflavin (mg.)	Niacin (mg.)	Vit. C (mg.)
STRING BEANS																	
Raw	90.1	32	1.9	.2	7.1	1.0	.7	56	44	.8	7	243	600	.08	.11	.5	19
Cooked in small amount of water, short time	92.4	25	1.6	.2	5.4	1.0	.4	50	37	.6	4	151	540	.07	.09	.5	12
Cooked in large amount of water, long time	92.4	25	1.6	.2	5.4	1.0	.4	50	37	.6	4	151	540	.06	.08	.3	10
BEETS																	
Raw	87.3	43	1.6	.1	9.9	.8	1.1	16	33	.7	60	335	20	.03	.05	.4	10
Cooked	90.9	32	1.1	.1	7.2	.8	.7	14	23	.5	43	208	20	.03	.04	.3	6
CARROTS																	
Raw	88.2	42	1.1	.2	9.7	1.0	.8	37	36	.7	47	341	11,000	.06	.05	.6	8
Cooked	91.2	31	.9	.2	7.1	1.0	.6	33	31	.6	33	222	10,500	.05	.05	.5	6
CAULIFLOWER																	
Raw	91.0	27	2.7	.2	5.2	1.0	.9	25	56	1.1	13	295	60	.11	.10	.7	78
Cooked	92.8	22	2.3	.2	4.1	1.0	.6	21	42	.7	9	206	60	.09	.08	.6	55
BROCCOLI																	
Raw	89.1	32	3.6	.3	5.9	1.5	1.1	103	78	1.1	15	382	2,500	.10	.23	.9	113
Cooked	91.3	26	3.1	.3	4.5	1.5	.8	88	62	.8	10	267	2,500	.09	.20	.8	90
CELERY																	
Raw	94.1	17	.9	.1	3.9	.6	1.0	39	28	.3	126	341	240	.03	.03	.3	9
Cooked	95.3	14	.8	.1	3.1	.6	.7	31	22	.2	88	239	230	.02	.03	.3	6
POTATOES																	
Raw	79.8	76	2.1	.1	17.1	.5	.9	7	53	.6	3	407	Trace	.10	.04	1.5	20
Baked in skin	75.1	93	2.6	.1	21.1	.6	1.1	9	65	.7	4	503	Trace	.10	.04	1.7	20
Boiled in skin	79.8	76	2.1	.1	17.1	.5	.9	7	53	.6	3	407	Trace	.09	.04	1.5	16
TOMATOES																	
Raw	93.5	22	1.1	.2	4.7	.5	.5	13	27	.5	3	244	900	.06	.04	.7	23
Cooked	92.4	26	1.3	.2	5.5	.6	.6	15	32	.6	4	287	1,000	.07	.05	.8	24

Food and description	Water (%)	Food Energy (calories)	Protein (gm.)	Fat (gm.)	Carbohydrate Total (gm.)	Carbohydrate Fiber (gm.)	Ash (gm.)	Calcium (mg.)	Phosphorus (mg.)	Iron (mg.)	Sodium (mg.)	Potassium (mg.)	Vit. A (I.U.)	Thiamine (mg.)	Riboflavin (mg.)	Niacin (mg.)	Vit. C (mg.)
ZUCCHINI																	
Raw	94.6	17	1.2	.1	3.6	.6	.5	28	29	.4	1	202	320	.05	.09	1.0	19
Cooked	96.0	12	1.0	.1	2.5	.6	.4	25	25	.4	1	141	300	.05	.08	.8	9
YELLOW SQUASH																	
Raw	93.7	20	1.2	.2	4.3	.6	.6	28	29	.4	1	202	460	.05	.09	1.0	25
Cooked	95.3	15	1.0	.2	3.1	.6	.4	25	25	.4	1	141	440	.05	.08	.8	11
BUTTERNUT SQUASH																	
Raw	83.7	54	1.4	.1	14.0	1.4	.8	32	58	.8	1	487	5,700	.05	.11	.6	9
Baked in skin	79.6	68	1.8	.1	17.5	1.8	1.0	40	72	1.0	1	609	6,400	.05	.13	.7	8
Boiled in skin	87.8	41	1.1	.1	10.4	1.4	.6	29	49	.7	1	341	5,400	.04	.10	.4	5
HUBBARD																	
Raw	88.1	39	1.4	.3	9.4	1.4	.8	19	31	.6	1	217	4,300	.05	.11	.6	11
Baked	85.1	50	1.8	.4	11.7	1.8	1.0	24	39	.8	1	271	4,800	.05	.13	.7	10
Boiled	91.1	30	1.1	.3	6.9	1.4	.6	17	26	.5	1	152	4,100	.04	.10	.4	6
ACORN SQUASH																	
Raw	86.3	44	1.5	.1	11.2	1.4	.9	31	23	.9	1	384	1,200	.05	.11	.6	14
Baked	82.9	55	1.9	.1	14.0	1.8	1.1	39	29	1.1	1	480	1,400	.05	.13	.7	13
Boiled	89.7	34	1.2	.1	8.4	1.4	.6	28	20	.8	1	269	1,100	.04	.10	.4	8
PUMPKIN																	
Raw	91.6	26	1.0	.1	6.5	1.1	.8	21	44	.8	1	340	1,600	.05	.11	.6	9
Canned	90.2	33	1.0	.3	7.9	1.3	.6	25	26	.4	2	240	6,400	.03	.05	.6	5
PEAS																	
Raw	78.0	84	6.3	.4	14.4	2.0	.9	26	116	1.9	2	316	640	.35	.14	2.9	27
Cooked	81.5	71	5.4	.4	12.1	2.0	.6	23	99	1.8	1	196	540	.28	.11	2.3	20
CORN (white and yellow)																	
Raw	72.7	96	3.5	1.0	22.1	.7	.7	3	111	.7	Trace	280	400	.15	.12	1.7	12
Cooked, kernels cut off cob	76.5	83	3.2	1.0	18.8	.7	.5	3	89	.6	Trace	165	400	.11	.10	1.3	7
Cooked, kernels on cob	74.1	91	3.3	1.0	21.0	.7	.6	3	89	.6	Trace	196	400	.12	.10	1.4	9
CUCUMBER																	
Raw, not pared	95.1	15	.9	.1	3.4	.6	.5	25	27	1.1	6	160	250	.03	.04	.2	11
Raw, pared	95.7	14	.6	.1	3.2	.3	.4	17	18	.3	6	160	Trace	.03	.04	.2	11

Food and description	Water (%)	Food Energy (calories)	Protein (gm.)	Fat (gm.)	Carbohydrate Total (gm.)	Fiber (gm.)	Ash (gm.)	Calcium (mg.)	Phosphorus (mg.)	Iron (mg.)	Sodium (mg.)	Potassium (mg.)	Vit. A (I.U.)	Thiamine (mg.)	Riboflavin (mg.)	Niacin (mg.)	Vit.C (mg.)
EGGPLANT																	
Raw	92.4	25	1.2	.2	5.6	.9	.6	12	26	.7	2	214	10	.05	.05	.6	5
Cooked	94.3	19	1.0	.2	4.1	.9	.4	11	21	.6	1	150	10	.05	.04	.5	3
RADISHES																	
Raw, common	94.5	17	1.0	.1	3.6	.7	.8	30	31	1.0	18	322	10	.03	.03	.3	26
Raw, Oriental	94.1	19	.9	.1	4.2	.7	.7	35	26	.6	—	180	10	.03	.02	.4	32
TURNIPS																	
Raw	91.5	30	1.0	.2	6.6	.9	.7	39	30	.5	49	268	Trace	.04	.07	.6	36
Cooked	93.6	23	.8	.2	4.9	.9	.5	35	24	.4	34	188	Trace	.04	.05	.3	22
LETTUCE (raw)																	
Butterhead	95.1	14	1.2	.2	2.5	.5	1.0	35	26	2.0	9	264	970	.06	.06	.3	8
Romaine	94.0	18	1.3	.3	3.5	.7	.9	68	25	1.4	9	264	1,900	.05	.08	.4	18
Crisphead	95.5	13	.9	.1	2.9	.5	.6	20	22	.5	9	175	330	.06	.06	.3	6
Looseleaf	94.0	18	1.3	.3	3.5	.7	.9	68	25	1.4	9	264	1,900	.05	.08	.4	18
GREEN PEPPERS																	
Raw	93.4	22	1.2	.2	4.8	1.4	.4	9	22	.7	13	213	420	.08	.08	.5	128
Cooked (boiled, drained)	94.7	18	1.0	.2	3.8	1.4	.3	9	16	.5	9	149	420	.06	.07	.5	96
SWISS CHARD																	
Raw	91.1	25	2.4	0.3	4.6	0.8	1.6	88	39	3.2	147	550	6,500	0.06	0.17	0.5	32
Cooked (boiled, drained)	93.7	18	1.8	.2	3.3	.7	1.0	73	24	1.8	86	321	5,400	.04	.11	.4	16
LIMA BEANS																	
Raw	67.5	123	8.4	.5	22.1	1.8	1.5	52	142	2.8	2	650	290	.24	.12	1.4	29
Cooked (boiled, drained)	71.1	111	7.6	.5	19.8	1.8	1.0	47	121	2.5	1	422	280	.18	.10	1.3	17
PARSLEY (raw)	85.1	44	3.6	.6	8.5	1.5	2.2	203	63	6.2	45	727	8,500	.12	.26	1.2	172
SPINACH																	
Raw	90.7	26	3.2	.3	4.3	.6	1.5	93	51	3.1	71	470	8,100	.10	.20	.6	51
Cooked (boiled, drained)	92.0	23	3.0	.3	3.6	.6	1.1	93	38	2.2	50	324	8,100	.07	.14	.5	28

Food and description	Water (%)	Food Energy (calories)	Protein (gm.)	Fat (gm.)	Carbohydrate Total (gm.)	Fiber (gm.)	Ash (gm.)	Calcium (mg.)	Phosphorus (mg.)	Iron (mg.)	Sodium (mg.)	Potassium (mg.)	Vit. A (I.U.)	Thiamine (mg.)	Riboflavin (mg.)	Niacin (mg.)	Vit. C (mg.)
KALE																	
Raw (leaves, incl. stems)	87.5	38	4.2	.8	6.0	1.3	1.5	179	73	2.2	75	378	8,900	–	–	–	125
Cooked (leaves, incl. stems)	91.2	28	3.2	.7	4.0	1.1	.9	134	46	1.2	43	221	7,400	–	–	–	62
COLLARD																	
Raw (leaves, incl. stems)	86.9	40	3.6	.7	7.2	.9	1.6	203	63	1.0	43	401	6,500	.20	(.31)	(1.7)	92
Cooked in small amt. water (leaves, incl. stems)	90.8	29	2.7	.6	4.9	.8	1.0	152	39	.6	25	234	5,400	.14	.20	1.2	46
MUSTARD GREENS																	
Raw	89.5	31	3.0	.5	5.6	1.1	1.4	183	50	3.0	32	377	7,000	.11	.22	.8	97
Cooked (boiled, drained)	92.6	23	2.2	.4	4.0	.9	.8	138	32	1.8	18	220	5,800	.08	.14	.6	48
CABBAGE (common)																	
Raw	92.4	24	1.3	.2	5.4	.8	.7	49	29	.4	20	233	130	.05	.05	.3	47
Cooked (boiled, drained):																	
Shredded, small amount water	93.9	20	1.1	.2	4.3	.8	.5	44	20	.3	14	163	130	.04	.04	.3	33
Wedges, large amount water	94.3	18	1.0	.2	4.0	.8	.5	42	17	.3	13	151	120	.02	.02	.1	24
BRUSSEL SPROUTS																	
Raw	85.2	45	4.9	.4	8.3	1.6	1.2	36	80	1.5	14	390	550	.10	.16	.9	102
Cooked (boiled, drained)	88.2	36	4.2	.4	6.4	1.6	.8	32	72	1.1	10	273	520	.08	.14	.8	87
OKRA																	
Raw	88.9	36	2.4	.3	7.6	1.0	.8	92	51	.6	3	249	520	(.17)	(.21)	(1.0)	31
Cooked (boiled, drained)	91.1	29	2.0	.3	6.0	1.0	.6	92	41	.5	2	174	490	(.13)	(.18)	(.9)	20
KOHLRABI																	
Raw	90.3	29	2.0	.1	6.6	1.0	1.0	41	51	.5	8	372	20	.06	.04	.3	66
Cooked (boiled, drained)	92.2	24	1.7	.1	5.3	1.0	.7	33	41	.3	6	260	20	.06	.03	.2	43

(Numbers in parentheses denote values imputed – usually from another form of the food or from a similar food.

Dashes denote lack of reliable data for a constituent believed to be present in measurable amount. Calculated values, as those based on a recipe, are not in parentheses.)

"The true gentleman should simply
stay out of the kitchen where animals
are killed and meals prepared."
— Confucius

COMFREY

Comfrey

Comfrey is truly a wonder plant that I urge everyone to learn more about. It is easy to grow and difficult to say enough good things about. In fact, there are books describing its many wonderful properties. One such book is **Comfrey & Chlorophyll** by Vincent Licapa. Most people who know about comfrey think of it as a tea or medicinal herb. Here in Hawaii, it is often found in the Oriental section of the supermarkets, for in its dried form it is made into a tea. But its uses go far beyond that.

The first time I saw a comfrey plant, it was growing near a spring flowing into a horse trough. Comfrey has fairly large, dark-green leaves that spread out in a big, circular cluster. The bigger, older leaves lie close to the ground and the younger, lighter green leaves—which are best for cooking due to their tenderness—come from the center of the plant. After finding out about all the many uses for comfrey, I decided to plant some in my yard to use for medicine and for meals.

A friend gave me one good-sized comfrey plant from his yard up in Kula where the soil is real rich and the weather is cool due to a high elevation. I was wondering if it was going to be able to live in my yard down in a very windy area only one block from the beach. But I was pleasantly surprised by what happened.

I took the big clump of roots and gently tore one root from another, making sure each root had a little

293

leaf stem coming from it, and buried it in the ground and cut off the leaves. In only a week's time, new leaves were starting to come up.

Comfrey will also grow from inch-long chunks of the root planted about an inch or so deep. The plant takes longer to grow when planted like this rather than from a clump of root. The soil at my home was not sandy even though we were so close to the beach. I'm mentioning this because the only place I know of where a person had a hard time growing comfrey was in very dry, sandy soil near the ocean. Actually, all I did to care for the plants was to water them at first to get them started. I never fertilized or gave them special attention or water after that first planting got started.

I would always use the leaves either singly or cut them off all at once and dry a bunch at a time by hanging them on a chicken wire fence, spread out so moisture would not cause them to mold. Within a few days of cutting them all off, tender, new leaves would come back fast. The only time I had a plant die was when I noticed a long stem turn into delicate, pale-purple flowers, and after the flowers wilted the whole plant died. But only one plant in the 20 or so I've grown in the past two years has ever flowered like that.

Another good thing about the comfrey plant is that it can grow to three feet across, acting almost as a ground cover to choke out the weeds. Usually the plant is only about a foot tall. So I would use it as a kind of living mulch under my banana trees and the papaya trees, too.

I would like to mention some of the healing properties of the herb since it has been traditionally used for healing (in recent years, primarily by naturopathic doctors).

The active ingredient in comfrey is allantoin, a substance known to aid granulation and cell formation. This is what the healing process is all about, so try some of these comfrey remedies.

To reduce swelling and inflammation and help heal cuts and bruises, it is best to make a poultice of comfrey. There are several ways of doing this. For a large poultice, use 10 to 12 medium-sized leaves. For open sores and cuts, you can steep fresh leaves in hot water and either cut or grind or smash them, squeezing out the excess water. Then apply the comfrey directly to the wound and cover with a hot, clean towel or wrap. The heat not only aids the healing effect of the allantoin, but also tends to draw out the poisons or toxins. The steeped leaves can be applied directly to the wound, though it is better to cut the leaves, as this releases the thick, mucilaginous substance.

For bruises, swelling or sprains, steep and drain the leaves, wrapping them in a clean cloth, and apply as warm as possible. Keep reapplying the leaves to keep the area warm.

Many herbs of healing benefit when used externally also can help internally. Comfrey is no exception. Both the leaves and the roots of the comfrey plant can be used for tea. It is a remedy for gastric ulcers, internal tumors, lung ailments, coughs, asthma and tuberculosis. It is also good for consumption and hemorrhaging, is very valuable in treating the ulceration of kidneys, stomach and bowels, and also helps get rid of boils.

A strong tea can be made with dried or fresh leaves or roots for dabbing with cotton onto a wound or for soaking a sore finger, toe, etc. Tea to drink can be made by steeping four small leaves per cup or one tablespoon of dried comfrey leaves or root for three to five minutes. This is a very soothing drink, especially when blended with equal parts peppermint and sweetened with honey. (It is a good idea never to boil herbs unless directed to do so since some lose their potency when boiled.)

Pure blood builds strong tissues, and comfrey leaves are very effective as a blood purifier when eaten like a vegetable similar to spinach, swiss chard, or beet greens. As a vegetable it is a very nourishing foodstuff.

COMFREY LEAVES (dried) 100 gm.	
Vitamin A	28 I.U.
Vitamin B$_1$ (Thiamine)	.5 mg.
Vitamin B$_2$ (Riboflavin)	1 mg.
Vitamin B$_3$ (Niacin)	.07 mg.
Vitamin C (Ascorbic Acid)	100 mg.
Vitamin E	30 I.U.
Allantoin	.18 mg.

It is an excellent source of vitamin C and the B vitamins: thiamine, riboflavin and niacin. The big leaves have a very high protein content of 22% to 33%, making this a very good source of protein. It is rich in potassium, phosphorus, and a fair source of vitamin A. What more could you ask for in a plant?

It is best to pick fresh, green comfrey leaves for cooking after a day in the full sunlight. This is when the leaf has its highest food value. You can stew or steam comfrey leaves (young and tender ones) briefly as you would spinach. The larger, tougher ones should be cooked longer—about 20 minutes. When cooking, use as little water as possible so as not to lose all the valuable nutrients in the cooking process. You will find that the leaves cook down quite a bit (almost as much as fresh spinach does). Comfrey leaves are also very good combined with other greens, sautéd lightly in oil with green pepper and served with home-grown sweet potatoes and/or brown rice. The young leaves are very good when cut into small pieces and tossed in salad or added to any blender drink. The dried comfrey leaves crushed to a powder are also a very good and healthy additive to soups and shakes.

It seems almost crazy with the price of medical bills these days not to use a little preventive medicine and start a few comfrey plants in your yard. You can't lose on these comfrey recipes because not only are they pleasant tasting, they're also very good for you.

COMFREY AND COCONUT   O

1/3 cup cooked comfrey
(about 1 cup chopped leaves)

2/3 cup spoon meat coconut
(save cocowater)
1½ - 2 Tbsp. honey

Steam comfrey in a little coconut water until tender. Whiz in blender with next 2 ingredients until smooth and serve. This is high in protein and vitamins; very good fed to an infant or adult. Yields 1 cup.

COMFREY ROOT CANDY ○

1 Tbsp. grated fresh comfrey root
1 Tbsp. finely grated coconut
1 tsp. carob powder
1 Tbsp. honey

Mix ingredients and let sit awhile. Roll into balls and roll in raw or toasted coconut.

COMFREY & PINEAPPLE DRINK ▢

4 small, fresh comfrey leaves
1 cup fresh (unsweetened) pineapple juice
2 tsp. honey
2 tsp. lemon juice

Whiz in blender and serve as a very refreshing, delicious and nutritious drink. Yields 1 serving.

HEALTHFUL COMFREY SMOOTHIE ▢

3 cups cold milk
3 fresh, young comfrey leaves
2 - 3 bananas
Handful of alfalfa sprouts
Handful of pitted dates
Handful of raisins
2 dashes of cayenne (opt.)

Combine ingredients and whiz in blender until smooth and creamy. Yields 4 servings.

HEALTHFUL COMFREY COCKTAIL #1

1½ - 2 cups apple cider
½ fresh apple, chopped
2 Tbsp. chopped comfrey
2 Tbsp. chopped celery leaves
¼ cup chopped escarole or lettuce
8 fresh mint leaves
¼ tsp. salt
1 tsp. honey

Combine ingredients. Blend in blender until smooth. Serve immediately for full benefit of the vitamins. Yields 1 to 2 servings.

HEALTHFUL COMFREY COCKTAIL #2

1½ - 2 cups tomato juice
½ fresh apple (opt.)
¼ cup chopped comfrey
2 Tbsp. chopped celery leaves
¼ cup escarole or lettuce
8 fresh mint leaves
1 tsp. fresh parsley
1/8 tsp. salt or ½ tsp. kelp
1 tsp. honey (opt.)

Combine ingredients. Blend in blender until smooth. Serve immediately also. These drinks are good served cold, so it is a good idea to have the ingredients chilled. They can also be served over ice. Yields 1 to 2 servings.

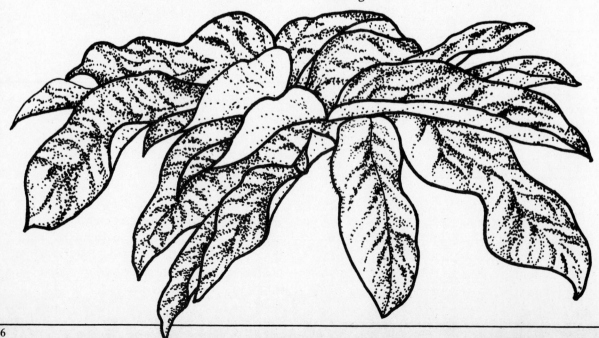

COMFREY VEGETABLE SOUP ○

4 cups water
2 Tbsp. barley
2 tomatoes, chopped
¼ cup diced carrot
½ cup small cubed potato
¼ cup small cubed beets
¼ cup slivered green beans
or ¼ cup chopped celery
2 cups washed, finely chopped comfrey
¾ tsp. salt or 2 tsp. kelp
½ tsp. summer savory powder
1/8 tsp. black pepper
1 tsp. basil
1 tsp. oregano
¼ tsp. thyme powder
1/8 tsp. asafetida

Combine ingredients. Bring to a boil, then simmer for about 45 minutes. Take 1 cup of soup and blend in blender until smooth. Add to the rest of the soup. Mix well and serve with crackers.

Variation: Soup broth can be left clear by not blending 1 cup of soup; and brown rice, lentils or mung beans can be used instead of barley.

COMFREY & TOMATOES WITH TOFU ○

4 cups chopped comfrey leaves
2 Tbsp. oil
1 tsp. grated fresh ginger
1 Tbsp. sesame seeds

2 tomatoes, chopped
Pinch of cayenne
½ tsp. curry powder
1 tsp. soy sauce
1 cup drained and crumbled tofu

Salt to taste

Combine first 4 ingredients and saute lightly. Combine with next 5 ingredients and cook, covered, stirring occasionally, for about 15 minutes. Remove cover and cook until liquid cooks off. Salt to taste and serve. Yields 2 to 4 servings.

COMFREY AND POTATOES ☆

4 cups diced potato or breadfruit

¼ cup milk
½ stick butter or margarine
1 tsp. salt or 2 tsp. kelp
½ tsp. black pepper

4 cups chopped comfrey leaves, steamed

Cook potatoes. Mash with next 4 ingredients. Toss in steamed, drained comfrey leaves. Mix well and serve. Sprinkle each serving with some paprika. Yields 2 to 4 servings.

GREEN POTATOES ☆

4 cups diced potato (or breadfruit)
4 cups chopped comfrey leaves

½ stick butter or margarine
2 tsp. salt or 4 tsp. kelp
½ tsp. black pepper

Cook first 2 ingredients with just enough water to steam-cook. When potatoes are soft, remove from heat and drain (save liquid). Combine next 3 ingredients with first 2 and mix in blender until smooth. Add liquid if necessary. (If not needed, save it for any soup broth.) Scrape from blender and serve. Yields 2 to 4 servings.

COMFREY SAMOSA ☆

Dough:
3 cups unbleached white flour
  + ¼ cup whole wheat flour
  or 3¼ cups whole wheat pastry flour
1 stick melted butter or margarine
6 Tbsp. warm water

Filling:
½ stick butter or margarine
¼ tsp. cumin seed
Dash red pepper

Pinch of ginger powder
Pinch of cloves
Pinch of nutmeg
Pinch of allspice
1/8 tsp. coriander powder
1/8 tsp. cinnamon
¾ tsp. salt
½ tsp. turmeric

3 cups finely chopped, steamed
and drained comfrey leaves

Soy sauce to taste

Ghee or light oil for deep frying

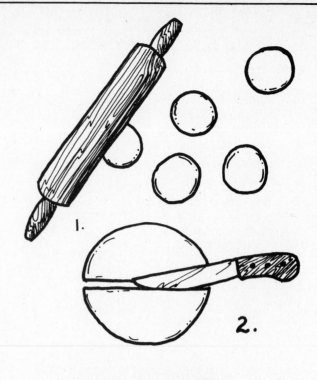

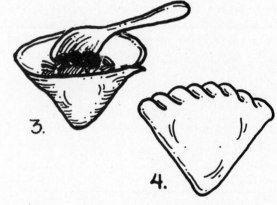

Combine first 3 ingredients to make a soft (not too wet) dough. Knead and cover with a damp cloth. Put next 3 ingredients in a skillet and fry until browning. Add next 8 ingredients. Stir and add cooked comfrey. Add soy sauce and fry for about 5 minutes. Let cool. Pinch off bits of dough. Roll on a smooth surface, not too thin. Slice in half. Bring the two corners together to form a cone shape, overlapping them and sealing well. Use water if necessary. Hold the cone in your hand and fill with a tablespoon of comfrey mixture. Seal top edge well, sealing as you go. Start folding the dough from the far right corner, bringing the point towards the center, then pressing. Repeat this pattern until pastry is sealed very securely. Gently drop in moderately hot ghee or light oil. Fry for about 15 minutes until light brown and a hollow sound is heard when lightly tapped on the outside. Drain and serve as soon as possible.

COMFREY POTATO PATTIES ☆

1 cup Green Potatoes
(see recipe this section, p. 297)
1 cup grated carrot
2 Tbsp. toasted sesame seeds
4 Tbsp. whole wheat flour
1 tsp. celery salt

Combine ingredients and mix well. Roll into balls about the size of golf balls. The mixture will be moist but will hold together. If necessary, add a bit more flour. Flatten and fry in a buttered skillet. Turn and flatten with spatula. Fry until crisp and browned. These are very good served with Tofu Dressing #2 spread over them (see recipe in Tofu Section, p. 374). Makes about 12 patties.

COMFREY FRITTERS ☆

1 cup whole wheat flour
1 tsp. salt or 2 tsp. kelp
1 tsp. baking powder
1 - 1½ cups water

Fresh comfrey leaves

Combine first 4 ingredients and blend until pancake batter consistency. Wash comfrey leaves, dry them and cut them in halves or thirds horizontally. Hold one corner and dip and swish back and forth in the batter until both sides are well-coated (prevents leaf from curling). Drop in hot ghee or oil and cook about 5 minutes, turning, until crisp and golden.

COMFREY VEGETABLE BURGERS ○

1 cup garbanzo flour (chickpea)
1 tsp. salt or 2 tsp. kelp
1/8 - 1/4 tsp. black pepper
1 tsp. parsley
1 tsp. thyme powder
1 tsp. oregano
1 tsp. basil
¾ cup water

½ cup grated carrot
½ cup slivered green beans
or ½ cup chopped celery
1 cup washed and finely chopped comfrey

Combine first 8 ingredients and mix until free from lumps to make a thick batter. Add next 3 ingredients and mix well. Roll into balls about the size of golf balls. Place in an oiled skillet and flatten into patties. Fry until golden and crisp. Good served with ketchup on a sandwich, etc. Yields about 2 dozen.

COMFREY CASSEROLE ○

1 cup bulgar wheat
2 cups water

1 cup diced carrot
½ cup slivered green beans
or ½ cup chopped celery
½ - 1 tsp. salt or 2 tsp. kelp
¼ tsp. black pepper
1 tsp. basil
1 tsp. oregano
½ tsp. thyme powder
½ tsp. savory powder
½ tsp. parsley flakes
2 Tbsp. oil

2 cups finely chopped comfrey

2 cups tomato sauce
½ cup grated cheese

Grated cheese for topping

Preheat oven to 350° F. Bring first 2 ingredients to a boil. Cover and cook on medium heat until water cooks off. In a skillet, sauté next 10 ingredients. Add comfrey and quickly stir-fry. Combine with 2 cups cooked bulgar and next 2 ingredients. Mix well and place in an oiled casserole dish. Cover and bake at 350° for 30 minutes. Remove cover, top with a good amount of grated cheese and return to oven until melted. Yields 6 hearty servings.

Variation: Brown rice could be used instead of bulgar wheat.

"Whatever my practice may be, I have no doubt that it is a part of the destiny of the human race, in its gradual improvement, to leave off eating animals as surely as the savage tribes have left off eating each other when they came in contact with the more civilized."
— Henry David Thoreau

FRESH
LEAVES

Leaves

At first I hesitated to include this section in the book because it's not dealing with foods that are growing here in abundance, but foods that could be grown here. I thought that if I started in on foods that could be grown here, that would be the beginning of another book. There are so many fruits and vegetables and trees that are grown in other tropical locations that we haven't even begun to know about! However, my enthusiasm for these three green leafy vegetables has overridden my intention to keep the book contained to fruits that are growing here and rotting on the ground.

I was introduced to amaranth, edible hibiscus and ong choy by Dr. Y. H. Yang at the Resource Systems Institute of the East-West Center. Dr. Yang has very kindly shared his knowledge with me on various edible plants that will do well in Hawaii, as he is willing to do with anyone and everyone. If you and your friends are interested in knowing more about nutrition and gardening, you can contact Dr. Yang at the Resource Systems Institute. He or someone there is always eager to come speak to clubs and community groups. But don't think it'll be a dry lecture! He's likely to show up with a slide show and plant cuttings for you to take home and plant in your backyard.

Even if you're one of those frustrated gardeners whose every attempt at gardening has withered before your eyes or been consumed by bugs, you will find that these plants are very easy to grow and require very little care. All you have to do is plant them in a place where they'll get sufficient sun and water. You don't have to worry about pests, since they don't seem to like these plants. These plants also make attractive potted plants for condominium "farmers."

Their hardiness and the ease with which these plants can be grown are just part of the wonderful qualities which make these plants so valuable. Another wonderful quality of these plants is their nutritional value. This is something we shouldn't ignore in today's society, where a surprisingly large percentage of American people suffer from some sort of malnutrition.

Two very common deficiencies are vitamin and iron deficiencies. Increased consumption of dark-green leafy vegetables can provide these nutrients as well as other nutrients and crude fiber.

"Eat your spinach, it's good for you."

Ever hear that before? My mom used to always say that to me and it's true. Among green leafy vegetables, amaranth, edible hibiscus and ong choy rank tops in nutritional value in comparison to other green leafy vegetables.

As can be seen in the comparison chart on pg. 306, the advantage of growing any or all of these three green leafies is that you get more nutrition per square inch of garden space than if you were to plant some other vegetable, except spinach. The advantage of growing any of these three green leafies in place of spinach is that they grow well in tropical climates, whereas spinach likes cool weather better.

Ong Choy (Chinese name) or **Kang kong** (Filipino name) is a very common vegetable in the Far East. There are two kinds of ong choy: the swamp kind and the dry kind. Many people here in Hawaii use ong choy in their cooking (it is commonly found on supermarket shelves), but most only know about the wetland variety. As a consequence, since most of us don't have swamps in our backyards, we don't think of it as something we can grow.

Dryland ong choy makes this possible. It is a desirable plant to grow because it grows so quickly. If you cut the plant down, about ten days later you'll have a growth about one foot tall to harvest again. It also requires little care and has very high nutritional value. Although ong choy will grow from seed, it is much easier and quicker to grow it from cuttings. All you have to do is find someone who has the plant growing and ask them for cuttings.

To plant ong choy, cut stems to about six inches long and remove all leaves except for one towards the top end. Now just bury two-thirds of each stem in the soil about one foot apart from the next one. Keep moist and you'll soon see new leaves and stems popping up.

ONG CHOY

Edible Hibiscus is a perennial plant that's not commonly known in Hawaii, but hopefully will be soon. It is a beautiful bush or shrub that resembles the common hibiscus bushes we have growing everywhere in Hawaii, but the leaves are edible and highly nutritious. (See nutrition table for information.)

The first time my kids had edible hibiscus leaves, they loved them — but they seem to like just about any vegetable. The leaves have the same taste and texture as malabar spinach but are more easily grown and don't require replanting.

All you have to do to plant the edible hibiscus is get a cutting about six inches long, stick two-thirds of it into the ground, keep moist and watch patiently! Once they take off, watch out! They can grow to be 10 to 12 feet tall.

Amaranth. Before Dr. Yang took me out to his garden plots, I had heard quite a lot about this wonderful new plant called amaranth. You can imagine my surprise when I was reintroduced to a weed that I — and probably many Island gardeners — had pulled out of the garden so many times. Whenever the kids and I pulled these weeds out of our gardens, we always used the leaves in salads or steamed them like spinach. Though I was aware that this plant was edible, I never imagined that it would be hailed as one of the most nutritious and efficient plants in the world. At that time, I recalled a quote from Henry David Thoreau which I had read some time ago:

"A plant is a weed only as long as we don't know its use."

Amaranth may be known to you as pigweed or Hawaiian spinach. The amaranth which Dr. Yang is cultivating and distributing is a hybrid strain. It is known as grain amaranth and is differentiated from the common, local amaranth by its larger leaves and large seed tassel. As is suggested by the name, the seed in the tassel can be ground as a grain and used like flour. I've heard that the seeds surpass soybeans nutritionally and the leaves are much like spinach in their nutritional value.

EDIBLE HIBISCUS

One use I've found for the seeds is in sprouting. You can sprout them just like alfalfa seeds and use them in the same ways you would use alfalfa sprouts. A few amaranth plants in your garden will provide enough seeds for a few months' worth of sprouts. Of course, you'll always want to save a few seeds to start new plants.

Here is a table showing the nutritional value of the previously described leaves as compared with some more commonly known green leaves.

Per 100 gm.	AMARANTH	ONG CHOY	HIBISCUS	SPINACH	CABBAGE	LETTUCE
Protein	2.4%	2.4%	3.1%	3.2%	1.1%	.8%
Calcium	177 mg.	80 mg.	62 mg.	84 mg.	35 mg.	44 mg.
Iron	2.8 mg.	2.5 mg.	1.3 mg.	3.1 mg.	.3 mg.	.9 mg.
Vitamin A	1830 I.U.	1755 I.U.	5000 I.U.	8100 I.U.	20 I.U.	365 I.U.
Vitamin C	61 mg.	36 mg.	30 mg.	51 mg.	36 mg.	12 mg.

Here are a few recipes in which you can use one or a mixture of those leaves. Eat your green leafies — they're good for you!

SUMMER SALAD

1 cup fresh leaves, chopped fine
10 - 15 fresh mint leaves, chopped fine
1 Tbsp. lemon juice
2 pinches asafetida
½ tsp. salt or 1 tsp. kelp
1 cup yogurt

Combine ingredients and refrigerate at least 1 hour before serving.

GARNISH

3 cups leaves, chopped very fine

½ Tbsp. toasted sesame oil
(available in grocery store Oriental section)
1 Tbsp. soy sauce
1 tsp. honey

Rinse leaves and chop very, very fine. Combine with other ingredients and toss into greens. Use as garnish on Crunchy Tofu Crisps (see recipe in Tofu Section, p. 384).

AMARANTH

CHINESE SALAD □

1 cup Crunchy Tofu Crisps
(see Tofu Section, p. 384, for recipe)
½ cucumber, sliced or grated very thin
3 cups leaves, chopped fine

1 Tbsp. toasted sesame oil
2 Tbsp. soy sauce
1 Tbsp. apple cider vinegar
1 Tbsp. dry mustard powder
1 Tbsp. honey

Combine first 3 ingredients and combine last 5 ingredients. Pour sauce onto salad and toss to mix in.

FLOWERS & LEAVES SALAD □

1 Tbsp. oil
2 Tbsp. parsley
1 tsp. tarragon
¼ tsp. oregano

2 cups watercress, chopped
6 cups leaves, chopped

2 cups drained, steamed cauliflower
¾ cup Eggless Soy Mayonnaise
(see Basic Recipes Section, p. 34)
1 Tbsp. lemon juice
Salt or kelp to taste

Sauté first 4 ingredients; add greens and stir-fry. Add to next 4 ingredients and chill. Sprinkle salt to taste. Be careful not to overdo and drown out the delicate taste of the tarragon.

BAKED CREAMED LEAVES ☆

6 cups slightly steamed leaves

1 cup sour cream
1 pkg. dried soup mix
or 1 Morga vegetable bouillon cube
1 Tbsp. butter or margarine

Preheat oven to 325° F. Mix steamed leaves with remaining ingredients and bake at 325° for 10 to 15 minutes.

RAVIOLI ○

Filling:
1 Tbsp. olive oil
½ tsp. asafetida

1 cup leaves, chopped, cut and drained well
½ cup cottage cheese
3 Tbsp. Parmesan cheese

Fine whole wheat dry bread crumbs
Salt and black pepper to taste
Nutmeg to taste

Ravioli Shells:
(or use Green Jao-Tze
recipe this section, p. 308)
1½ cups whole wheat flour
1½ cups unbleached white flour
1½ cups warm water

Filling: Sauté asafetida in heated oil. Add leaves, cottage cheese and Parmesan and mix well. Add enough bread crumbs to thicken mixture, and season with salt, black pepper and nutmeg. Set filling aside.

Ravioli Shells: Mix together all ingredients. Gather into ball with fingers, kneading lightly. Flour surface and roll out dough 1/8" thick with rolling pin, using more flour as necessary so it will not stick. Roll out and cut into 3" squares. On each square put seasoned ravioli filling. Cover with another square. Seal all around edges with a fork — sealing well to keep filling inside. Drop in boiling, salted water or directly into tomato sauce and cook until tender — 8 to 10 minutes. Remove and serve with tomato sauce for Breadfruit-Cauliflower Patties (see recipe in Breadfruit Section, p. 110).

GREEN JAO-TZE ⭘

Dough:
1 cup boiling water
3 cups raw leaves

3 cups whole wheat flour

Filling:
2 Tbsp. grated fresh ginger
¼ tsp. asafetida
1 Tbsp. oil

2 cups tofu
2 cups chopped vegetables

3 Tbsp. soy sauce
2 Tbsp. honey
3 Tbsp. whole wheat flour

Dough: Bring water to boil. Add raw leaves and cook a few minutes. Pour 1 cup of boiling water into blender and add 1 cup of well-packed, cooked leaves. Blend thoroughly. Put flour in bowl, make a crater in the middle, and pour blended water into middle. Mix in with a fork. When cool enough to handle, knead 5 to 10 minutes; you may have to add flour to make it more firm. Cover with bowl and let sit about 30 minutes. Break off balls about 1" in diameter. Roll on oiled surface. Put about 1 heaping teaspoon of filling in middle and fold over and seal dough as you would a turnover. Place on oiled steamer and steam for 45 to 60 minutes. The dough batter can also be used to make noodles. For noodles, just roll thin and cut to desired shapes and boil either in salted water first or directly in tomato sauce. Can also be used for ravioli noodles (see recipe this section, p. 307).

Filling: Toast spices in oil. Quick-fry next 2 ingredients for a few minutes. Mix together last 3 ingredients until flour is thoroughly blended. Pour into tofu and vegetables and stir until thickened.

KOREAN STYLE LEAVES ⭘

1 Tbsp. sesame oil (dark sesame)
3 Tbsp. honey
¼ tsp. cayenne
2 Tbsp. grated fresh ginger
¼ tsp. fresh red pepper, chopped fine
2½ Tbsp. lemon juice
¼ tsp. salt or ½ tsp. kelp

1 lb. leaves

Sauté first set of ingredients a few seconds to bring out the spices' flavor, then stir in leaves until wilted.

GREEN NUGGETS

1 Tbsp. oil
¼ tsp. dried chilies or 1/8 tsp. cayenne
¼ tsp. asafetida
½ tsp. cumin powder
½ tsp. turmeric
2 pinches clove powder

1½ cups milk
¾ cup uncooked cream of wheat (farina)

2 cups leaves
1 cup grated cheese

½ cup grated cheese

Sauce:
½ cup milk
1 Tbsp. whole wheat flour
¼ tsp. nutmeg

Preheat oven to 350° F. Toast chili peppers in oil. When they begin to brown, add powdered spices and toast (be careful not to burn). Add milk and cream of wheat. Bring to boil, stirring constantly until thickened. Remove from heat and mix in next 2 ingredients. Drop by tablespoon onto greased cookie sheet so that lumps are touching each other. Sprinkle with grated cheese. Cook last 3 ingredients (sauce) together in a pan to make a gravy. Pour over balls or use Mock Turkey Gravy (see Tofu Section, p. 379). Bake at 350° for about 35 minutes.

CREAM OF "SPINACH" SOUP ○

6 cups water
3 cups fresh chopped leaves

1 cup milk powder
¼ cup whole wheat flour
½ tsp. salt or 1 tsp. kelp
1 Morga vegetable bouillon cube
¼ tsp. black pepper

4 cups water

Cook first 2 ingredients until leaves are tender. Blend next 5 ingredients in blender with leaves and water they were cooked in. Blend until leaves are completely liquified. Pour back into pan and cook; add more water, stirring constantly until thickened.

CREAMED GREENS ☆

3 Tbsp. butter or margarine
¼ tsp. asafetida

3 Tbsp. whole wheat flour
1 cup milk

3 cups finely chopped leaves

¼ cup grated cheese
Salt to taste

Toast asafetida in butter. Remove from burner and pour in milk and flour and stir until all lumps of flour are gone. Put on heat and stir constantly, adding leaves a little at a time. Cook, constantly stirring, until leaves are tender. Add last 2 ingredients and mix in. Serve by itself or in crepes, or stuff tomatoes or bell peppers.

QUICK 'N EASY ○

2 Tbsp. oil
½ tsp. ground coriander
¼ tsp. ground cumin
1 tsp. fresh grated ginger
1/8 tsp. asafetida
1/8 tsp. cayenne pepper
2 - 3 pinches cloves

2 qts. leaves, chopped fine

½ block tofu, cut in ½" cubes

2 Tbsp. lemon juice
2 Tbsp. soy sauce

Toast spices in oil in wok or large frying pan. Toss in leaves and stir-fry until tender. Pour into serving bowl. Top with cubes of tofu. Pour lemon juice and soy sauce over it.

SWEET & SOUR LEAVES ○

4 Tbsp. olive oil
½ tsp. asafetida

2 large tomatoes, peeled & chopped
8 cups chopped fresh leaves

1 Tbsp. mustard powder
2 cups plain yogurt
1 cup diced Crunchy Tofu Crisps
(see recipe in Tofu Section, p. 384)
3 tsp. lemon juice
3 Tbsp. soy sauce

Cottage cheese

Sauté first 2 ingredients. Add next 2, stir, cover and cook about 5 minutes until soft and mushy. Add remaining ingredients and cook about 5 minutes longer until flavors blend. Serve with cottage cheese on the side.

CURRIED CUSTARD PIE

Flaky Pie Shell
(see Basic Recipes Section, p. 33)

1 cup fresh leaves, steamed,
drained and chopped

2 cups milk
1 cup grated cheese
¼ cup whole wheat flour
¼ cup arrowroot
½ tsp. salt
¼ tsp. black pepper
½ tsp. baking powder
1 Tbsp. curry powder (opt.)

Preheat oven to 350° F. Half-bake pie shell. Lay leaves in bottom of shell. Blend together remaining ingredients and pour over leaves. Bake at 350° for 30 to 45 minutes.

SLIGHTLY TENDER

2 cups grated zucchini
3 cups finely chopped leaves

¾ cup grated cheese
¼ cup fresh parsley
½ cup whole wheat bread crumbs
1 cup lentil, soy or wheatberry sprouts
2 Tbsp. butter or margarine
1 - 2 tsp. soy sauce

Preheat oven to 375° F. Quick-fry vegetables until half-cooked. Mix together other ingredients in separate bowl. Put half of the vegetables in a baking pan and then half of the cheese mixture on top. Layer again with other half of vegetables and top this with rest of the cheese mixture. Bake at 375° for 15 minutes.

CASSEROLE

1 Tbsp. olive oil
½ tsp. asafetida

2 cups cooked brown rice
1½ cups grated cheese
4 Tbsp. parsley
1½ tsp. salt (or more to taste)
½ tsp. black pepper
1 lb. fresh leaves, chopped small
2 Tbsp. nutritional yeast

1 cup milk or tomato sauce
1 cup toasted sesame or sunflower seeds
¼ cup arrowroot
½ cup wheat germ

Preheat oven to 350° F. Toast asafetida in oil. Add next 7 ingredients and mix together well. Blend last 4 ingredients in a blender until seeds are completely blended. Pour in with other ingredients and mix thoroughly. Bake at 350° for 35 minutes.

SCRAMBLED GREENS O

3 cups chopped leaves
1 Tbsp. sesame oil
2 tsp. Eggless Soy Mayonnaise (opt.)
(see Basic Recipes Section, p. 34)
2 Tbsp. tofu, crumbled
2 tsp. miso
1 tsp. honey
½ tsp. lemon juice

Put all ingredients in frying pan and sauté until leaves have wilted.

MA'S STUFFED TOFU ○

1 block tofu, cut into quarters
Soy sauce

1 Tbsp. oil
¼ tsp. asafetida
2 Tbsp. fresh coriander leaves, chopped fine
2 cups leaves, chopped fine
2 Tbsp. toasted sesame meal

Soak tofu in bowl with soy sauce in it. While soaking, toast asafetida in oil and quick-fry leaves. Remove from heat and add sesame meal. Hold tofu firmly but gently (so it doesn't squash) and slit with a knife, leaving about ½" from all edges, so the tofu is like a pocket. Stuff pockets with leaves by wrapping fingers around tofu to prevent tearing. These pockets can now be either steamed 10 to 15 minutes or fried in 1 Tbsp. oil, then covered with one of the following two sauces.

STUFFED TOFU SAUCE #1 □

1 Tbsp. toasted sesame oil
1/8 tsp. asafetida
1 fresh red pepper, chopped fine,
or 3 - 4 shakes cayenne

3 Tbsp. soy sauce
2 Tbsp. apple cider vinegar
2 tsp. honey

Toast spices a few seconds. Add last 3 ingredients. Pour over cooked, stuffed tofu just before serving.

STUFFED TOFU SAUCE #2 □

2 Tbsp. oil
¼ cup fresh grated ginger
1 fresh red pepper, chopped fine,
or a few shakes cayenne
1 lemon, sliced paper thin (including peels)

1 Tbsp. toasted sesame oil
¼ cup honey
½ cup lemon juice

Sauté first 4 ingredients together a few seconds. Add remaining ingredients. Bring to boil and add the stuffed tofu and cook on both sides just long enough to heat through. Take the stuffed tofu out and arrange on platter. Pour rest of sauce over tofu and serve.

GREEN CRESCENTS ○

Use Basic Bread Dough
(see Basic Recipes Section, p. 31)
Italian salad dressing
Parmesan or grated cheese

2 cups leaves, steamed,
drained and chopped fine
¼ cup baco-bits

Roll out Basic Bread Dough on a well-oiled counter to ¼" thickness. Rub surface with salad dressing and sprinkle with cheese. Cut dough into triangles. Mix together last 2 ingredients and put about 1 to 2 Tbsp. (depending on size of triangle) on base of triangle and roll up. Place on well-oiled cookie sheet about 1 inch apart. Bake at 375° for 15 minutes.

NUTTY PROTEIN GRAVY & LEAVES ○

½ cup peanut butter
¼ cup soy sauce
1 cup water (more water if desired)
2 Tbsp. sunflower seeds
½ tsp. curry powder
¼ tsp. nutritional yeast
2 tsp. fresh lemon juice

1 quart steamed leaves

Combine all 7 ingredients and blend in blender. Heat to warm or serve at room temperature over steamed leaves. Very nutritious. Delicious as a gravy or salad dressing.

SAN FRANCISCO-STYLE MANAPUA WITH LEAVES

Use Basic Bread Dough
(see Basic Recipes Section, p. 31)
1 lb. leaves

2 tsp. oil
½ tsp. asafetida
¼ tsp. black pepper
¼ tsp. salt

2 Tbsp. French dressing or tomato sauce
4 Tbsp. hulled sunflower seeds

Preheat oven to 350° F. Slightly wilt leaves and set to drain. Sauté next 4 ingredients. Add leaves and quickly stir-fry to mix well. Remove from heat. Add next 2 ingredients and mix well. Take ½ cup dough and pat between hands. May need to rub hands with oil to prevent sticking. Place ¼ of the filling (about ¼ cup or a little more) into center. Bring up sides, folding over one another, and pat. Dough should stick and seal very well. Place smooth side up in a baking pan and bake at 350° for 15 to 20 minutes. Serve warm. (This filling is enough for 4 to 5 manapuas.)

LEAFY NUT LOAF WITH SAUCE O

2 cups wilted leaves
¾ cup chopped walnuts
1 pinch asafetida
1 cup graham crackers or
sesame cracker crumbs
2 Tbsp. butter or margarine
1 tsp. vegetable salt
2 tsp. nutritional yeast
½ cup milk with ¼ tsp. arrowroot and
1 tsp. whole wheat flour stirred in

Preheat oven to 350° F. Stir all ingredients together. Place in baking loaf pan and bake at 350° for 20 to 30 minutes. Pour sauce on top of individual loaf slices.

Sauce:
2 Tbsp. baco-bits
Juice of ½ lemon
¼ tsp. vinegar
1/3 cup prepared chili sauce
½ tsp. oregano
1 pinch black pepper
1 tsp. vegetable salt
½ tsp. asafetida

Cook over low heat until hot. Use for loaf.

SWEET POTATOES

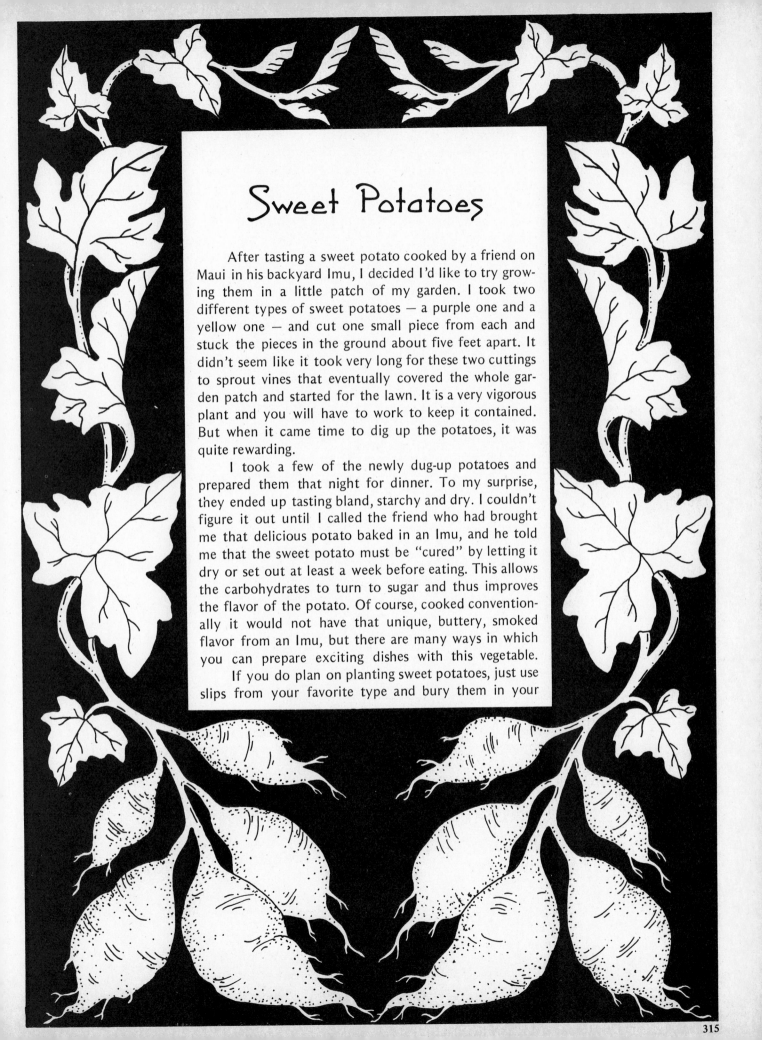

Sweet Potatoes

After tasting a sweet potato cooked by a friend on Maui in his backyard Imu, I decided I'd like to try growing them in a little patch of my garden. I took two different types of sweet potatoes — a purple one and a yellow one — and cut one small piece from each and stuck the pieces in the ground about five feet apart. It didn't seem like it took very long for these two cuttings to sprout vines that eventually covered the whole garden patch and started for the lawn. It is a very vigorous plant and you will have to work to keep it contained. But when it came time to dig up the potatoes, it was quite rewarding.

I took a few of the newly dug-up potatoes and prepared them that night for dinner. To my surprise, they ended up tasting bland, starchy and dry. I couldn't figure it out until I called the friend who had brought me that delicious potato baked in an Imu, and he told me that the sweet potato must be "cured" by letting it dry or set out at least a week before eating. This allows the carbohydrates to turn to sugar and thus improves the flavor of the potato. Of course, cooked conventionally it would not have that unique, buttery, smoked flavor from an Imu, but there are many ways in which you can prepare exciting dishes with this vegetable.

If you do plan on planting sweet potatoes, just use slips from your favorite type and bury them in your garden. Within four to six months, you will have plenty of potatoes and even more vines and leaves than you'll know what to do with. You can eat the sweet potato tops, and I have included some recipes for those, too.

Be careful when you spade up the potatoes to try to avoid cutting or breaking them; dig carefully! If you decide you want to dig up your sweet potatoes to plant something else, good luck! Trying to get all the vines and parts of roots out of the soil is very difficult; they will just keep on sprouting. For this reason, you may want to give them their very own edged-in spot in the garden. If the outer growing end of the vine finds a nice piece of soil, it will put down roots, produce a few sweet potatoes and start new vines, heading for new locations.

In comparison to other foods, sweet potatoes are an excellent source of vitamin A, a good source of calcium and phosphorus, a fair source of thiamine and iron, but a poor source of riboflavin, niacin and vitamin C.

Most of the vitamins are near the skin and boiling removes many of its nutrients, so it is best not to boil them. Cook them by steaming or baking in the skins. Sweet potatoes are excellent either steamed, baked or fried. The flourishing leaves are quite palatable and serve nicely as a green added to soups and salads.

Recently, I headed a workshop at the International Women's Year Conference here in Hawaii. The topic discussed in my workshop was "Basic needs and self-sufficiency in Hawaii." We discussed the reasons why

(From U.S.D.A. Agriculture Handbook #8) SWEET POTATO 100 gm. edible portion				
	Raw	Baked in skin	Boiled in skin	* Leaves
Water	70.6%	63.7%	70.6%	86.7%
Food energy	114 calories	141 calories	114 calories	42 calories
Protein	1.7 gm.	2.1 gm.	1.7 gm.	3.2 gm.
Fat	.4 gm.	.5 gm.	.4 gm.	.7 gm.
Carbohydrate	26.3 gm. (Total) .7 gm. (Fiber)	32.5 gm. (Total) .9 gm. (Fiber)	26.3 gm. (Total) .7 gm. (Fiber)	8 gm. (Total) 1.6 gm. (Fiber)
Ash	1.0 gm.	1.2 gm.	1.0 gm.	1.4 gm.
Calcium	32 mg.	40 mg.	32 mg.	86 mg.
Phosphorus	47 mg.	58 mg.	47 mg.	81 mg.
Iron	.7 mg.	.9 mg.	.7 mg.	4.5 mg.
Sodium	10 mg.	12 mg.	10 mg.	5 mg.
Potassium	243 mg.	300 mg.	243 mg.	562 mg.
Vitamin A	8,800 I.U.	8,100 I.U.	7,900 I.U.	2,700 I.U.
Thiamine	.10 mg.	.09 mg.	.09 mg.	.13 mg.
Riboflavin	.06 mg.	.07 mg.	.06 mg.	.26 mg.
Niacin	.6 mg.	.7 mg.	.6 mg.	.9 mg.
Vitamin C	21 mg.	22 mg.	17 mg.	21 mg.

* (From Food Composition Table for Use in East Asia)

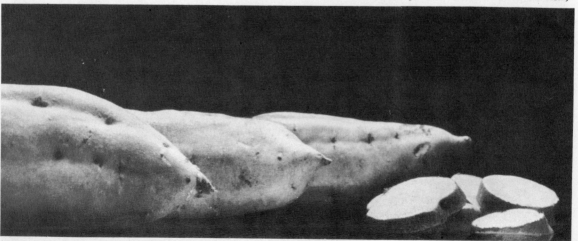

Hawaii should become self-sufficient and the different things that both government and individuals can do to make self-sufficiency a reality.

In one workshop, we discussed in depth how self-sufficiency means developing a self-sufficient mentality. Such a mentality means that we mustn't be controlled by television and advertisers, who want people to be controlled by them and made to want this thing and that. This can be done in many ways, large and small.

One way was practically demonstrated by a woman at the workshop who wondered out loud whether rice would grow in Hawaii. Another woman remarked that rice used to be grown and milled here, but pointed out that it's not a particularly profitable or practical crop because of the amounts of water required.

The first woman shrugged her shoulders and said, "Oh well, I guess that means I have to change my eating habits. I guess I could eat something else, besides rice, that grows here. Like sweet potatoes . . ."

Especially for that woman, and for all of you, too, here are some favorite uala (sweet potato) recipes.

HONEYED SWEET POTATOES ○

3 medium sweet potatoes, baked
1 Tbsp. honey
1 Tbsp. date sugar
Butter or margarine

Preheat oven to 350° F. Let potatoes thoroughly cool. Slice and place them in a buttered casserole dish. Place them in two layers, drizzling honey and sprinkling date sugar evenly on each. Dot the top with butter and bake at 350° for about 25 minutes. They should be slightly browned. Yields 3 to 4 servings.

SWEET POTATO PUDDING ○

1½ cups diced, firm coconut
1½ cups hot milk or water

¾ cup honey
1 tsp. cinnamon
½ tsp. salt
½ tsp. nutmeg
½ tsp. ginger or allspice

1½ cups diced sweet potatoes, raw

¾ cup chopped raisins
¾ cup coconut pulp
2 Tbsp. butter or margarine

Preheat oven to 350° F. Put hot liquid in blender. Gradually add coconut and blend until grated. Let set a few minutes. Strain and save ¾ cup dry pulp. Combine milk in blender with next 5 ingredients, gradually adding the sweet potato, and blend until smooth. Add last 3 ingredients. Mix well and pour into buttered casserole dish. Bake at 350° for 1½ hours, until knife comes out clean. This can be served hot as a vegetable or cool as a dessert. Good topped with Coconut Cream (see Coconut Section, p. 122).

SWEET POTATO PIE #1 ☆

Preheat oven to 350° F. Follow instructions for sweet potato pudding (see previous recipe). Pour into your favorite uncooked pie shell (Flaky Pie Crust is good — see Basic Recipes Section, p. 33). Drizzle top well with honey and bake at 350° for 1½ hours, until knife comes out clean. Let cool and serve with whipped cream or ice cream. Delicious!

SWEET POTATO PIE #2 ☆

Crust:
Use Crumbly Crust recipe
(see Basic Recipes Section, p. 33)

Filling:
5 to 6 cups mashed sweet potato
¼ cup butter or margarine
1 Tbsp. grated ginger, sautéd in butter
½ to ¾ cup canned or thick, creamy milk
1 cup honey
1 tsp. cinnamon
½ tsp. nutmeg
¼ tsp. ground cloves or allspice

Preheat oven to 375° F. Combine cooked, mashed sweet potatoes and remaining ingredients. Mix well and spread in unbaked pie shell. Sprinkle on topping and bake at 375° for 20 minutes until browning on top. Serve warm or cold.

POTATO SWEET BALLS ○

4 medium sweet potatoes, mashed
A little whole wheat flour
½ tsp. nutmeg

1 cup water
2 cups honey

Ghee or light oil

Steam potatoes. Cool, peel and mash them, mixing with next 2 ingredients. Combine next 2 ingredients and boil about 5 minutes. Roll sweet potatoes into olive-sized balls and deep fry in medium-hot ghee until browned and firm. Remove, drain, and soak in hot honey syrup. Yields 4 to 6 servings.

SWEET POTATOES & ORANGE ○

3 cups boiled sweet potato
¼ cup orange juice
1 Tbsp. grated orange rind

This is a very simple recipe and tastes good. Either sauté sweet potatoes in a little butter and then sprinkle with orange juice and rind, or mash sweet potatoes and mix in orange juice and rind.

HAWAIIAN STYLE SWEET POTATOES ○

4 cups cooked, mashed sweet potato
1 cup fresh, crushed pineapple
2 Tbsp. pineapple, lemon or orange juice
2 Tbsp. butter or margarine
½ tsp. salt
Dash of black pepper

½ cup dry whole wheat bread crumbs
4 Tbsp. butter or margarine
2 Tbsp. honey
1 Tbsp. date sugar
Dash of cinnamon, nutmeg and cloves

Preheat oven to 375° F. Combine first 6 ingredients and mix well. Place in a buttered casserole dish (1 quart). Combine last 5 ingredients. Mix well and sprinkle evenly on top of sweet potato. Bake at 375° for 25 to 30 minutes. Yields 6 servings.

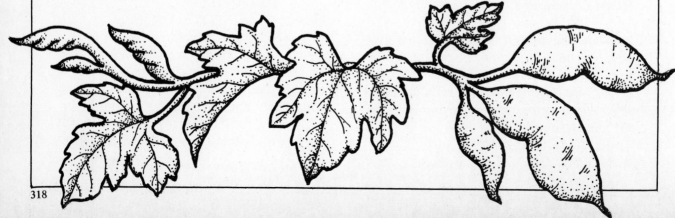

CREAM OF SWEET POTATO SOUP

1½ potatoes, cut in cubes (2½ - 3 cups)
1 cup water
1 tsp. sweet basil

1 Tbsp. oil
1 Tbsp. whole wheat flour
¼ tsp. asafetida

2 cups milk or coconut milk

½ cup minced celery
1½ - 2 tsp. vegetable salt
¼ tsp. black pepper
¼ tsp. allspice
1 cup finely chopped sweet
potato leaves (firmly packed)

Combine first 3 ingredients. Cover and cook until tender. Drain any water that is left and mash thoroughly. Fry next 3 ingredients, stirring constantly. Continue stirring and gradually add milk. Add next 5 ingredients and sweet potatoes. Mix well and cook until thick. Yields 2 to 4 servings.

SWEET POTATO CASSEROLE

½ cup hot milk
1 Tbsp. butter or margarine
1 tsp. salt
4 cups mashed sweet potato

½ cup raw peanut butter (chunky style)
¼ cup honey
½ tsp. cinnamon (opt.)

Preheat oven to 375° F. Combine first 4 ingredients. Cream next 3 together; add to sweet potato. Mix well and spread into a greased baking dish. Bake at 375° for 35 minutes. Yields 6 servings.

BAKED SWEET POTATO

Preheat oven to 375° F. Bake whole sweet potatoes with skins at 375° for 50 to 60 minutes. When fork can be easily inserted, they are done. Turn off heat and let sit in oven until serving time. Serve with butter, salt and black pepper.

SWEET POTATO CASSEROLE #1

2 cups boiled sweet potato, sliced very thin
1½ cups crushed pineapple

¼ cup whole wheat flour
½ cup honey
¼ cup butter or margarine
¼ tsp. cinnamon
¼ tsp. nutmeg

½ cup grated coconut

Preheat oven to 350° F. Combine second group of 5 ingredients. In a casserole dish, place one layer of sweet potatoes, one layer of pineapple and one layer of mixture; then repeat layering in same order. Top with grated coconut and bake at 350° for 30 minutes.

SWEET POTATO CASSEROLE #2

3 cups mashed sweet potatoes

1 cup applesauce
½ cup honey
1 Tbsp. lemon juice
½ tsp. nutmeg
¼ cup butter or margarine
½ cup chopped nuts
¼ cup raisins

Preheat oven to 375° F. Combine last 7 ingredients and pour over the mashed potatoes in a casserole dish. Bake at 375° for 35 minutes.

319

SWEET POTATO CASSEROLE #3 ☆

3 cups boiled sweet potatoes, sliced thin
½ lb. apricots, soaked overnight
½ cup date sugar

¼ cup butter or margarine
1 Tbsp. orange rind
½ cup orange juice
2 Tbsp. arrowroot
¼ cup sunflower seeds

Preheat oven to 350° F. In a casserole dish, layer first 3 ingredients two times over. Combine last 5 ingredients and pour over layers. Bake at 350° for 30 minutes.

SUN SWEET BREAD ◯

1 cup cooled, mashed sweet potato
¾ cup whole milk
1/3 cup honey
1 tsp. oil or melted butter
1 tsp. salt

½ cup lukewarm water
1 envelope yeast
or 1 Tbsp. bulk baking yeast

3¼ cups whole wheat flour
1 tsp. cinnamon

½ cup sunflower seeds

Preheat oven to 425° F. Combine first 5 ingredients and blend until smooth. You can use a blender or an electric mixer. Combine next 2 ingredients and let sit until dissolved. Scoop potato mixture into a bowl and mix in yeast. Sift in next 2 ingredients. Add sunflower seeds and mix with a fork until you need to use your hands. Knead for 3 to 5 minutes. Roll into a loaf and set in a buttered and floured loaf pan. Cover with a dampened cloth and set in a warm place for one hour to rise. Put in oven to bake at 425° for 10 minutes. Baste with milk and lower heat to 375°. Continue baking for 35 to 40 minutes. Remove from pan; let cool, and slice. Delicious!

SWEET POTATO CHIPS ☆

Lightly peel and slice potatoes crosswise into very thin slices. Soak them in cold water for about 15 minutes. Drain thoroughly and deep fry in ghee or light oil until delicately browned. Drain well (on paper) and serve with salad as a main course, or as a snack.

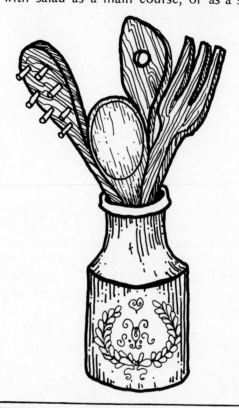

SWEET POTATO TEMPURA ☆

1 cup flour (whole wheat or garbanzo)
1 tsp. ground cumin
1 tsp. turmeric
1 tsp. ground coriander
½ tsp. allspice
½ tsp. cinnamon
½ - ¾ tsp. salt
¼ tsp. chili powder
2 Tbsp. yogurt
1 cup water (a little less)

Sweet potato slices, ½" thick

Sift flour and spices into a bowl. Add yogurt and water (a little at a time), mixing well to avoid lumps. Dip sweet potatoes until well coated with batter and deep fry in hot ghee or light oil until golden brown. Remove and drain.

SWEET POTATO SQUARES ☆

4 large sweet potatoes

3 Tbsp. butter or margarine
½ cup water blended with
¼ cup buttermilk powder
1½ tsp. cinnamon
Egg replacer equal to 1 egg
2 tsp. salt
½ tsp. black pepper
½ cup honey
1 cup chopped walnuts
½ cup ground walnuts
1 cup whole wheat flour, dry toasted

Graham crackers, finely crushed
Ghee for deep frying

Boil potatoes in skins. Cool, peel and press through a sieve. Whip together next 11 ingredients. Add to sweet potatoes and mix well. Roll into balls and refrigerate until firm. Press between fingers to form small squares. Deep fry in oil or ghee. Remove and immediately roll in crumbs. These are good served warm or cool and especially good served the following day.

SWEET POTATO CARROT MALPOURA ☆

1 cup whole wheat pastry flour
½ cup honey

½ cup grated sweet potato
½ cup grated carrot
1/8 tsp. cardamom

½ cup water

Ghee or oil for deep frying

Mix first 2 ingredients. Add next 3 and mix well. Add water to make a fairly thick batter. Drop by tablespoonfuls (in one clean drop) into hot ghee and fry until golden brown. Drain and serve.

RICE & SWEET POTATOES ○

1½ cups brown rice
(washed and well-drained)
1½ Tbsp. oil

1 lb. sweet potatoes,
cut into ½" x ¾" cubes
3 cups water
1 tsp. salt

Combine first 2 ingredients and fry, stirring frequently, until lightly toasted. Combine with last 3 ingredients. Cover tightly and bring to boil. Reduce to simmer and cook about 35 minutes until rice is tender and water has cooked off. Turn off heat and let sit covered a few minutes. Top each serving with a dab of butter and sprinkle with cinnamon. Yields 6 servings.

SWEET POTATO AND TOASTED COCONUT ○

2½ lbs. sweet potato, cooked and mashed

1½ cups fresh coconut, grated and toasted
½ stick butter or margarine
½ tsp. cinnamon
½ tsp. allspice
1 tsp. cumin powder
1½ tsp. salt or 1 Tbsp. kelp
1/8 tsp. cayenne

Cook potatoes. Mash and mix well with remaining ingredients. Serve hot as a vegetable. Yields 6 servings.

HASH BROWN SWEET POTATOES ○

Wash and peel sweet potatoes. Grate and drop by large spoonfuls onto a griddle or heavy skillet. Fry in sesame or other light oil on medium heat until brown and crusty. Turn with spatula and fry other side.

Suggestion: Try serving them with cooked comfrey leaves with butter and Scrambled Eggs Tofu (recipe in Tofu Section, p. 376).

Sweet Potato Pie #2, p. 318   Cream of Sweet Potato Soup, p. 319   Homemade Whole Wheat Buns, p. 415

SWEET POTATO LEAVES ○

2 Tbsp. ghee or oil
3 cups finely chopped leaves,
washed and well drained

1 cup grated coconut
½ cup chopped green pepper
1 tsp. salt or soy sauce (or less)
½ tsp. turmeric
½ tsp. mustard powder (opt.)
¼ tsp. black pepper (or more)

1 tsp. lemon juice

Heat oil in a skillet. Add leaves and cook a few minutes over high heat, stirring well. Add next 6 ingredients. Mix well and cook on low heat for 5 minutes more, being careful not to overcook. Remove from heat. Mix in lemon and serve. Yields 2 to 3 servings.

SWEET POTATO GREENS IN COCONUT MILK ○

1 large bunch of sweet potato leaves
1 cup coconut milk

Pinch of asafetida (opt.)
Pinch of black pepper
Pinch of salt or soy sauce to taste

Wash, drain and chop leaves. Steam with coconut milk until tender. Turn up heat; cook on high heat, stirring constantly, until coconut milk cooks off. Add remaining ingredients. Mix well and serve.

Variation: This may also be done with Coconut Cream (see Coconut Section, p. 122).

322

TARO

Taro

I really like the flavor and texture of taro. But until I discovered dryland taro, I figured it would be nearly impossible for me to grow it. For most people, dryland taro is more feasible to grow than the water varieties. But if you're lucky enough to be near one of the few fresh water streams left here in Hawaii and have water rights, then try diverting some for a patch of taro.

There is a valley on Maui where interest has been renewed in taro farming. The valley was becoming barren because the young people were going off to the cities for some excitement. But recently, due to getting burned out on the emptiness and hardness of city life, many of the young people are returning with a new pioneering spirit. They're returning to work the land with a greater appreciation and love for the aina (land). To protect their right to the land and water, they are starting taro patches again.

They are fortunate, since they can tap into one of the few remaining untampered-with mountain streams. I say one of the few because although there are 17 stream valleys in West Maui alone, today only two of these streams follow their natural course to the ocean. The other streams have been diverted. Once again, we see a result of man's arrogant attitude of thinking he can play God by dominating and conquering nature. But these young people (and others) are seeing how the environment and the people are being betrayed by a society based on this attitude. They are starting wet taro patches. Even though most of us don't have a mountain stream, we can still plant taro.

To plant both dry and wetland taro, all you have to do is cut the leaves and some of the stem off, so that some of the stem is left sticking up from the bulb. Next, cut the root bulb off about one inch down from where the stem joins the bulb. Keep the root bulb and leaves with stems for cooking, and stick the piece of bulb with stem back into the ground. In about six months you'll be able to harvest another bulb, not to mention all the leaves you can harvest in between.

As for the part you didn't plant, this should be made into a meal! Taro was the favorite food of the native Hawaiians, preferred over breadfruit and sweet potatoes. The Hawaiians were akamai (smart; full of common sense) in this way. Having no supermarkets or refrigerators to take shelter in, they had the ingenuity to collect the taro and eat it when breadfruit was not in season. Such a simple, common sense thing to do — probably something I would never have thought of doing!

It's said that the native Hawaiians could recognize over 150 different kinds of taro. Myself, I only know of a couple of kinds.

The Tahitian taro that I planted is especially good because of the sweetness of its leaves and stems.

Whether it's the leaves and stems or the root bulb itself, you must boil it for a long time to break down the needlelike crystals (calcium oxalate) contained in taro which are extremely irritating to the lining of the mouth and throat. Anyone who has ever had the misfortune of eating taro or the leaves that haven't been cooked sufficiently can tell you about the "pins and needles" sensation in the mouth and throat.

Ridiculously, though, I was only able to find nutrition tables in the U.S.D.A. Agriculture Handbook #8 for raw taro and leaves, so these tables are more or less useless. I've included them because they give you some idea of the nutritional content, and the table from the Food Composition Table for Use in East Asia will give you some idea of how the nutrients change when taro is cooked.

Next year after breadfruit season, give taro a try! Here are some recipes you can try. Especially good tasting (one of my favorites) and also symbolic, is the Waiahole-Waikane Special. I first tasted this preparation when people from all over Hawaii were camping out in the Waiahole-Waikane Valley

to give their support to the residents there who refused to move off of the land they had been farming for generations to make way for land developers. This simple dish was one that residents of the valley served to all the thousands of people who came to give their support. To me it symbolizes how people can work together to preserve prime agricultural land (an unrenewable resource), the quality of life, and the hope that we can keep buying taro and other produce that's grown in these valleys and others like it. Hoping that by the time this book is published more valleys aren't covered with concrete, I would like to offer these recipes aimed at utilizing locally grown produce.

(From U.S.D.A. Agriculture Handbook #8) TARO 100 gm. edible portion		
	Tubers	Leaves and stems
Water	73.0%	87.2%
Food energy	98 calories	40 calories
Protein	1.9 gm.	3.0 gm.
Fat	.2 gm.	.8 gm.
Carbohydrate	23.7 gm. (Total)	7.4 gm. (Total)
	.8 gm. (Fiber)	1.4 gm. (Fiber)
Ash	1.2 gm.	1.6 gm.
Calcium	28 mg.	76 mg.
Phosphorus	61 mg.	59 mg.
Iron	1.0 mg.	1.0 mg.
Sodium	7 mg.	–
Potassium	514 mg.	–
Vitamin A	20 I.U.	–
Thiamine	.13 mg.	–
Riboflavin	.04 mg.	–
Niacin	1.1 mg.	–
Vitamin C	4 mg.	31 mg.

(From Food Composition Table for Use in East Asia) TARO 100 gm. edible portion		
	Tubers, raw	Tubers, boiled
Water	75.4%	67.8%
Food energy	94 calories	124 calories
Protein	2.2 gm.	1.9 gm.
Fat	0.4 gm.	0.3 gm.
Carbohydrate	21.0 gm. (Total)	28.8 gm. (Total)
	0.8 gm. (Fiber)	– (Fiber)
Ash	1.0 gm.	1.2 gm.
Calcium	34 mg.	48 mg.
Phosphorus	62 mg.	48 mg.
Iron	1.2 mg.	0.9 mg.
Sodium	10 mg.	11 mg.
Potassium	448 mg.	498 mg.
Vitamin A	Trace	Trace
Thiamine	.12 mg.	.08 mg.
Riboflavin	.04 mg.	.05 mg.
Niacin	1.0 mg.	0.6 mg.
Vitamin C	8 mg.	4 mg.

BOILED OR STEAMED TARO ROOT ○

Scrub taro root thoroughly. Cut into cubes and pour enough salted, boiling water over them to half-cover them. Cover pan and boil for 1 to 1½ hours, until tender. Peel and serve in cubes or mashed with butter, salt and black pepper.

BAKED TARO ○

Preheat oven to 350° F. Scrub root thoroughly. Cut in half (if very large). Bake at 350° for 1 to 1½ hours, until tender. Peel and serve hot with butter, salt and black pepper.

FRIED TARO ○

Cut cooled, boiled taro into thin pieces. Sprinkle with salt and fry in butter.

POI ○

2½ lbs. taro, cubed and cooked
2½ cups water

Place taro in wooden bowl and pound until smooth and pasty. Gradually add some of the water and work in with hands. Strain through a double thickness of cheesecloth (or poi cloth) to remove fibers and lumps. Add more water and mix with hands until desired thickness is reached. Serve immediately or mix with a little extra water and refrigerate. Poi that has been mixed with water is called "paiai" and can also be left in a bowl covered with a damp cloth for 2 or 3 days at room temperature to develop a sour taste. Store-bought poi should be mixed with water before using. Poi is sometimes used instead of flour to thicken gravy, or sweetened and diluted with milk and served as a pudding.

TARO & BANANA POI

1 cup poi
1 cup mashed banana

¼ cup scorched coconut milk
¼ cup coconut milk
¼ tsp. cinnamon
2 Tbsp. honey

Toasted coconut

Press first 2 ingredients through a sieve or run through a juicer. Add next 4 ingredients and mix well. Top with toasted coconut and chill before serving. Yields 2 servings.

TARO CHIPS ☆

Scrub taro well. Peeling is optional. Cut in thin slices. Deep fry in oil or ghee. Drain and salt. About 2½ cups sliced taro yields 6 servings.

TARO BALLS ☆

Bake a taro root. When done, mash it well and mix with milk, salt, black pepper and sesame seeds. Roll into balls and deep fry in hot ghee or oil. These puff up a bit and are light and crispy.

TARO PUFFS ◯

2 cups hot, mashed taro
2 tsp. baking powder
1 tsp. salt or 2 tsp. kelp
¼ cup flour

Butter or margarine

Preheat oven to 450° F. Combine first 4 ingredients and mix well. Roll into small balls and place in buttered muffin tins. Press a dab of butter in the top of each and bake at 450° for 10 to 15 minutes, until brown and puffy.

BAKED OR FRIED TARO PATTIES ◯

2 cups cooked, mashed taro
1 Tbsp. milk
1 Tbsp. butter or margarine
1 tsp. salt or 2 tsp. kelp

Mash taro well. Combine ingredients and mix. Form into small, flat patties and place in buttered pan. Bake at 350° F for 30 minutes or fry in butter. Yields 6 servings.

TARO & TOFU SALAD ◯

2 cups taro, cubed

¼ cup finely grated carrot
¼ cup thinly sliced celery
½ large bell pepper, diced
1 cup firm tofu, cubed

2 Tbsp. hulled sesame seeds
¼ tsp. asafetida

½ cup Eggless Soy Mayonnaise
(see Basic Recipes Section, p. 34)
¼ cup sour cream
1 - 1½ tsp. salt
½ tsp. black pepper

Cook taro; cool and mix with next 4 ingredients. Toast next 2 ingredients. Combine with next 4 ingredients and mix well. Add to taro mixture. Mix well and chill before serving. Yields 4 servings.

TARO WITH OTHER GARDEN VEGETABLES ○

4 cups raw taro, peeled and chopped
Water to cover

2 cups beets, sliced in ¼" discs
2 tsp. oil

2 cups sweet potato, sliced or chopped
2 cups chopped greens (beet tops,
kale, squash leaves, wom bok, etc.)

¼ cup butter or margarine
1 tsp. turmeric
½ tsp. chili powder
½ tsp. curry powder
½ tsp. Spike seasoning (opt.)
Salt and black pepper to taste

Start boiling taro. Sauté beets in oil. When taro begins to get mushy, add beets and next 2 ingredients. Continue cooking until done. Mix in remaining ingredients and serve. Simple and delicious. Yields 4 to 6 servings.

TARO & CHEESE BAKE ○

2 Tbsp. butter or margarine
4 Tbsp. whole wheat flour

2 cups milk
¾ tsp. salt
¼ tsp. black pepper

3 cups boiled taro, sliced thin
½ cup grated cheese

1 Tbsp. butter or margarine
¼ cup dry whole wheat breadcrumbs

Preheat oven to 350° F. Melt butter, add flour and stir to toast, making a smooth paste. Gradually add milk, stirring until it thickens. Add salt and black pepper. Combine in alternate layers with taro and cheese in an oiled casserole dish (taro, sauce, cheese, etc.). Combine next 2 ingredients. Mix thoroughly and sprinkle over top of casserole. Bake at 350° for about 20 minutes until crumbs are golden brown. Yields 6 servings.

TARO & GREEN BANANAS ○

1 lb. taro root, cubed
½ lb. green banana, peeled & sliced
2 cups water
1 tsp. salt
½ tsp. black pepper
1 tsp. turmeric

1 Tbsp. oil
1 tsp. mustard seeds

1 fresh coconut, grated

Cook taro until half-done. Drain. Put in a large skillet with next 5 ingredients; cover and boil until tender (add extra water if necessary). Lightly toast next 2 ingredients and add to vegetables with coconut. Mix well and cook for 10 minutes more. Yields 2 to 4 servings. Good served with sour cream or yogurt.

TARO MALPOURA ☆

1 cup whole wheat pastry flour
½ cup honey

1 cup grated, raw, peeled taro
¼ - ½ tsp. cinnamon

½ cup water

Ghee for deep frying

Mix first 2 ingredients. Add next 2 and mix well, adding water to make a fairly thick batter. Drop by tablespoonfuls (in one clean drop) into hot ghee and fry until golden brown. Drain and serve.

TARO WON TUNS ☆

½ cup whole wheat flour
½ cup unbleached white flour
½ tsp. salt
¾ stick of butter or margarine

Filling:
3 cups diced and peeled taro root

1/3 - 1/2 cup thick coconut cream
2 Tbsp. butter or margarine
½ tsp. asafetida
½ tsp. salt
1 cup chopped, steamed kale
or 1 cup finely chopped string beans
or 1 cup finely chopped Chinese peas

Combine first 4 ingredients well. Add a little water if necessary. Roll out 1/8" thick (or thinner) on an oiled counter. Cut into 2" squares with sharp knife or pastry wheel. Steam taro until tender. Cool and slightly mash. Combine with next 5 ingredients and mix well. Place 1 tsp. filling on pastry squares, dot edges with water, place another pastry over the top and press edges to seal. Drop gently in hot ghee or oil; deep fry for 5 minutes until golden. Drain and serve. The raw won tuns can also be dropped into soups and cooked that way.

TARO LEAVES WITH EVAPORATED MILK

80 leaves
2 cups water

1 cup evaporated milk
2 Tbsp. butter or margarine
1 tsp. salt
Black pepper to taste

Wash leaves well. Remove stems and membrane from the back of each leaf. Divide into several pieces. Boil in 1 cup water for 10 minutes and drain. Add 1 cup water, milk and butter. Partially cover pot and bring to a boil. Lower heat and simmer for 45 minutes. Remove cover and cook until most of the liquid has cooked off. Add salt, mix and serve. Yields 6 servings.

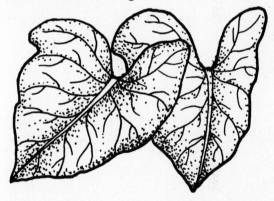

TARO LEAVES WITH COCONUT MILK ☆

60 leaves
1 cup water

¾ cup cooked chickpeas
2 cups thick coconut milk
1 tsp. turmeric
1 tsp. ground coriander
2 Tbsp. butter or margarine
1 tsp. salt
Black pepper to taste

Prepare leaves for cooking by washing well. Remove stems and membrane from the back of each leaf. Divide into several pieces. Boil in 1 cup water and cook until very tender, about 45 minutes. Drain well; add remaining ingredients and simmer for a few minutes and serve. Yields 6 servings.

KULOLO (Haole Style) ○

2 cups grated taro root
½ cup coconut milk
½ cup honey
4 Tbsp. finely grated coconut

Preheat oven to 300° F. Combine ingredients. Mix well and pour into an 8" baking pan well covered with aluminum foil, not allowing any steam to escape. Bake at 300° for 2½ to 3 hours.

POI MUFFINS ○

2/3 cup poi
½ cup coconut milk
3 Tbsp. melted butter or oil
2 Tbsp. honey
Egg replacer equal to 1 egg

1½ cups whole wheat flour
½ tsp. salt
1 tsp. baking powder
1 tsp. baking soda

Preheat oven to 350° F. Combine first 5 ingredients in a mixing bowl and mix well with a whisk or fork. Sift in last 4 ingredients and mix well. Fill buttered and floured muffin tins three-fourths of the way and bake at 350° for 30 to 35 minutes. Good served as a dinner roll. Makes about 8 muffins.

POI SHAKE □

1 cup cold milk
2 tsp. poi
2 tsp. honey
Dash of cinnamon

Combine ingredients. Whiz in blender and serve. Yields 1 cup.

WAIAHOLE-WAIKANE SPECIAL ☆

4 cups peeled and cubed taro (1½" cubes)
½ tsp. salt

4 cups cubed sweet potato

2 cups coconut milk
½ to ¾ cup honey

Bring salted water (enough to cover taro) to a boil and add the taro. Stir occasionally to keep it from sticking. When taro is soft enough to be cut, add sweet potato and more water if necessary. When sweet potatoes are tender, drain off water (save water for adding to soup stocks and for cooking rice because any water that is left after the vegetables are boiled is full of vitamins). Add coconut milk and honey, mix well, and let cook 5 to 10 minutes before serving. Ono! Yields 6 servings.

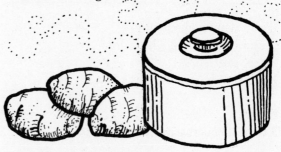

CAROB POI PUDDING ○

1 cup coconut milk or ½ cup water
1 cup noninstant dry milk powder

4 - 6 Tbsp. carob
8 Tbsp. honey

1 small package poi

½ cup raw coconut
½ cup toasted coconut

Combine first 2 ingredients in blender at low speed until smooth and pasty. Pour into a saucepan. Combine carob and honey and mix until smooth. Mix with milk. Add remaining ingredients and blend well. Cook over medium flame for about 5 to 10 minutes, stirring frequently. Pour into a cake or pie tin and refrigerate until cool.

SEAWEED

Seaweed

Harvesting vegetables from the sea is one way you can think of seaweed. Unfortunately, people in the West who haven't had, through culture, the use of seaweed as a food, are often squeamish about the thought of eating sea vegetables. Yet almost all of us have unknowingly partaken of them. Any label reader may remember the terms agar, carrageenan or algin on their ice cream, yogurt, salad dressing and many other labels. These all mean that you've eaten seaweed. It wasn't all that bad, was it?! Not only is it "not bad," it's actually great for you.

Seaweed is a great natural tonic. It is very rich in chlorine, potassium, calcium, and is a very good source of iodine. Iodine helps provide the body with energy and endurance. It aids the body in relieving nervous tension, in improving circulation and in promoting function of the thyroid gland. It helps burn off food we take in every day and has long been used as an aid to reducing.

Seaweed has many other minerals including magnesium, phosphorus, iron, copper, sodium, sulphur and natural salt from the sea. It contains all the mineral elements that are required for growth. It contains little fat and a fair amount of protein and vitamin C. It is a good source of vitamins, and it has been estimated that 100 grams (about 3 oz.) of certain seaweeds provide more than the necessary daily requirements of vitamin

A, riboflavin and vitamin B_{12}, and about half the daily requirement of vitamin C.

Here in Hawaii, we have the largest variety of edible seaweeds available, but we have less quantity in comparison to Japan and other parts of the world. Seaweed has been a long-time favorite of the native Hawaiians and the Orientals. The Hawaiians probably know the most about how to use the seaweeds that grow here. Early Hawaiians used seaweed as a staple in their diets, especially when taro, sweet potatoes and yams were short.

Here is a list of seaweed most easily found and commonly used in Hawaii:

Limu kohu. Also called **kohu lipehe** (light-colored kohu) and **kohu koko** (dark-red kohu) on Kauai.

They can be found growing on edges of reef where there is water in constant motion. Found especially in the Anahola district of Kauai. Also found in Waianae and Kahuku, Oahu; Hana, Maui; Kohala, Hawaii; and around Molokai.

The straight parts of the plant are collected by diving; the creeping base portions are never taken or used. The plants are cleaned, pieces of coral and sand removed, and then soaked in fresh water for half a day or overnight. They are then lightly salted, upper branches pounded and rolled with stems into balls about the size of a walnut. Prepared in this way, they will keep indefinitely. Portions are taken for use as needed. Due to its strong flavor when added to soups and stews, only a small amount is needed.

Limu lipoa. This name is used on all the Islands.

They are found at Nomilu, Kauai; Kaneohe and Waikiki, Oahu; Olowalu and Lahaina, and Waihee to Sprecklesville, Maui; and Kohala, Hawaii. They are subtidal but are sometimes cast ashore in strong winds and are plentiful where found.

They are found growing from 3 to 15 feet deep in meadows beyond the reef. They are fairly tall and coarse and easy to pick. The leafy branches are washed and heavily salted so that they keep indefinitely without refrigeration. The younger leaves can be chopped or pounded, lightly salted and refrigerated. This seaweed has a unique odor and spicy flavor and is a favorite in vegetable stew.

Limu manauea. This name is used on all the Islands. Another common name is **ogo.**

This seaweed comes in small bunches and is easily collected. Other seaweeds and

clinging objects are removed. It is then washed well in fresh water and chopped into fine pieces or eaten in long pieces. This seaweed freezes well or may be lightly salted and refrigerated until needed.

Limu pahe'e. Also called **paheehee** and **luau** on Kauai. Another most common name is **nori**.

They are usually found in winter or early spring growing on large, rounded rocks in heavy surf. They can be found at Moloaa and Kalihiwai, Kauai; Waimea and Maile, Oahu; Honolua and Hana, Maui; Kohala, Kona and Waikapuna and Lalae, Hawaii.

They should be carefully scraped from the rocks and washed well. To serve, cut into small pieces, mix with a little salt and let stand for a few hours before serving. This seaweed doesn't keep as well as others do. It may also be quickly sun-dried and stored for using in its most common way — nori.

Collecting seaweed was always one of the chores that my children had the most fun doing. Sometimes we would all pile into a friend's pickup truck and drive down to a beach by the Kahului Airport to gather seaweed for the garden. Seaweed would be washed up on the beach and we'd shovel the seaweed into the truck. The kids would throw handfuls in the truck and at each other. I would take this seaweed home, give it a quick hose off, and then put it in the compost pile and the garden itself. Seaweed

has been used for thousands of years as an agricultural fertilizer to replenish worn-out soil. It helps reduce fungus diseases in the soil, it is free from weeds and seeds carrying crop diseases, it is high in potassium and nitrogen content, has numerous trace elements — and it's free.

A last word about seaweed as a garden fertilizer — be sure to rinse it off well so you won't be putting too much salt into the soil. Hosing the seaweed was always fun for the kids too. We'd squirt each other with the hose and jump and dance up and down on the seaweed to wring it out. Everyone would get a lot of exercise, have fun, and get a chore done all at the same time.
time.

Picking edible seaweeds was another of the kids' favorite activities. My oldest son would always beg to go to Kihei and pick seaweed. We'd usually take goggles and an inner tube for the baby and just go swimming, diving and picking seaweed. I always wondered, while we were picking, if it mattered how seaweed was picked. I finally contacted someone at the Oceanography Department at the University of Hawaii and asked. I'm sure glad I did!

I found out how to pick seaweed so the plant wouldn't be killed and would still be able to continue growing. I was told to carefully break or snip the seaweed off at the stem. If the seaweed is pulled off from

---

(From U.S.D.A. Agriculture Handbook #8)
SEAWEED
100 gm. edible portion

	Agar	Dulse	Kelp	Laver
Water	16.3%	16.6%	21.7%	17.0%
Food energy	–	–	–	–
Protein	–	–	–	–
Fat	.3 gm.	3.2 gm.	1.1 gm.	.6 gm.
Carbohydrate	– (Total)	– (Total)	– (Total)	– (Total)
	.7 gm. (Fiber)	1.2 gm. (Fiber)	6.8 gm. (Fiber)	3.5 gm. (Fiber)
Ash	3.7 gm.	22.4 gm.	22.8 gm.	11.0 gm.
Calcium	567 mg.	296 mg.	1,093 mg.	–
Phosphorus	22 mg.	267 mg.	240 mg.	–
Iron	6.3 mg.	–	–	–
Sodium	–	2,085 mg.	3,007 mg.	–
Potassium	–	8,060 mg.	5,273 mg.	–

(Dashes denote lack of reliable data for a constituent believed to be present in measurable amount.) The following data for two kinds of dried seaweed is from the "Food Composition Table for Use in East Asia" (vitamins and minerals in milligrams):

100 gm.	Calories	Protein	Carbohydrate	Calcium	Phosphorus	Iron	Sodium	Potassium	B_1	B_2	B_3	Vit. C
Laver	235	22.2 gm.	44.3 gm.	434	350	28.3	1,294	3,503	.24	1.3	5.5	14
Hijiki	173	4.5 gm.	42.8 gm.	1,400?	56	29.0			.01	.20	4.0	0

where it's connected to the rock or sand, it's like uprooting a plant. I taught the kids how to pick seaweed, and we always try to be careful so the seaweed can continue to grow and be there for others. We usually pick ogo and make namasu out of it. That seems to be the most common way of using seaweed in the Islands.

Seaweeds, as food for humans, contain all minerals and elements required by the body for nutrition. It should be eaten more often but tends to be ignored because of being a bit less palatable than vegetables we are used to eating. It can be prepared nicely and is most commonly used by the Japanese in salads and as soup stock base or flavoring. Two kinds they use most are nori, which is dried in sheets, toasted, stuffed with rice and vegetables and called sushi; and kombu or kelp, which is dried and used as a soup stock or as a flavoring in place of salt, pepper or curry. Most limu used by early Hawaiians was lightly salted, chopped into small pieces and eaten raw like salad or relish. A favorite relish was made by roasting the kernels of kukui nuts, chopping them fine, mixing them with chopped limu and salt, and serving this with bread and butter or poi. They would also use limu manauea or ogo and add it to soups and stews for thickening or add it to cooked foods just before serving to add to the flavor.

Here are some common derivatives:

Agar is a gelatinous extract of seaweed coming mostly from seaweeds of the East Coast of the U.S. and some from the West. The industrial grade is used for stabilizing sherbets, cheeses, bakery products, making candy and preserves, and for all gelatin uses requiring a nonanimal stabilizer. It is low in carbohydrates and calories and is not derived from animal sources; it is therefore useful in the healthful, vegetarian diet. It is a good jelling agent in home cooking and can be found in most any natural food store.

Dulse is one of the red seaweeds. It is found in a rough, dried state in Boston and New York and other seaports of the U.S. and is shipped to many places. In Ireland it is used with potatoes. It is usually eaten dried or raw and is very good added to salads.

Kelp or **kombu** is one of the brown seaweeds and is a principal source of iodine. It is available in tablet or powdered form and is very good used in place of salt, added to any soup, salad or vegetable dish.

When I was little, I liked seaweed — especially nori — so much that my parents served it as dessert. They would say that I could have some seaweed if I ate all my vegetables! You may or may not like seaweed that much, but here are some ono (delicious) ways to prepare different kinds of seaweed that anyone would like.

LIMU-OGO SALAD □

2 cups ogo

½ carrot, grated
1 cucumber, sliced thin

¼ cup lemon juice or apple cider vinegar
2 Tbsp. honey
2 Tbsp. soy sauce

2 Tbsp. toasted sesame seeds or sesame meal

Wash ogo and clean well. Some people prefer blanching the ogo and others prefer not to. This is up to you. After ogo is ready, chop fine. Add vegetables and sauce made of next 3 ingredients. Refrigerate about 1 hour. Sprinkle with sesame seeds or meal right before serving.

AGAR-AGAR SALAD □

2 sticks agar-agar (1 cup flakes)
1½ cups cabbage, sliced thin
½ carrot, grated
2 cups bean sprouts
¾ head of lettuce (about 3 cups)

Dressing:
1 Tbsp. toasted sesame oil
1 Tbsp. vegetable oil
1 Tbsp. honey
2 Tbsp. soy sauce
Pinch each of asafetida and cayenne

Soak agar sticks in water until soft. Tear or cut into pieces and toss in with other vegetables. At last minute before serving, toss in dressing.

LAND & SEA VEGETABLE SALAD □

Your favorite garden fresh salad
Handful of dried dulse

Make your favorite garden fresh salad. Rinse dulse off and tear into small pieces. Toss into salad and serve with your favorite dressing. Adds a wonderful flavor as well as much nutrition to your salad.

TOSSED HAWAIIAN GREEN SALAD □

½ cup finely chopped ogo
1 small head Manoa lettuce
3 large stalks watercress, chopped
½ cup firm tofu, cubed
½ cup alfalfa sprouts

¼ cup finely grated carrot (opt.)

1 Tbsp. toasted sesame oil
1/8 tsp. asafetida

1 Tbsp. salad oil
1½ Tbsp. soy sauce
Juice of half a lemon
1 tsp. honey

Combine first 5 ingredients and toss until blended. Sprinkle carrot over the top. Combine next 2 ingredients in a saucepan and toast asafetida. Cool and combine with next 4 ingredients. Serve over tossed greens. Yields about 4 servings.

OGO CHICKPEA SALAD ○

½ cup garbanzo beans (chickpeas)
Boiling, salted water

½ cup finely chopped ogo

2 Tbsp. tahini
2 Tbsp. water
1 Tbsp. lemon juice
¼ tsp. salt (or more) or ½ tsp. kelp
3 pinches asafetida toasted in ½ tsp. butter

Soak chickpeas for 6 to 8 hours. Drain and then boil in salted water for about 1 hour until tender (will mash between fingers). Rinse, drain and cool. Rinse ogo, drain and chop fine. Toss with garbanzo beans. Combine last set of ingredients, mix well and serve over ogo and chickpeas. Serves 2.

OGO CHEESE SALAD

1 tsp. oil
1/8 tsp. asafetida

¼ tsp. salt or ½ tsp. kelp
1/8 tsp. black pepper
2 tsp. apple cider vinegar

1 cup finely chopped limu
2 Tbsp. toasted sesame seeds

½ cup creamed cottage cheese
3 radishes, grated
1 Tbsp. finely grated carrot

Toast first 2 ingredients. Mix with next 3 ingredients and toss with next 2 ingredients. Place in a salad bowl and set aside to marinate. Combine next 3 ingredients. Mix well and place on top of ogo in the center. Spread it out to not quite cover the ogo. Sprinkle grated radish and toasted sesame seeds over the top. Cover and set in refrigerator to chill. This makes an attractive-looking salad that yields about 4 servings.

Variation: This can also be served with a little creamy French dressing over each serving.

ALMOST POKI ☐

½ cup firm tofu, cut in 1" cubes
¼ cup rubber coconut, cubed
Soy sauce

1 cup finely chopped ogo
1 small chili pepper, minced
1 Tbsp. sesame meal
1 tsp. apple cider vinegar (opt.)

Cover first 2 ingredients with soy sauce and soak for about 30 minutes until well-coated and dark. Pour through sieve and drain well. (Soy sauce can be used again.) Combine next 4 ingredients. Mix well; toss in tofu and coconut. Mix well and set in refrigerator to marinate and chill. Serve cold. Yields 2 servings.

WAKAME SALAD ☐

1 cup wakame, soaked and cut up
1 large cucumber, cut in half
and grated into thin slices
¼ cup vinegar
2 Tbsp. honey
1 Tbsp. soy sauce

¼ cup toasted sesame seeds or sesame meal

Combine first 5 ingredients and refrigerate about 1 hour. Sprinkle sesame seeds or meal over salad right before serving.

MINERAL BOWL ☐

10 sheets nori seaweed

Dressing:
1 Tbsp. toasted sesame oil
1 Tbsp. safflower or sunflower
or other light oil
1 Tbsp. honey
Pinch cayenne pepper
1 tsp. soy sauce
2 Tbsp. sesame seeds
1 tsp. grated ginger

Toast seaweed by running sheets over a flame (but not touching the flame) until crisp and greenish. Crumble with hands or cut with scissors into bite-sized pieces. Toss in with dressing made of next 7 ingredients and serve immediately before the seaweed gets soggy.

Note: Use nori cut in strips or toasted and crumbled on top of rice, entrees, salads or vegetables.

FAVORITE RICE BALLS ○

6 cups cooked brown rice
(good way to use leftovers)
1 Tbsp. soy sauce
¼ cup nutritional yeast

3 sheets nori seaweed

Combine first 3 ingredients and mix well.
Cut nori sheets in quarters across the width.
Dip hands in a bowl of water and take about
½ cup of brown rice mixture out at a time,
form into ball shape and wrap with nori
strip.

KOREAN STYLE SEAWEED CRISP ○

10 sheets nori seaweed

3 Tbsp. toasted sesame oil
3 Tbsp. soy sauce
Pinch cayenne (opt.)

Combine last 3 ingredients and brush mixture with basting brush onto one side of
seaweed. Only do as many as will fit on a
cookie sheet at once. Place on cookie sheet
and bake at 350° for about 2 minutes until
seaweed is crispy. Continue until all sheets
are used. Serve in place of chips, on rice, or
as hors d'oeuvres.

NORI – LUMPIA STYLE ○

10 nori sheets

3 cups finely chopped
or grated fresh vegetables
1 cup bean sprouts
1 Tbsp. toasted sesame oil
1 Tbsp. honey
1 tsp. grated ginger
Dash of cayenne

Mix last 6 ingredients together. Lay one
sheet of nori out flat. Place about 1/3 cup
of vegetables in a strip in the middle of the
seaweed, leaving about 2 inches at the end
edges. Fold opposite lengthwise edges over
each other. Then fold open ends under
(should look like a burrito). Fold all in this
way, then heat skillet and pour a few tablespoons of oil in skillet. Fry each roll on both
sides until seaweed becomes crisp.

STUFFED NORI TEMPURAS ☆

½ cup mashed tofu
1/8 tsp. asafetida
¼ cup celery, diced fine
1 heaping tsp. arrowroot
2 tsp. soy sauce
½ tsp. grated, fresh ginger
2 Tbsp. sesame seeds

4 sheets nori

Tempura Batter (see recipe
in Basic Recipes Section, p. 36)

Combine first 7 ingredients and mix well.
Cut nori sheets in half. Place heaping 2 Tbsp.
of this in middle of nori sheet. Fold edges
over each other and then fold the two other
open ends over. Dip in tempura batter and
deep fry until batter is crisp. Remove from
oil and drain on paper towels.

NORI RICE OR VEGETABLE SPREAD ○

6 sheets of nori seaweed
1 cup water
2 Tbsp. soy sauce
1 Tbsp. honey
1/8 tsp. cayenne (opt.)

Combine all ingredients in a pot off the heat
and let sit until seaweed becomes soggy and
falls apart. Place on burner and cook over
medium heat, stirring occasionally, until
water cooks out and seaweed is a pasty texture. Use as a spread on top of brown rice
or vegetables. Refrigerate extra for use on
another day.

TRADITIONAL NORI SUSHI ○

2½ cups raw brown rice
6 cups water

¼ cup vinegar
2 Tbsp. honey

½ cup gomasio
(see Basic Recipes Section, p. 38)

1/8 tsp. asafetida	10 nori sheets
1 tsp. oil	
1 cup okara	Grated carrot with a little honey and salt
1 Tbsp. beet juice	
½ tsp. gomasio	2 or 3 watercress or thin celery strips per sushi
1 Tbsp. honey	
¼ tsp. salt	

remove filled nori. Place seamside down and let set a few minutes. Cut into sixths with a sharp knife, place on their sides and serve.

Bring water and rice to a boil. Cover and simmer 40 minutes until tender and water cooks off. Rice should be soft. Add next 2 ingredients and mix well. Add gomasio and mix well. If making rice the night before, cover the pot with a damp cloth overnight and add gomasio in the morning when rice is cool. Toast asafetida in oil. Add okara and more oil, if necessary, and stir-fry until drying out. Add next 4 ingredients and mix well. Cool and set in freezer until needed. Place nori sheet at the edge of the bamboo roller. Place 1 cup rice ½" away from the opposite edge. One-third of the way down the rice, place a nice layer of seasoned okara. On top of that, place the watercress or celery strips and then the grated carrot. Gently start to roll. When one-eighth of the way rolled, gently press nori to make it stick together. Lift edges of bamboo roller a tiny bit and gently pull the bamboo to the opposite edge and over enough until the nori is rolled. Gently roll the nori in the bamboo back (toward your body) and roll up inside bamboo. At this time, apply gentle, even pressure by squeezing with hands up and down the bamboo roll with nori sushi inside. Press filling in ends before taking out of bamboo. It is good to have a bowl of vinegar water on the side to dip fingers in while filling and rolling. Gently unroll bamboo to

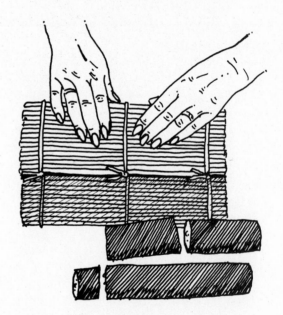

HAOLE NORI SUSHI ○

1 cup brown rice
1½ Tbsp. sesame oil
¼ cup sesame seeds

2 cups water
1 tsp. celery salt

½ cup grated, raw beets
½ cup chopped walnuts
3 tsp. sesame oil

1 cup grated carrot
2 tsp. grated ginger
3 tsp. sesame oil

Nori sheets

Wash rice and drain well. Fry with sesame seeds in oil until lightly toasted. Place in a pan with water and salt and bring to boil. Turn to simmer and cook with cover for 30 to 40 minutes until rice is tender and water evaporated. Set aside to cool. Sauté next 3 ingredients and set aside. Sauté last 3 ingredients and set aside. Fill each nori sheet with about 4 Tbsp. of rice and spread evenly. Top with about 2 Tbsp. of carrot mixture and spread; then 2 Tbsp. of beet mixture and spread. Roll it up tightly by hand or with a bamboo rolling sheet. Cut in half with a sharp knife and toast in oven at 375° for a few minutes so that nori can get a little crispy. Cool before serving. The size and shape of each sushi and amount of filling added is up to the individual. For a wider, more round sushi, you can double or triple the amount of rice and vegetables added; slice the roll in quarters, etc.

UMEBOSHI RICE BALLS "ONIGIRI" ○

5 cups seasoned rice from Traditional Nori Sushi (see previous recipe, p. 342)

¼ of an umeboshi plum per rice ball

¼ of a nori sheet per rice ball

Have a bowl of salt water for dipping fingers.

Measure ½ cup rice, wet fingers and roll rice into a ball. Indent the center and place the plum. Reseal. Then fold nori sheet in half and cut into four strips. Wrap strip around rice ball, seal edge with salt water and serve.

MOCK FILLETS OF FISH IN NORI ○

½ cup whole wheat flour
½ cup bran
1 tsp. chili powder

10 sheets nori
40 tofu fillets
Tamari (soy sauce)
Oil for frying

Mix together first 3 ingredients. Set aside in bowl. Cut nori sheets in fours. Cut ¼" slices of tofu and cut each slice in half. Dry them on paper towels; then brush with tamari on both sides. Place each tofu slice in a piece of nori and fold nori over tofu. Seal with a little water. Brush both sides of stuffed nori with tamari. Roll in flour mixture until well coated. Fry in hot oil until golden brown. Turn and fry other side.

JELLED CONSUMÉ ○

½ recipe of Basic Broth
(see Basic Recipes Section, p. 31)

1 tsp. agar-agar powder
(about 1/6 stick of agar-agar)

Bring broth and agar to boil and simmer until agar is dissolved. Allow to cool and chop or cube jelled consumé. Serve with a favorite garnish in individual chilled glass bowls brought to the table on a platter of ice.

TOMATO ASPIC ○

2 Tbsp. butter or margarine
1 Tbsp. asafetida
2 cups finely chopped celery

12 cups puréed tomatoes
6 bay leaves
2 tsp. sweet basil
1 Tbsp. + 1 tsp. marjoram
2 tsp. soy sauce
4 whole cloves

1 Tbsp. + 1 tsp. apple cider vinegar
1 Tbsp. + 1 tsp. honey
2 sticks agar-agar (1 cup flakes)

Blend fresh tomatoes in blender to make 12 cups of purée and reserve in a bowl. In a large pot, sauté first 3 ingredients together until asafetida toasts and celery is browned. Add next 6 ingredients, cover and simmer for 15 minutes. Pour this mixture through a strainer and squeeze as much liquid out of the pulp as possible. You can keep pulp to make soup broth, or add to other cooked vegetable. Pour strained liquid back into pot and add last 3 ingredients and let sit until agar-agar softens. Then put onto heat and boil until agar dissolves. Pour into a ring mold and refrigerate until set. Pour aspic out onto a bed of sprouts or watercress. Fill the middle with your favorite guacamole or vegetable stuffing (recipes in Avocado and Garden Vegetables Sections, pp. 66, 259). Sprinkle and decorate sides with parsley.

CHINESE NECTAR DRINK ○

2 sticks agar-agar (1 cup flakes)

4 cups favorite fruit juice

4 cups (or more) other flavor fruit juice aside from the one cooked in agar
Honey to taste

Combine the first 2 ingredients by breaking agar and soaking until soft. When soft, cook until agar-agar is dissolved. Pour into a cake or baking tray. Cool and then refrigerate a few hours to allow setting. Blend the last 2 ingredients (so you can mix in the honey without having to heat the juice). Cut the agar-agar jell into ¾" cubes and float in sweetened juice. You can also make the nectar juice part more like a liquid fruit salad by adding fruits in season and then adding agar-agar.

SEAMEAL CUSTARD ○

6 cups milk (soy, nut or dairy)
2 sticks agar-agar (1 cup flakes)
1 vanilla bean
¾ cup honey
Pinch cardamom
1/8 tsp. turmeric
1/8 tsp. cinnamon

Combine all ingredients in pot. Let agar-agar soak until softened. Bring to boil, stirring often to prevent sticking and burning. Cook until agar-agar dissolves. Pour mixture in mold or on top of a layer of your favorite fruit. Sprinkle a little more cinnamon on top and let cool. Refrigerate for a few hours after custard has cooled.

LEMON CHIFFON PIE ○

3 cups milk (soy, nut or dairy)
1 stick agar-agar (½ cup flakes)

1/3 cup honey
¼ cup lemon juice
¼ tsp. grated lemon rind
2 Tbsp. liquid lecithin
½ tsp. lemon extract

(See directions on next page.)

Combine first 2 ingredients in a pot off the heat. When the agar-agar softens, put pot on burner and bring to a boil over medium heat, stirring occasionally, cooking until agar dissolves. Set aside and let cool until this jells. Then chop into pieces and put into a blender with next 5 ingredients. Blend until smooth and creamy. Pour this into an already baked pie shell or a raw foods pie shell that requires no baking (see Basic Recipes Section, pp. 32, 33), layering with or pouring over a layer of chopped fruit if you desire. You can also make other flavored variations of chiffon pies by eliminating lemon juice, rind and extract and adding any of the following:

1) 1/3 cup carob powder, 2 tsp. vanilla, 1 tsp. Pero
2) ½ cup of fruit in season, cutting down on honey according to sweetness of fruit
3) Replace honey with ¼ cup molasses (barbados) and fold into mixture that has been blended smooth. Add 1/3 cup chopped and softened dried fruit and ¼ cup finely chopped pecans.
4) Use your imagination with your favorite ingredients, or ingredients on hand!

RICE CAKE WITH DRIED FRUIT　　　O

2 cups cooked rice
4 cups milk
1 stick agar-agar (½ cup flakes)
1 tsp. cardamom
½ cup honey
¾ cup dried fruit and nuts

2 Tbsp. butter or margarine
½ cup honey, cooked down (caramelized)

Combine first 6 ingredients in a pot (break stick of agar into smaller pieces) and let set until agar softens. Place over medium heat and bring to a boil, stirring occasionally, and cook until agar totally dissolves. Remove from heat and set aside to cool. As the agar-agar mixture begins to cool but not set, melt next 2 ingredients in a saucepan and cook until it forms a caramel (soft ball stage—drop a bit in a bowl of ice-cold water and if a soft, squishy ball forms, it's ready. Be very careful not to let it cook to the hard ball stage). Pour the caramel into a buttered mold and turn mold so caramel coats all sides. Dip outside of mold into a large bowl filled with cold water and ice cubes so caramel will instantly harden on sides of mold. Be careful while doing this not to get water on the inside of the mold. Pour agar mixture that has cooled down a bit into the mold and refrigerate 'til set. Turn out onto a platter. refrigerate until set. Turn out onto a platter. Decorate with imagination and serve. Especially good served with a dollop of real or Soy Whipped Cream (see Basic Recipes Section, p. 34).

ONO OGO CASSEROLE　　　O

2 cups whole wheat bread, cut in cubes (may be dried out in oven)

2 cups ogo, chopped fine
4 tsp. sesame butter
2 tsp. soy sauce
2 tsp. miso
1/8 tsp. black pepper

½ cup tomato sauce
½ cup grated cheese

Preheat oven to 350° F. Rub bread between hands to crumble it. Combine with next 5 ingredients; mix well and press into a small casserole dish. Leave a little room on each side for the sauce. Pour sauce over the loaf and bake at 350° for 15 to 20 minutes. Place grated cheese on top and return to oven until melted. Cut in slices and serve. This is also good served cold. Tastes almost like meatloaf! Yields 2 to 4 servings.

STIR-FRY LAND & SEA VEGETABLES ○

2 Tbsp. toasted sesame oil
3 cups assorted hard vegetables (celery, carrots, string beans, cauliflower, etc.)
¼ tsp. asafetida

½ cup dry hijiki seaweed

2 Tbsp. miso
1 Tbsp. honey
½ cup water
Dash cayenne

Soak hijiki in hot water 10 to 15 minutes. In the meantime, cut vegetables. Sauté first 3 ingredients together until vegetables become translucent. Drain and rinse hijiki seaweed and add to sautéing vegetables. Add last 4 ingredients, mixing until miso dissolves. Cover and simmer about 7 minutes. This is good served hot or cold with brown rice.

OGO WITH FRIED RICE ○

2 Tbsp. sesame seeds
1 cup cooked brown rice, cooled
1 Tbsp. oil

1 cup ogo, chopped fine
2 tsp. vinegar
4 tsp. soy sauce
1 tsp. honey

Toast sesame seeds. Add next 2 ingredients and fry, stirring occasionally, until grains are separated and a little golden. Combine next 4 ingredients and mix well. Let marinate a few minutes. Add to fried rice. Mix and stir-fry over a medium-high heat until blended and excess liquid has evaporated. Be careful not to overcook — will get too mushy. Delicious! Yields 2 servings.

TERIYAKI OGO COCONUT RELISH ○

½ cup rubber coconut strips, sliced thin
1 tsp. oil

2 Tbsp. honey
2 Tbsp. soy sauce
1 Tbsp. water
1/8 tsp. asafetida
1 tsp. finely grated ginger

1 cup finely chopped ogo

Combine first 2 ingredients in a skillet and fry a few minutes. Add next 5 ingredients. Mix well and cook over medium flame, stirring occasionally until thick. Add well-drained ogo. Cook and stir until thickened. Good served with brown rice. Yields 2 servings.

OGO TOFU STEAM CAKES ○

1 cup tofu, drained well and mashed
1 Tbsp. sesame butter
1 tsp. honey
1 tsp. soy sauce
2 tsp. miso
1 tsp. grated ginger
2 Tbsp. finely grated carrot
2 Tbsp. slivered green beans
½ cup ogo, washed and chopped

Combine ingredients and mix well. Divide into half. Press into oblong cakes. Place each of them on a piece of aluminum foil and place on top of a steamer rack. Cover and steam for 20 to 30 minutes. Good served warm or cold. Also good served with an eggless tartar sauce. Yields 2 servings.

FRIED KOMBU ○

Soak kombu a few hours, then cut kombu in bite-sized pieces and freeze (freezing helps break down the toughness). When frozen, take out and thaw. Dip kombu in soy sauce and fry in sesame oil until crisp. Toss chips in 1 tsp. flaky nutritional yeast.

BAKED KOMBU　　　　　○

Prepare kombu by soaking and freezing as for Deep-Fried Kombu. Dip thawed kombu in soy sauce and bake in oven at 220° for 30 minutes on a cookie sheet. Remove from oven and sauté over medium heat in a dry skillet with enough flaky nutritional yeast to coat the kombu. Stir until completely coated with yeast and kombu pieces are quite crisp.

KOMBU CHILI　　　　　○

2 cups dry pinto beans
10 strips of kombu 6" long

½ tsp. asafetida
2 Tbsp. olive oil

1 tsp. basil
1 tsp. kelp
½ tsp. marjoram
¼ tsp. black pepper

3 Tbsp. lemon juice
¼ cup soy sauce

Soak beans and kombu overnight. Cut kombu into ½" wide strips. Simmer beans and kombu together over medium heat for about 2 hours. In a pan, toast asafetida in olive oil on medium heat. Add next 4 ingredients. Combine with beans and seaweed. Mix well, then add last 2 ingredients and simmer for 45 minutes to 1 hour, until beans are tender.

DEEP-FRIED KOMBU　　　　　○

Soak kombu strips in water at least 3 hours, then freeze. Freezing helps break down some of the toughness. Soak frozen kombu in soy sauce until kombu is thawed out. Cut kombu into bite-sized pieces. Deep fry prepared kombu plain and you will have a crisp seaweed chip. You can dip kombu in Tempura Batter (see Basic Recipes Section, p. 36) and deep fry, or use the following batter.

Batter:
¼ cup whole wheat flour
¼ cup + 1 Tbsp. water
1 tsp. sesame seeds
1½ tsp. fresh finely chopped parsley
¼ tsp. asafetida

NISHIME　　　　　○

1 yd. of nishime kombu
1 qt. hot water

4 cups assorted hard vegetables, chopped
2 tsp. honey
1 Tbsp. + 1 tsp. soy sauce

Soak first 2 ingredients together for about 1 hour. With scissors, cut nishime kombu (if necessary) so the yard-long strip is about 1" wide. If you have a wide strip of nishime kombu, you may end up with 3 or 4 yard-long strips. Now tie single knots 2" apart all the way down the strips (use all the kombu). Be sure to tie knots tight so they won't come undone while cooking. Cut kombu halfway between each knot. This will give you a bunch of bow-tie-shaped nishime. Set the bow ties aside. Chop hard vegetables (such as taro, carrots, potatoes, broccoli stems, cauliflower, radish or daikon) into 1" chunks to make about 4 cups of chopped vegetables. If you wish to use vegetables like string beans, mushrooms, etc., which don't require such a long cooking time, just chop them and add them later in the cooking when you add the nishime bow ties. Put hard vegetables, honey, soy sauce and the remaining soaking water in a large pot and cover and simmer over medium heat until vegetables are tender enough to pierce with a fork. When the hard vegetables are tender, add nishime bow ties and softer vegetables (if you're using any). Cover and continue simmering until water is nearly cooked out and is like a thick gravy, coating the vegetables and the nishime (this doesn't take long, as the nishime kombu absorbs water as it cooks). As the nishime reaches completion, stir it occasionally to avoid sticking and burning. Cool and refrigerate. Serve cold as a refreshing summer dish.

"Lo, there are some who can call themselves nothing more than a passage for food, producers of dung, fillers up of privies, for of them nothing else appears in the world, nor is there any virtue in their work, for nothing of them remains but full privies."

— Leonardo da Vinci

SOYBEANS

Soybeans

Soybeans are such a superfood that they deserve a whole chapter to themselves, since they are one of the more valuable, yet unappreciated foods on the planet. It's really quite amazing to think that soybeans: 1) offer a healthful (cholesterol and saturated fat-free), cheap, high-quality source of protein; 2) if utilized, can make possible self-sufficiency in food needs almost anywhere in the world, thereby eliminating the world hunger problem; 3) at the same time, enrich the soil where they are grown by fixing in nitrogen. Considering all of this, it's really amazing that in many parts of the world — especially in the Western hemisphere — most people have never even tasted soybeans.

In the United States this certainly holds true. Very few people in the United States have tasted soybeans or foods made with soybean by-products, even though soybeans are one of our major crops (we harvest an average of 50 million tons a year).

The nutritional value of such a harvest may be hard to imagine. Akiko Aoyagi and William Shurtleff put it in a nutshell in their **Book of Tofu:**

"The 47 million tons of soybeans harvested in 1973 is enough to provide every person in the United States with 165 pounds of pure, high-quality protein. If all of this protein was used directly as food — in the form of tofu, for example — it would be sufficient to fulfill the average adult protein requirement for about three years."

This may sound like an extreme exaggeration, but when we consider that the amount of usable protein in a half cup of soybeans is equal to the amount of protein contained in a five-ounce steak, it's more easily understood. Of course, when we're speaking of nutrition, protein isn't the only factor. As can be seen in the following table, which was taken from an **El Molino Cookbook** printed 10 years ago (which accounts for the difference in price), soybeans are equal or superior to meat in providing other nutrients as well.

Mrs. Smith spent $5.40 for 4½ pounds of beef and 25 pounds of soybeans. Mrs. Smith received:

	Beef	Soybeans
Servings	6	150
Days of protein	13	180
Total protein	355 gm.	4,540 gm.
Calories	5,659	37,765
Calcium	2,841 mg.	25,765 mg.
Phosphorus	2,841 mg.	66,511 mg.
Iron	53 mg.	908 mg.
Vitamin A	0 I.U.	15,890 I.U.
Vitamin B_1	2 mg.	121 mg.
Vitamin B_2	3 mg.	35 mg.

And just think . . . all these nutrients can be gotten inexpensively through soybeans with the added healthful plus of not consuming any cholesterol or saturated fat to get them! Considering all this, it's quite amazing that soybeans aren't a staple in our diet, isn't it?

If so few Americans eat soybeans, then where do all the soybeans go? We export some, but 95% of unexported soybeans (as well as 78% of our total grain crop) is fed to livestock. In **Diet for a Small Planet**, Frances Moore Lappe points out that we feed 14 to 21 pounds of protein in the form of legumes and grains to a cow to get one pound of protein in return in the form of meat.

By getting protein indirectly through meat, poultry, fish and eggs, rather than getting protein directly from plant sources, the average American manages to consume the equivalent of 2,000 pounds of grains and soybeans annually. On the other hand, in countries where the primary protein source is grains and legumes, the average person consumes only 400 pounds of these foods a year. This means that one meat-eater consumes as much grains and legumes as about five vegetarians.

In this way, our eating habits affect more than just our personal health. They actually affect the ability or inability of a particular community to be self-sufficient for its food needs, as well as having an effect on the world's food resources.

As can be seen, self-sufficiency for our food needs in Hawaii, as well as any community or developing country in the world, depends a great deal on consumption habits. For example, growing soybeans here in Hawaii and using them as a direct source of protein would be an important step towards self-sufficiency. Because we live on an island with a limited amount of resources, self-sufficiency requires using those resources in the most efficient and productive way possible. As can be seen by the following figures, soybeans could provide more usable protein per acre than is now being provided by beef cattle, the source of protein presently produced on a large scale in the Islands.

*** Every two years in Hawaii
NPU = Net Protein Utilization**

---

1 acre of land = 1 beef steer = 400 to 500 pounds of meat.
20% protein by weight = 100 pounds
NPU = 67 pounds

1 acre of land = 25½ bushels of dry soybeans at 60 pounds per bushel. Two years (figuring three harvests a year on one acre) = 9,180 pounds of dry soybeans.
35% protein by weight = 3,213 pounds
NPU = 1,960 pounds

* A two-year period is used because steers are usually slaughtered when two years old.

Of course, these figures hold true for Hawaii, but would vary from place to place according to whether or not there was a year-round growing season and other variables. But in any situation, the growing and eating of soybeans for protein has pluses all along the way. Soybeans use resources more efficiently, which means economic savings for individuals as well as for the state and the world. They also offer more nutritional value which means better health for everyone.

Furthermore, making this substitution by no means has to be an unpleasant or distasteful experience. Here are a few recipes you can try so you can see for yourself!

These are just an introduction to what you can do with soybeans and their byproducts. If you want more recipes and more detailed information on nutrition, etc., a few excellent books you can look into are **The Book of Tofu, The Book of Miso** and **The Book of Tempeh** by Akiko Aoyagi and William Shurtleff; and **Diet for a Small Planet** by Frances Moore Lappe.

SOYBEANS

Soybeans are a very versatile food and lend themselves to be used in many ways. You can soak a lot of beans at once, then freeze them. This cuts down on the amount of time the beans must be boiled to be cooked. These recipes are made with beans that have been soaked but not yet cooked.

SOY NUTS ☆

Soak beans overnight. Drain, rinse and let sit in a colander for 15 to 20 minutes so water can drain out. Deep fry in medium-hot oil (300° to 350°) until light golden. Sprinkle with salt, nutritional yeast, kelp, etc.

DRY ROASTED SOY NUTS ◯

4 cups soaked soybeans

Soak soybeans overnight. Drain water off thoroughly and let sit on towel for a while to make sure excess water is soaked up. Spread soybeans on an unoiled baking pan only 1 layer thick and bake at 200° for 2 to 3 hours. Stir beans in pan every 20 minutes. They are done when beans are golden brown and slightly soft. The beans will harden as they cool. Don't try to bake them until they are hard, as they will probably burn. (If beans turn dark-brown, they are burned.) While still warm, sprinkle with vegetable salt or nutritional yeast and/or other spices.

The following recipes are made with soybeans that have been boiled and mashed (a done bean should mash easily between the tongue and roof of the mouth). You can make a whole lot at once and freeze in little containers, taking them out as needed.

SOY SPREAD #1 ◯

2 cups cooked, mashed soybeans
2 small red chili peppers
1 small chunk ginger
½ tsp. asafetida
1 Tbsp. soy sauce
¼ cup olive oil
½ cup lemon juice
1 cup water

Blend all ingredients in a blender. Use on top of pita bread, chapatis with sprouts, salad, etc.

SOY SPREAD #2 ◯

2 cups tomato sauce
2 cups cooked, mashed soybeans
1 cup nutritional yeast
¼ cup soy sauce
1 cup water

try

Blend ingredients. Use as sandwich spread, etc.

SOY SPREAD #3 ◯

2 Tbsp. oil
¼ tsp. asafetida
2 - 4 small chilies

1 cup diced celery

2 cups cooked, mashed soybeans
6 medium tomatoes, diced

½ tsp. turmeric
1 Tbsp. gomasio (see Basic Recipes Section, p. 38)
2 tsp. honey

½ cup coriander leaves (Chinese parsley)

Sauté first 3 ingredients. Add celery and sauté. Add next 2 ingredients and cook until a smooth mush. Add next 3 ingredients. Remove from heat and add coriander leaves.

SOY-COCONUT CHUTNEY ○

1 cup water
1 cup cooked, mashed soybeans
2 cups grated fresh coconut
(can use pulp from coconut milk)
4 - 6 small red chilies
1 cup coriander leaves
2 tsp. salt
½ tsp. asafetida
2 Tbsp. lemon juice

2 Tbsp. oil or ghee
1 Tbsp. mustard seeds

Combine first 8 ingredients. Toast mustard seeds in oil and pour into other ingredients.

SOYBEAN LENTIL LOAF ○

2 - 3 Tbsp. whole wheat
or garbanzo bean flour
3 Tbsp. oil

1½ cups milk or soy milk
1 Morga bouillon cube
½ tsp. vegetable salt
½ tsp. celery seed
1 tsp. parsley
½ tsp. black pepper
½ tsp. sage
½ tsp. thyme
¼ tsp. asafetida

1 cup whole wheat bread crumbs
1 cup whole wheat cracker crumbs
½ cup cooked, mashed soybeans
½ cup cooked, mashed lentils
¼ cup finely chopped pecans
¼ cup finely chopped walnuts

Preheat oven to 350° F. Toast first 2 ingredients in small pot. In a saucepan, bring milk to a boil and add next 8 ingredients. Mix in next 6 ingredients and the toasted flour. Spread mixture in an oiled casserole dish and bake at 350° for 20 to 30 minutes. Cool enough to cut into slices or squares and serve with Mock Turkey and Gravy (see recipe in Tofu Section, p. 379).

NUT LOAF ○

¼ tsp. summer savory
¼ tsp. marjoram
1/8 tsp. sage
1/8 tsp. thyme
½ tsp. sweet basil
1½ cups cooked, mashed soybeans
1 cup bread crumbs
1 cup chopped walnuts
½ cup soy milk
½ Tbsp. nutritional yeast
1/8 tsp. asafetida
1 Tbsp. green pepper
4 Tbsp. tomato sauce

Combine ingredients. Put into greased loaf pan and bake at 325° for 20 to 30 minutes. Garnish with parsley and gravy, if desired.

SOYBEAN HALVAH ☆

2 Tbsp. butter or margarine
1 cup cooked, mashed soybeans
1½ cups grated coconut
1 cup honey

2 pinches cardamom
2 tsp. nutmeg
2 tsp. vanilla

Cook first 4 ingredients on medium-high heat until they form a lump in the pan. Add last 3 ingredients, pour into a buttered dish and cool.

SOY CANDY ☆

6 Tbsp. butter or margarine
1 cup cooked, mashed soybeans

1½ cups honey
1/8 tsp. cardamom

1 cup dried fruits and nuts

Sauté first 2 ingredients together until beans turn brown. Add next 2 ingredients and cook on medium-high heat until honey candies and ingredients form a lump. Add dried fruit and nuts and pour into a buttered dish.

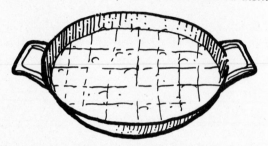

SOY SAUSAGE ○

2 cups cooked, mashed soybeans
2 slices whole wheat bread crumbs
½ cup nutritional yeast
1 Morga bouillon cube
1/8 tsp. thyme
½ cup tomato sauce

Mix all ingredients. Roll in hands into sausage shape. Dip in whole wheat flour and either panfry in oiled skillet or broil in oven on oiled baking sheet.

SOY PILAF ○

¼ cup oil or ghee
1/8 tsp. black pepper
2 bay leaves, crumbled
1 pinch cloves
¼ tsp. cinnamon
¼ tsp. asafetida
½ tsp. grated fresh ginger
1/8 tsp. cayenne

½ cup raw brown rice
1 cup soaked soybeans, uncooked

2 cups diced celery

Toast first 8 ingredients. Add grain and beans and toast. Add celery. Cover with 1½" of water and simmer until rice is cooked. Add vegetable salt to taste.

SOYBURGER ○

2 cups soaked soybeans (½ lb. dry)
2 Tbsp. vegetable oil
½ cup water
1 tsp. celery salt
2 tsp. oregano
1 tsp. Spike
¼ tsp. asafetida
1 tsp. basil
2 Tbsp. soy sauce

¼ cup nutritional yeast
½ cup finely grated carrot
½ cup finely chopped celery
½ cup chopped walnuts
2 Tbsp. dried parsley
¼ cup whole wheat flour

Combine first 9 ingredients in blender and blend until smooth. May need to stop blender and mix with spoon a few times. Scrape into a bowl and mix in next 6 ingredients. Mix well, form into patties and fry in well-oiled skillet on medium heat until browned and crispy. Serve on whole wheat bun with eggless mayonnaise, lettuce, tomato, sprouts, etc. Makes 12 patties.

SOYBURGER #2
(using cooked beans)　　　　　　　　　○

4 cups cooked soybeans
¾ cup water or tomato sauce
¼ - ½ tsp. asafetida
¼ tsp. black pepper
2 Tbsp. nutritional yeast
¼ cup soy sauce
¼ - ½ tsp. liquid smoke
1 tsp. Spike

try

½ - 1 cup bran and/or rolled oats

Blend first 8 ingredients in a blender until smooth, using only 2 cups of soybeans. Pour into a bowl. Grind remaining 2 cups of soybeans in blender without any liquid so they are coarsely chopped. Add to mixture in the bowl and add grains. Mix well and let sit 10 to 15 minutes so grains can absorb moisture. Shape ½ cup of mix at a time into patties and fry on medium-high heat in an oiled skillet. Cook until browned on one side, then flip over and cook on other side until browned. Serve between whole-grain buns (made out of Basic Bread Dough recipe in Basic Recipes Section, p. 31) or as an entree with gravy or dressing.

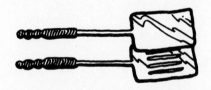

SOYBEAN PATTIES IN SAUCE　　　○

2 cups uncooked soybeans
1/8 tsp. cinnamon
½ tsp. ground coriander
1 Tbsp. sage, crushed
1½ tsp. ground cumin
1½ tsp. turmeric
¼ tsp. cayenne
¾ tsp. salt
1/8 tsp. allspice
¼ tsp. asafetida

Soak beans overnight, then drain and grind in a food grinder. Add all spices and mix well. Heat oil or ghee in deep pot or wok.

Shape ground beans into flat cakes the size of a half dollar. Gently place in medium-hot oil and deep fry until hard but not too brown. Remove and drain. Place them in either buttermilk (at room temperature) or Tomato Chutney (see recipe in Garden Vegetables Section, p. 263) and serve.

KINAKO　　　　　　　　　　　○

Kinako (roasted soybean flour) is best when homemade and fresh. Toast desired amount of whole, dry, uncooked soybeans in a wok over low heat for about 20 minutes. Stir often. When beans are light brown and fragrant, grind in a flour mill or grind small amounts at a time in a blender. Sift to remove hulls. If this is too time-consuming, you can bake soy flour at 350° to 400°, stirring often until it's toasted golden, although the nutlike sweetness isn't the same. Also, bottles or bags of kinako are usually available in Japanese markets or Oriental food sections of grocery stores.

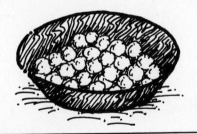

KINAKO LADDU　　　　　　　　○

2 cups kinako
½ cup peanut butter
½ cup honey

Combine all ingredients and roll into balls or press onto cookie sheets and cut in squares.

SOY MILK

The potential of soybeans is so great because they're such a versatile food. One way that soybeans can be used is already familiar to people who are allergic to dairy products; that is, they can be made into soy milk.

Soy milk has a unique flavor all its own, and I use it in my cooking in place of dairy milk. (You can substitute soy milk for any recipe in this book which calls for dairy milk.) I sometimes make nut milks and use them also, but soybeans offer a good quality protein at such a reasonable cost. Whereas nuts are so expensive, soybeans are still a bargain in these days of rising costs!

As can be seen in the table below, soy milk stands out well when compared with dairy milk and mother's milk.

(From U.S.D.A. Agriculture Handbook #8)
MILK
100 gm. edible portion

	Soy milk	Cow's milk	Human milk
Water	92.4%	87.4%	85.2%
Food energy	33 calories	65 calories	77 calories
Protein	3.4 gm.	3.5 gm.	1.1 gm.
Fat	1.5 gm.	3.5 gm.	4.0 gm.
Carbohydrate			
(Total)	2.2 gm.	4.9 gm.	9.5 gm.
(Fiber)	0	0	0
Ash	.5 gm.	.7 gm.	.2 gm.
Calcium	21 mg.	118 mg.	33 mg.
Phosphorus	48 mg.	93 mg.	14 mg.
Iron	.8 mg.	Trace	.1 mg.
Sodium	–	50 mg.	16 mg.
Potassium	–	144 mg.	51 mg.
Vitamin A	40 I.U.	140 I.U.	240 I.U.
Thiamine	.08 mg.	.03 mg.	.01 mg.
Riboflavin	.03 mg.	.17 mg.	.04 mg.
Niacin	.2 mg.	.1 mg.	.2 mg.
Vitamin C	0	1 mg.	5 mg.

(Dashes denote lack of reliable data for a constituent believed to be present in measurable amount.)

It's amazing that a humble seed, when ground and cooked with water, offers nutrition almost equal to that given by mammals to their offspring.

The only thing in which soy milk is a little deficient is calcium, and this is easily remedied by grinding and cooking in some sesame seeds which are loaded with calcium.

Unfortunately, canned soy milks which are readily available on store shelves (usually in the form of baby formula) are often full of other undesirable ingredients that have been added to them. I have never bought one of these canned soy milks, since I have never gotten past the label. Rather, I go to a local tofu factory and buy soy milk as it pours out of the grinding machine. If you are fortunate enough to live in an area where there is a tofu factory, you can probably do the same thing and have lots of soy milk to use as a drink, for baking, puddings, gravies or anywhere else dairy milk is usually used.

But just in case there isn't a tofu factory in your neighborhood yet, I've included a few recipes for making your own home-made soy milk. Once you've tried it, I'm sure you'll like it, and you may want to try one of the other recipes for using soy milk. (Don't forget, you can substitute soy milk in any recipe calling for dairy milk!)

HOMEMADE SOY MILK ○

2 cups soaked soybeans
6 cups boiling water

Soak soybeans overnight. Pour out water and rinse. Blend beans in 4 cups of boiling water. Strain through thin muslin. Pour remaining 2 cups of boiling water through cloth. (Don't throw the pulp away, as it still contains much nutrition. There are recipes for using this pulp, called **okara**, also included in this section.) Bring milk to a boil. While coming to a boil, stir occasionally to prevent sticking on bottom. After milk starts to boil, stirring isn't necessary. Boil over medium-high heat for ½ to 1 hour. The longer it's boiled, the thicker and richer the milk will be. Makes about 1 quart.

SESAME SOY MILK ○

Make as in Homemade Soy Milk, except add 1 cup of sesame seeds when soaked beans are blended and blend until the sesame seeds are finely ground.

MORE INSTANT SESAME SOY MILK ◯

4 cups soy milk
½ cup sesame butter or sesame tahini
1 Tbsp. honey

Blend ingredients together in blender and use anywhere dairy milk or soy milk are called for.

SOY MILK FROM SOY MILK POWDER ◯

This is a quicker way to make soy milk if you don't have the time to grind the beans yourself. The whole thing will take only about 10 minutes. But as with most convenience foods, you have to pay for the convenience. Most boxes have instructions on them for making soy milk, but I'm including this recipe in case you get some soy milk powder in bulk, which is cheaper.

1¼ cups soy milk powder
3 cups water

Mix small amount of water in a small bowl with the soy milk powder until it's dissolved. Pour into a pot with the rest of the water and bring to a boil, stirring constantly so the soy milk won't stick and burn. Once it has come to a boil, lower heat and allow to simmer 5 minutes or more (the longer it's allowed to simmer, the richer the milk gets).

SOY MILK BANANA SHAKE ◯

4 cups chilled soy milk
4 bananas
1 tsp. lemon juice
1 tsp. vanilla or almond flavoring
1 Tbsp. honey
¼ tsp. cinnamon

Blend and serve.

CAROB SOY MILK ◯

4 cups soy milk
½ cup honey (or less)
¼ cup carob powder
1 tsp. Pero
1 tsp. vanilla

Blend and serve. Good hot or cold.

SOY MILK ICE CREAM ◯

3 cups soy milk
1 stick agar-agar (½ cup flakes)

2/3 cup honey
2 Tbsp. liquid lecithin
1 tsp. almond extract
2 tsp. vanilla extract

Combine first 2 ingredients in a pot and let sit off heat until agar-agar softens. Put on heat and slowly bring to a boil, stirring occasionally until agar completely dissolves. Remove from heat and cool until soy milk jells. Chop the jelled soy milk up into small pieces and put them in the blender with last 4 ingredients. Blend until smooth. Pour into a covered container and freeze.

Variation: To make Carob Soy Milk Ice Cream, add ¼ cup carob at the end (when blending) and replace the 1 tsp. of almond extract with 1 tsp. peppermint extract.

SOY-COCONUT MILK ☐

2 cups soy milk
2 cups coconut milk
1 Tbsp. honey
½ tsp. cinnamon
1/8 tsp. cloves
1 pinch cardamom
1 tsp. vanilla

Blend and serve.

SOYBEAN FUDGE ◯

1½ cups soy milk

¼ cup carob powder
1 cup honey

2 Tbsp. butter or margarine
½ cup cooked, mashed soybeans

Nuts and/or dried fruit (opt.)

Bring soy milk to a boil, stirring constantly to prevent sticking. Boil on medium-high heat, stirring occasionally, until milk becomes thick and begins forming a lump in pan. Remove from heat, add carob powder and stir well to get lumps out. Add honey and return to heat. Cook on medium-low heat, stirring occasionally until mixture begins leaving side of pan. Add butter and mashed soybeans (and last ingredient, if desired). Pour into a greased dish and cool.

SOY CREAM ☐

1 Tbsp. honey
1 cup soy milk
1 cup tofu

Blend in blender until smooth. Use any-where rich dairy cream would be used: on desserts, fruit, etc.

RICE PUDDING ☐

2 cups cooked and cooled brown rice
(good way to use leftovers)
1 cup soy milk
¼ cup honey
1 tsp. vanilla
1 tsp. cinnamon

¼ cup raisins

Blend first 5 ingredients until fairly smooth. Add raisins and chill a few hours before serving.

MOCHI ◯

¼ cup honey
4 cups soy milk
1 cup arrowroot

Kinako flour (see p. 357, this section)
Date sugar (opt.)

Put ingredients in pot and mix well until arrowroot dissolves. Put on heat and stir constantly, because arrowroot lumps as it cooks. Bring to a boil and lower heat to medium-high. Continue to stir constantly until it's like one lumpy lump in the pot. Use back of spoon and continue stirring while mashing and smoothing out lumps. When it is all a smooth lump in the pot, remove from heat and let cool. Slice in 1" by 2" pieces and roll in kinako flour (or kinako flour and date sugar combined).

SUMMER NOODLES ○

2 cups soy milk
1 stick agar-agar (½ cup flakes)

Break agar-agar stick into pieces and let soak in soy milk until softened. When agar-agar softens, put pot on heat and bring to a boil. Stir to keep from boiling. Cook until agar-agar dissolves. Pour into a loaf pan or other container so that soy milk is about 2" deep. Cool. Then cut into thin, noodlelike strips with a Japanese noodle slicer (usually available at Japanese markets — ask for a "konyaku" noodle slicer) or with a knife. If using a knife, cut a 2" slice from the loaf and lay it flat. Slice horizontally into 1/8" slices, then slice vertically into 1/8" strips. You'll have "noodles" about 1/8" wide. The "noodle" can be served in any of the following ways, or in any place you would use cold noodles.

BRAHMIN SPAGHETTI ☆

2 cups ice water
½ cup honey
Rose water to flavor

Summer Noodles
(see recipe above)

Blend first 3 ingredients in blender. Place Summer Noodles in a shallow bowl and add enough sweet liquid to just cover. Top with fresh fruit and/or slivered almonds. The Summer Noodles are also good served in this way in your favorite lemonade and topped with grated lemon rind.

SOBA ○

1 quart ice water
¼ cup miso
2 Tbsp. molasses
1" chunk fresh ginger
Pinch asafetida
2 Tbsp. soy sauce

Summer Noodles
(see recipe this page)

Blend first 6 ingredients in blender until ginger is chopped fine. This is the soup stock. Put ice-cold stock in bowls. Place Summer Noodles in the bowl so they're covered by stock. Top with fresh chopped vegetables or stir-fried vegetables. This is also good served in a cold spaghetti sauce.

CORN CHOWDER AND DUMPLINGS ○

2 Tbsp. oil
¼ tsp. asafetida
1 cup chopped celery
1 potato, diced
¼ cup chopped, fresh parsley

1 cup corn kernels
4 cups soy milk
¼ tsp. black pepper
½ - 1 tsp. vegetable salt or Spike

Sauté first 5 ingredients together until potatoes get a little browned and translucent-looking. Add next 4 ingredients and bring to boil, stirring occasionally. While the chowder is coming to a boil, make dumplings.

Dumplings:
1 cup whole wheat flour
½ cup milk
1 tsp. parsley
½ tsp. vegetable salt or Spike
1½ tsp. baking powder

Stir all ingredients together to form dough. When soup comes to a boil, drop dumpling dough in by tablespoonfuls. Put lid on and turn heat down to simmer. Allow to simmer 25 minutes without lifting the lid.

BASIC RICH SAUCE ☆

2 Tbsp. vegetable oil (opt.)
¼ cup whole wheat flour or other
whole grain or legume (garbanzo
bean flour is especially good)

2 cups soy milk (more for a thinner sauce)

1 Tbsp. soy sauce
1 Tbsp. nutritional yeast
1 tsp. lemon juice
1/8 tsp. black pepper
1/8 tsp. asafetida

Sauté first 2 ingredients until flour is toasted (optional). Add soy milk a little at a time, stirring all the while to keep from lumping. When the soy milk is thickened, add last 5 ingredients. This is good served as is or in any number of variations, such as those following, or use your imagination.
* Mix in 1 Tbsp. curry powder and 1 Tbsp. honey and a handful of raisins.
* Add about ½ cup of your favorite cheese (grate first).
* Add ½ cup cooked lentils or split peas and ¼ cup nutritional yeast.
* Mix in 1 tsp. each of mustard powder, honey and apple cider vinegar or ketchup.
* Chop in fresh or dried herbs such as parsley, basil, thyme, summer savory, rosemary.
* Blend in your favorite steamed vegetable such as broccoli, spinach, sweet peas, pumpkin, carrots, etc.

DILL SAUCE ○

1 Tbsp. oil
¼ tsp. asafetida
3 potatoes, cubed

2 cups soy milk
2 tsp. dill weed

1/8 tsp. black pepper
Few clusters parsley
1 tsp. soy sauce
1 tsp. lemon juice

Sauté first 3 ingredients to brown potatoes a bit. Then add next 2 ingredients. Stir until soy milk comes to a boil. Cover and simmer about 15 minutes until potatoes are tender.

Put in a blender with last 4 ingredients and blend until smooth. Delicious over green vegies.

VEGETABLE CASSEROLE ○

5 - 6 potatoes
6 cups green leafies, chopped
(spinach, chard, sweet potato leaves, etc.)

Nutritional yeast
Spike

White Sauce:
¼ cup butter or margarine
¾ cup whole grain flour
6 cups soy milk

Preheat oven to 350° F. Slice potatoes as for scalloped potatoes, about 1/8" thick. Make alternating layers of potatoes and green leafies. Between each layer sprinkle with nutritional yeast (gives a nice, cheesy flavor) and lightly with Spike. Boil ingredients for white sauce together and pour over vegetables. Cover and bake at 350° for 30 to 45 minutes. Uncover and bake another 15 to 20 minutes until golden.

CREAMED VEGETABLE SOUP ○

½ tsp. asafetida
¼ cup oil
½ cup whole wheat flour
1 cup chopped celery
1 potato or other hard vegetable, chopped

6 cups soy milk
2 cups water
3 cups assorted vegies

1 tsp. Spike or vegetable salt
1 tsp. basil

Sauté first 5 ingredients until the flour is browned. Add next 3 ingredients and bring to a boil. Turn heat down and simmer until potato is done. Take about half of the vegetables out of the liquid and some of the liquid and blend until smooth with last 2 ingredients. Pour into soup and serve.

YUBA

Yuba, also called "Jai" or "Monk's food," is yet another by-product of soybeans. If you make soy milk at home, or if you have ever heated dairy milk, you can easily understand how yuba is made. When heated, dairy milk and soy milk have a thin film that forms on the surface. This is the making of yuba.

When lifted fresh off the milk, this melt-in-the-mouth, protein-rich, sweet-tasting film is a real delicacy! In today's world of convenience foods and hurried living, probably few of us will have the time and patience to stand over a pot of soy milk and lift pieces of this film off the top of the milk — especially layer after layer until the soy milk is totally gone!

But this doesn't mean you'll never be able to sample the flavor of yuba or receive the benefit as well. Just as there are tofu shops in the Far East, there are many shops where yuba is made. Yuba is available there fresh, half-dried, and completely dried. The dried form is available to us here in most Chinese food stores or in the Oriental food section of supermarkets, although it's generally called "dried bean curd" (available in sheets or rolls). These are not only tasty, but nutritious as well. The dried yuba is about 50% protein, and rich in minerals that are very easily digested in this form. In Japan, yuba is given to mothers before and after birth to stimulate the flow of mother's milk, and doctors credit it with being able to aid in removing cholesterol from the system, which helps high blood pressure and other related conditions.

In the dried form, yuba loses its melt-in-the-mouth quality and becomes tough and rubbery. The rubbery-textured yuba has been used for centuries by Buddhist monks — whose spiritual disciplines and philosophy require a vegetarian diet — as a meat substitute. I have included some recipes you can try (using sheets of yuba) for monk food types of meat substitutes. As for the delicate flavor of warm, fresh, melt-in-your-mouth yuba, you'll have to make your own soy milk for that, and the yuba will make its appearance in the process!

YUBA CHIPS ☆

Deep fry unsoaked yuba sheets in heated oil. It should fry in a matter of seconds and bubble up. Remove from oil and place on paper towels to drain. While chips are still warm, sprinkle with nutritional yeast, vegetable salt and/or any spicing desired.

MOCK BACON ○

Yuba sheets (flat kind)

1 Tbsp. liquid smoke
1 cup soy sauce

Oil for frying

Soak yuba sheets in warm water until soft. Remove from water and drain. Cut into pieces the size of bacon and soak in next 2 ingredients for 5 to 10 minutes. Fry in oiled skillet on medium-high heat until both sides get crisp. Be careful not to burn. Serve with Scrambled Eggs Tofu (see Tofu Section, p. 376).

YUBA SEAWEED ROLLS ☆

Soak dry yuba sheets in water. When yuba is rubbery, remove from water. Lay yuba sheet out flat and top with a sheet of nori seaweed. Roll from one end to form a cylinder. Fasten with toothpicks and deep fry until yuba is golden brown.

MOCK PEKING DUCK

Flat sheets dried yuba

2 tsp. soy sauce
½ cup whole wheat flour
½ cup mashed tofu
½ cup water
2 tsp. honey
4 tsp. toasted sesame oil
¼ tsp. asafetida

Wet yuba until it softens. Combine next 7 ingredients. Spread thin layer inside of yuba, fold in half, spread again, fold again. Brush top with soy sauce. Steam for 30 minutes. Deep fry or fry in oil until golden brown and crisp on outside. Serve in Peking Duck Sauce or Hoisin Sauce thinned with a little sesame oil.

Peking Duck Sauce:
¼ cup bean sauce (see Hoisin Sauce recipe in Miso Section, p. 389)
1 Tbsp. water
2 tsp. - 1 Tbsp. honey
2 Tbsp. oil

1 tsp. sesame oil
1 pinch dried hot pepper

Combine first 4 ingredients. Toast last 2 ingredients in skillet. Pour into first 4 ingredients. Put cooked pieces of Mock Duck into sauce so that they're lightly covered. Serve over vegetables, noodles or in Chinese pancakes.

MONK'S HAM

2 Tbsp. oil
½ cup grated carrots
2 cups dried yuba trimmings
(soaked and packed into cup well)
6 drops liquid smoke
1 Tbsp. honey
2 Tbsp. soy sauce

1 Tbsp. arrowroot

Prepare yuba by smashing dry sheets into tiny pieces and then soaking in water until rubbery (about 5 minutes). Sauté first 6 ingredients until carrots are very tender. Sprinkle in arrowroot powder a little at a time while stirring with the other hand to prevent lumps from forming. Place in a small container that another container will fit in (tupperware storage bins that come in sizes that fit in each other are ideal). Place a container that will fit inside the one with the yuba in it, on top. Now put about 5 to 10 pounds of weight (a bag of rice or something of the sort) on top to press the yuba. Let stand 2 hours. Slice and serve on top of stir-fried vegetables, in salads, as hors d'oeuvres.

YUBA SAUSAGE

2 cubes red bean curd (1 Tbsp.)
2 Tbsp. red bean curd water
2 cups okara
3 - 4 drops liquid smoke
2 Tbsp. honey
2 Tbsp. arrowroot

Soaked yuba sheets

Mix first 6 ingredients in pot. When well mixed, put on heat and stir constantly until arrowroot thickens a little (after boiling). Roll okara mixture like sausages and wrap with yuba. Steam 20 minutes or fry in a little oil in skillet.

SOUTHERN FRIED MOCK CHICKEN

5 large yuba pieces
Water for soaking

½ block frozen tofu, thawed
(spongelike consistency)
½ cup whole wheat flour
1/8 tsp. asafetida
2 tsp. nutritional yeast
1 tsp. soy sauce
1/8 cup water

1/8 cup soy sauce
(Continued next page.)

½ cup whole wheat flour
3 tsp. black pepper
1 tsp. salt

Oil for frying

Put yuba in a pan and cover with water. Combine next 6 ingredients together in another bowl and mix well. When yuba sheets have soaked long enough to be flexible, divide yuba sheets in fourths and dip one at a time in a bowl of soy sauce. Take a piece of yuba and place about 2 Tbsp. of mixture in the center of it. Fold the sides up and under like wrapping a package. Mix last 3 ingredients in a bowl. Coat the Mock Chicken pieces by dipping in this mixture. Deep fry in medium-hot oil until golden brown.

FESTIVE MOCK STUFFED TURKEY

1 block solid tofu

½ cup soy sauce
2 Tbsp. water

½ recipe Festive Holiday Stuffing
(see recipe in Dried Fruit Section, p. 249)
or
½ recipe Thanksgiving Stuffing
(see recipe in Grain Section, p. 418)

6 large pieces yuba

Mock Turkey Gravy
(see recipe in Tofu Section, p. 379)

Cut block of tofu in half across the width of the block. (Some tofu comes already cut this way.) Then cut each half into thirds by cutting across the width. Combine next 2 ingredients and soak the 6 tofu pieces in the liquid for a few minutes. Remove tofu from liquid. Split each block in half so the pieces of tofu are like a sandwich. Divide stuffing into sixths and put one part on a piece of tofu and top with the other half of the split block. Repeat until all 6 are stuffed. Lay yuba in a large pan and cover with water. Soak about 5 minutes or until flexible. Re-

move one sheet and dip in soy sauce and water. Lay sheet out and put one stuffed block of tofu in the middle of yuba. Take one end of yuba and fold it over, tucking it under the tofu. Fold both side pieces in to the middle and roll it up like wrapping a package. Repeat until all are done and you have 6 bundles. Place in a steamer and steam for 10 minutes. Remove and dip in soy sauce liquid again. Put in a pan and bake at 350° for 10 minutes or until yuba starts to get hard and browned. Serve topped with Mock Turkey Gravy.

SOAKING SAUCE

2 Tbsp. honey
2 Tbsp. toasted sesame oil
¼ cup soy sauce

Mix ingredients together. This sauce is for soaking yuba to be used in any of the following ways.

YUBA VEGETABLE ROLLS ○

Make your favorite stir-fry vegetable or use leftover steamed vegetable. Fill yuba sheet (soaked in soaking sauce) with vegetables and cook same as Monk's Chicken #1.

MONK'S CHICKEN #1

First soak yuba sheets in water. Then soak yuba in the above sauce — a few whole sheets as well as pieces and flakes that have broken off and won't be usable as a wrap. After soaking in sauce for about 15 minutes, wrap as tightly as possible, pieces of soaked yuba in the soaked yuba sheet. Place pieces on the yuba sheet so that they cover the top 1/3 section of the sheet. Fold side edges over pieces so they won't fall out. Then roll from end with the pieces in it to form a log shape. Fasten with toothpicks or tie with sewing thread along seam to hold together while cooking. The cylinder can be deep-fried until golden brown or simmered in the soaked sauce and water for 20 to 30 minutes. Serve as is or cut and serve on top of salads or stir-fried vegetables.

MONK'S CHICKEN #2 ☆

Prepare the same way as with Monk's Chicken #1, except use the following mixture combined with yuba pieces as the filling:

1 cup mashed tofu
1 tsp. soy sauce
2 Tbsp. nutritional yeast

Cook same as Monk's Chicken #1.

OKARA

If you make your own soy milk, you're going to end up with a lot of what the Japanese call "okara." Okara is the fibrous pulp that is left after the liquid is strained out of the ground soybeans. As I mentioned in the "Homemade Soy Milk" recipe, this is a nutritious food, so don't throw it away! There is still enough nutrition left in okara that it should actually be considered a food and not waste or pig food (which is what okara is to many tofu factories — in the United States, at any rate).

The Japanese have placed the honorific "o" in front of the word "kara," which means "husk" or "hull," and rightfully so. Okara is a good source of fiber, or what grandma called "roughage," which we now know is an essential part of a well-balanced, healthful diet. Unfortunately, in the United States we have come to learn this the hard way, by masses of people having to suffer degenerative diseases such as cancer of the colon, heart disease, diverticulosis and even obesity from a diet lacking in fiber.

Okara is a way you can increase your fiber intake that rivals bran flakes. Bran flakes are a highly nutritious, inexpensive source of fiber, and so is okara. It is a natural by-product from making soy milk or tofu, so in a sense it is available for free and is obtained by making a healthful product rather than an unhealthful product like refined white flour. Besides fiber, okara contains about 3.5% protein by weight (about the same proportion by weight as milk or cooked brown rice).

Here are a few recipes you can try so that you can make use of okara!

TRADITIONAL OKARA O

2 Tbsp. oil
¾ cup assorted vegetables, chopped fine
Soaked, dried mushrooms

1 cup okara

1½ cups water mushrooms were soaked in
2 Tbsp. honey
2 Tbsp. soy sauce
½ Tbsp. vinegar
¼ cup toasted, ground sesame seeds

Stir-fry vegetables in oil a few minutes. Take vegetables out of pan and set aside. Put okara in pan and stir-fry until dry and flaky. Add vegetables and stir-fry a few more minutes. Add last 5 ingredients. Mix well. Remove from heat. Best served cool.

OKARA LOAF O

2 cups okara
½ cup whole wheat flour
½ cup sesame seeds
½ cup soy milk
2 cups nutritional yeast
2 Tbsp. soy sauce
1 tsp. salt

2 Tbsp. oil
½ tsp. black pepper
¼ tsp. asafetida
¼ tsp. cayenne
Pinch clove
½ tsp. thyme
2 tsp. oregano leaves
2 bay leaves, crumpled

Combine first 7 ingredients. Toast last 8 ingredients together in a skillet. Pour into okara mixture and mix well. Press into a greased baking dish and bake at 325° or steam for 30 minutes. This can be served as is or refrigerated, then sliced and fried to be used as an entree or put in sandwiches.

MOCK SEAFOOD ☆

4 cups okara
1 cup Eggless Soy Mayonnaise
(see Basic Recipes Section, p. 34)
¼ cup nutritional yeast
1 Tbsp. soy sauce
1 Tbsp. pickle relish
¼ cup chopped celery
½ tsp. asafetida
½ tsp. mustard (dry powder)
½ tsp. black pepper
1 Tbsp. plus 1 tsp. kelp powder

Combine ingredients. Mix well. Serve in sandwiches, on crackers, cucumber sticks or like a dip. Good on salads or as stuffing for fresh tomatoes and bell peppers.

OKARA BURGER ◯

1 cup okara
1 cup brown rice
½ cup Homemade TVP (see p. 383)
or soaked Granburger (about ¼ cup dry)
¼ cup chopped celery
¼ tsp. asafetida
1 Tbsp. soy sauce
¼ tsp. black pepper
½ cup rolled oats

Combine ingredients. Shape into patties and fry in skillet that has heated oil 1/8" deep. Let fry a few minutes until golden brown and gently turn over. These don't hold together like a hamburger, so handle gently. Serve as patty with tartar sauce or in sandwich or burger bun.

MOCK SEAFOOD & RICE LOAF ☆

2 cups prepared Mock Seafood
(see recipe this page)
2 cups cooked and cooled brown rice
½ cup presteamed, chopped potato, cooled
¼ cup nutritional yeast flakes
2 Tbsp. soy sauce
2 tsp. Spike

Combine all ingredients and mix well. Vegetables should be totally mashed. Spread evenly in an 8" oiled baking pan and bake at 350° for 45 minutes. Serve hot or cold, in sandwiches, or as an entree.

OKARA ROAST ◯

2 cups okara

1 cup dry beans, soaked
¾ cup water
3 Tbsp. soy sauce
¼ tsp. black pepper
1 tsp. basil
1 tsp. rosemary
1 bay leaf

¼ cup wheat germ
½ cup celery
½ cup chopped sunflower seeds
½ cup gluten flour

Sauce:
2 Tbsp. oil
2 Tbsp. soy sauce
1 Tbsp. nutritional yeast

Put okara in bowl. In blender, blend next 7 ingredients until herbs are chopped fine. Pour into bowl and add next 4 ingredients. Mix thoroughly for a few minutes to develop the gluten. Pour into oiled casserole dish, top with chunks of assorted vegetables (like celery, carrots, potatoes, etc.) and baste with sauce. Bake covered for 45 minutes at 350°. Uncover, baste again and bake another 15 minutes uncovered.

OKARA PATÉ ⭕

1 vegetable bouillon cube
2 cups okara
1 Tbsp. oil
1 tsp. soy sauce
¼ cup wheat germ
½ cup nutritional yeast
1 tsp. poultry seasoning
¼ tsp. asafetida
¼ tsp. thyme
¼ tsp. summer savory

Combine all ingredients in a bowl and mix well. Pour into oiled baking pan and bake, covered, at 350° F for 30 minutes.

OKARA MOCHI ⭕

½ cup okara
½ cup arrowroot powder
¼ cup soy milk or water
½ tsp. salt

Combine ingredients and knead a little. Oil a skillet and fry on a medium-high heat so outside hardens. Lower heat to medium-low and cook until brown on both sides. Should be gooey inside like mochi; if not, they must cook more. Take out of pan and squash with front of chopsticks into a mixture of equal parts soy sauce and honey. Serve while still hot.

OKARA OATMEAL COOKIES ⭕

¼ cup oil
½ cup honey
½ tsp. vanilla
1 cup okara
½ cup whole wheat flour
1½ cups rolled oats
¼ cup raisins and/or carob chips
¼ cup sunflower seeds

½ tsp. baking soda

Preheat oven to 350° F. Combine first 8 ingredients in mixing bowl. Mix in leavening and drop on oiled cookie sheet. Flatten to about ½" thick and bake 12 to 15 minutes.

OKARA ALMOND COOKIES ⭕

1 cup okara
1 cup whole wheat flour
¼ cup oil
2/3 cup honey
2 tsp. almond extract

½ tsp. baking soda

Preheat oven to 350° F. Combine first 5 ingredients. Add baking soda and mix. Drop by tablespoon or ice cream scoop onto oiled cookie sheet. Flatten to about ½" thick. Place whole or slivered almond in center. Bake 12 to 15 minutes until golden brown.

OKARA BREAD PUDDING ⭕

3 apples or 4 bananas, sliced
½ loaf whole-grain bread, broken
4 cups okara
½ cup raisins
½ cup sunflower seeds

1 cup honey
1 cup soy milk
1 tsp. cinnamon
½ tsp. vanilla

1½ tsp. baking soda
1½ tsp. baking powder

Mix first 5 ingredients well, making sure bread is broken into crumbs. Add next 4 ingredients and mix thoroughly. Mix in leavening and mix thoroughly. Pat into oiled baking pans and bake at 350° for 1 hour.

OKARA CARROT CAKE ◯

1 cup okara
2 cups whole wheat flour
¾ cup honey
1 tsp. cinnamon
1 tsp. vanilla
¼ cup raisins or chopped dates

try

½ cup oil
3 carrots (enough to make 1¼
to 1½ cups chopped in blender)

1½ tsp. baking soda
1½ tsp. baking powder

Preheat oven to 350° F. Combine first 6 ingredients in bowl. Blend next 2 ingredients in blender, dropping small chunks of carrot in blending oil one at a time until the blender shows that there's about 1¼ to 1½ cups. Pour in with first 6 ingredients. Add leavening. Mix enough to blend together and immediately pour into oiled cake pan. Bake for 45 minutes or until knife inserted comes out clean.

OKARA CRUMBLE ☆

¼ cup butter
½ cup honey
1 cup okara
¼ cup whole wheat flour
1 cup bran or oatmeal
¼ cup sesame seeds
½ tsp. vanilla

Preheat oven to 325° to 350° F. Mix ingredients together in a bowl. Put 2/3 of crumble mixture on bottom of cake pan. Pour in tapioca or other type of pie filling or pudding about ½" thick. Crumble remaining 1/3 onto top of filling. Bake until crumble is golden brown.

OKARA MUFFINS ◯

2 cups whole wheat flour
2 cups okara
½ cup oil
1 cup honey
1 tsp. vanilla

4 tsp. baking powder
½ cup berries in season or raisins (opt.)

Preheat oven to 400° F. Mix first 5 ingredients. Add leavening and berries (opt.) and stir a few strokes to mix in leavening. Immediately pour into oiled muffin tins or drop by ¼ cupfuls on oiled cookie sheet. Bake for 20 minutes until golden brown.

CAROB-OKARA BROWNIES ◯

2/3 cup whole wheat flour
1/3 cup soy milk powder
1-1/3 cups carob powder
1 Tbsp. + 1 tsp. baking powder

2/3 cup oil
1-1/3 cups honey
1½ cups water
1½ cups okara
2 tsp. vanilla

1 cup peanuts (opt.)

Sift first 4 ingredients together. Add next 5 ingredients and mix well. Add nuts if desired. Pour into an oiled baking pan and bake at 350° for 30 minutes. Allow to cool and cut into squares. Good frosted with Carob Icing (see Dairy Section, p. 456).

Soybean Products (clockwise): Miso, Yuba (sheets), Aburage Shells, Okara, Tofu (center)

TOFU

No book on Island cooking would be complete without tofu, which was brought here by people from the Far East where it has been eaten for at least 2,000 years. This superb soybean product has been making its way westward into more and more homes and looks like the next healthy food to sweep the nation, following the footsteps of yogurt.

Over a dozen years ago, when I first started thinking about putting healthy foods into my body, yogurt was not commonly found in supermarkets. It was mostly a health food store item. Today, yogurt can be found in any supermarket, as well as in little booths or shops that serve only yogurt (frozen in particular). Tofu seems to be the next healthy food to do this.

And no wonder! Nutritionally, tofu contains easily digestible protein with no cholesterol and hardly any trace of saturated fat. Whole, cooked soybeans are 68% digestible, whereas tofu is 95% digestible. An 8-ounce serving of tofu supplies 27% of the adult male daily protein requirement (which can be increased when tofu is used with whole grains and/or nuts and seeds), and 38% of the adult daily requirement of calcium, as well as a good supply of B vitamins, and minerals like iron, phosphorus and potassium. All this pound for pound at half the price of cheap hamburger.

Tofu's good qualities don't end there, though. It's not one of those foods that you have to hold your nose and wince down because it's good for you. Tofu's bland flavor makes it somewhat like the loveable "shmooo" of "Li'l Abner" fame. It can take any shape or form and be loveable in every situation.

Here are a few recipes to introduce you to the versatility of tofu. Once you get the hang of using it, you're on your way to as many intriguing and delicious dishes as you can imagine! And, if you make your own tofu, you're on your way to cheap meals and self-sufficiency!

Tofu produced in the home will enable you and your family to be more self-sufficient, and produced in the community can make for a more self-sufficient economy and community (especially if soybeans are also locally grown). The production of tofu provides the possibility for many cottage industries to spring up.

In Hawaii, although tofu is produced locally, dependence on imported soybeans prevents the tofu business from becoming a truly self-sufficient cottage industry.

Soybean plants grow very well here in Hawaii, and all year long at that! If land were made available, it would be feasible to grow them in large quantities as a prime source of protein. Per acre, soybeans provide more usable protein than beef (see figures in the introduction to the Soybean Section, p. 353), and the versatility of the soybean suggests the possibility of a variety of cottage industries.

"There is no answer to the evils of mass unemployment and mass migration into cities, unless the whole level of rural life can be raised, and this requires the development of an agro-industrial culture so that each district, each community, can offer a colorful variety of occupations to its members."

E. F. Schumacher — **Small Is Beautiful**

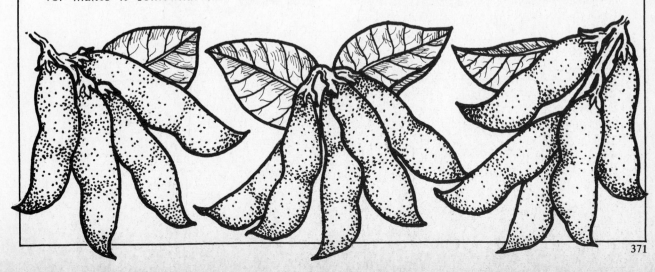

HOMEMADE TOFU ○

2 cups dry soybeans

1 Tbsp. (heaping) Epsom salt
¼ cup warm water

Wash beans. Soak in cold water overnight (6 to 8 hours). Rinse well and liquify in blender with 1 to 1½ cups water and 1 cup beans until very smooth. Do this twice. Then mix pulp with 8 cups water and blend in batches. Strain through a clean dish towel or muslin cloth, squeezing out as much milk as possible. Bring milk to boil and boil for 3 minutes. Turn off heat; gradually add Epsom salt (dissolved in water), stirring evenly but not too much. Let sit 5 to 10 minutes until milk curdles well. Gently pour curd into muslin cloth and rinse. Apply a little pressure, extracting excess liquid, and let drain 2 to 3 hours. There are wooden molds with fine screen bottoms for drainage and weights for the top to apply pressure that can be used specifically for molding the tofu into blocks. Put curd into a container with water and refrigerate. Yields about 1½ lbs. of tofu.

RAW TOFU WITH DRESSINGS □

One of the most basic, simple, yet elegant ways to serve tofu is to cut the cold block of tofu into bite-sized cubes and serve with any of the following sauces poured over the block, or else serve the sauce in small individual bowls for tofu to be dipped in.

KOREAN STYLE □

3 Tbsp. soy sauce
1 tsp. toasted sesame oil
2 Tbsp. honey
Pinch of asafetida
Pinch of cayenne or red chili pepper

Mix together and use as a dip or sauce.

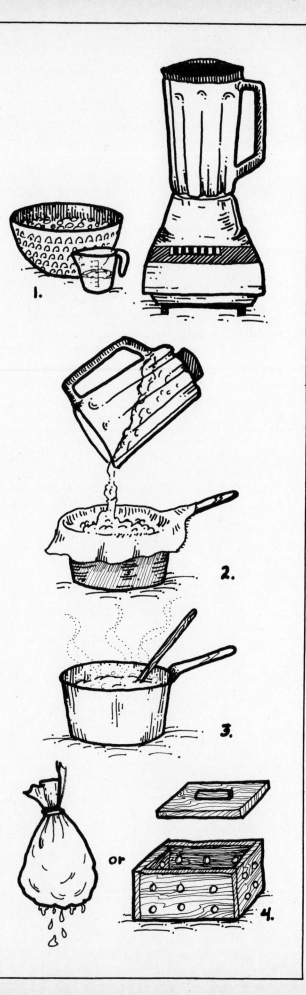

THIN DIPPING SAUCE ☐

½ cup water or soup stock
2 Tbsp. honey
3 Tbsp. soy sauce
¼ cup grated daikon or radish
3 Tbsp. grated fresh ginger root

Mix ingredients together. Use as a dip or sauce.

GINGER SOY SAUCE ☐

2 Tbsp. soy sauce
1 Tbsp. fresh grated ginger root

Pour soy sauce over cubes of tofu and sprinkle with grated ginger, or use as a sauce.

CREAMY SAUCE ☐

½ cup Eggless Soy Mayonnaise
(see Basic Recipes Section, p. 34)
1 Tbsp. soy sauce
2 Tbsp. tomato sauce

Mix together and use as a dip or sauce for tofu and vegetables.

THE BOYS' FAVORITE ☐

Pour soy sauce over cubes of tofu and sprinkle with nutritional yeast to taste.

HOT SOY SAUCE ☐

½ tsp. dry mustard powder
Enough water for right consistency
Soy sauce to taste

Measure out mustard powder into a small bowl and add water, drops at a time, to form a paste about as thick as ketchup (the longer you mix it, the hotter it seems to get). Pour in soy sauce to taste.

SESAME SOY SAUCE ☐

2 Tbsp. soy sauce
1 Tbsp. honey
2 Tbsp. water
2 Tbsp. toasted, ground sesame seeds

Mix together and use as a sauce or a dip.

RADISH ROOT SOY SAUCE ☐

2 Tbsp. soy sauce
¼ cup finely grated daikon or radish

Combine and let sit a few hours so flavor of radish can mix into soy sauce. Use as a dip or a sauce.

TOFU SALAD DRESSING #1 ☐

2 cups mashed tofu
½ cup oil (safflower or soy)
2 tsp. honey
1 tsp. curry powder
½ tsp. turmeric
1 tsp. salt or 2 tsp. kelp
Juice of 2 lemons
Water

Combine ingredients and blend in blender until smooth and creamy. May have to turn off blender, mix with spoon to distribute oil evenly and blend again. Add a little water if necessary. Serves nicely as a sandwich spread, as a salad dressing and also very good served over steamed vegetables. Yields about 2 cups.

TOFU SALAD DRESSING #2 □

2 cups mashed tofu, well-drained
2 Tbsp. toasted, ground sesame seeds
2 tsp. honey
2 tsp. soy sauce
¼ tsp. salt or ½ tsp. kelp
1 tsp. grated ginger
Dash of black pepper

Combine ingredients and mix well. (Tofu can be drained by placing it in cheesecloth, slightly squeezing out excess liquid.) This dressing is very good tossed with drained, steamed vegetables, especially with green, leafy ones. Also very good served with Comfrey Potato Patties (see recipe in Comfrey Section, p. 298). Yields 2 cups.

TOFU DRESSING #3
CREAMY ITALIAN □

½ block tofu, mashed and well-drained
1 cup oil or ½ cup oil with ½ cup water
(use safflower or olive oil)
2 Tbsp. vinegar
1/8 tsp. cayenne
¼ tsp. turmeric
2 tsp. celery salt
½ tsp. crushed dill seed
¼ tsp. basil
½ tsp. oregano leaves

Combine all ingredients and mix in blender until creamy and smooth. This makes a thick, creamy Italian dressing which covers a large bowl of tossed greens, etc.

THOUSAND ISLE DRESSING □

2 cups tofu
12 oz. V-8 juice
¼ cup vinegar
½ cup oil (safflower or soy)
½ cup water
2 Tbsp. Spike
2 Tbsp. honey

Blend ingredients together in blender until smooth.

MOCK CHICKEN NOODLE SOUP ○

Instant Mix:
¾ cup uncooked barley
4 dried mushrooms (found in the
Oriental section of the grocery store)

½ cup broken buckwheat soba noodles
½ tsp. asafetida
1 tsp. turmeric
1 tsp. parsley flakes
1 tsp. nutritional yeast
1 tsp. kelp powder
Pinch black pepper
Pinch cumin powder

Blend barley for a few minutes until powdered. Add mushrooms and blend a few more seconds. Combine with next 8 ingredients; mix well. Store in a jar until needed.

Soup:
4 cups water

1 Morga bouillon cube
1/3 cup homemade instant soup mix
1 cup tiny tofu cubes

Bring water to a boil. Turn heat down and add next 3 ingredients. Simmer about 20 minutes. Serve hot with whole wheat crackers.

TOFU CHOWDER ○

2 cups corn kernels and other
assorted, chopped vegetables
4 cups water

1 block tofu
¼ cup nutritional yeast
¼ cup dulse
1/8 tsp. cayenne (opt.)
½ - 1 tsp. curry powder

Steam first 2 ingredients until vegetables are tender. Using water from steaming, blend next 5 ingredients until smooth. Mix in steamed vegetables and heat up a bit if necessary.

BROILED TOFU

1 block tofu
Soy sauce
Nutritional yeast

Cut tofu into cutlets about ½" thick and place side by side on an oiled cookie sheet (or other large baking pan — oiling is unnecessary with a teflon pan). Put sheet with tofu under the broiler and broil until tofu begins to turn golden brown. Remove sheet from oven, turn tofu over with a spatula and broil again until second side is golden brown. Remove sheet of tofu from the oven and sprinkle with soy sauce, then sprinkle on nutritional yeast. Place back under broiler and broil until a little browned; flip tofu over and repeat on other side. Serve as is or topped with your favorite gravy.

BROILED AGÉ TOFU

1 lb. agé tofu cakes
(not aburage or agé pouches)

1/3 cup soy sauce
3 Tbsp. honey
2 Tbsp. water

Drop agé in boiling water and let boil 5 to 10 minutes to remove excess oil. Remove from water, drain and pat dry if necessary. While the agé tofu is boiling, prepare the sauce with the next 3 ingredients. Place boiled and drained agé tofu in the sauce and marinate for about 5 minutes so the tofu is evenly coated with the sauce. Turn on the broiler and arrange agé tofu in a baking dish and baste with the sauce. Broil until the agé tofu browns. Remove the pan from the broiler, turn the tofu over, baste again and broil until browned. Remove, drizzle on remaining sauce and top with a garnish if you like.

BROWNED TOFU

½ block tofu

1 tsp. grated fresh ginger
Oil
Soy sauce

Drain tofu well. Cut into ¼" slices and brown in last 3 ingredients. Serve alongside rice, vegetables or salad. Also can be served between toasted whole wheat bread with tomatoes, lettuce and dressing. Very good!

FRIED TOFU

1 firm block tofu
½ cup whole wheat flour
½ cup oil or ghee

½ cup soy sauce
2 Tbsp. honey
1 Tbsp. grated fresh ginger

Drain tofu well. Cut into 4 slices (the long way). Dredge each piece in flour until well coated and fry in oil until crispy. Combine last 3 ingredients. Cook about 10 minutes and serve over fried tofu slices. Serves 4.

FRIED TOFU & SWEET-SOUR SAUCE

12 slices firm tofu
Whole wheat flour
Oil

Dredge tofu in flour and fry in oil. Top with Pineapple Sweet-Sour Sauce (see Pineapple Section, p. 214). Yields 6 servings.

TERIYAKI TOFU ○

½ cup soy sauce
½ cup honey
½ tsp. asafetida
2" - 3" chunk of fresh ginger

12 cups tofu, sliced

Blend first 4 ingredients together in a blender. Pour over slices or pieces of tofu that have been placed in a large baking tray (teflon preferred). Cover with foil and bake at 450° to 500° for about 20 minutes. Lift up corner of foil to see if tofu is boiling and swollen. If not, cook longer until it is; if it is, remove foil and flip tofu over with a spatula and cover again with same piece of foil. Bake another 20 minutes. Remove foil and let bake in oven until sauce dries out and tofu is browned. You will have to stir a few times in between.

MOCK CHICKEN TOFU ○

12 cups tofu slices

Gravy:
1 cup water
1 heaping Tbsp. Dr. Bronner's Balanced Protein Seasoning or 2 Tbsp. soy sauce
2 tsp. poultry seasoning
½ tsp. thyme
½ tsp. summer savory
½ tsp. asafetida
2 Tbsp. nutritional yeast

Prepare and cook in the same way as Teriyaki Tofu.

STIR-FRIED TOFU ○

1 block tofu, crumbled
Soy sauce to taste
Enough oil to keep from sticking to pan

Crumble tofu into frying pan with soy sauce and little bit of oil. Stir-fry until soy sauce is evenly distributed and warm and browned a bit from frying. Sprinkle nutritional yeast in if you like.

SCRAMBLED EGGS TOFU ○

2 Tbsp. oil
½ tsp. turmeric
1 Tbsp. soy sauce
½ tsp. salt or 1 tsp. kelp
Dash of black pepper

2 cups tofu, well-drained and mashed

2 Tbsp. cream cheese (opt.)

Combine first 5 ingredients in a skillet and lightly cook. Add tofu and scramble for about 5 to 10 minutes. Mix in cream cheese until it melts and serve like scrambled eggs with toast. Yields 2 to 4 servings.

SIMPLY DELICIOUS TOFU ○

1 block tofu
Soy sauce

2 Tbsp. grated fresh ginger
2 Tbsp. grated radish or turnip

2 Tbsp. oil
¼ tsp. asafetida

Chinese parsley, chopped fine
Nut or seed meal

Slice tofu into ½" to ¾" fillets and soak each piece in soy sauce a few minutes on each side to absorb soy sauce. Place tofu on steam rack so no fillet is covering another. Sprinkle surface of fillets with next 2 ingredients and steam about 10 minutes. Remove steamer from pot and place over large platter. Heat oil to very hot and add asafetida. When oil bursts into flames, take container by handle and pour a little oil very carefully over each tofu fillet. It should sizzle or even flame when the oil hits the tofu. Sprinkle a little soy sauce on fillets and garnish with last 2 ingredients.

TOFU CUTLETS ○

Slice a block of tofu into ½" slices. Dip in soy sauce and then into nutritional yeast (optional) and fry or broil. Serve as is or top with melted cheese or serve with gravy, catsup or your favorite topping.

STUFFED TOFU LOAF ○

6 cups mashed tofu
¼ cup soy sauce
2 Tbsp. oil (sunflower or safflower)
2 Tbsp. whole wheat flour
½ tsp. thyme
½ tsp. savory
½ tsp. asafetida
2 tsp. basil
½ cup nutritional yeast

Preheat oven to 350° F. Combine all 9 ingredients together in a bowl. Press about 2/3 of mixture in an oiled bread pan so tofu is about 1" thick all the way around. Stuff the center with stuffing and top with remaining tofu mixture. Bake at 350° for 30 minutes. Serve topped with gravy or cranberry sauce. Save leftovers to slice and use in sandwiches.

Stuffing:
½ cup chopped walnuts or seeds
2 cups bread cubes
2 cups cooked brown rice

2 - 3 Tbsp. butter or margarine
¼ tsp. asafetida
1 cup chopped celery

½ cup tomato sauce
1 tsp. sage
½ tsp. thyme
½ tsp. vegetable salt
Some sprigs chopped parsley

Combine first 3 ingredients in a bowl. Sauté next 3 ingredients together in a large skillet. Add next 5 ingredients and simmer together a few minutes. Add first 3 ingredients and stuff tofu immediately. Good served with Mock Turkey Gravy (see recipe, p. 379).

TOMATO CHUTNEY WITH TOFU CURD BALLS ○

Sauce:
Tomato Chutney (see recipe in Garden Vegetables Section, p. 263)

Curd Balls:
1 cup tofu, mashed and well drained
2 Tbsp. noninstant dry milk

Prepare curd balls by draining tofu well. Press it through a sieve into a bowl and mix in milk powder so that it will hold together. Roll into nice balls and deep fry in ghee, olive oil or sesame oil on medium heat until golden. Add to Tomato Chutney just before serving. Delicious!

TOFU BALLS ○

1½ cups well-drained, mashed tofu
¼ cup sunflower seeds
¼ cup whole wheat flour
2 Tbsp. parsley flakes
1/8 tsp. black pepper
½ tsp. salt
½ tsp. asafetida toasted in a bit of oil
2 Tbsp. nutritional yeast

Soak sunflower seeds. Meanwhile, mash and measure tofu. Drain and chop sunflower seeds. Mix all ingredients together well and roll into small balls (1" to 1½" in diameter). Deep fry in ghee or hot oil for about 10 to 15 minutes. Drain on paper towels. Can make a lot at once and freeze for future use. Makes about 24 balls. Tofu balls can be served in place of meat balls in spaghetti, etc., or in Nutty Protein Gravy (see recipe in Fresh Leaves Section, p. 311).

TOFU PIZZA ○

Basic Bread Dough
(see Basic Recipes Section, p. 31)

Sauce:
2 tsp. olive oil
2 green peppers, sliced thin
1 large zucchini, sliced thin

½ block tofu, drained and mashed
1 tsp. butter or margarine
1 tsp. sweet basil
1 tsp. oregano leaves

2 cups tomato sauce

2 cups grated cheese
or 1 cup nutritional yeast

Or use Basic Italian Sauce instead
(see Garden Vegetables Section, p. 263)

Preheat oven to 350° F. Prepare dough using Basic Bread Dough recipe. This is enough for two 10" x 14" cookie sheets. Roll out between wax paper, place on cookie sheets and mold into shape. Bake at 350° for 10 to 15 minutes. Meanwhile, combine first 3 ingredients for sauce and sauté lightly. In another pan, combine next 4 ingredients. Scramble until water has evaporated. When crust is done, spread each with half of the tomato sauce, scrambled tofu and vegetables. Then sprinkle 1 cup of grated cheese or ½ cup nutritional yeast on each. Return to oven and bake until cheese is melted. Delicious!

TOFU AND VEGETABLE CASSEROLE ○

4 cups carrot pulp (or finely grated carrot)
1½ blocks tofu, well drained and mashed
1 cup walnut or cashew meal
or peanut butter

Little oil for frying
2 cups diced celery (small)
4 cups diced eggplant (small)

4 cups potato chips, finely crushed
2 tsp. nutritional yeast
2 tsp. salt
4 tsp. soy sauce
1 tsp. thyme

Grated cheese

Preheat oven to 350° F. Carrot pulp can be obtained by running carrots through a juicer (using juice also), a food grinder, or grating on a fine grate. The walnut or cashew meal can be obtained by grinding nuts in a blender or food grinder until smooth. Natural peanut butter may be used (walnuts are first choice). Combine first 3 ingredients and mix well with hands. Lightly sauté vegetables in a little oil. Combine with tofu mixture and remaining ingredients. Mix well and spread into an oiled 10" x 14" cake pan and bake at 350° for 25 to 30 minutes. Top with grated cheese and return to oven until cheese melts. This is very good served as is or with Mock Turkey Gravy (see recipe this section, p. 379). Yields 8 to 10 servings.

TOFU QUICHE ○

1½ cups tofu
½ cup water
¼ cup nutritional yeast
¼ cup egg replacer
2 Tbsp. honey
2 Tbsp. sesame butter or tahini
1 Tbsp. soy sauce or 1 tsp. vegetable salt
1 tsp. curry powder
¼ cup diced onion or 1/8 tsp. asafetida

1 cup of your favorite vegetable
or a combination of them

Blend first 9 ingredients together in a blender until smooth. Fold in the vegetable and pour into your favorite unbaked pie crust (see Basic Recipes Section, p. 33). Bake at 375° for 30 to 40 minutes, until top is puffed and golden brown and filling has set.

MOCK TURKEY AND GRAVY ○

Mock Turkey:
1 firm block tofu, well-drained
½ cup soy sauce

Gravy:
¼ cup butter or margarine
1 cup garbanzo flour (chickpea)
1 tsp. basil
½ tsp. thyme
½ tsp. black pepper

3 cups water

¼ cup soy sauce
2 tsp. lemon juice
2 - 3 Tbsp. nutritional yeast

Place tofu in bowl with soy sauce and let sit a few minutes on each side to soak up soy sauce and turn brown. Place on top of steamer rack with small amount of water and steam with cover for 20 minutes. Prepare gravy by combining next 5 ingredients, stirring constantly over medium-high flame until lightly toasted. May have to mash it with back side of the spoon. When toasted, gradually add water, stirring constantly to prevent lumping. (A whisk is ideal.) When blended, add last 3 ingredients and mix well. When tofu is done, remove from steamer. Slice in ¼" to ½" slices. Place in a baking pan, top with gravy and broil in oven a few minutes. Tofu can also be fried in a little butter before topping with gravy. Yields about 4 servings.

VEGETARIAN TOFU CHOW MEIN ○

¼ cup water
½ tsp. salt
¼ tsp. black pepper

3 cups celery, thinly sliced
2 cups bean sprouts (soy or mung)
1 cup tofu, cubed

½ cup Chinese peas or sweet peas
1 cup chestnuts, thinly sliced,
or bamboo shoots or banana heart

¼ tsp. salt
1 tsp. soy sauce

1¼ Tbsp. arrowroot, made into paste

Combine first 3 ingredients in a skillet. Add next 3 ingredients and cook about 15 minutes with a tight lid. Add next 2 ingredients the last 5 minutes of cooking. Drain liquid from vegetables to measure 1¼ cups (if necessary, add tap water). Mix with next 2 ingredients, heat and gradually add arrowroot paste. Stir until thickened, pour over vegetables and serve with steaming, fluffy brown rice. Yields 6 servings.

TOFU ESPAÑOL ○

2 lbs. tofu
3 Tbsp. oil

1 tsp. asafetida
½ cup minced celery
¼ cup minced green pepper
¼ tsp. oregano
1 Tbsp. honey
½ tsp. vegetable salt
¼ tsp. black pepper
1½ cups tomato sauce

½ cup bread crumbs
½ cup nutritional yeast

Melt oil in large skillet. Sprinkle tofu slices with vegie salt; brown quick on both sides. Combine next 8 ingredients and pour into skillet around, but not on top of, slices. Sprinkle crumbs and yeast over tops of slices. Bake uncovered in 375° oven for 20 to 30 minutes or until slices are brown.

TOFU PATTIES WITH SWEET-SOUR SAUCE

Patties:
1 block tofu, mashed

2 cups Homemade TVP (see p. 383)
or soaked Granburger (about 1 cup dry)

1 cup whole wheat flour
1/3 cup sesame seeds
½ tsp. asafetida
2 tsp. salt
1 tsp. black pepper
½ tsp. turmeric
½ tsp. cumin powder

1 diced bell pepper
1 medium-sized, round eggplant, diced
3 sticks celery, diced
½ cup finely chopped cauliflower,
green beans or most any fresh vegetable
Butter or margarine

Sweet-Sour Sauce:
1 cup soy sauce
Juice of 1 lemon
4 Tbsp. honey
1 Tbsp. oil
½ tsp. asafetida
½ tsp. mustard powder
½ tsp. ground coriander
Dash of chili powder
Dash of curry powder

2 Tbsp. arrowroot powder
or unbleached white flour

¼ cup chopped raisins
¼ cup chopped dates

Or use Pineapple Sweet-Sour Sauce
(see recipe in Pineapple Section, p. 214)

Quick-fry tofu to evaporate excess water. Add Homemade TVP or moistened Granburger and next 7 ingredients. Mix well and toss in vegetables that have been lightly sautéd in butter. Mix well and form into flat patties, adding extra flour if needed to hold them together. Fry in butter until lightly browned. Blend first 9 sauce ingredients and cook on medium heat. Make a paste with arrowroot and a little water. Pour into sauce, stirring constantly until thickened. Add last ingredients. Cook a few minutes and serve over patties.

CURRIED TOFU

1 block tofu
Soy sauce

3 Tbsp. oil
½ tsp. lemon rind
¼ tsp. asafetida
2 tsp. grated fresh ginger

1 Tbsp. Sri Lanka curry powder
(see Basic Recipes Section, p. 37)
¼ tsp. cayenne pepper (or to taste)
1 large tomato, cubed
1 Tbsp. fresh mint, chopped
1 tsp. lemon juice
¾ cup water

½ cup coconut milk

Soak ½" slices of tofu in soy sauce. Heat a large skillet and add oil to skillet. Fry soaked tofu cutlets in oil. Remove when browned on both sides. In same skillet with oil, add next 3 ingredients and toast. When toasted, add next 6 ingredients and cook until thick; then add coconut milk. Mix well and then place fried tofu cutlets in gravy. Cover, lower heat and simmer for 10 minutes.

TOFU FRITTATA ○

2 Tbsp. oil
1 cup celery + ¼ tsp. asafetida
                or
¾ cup celery + ¼ cup onion, diced

1 potato, sliced
1 large, juicy tomato, sliced
2 tsp. dried basil
or ¼ cup fresh basil, chopped
¼ cup fresh parsley
¼ cup bell pepper
Couple sprinkles of cayenne

1 block tofu
1 Tbsp. soy sauce
1 tsp. curry powder
¼ cup nutritional yeast
1 Tbsp. liquid lecithin or 2 Tbsp. granular
½ cup water

In a skillet, saute first 3 ingredients together until vegetables become translucent. Turn down heat to simmer. Add next 6 ingredients one layer at a time in the order listed (no need to stir them). Blend last 6 ingredients together until smooth and pour over layered vegetables. Cover the skillet and let simmer 20 to 30 minutes (until tofu mixture puffs and rises and is no longer gooey to the touch). The tomato must be very ripe and juicy for the long simmering, so if there isn't much juice, you may want to add a few tablespoons of water or diluted tomato sauce. When the simmering is done, flip frittata over (tofu side down) onto a platter. You can sprinkle with grated cheese or nutritional yeast if you like.

TOFU YUM ○

½ block tofu (1 cup)
2 Tbsp. soy sauce
¾ cup water
2 Tbsp. arrowroot
½ cup nutritional yeast
2 Tbsp. liquid lecithin
Pinch black pepper
Pinch asafetida
¼ tsp. turmeric

1 cup finely chopped, assorted vegetables

Blend first 9 ingredients together until smooth. In bowl, mix with vegetables. Fry in oiled skillet, as you would an omelet, until golden brown on both sides. Serve topped with Pineapple Sweet-Sour Sauce (p. 214).

VEGETARIAN STROGANOFF ○

¼ cup butter or margarine
2 bell peppers, slivered
5 - 6 tomatoes
2 zucchini, sliced
1 cup diced celery
1 eggplant, diced
1 cup chopped string beans

½ tsp. asafetida
1 tsp. chili powder
2 tsp. vegetable salt
½ cup nutritional yeast
½ tsp. cumin powder
¼ tsp. black pepper
1 - 2 Tbsp. chopped, fresh parsley

1 cup Homemade TVP (see p. 383)
or soaked Granburger (about ½ cup dry)

1 lb. whole wheat noodles
8 oz. sour cream
8 oz. yogurt

Sauté vegetables in butter until just tender. Then add next 7 ingredients and Homemade TVP or moistened Granburger. Stir in boiled and drained noodles with yogurt and sour cream. This makes a hearty dinner entree which serves about four.

FROZEN TOFU

I was first introduced to frozen tofu by my mother. Once, after we had decided to leave meat out of our diet, she invited us to dinner and had used frozen tofu in place of meat in a Japanese sukiyaki dish. The tofu she fed us was bought at a Japanese import store and was quite expensive, as it was snow dried in Japan, where it is considered to be quite a delicacy.

The texture of the tofu changes once it is frozen. It becomes tough and rubbery, much resembling the texture of meat. When I got home, I thought that maybe we could get a similar product to the snow frozen tofu at a cheaper price, so I threw a block of tofu into the freezer and left it a few days. And it worked! You can make the delicacy of frozen tofu so easily and cheaply right in your own freezer; and it's an excellent way to use extra tofu that might go bad otherwise.

You can freeze a whole block at a time, or else cut cubes or slices and freeze them. If you want the frozen tofu to be able to be cooked as a cube or chunk, you will have to bring some water to a boil and drop the still frozen tofu into the boiling water and boil until it's thawed. Otherwise, you can let the frozen tofu thaw and it will crumble apart (as in the Homemade TVP recipe). Either way, here are a few recipes you can try for using tofu in a different way.

FROZEN TOFU STRIPS ○

Cut tofu in cubes or strips and freeze. Drop in boiling water to thaw, boiling until completely thawed. Rinse with cold water and squeeze out excess water. The frozen tofu will be so tough and spongy that you can wring it out like a sponge. Stir-fry in a little oil, soy sauce, black pepper and asafetida to taste. This can be used as is, in stews or stir-fried vegetables.

VEGETABLE TOFU STEW ○

2 blocks tofu, cut in ½" slices and prepared as described in Frozen Tofu Strips (see previous recipe)
3 Tbsp. soy sauce

½ cup chopped carrots
1 cup chopped string beans
1 cup chopped beets
1 - 2 potatoes, chopped
1 squash, chopped
½ cup corn
½ cup sliced celery
3 bay leaves

½ cup whole wheat flour
¼ cup butter or margarine

¾ tsp. asafetida
1 tsp. black pepper
¾ tsp. basil
¾ tsp. thyme
¼ tsp. sage
½ tsp. turmeric
½ tsp. chili powder
2 Tbsp. nutritional yeast
1 Morga vegetable bouillon cube
Liquid from steamed vegetables

Prepare tofu same as for Frozen Tofu Strips. Steam vegetables with bay leaves until tender in enough water to cover vegetables (save liquid). In same skillet that tofu was prepared in, toast whole wheat flour (or any other whole grain flour). Add next 10 ingredients to make a thick gravy. Pour into steamed vegetables along with prepared tofu and mix well. Served on top of millet or long grain brown rice, it makes a hearty main meal.

HOMEMADE TEXTURIZED VEGETABLE PROTEIN (TVP) ○

1 block frozen tofu (thawed, then squeezed and crumbled)
2 Tbsp. oil
1 Tbsp. tomato sauce
1 Tbsp. soy sauce
1 Tbsp. Spike
1/8 tsp. asafetida
1/8 tsp. black pepper
1 tsp. honey

Take block of frozen tofu out early in the day and let sit at room temperature to thaw out. When thawed, break into quarters or so and wring the water out of the tofu, like wringing out a sponge. Crumble with your hand into a skillet and fry with all other ingredients until browned. This can be used as is or dried in an oven for 5 to 6 hours at 200° to 250°. The dried TVP is like the commercial TVP that can be kept on a kitchen shelf and soaked in equal parts water before use. However, as with any commercial TVP, it can go stale after some time.

ALMOST STROGANOFF ○

2 cups frozen tofu cubes
2 Tbsp. soy sauce
1 Tbsp. oil

1 cup garbanzo flour
½ cup oil or melted butter

1½ tsp. nutritional yeast
1 tsp. basil
¼ tsp. black pepper
½ tsp. thyme

4 cups water
¼ cup soy sauce
2 Tbsp. lemon juice

1 cup cooked whole wheat spinach noodles (more can be added)

1 cup grated cheese

Cut tofu into cubes. Measure 3 cups. Put in plastic bag and freeze (this should be done the day before). Preheat oven to 350° F. Remove from freezer; rinse with hot water to defrost. Squeeze out excess water, measure 2 cups, mix with soy sauce and squeeze to distribute it evenly. Fry in butter until getting crispy. Remove from skillet and set aside. In skillet, add next 2 ingredients, mix well and stir frequently, smashing it with back of spatula or spoon until it starts to dry out and get toasty. Add spices and stir. Gradually add next 3 liquid ingredients, stirring constantly until smooth and thickening. Combine noodles and fried tofu. Place in a baking pan, mix in gravy and bake at 350° for 25 minutes. Top with grated cheese and return to oven for about 5 minutes until cheese is melted.

CHILI ○

1 tsp. oil
¼ tsp. asafetida
2 tsp. chili powder
2 cups chopped celery or other chopped vegetable

3 cups tomato sauce
1 tsp. honey
½ tsp. salt
2 cups cooked beans
2 Tbsp. nutritional yeast
¼ tsp. black pepper

2 cups Homemade TVP (see recipe this page) or soaked Granburger (about 1 cup dry)

Cooked brown rice

Sauté first 4 ingredients. Add next 6 ingredients and TVP or moistened Granburger. Simmer a few minutes. Serve over brown rice.

MOCK SLOPPY JOE

1 Tbsp. oil
½ cup diced bell pepper
¼ tsp. asafetida
½ tsp. turmeric
½ tsp. cumin powder
1 tsp. mustard powder
¾ tsp. chili powder
½ tsp. salt
1/8 tsp. black pepper

3-1/3 cups Homemade TVP (see p. 383)
or soaked Granburger (1-2/3 cups dry)

1½ cups tomato sauce
¼ cup molasses
2 Tbsp. apple cider vinegar

Sauté first 9 ingredients together for about 5 minutes. Add Homemade TVP or soaked Granburger and last 3 ingredients. Mix well, cover and simmer for about 15 minutes. Serve over a whole wheat bun.

STIR-FRIED TACO

1 Tbsp. oil
2 cups Homemade TVP (see p. 383)
or soaked Granburger (about 1 cup dry)
1 - 2 Tbsp. chili powder
1 cup fresh corn, uncooked
1 lb. fresh tomatoes, chopped
1 tsp. honey
¼ cup diced bell pepper
¼ tsp. asafetida
½ tsp. oregano

1 cup grated cheese
9 oz. package corn chips
Salt and black pepper to taste

2 small heads of lettuce, shredded
1 large avocado, sliced

Stir-fry first 9 ingredients; cover and let simmer about 10 minutes. Stir in cheese and chips. Spoon over lettuce and garnish with avocado.

CRUNCHY TOFU CRISPS

4 aburage shells
2 Tbsp. oil
1 tsp. soy sauce

Cut up aburage. Lay them flat in a pan with oil and soy sauce and fry over low heat until crisp. Can be used in soups, salads, sandwiches and vegetable entrees.

SUSHI VARIATION #1

3 - 4 aburage (6 - 8 halves)

½ block tofu, mashed
½ cup grated carrots
½ cup slivered green beans
¼ cup water chestnuts, diced
4 tsp. miso
1 tsp. sesame salt
1 tsp. grated ginger

Prepare aburage in same manner as in Vegetable Stuffed Sushi (see recipe in Legume Section, p. 402). Set aside. Combine remaining ingredients and mix well. May need to use hands. Fill prepared aburage and steam on a rack for 15 minutes. Serve. Yields 6 to 8 sushi.

SUSHI VARIATION #2 ○

1 cup brown rice
2 cups water

½ cup oil
½ cup diced celery
½ cup grated carrots
½ cup diced green pepper
½ tsp. cumin powder
½ tsp. turmeric
1 tsp. curry powder
1½ tsp. salt or 3 tsp. kelp
½ tsp. grated fresh ginger
¼ tsp. cinnamon
1/8 tsp. allspice

1 cup tofu, well-drained and mashed

Combine washed rice with water and cook until tender (about 40 to 45 minutes); let sit with cover on. Combine next 11 ingredients in a skillet and cook for a few minutes. Mix in rice and sauté 5 minutes. Add tofu, mix well, cooking a few minutes longer. Place filling in prepared aburage shells or in nori sheets and roll.

SUSHI VARIATION #3 ○

3 cups cooked rice with grated carrot

4 Tbsp. vinegar
3 Tbsp. honey
2½ tsp. sesame salt

Prepare aburage in same way as Vegetable Stuffed Sushi (see recipe in Legume Section, p. 402). Mix first 2 ingredients, toss in last 3 ingredients and stuff into cones.

TOFU SHAKE □

3 cups cold soy milk
¾ cup tofu
2 bananas
2 cups fresh fruit (berries, peaches, apricots, etc.)

3 Tbsp. honey
¼ cup wheat germ (opt.)

Blend ingredients in blender until smooth and serve.

BREAKFAST TOFU PUDDING □

1½ cups mashed, ripe papaya
½ cup mashed tofu
¼ cup raisins
2 tsp. honey
Dash of cinnamon

Combine ingredients. Blend in blender until creamy and smooth. Yields 1 to 2 servings.

BET YA' THOUGHT IT WAS CHOCOLATE PUDDING □

1 cup tofu, well-drained and mashed
1 average banana
1 Tbsp. peanut butter
1 Tbsp. carob powder
3 Tbsp. honey

2 Tbsp. chopped sunflower seeds
Toasted, grated coconut

Combine first 5 ingredients and mix in blender on low speed until smooth. Scoop into a bowl, add sunflower seeds and mix. Top with coconut and set in freezer or refrigerator to chill. This pudding is very good when placed in little tarts made from Flaky Pie Crust recipe (see Basic Recipes Section, p. 33). Delicious!

CAROB SHAKE □

2 cups cold soy milk
2 cups orange juice
½ cup tofu
¼ cup carob
¼ cup honey

Blend ingredients in blender until smooth and serve.

TOFU CHEESECAKE ○

Crust:
Use Graham Cracker Crust or
Oilless Cracker Crust (see Basic
Recipes Section, pp. 32, 33)

try

Filling:
2 cups drained and mashed tofu
1 average-sized banana
½ cup honey
2 Tbsp. lemon or lime juice

Topping:
1 cup fresh strawberries, sliced
1 Tbsp. honey
½ tsp. arrowroot

Preheat oven to 350° F. Prepare crust. Press into 8'' pie pan and refrigerate. Combine next 4 ingredients and mix in blender until smooth. Pour into pie shell and bake at 350° for 25 to 30 minutes. Chill 4 to 6 hours. Prepare topping by combining last 3 ingredients and cooking lightly and quickly over flame until thickened. Spread evenly over set cheesecake. Refrigerate until cool; cut and serve. Cheesecake can also be topped with fresh fruit mixed with honey or any flavor of your favorite preserve. Also good without topping.

EGGLESS FRENCH TOAST ○

Tofu Batter:
½ cup mashed tofu
½ cup milk (soy or dairy)
½ tsp. vanilla
½ tsp. grated orange rind
1/8 tsp. turmeric
1/8 tsp. cinnamon

1 Tbsp. egg replacer
1 tsp. baking powder

Combine first 6 ingredients in a blender and blend until smooth. Pour into wide-mouthed bowl and whisk in last 2 ingredients with a fork or wire whisk. Quickly dip in whole-grain bread. Fry in lightly oiled skillet until golden and crisp on both sides. Serve topped with honey or your favorite jam. This recipe is very nutritious, and you get a complete protein with the tofu and whole-grain bread, without any cholesterol. The Fancy French Toast recipe (see Grain Section, p. 425) makes the kind of French toast which is available in pancake houses, I've been told. However, the egg replacer isn't a protein source, so you may want to serve some kind of milk (soy or dairy) to complement the protein in the whole-grain bread.

Tofu Yum, p. 381

CAROB TOFU "MUD" PIE

1 block tofu (2 cups)
2 ripe bananas
½ cup honey
1 tsp. vanilla
½ cup carob powder
1 Tbsp. egg replacer
1/3 cup water

Topping:
¼ cup honey
1 Tbsp. liquid lecithin
½ tsp. vanilla and/or almond extract
¼ cup carob powder
¼ cup powdered milk
¼ cup water

Blend ingredients until smooth. Pour into Graham Cracker or Oiless Cracker Crust (see Basic Recipes Section, pp. 32, 33). Bake at 350° for 20 minutes. Mix topping ingredients and put on cooled pie.

TOFU DESSERT BALLS ☆

1 cup tofu, drained well
1 Tbsp. tahini
Pinch of salt
Pinch of black pepper

3 Tbsp. finely chopped cashews or almonds
3 Tbsp. shredded coconut
¼ tsp. cinnamon
¼ tsp. grated lemon rind
½ tsp. vanilla extract
1 Tbsp. honey

2/3 cup chopped nuts

Press tofu through a sieve. Combine with next 3 ingredients and mix well. Add 3 Tbsp. of chopped nuts and remaining ingredients. Mix well. Roll into balls and roll in remaining nuts. Chill for about one hour and serve.

MISO

Miso happens to be just another wonder food which is a by-product of soybeans! Yet its taste and qualities set it apart and distinguish it from tofu or any of the other by-products of the supersoybean. Adding miso to your favorite recipe means adding an ingredient that is a complete protein, full of healthy microorganisms and enzymes, and which has a rich, full-bodied flavor as well.

From the health and nutrition standpoint, this concentrated mass of fermented soybeans (yes, that's what miso is) offers quite a bit.

1) Since miso is usually combined with a whole grain in the fermenting process, it forms a whole protein. It is important that the grain is a whole unrefined one, though. For this reason, I pick the darker misos. As a rule, the darker the miso the more natural or unrefined it is. If you read the labels closely on light misos, you'll find that they are made with refined white rice, etc., and are usually lighter tasting or are a synthetically aged miso containing preservatives.

2) As a fermented product (like yogurt and kefir, to name a couple of the more popular fermented foods), miso is a "live" food that's so good for replenishing friendly bacteria in the intestines and aiding digestion. (Just a note: Because miso is a live food, add it to the cooking as late as possible to avoid destroying the friendly bacteria.) As with all naturally fermented foods, miso also contains vitamin B_{12}, which makes miso one important vegetarian source of this vitamin.

3) Miso has an alkalizing effect in the body.

4) Miso contains only 5% fat, which is totally cholesterol-free.

5) And, unfortunate but true, miso may be a most important food in this day and age. Miso can be an especially beneficial addition to our diets because it contains zybicolin. What is zybicolin, you ask? It is a substance that attracts and absorbs undesirables in the environment (such as cigarette smoke, air pollution and even radioactive elements) which have been inhaled or have

made their way into the body somehow or other. Zybicolin absorbs these poisonous elements and carries them out of the body through the body's eliminating process.

Certainly something this good for the body is worth a try, and you'll find that it is not an unpleasant austerity either, by trying one of the recipes that follow, or even by using miso to replace salt in your favorite recipe. Miso may taste salty, but surprisingly, it contains only 12% salt. Use of miso, like soy sauce, can actually help cut down on overall salt intake when it's used to replace salt. So please experiment with miso, perhaps first trying some recipes here, and then in your own recipes.

YUMMY HI-PROTEIN DRESSING □

¼ cup miso
¼ cup sesame butter (raw)
½ cup nutritional yeast
¾ cup water

Combine all ingredients and stir until smooth and creamy. Use as a salad dressing or a creamy gravy.

MISO SALAD DRESSING □

1/3 cup miso
1/3 cup lemon juice or vinegar
1/3 cup toasted sesame oil
1½ cups water
¼ tsp. asafetida
½ tsp. grated fresh ginger

Mix all ingredients together and use as a salad dressing.

MISO CHEESE DRESSING ☆

2 Tbsp. miso
¾ cup olive oil
1/3 cup Parmesan cheese
1½ tsp. lemon juice
½ tsp. finely grated ginger

Mix all ingredients together well and toss in salad.

MISO SWEET & SOUR SAUCE ○

¼ cup vinegar
½ cup fresh lime juice
¼ cup frozen orange juice
½ cup honey
2 tsp. finely chopped, packed dates
¼ - ½ tsp. cayenne
1/8 tsp. asafetida
¼ cup diced celery
¼ cup diced bell pepper

¼ cup water
1½ tsp. arrowroot

1 Tbsp. + 1 tsp. miso

Combine first 9 ingredients and cook over low heat for 10 to 15 minutes. Mix next 2 ingredients together in measuring cup until arrowroot dissolves. Stir into cooked ingredients and stir constantly over low heat until sauce thickens. Remove from heat and mix miso in well. Serve this sauce over deep-fried noodles (noodles which have been boiled, drained and deep fried) and vegetables, or in place of sweet-sour sauce used with recipes in other chapters.

MISO HERB SAUCE □

1 cup water
1 Tbsp. + 1 tsp. miso
2 Tbsp. raw sesame tahini
¼ tsp. fresh thyme
2 Tbsp. fresh parsley
¼ tsp. rosemary
1 Tbsp. olive oil
½ tsp. cilantro (Chinese parsley)
1 Tbsp. butter or margarine

Combine all ingredients in a pan. (Be sure herbs are chopped fine. If you don't have fresh herbs, use about half the amount of dried herbs.) Simmer over low heat for 20 minutes. Serve over whole-grain noodles or use as a gravy for your favorite entree.

HOISIN SAUCE ☐

¼ cup miso
2 tsp. toasted sesame oil
¼ cup honey
1 tsp. soy sauce
2 Tbsp. water
1½ tsp. apple cider vinegar

Combine all ingredients and mix well. Use for Mock Peking Duck (see recipe in Tofu Section, p. 364) or Stuffed Buns or for Chinese Dumplings (see recipes in Grain Section, pp. 417, 424). The extra sauce can be stored in the refrigerator for future use.

SIMMERED TOFU ○

6 cups water
2 Tbsp. miso
2 strips of kombu, 6" long
or 2 Tbsp. hijiki seaweed

1 block tofu cut in 2"x 2"x 1" cubes

Bring first 3 ingredients to a boil and mix to dissolve miso. Turn down to simmer. When broth is no longer boiling, add tofu cubes and simmer until tofu floats to the top. Serve in a chafing dish and give each person a pair of chopsticks and a small bowl of dipping sauce (see sauces to serve with raw tofu in Tofu Section, pp. 372, 373) so they can pick the tofu out of the broth and dip it steaming hot into dipping sauce. Also good to provide a tray of garnishes the tofu can be dipped in after dipping in the sauce, such as grated ginger, grated radish, crisped and crumbled nori seaweed, toasted sesame seeds, nut meals, etc. Save the broth and serve as miso soup (hot or cold), or use as a soup or gravy base.

MEXICAN SAIMIN ○

6 tortillas
2 Tbsp. + 1 tsp. oil

¼ tsp. asafetida
½ cup diced celery

1 cup tomato purée

1½ qts. water
2 Tbsp. miso
1 bay leaf
½ tsp. oregano
¼ tsp. cinnamon
¼ tsp. mustard
1 Tbsp. chopped cilantro (Chinese parsley)

½ cup flaky nutritional yeast

Slice tortillas into strips ¼" to 3/8" wide. Fry in 2 Tbsp. oil until crisp. Remove from pan and let drain. In same pan, add 1 tsp. oil. Sauté next 2 ingredients until celery is translucent. Blend one large tomato until puréed to make about one cup. Add along with last 7 ingredients to celery in pan. Bring to boil, simmer 30 minutes and remove from heat. Add nutritional yeast, whisking as you add. Just before serving add tortilla strips.

SAUTÉD VEGETABLES IN MISO ○

1½ Tbsp. toasted sesame oil
1½ Tbsp. vegetable oil
8 cups assorted, chopped vegetables

3 Tbsp. miso
3 Tbsp. honey

Sauté first 3 ingredients together until vegetables are tender. If you are using some vegetables that cook faster than others, sauté those which will take longer to cook first and when they become translucent, add the quicker-cooking vegetables. Turn off heat. Add last 2 ingredients when vegetables are done and mix in well.

MISO-POTATO SAUTÉ

1 Tbsp. oil
4 cups diced potatoes
½ tsp. cumin powder
Pinch cloves

2 Tbsp. miso
1 tsp. honey
1 Tbsp. lemon juice
½ cup water

Sauté first 4 ingredients together for about 5 minutes. Add next 4 ingredients, stirring miso in until dissolved. Cover and simmer another 5 minutes until potatoes are tender.

MISO SPAGHETTI

2 Tbsp. oil
2 cups diced celery
1 cup diced bell pepper
½ tsp. asafetida

4 cups diced tomato
2 tsp. honey
1 tsp. basil
½ tsp. oregano

¼ cup miso
1 cup chopped walnuts (pecans or brazil nuts will add a similar flavor)

½ lb. uncooked whole grain spaghetti

Sauté first 4 ingredients together until vegetables are translucent. Add next 4 ingredients, bring to a boil, then turn heat down and simmer on lowest heat about half an hour, stirring occasionally. Add last 2 ingredients; mix until miso is dissolved. Remove from heat, cool and refrigerate overnight. For dinner, simply reheat the sauce and serve over already cooked spaghetti noodles.

MISO PATÉ

3 Tbsp. miso
¼ cup nutritional yeast
¼ cup grated Monterey Jack cheese (packed)
2 Tbsp. chopped olives
2 Tbsp. raw sesame tahini
(or other nut butter)
¼ cup water
2 Tbsp. sour cream or yogurt
¼ cup finely chopped walnuts
2 Tbsp. diced bell peppers
2 Tbsp. diced celery

½ cup water
3 slices of wheatberry bread, crumbled

Mix first 10 ingredients together well. Mix next 2 ingredients together in a separate bowl and let sit until bread crumbs absorb water, then mix in with all other ingredients. Pour into an oiled baking pan and bake at 350° for 30 minutes.

MISO MOCHI

2 cups brown rice flour
1 cup honey
1 cup okara or grated coconut
1 cup nut milk or coconut milk
1 cup water
1 Tbsp. miso

Kinako flour (see p. 357)
or toasted, ground sesame seeds

Combine first 6 ingredients and mix out all lumps. Pour into an oiled baking pan so it is at least ¾" thick. Cover pan with foil and bake at 350° for 1 hour and 10 minutes. Cool overnight. Cut into bite-sized slices and roll in kinako flour or in toasted, ground sesame seeds.

MISO NUT BALLS ○

½ cup nut butter
½ cup honey
¼ cup carob powder
¼ cup milk powder
¼ cup chopped pecans
¼ cup chopped almonds
½ cup chopped cashews
1½ tsp. miso
1 tsp. cinnamon

Combine all ingredients and mix thoroughly. Roll into balls or other desired shapes. If you don't have specific nuts called for, just use any combination of nuts or seeds to equal about 1 cup total.

MISO SURPRISE PIE ○

Crust:
Use any pie crust from
Basic Recipes Section, p. 33

Filling:
¼ cup sesame oil
¼ cup olive oil
¼ cup miso
2/3 cup chopped raisins
½ cup chopped walnuts
½ cup honey
3 Tbsp. grated orange rind
2 Tbsp. fresh oregano
1 tsp. fresh thyme
½ tsp. fresh sage
¼ cup fresh parsley
¼ cup nutritional yeast
¼ cup whole wheat flour
4 cups water
¼ cup cornmeal

Mix all ingredients together. (Make sure to chop up herbs fine. If you don't have fresh herbs, use half the amount of dry herbs.) Simmer for 20 minutes, stirring occasionally. When the filling is thickened, pour it into an unbaked pie crust and bake at 350° for 20 to 30 minutes until crust is golden brown.

Variation: Add 1 Tbsp. honey and 1½ Tbsp. carob powder to the pie filling ingredients.

SWEET SANDWICH SPREAD □

1¼ cups mashed banana
¼ cup carob powder
2 Tbsp. honey
1/3 cup chopped dates (pack to measure)
½ cup raw tahini
¼ cup miso
¾ cup water
2 Tbsp. frozen orange juice concentrate
1½ Tbsp. finely grated lemon peel (packed)
1½ Tbsp. finely chopped raisins
(pack to measure)
2½ tsp. lemon juice

Mash all ingredients together and mix well. Refrigerate at least 1 hour to allow flavors to blend. Use as sandwich spread between whole grain bread. You may want to add banana slices, raisins, chopped nuts and/or seeds on top of the spread when you make the sandwich.

MISO CHEESE NUT BALLS ☆

8 oz. package cream cheese, softened
1 tsp. red (or dark) miso
1 pinch asafetida
6 Tbsp. finely chopped celery
½ cup chopped walnuts

1 cup grated cheddar cheese

Finely chopped walnuts

Mix together first 5 ingredients until well-blended. Then add grated cheese and blend together. Roll into balls, then roll in finely chopped walnuts. Serve as an hors d'oeuvre.

SESAME MISO APPLE BAKE ○

8 apples

Filling:
3 Tbsp. sesame butter (tahini)
or sesame seeds ground in blender
2 Tbsp. dark miso
2 Tbsp. butter or margarine
3 Tbsp. honey
1 tsp. lemon juice
2 Tbsp. water
½ tsp. cinnamon

¼ cup chopped raisins,
dates or other dried fruit
¼ cup chopped walnuts,
sunflower seeds or other nuts

3 Tbsp. honey
1 cup water

Preheat oven to 350° F. Wash and core apples, leaving a bit of core in the bottom to hold the filling. Place apples in a baking dish. Mix next 7 ingredients and partially fill the cored center of each apple. Finish filling apples with next 2 ingredients. Mix last 2 ingredients and pour on bottom of baking dish. Cover with foil and bake at 350° for 30 to 40 minutes or until apples are fork tender but not overdone and mushy. About 10 minutes before apples are done, remove foil and baste with the juice in bottom of pan. Return uncovered to oven and finish baking. Good served with Soy Whipped Cream (see Basic Recipes Section, p. 34).

"Immortal upon earth no longer now,
He slays the lamb that looks him in the face,
    And horribly devours his mangled flesh,
Which, still evenging nature's broken law,
    Kindled all putrid humours in his frame,
All evil passions, and all vain belief,
    Hatred, despair, and loathing in his mind,
The germs of misery, death, disease and crime."

— Shelley

LEGUMES

Legumes

As more people in the United States are cutting back or turning away from meats and even excessive dairy products as expensive cholesterol and saturated fat-laden sources of protein, we can look to a lot of little seeds as affordable, nutritious and palatable alternatives. In general, these little seeds are divided into three categories: legumes, grains and nuts. Each one of these categories is featured in a separate chapter, although you'll probably notice the recipes usually contain a combination of legumes, grains and/or nuts or seeds. If not combined together in a recipe, they should be combined when served at the meal to balance amino acids.

Legumes are seeds that are characterized by a single-cavity ovary which is split along two seams. Legume plants are also unique in that they fix nitrogen from the air into the soil. Because they add so much to soil fertility and structure, legumes have always been a regular in our garden for the sake of the soil as well as our family's meals.

We have never grown them for drying, though. Rather, we use them fresh and raw in salads or lightly steamed. When used in the dried form, legumes are a low-cost source of protein. Legume prices and nutritional content vary a great deal from one kind to the next, so you may want to study the table on page 468 to check for the best nutritional bargain when shopping for beans. As can be seen, some legumes actually have a protein content equal to or even greater than meat, without the drawbacks of cholesterol and saturated fat.

The king of the legumes, nutrition and cost-wise, is the soybean. But because it's such a super-bean, I have reserved a whole separate section just for the soybean and its by-products.

Legumes as a group include some of the highest quality plant protein there is. But the amount of protein digestible by the body (NPU = Net Protein Utilization) is lower than other food groups which are recommended as protein sources. This is due to the fact that legumes tend to be short on two of the essential amino acids — tryptophan and sulphur-containing amino acids, to be exact. Yet, this shortage can be complemented by serving a grain with legumes or a nut and/or seed with legumes. (See protein information in the Dairy Section of this book; or for an in-depth informative study, see **Diet for a Small Planet** by Frances Moore Lappe.) By combining foods in this way, legumes will give you as much digestible protein pound for pound as foods which are thought of as being high-protein foods.

The major reasons people usually give for not using legumes more consistently as a protein source are 1) they take so much time to prepare, and 2) "Beans are so blah." Both of these reasons could definitely be negative factors, but they can be overcome!

Let's take the first one. Yes, it's true that dry beans do take a long time to cook. But this can be overcome with a little planning. First of all, soaking the beans overnight cuts actual cooking time at least in half. (The soaking water from beans should be thrown out because toxic elements come off in the water. This doesn't take away from the nutritional value of the bean.) Before soaking beans overnight, boil them in the soaking water for about two minutes to prevent the hard skins from getting sour in warm weather. Another way I cut down on cooking time is that rather than cooking a new pot of beans every day, I just presoak and boil five, ten, or fifteen pounds of beans at a time. If you are going to add salt at all, don't add it until after the beans have been cooked, since salt toughens the skin around the bean and will increase cooking time.

After the beans are cooked, I put them in airtight containers in portions my family normally goes through in a meal and freeze some and refrigerate some. I have found that changing the kind of bean I use every week helps to add some variety to our diet. A whole week of soybeans, followed by a whole week of split peas, followed by a whole week of lentils, etc., may not exactly sound exciting and may even border on sounding out and out blah. But I think trying some of the following recipes will disprove that very quickly. And that takes care of the second reason for not using legumes more often!

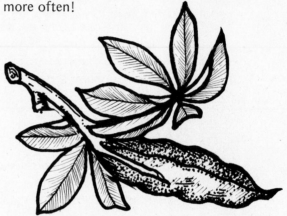

SPLIT PEA-VEGETABLE SOUP ○

2 cups split peas soaked in water overnight
(will amount to about 4 cups soaked peas)
10 cups water

3 Tbsp. oil or ghee
2 tsp. cumin seeds
1 pinch red pepper
¼ tsp. ground coriander
¼ tsp. asafetida
2 tsp. basil
Pinch cloves

2 cups chopped vegetables
3 Tbsp. nutritional yeast

Boil first 2 ingredients over medium heat for about 1½ hours. Do not remove lid until 1½ hours are up. Toast next 7 ingredients together in small skillet and throw into the cooked soup. Turn off heat, add last 2 ingredients and let sit a while on burner.

POPPERS

Even though this is not a recipe to be prepared by you, I had to include the mention of these tasty, spicy legume wafers! They make a delicious discovery. These are round, paper-thin crackers, usually about the size of tortillas, that are made from legume flours and spices. It would be very difficult for you to make these delicately paper-thin wafers which, as I've been told, are usually dried in the sun for a few days, so it'll be easier to look in the closest Indian food import store (sometimes found in Mid-Eastern food stores).

If you do go out and buy a package of these poppers, which come spiced in a variety of ways, the rest is simple . . . and quite tasty. Just heat ghee or oil about 1" deep in a skillet for deep frying. The skillet must be large enough to fit one popper in at a time with room for the popper to expand almost one-half time more in diameter. When the ghee is so hot it's beginning to smoke, drop one popper in. In 2 to 3 seconds it should have expanded in diameter and turned a light color. Take tongs and immediately flip over in oil for 1 to 2 seconds, then lift out of the oil with tongs and place on paper toweling to drain. While draining poppers, it's better to stand them in a row on their sides rather than laying them on top of one another, as they get soggy when stacked on top of each other.

Minestrone Soup, p. 398

MINESTRONE SOUP

¼ cup olive oil
1 cup diced celery
½ tsp. asafetida

1½ qts. water
1 cup flaky nutritional yeast
1 cup diced tomatoes
½ tsp. Dr. Bronner's Seasoning
1 cup diced carrots
1 cup diced potatoes
½ cup diced green beans
½ tsp. basil
1 tsp. oregano
1 cup whole wheat noodles, broken up

1 cup cooked pink beans

Sauté first 3 ingredients together. Put the next 10 ingredients in a pot and add the sautéd ingredients to the pot also. Put the beans in a blender and pureé them. Add the beans to the pot. Bring to a boil, then turn heat down and simmer for 20 minutes. Serve topped with Parmesan cheese.

MUNG BEAN DAHL SOUP

1 cup mung beans
6 cups water
½ tsp. fresh ginger, chopped fine

1 tsp. turmeric
1 tsp. vegetable salt
1 large, fresh tomato, sliced

3 Tbsp. ghee or oil
½ tsp. cumin
Tiny pinch crushed red pepper (opt.)

Wash beans and put into saucepan with water and ginger. Cook until beans are soft and broken up. Add next 3 ingredients and simmer for 15 minutes. Then heat ghee and add cumin seeds. When browned, add the crushed chilies, if desired. Add spices to soup and remove from heat.

SPICY BEANS

3 Tbsp. butter or margarine
½ tsp. asafetida
1 chopped green bell pepper
1 cup diced celery
3 tsp. vegetable salt
3 tsp. ground cumin
2 tsp. celery seed
1 tsp. chili powder
1 tsp. basil
2 Tbsp. soy sauce

2½ cups fresh tomatoes, cut in eighths

4 cups kidney beans, cooked

try

Sauté first 10 ingredients in butter or margarine until slightly tender. Add tomatoes and simmer until they begin to cook down (about 15 minutes). Add cooked kidney beans and cook 15 minutes more, adding a little more water if necessary. Good served with steamed brown rice.

STOVE-TOP BAKED BEANS

2 cups dry pinto, navy or
kidney beans, soaked overnight
5 cups water

2 Tbsp. oil
¼ tsp. asafetida

¼ cup molasses
1½ tsp. vegetable salt
1 tsp. dry mustard powder
1 tsp. chili powder
¼ cup tomato sauce (opt.)

Soak beans overnight. Rinse and add new water. Bring to boil, reduce heat, cover and simmer 2 to 3 hours or until tender. In a small skillet, toast next 2 ingredients. Add to beans when tender with remaining ingredients. Simmer the beans until desired thickness is reached. This is much faster than baking in the oven. The beans may also be pressure-cooked; then add other ingredients and simmer a few minutes.

GARBANZO PATÉ ○

1 vegetable bouillon cube
2 cups soaked garbanzo beans
1 Tbsp. oil
1 cup water
1 tsp. soy sauce

¼ cup wheat germ
½ cup nutritional yeast
1 tsp. poultry seasoning
¼ tsp. asafetida
¼ tsp. thyme
¼ tsp. summer savory

Blend first 5 ingredients in blender until smooth. Then add last 6 ingredients and mix well. Pour into an oiled baking pan, cover and bake at 350° for 1 hour.

CREAMY BEAN DIP ○

2 cups cooked pinto beans, mashed
½ cup water
1/8 tsp. asafetida
½ tsp. cumin seed
1 jalapeño pepper, chopped
½ Tbsp. molasses
2 large tomatoes

Juice of ½ lemon
1½ Tbsp. chili powder
½ Tbsp. soy sauce

¼ lb. cheddar cheese, grated

In a saucepan, simmer first 7 ingredients for 30 minutes. Then add next 3 ingredients. While beans are still hot, add the grated cheddar cheese. Mash or blend until smooth. May be served either hot or cold with chips or crackers.

GARBANZO CROQUETTES ○

1½ cups cooked garbanzo beans, ground
2½ cups cooked brown rice or millet
3 Tbsp. sesame tahini, peanut
butter or other nut butter
½ cup finely chopped celery
½ cup finely chopped walnuts
¼ tsp. asafetida
2 Tbsp. soy sauce
2 Tbsp. light oil

Corn meal

Mix first 8 ingredients well with hands and form into croquettes (three-sided patties). Roll in corn meal. Bake at 375° for 30 minutes or fry in a little oil until browned on all three sides. May be served with gravy or sauce.

LEGUME PATÉ ○

2 Tbsp. butter or margarine
½ cup diced celery
½ tsp. asafetida
1 tsp. basil
1 tsp. oregano
1 cup diced tomatoes
Pinch cayenne

1 cup cooked lentils
1 cup cooked split peas
1 cup flaky nutritional yeast
½ cup finely grated carrots
2 tsp. olive oil
1 tsp. Spike
2 Tbsp. bran flakes
¼ cup whole wheat flour
2 Tbsp. ground oat flakes
½ cup ground peanuts
½ cup ground cashews

Sauté first 7 ingredients for 2 minutes. Put in a bowl and add the next 11 ingredients. Mix together thoroughly. Bake at 400° for 35 minutes. Allow to cool completely before removing from pan. Serve chilled.

GARBANZO DIP

2 cups garbanzo beans, cooked and drained
3 - 4 Tbsp. tahini
¼ cup lemon juice
½ cup finely chopped celery
¼ tsp. asafetida
1 tsp. soy sauce

Grind garbanzo beans in food grinder. Add remaining ingredients to make a thick dip. Serve as a dip with raw vegetables or as a sandwich spread.

LENTIL SOUP

1½ cups lentils, washed
1½ qts. cold water

1 Tbsp. butter
2 Tbsp. sesame oil or soy oil

½ tsp. asafetida
1 large rib celery, chopped
¼ cup celery leaves
2 carrots, thickly sliced
1/3 cup brown rice
2 Tbsp. parsley, chopped

Black pepper to taste (opt.)
2 Tbsp. vegetable salt
3 Tbsp. nutritional yeast

1½ Tbsp. miso

Place lentils in water and cook on medium heat while preparing other vegetables. Heat butter and oil in heavy skillet and sauté next 6 ingredients. Add to your kettle of lentils. Add next 3 ingredients and cook until all vegetables are tender and the lentils have opened up and softened, about 1 hour. Remove ½ cup of soup broth and mix with miso until smooth. Return to soup kettle. Yields 6 servings.

Variation: Barley or millet can be used instead of rice, or 2 cups of green, leafy vegies such as kale, spinach, escarole, etc.

LENTIL LOAF

1 cup cooked lentils
1 cup finely chopped walnuts
1 cup whole wheat bread crumbs

1 cup garbanzo flour
4 Tbsp. butter or margarine

1 cup diced celery
1 cup chopped black olives
½ cup tomato sauce
½ cup grated cheddar cheese
½ tsp. asafetida
2 tsp. sage powder
1 tsp. thyme powder
1 tsp. vegetable salt

Combine first 3 ingredients. Toast flour in butter or margarine. Add to first 3 ingredients and mash together well. Add remaining 8 ingredients and mix well. Place into a well-oiled loaf pan (bread loaf size) and press into shape. Cover with aluminum foil and bake at 350° for 30 minutes. Remove foil and continue to bake for 30 minutes longer. Cool a bit, cut into thick slices and serve plain or with gravy. Serves 4 to 6.

SWEET AND SOUR LENTILS

2 cups vegetable broth or soup stock
(see Basic Recipes Section, p. 31)
1 cup dried lentils or yellow
or green split peas (washed)

1 tsp. grated fresh ginger
¼ tsp. asafetida
¼ tsp. ground cloves
¼ tsp. nutmeg
1 tsp. soy sauce
4 tsp. apple cider vinegar
4 tsp. honey or molasses
3 Tbsp. oil

Bring the broth to a boil in a pot and add the lentils or peas. Cover and simmer gently for 30 minutes. Check after 20 minutes and add a little more water if necessary. Add remaining ingredients. Stir and cook 5 more minutes or until lentils or peas are tender. Yields 4 servings.

HEALTHY HOLIDAY MOCK TURKEY ○

2 cups chickpeas, cooked and mashed
2 cups brown rice, cooked soft
½ cup vegetable bouillon liquid
1 cup finely diced bread crumbs
½ cup whole wheat flour
1/3 cup chopped walnuts

2 Tbsp. butter or margarine
½ tsp. celery seed
½ tsp. vegetable salt
½ tsp. black pepper
½ tsp. sage
½ tsp. thyme
1 tsp. asafetida

Cook and mash chickpeas. Cook and cool rice. Dissolve bouillon in hot water. Toast spices in butter. Combine all ingredients and mix and mash together well. Shape into slices or patties. Place on oiled baking sheet, sprinkle with paprika and bake at 375° for for 45 minutes or until browned.

MOCK TUNA SALAD ○

¼ lb. uncooked garbanzo beans
¼ lb. uncooked soybeans

½ cup diced celery
½ cup pickle relish
½ cup Eggless Soy Mayonnaise
(see Basic Recipes Section, p. 34)
½ tsp. salt
2 tsp. soy sauce
¼ cup nutritional yeast
1 tsp. kelp powder
1/8 tsp. asafetida
1/8 tsp. black pepper

Soak beans overnight. Rinse, drain and boil in fresh water until tender. When they mash easily between fingers, rinse and drain. Mash well with a potato masher or run through a food grinder or Champion juicer. Combine with next 9 ingredients and mix thoroughly. Chill in refrigerator. Serve as a side dish, on crackers, in a sandwich, or on a salad.

CRUNCHY SAVORIES ☆

1 cup garbanzo (chickpea) flour
1 Tbsp. soy sauce
1 tsp. turmeric
1/8 tsp. asafetida
1/8 tsp. cayenne
A shake of clove powder
½ - ¾ cup water

Ghee or oil for deep frying

Combine all ingredients to form a fairly wet dough. Heat ghee or oil until very hot and almost smoking. Place dough in a colander or a pie tin with holes punched in it with nails. Push dough batter through the holes using the back of a spoon or your hand. The drips that fall into the heated oil or ghee will cook in a matter of a few seconds. As soon as they look golden brown, take a strainer and scoop all the driplets out at once. Set on a paper towel to drain. Repeat this process until dough is gone. This is good served as a snack by itself or with nuts. Also good sprinkled on salads or over your favorite entree. Or try making a vegetable crisp (much like an apple crisp) using these Crunchy Savories as the crumble on the bottom and top and using vegetables and your favorite sauce or gravy as the filling (a good way to use up those leftovers!).

SIMPLE SUCCOTASH WITH BEANS ○

3 Tbsp. oil
¼ tsp. asafetida
½ green pepper, chopped

2 cups corn, cooked
2 cups beans, cooked
1 Tbsp. soy sauce
½ tsp. vegetable salt
¼ cup nutritional yeast
1 tsp. savory
Vegetable or bean stock

Sauté first 3 ingredients. Add remaining ingredients, using just enough stock to moisten. Cover pot and simmer for 20 minutes. Makes 6 servings.

VEGETABLE STUFFED SUSHI ○

10 aburage shells
½ cup honey
¼ cup soy sauce
Water

2 cups lentils, cooked

½ cup oil
½ tsp. cumin powder
½ tsp. turmeric
1 tsp. curry powder
½ tsp. fresh grated ginger
1½ tsp. salt
Dash of cayenne pepper

½ lb. celery, diced
½ bell pepper, diced

½ lb. carrots, grated

1 cup okara

Slice triangle-shaped aburage in half across the middle. Then slice each half once through the open end so knife never cuts through the shell itself. Place in boiling water for 10 minutes. Pour water off and boil again in new water to get rid of excess oil. Then drain again and place aburage shells in 1½ inches of water and ½ cup honey. Cover and cook 5 minutes. When 5 minutes is up, add ¼ cup soy sauce. Let set a minute, then drain and set shells aside. (Keep water for soup stock or to cook vegetables in, etc.) Measure lentils and set aside. Toast next 7 ingredients. Add next 2 ingredients, cover and cook until almost tender. Add carrots and cook a few minutes longer. Add last ingredient and stir-fry for a few minutes. Toss in lentils, mix well and stuff aburages with mixture.

SPLIT PEA BARATS ☆

2 cups uncooked, green split peas
(may use half lentils, mung bean sprouts or any other bean)

1/8 tsp. cinnamon
½ tsp. ground coriander
½ tsp. ground cumin
½ tsp. turmeric
1/8 tsp. cayenne (opt.)
1/8 tsp. asafetida
½ tsp. vegetable salt

Ghee or oil for deep frying

2 cups plain yogurt or buttermilk

Wash peas well. Soak overnight or for at least 4 hours. Drain. Grind with food grinder into a bowl. Place another pan under grinder to catch excess water. Grind a second time. Add next 7 ingredients to ground peas and mix well. Heat ghee (or oil) in a deep pot or wok. Shape ground peas into flat cakes the size of a half dollar. Deep fry until hard. Should be very crisp. Drop sizzling into plain yogurt or buttermilk. Delicious!

LIMA BEANS 'N CREAM BAKE ○

4 cups cooked lima beans
2 cups whole grain bread crumbs
or toasted, rolled oats
½ cup finely chopped green bell peppers
½ cup finely chopped celery
¼ tsp. vegetable salt
½ tsp. asafetida
½ tsp. basil
¾ cup chopped walnuts
1½ cups heavy cream

Preheat oven to 350° F. If you decide to use toasted, rolled oats instead of bread crumbs, spread 2 cups rolled oats on a cookie sheet and toast in 350° oven for 15 to 20 minutes or until golden brown. Combine all ingredients and bake in covered, oiled casserole dish for 45 minutes. Yields 6 servings.

BAKED LENTIL SURPRISE ○

2 cups lentils, cooked
1 cup bulgar, cooked
1 cup sunflower seed meal
(or other nut meal)
3 Tbsp. nutritional yeast
1 Tbsp. soy sauce
1 Tbsp. oil
¼ tsp. basil

Thoroughly blend all ingredients. Turn into oiled muffin pans. Bake at 300° F for 30 to 40 minutes. Serve with sauce, if desired. Yields 6 servings.

FALAFEL (A Mid-Eastern Sandwich) ☆

½ lb. chickpeas, soaked

1 Tbsp. bread crumbs
or whole wheat flour
½ tsp. baking soda
¼ tsp. cumin powder
½ tsp. salt (or more)
¼ tsp. black pepper
Chopped parsley
Pinch cayenne
¼ tsp. turmeric
1 tsp. coriander
¼ tsp. asafetida

Tahini Sauce:
½ cup tahini
¼ cup lemon juice
¼ tsp. black pepper
½ tsp. salt
¼ tsp. asafetida
¼ cup cold water

Bible bread
Grated carrot
Tomatoes
Alfalfa sprouts

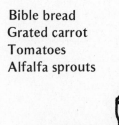

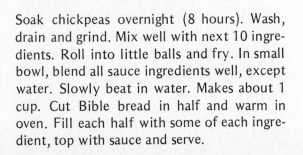

Soak chickpeas overnight (8 hours). Wash, drain and grind. Mix well with next 10 ingredients. Roll into little balls and fry. In small bowl, blend all sauce ingredients well, except water. Slowly beat in water. Makes about 1 cup. Cut Bible bread in half and warm in oven. Fill each half with some of each ingredient, top with sauce and serve.

FALAFEL #2 ☆

¼ cup uncooked bulgar (also called pilaf)
½ cup hot water

2 cups cooked garbanzo beans, mashed
1 slice whole-grain bread broken into crumbs
¼ cup water
2 Tbsp. arrowroot
1 Tbsp. soy sauce
2 Tbsp. parsley
1 tsp. coriander powder
1 tsp. cumin powder
1 tsp. turmeric
¼ tsp. black pepper
½ tsp. asafetida
¼ tsp. cayenne

Ghee or oil for frying

About 1 hour before preparation time (or in the morning before leaving for work), soak first 2 ingredients. Grind 2 cups of cooked garbanzos in food grinder or grind 1 cup at a time in a blender. Combine all ingredients and mix thoroughly. Shape into small patties or balls and deep fry in hot oil. (It must be hot; if it is too cool, the patties will begin to fall apart in the oil. The oil must be hot enough to cook the patty hard on the outside so it won't fall apart). Fry until golden brown and remove from oil with a slotted spoon. Serve in pita bread with fresh vegetable salad and topped with the following dressing.

FALAFEL DRESSING □

½ cup sesame tahini
¼ cup lemon juice
¼ tsp. asafetida
¼ tsp. black pepper
½ tsp. mustard powder
1/8 tsp. cayenne (opt.)
1 tsp. soy sauce

¼ - ½ cup water

Combine first 7 ingredients and mix well. Slowly add water to desired consistency.

MANJU

1 cup uncooked beans
(adzuki or black beans traditionally)

1¼ cups butter or margarine
2½ cups whole wheat flour
¼ cup milk

¼ cup honey

Soak beans overnight. Traditionally adzuki or black beans are used, but this is delicious using other beans for filling as well. Drain and rinse beans well. Cover beans with 2 to 3 times as much water and bring to a boil. Cover the pot, turn heat down to medium and gently boil beans until they begin falling apart. Remove lid of pot; cook until water is just covering the top of the beans. While beans continue to cook, take a potato masher and mash the beans. Some people like the filling completely smooth. To do this, instead of mashing with a potato masher, pour soft beans and cooking water into the blender and blend until smooth; then pour back into the pot. Cook mashed or blended beans with honey, stirring occasionally until they reach the consistency of mashed potatoes. Remove from heat and set aside to cool. If you're using already cooked beans, use 2 cups of beans, ¼ cup of honey and enough water to mash or blend them and then cook down. While beans are cooling, make the Manju dough by combining last 3 ingredients as you would pie dough. (Cut butter or margarine into the flour until a sandy texture. Then mix in milk.) Pinch walnut-sized balls of dough off and flatten one at a time in the palm of the hand to about 1/8" thick. (This will not work rolled out on a counter. The Manju dough must be formed in the palm of your hand.) Spoon about a tablespoon of the bean filling into the center of the flattened dough and gently and carefully fold all edges of the dough over the bean filling so they meet in the middle. Pinch the edges of the dough together to seal filling in. Place seam side down on an unoiled cookie sheet and bake at 425° for 20 to 25 minutes. You can also use Date Pudding (see Dried Fruit

Section, p. 247) or nut butter and chopped dates as a filling in place of beans.

BEAN NECTAR ○

1-1/3 cups Manju bean filling
(see recipe this page)
3 cups milk
2 bananas
1/8 tsp. cardamom

Blend all ingredients in a blender until smooth. Serve chilled.

LADDU

¼ cup butter or margarine
¾ cup garbanzo (chickpea) flour

¼ cup nut butter
½ cup honey
1/3 cup noninstant powdered milk

Combine first 2 ingredients in a skillet and toast over medium heat, stirring constantly. Toast until flour is golden brown (this can be done using whole wheat flour or other flours if you like). Remove from heat and allow to cool. Add next 3 ingredients and mix together well. Press into a pan and cut into squares or roll into balls.

GRAINS

Grains

Grains, also known as cereals (the name coming from the Roman Goddess Ceres, the provider of plentiful gifts from the earth), have been in the past and are presently the most important food staple around the world.

In the past, the staple grain of a particular people depended on geographical location. In the West (Europe), wheat, rye, oats, barley and millet were the staples; rice and millet in the Orient; and maize and sorghum in Africa and the Americas. Although such geographical distinctions still exist today, it's mostly due to traditional tastes that have developed.

Although wheat and rice are the two grains most commonly consumed in America today, there is a whole fascinating spectrum of grains which offer diversity in taste, texture and nutritional value.

As can be seen in the nutritional table on page 410, the nutritional value of each grain is quite distinct from the others. And you will note (on pages 49 and 51) the difference in nutritional value between grain in its whole, natural state and its refined state.

Grains have been refined for centuries, but only in recent years has the science of nutrition clearly established that refined grains are indeed inferior to unrefined grains. In the past, refined grains were quite a status symbol. In Japan, only the Japanese princesses were fed this "pure" food. And in the Middle Ages in Europe, only the rich class could afford white bread. (In those days, whitening was accomplished by adding chalk, alum, or even bone meal obtained from corpses in graveyards, or even arsenic powder.)

Today, our methods of whitening and refining wheat, rice and other grains are quite different. But the detrimental effect on nutritional value is still there. During the refining process, the bran and endosperm are removed. These are the two parts of the grain that contain the most nutrients, amino acids, vitamins, minerals, protein, natural oils, and essential fiber needed by the body. So much in nutritional value is lost that no amount of "enriching" or "fortifying" replaces it all. Nor does it even make sense to go through all the extra steps to remove the nutrition which nature has bountifully put in the whole grain, and then turn around and throw in synthetic replacements to try to make up for it!

Wheat is a good example of what I'm talking about. In wheat, nature has made an almost nutritionally perfect package. The interior part of the wheat kernel, called the endosperm, contains carbohydrates (starch) and a small amount of protein (gluten). White flour is made from this part of the kernel. In the hull and germ of the wheat kernel (which are removed in the refining process) are contained, among other vitamins and minerals, B vitamins, iron, zinc, and the amino acid lysine, which the body needs to be able to fully utilize protein and starch, as well as essential fiber. "Enriched" or "fortified" flour replaces only three of the B vitamins. Not only are all the nutrients removed in the refining process not replaced, but there is a great possibility that refining removes nutrients still unknown to nutrition science, which obviously aren't replaced because we don't know about them yet.

During World War II, governments of warring nations found it imperative to determine ways to supply food nutrition in the face of a shortage. In Canada, the government wisely decided the best thing to do

with wheat was to leave all the natural nutrients as they were, as they concluded only two or three vitamins of the many natural vitamins present could be replaced by chemical laboratories. In England, a special wartime bread consisting of 85% whole wheat flour was included in rationing. (It's interesting to note that the health of the English people actually improved during this time, largely because the 85% whole wheat bread was a great improvement over white bread.) Meanwhile, in America, the accepted standard was that only three vitamins (B_1, B_2 and niacin) were necessary to be added to white flour to make it "enriched" enough.

Unfortunately, it took the U.S. government and "experts" until the 1970's to recognize the health detriments directly linked with consumption of refined grains. And this was only due to a "wave of malnutrition," as described in the U.S. Senate Dietary Goals report, which was sweeping the country.

Using whole grains is healthier for the body and much superior in taste to refined grains. After getting used to the full, nutty flavor of whole grains, white refined grains are like biting into sponges. I think you'll find that the taste of whole grains simply "makes" the recipes! Hope you like them!

BROWN RICE ○

Use 2 parts water to 1 part rice. Cover pot with lid and do not remove for the following: Bring to boil over high heat and allow to boil 2 to 3 minutes; turn down to medium-high and softly boil for 10 to 15 minutes; turn heat to simmer or off and allow rice to steam at least 15 to 20 minutes.

SIMPLE FRIED RICE ○

2 Tbsp. oil
½ tsp. finely grated ginger
2 cups cooked, cooled rice
1 Tbsp. soy sauce

Sauté ginger in oil, add rice and stir-fry on medium-high heat for 5 to 10 minutes. While stirring, add soy sauce and continue to fry and stir constantly for 5 minutes; then serve.

GRAINS
(From U.S.D.A. Agriculture Handbook #8)
100 gm. edible portion

Food and description	Water (%)	Food Energy (calories)	Protein (gm.)	Fat (gm.)	Carbohydrate Total (gm.)	Fiber (gm.)	Ash (gm.)	Calcium (mg.)	Phosphorus (mg.)	Iron (mg.)	Sodium (mg.)	Potassium (mg.)	Vit. A (I.U.)	Thiamine (mg.)	Riboflavin (mg.)	Niacin (mg.)	Vit. C (mg.)
BROWN RICE (cooked)	70.3	119	2.5	.6	25.5	.3	1.1	12	73	.5	282	70	(0)	.09	.02	1.4	(0)
WHOLE WHEAT FLOUR	12.0	333	13.3	2.0	71.0	2.3	1.7	41	372	3.3	3	370	(0)	.55	.12	4.3	(0)
CORNMEAL (whole ground)	12.0	355	9.2	3.9	73.7	1.6	1.2	20	256	2.4	(1)	(284)	510*	.38	.11	2.0	(0)
RYE (whole grain)	11.0	334	12.1	1.7	73.4	2.0	1.8	(38)	376	3.7	(1)	467	(0)	.43	.22	1.6	(0)
BUCKWHEAT (whole grain)	11.0	335	11.7	2.4	72.9	9.9	2.0	114	282	3.1	–	448	(0)	.60	–	4.4	(0)
ROLLED OATS (cooked)	86.5	55	2.0	1.0	9.7	.2	.8	9	57	.6	218	61	(0)	.08	.02	.1	(0)
BARLEY (pearled, light)	11.1	349	8.2	1.0	78.8	.5	.9	16	189	2.0	3	160	(0)	.12	.05	3.1	(0)
MILLET (whole grain)	11.8	327	9.9	2.9	72.9	3.2	2.5	20	311	6.8	–	430	(0)	.73	.38	2.3	(0)
BULGAR (dry)																	
Club wheat	9.0	359	8.7	1.4	79.5	1.7	1.4	30	319	4.7	–	262	(0)	.30	.10	4.2	(0)
Hard red winter wheat	10.0	354	11.2	1.5	75.7	1.7	1.6	29	338	3.7	–	229	(0)	.28	.14	4.5	(0)
White wheat	(9.0)	357	10.2	1.2	78.1	1.3	1.4	36	300	(4.7)	–	310	(0)	(.30)	(.10)	(4.2)	(0)
SOY FLOUR																	
Full-fat	8.0	421	36.7	20.3	30.4	2.4	4.6	199	558	8.4	1	1,660	110	.85	.31	2.1	0
Low-fat	8.0	356	43.4	6.7	36.6	2.5	5.3	263	634	9.1	1	1,859	80	.83	.36	2.6	0

* Based on yellow varieties; white varieties contain only a trace of cryptoxanthin and carotenes, the pigments in corn that have biological activity.

(Numbers in parentheses denote values imputed — usually from another form of the food or from a similar food. Zero in parentheses indicates that the amount of a constituent probably is none or is too small to measure. Dashes denote lack of reliable data for a constituent believed to be present in measurable amount. Calculated values, as those based on a recipe, are not in parentheses.)

Danish Pastry, p. 434 - 436

FRIED RICE

2 Tbsp. oil
3 Tbsp. grated fresh ginger root

3 carrots, grated
2 sticks celery, diced
½ cup cooked peas

3 cups cooked brown rice
2 tsp. salt

4 oz. raisins
½ cup cashews
1 tsp. soy sauce

Gomasio (see Basic Recipes Section, p. 38)
Grated cheese
Parsley

Heat the oil in a large frying pan and fry grated ginger root. Then add the vegetables and sauté slightly. Add the rice and salt, mixing all ingredients together well. Then add the raisins and cashews and mix with soy sauce. Place in a serving dish and sprinkle generously with gomasio, fresh grated cheese and parsley.

GINGER RICE BALLS

2 cups uncooked brown rice
½ cup uncooked barley
5 cups water

1 tsp. butter or margarine
1 Tbsp. finely grated ginger
¼ cup chopped mung bean sprouts
¼ cup grated coconut or
other seed or nut meal
¼ cup shredded nori seaweed
1½ Tbsp. soy sauce (or to taste)

Juice of ½ lemon

1½ cups toasted sesame seeds

Cook first 3 ingredients together as you would normally cook brown rice (see directions on p. 409, this section). Sauté next 6 ingredients together in frying pan. Squeeze in lemon juice. Add rice. Stir-fry until rice starts to hold together. Wet hands (to prevent sticking) and make rice into ball shapes. Roll in toasted sesame seeds.

SIZZLING RICE SOUP

1 cup slivered dried mushrooms
2 qts. water
2 tsp. finely grated ginger root
¼ cup soy sauce
2½ Tbsp. lemon juice
2 tsp. cayenne
1½ Tbsp. vinegar

¾ cup brown rice
3 cups water

Sesame or other vegetable oil
(enough for 1" deep in pan)

Put first 7 ingredients in pan and bring to a boil. Turn down to lowest heat and simmer for 30 minutes. In a separate pan, bring next 2 ingredients to boil. Turn down to a low heat and cook covered for 30 minutes, stirring occasionally. (You want the rice to become sticky and stirring makes the rice sticky.) In a separate pot, heat oil for deep frying to medium-high. When rice is cool enough to handle, pinch into small bunches (about tablespoon size) and deep fry in oil. When crisp on all sides, drop these rice cakes into hot soup. Serve hot immediately. Usually the frying rice is removed from the oil and dropped into the soup right at the table so everyone can see the "excitement" of the rice sizzling when it hits the soup.

SPANISH RICE WITH PEAS

1 cup brown rice
1½ cups water
1 cup tomato sauce
¼ cup oil
1 cup peas
Pinch of asafetida

Fry rice in oiled skillet until toasted. Then add tomato sauce and 1½ cups water. Bring to a boil, then turn to simmer. Add peas, cover and cook for 45 minutes or until done.

POPCORN SNACK

8 cups popped corn
2 - 4 Tbsp. melted butter (or else put seasoning on while popcorn is still hot)

2 Tbsp. nutritional yeast
1 Tbsp. Dr. Bronner's Balanced Protein Seasoning or vegetable salt

Pop the corn. Toss in melted butter. Add last 2 ingredients, mix well and serve. Tastes like cheese popcorn.

SPICY POPCORN SNACK

½ cup oil
¼ tsp. chili powder
1 tsp. cumin powder
¼ tsp. turmeric powder
1/8 tsp. black pepper
¼ tsp. asafetida
1 cup popcorn

¼ cup melted butter (or more)

4 Tbsp. nutritional yeast
½ - 1 tsp. salt

Combine first 7 ingredients in a pan. Mix well and place on medium-high heat. Cover and allow to start popping and shake pan until done. Pour on melted butter and mix well. Add yeast and salt. Mix well and serve. Spices can also be lightly toasted in melted butter and poured over popped corn instead of popping corn in the spices. The amount of spices can also be increased according to desired taste.

HERB BREAD

2 Tbsp. active yeast
2 cups warm water
1 tsp. honey
½ tsp. salt

4 cups whole wheat flour

6 Tbsp. butter or margarine

2 Tbsp. dry parsley
1 tsp. powdered sage
½ tsp. asafetida
2 tsp. dill leaves
2 tsp. basil
2 tsp. thyme
1 tsp. marjoram
¼ tsp. black pepper

2 cups grated cheese (opt.)

Make bread dough by combining first 4 ingredients and let sit until yeast dissolves. Add flour and knead (for about 10 minutes) into a firm ball. Place in a bowl, cover with a damp cloth and allow to rise in a warm place for about 1 hour or until doubled in size. Punch the dough down and oil the counter. Roll dough out on oiled counter into a ¼" thick rectangle. Spread half the butter over surface of the dough and then sprinkle half of the dry herbs (which have been mixed together) over the surface of the dough. At this point add half the grated cheese if you're going to use it. Fold one edge of rectangle one-third of the way over the edge already folded over. Seal ends. Roll dough out into a rectangle again and repeat steps using up all the remaining ingredients. Fold under as before. Place dough in a large oiled bread pan, press it down and crisscross the top with a sharp knife. Oil the top of the bread, cover with a damp cloth and allow to rise in a warm place until double in volume. Bake at 400° for 30 minutes. This can also be made into muffins or rolls by cutting off small pieces of dough, allowing to rise and then baking.

YEAST BISCUITS   O

½ cup whole wheat flour
¼ cup nutritional yeast
½ tsp. baking powder

1/6 cup frozen butter

3 Tbsp. yogurt
1 Tbsp. water

Preheat oven to 450°. Stir together first 3 ingredients. Then grate frozen butter into bowl with flour mixture. Mix with fingers or fork **only until** butter is well mixed, just before flour mixture starts looking like cornmeal. Speed and cold ingredients are an asset in biscuit making. Use fork to mix in last 2 ingredients. Add yogurt first, then water, only until mixture is no longer dry but clumps up on your fork. You should just be able to lift the whole clump up on the fork out of the bowl. For rolled biscuits, pat into ball, roll out ¾" thick, cut with 3" cutter, and bake 12 to 15 minutes until golden brown. For drop biscuits, use your big serving spoon to drop good-sized spoonfuls on the sheet. Then bake 12 to 15 minutes or until golden brown.

WHOLE WHEAT BISCUITS   O

2 cups whole wheat flour
2½ tsp. baking powder
½ tsp. salt

½ cup frozen butter or margarine

¾ cup milk

Mix together first 3 ingredients in a bowl. Grate frozen butter into flour mixture and mix well. Mix in milk with a fork only until flour is moistened and dough pulls away from sides of bowl. Turn out onto floured counter and knead lightly 30 seconds. Roll out to ¾" thickness and cut into rounds. Place on lightly greased pan. May brush tops with butter or margarine. Bake at 450° for 15 to 18 minutes.

BROWN GRAVY   ☆

1 cup whole wheat flour
½ cup butter or oil

½ tsp. salt
¼ tsp. black pepper
¼ tsp. chili powder

2 cups water

Toast flour in butter or oil. Add next 3 ingredients and toast a few minutes. Slowly whisk in water and cook on medium heat until thickening. Serve over Mock Turkey slices (see Tofu Section, p. 379) or other entrees.

ENGLISH MUFFINS   O

1 Tbsp. honey
1 Tbsp. yeast
½ cup warm water

½ cup yogurt
½ cup hot water

3 cups whole wheat flour
½ tsp. baking powder

½ cup coarse cornmeal

Dissolve yeast in warm water. Add honey and mix. Continue mixing and add 2 cups of the flour to yeast mixture. Then combine yogurt and hot water and add this mixture to the dough. Cover and let rise until double in size. Mix in remaining flour and baking powder. Mix thoroughly. If sticky, add a little more flour. Knead until soft. Cover and let rise again until double in size. Punch dough down and roll out to ½" thickness. Cut into 4" circles. Coat each side of dough with cornmeal. Put on cookie sheet and let double in size. Heat an iron skillet. Put a few muffins in the skillet on low heat and cook 10 minutes on both sides.

HOMEMADE WHOLE WHEAT BUNS ○

6 cups warm water
6 Tbsp. yeast
¼ cup honey

½ cup oil or butter
12 cups whole wheat flour
          or
10 cups whole wheat flour and 2 cups bran
2 tsp. salt
3 tsp. baking powder

Combine first 3 ingredients. Stir until dissolved and let set a few minutes. Add oil and sift in flour with salt and baking powder. Mix well to consistency of soft dough (may need to add more flour). Break off pieces of dough. Roll into balls, place on cookie sheet, slightly flatten, place in oven set at warm and let rise 15 minutes. Turn oven up to 400° and bake for 15 to 20 minutes. Check bottom; when very brown they are done.

PITA BREAD ○

1 package active dry yeast
2 cups warm water
1 tsp. honey

1 tsp. vegetable salt or Spike
4 cups whole wheat flour

½ - ¾ cup whole wheat flour

Mix first 3 ingredients together; then add the last 2 ingredients and mix well. Put in a bowl and cover. Let rise until double in size. Punch down and divide into 12 balls. Put ½ cup flour on counter, put the ball in flour lightly and roll out into circles about 1/8" thick. Place on ungreased cookie sheets. Turn bread over gently with both hands while rising. Bake at 450° for 5 minutes.

BAGELS ○

2 cups warm water
2 Tbsp. active dry yeast

1 Tbsp. honey
¼ cup oil
1½ tsp. salt

5½ cups whole wheat flour

Dissolve yeast in warm water and add next 3 ingredients. Mix in flour a cup at a time. When your dough is mixed it will be soft and somewhat sticky. Put ½ cup of flour on the corner of your counter. Put your hands in the flour and begin to knead your dough. Only add flour to your hands when kneading. You want the dough to remain light. Put dough in an oiled bowl and let rise in a warm place until double in size. Punch the dough down and knead it a few times. Put again in a warm place to rise. Preheat oven to 375° and put a large pot of water on stove top to bring to a boil just before you have to punch down the dough for the second time. Punch dough down when it has doubled and divide the dough into 16 to 18 pieces. Roll each one into a rope shape about 6" to 8" long and 1" in diameter. Form them into rings by pinching the ends together. Drop each ring into the boiling water as soon as each is made and boil each ring for only 1 minute. Remove each ring from water after boiling for 1 minute and place on an oiled cookie sheet. When all bagels are done boiling, bake them at 375° for 20 minutes. You can make variations by adding caraway seeds, sesame seeds, poppy seeds, garlic and onion, or raisins and cinnamon to the dough as you mix it. You can also substitute a cup of whole wheat flour with another grain of your choice.

HERB CHEESE ROLLS ☆

3 cups warm water
2 Tbsp. active dry yeast
½ cup honey

3 cups whole wheat flour

¼ cup sesame oil
1 Tbsp. Spike
2 Tbsp. basil
1 Tbsp. oregano
2/3 cup diced celery
1 tsp. asafetida
2 Tbsp. poppy seeds

½ cup grated cheese
4 - 5 cups whole wheat flour

Suggested filling for stuffed roll variation:
1 cup grated carrots
¼ cup soy sauce
¼ cup honey
2 tsp. finely grated ginger
1 tsp. sesame oil
1 block tofu, crumbled

Combine the first 3 ingredients and stir until yeast is dissolved. Add the flour and stir until mixed thoroughly. Cover bowl and set in a warm place for 30 minutes or until doubled in size. Sauté next 7 ingredients together for 2 minutes, allow to cool and then add to dough along with the next 2 ingredients. Mix all ingredients together thoroughly. Put dough on counter and knead 5 minutes. Put in a bowl in a warm place and let sit until dough has doubled in size. Remove dough from bowl and knead a few times. Divide dough into 24 balls. Set rolls on oiled cookie sheet and allow to rise in a warm place until double in size. Bake at 375° for 20 minutes.

If you want to make stuffed rolls, here's how:

Sauté filling ingredients for a couple of minutes and allow to cool while dough is rising. Make dough as described and divide into 24 balls. Roll each ball to ¼" thick on an oiled counter or flatten in the palms of your hands. Place a tablespoon or so of sautéd ingredients in the center of the dough. Gather up the sides of dough over the filling and pinch dough together with fingertips to seal. Set rolls on a buttered cookie sheet with sealed side down. Let double in size. Bake at 350° for 20 minutes.

FRENCH BREAD ◯

1 pkg. yeast
1¼ cups warm water
1 Tbsp. honey
1 Tbsp. oil
1 tsp. salt (opt.)

3½ cups whole wheat flour

Combine first 5 ingredients and let sit until yeast dissolves. Add 2 cups of flour and mix. Then add remaining flour and mix with hands. Turn dough out onto slightly floured surface. Pour a little bit of flour on the corner of the counter. If your dough becomes sticky, pat the dough with flour. Knead your dough for 5 minutes. Then put in a covered, oiled bowl to rise until doubled in size. Punch dough down (if needed, pat with flour) and let rise again until doubled. Punch down again and let rise 5 minutes. Put 1 Tbsp. of cornmeal on counter and knead. Divide dough in half and roll into a 15"x10" rectangle. Roll up tightly, place in baking pan and slit the loaf across the top every 4" to 5". Let rise until size has doubled. Meanwhile, boil some water in a pot and preheat oven to 350°. Put pan of boiling water on bottom shelf of oven. (This helps to keep dough from drying out.) Bake 20 minutes. Then make a mixture of 2 Tbsp. oil and 2 Tbsp. milk. Remove loaf from oven and brush generously with oil-milk mixture. Return to oven and bake 25 minutes longer.

BUTTER ROLLS ☆

1 Tbsp. baking yeast
2 cups warm water
½ cup butter or margarine
¼ cup honey

4 cups whole wheat flour
1 heaping tsp. baking powder

Combine first 4 ingredients and let sit until yeast dissolves. Mix in flour and baking powder and knead 5 to 10 minutes. Place dough on an oiled counter and cover with a mixing bowl. Allow to rise 15 minutes. Punch dough down, knead a few more minutes and make shapes to go in muffin tins. Liberally butter the muffin tins before dough is put in. Dough can be broken into walnut-sized pieces and 3 to 4 balls placed in each tin. Brush tops with melted butter and allow to rise 30 to 45 minutes in a warm place until almost double in size. Bake at 350° for 15 - 20 minutes until golden brown.

MILLET VEGETABLE LOAF ○

1 cup cooked millet
¼ cup chopped bell pepper
¼ cup diced celery
¼ cup grated carrot
¾ cup sunflower seed meal
½ cup grated cheese
1 cup whole wheat bread crumbs
½ cup milk
2 tsp. lemon juice
1 Tbsp. soy sauce
½ tsp. black pepper
2 tsp. sweet basil
1/8 tsp. asafetida

Mix above ingredients together well and press into an oiled loaf pan. Bake at 350° for 45 to 50 minutes. Slice and serve like a meat loaf. This is good topped with a gravy or ketchup. It's also good cold.

STUFFED BUNS ○

Basic Bread Dough recipe
(see Basic Recipes Section, p. 31)

¼ cup water
3 Tbsp. soy sauce
3 Tbsp. honey
1½ Tbsp. grated ginger
¼ tsp. asafetida

2 cups tofu, cubed
½ cup celery, chopped
½ cup carrots, chopped
½ cup broccoli, chopped

1 Tbsp. whole wheat flour

Make bread dough. Sauté first 5 ingredients. Add next 4 ingredients and saute for a minute. Don't cook vegetables too long, as they will get tender when cooked inside the buns. Sprinkle in whole wheat flour to thicken the vegetable juices that have cooked out. Measure dough into ½-cup balls. Roll flat to about ¼" thick. Holding flattened dough, put 1/3 cup of filling in very middle of flattened dough. Bring edges over filling to meet in the middle. Pinch together to seal. Place pinched side down on: 1) oiled cookie sheet to bake at 350° for 20 to 25 minutes; or 2) wax paper to steam for 30 to 45 minutes.

SPAGHETTI ○

1 pkg. soba noodles or whole grain pasta
Boiling water

Basic Italian Sauce
(see Garden Vegetables Section, p. 263)

2 cups grated cheese
or ½ - 1 cup nutritional yeast

Put noodles into boiling water and start preparing Basic Italian Sauce. When noodles are tender, drain in colander and rinse under running water. Pour sauce over noodles on a platter and top with cheese or nutritional yeast. Served with a salad, this makes a whole meal!

THANKSGIVING STUFFING

2 cups whole wheat or other
whole-grain bread cubes
½ cup cooked lentils
½ cup finely chopped walnuts

2 - 3 Tbsp. butter or margarine
¼ tsp. asafetida
½ cup diced celery

½ cup blended and strained tomatoes
1 tsp. sage, crushed fine
½ tsp. thyme
½ tsp. vegetable salt

½ cup chopped black olives
2 Tbsp. arrowroot mixed in 4 Tbsp. water

Combine first 3 ingredients and set aside.
Sauté next 3 ingredients in a skillet. Add
next 4 ingredients and cook for about 5 minutes. Add next 2 ingredients. Stir in well,
then pour into mixture of dry ingredients.
Place in oiled loaf pan and bake at 350° for
1 hour. Baste the top every 15 minutes with
melted butter. Good served with Mock Turkey and Gravy (see Tofu Section, p. 379).

BRAISED GLUTEN

1½ cups raw washed gluten

¼ cup oil
¼ cup soy sauce

5 - 6 star anise
Water to cover

Cut or break and flatten raw gluten into ½"
thick slabs. Fry in oil and soy sauce until
browned on both sides. When browned —
even a little burned — cover with water and
add anise. Cover and boil until water boils
out. Remove from pan. A large amount can
be made and frozen for future use. Cut into
thin slices and garnish Stir-fry Chinese Style
(see recipe in Garden Vegetables Section,
p. 275).

LASAGNE

Basic Italian Sauce (see Garden
Vegetables Section, p. 263)

1 lb. whole-grain lasagne noodles

2 blocks tofu, crumbled

Vegetable Filling:
2 Tbsp. oil
1 eggplant, diced
2 zucchinis, diced
1 bell pepper, diced

½ tsp. black pepper
1 tsp. oregano
1 tsp. turmeric
1½ tsp. chili powder
1 tsp. basil

1 cup grated cheese
or ½ cup nutritional yeast

Bring a pot with 1 gallon of salted water to
a boil and place lasagne noodles in to boil
for 20 minutes, or until tender. (When
noodles are done, drain through a colander
and rinse with cold water.) While they're
boiling, prepare filling by mashing the blocks
of tofu and sautéing the first 4 ingredients of
the vegetable filling until the vegetables get a
little translucent. Add the next 5 ingredients
to the sautéing vegetables, cover and simmer
a few minutes until vegetables get a little
tender. Pour the vegetable filling in the Basic
Italian Sauce. Spread a thin layer of sauce
in the bottom of an oblong baking pan.
Sprinkle crumbled tofu into sauce. On top
of that, lay strips of lasagne noodles side by
side. Then add more sauce, sprinkle with
crumbled tofu and repeat alternating layers
until you run out of ingredients or room in
the baking pan. End with tomato sauce on
top. Sprinkle with grated cheese or nutritional yeast. Bake at 350° for 20 minutes.
Cut into squares and serve.

NOODLE CAKES IN SOUR SAUCE ☆

12 oz. of buckwheat soba noodles
(or whole-grain ramen noodles or
other thin whole-grain noodles)

Oil for deep frying (about 1" deep)
Soy sauce
Arrowroot

3 Tbsp. oil
1 tsp. asafetida
1 block tofu

1 cup chopped celery
1 cup chopped tomato
1 cup chopped summer squash

1 recipe Sizzling Rice Soup
(see recipe this section, p. 412)
1 Tbsp. + 1 tsp. arrowroot

Boil noodles until done, drain and rinse in cold water in a colander (or use leftover noodles that have been refrigerated). On a platter, lay lumps of noodles equivalent to about ½ cup, apart from each other. Heat oil until almost smoking. While oil is heating, sprinkle a little soy sauce on each mound of noodles and toss each mound of noodles with enough arrowroot to help hold them together. When oil is hot and all noodles have been prepared, deep fry each mound of noodles separately until golden brown on one side. Flip over and fry until golden brown on the other side. Remove each crisp noodle cake (shouldn't be crisp all the way through — just on the outsides) and layer on the bottom of a large serving platter. In a large skillet, sauté oil, asafetida and tofu together over high heat until tofu begins to brown a little. Add chopped vegetables and stir-fry a few minutes. Dissolve arrowroot in the soup (from Sizzling Rice Soup). If the soup is cold, just mix until arrowroot dissolves; if the soup is hot, dissolve arrowroot in a tiny bit of cold water and mix into the hot soup, stirring constantly until the soup thickens. Pour soup over sautéed tofu and vegetables and cook, stirring constantly, until thickened. Pour over noodle cakes. Serve so each person gets a noodle cake.

GLUTEN CHAR SIU WITH CHINESE VEGETABLES ○

3 cups gluten flour
1½ cups water

2 Tbsp. red bean curd (red rice water mixed with tofu and found in Chinatown)
3 Tbsp. char siu seasoning

Oil for frying

Combine first 2 ingredients and form into a ball. Place in bowl, cover with water and let soak overnight. Rinse and knead under water to remove excess starch. Continue kneading and rinsing until water is nearly clear. Drain. Cut off chunks and drop into boiling water. Boil until they float to the top like dumplings. Continue to cook a few more minutes. Remove. Combine next 2 ingredients and mix well. Pour over dumplings. Let set in refrigerator overnight. Next day, heat wok with some oil and stir-fry dumplings until they are dark red and appear charred in spots. Remove, drain and cool a bit. Cut into thin slices and serve over Stir-fry Chinese Style (see recipe in Garden Vegetables Section, p. 275).

QUICK PIZZA ○

Basic Italian Sauce
(see Garden Vegetables Section, p. 263)

1 pkg. whole wheat pita breads
½ block tofu, mashed
2 cups grated cheese or nutritional yeast
Olive slices

Prepare Basic Italian Sauce. Pour ¼ to ½ cup on top of each pita bread and spread evenly. Sprinkle on mashed tofu, grated cheese or nutritional yeast and olives. Set under broiler or in 425° oven until warmed and cheese melts. Use leftover sauce for spaghetti!

CHAPATIS   ○

3 cups whole wheat flour
1 cup water

Mix both ingredients together and knead a bit until dough is earlobe consistency. Cover the ball of dough with the bowl inverted on the counter and let dough sit 20 to 30 minutes (you can be making the rest of the dinner in the meantime). Flour counter liberally, heat a skillet to medium-high heat and break balls of dough about 1½" to 2" in diameter. One at a time, roll the balls out to about 4" to 5" in diameter and put the rolled chapati into the heated dry skillet. The chapati should get little bubbles on the top surface in 15 to 20 seconds. Using tongs, flip the chapati over to the other side and cook a few seconds. Remove chapati from skillet and immediately put it directly over a flame by holding an edge of the chapati with tongs. (Try not to touch the chapati to the grill or a hole may burn which releases the steam and prevents the chapati from ballooning up.) It should puff up like a balloon in a few seconds. Flip over to the other side as soon as it bubbles and let cook a few seconds on the other side. This ballooning up steams the chapati from the inside. Remove the chapati from the flame and put onto a platter. The chapati will deflate. At this point you can rub a little butter on one surface of the chapati or leave it dry and put the next chapati in the skillet. This recipe makes about a dozen chapatis. (You can cook a stack of chapatis and freeze them for future use if this whole process takes too long to consider doing often.) A few crucial hints for making successful chapatis:

1) The skillet must be the right temperature. Too cool and the chapati will get hard and brittle before it gets little bubbles, and won't balloon up. If you notice the chapati is turning a golden brown on the first surface, the heat is up too high and the chapati may burn, which prevents ballooning also.

2) You may want to periodically wipe the burned excess flour out of the skillet to prevent burning.

3) Gas stoves work best for this, but it is possible to balloon the chapati over an electric element turned to high.

QUICK & ONO CHAPATI LUNCHES OR DINNERS   ○

Out of your homemade chapatis (or store-bought ones if you just don't have the time) you can make quick, ono dinners. All you need is:

Whole wheat chapati
(or Bible bread or tortilla)
Melted cheese and/or tofu
Tossed salad
Dressing
Seeds (sunflower, sesame) and/or nuts

Use a chapati (Bible bread or tortilla can also be used as a base for this meal — always use a whole-grain product, staying away from refined grains). Usually they're sold in the freezer section of natural food stores. If not, your store-bought or homemade chapatis can be frozen at home if you think you won't use them all before they mold. Take out one at a time as you need them. They will need to be heated — Bible bread usually in the toaster, chapatis and tortillas in a skillet. Let warm on one side, flip over and grate cheese onto it while the other side is heating. Top this with tofu that has been prepared prior to heating the bread. Tofu can be prepared in a number of ways. Stir-fried Tofu, Mock Scrambled Eggs, Teriyaki Tofu, Mock Chicken Tofu, or Tofu Cutlets are some suggestions (see Tofu Section for recipes). Top tofu with a tossed salad, your favorite dressing (some suggestions: Tofu Dressing, Sesame Seed Dressing, Yogurt Dressing or Nutty Protein Gravy) and a generous sprinkling of nuts and/or seeds.

PURIS

2 cups whole wheat flour
2 Tbsp. ghee, butter or margarine
¾ cup cold water

Ghee or oil for deep frying

Add butter to flour and use fingertips or pastry cutter to break butter up and mix into flour until flour is crumbly or has a sandy texture. Add water a little at a time, mixing while adding. Knead dough a few minutes, invert mixing bowl and cover ball of dough. Let dough sit for 10 minutes. Pinch off balls of dough about 1½" in diameter. Roll each ball with a rolling pin on an oiled counter to a flat shape (about 1/8" thick). Place in hot ghee or oil (almost smoking), push puri to bottom and bathe in ghee. It will pop up immediately to the surface of the ghee and puff up like a balloon. Turn over quickly using tongs on the edge of the puri. Be careful not to poke a hole in the puri with the tongs. Let fry a few seconds. Remove and drain on paper towel. The whole cooking time of one puri should be about 10 to 15 seconds. Serve immediately either plain or sprinkled with date sugar, or filled with your favorite filling and rolled up.

RAVIOLI WITH TOFU FILLING

Shells:
2 cups whole wheat flour
or 1 cup whole wheat and 1 cup soy flour
1 cup water

Combine water and flour and mix well. Gather into a ball and knead on a floured surface until consistency of bread dough. Roll out with rolling pin on floured surface to 1/8" thickness. Cut into 3" squares. On each square place Tofu Filling. Fold over and seal well all around edges with a fork. Gently drop in lightly salted, boiling water and cook 8 to 10 minutes. Remove and serve with Ravioli Sauce.

Tofu Filling:
½ block firm tofu, mashed

½ tsp. salt
½ tsp. turmeric
½ tsp. basil
½ tsp. oregano
½ tsp. chili powder

Combine ingredients in a skillet and mix. Cook until the water is gone. Set aside to cool.

Ravioli Sauce:
8 cups tomato sauce
½ tsp. salt or 1 tsp. kelp
¼ tsp. black pepper
2½ tsp. oregano
2½ tsp. basil
¼ tsp. chili powder

¼ - ½ cup nutritional yeast
3 cups chopped, assorted vegetables
(celery, bell pepper, carrot, broccoli, etc.)
½ tsp. salt or 1 tsp. kelp

Combine first 6 ingredients and bring to a boil. Add yeast and vegetables and cook 5 to 10 minutes until vegetables are cooked but not overdone — still a bit crispy. Add cooked ravioli and serve.

POTATO SOUP WITH DUMPLINGS

1 cup celery and other vegetables
6 potatoes
2 tsp. salt
4 - 6 cups of soup stock

3 cups milk

Cook first 4 ingredients until potatoes are done. Add 3 cups milk. Bring to boil and add dumplings. Turn heat down and simmer for about 25 minutes. Don't lift lid.

Dumplings:
1 cup whole wheat flour
1½ tsp. baking powder
½ tsp. salt
1 tsp. parsley
½ cup milk

Mix all ingredients together and drop by tablespoonfuls into soup.

TAMALE PIE ○

Filling:
1 cup Homemade TVP (see p. 383)
or soaked Granburger (about ½ cup dry)
1 cup mashed tofu
or 2 cups cooked, mashed beans

2 Tbsp. oil
¼ tsp. asafetida

2 tsp. chili powder
2 Tbsp. soy sauce
½ cup tomato sauce
¼ cup sliced olives
½ cup corn (frozen or fresh)
½ cup chopped bell pepper
¼ cup chopped parsley
¾ cup chopped celery

Crust:
2½ cups cold water
1½ cups cornmeal
1 tsp. salt
1 tsp. chili powder

½ - ¾ cup grated cheese (opt.)

Prepare bulk of filling by mashing 1 cup of tofu or 2 cups cooked beans into 1 cup Homemade TVP or soaked Granburger. Brown next 2 ingredients in a skillet, then add next 8 ingredients and sauté a few minutes until ingredients are well mixed. Remove from heat. Prepare crust by bringing last 4 ingredients to a boil, stirring constantly until thickened. When thickened, remove from heat and pat 2/3 of cornmeal into an oiled 8" square baking pan. (Wetting your hands with cold water will keep the cornmeal from sticking to them.) Pat in evenly and up the sides. Pour in filling. Cover filling with remaining 1/3 of cornmeal. The easiest way to lay on the cornmeal top crust is to roll it out between sheets of wax paper with a rolling pin and flip the topping on straight off of the wax paper. Sprinkle the cheese on top if you wish to use it. Bake at 350° for 30 minutes.

SOBA (A Japanese Soup) ○

1 pkg. buckwheat soba noodles

1 Tbsp. oil
1½ cups sliced tofu and/or aburage shells fried in oil and soy sauce
2 cups chopped, assorted vegetables

1½ quarts water
4 Tbsp. miso
2 Tbsp. molasses
Soy sauce to taste

Boil noodles in separate pot of water until done. Meanwhile, sauté vegetables and tofu. In another pot, bring last 4 ingredients to a boil. Drain noodles and add directly to soup if served hot. Serve in bowls and garnish with vegetables. Soba is often served cold as a summer soup. For cold soba, refrigerate stock and lay cooked noodles over ice cubes. Dish cooled noodles into cooled stock and garnish.

TABOULI SALAD WITH TOFU ○

1 cup dry cracked wheat
1-1/3 cups water

1 cup watercress, chopped
1 cup finely chopped celery
2 tomatoes, diced
10 mint leaves, chopped fine
2 cups finely chopped parsley
1 cup small cubes firm tofu

Dressing:
6 Tbsp. olive oil
2 Tbsp. lemon juice
2 Tbsp. soy sauce
Dash of cayenne or asafetida (opt.)

Combine water and cracked wheat. Bring to boil, then lower to simmer and cover until done. Cool completely and combine with next 6 ingredients. Combine dressing ingredients and whiz in blender. Pour dressing over salad and mix lightly and thoroughly. Delicious served with crackers and cheese. Makes a complete meal.

STIR-FRIED TACO SALAD ○

1 Tbsp. oil
2 cups Homemade TVP (see p. 383)
or soaked Granburger (about 1 cup dry)
1 Tbsp. chili powder
2 cups chopped fresh vegetables
(celery, green pepper, carrot, broccoli, etc.)
1½ cups tomato sauce or 1# fresh tomatoes
1 tsp. honey
¼ tsp. asafetida
½ tsp. oregano

1 cup grated cheese
or ¼ cup nutritional yeast
9 oz. package corn chips
Salt and black pepper to taste

Chopped lettuce, sprouts
and other salad greens
1 large avocado, cubed (garnish)

Stir-fry first 8 ingredients. Cover and let simmer for 10 minutes. Stir in cheese and chips and mix well. Spoon over tossed salad greens and garnish with avocado cubes. This salad is a whole meal in itself. Delicious!

CREAMED NATURAL GRAINS ○

1 Tbsp. oil
¼ cup cubed celery
¼ tsp. asafetida

3 cups water
¾ cup bulgar (or other whole grain
like brown rice, millet, etc.)
2 tsp. soy sauce
¼ tsp. mustard
1/8 tsp. sage powder
¼ tsp. grated fresh ginger root

2 Tbsp. water
2 tsp. arrowroot

1½ cups fresh or frozen peas
1/3 cup nutritional yeast
1 Tbsp. butter or margarine

Sauté first 3 ingredients. When vegetable gets translucent, add next 6 ingredients, cover pot and bring to a boil. Turn heat down and simmer 20 to 25 minutes. Turn off heat. Stir water and arrowroot together until arrowroot dissolves. Pour this mixture into the cooked grain and mix immediately and quickly so grain water thickens to a gravy consistency. Add last 3 ingredients, cover pot and let steam on heat already in the pot for 5 to 10 minutes.

CHOW FUN ○

1 block tofu

½ cup chopped green onions
3 cups chopped vegetables
(such as broccoli, carrots, etc.)
¼ cup soaked hijiki seaweed
(approximately 2 tsp. dry seaweed)

2 Tbsp. toasted sesame oil + 2 Tbsp. butter
1½ tsp. black pepper
1/8 tsp. asafetida
2 Tbsp. baco-bits
2 Tbsp. nutritional yeast
2 Tbsp. soy sauce

8 oz. uncooked medium ribbon noodles
(sesame wheat or plain sesame)

Fry slices of tofu until browned and crisp. Smash the tofu up into small pieces and fry in some sesame oil, adding green onions the last 5 minutes of frying. On other burners, boil water for noodles and cook noodles until soft (about 10 minutes), then drain and steam vegies in steamer. Stir-fry all ingredients together — the tofu, noodles, seaweed, steamed vegies, spices and oil — over warm heat a few minutes and the meal is ready to serve. You can add more soy sauce or oil to suit your taste.

SPICY MACARONI SALAD ☆

2 cups uncooked macaroni
(vegetable, whole wheat or soy macaroni)

¼ cup chopped bell pepper
½ cup diced celery
½ cup Eggless Soy Mayonnaise
(see Basic Recipes Section, p. 34)
¼ cup yogurt or sour cream
½ cup grated cheese
1 Tbsp. wet mustard
1 Tbsp. soy sauce
1 Tbsp. finely chopped parsley
½ tsp. asafetida
¼ tsp. cumin powder
¼ tsp. chili powder
1/8 tsp. dill seed
¼ tsp. oregano
¼ tsp. black pepper

2 tomatoes
Lettuce leaves

Boil noodles, drain and rinse under cold water. Combine with next 14 ingredients and mix well. Line salad bowl with lettuce leaves, put salad into bowl and top with tomato wedges. Chill before serving.

TOASTED GRAINS & VEGETABLES O

3 Tbsp. oil
1 tsp. asafetida
1 tsp. marjoram powder
1 tsp. cumin powder
Pinch clove powder
2 tsp. turmeric
2/3 cup uncooked millet, rice,
cracked wheat, pilaf, etc.

6 cups assorted chopped vegetables
(bite-sized chunks)
2 cups water
3 Tbsp. soy sauce

Toast first 7 ingredients together over medium-high heat until grain gets toasted golden brown. Add next 3 ingredients, cover pot and turn heat up to high. Bring to a boil. When it's boiling, turn the heat down to medium-high and let boil about 20 minutes. Turn down to simmer for about 15 minutes. This can be served as a main dish or the grain dish. You will find that pretoasting the grain adds a unique flavor, and you might enjoy experimenting with different grains and spices. This is delicious topped with chopped nuts or seeds.

CHINESE DUMPLINGS O

½ cup arrowroot
¾ cup brown rice flour

½ cup boiling water

Combine first 2 ingredients in a bowl and mix well. Add boiling water and with a spoon (you'll burn your fingers if you use your hands), mix quickly until a ball of dough forms that leaves the sides of the bowl. Invert the bowl over the dough and let sit on the counter until the dough cools off. Oil counter and a rolling pin and break balls of dough off that are about walnut-size or a little larger (depending on how large a dumpling you want). Roll ball of dough out, one at a time, to rounds about 1/8" thick. Handle the dough very gently or it will tear. Lift off of oiled counter and place a good teaspoonful of filling (like the one given below) in the center of the dough. Fold half the dough over the filling to make a turnover shape and press edges in at least ¼". Make each dumpling immediately after rolling the dough out so the dough won't dry or crack. Depending on how you plan to cook the dumpling, you need to set it in the proper container. If you are going to steam the dumplings, place each one as you finish it onto a steamer rack and bring a pot full of water to a boil. When the water boils, place steamer rack full of dumplings over or in pot and cover. Allow to steam 20 to 30 minutes. Remove and serve hot with a soy sauce mix (see sauces for raw tofu in Tofu Section, p. 372). These dumplings can also be cooked by coating the bottom of a skillet or pot with oil 1/8" to 1/4" deep and sprinkling with asafetida. When the oil is sizzling hot, lay dumplings in skillet so there

(Continued next page)

is one layer of dumplings lying flat on the bottom of the skillet. Fry until golden brown on one side and gently turn over to fry until golden brown on the other side. Pour water over the dumplings to about 1" deep and cover pot. Lower heat to medium-high and boil until water cooks out. Water will thicken and make a gravylike coating over the dumplings.

FILLING:

1 Tbsp. oil
½ tsp. asafetida
½ cup celery

2 Tbsp. miso
2 cups tofu

1 Tbsp. arrowroot
¼ cup water

Sauté first 3 ingredients together until celery is translucent. Add next 2 ingredients. Mix last 2 ingredients together in a separate cup until arrowroot dissolves. Add to other ingredients and cook, stirring constantly until gravy thickens.

SOUTH OF THE BORDER CHILI BREAD

½ cup butter or margarine
1 tsp. asafetida

1 cup diced celery

½ cup chopped jalapeño chilies

1 cup whole wheat flour
1 cup cornmeal
1 Tbsp. chili powder
1 Tbsp. baking powder

1 cup cream of corn:
   ½ cup milk
   1 cup corn
   ½ tsp. honey
   ¼ tsp. vegetable salt
   1½ tsp. arrowroot
1 cup milk

1 tsp. egg replacer
2 Tbsp. water
1 cup grated cheddar cheese

½ cup grated cheese
¼ cup olives
¼ cup pimientos

Melt butter in a skillet and toast asafetida. Add celery and sauté until tender. Add jalapeño chilies and mix well. Remove from heat and set aside. Combine next 4 dry ingredients in a separate bowl. Then add next 5 ingredients and the sautéd vegetables and mix well. (To make the cream of corn, just combine ingredients off heat and mix until arrowroot dissolves. Put on heat and cook, stirring constantly, until milk thickens.) Pour batter into an oiled baking pan and sprinkle last 3 ingredients over top. Bake at 400° for 25 minutes or until knife inserted in the middle comes out clean. This served with a fresh salad makes a whole meal.

FANCY FRENCH TOAST

3 Tbsp. egg replacer (heaping)
¾ cup water
½ tsp. vanilla
¼ tsp. cinnamon
¼ - ½ cup milk (soy or dairy)

Slices of whole-grain bread

Whisk first 5 ingredients together in a bowl with a fork or wire whisk. Dip whole-grain bread into batter and coat well. If you want a thick batter coating, use ¼ cup milk; for thinner batter, up to ½ cup. Fry dipped bread in a skillet which has about ¼" of oil in the bottom heated to medium-high. (If the oil is too cool, it will soak into the bread. Test the oil by dripping some batter into it. If the oil sizzles, it is hot enough.) Fry on both sides until golden brown.

CARROT-GINGERBREAD ROLL O

3½ - 3¾ cups whole wheat flour

¼ cup nonfat dry milk powder
2 Tbsp. wheat germ
1½ tsp. dry yeast

1-1/3 cups water
1 tsp. lecithin
4 tsp. oil
1 tsp. salt (opt.)
2 Tbsp. honey

Filling:
2 Tbsp. grated fresh ginger
½ cup honey

2 cups grated carrots

A few threads of saffron
or 1/8 tsp. powder (opt.)

In mixing bowl, combine 1½ cups of the whole wheat flour and next 3 ingredients. Heat together the next 5 ingredients in a saucepan until warm (115° to 120°), stirring constantly. Add to dry mixture and beat on low speed of electric mixer for 30 seconds.

Beat 3 minutes more at high speed. Stir in enough of the remaining whole wheat flour to make a moderately stiff dough. Knead on a floured surface (using remaining whole wheat flour) for 5 to 7 minutes. Place in a greased bowl, turning once to grease surface. Cover and let rise until double in size (about 40 to 50 minutes). As the bread is rising, prepare the filling. Boil the first 2 filling ingredients together for 5 minutes, stirring

constantly. (Be careful to use a deep enough pot so that it won't boil over.) Then add the carrots and cook for another 5 minutes to cook out some of the liquid. Add the saffron if desired. After dough has risen to double in size, punch down. Roll dough out in an approximate 9"x 18" rectangle. Spread filling evenly over dough and roll it up, sealing the ends. Place seam side down in a greased 9" x 5"x 3" loaf pan. Cover and let rise until double. Bake at 375° in a preheated oven for 35 to 45 minutes. Remove from pan and cool on rack. This is nice to serve for breakfast or brunch. Makes one loaf.

POPCORN BALLS O

¾ cup honey
2 Tbsp. butter or margarine (opt.)
2/3 lb. pitted dates

6 cups popped corn
½ cup raisins
½ cup sunflower or sesame seeds
½ cup roasted nuts

Combine first 3 ingredients and cook, stirring often, over medium heat until dates melt. Pour over last 4 ingredients and mix well. Butter or oil hands to prevent sticking and roll mixture into balls while still warm.

NUTS 'N HONEY POPCORN SNACK ☆

½ cup melted butter
½ cup honey

3 - 3½ qts. popped popcorn
(approximately ¾ cup unpopped)
1 - 1½ cups seeds and chopped nuts

Preheat oven to 350° F. Combine butter and honey and heat until liquid enough to pour. Mix together the popcorn, nuts and seeds. (Sunflower seeds and walnuts or peanuts are two good combinations.) Then pour the butter-honey mixture over it and toss well, making sure that the popcorn and nuts are evenly and lightly coated. Spread on a cookie sheet in a thin layer. Bake 10 to 15 minutes or until crisp, stirring occasionally.

HONEY COOKIES ☆

½ cup butter or margarine
½ cup honey
1 cup whole wheat flour

Mix all ingredients well. Spoon by tablespoons onto oiled cookie sheet and flatten a bit, leaving room for cookies to spread. Bake at 350° for 10 to 12 minutes or until golden brown on edges and bottoms. This recipe makes a very thin, crisp cookie, but as with most honey cookies, it loses its crispness in a day. (For breadier, thicker cookies, just add more flour to the recipe.) If the thin cookies get a little soggy, you can use them like little crepes to wrap your favorite custard or sweet sauce in, or fill them with jam or cream cheese. This recipe can be varied in a number of wonderful ways. Here are some ideas. Use your imagination for more. Add one of the following to the above recipe while mixing:

1) ½ cup carob chips
2) ½ cup chopped nuts or seeds
3) ¼ cup carob + ½ cup chopped nuts or raisins
4) ½ cup chopped dried fruit
5) ½ tsp. almond extract and top with a split almond
6) 1¼ cups oatmeal, ½ cup pitted dates and ½ cup chopped nuts
7) Roll balls of batter in sesame seeds and then flatten on cookie sheet

You can even make a batch of the basic cookie dough, split it up and make four or more different variations at once. You can also combine different doughs. For example, drop a glob of carob dough into the middle of a thin, flat, plain batter.

RAISIN BRAN COOKIES ○

¼ cup butter or margarine
½ cup honey
½ tsp. vanilla
½ tsp. baking powder

1 cup bran
½ cup whole wheat flour
¼ cup chopped raisins

Cream first 4 ingredients. Add last 3 ingredients and mix well. Scoop ¼ cup of cookie batter at a time, roll each ¼ cupful into a ball and slightly flatten on an oiled cookie sheet. Bake at 350° for 12 to 15 minutes.

ALMOND COOKIES ☆

1 cup butter or margarine
1 cup honey
4 tsp. almond extract

3 cups whole wheat pastry flour
1 tsp. baking soda

Cream first 3 ingredients with an electric mixer until very fluffy. Sift in next 2 ingredients and mix well with mixer until too thick, then use fork. Roll into tablespoon-sized balls and press down a bit. Make an indentation in center with thumb and a few on the side with a straight edge. Bake at 350° for 7 to 10 minutes until golden. Cool and serve.

CAROB COOKIES ☆
(Little Carob Cakes)

½ cup butter or margarine
¼ cup water
½ cup honey
1 Tbsp. vanilla

1½ cups whole wheat flour
½ cup carob
½ cup bran
½ tsp. baking powder
2 Tbsp. chopped, pitted dates
¼ tsp. cinnamon
1/3 cup date sugar

Combine first 4 ingredients and cream well. Add next 7 ingredients and mix well. Measure ¼ cup or 1/3 cup of batter onto oiled cookie sheet and pat to about ½" flat. Bake at 350° for 12 to 15 minutes. Remove from oven, cool and frost with Carob Frosting (see recipe in Dairy Section, p. 464).

CAROB WALNUT DROPS (Wheatless)

1 cup butter or margarine
¾ cup honey

1 cup mashed potatoes

1 cup oat flour
½ cup carob powder
1 tsp. cream of tartar
½ tsp. baking soda
2 tsp. vanilla
½ cup walnuts, chopped

Cream the first 2 ingredients until smooth. Add mashed potatoes and blend. Now add next 6 ingredients and mix together until well-blended. Drop batter by the spoonful onto oiled cookie sheets and bake at 350° for 10 minutes.

OATMEAL CAROB CHIP COCONUT COOKIES

¾ cup butter or margarine
1 cup honey
1 tsp. vanilla
1 tsp. salt

½ tsp. baking soda
1 cup whole wheat flour

3 cups oats
2 cups carob chips
1 cup finely grated coconut

Cream together first 4 ingredients. Sift in next 2 and mix well. Add last 3 ingredients. Mix well and drop by teaspoonfuls onto oiled cookie sheet. Bake at 350° for 10 to 12 minutes. Makes about 60 cookies.

POTATO PECAN COOKIES (Wheatless)

1 cup butter or margarine
¾ cup honey

1 cup mashed potatoes

1½ cups brown rice flour
1 tsp. cream of tartar
½ tsp. baking soda
2 tsp. vanilla
½ cup pecans, chopped
1½ Tbsp. yogurt

Cream the first 2 ingredients until smooth. Add mashed potatoes and blend. Now add next 6 ingredients and mix together. Drop batter by the spoonful onto oiled cookie sheets and bake at 350° for 10 minutes until golden.

CAROB CHIP COOKIES

½ cup butter or margarine
¼ cup crystallized honey (lehua, etc.)
2 tsp. vanilla

1 cup whole wheat pastry flour
½ tsp. baking soda

½ cup chopped walnuts
1 cup carob chips

Cream together first 3 ingredients with an electric mixer until light and fluffy. Sift in next 2 ingredients. Add nuts and carob chips and mix well. Roll into small balls (about the size of a walnut) and flatten on lightly greased baking sheet. Bake at 350° for 10 to 12 minutes. Makes 1 dozen.

CAROB CHIP SQUARES

½ cup butter or margarine
½ cup honey
½ cup milk
1 tsp. vanilla

½ cup whole wheat flour
½ cup unbleached flour
1 cup carob chips
1 cup chopped walnuts
1 tsp. baking powder

Combine first 4 ingredients. Add last 5 and mix until smooth. Pour into an oiled baking sheet so batter is about ½" thick. Bake at 350° for 10 to 15 minutes. Allow to cool, cut into squares and remove from baking sheet.

CAROB CAKE

½ cup butter or margarine
1 cup honey
1 cup milk or water
1/3 cup yogurt
1 tsp. vanilla, mint, almond
or orange extract

½ cup carob powder
2½ cups whole wheat flour
½ tsp. salt
1 tsp. baking powder
1 tsp. baking soda

Preheat oven to 350° F. Combine first 5 ingredients in mixing bowl. When creamed together and smooth, add last 5 ingredients. Mix until all ingredients are thoroughly blended. Pour into an oiled, floured cake pan and bake at 350° for 30 minutes, until toothpick inserted in middle of cake comes out clean. Cool and frost.

BRAN CAKE

1 cup butter or margarine
1 cup honey
2 tsp. vanilla
1 cup grated coconut
3 cups canned milk

2 cups bran
2 cups whole wheat flour
1½ Tbsp. baking powder

Combine first 5 ingredients. Mix in last 3 and stir until all lumps are gone. Pour into an oiled cake pan and bake at 350° for 30 minutes.

ANY-KIND-OF-FRUIT SAUCE CAKE   O

1½ cups mashed fruit (any kind —
bananas, mango, applesauce, etc.)
½ cup butter or margarine
½ cup yogurt
1½ cups honey

3 cups whole wheat pastry flour
2 tsp. baking soda
2 tsp. baking powder
1 tsp. cinnamon
1 tsp. cloves

Preheat oven to 350° F. Cream first 4 ingredients together. Sift in next 5 and mix well. (Add 1 cup nuts, seeds and/or raisins, if desired.) Mix well and pour into a greased, floured cake pan. Bake at 350° for 25 to 30 minutes. Cool, remove from pan and frost.

CAROB BROWNIES

½ cup butter or margarine
¾ cup honey
½ cup carob powder
1 tsp. vanilla

¼ cup yogurt

1 cup whole wheat flour
1 tsp. baking powder
½ cup sunflower seeds or chopped nuts

Cream first 4 ingredients together until smooth. Add yogurt and stir in. Add next 3 ingredients. Pour into an oiled 8" square baking pan and bake at 350° for about 25 to 30 minutes or until a toothpick inserted in the center comes out clean. Frost with Carob Frosting (see recipe in Dairy Section, p. 464).

DOUGHNUTS ☆

1 Tbsp. yeast
7/8 cup warm water
½ tsp. salt
3/8 cup honey

¼ cup butter or margarine
1½ cups whole wheat flour
1½ cups gluten flour

Oil or ghee for deep frying

Combine first 4 ingredients and let sit until yeast dissolves. Mix in next 3 ingredients and knead well (5 to 10 minutes). Allow to rise in a warm place — by inverting mixing bowl over dough — until almost double in size. Oil a counter and a rolling pin and roll dough out to about ½" thick. Cut doughnuts with a doughnut cutter, or if you don't have one, a round cookie cutter. Heat oil or ghee to a medium heat. Allow dough to rise until almost double in size. Gently pick doughnuts up and slide them into cooking oil (doughnuts are especially delicious cooked in ghee). Cook on one side until golden brown. Turn over and cook other side. Remove from oil and immediately drop in date sugar to coat, or allow to cool and ice with your favorite icing. If you don't have a doughnut cutter, you can cook the whole round (in Hawaii these are called malasadas or Portuguese doughnuts). Roll in date sugar and after they cool you can slit a hole in the top and use a pastry bag to squirt jam or a custard filling in them.

WHOLE-GRAIN PANCAKES ◯

2 Tbsp. vegetable oil
2 cups whole wheat flour
(or combination of whole-grain flours)

1 Tbsp. honey
¼ cup yogurt or 2 Tbsp. egg replacer
1 Tbsp. baking powder

2 - 2½ cups milk or water

½ cup wheat germ, bran,
chopped nuts or seeds, etc. (opt.)

Mix oil into flour with fingertips until flour is a sandy texture. Add next 3 ingredients and milk or water. Mix until all lumps are out. Mix in optional ingredients if desired. Pour batter into preheated, oiled skillet on medium heat. The heat of the skillet is crucial for pancakes. It should be hot enough that the batter sizzles when it's poured in, but not so hot that the surface against the skillet burns before the pancake is ready to flip. Cook pancake until the outside edges dry and air bubbles in the middle of the pancake pop and cook firm to form little craters in the surface of the pancake. Flip the pancake over and cook on other side a few minutes and remove from heat. Lightly oil skillet each time you cook another pancake.

QUICK 'N EASY FANCY PANCAKES ◯

½ cup pancake mix (see recipe this pg.)
1 cup milk
2 tsp. egg replacer
Grated peel from ½ lemon
Grated peel from ½ orange
¼ tsp. vanilla
1 tsp. honey

2 Tbsp. honey
1 Tbsp. butter or margarine

2 Tbsp. chopped raisins or figs
2 Tbsp. finely chopped almonds

2 Tbsp. strawberry jam or date butter

Combine first 7 ingredients and mix to a fairly thick batter. Heat on medium heat 2 tsp. butter in an 8" skillet until it turns brown. Add half the pancake mixture and cook until bubbles pop on top, then turn and cook until brown. Remove and repeat with remaining mixture. Heat a large skillet with honey until it caramelizes. Quickly add butter and stir. Add pancakes and next 2 ingredients. Using forks, tear pancakes in about 1" pieces while cooking on medium heat. Remove from heat and mix in jam. Place in serving dish and top with date sugar (opt.) and Soy Whipped Cream (see Basic Recipes Section, p. 34).

BREAD PUDDING ○

2 loaves whole wheat bread

1 quart milk (soy or dairy)
1½ cups honey
1 Tbsp. cinnamon
2 tsp. vanilla

½ lb. raisins
½ lb. seeds or nuts, chopped

2 tsp. each: baking powder and baking soda

½ cup butter or margarine, melted (opt.)

Break bread crumbs up and dry out. Blend next 4 ingredients and pour over dry bread crumbs. Add raisins and seeds and/or nuts. Let soak a few minutes. Sift in leavening and mix well. Pour into oiled baking pan and bake at 300° for 1 hour. While still hot pour melted butter over top, if desired.

MILLET-BANANA-DATE PUDDING ○

1 cup raw millet
3 cups water

½ cup pitted dates, chopped
1 cup milk

1 or more bananas, sliced
2 Tbsp. honey
1 tsp. cinnamon

Bring first 2 ingredients to boil in a covered pot, lower heat and simmer for at least 30 minutes. Add next 2 ingredients and cook uncovered for another 15 minutes, stirring occasionally to prevent sticking and burning on the bottom of the pot. Stir in last 3 ingredients and serve warm for breakfast topped with milk, or chill and cut into squares for dessert.

GINGERBREAD ☆

½ cup butter or margarine
1 heaping Tbsp. grated fresh ginger root
½ cup honey
2 Tbsp. carob powder
1 tsp. vanilla
1 tsp. maple flavoring (opt.)
1/3 cup molasses
½ tsp. clove powder
1 tsp. cinnamon
¼ tsp. nutmeg
¼ cup powdered milk
2 heaping tsp. baking powder

2 cups boiling water

3 cups whole wheat flour

try

Combine first 12 ingredients and mix well. Pour in the boiling water and mix well. Add flour and mix quickly and immediately. Pour into an oiled bread pan and bake right away at 350° for 30 minutes or until a toothpick inserted in the center comes out clean. Serve as is or with a scoop of yogurt, or make it special with the following icing.

Icing:
½ cup honey
½ cup nut milk or coconut milk
¼ cup butter or margarine
1 Tbsp. arrowroot
½ tsp. vanilla
Mix all ingredients in a pot until arrowroot is dissolved. Cook over heat, stirring constantly until thickened. Allow to cool. Frost gingerbread with this and sprinkle with date sugar and/or grated coconut.

BRAN MUFFINS ○

1 cup bran
1 cup whole wheat flour
2 tsp. baking powder

try

¼ cup honey
1 cup milk

Combine first 3 ingredients. Mix in last 2. Pour into oiled muffin tins and bake at 350° for about 30 minutes.

CAROB CREPES

1 cup whole wheat flour
2 cups milk (soy or dairy)
1 Tbsp. oil
3 Tbsp. carob powder
¼ tsp. Pero
2 Tbsp. honey

Blend ingredients in blender until smooth. Let sit at room temperature about 1 hour or all day/overnight in refrigerator. This is crucial; it allows the flour to absorb the liquid. You may or may not have to add water (depending on how long the batter sits) to make the consistency of thick cream. In a small 8'' or 10'' heated T-fal skillet or cast iron skillet (do not oil T-fal skillet; brush cast iron skillet with oil), pour 1/4 to 1/3 cup batter with one hand, turning skillet with the other hand so batter spreads evenly on bottom of the skillet.

Mint Filling:
1 cup apple juice
2 Tbsp. honey
2 Tbsp. arrowroot
¼ tsp. mint extract

Combine ingredients in a saucepan and mix together away from heat until arrowroot dissolves. Then place on heat and bring to boil, stirring until thickened. Remove from heat, cool and refrigerate. Put mint filling inside of Carob Crepes using the Traditional Crepe Fold-over (see Basic Recipes Section, p. 40) and top with Soy Whipped Cream (see Basic Recipes Section, p. 34) or real whipped cream. Then sprinkle with chopped, toasted almonds and carob chips.

CREAM PUFFS

¾ cup egg replacer
¾ cup water
¼ cup butter or margarine

¼ cup brown rice flour

Preheat oven and cookie sheet to 450°. Whip first 3 ingredients together until stiff like whipped egg whites. Gently fold in rice flour. Spoon ¼ cup of batter onto heated cookie sheet in ball shape or log shape (for eclairs). Bake at 450° for 10 minutes, then turn the oven down to 350° and bake for 20 minutes more. Remove from oven, cool and split in half. Fill with whipped cream or Soy Whipped Cream (see recipe in Basic Recipes Section, p. 34). Put top on and either dust with fructose or dextrose, or spread with Carob Icing (see recipe in Dairy Section, p. 456).

FARINA HALVAH

1 cup farina (Cream of Wheat)
½ cup butter or margarine

1½ cups water
¾ cup honey

Combine first 2 ingredients in a large skillet. Combine last 2 ingredients in a pot. Put the pot of water on medium-high heat while toasting the grain and butter in the skillet over medium heat, stirring constantly. When the grain is golden brown and toasty smelling, pour the heated water into the skillet (warning: it will probably bubble and splash a lot), take spatula and stir constantly 'til mixture thickens to prevent lumping of the grain. Stir until grain is translucent and sticking together in a mass because it's thickened so much. Delicious served hot or cold. If served cold, you can even press the halvah flat into a baking sheet and, when cool, cut squares or diamond shapes. For variations, you can add any of the following to the water and honey as they are heating:
1) 2 - 3 Tbsp. grated orange rind
2) ½ cup dried fruit
   (raisins, chopped apricots, dates, etc.)
3) 1 cup pieces of fresh or frozen fruit
   (berries, pineapple, etc.)
4) 1 tsp. vanilla extract
5) Pinch of cardamom
6) ½ tsp. almond extract
   + ½ cup chopped almonds
7) ½ cup any nut, chopped

ROSE PETAL HALVAH

Rose petal syrup:
2 cups cut rose petals
1 cup water
1 cup honey
¼ cup lemon or orange juice

Halvah:
1 cup farina (Cream of Wheat)
½ cup butter or margarine

1¼ cups water
¾ cup honey or ½ cup rose petal
syrup and ¼ cup honey

Bring water to a boil, remove from heat, add rose petals and cover. Steep petals with water for 15 minutes. Strain, add honey and boil rapidly for 5 minutes. Add juice and cook slowly for 40 minutes. Toast farina in butter, stirring frequently for about 20 minutes until golden. Combine water and honey and bring to a boil. Gradually add farina, stirring constantly to prevent lumping. Cook for about 5 minutes or until thick. If just honey is used instead of rose syrup, the halvah is very good sprinkled with rose water. Delicious served warm or cold.

CINNAMON ROLLS ○

Dough:
Use Basic Bread Dough
(see Basic Recipes Section, p. 31)

Filling:
5 Tbsp. nut butter
5 Tbsp. honey
        or
5 Tbsp. butter or margarine
5 Tbsp. honey
1 Tbsp. cinnamon
1 tsp. nutmeg

Raisins and/or chopped nuts, seeds

Preheat oven to 350° F. Roll out dough on oiled counter into oblong shape. Spread filling on dough and sprinkle raisins and/or nuts evenly, leaving 1" on one edge bare. Begin rolling dough from edge opposite the bare edge towards bare edge. Place seam side down. Slice across log-shaped roll into about 1" sections. Place on oiled baking sheet with swirl facing up, leaving ½" space between rolls. Bake at 350° for 15 minutes. Top with icing if you like after rolls are cooled, or brush with honey while still warm.

STUFFED CREAM LOAF

1/3 pkg. active yeast
½ cup warm water
1/3 cup honey

1 Tbsp. plain yogurt
1 Tbsp. baking powder
1/3 cup oil
1/3 cup mashed potatoes (with skins)
2-1/3 cups whole wheat flour

Filling:
¼ cup honey
2 Tbsp. whole wheat flour
2 Tbsp. vanilla yogurt
1 Tbsp. grated lemon peel
1 Tbsp. lemon juice
¾ tsp. vanilla
8 oz. cream cheese (softened)

Combine first 3 ingredients and let sit until yeast dissolves. Add next 5 ingredients and mix well. Place dough on a lightly floured counter and knead for 5 minutes. Place in an oiled bowl and cover. Refrigerate overnight or at least 8 hours. Punch dough down, roll dough into a 15" circle and place over an oiled 9" ring mold. Fit it in mold. Then mix filling ingredients together and spoon into ring mold. Bring sides of dough down to cover filling. Cut a cross in center of dough, fold dough over ring and pinch to seal. Let rise until doubled in size. Meanwhile, preheat oven to 350°. Bake for 30 minutes, then remove from pan and place topside up on plate to cool. Turn out of ring mold when cooled and top with your favorite thickened fresh fruit sauce, or a natural honey preserve which has been heated and melted down, or your favorite icing.

DANISH PASTRY ☆

2 Tbsp. baking yeast
1/3 cup honey
½ cup warm water
1¼ cups warm milk

2 tsp. egg replacer in ¼ cup water
½ tsp. salt
2 cups whole wheat flour
2 cups gluten flour

1 cup softened butter or margarine

Place softened butter (butter which has been left at room temperature) between two sheets of wax paper cut to 10" x 12". Then with a rolling pin, roll butter out so it is spread evenly under the paper out to the edges. Place in the freezer to harden. Meanwhile, make the dough by letting first 4 ingredients sit together until yeast dissolves. Add next 4 ingredients but only half of the flour. Beat for 3 minutes. Add remaining flour, mix well and knead. Cover the mixing bowl and let dough sit in a warm place about 15 minutes. Flour the counter and roll dough out to form a rectangle about 13" x 18". Take butter between wax paper from freezer. The butter should be so hard that it is stiff like a piece of glass. Peel off one of the sheets of wax paper and place butter side down in the middle of the dough. Remove other piece of wax paper from the butter. All this must be done quickly, as the batter will stick to the wax paper if it starts to soften. The dough should have the butter in the middle with two outside edges bare. Fold the outside edges one at a time over the buttered center (as if folding the rectangle into thirds across the 18" length). Seal the open ends by pinching them together (to prevent the butter from leaking out) and fold the dough in half by meeting the two sealed edges. Roll the dough out again on the floured surface to form a 13" x 18" rectangle and fold the dough exactly as above. Repeat this process twice. Cover and refrigerate the dough overnight or at least 1 hour to allow butter to harden. Then remove from refrigerator, roll dough out on an oiled counter to ¼" thick and cut into 5" squares.

Fill with desired fillings (such as Elephant Ear Filling or Almond Filling that follow, or any fruit jam or Custard Pie filling as in the Dairy Section, p. 465) and fold into desired shapes. Some shapes are as follows:

1) Turnover Triangle

Put filling in the middle and fold over to form a triangle. Seal edges by pinching with edge of a fork.

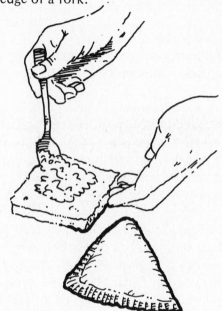

2) Bearclaws

Put filling in middle and fold edges over to form a rectangle. Seal edges by pinching together. Make slits with a butter knife that don't go past the sealed edges (if you do, the filling will leak out). Bend folded edge into an arch so slit edges will fan out.

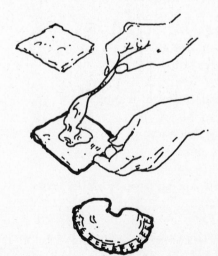

1.

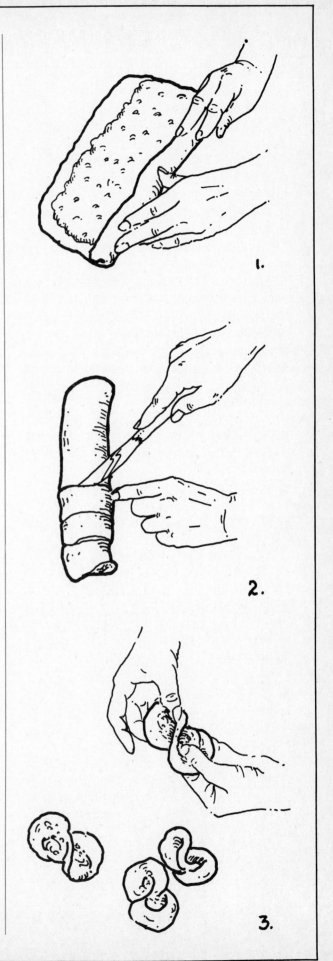

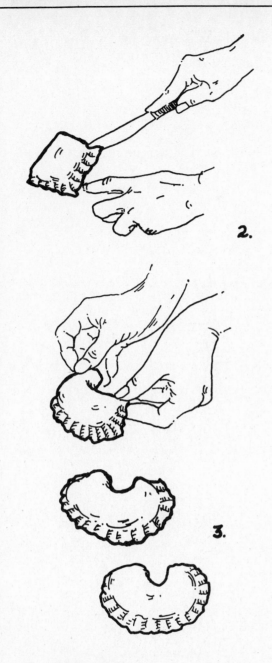

3) Elephant Ear

Handle dough as if you were going to make cinnamon rolls. Roll out a rectangle the desired length and width and spread filling in a thin film over the entire surface of the rectangle, leaving 1" to 2" of one of the lengthwise edges bare. Sprinkle with raisins and/or chopped nuts if you like. Start rolling lengthwise edge opposite the one that was left bare until a cylinder-shaped roll is made. Put sealed edge on the bottom. Take a knife and cut across the cylinder every inch so you will get what looks like cinnamon rolls. Take each roll and twist in the middle once over so a figure 8 is formed.

4) Sweet Rolls

Cut 5" squares in half and roll each half into snakelike strips about 8" long. Twist two strips around each other like a braid and pinch together at both ends. Twist this into a figure 8, bringing ends up into holes of the 8 and pressing them in place so the filling can be put in the holes and won't leak out the bottom. Fill holes of figure 8 with custard and/or fruit jam. Place desired filled shapes on an oiled cookie sheet. (At this point, Danishes may also be frozen and taken out later at an appropriate time for baking. You can make a big batch at once and freeze the Danishes for future use.) Allow the Danishes to rise in a warm place until almost double in size. Place in a 400° oven and immediately turn down to 350°. Bake 15 to 20 minutes. Five minutes before removing from the oven, brush the tops with a mixture of milk and honey and sprinkle with date sugar and finely chopped nuts. Bake 5 minutes more until a golden brown. Remove from oven, allow to thoroughly cool and frost with icing (see Basic Recipes Section, p. 35, or use your favorite). To bake frozen Danishes, remove from freezer, allow to thaw and rise, then bake as instructed above.

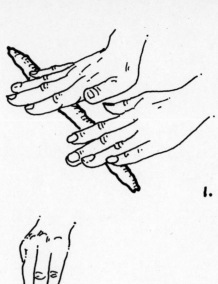

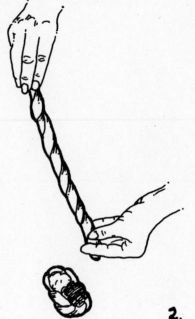

ELEPHANT EAR FILLING ☆

½ cup butter or margarine
1 cup honey
1 tsp. cardamom
1 tsp. cinnamon
1 cup nuts
½ cup raisins

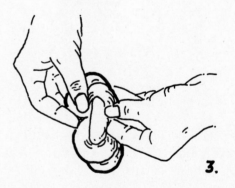

ALMOND FILLING ☆

½ cup almond butter
½ cup peanut butter
¼ cup butter or margarine
1 cup honey
1 tsp. almond extract

Combine ingredients and use as filling for Danish Pastries.

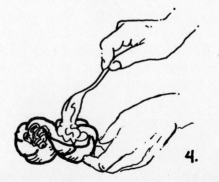

NUTS & SEEDS

Nuts & Seeds

This group of little seeds follows legumes in our home as a protein source. Some are actually higher or about equal to legumes in protein content (as can be seen in the table on page 468).

One main reason we use less of them is cost. Nuts and seeds cost a great deal more pound for pound of usable protein than almost any other protein source. Legumes, in contrast, are priced very reasonably. I personally tend to use sunflower seeds a lot because they offer the best nutritional bargain in this category. They also add the nice nutty flavor and texture to meals that make nuts such a plus to the flavor of a meal.

Another reason I don't use them as much as legumes is that proportionwise, nuts must be used in smaller quantities than other protein sources because of their high fat content. They are a very concentrated form of calories. While the fat in nuts and seeds has a healthy balance of unsaturated and saturated fats, there is so much in each nut and seed that it makes them a very rich food.

One minor drawback in using nuts and seeds is the fact that one must chew them very well to be able to digest the nutrients contained in them. This may be a great incentive for very young children to learn to get into the good habit of chewing well; but while they're in the process of learning, a lot of good nutrition goes in one end and out the other. For this reason I usually

use nuts in the form of nut butters, or grind them into a meal or a drink. Our daily breakfast drink (please see following recipe) has a base of nuts and seeds which I sprout a bit first.

Other than that, I sometimes use nuts and/or seeds to add flavor and crunch to a dish, and most importantly to complement low or missing amino acids in grain or legume dishes.

I have never grown a nut tree in a backyard (except coconuts!) but have always bought them. Nuts in the shell are definitely fresher, but I don't have the time to sit and shell them. It is a chore the children like doing, though. The main thing in buying nuts that are already shelled is to try to get the freshest ones possible in whole pieces. This is because the oil in nuts goes rancid very easily, especially when the nut kernel is broken. Then once the nuts are at home, I keep them stored in the refrigerator in airtight containers. It's always interesting to get different varieties of nuts and try them in different recipes, like the ones following.

BREAKFAST DRINK ☐

2 cups soaked seeds, nuts and raisins
4 - 5 cups soaking water or rejuvelac (liquid that wheatberries have soaked in overnight)
4 heaping Tbsp. lecithin granules
2 tsp. Pero
¼ cup honey
½ cup carob powder

Blend all ingredients together until smooth.

NUT AND/OR SEED MILK ☐

1 cup nuts or seeds (preferably whole ones soaked overnight and sprouted a bit)
4 cups water (if nuts were soaked, use water they were soaked in)
1 Tbsp. honey (opt.)

Nut milks can be used in any recipe calling for milk or soy milk. You can use any nut to make nut milk with, or any combination of nuts and/or seeds. Whole nuts or seeds blend up easier and are more digestible and increase in nutritional value when they are soaked overnight and sprouted a bit. To make the nut milk, just blend all ingredients together in a blender until smooth. If you are going to be making a gravy or baking with the nut milk, just leave the honey out. After ingredients are blended you can leave the pulp in for a smoothie textured nut milk, or pour blended milk through a strainer to strain pulp out. Pulp should be saved and frozen for use in vegetable loaves, baking, candies, etc.

NUT AND/OR SEED MEAL ☐

Take raw or roasted nuts and/or seeds and blend in blender to a fine powder. You can also use a fine head on a food grinder or a heavy mortar and pestle. Make nut and/or seed meal as you need it to prevent oils from going rancid.

DRY ROASTED NUT CHUTNEY ☐

1 cup toasted nuts of your choice or combination
¼ cup toasted sesame or sunflower seeds
1 tsp. chili powder
½ tsp. cumin powder
¼ tsp. asafetida
1/8 tsp. clove powder
2 Tbsp. nutritional yeast

Blend all ingredients in blender until nuts make a nut meal. Use to sprinkle on grain, vegetable or salad dishes.

NUTTY CRUST WHIPPED PIE

Crust:
3 cups finely crushed graham crackers
(Midel Honey Grahams are good)

2½ cups finely chopped nuts or seeds

1 cup peanut butter
¾ cup honey

Filling:
1 cup soy milk
1 tsp. vanilla
2 Tbsp. honey

1½ cups cold-pressed, unsaturated oil

1 Tbsp. lemon juice

3 - 4 ripe bananas, sliced
1 cup raisins

Blend graham crackers in blender until like flour. Blend second ingredient until chopped fine, or do it by hand. Add last 2 crust ingredients to stick together. Pat, with hands dipped in water (to keep crust from sticking to hands), into a cake pan. Then make filling by blending first 3 filling ingredients on low speed of blender. Open up top and pour oil in slowly. Pour out of blender into a bowl. Add lemon juice and whip in with wire whisk or fork. Mixture will thicken like whipped cream. Fold in last 2 ingredients and refrigerate a few hours. A refreshing, special dessert.

TANGY NUT DIP

2 cups unsalted peanuts
1½ Tbsp. chopped olives

¾ cup prepared horseradish
2 cups cream cheese, softened
1 cup yogurt
1/8 tsp. asafetida
1/8 tsp. cayenne

Put first 2 ingredients in a blender and blend until chopped into smallish pieces. Put next 5 ingredients in a bowl and cream together. Mix in chopped ingredients. Chill before serving.

SEED SOUP □

12 almonds
½ cup sunflower seeds
½ cup sesame seeds

2 cups fresh carrot juice or water
2 Tbsp. nutritional yeast
2 tsp. Spike
1½ tsp. soy sauce
1/8 tsp. cayenne
1/8 tsp. asafetida

1 cup grated summer squash
1 cup sprouts

Blend first 3 ingredients in blender into a fine nut meal. Add next 6 ingredients and blend until smooth.

FRUIT SALAD DRESSING ☐

¼ cup untoasted sesame tahini
1 Tbsp. honey
2/3 cup fruit juice or water
3 Tbsp. sunflower seeds
5 Tbsp. raisins
½ tsp. lemon juice

Mix ingredients together and pour over chopped fruit of the season.

SESAME SEED DRESSING ☐

1 cup water
1½ cups sesame seeds
1 cup oil
1 - 2 Tbsp. Spike

Put ingredients in blender and blend until smooth. Keep in refrigerator.

NUT BUTTER SAUCE ☐

4 Tbsp. nut butter (almond or peanut)
4 Tbsp. water
1 tsp. soy sauce
½ tsp. lemon juice

Combine and mix until smooth. Spoon over Raw Vegetable Nut Loaf slices (see recipe in Garden Vegetables Section, p. 256) or use as a salad dressing.

NUT CREAM ☐

2/3 cup nuts
1/3 cup water

2 tsp. honey
½ tsp. vanilla
¼ tsp. cinnamon (opt.)

Blend first 2 ingredients together until smooth. This is a nut cream you can use for vegetables, sauces, etc. If you want a sweet nut cream for desserts, just blend in next 3 ingredients along with nuts.

STUFFED NUT BUTTER CONFECTIONS ☐

1 cup mild-tasting seed or nut butter
1/3 cup honey
1/3 cup finely grated coconut or bran,
or seed or nut meal

Whole strawberries or 1" cubes
of fresh fruit in season

More grated coconut or bran,
or seed or nut meal

Mix first 3 ingredients together well. Pinch off balls about 1" in diameter (wet your hands if necessary to keep mixture from sticking to them). Flatten each ball a bit and press and wrap around chunk of fresh fruit until the whole piece of fruit is covered with the nut butter. Roll in loose coconut, bran or nut meal and refrigerate until firm. I prefer to use raw nut butters for this, as they are milder tasting. You can use different combinations of nut butters and seed meals, etc., and will find certain fruit-nut butter combinations especially delicious (peanut butter and banana, and strawberry-coconut-almond are especially good!).

PEANUT BUTTER CUPS ☐

1 lb. (about 2 cups) peanut butter
2/3 cup hard, crystallized honey
2/3 cup bran and/or coconut
1/3 cup raisins
Vanilla (opt.)
Cinnamon (opt.)

Mix ingredients together thoroughly. Roll into balls or make cups with a 2 Tbsp. ice cream scoop. Lay on a tray and allow to sit overnight to harden (bran will absorb moisture). For a special touch, dip in heated Carob Coating (see Dairy Section, p. 466).

RAW CAROB NUT PUDDING □

2 cups water
¼ cup noninstant milk powder
½ cup sunflower seeds
½ cup pitted dates
1 Tbsp. vanilla

4 - 6 Tbsp. carob
4 Tbsp. almond butter

Blend first 5 ingredients in blender until smooth. Add last 2 ingredients and blend until well mixed. Scoop into small dessert bowls and chill at least 1 hour before serving. Good as filling for a raw pie crust (see Basic Recipes Section, p. 32).

ROASTED NUTS ○

Always roast nuts of your choice, or a nut and seed mix at a low oven temperature — 220° to 250°. Just spread nuts out on a cookie sheet one layer deep and put in oven. Stir every 20 to 30 minutes until nuts and/or seeds are a light gold. This takes a longer time than at a high temperature, but the nuts are less likely to burn and retain more of their nutrients this way. If you are going to serve the nuts as a snack, you may want to try flavoring them in one of the following ways. While nuts are still hot and the natural oils are on the surface of the nut, sprinkle any of the following seasonings on the nuts. The flavorings should stick to the oil on the nuts.
1) Sprinkle with enough nutritional yeast to coat nuts.
2) Sprinkle a mix of ½ tsp. cumin powder, ¼ tsp. asafetida, 1/8 tsp. clove powder, ½ tsp. coriander powder, and 2 tsp. chili powder to every 2 cups of nuts.
3) Curry powder mixed with nutritional yeast.
4) About 30 minutes before nuts are done, add soy sauce — about 1 Tbsp. for every 2 cups of nuts — and mix so all are coated.

VEGETABLE-NUT LOAF ○

2 Tbsp. butter or margarine
½ cup chopped celery
½ cup diced zucchini
¼ cup finely grated carrots
2 Tbsp. chopped olives
¼ cup sesame seeds
½ cup chopped sunflower seeds
¼ cup chunky peanut butter
¼ cup diced walnuts
¼ cup diced almonds
½ tsp. asafetida

1 cup milk
1½ cups cooked, mashed garbanzo beans
½ cup cooked, drained lentils
½ tsp. Spike

1 cup whole-grain bread crumbs

Sauté first 11 ingredients together in wok or frying pan over medium-high heat for 5 minutes. Add next 5 ingredients and continue stirring and cooking in wok another 5 minutes. Remove from heat and add bread crumbs. Mix thoroughly. Butter a medium-sized loaf pan and pour ingredients into the loaf pan. Bake 1 hour at 350°. Remove from oven and let set at least 15 minutes before slicing. Serve with heated Nut Butter Sauce for gravy (see recipe this section, p. 443).

CASHEW GRAVY ○

2 cups water
½ cup cashew pieces
2 Tbsp. arrowroot powder
2 Tbsp. oil
½ tsp. salt
¼ tsp. black pepper

Blend ingredients until smooth. Pour into a pot and stir constantly over medium flame until thick.

MOCK CHEESE ROULADE ○

Roulade Filling:
1½ cups diced celery
½ cup diced bell pepper
½ tsp. asafetida
3 Tbsp. olive oil

3 Tbsp. whole wheat flour

1¼ cups water
½ cup almonds
¼ cup sunflower seeds

½ cup chopped walnuts
¼ cup chopped cashews
1½ tsp. Spike
½ tsp. nutmeg
1/8 tsp. cinnamon
¼ tsp. coriander
¼ tsp. basil
½ tsp. dry mustard
1/8 tsp. sage
1 Tbsp. flaky nutritional yeast
1/8 tsp. vanilla

Shell:
1 cup flaky nutritional yeast
4 Tbsp. whole wheat flour
¼ tsp. fresh diced thyme
¼ cup chopped parsley
¼ tsp. coriander
¼ tsp. Spike
Pinch cayenne
½ tsp. baking powder
4 Tbsp. water
4 Tbsp. yogurt

1 Tbsp. olive oil

Saute first 4 ingredients together until vegetables become translucent. Remove from heat and add whole wheat flour to the sautéd vegetables in the skillet and mix well. Put next 3 ingredients in blender and blend until smooth. Put skillet with sautéd vegetables and whole wheat flour back on the heat and add 3 blended ingredients over low heat. Stir until this thickens. Add the next 11 ingredients to the thickened mixture and stir. Put on top of double boiler to keep warm while you make the roulade shell. Mix all 10 shell ingredients together. Line a 12" x 8" jelly roll pan with wax paper and butter the wax paper generously. Pour roulade shell ingredients onto wax paper and spread out evenly over the wax paper. Dribble olive oil over the spread out roulade shell ingredients. Bake at 400° for 10 minutes. Remove roulade shell from pan by lifting wax paper out of jelly roll pan. Then peel wax paper off. Put stuffing (waiting in the double boiler) on roulade shell by placing along one lengthwise edge. Begin rolling jelly roll fashion from the end stuffing is on to form a log-shaped roll. To serve, just slice across the log-shaped roll.

SWEET-SOUR DEEP-FRIED NUT GEMS ☆

¾ cup walnut halves or other large nuts (almonds or whole cashews are good)

Tempura Batter #1 or #2
(see Basic Recipes Section, p. 36)

6 cups steamed or stir-fried assorted chopped vegetables (carrots, broccoli, string beans, celery, etc., to name a few)

1 recipe Pineapple Sweet-Sour Sauce
(see Pineapple Section, p. 214)

Oil for frying

Soak nuts overnight or a few hours in hot water. Heat tempura frying oil. While it is heating, make the tempura batter using the water the nuts were soaking in and keep extra water for drinking or other use. Put vegetables on to steam or stir-fry. While the vegetables are cooking, dip the nuts one at a time into the tempura batter and fry them in the heated oil as you do tempuras. After the nuts are cooked, put them on a paper towel to drain off excess oil. Make the sweet and sour sauce. Put cooked assorted vegetables on a large serving platter, top with deep-fried nut gems and pour the sweet-sour sauce over all of this. Served with brown rice this makes a delicious gourmet Chinese-style entree.

NUT STUFFING

1 cup diced celery
1 tsp. asafetida
1 Tbsp. butter or margarine
¼ cup diced bell peppers
1 tsp. Spike

½ cup flaky nutritional yeast
½ cup ground walnuts
½ cup ground cashews
½ cup ground pecans
½ cup ground almonds
½ tsp. thyme
1 Tbsp. diced fresh parsley
¼ cup finely grated carrots
1½ tsp. basil
1 Tbsp. milk
Pinch cayenne

Sauté first 5 ingredients together for 3 minutes. Remove from heat. Add the next 11 ingredients to sautéd ingredients and mix together well. Use to stuff raw vegetables or use as a stuffing in bell peppers or squash, etc., and bake. This can also be pressed into a loaf pan and used as a raw or baked nut loaf.

MATMA'S QUICK & EASY CASSEROLE FAVORITE

6 - 8 cups chopped vegies, steamed lightly

1 cup nuts
1½ cups water
½ cup nutritional yeast
¼ cup soy sauce
½ cup tomato sauce
2 tsp. arrowroot

½ - ¾ cup grated cheese

Take half of the steamed vegies and layer bottom of oiled casserole dish. In blender, combine next 6 ingredients and blend until smooth. Put in saucepan and stir on medium heat until thickened. Pour half of this gravy over first layer of vegies, then repeat with the rest of ingredients and top with grated cheese. Bake at 350° for 8 to 10 minutes.

CURRIED NUT SOUP

4 cups water
1½ cups chopped raw nuts

1 tsp. fresh grated ginger
2 tsp. Madras curry or other curry powder
¼ tsp. asafetida
¼ tsp. cinnamon

¼ tsp. nutmeg
1/3 cup yogurt

Soak first 2 ingredients overnight. Add next 3 ingredients and bring to a boil, then turn heat down. Cover and simmer nuts over a low heat about 20 minutes. Blend nuts and broth until smooth. Set blended nut broth aside to cool, then refrigerate until chilled. Just before serving, fold in the last 2 ingredients. Serve cold as a summer soup or heat until just hot (do not boil) and serve warm.

CHILLED ALMOND-YAM SOUP

2 cups almonds
4 cups cold water

2 cups cooked, mashed yams
or sweet potatoes

Pinch cardamom or a few drops
of rose water (opt.)

Soak first 2 ingredients together overnight. Put soaking water and almonds in blender and blend until smooth. Pour ingredients into cheesecloth or strainer and wring the milk out of it. Repeat twice to get as much pulp out as possible. (The pulp can be saved for use in baking, candies, etc.) Put almond milk back in blender and blend with yams or sweet potatoes that have been prepared as follows. Cook yams in their skins. Remove skins after cooking and mash the yam or potato. Put cooked yams in blender with almond milk and blend until smooth. Add subtle flavoring (either the cardamom or rose water) and chill at least 1 hour.

NUTTY HERB PATTIES ○

2 Tbsp. butter or margarine
1 tsp. asafetida
¾ cup diced celery

¼ cup butter or margarine

6 Tbsp. whole wheat flour

1 cup milk

3 Tbsp. flaky nutritional yeast
1/8 tsp. cayenne
1 tsp. Spike
1/8 tsp. ground cloves
1/8 tsp. cinnamon
1/8 tsp. nutmeg
½ tsp. fresh diced thyme
¼ tsp. fresh diced sage
1 cup bread crumbs
1 cup corn bread, crumbled
¾ cup ground walnuts
¼ cup ground pecans

Sauté first 3 ingredients together for 3 minutes. When celery turns translucent, add extra butter to ingredients. When butter is melted, remove from heat and add flour. When thoroughly mixed, add milk, mix together well and return to heat to bring to a boil, stirring constantly until it thickens. Then remove from heat, add next 12 ingredients and mix together well. Form into balls and flatten with palms to ¼" to ½" thick. Put on ungreased cookie sheet and bake at 350° for 30 minutes.

NUT SALAD PATTIES □

½ cup ground walnuts
½ cup ground sunflower seeds
½ cup ground cashews
½ cup ground almonds
2 cups crumbled corn bread
½ tsp. finely grated lemon rind
½ tsp. grated ginger
1 tsp. flaky nutritional yeast

¼ cup diced celery
½ tsp. asafetida
¼ tsp. fresh diced thyme
Pinch cayenne
1 tsp. cilantro (Chinese parsley)
2 Tbsp. melted butter or margarine

¼ cup finely chopped parsley

Mix first 14 ingredients together well. Roll into balls. Roll balls in parsley and pat parsley on balls so it will stick. Flatten balls between palms of your hands to form ¼" thick patties. Refrigerate at least 1 hour before serving. Serve as an entree or a few small patties on a bed of greens topped with a nice dressing.

CHESTNUT DRESSING ☆

¼ cup butter or margarine
1½ tsp. grated fresh ginger
2 Tbsp. celery, diced
2 Tbsp. green pepper, diced
½ cup cooked chestnuts, diced

4 slices bread, crumbled
½ tsp. salt
½ tsp. black pepper
1 Tbsp. parsley
1 Tbsp. basil
1½ tsp. thyme
½ tsp. rosemary

1½ tsp. lemon juice
1/3 cup water

Sauté first 5 ingredients in a skillet about 5 minutes. Add next 7 ingredients and mix thoroughly. Add lemon juice and water. Remove from skillet, place in a loaf pan and bake 20 minutes at 425° F. Cut into squares and serve with or without gravy.

PEANUT BUTTER FUDGE □

5 Tbsp. honey
¾ cup natural peanut butter
1½ cups nonfat, noninstant
powdered milk or protein powder
½ tsp. vanilla

Mix ingredients together well. Press into a 13" x 22" baking pan and cut into 1" x 2" shapes. Store in refrigerator. For Carob Peanut Butter Fudge, replace half of the milk powder with carob powder.

SESAME CHEWS
(A good source of calcium) ○

¼ cup butter or margarine
1½ cups hulled (white) sesame seeds

¾ cup milk powder (whole or nonfat)
or protein powder

½ cup honey
1 tsp. vanilla (opt.)

Melt butter in skillet. Add sesame seeds and toast lightly, stirring often. Sift in milk powder. Stir until mixed. Add honey and vanilla and mix well. Continue to cook for about 7 to 8 minutes, stirring constantly. Scoop and press into a greased cookie sheet. Cool and cut into squares.

CARAMEL CANDY ○

1 Tbsp. Pero
2½ cups honey

3 Tbsp. butter or margarine

1 tsp. vanilla
½ cup chopped nuts

Cook first 2 ingredients to 238° or soft ball stage (test by dropping drops of candy into a cup of cold water; if a soft ball forms, it is done). Add butter and cool to 110°. Add last 2 ingredients and beat. Drop by spoonfuls onto an oiled surface and allow to cool.

CAROB PEANUT CLUSTERS □

1½ cups roasted peanuts

½ cup honey
2 Tbsp. butter or margarine

¼ cup carob chips

Roast raw, blanched peanuts in oven. Combine honey and butter in saucepan and boil on medium-high heat to soft crack stage, using a candy thermometer. Mix in roasted peanuts and drop by teaspoons onto greased cookie sheet. Melt carob chips in a double boiler. Spoon a thin layer over peanut clusters and chill.

PEANUT BUTTER COOKIES ☆

½ cup butter or oil
1 cup peanut butter (crunchy)
1 cup honey
2 cups whole wheat flour
1 tsp. vanilla
1 tsp. baking powder

Filling:
½ cup peanut butter
¼ cup honey

Mix together 6 cookie ingredients. Drop with a 2 Tbsp. scoop onto oiled cookie sheet and flatten to about 1" thick. Make depression in the middle of each lump of batter with thumb and fill with peanut butter filling. Bake at 350° for 15 minutes. Frost with Carob Frosting (see recipe in Dairy Section, p. 464).

DAIRY FOODS

Dairy Foods

In the world of "vegetarianism" there are many different ways of grouping or categorizing a vegetarian. To some people, just cutting out red meat makes them a vegetarian. I remember my oldest son's bewilderment one day when we met a woman who told us she was a vegetarian. She invited us to her house for a visit, and when we got there my son found a package of dead chicken body pieces on her table. He was very puzzled and asked her whose they were. "Oh, they're mine," she replied. My son looked at her with a puzzled expression and said, "But I thought you said you were a vegetarian." To which she replied, "Yes, I am. I don't eat meat; that's not meat, that's bird."

At any rate, there are those just described who somehow or other consider themselves vegetarians but still actually eat the flesh of other living entities. Then there are the ovo-lacto vegetarians who have cut out all flesh food but still include eggs and dairy products in their diet. Then there are the lacto vegetarians who include dairy but exclude eggs. And then there are the vegans who consume only foods from the plant world.

I went through that whole explanation so I'd be able to tell you how my family and I eat and you'd be able to understand! We are somewhere between the last two. Although we eat primarily a vegan diet, we sometimes do include dairy products in our diet. That sometimes is very, very sometimes! Probably once every few months we have something with dairy in it.

Dairy products are so expensive; this is a big factor in our not using them much. There is also the fact that most dairies nowadays are run in such a way that the cow is subjected to all kinds of unnatural and cruel treatments and even slaughtered when it can no longer give any milk. This makes the "dairy," in essence, a slaughterhouse. There are also many dairy products on the supermarket shelves which contain pieces of slaughtered animal in them, such as gelatin (ground up cow bones and hoofs, etc.) and rennet (enzymes from the juice of a baby calf's stomach used to curdle milk to make curds and cheeses). Add all this to the fact that the milk available in most stores today is not really milk anymore. It is full of toxic chemicals from the different antibiotics that are used on cows to prevent different diseases, as well as pesticides accumulated in the cow's body from eating plants that were sprayed with pesticides. And as a final blow, pasteurization and homogenization are, in a sense, refining processes (like refining whole grains) that deplete the nutritive value in milk.

All these factors combined make it very difficult to find milk that is suitable for human consumption. Yet taking all this into consideration, milk is still by far a superior source of protein when compared to meat or other forms of animal protein. At least milk doesn't contain uric acid and purines as meat does, while it does contain a high-quality protein with all eight essential amino acids for easy digestibility. Because unpasteurized milk and milk products that don't contain dead animal by-products and which are produced from lovingly cared-for, organically raised animals, are few and far between (and usually quite expensive), we end up not using dairy products regularly.

"If you see them in life, you can't bear to watch their death.
If you hear their screams, you can't bear to eat their flesh.
This is the nature of true benevolence."
— Mencius

YOGURT CUCUMBER SALAD ☐

2 large cucumbers
2 cups yogurt
½ cup finely chopped walnuts
½ tsp. cumin powder
½ tsp. salt
Pinch of cayenne
Black pepper

Cut off ends of cucumbers and rub them to remove any bitterness; then peel and thinly slice. Add remaining ingredients and toss. Chill and serve. A cool, refreshing salad.

CREAMY COCONUT MARVELS ☆

½ cup + 3 Tbsp. butter
1 lb. grated coconut (unsweetened)

¾ cup honey

8 oz. cream cheese
8 oz. cottage cheese

Melt butter in a frying pan. Add grated coconut and fry over low heat, stirring constantly until coconut is light brown. Mix in honey and set aside. When cool, fold in last 2 ingredients. Roll into balls and refrigerate overnight or at least 2 hours before serving.

YOGURT CHEESE ☐

Mix yogurt with equal parts water and hang in a thin muslin or doubled cheesecloth for 8 hours. Do not squeeze, but just let hang. Turn out of cheesecloth and refrigerate. A lot of yogurt makes a little cheese. You will start with a lot and end with a little, so be sure to hang an ample amount.

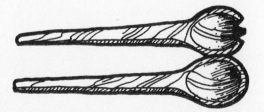

WALDORF SALAD ☐

3 cups apples, chopped
1 Tbsp. lemon juice
1 cup diced celery
½ cup chopped raisins
½ cup walnuts

Dressing:
2 Tbsp. honey
1 cup yogurt
Dash of salt and black pepper

Combine first 5 ingredients in a bowl. Mix together dressing ingredients, pour over salad and chill. You can also use Eggless Soy Mayonnaise instead of yogurt dressing (see Basic Recipes Section, p. 34).

YOGURT COLESLAW ☐

1 cup yogurt
1½ tsp. lemon juice
½ tsp. celery seed
2 Tbsp. chopped parsley

1 large apple, chopped
4 cups finely shredded cabbage
½ cup chopped celery
1 cup shredded carrot
2 tsp. honey
Dash of salt and black pepper

Combine first 4 ingredients. Mix together remaining 6 ingredients in a bowl and pour yogurt dressing on top. Mix well and serve. Yields 6 servings.

SONG OF PEACE

We are the living graves of murdered beasts,
Slaughtered to satisfy our appetites.
We never pause to wonder at our feasts,
If animals, like men, can possibly have rights.
We pray on Sundays that we may have light,
To guide our footsteps on the paths we tread.
We're sick of war, we do not want to fight,
The thought of it now fills our hearts with dread
And yet we gorge ourselves upon the dead.
Like carrion crows, we live and feed on meat,
Regardless of the suffering and pain
We cause by doing so. If thus we treat
Defenceless animals for sport or gain,
How can we hope in this world to attain
The PEACE we say we are so anxious for?
We pray for it, o'er hecatombs of slain,
To God, while outraging the moral law,
Thus cruelty begets its offspring – War.

– George Bernard Shaw

CHEESE MOUND ☆

2¼ cups grated cheese
(jack or mild cheddar, etc.)

½ cup pecans

¼ tsp. black pepper
Dash cayenne
2 Tbsp. Eggless Soy Mayonnaise
(see Basic Recipes Section, p. 34)

Leave cheese at room temperature until it softens. Blend pecans in blender or grate into a nut meal. Add cheese and last 3 ingredients and mix in a bowl with the back of a heavy spoon until smooth. Shape with hands into a mound and sprinkle with pecan meal to serve with crackers as an hors d'oeuvre. Or, pat with hands flat onto a large platter to about ½" thick with a higher rim along the edge (or make small, individual tart-sized patties with raised edges). Fill center with cold vegetable entree, fresh vegetable salad or a cold chutney (like apple, mango, etc.) and serve encircled by a bed of sprouts.

BUTTERMILK ○

½ cup buttermilk
4 cups milk

Pour buttermilk into milk and let sit at room temperature about 12 to 16 hours. Check from time to time and refrigerate when it reaches buttermilk consistency.

BASIC CANDY ☆

¼ cup butter or margarine
½ cup honey

1 cup noninstant powdered milk

Cream first 2 ingredients together. Mix in powdered milk. Roll into balls or shape into desired shapes.

DILL DIP ☐

½ cup sour cream or yogurt
1 avocado
1 Tbsp. dried dill leaves
1 Tbsp. parsley
Pinch asafetida

Mix together all ingredients and refrigerate a few hours so flavors can blend. Serve as a dip for chips, or especially good as a refreshing summer dinner with sticks and slices of crisp, fresh vegetables.

YOGURT DRESSING ☐

3 cups yogurt
1½ Tbsp. turmeric
3 Tbsp. honey
3 Tbsp. soy sauce

Whiz in blender. Serve over salads or brown rice.

BENEDICTINE CHEESE SPREAD ☆

8 oz. cream cheese
¼ tsp. asafetida
½ cup grated cucumber (more if desired)

Peel cucumber and slice in half lengthwise. Remove seeds with a spoon and grate on fine part of grater. The results will be cucumber juice and pulp. Add this and the asafetida to the cream cheese and combine well. If used for a dip, add a few extra tablespoons of cucumber juice.

KEFIR

½ cup plain kefir
1 qt. milk

Add kefir to milk and let sit at room temperature for 12 to 16 hours. Refrigerate when it is the consistency of kefir.

BANANA YOGURT SMOOTHIE

2 Tbsp. honey
2 cups low-fat yogurt
2 medium-ripe bananas
½ cup apple or pineapple juice
½ cup strawberries
6 ice cubes

Whiz in blender. Makes 4 servings.

FRUIT SMOOTHIE

1 cup orange juice
½ medium papaya
1 banana
¼ cup yogurt
2 tsp. honey

Whiz in blender and serve over ice; or chill and whiz again before serving.

ORANGE DAHI

2 cups orange juice
2 cups yogurt
2 Tbsp. honey

Blend ingredients together in blender. Chill and serve. The amount of honey desirable will depend on the sweetness of the orange juice.

HOLIDAY LASSI

2 cups yogurt
2 cups fresh unsweetened orange juice
¼ cup of honey (or less)
1 tsp. vanilla
1½ tsp. nutmeg
¼ cup noninstant, nonfat milk powder

Combine ingredients in blender and whiz until fluffy and smooth. Serve over ice.

LEMON LASSI

2 cups low-fat yogurt
2 cups water
¼ cup fresh lemon juice
¼ cup honey
½ tsp. ground cardamom

Combine ingredients in blender and whiz until smooth. Refrigerate to chill, then shake well and serve. Refreshing!

CAROB ICING

½ cup butter or margarine
1 tsp. vanilla
1 cup honey
1 cup water

¾ cup noninstant, nonfat powdered milk
¾ cup buttermilk powder
½ cup carob powder
1 tsp. Pero

Cream first 4 ingredients together. Add next 4 and mix until smooth. Frost cooled cakes, cookies, etc.

Variations:
1) Use mint oil instead of vanilla.
2) Add 2 tsp. grated orange rind, and use orange juice in place of water.

SWEET BALLS

¼ cup butter or margarine
½ cup honey
1 cup whole milk powder
½ tsp. vanilla
½ cup shredded unsweetened coconut

Cream butter, honey and vanilla. Add one heaping cup of milk powder and mix well. Add coconut and mix again. Add natural food coloring of your choice (beet juice, carrot juice, etc.) and mix well. Roll into balls and roll in coconut. Place on a clean surface or cookie sheet and let set. Makes 20 large balls.

GINGER-DATE SWEETBALLS ☆

1 cup honey
1 cup butter or margarine
1 Tbsp. vanilla
¾ cup chopped dates
½ cup sunflower seeds
2 Tbsp. ginger powder
3 cups buttermilk powder
1 cup milk powder

Mix ingredients thoroughly and roll into balls or press onto a cookie sheet and cut into desired shapes.

CAROB CONFECTIONS ☆

½ cup butter or margarine
2/3 cup honey
2 tsp. vanilla
2/3 cup carob
½ cup water
2/3 cup whole milk powder
1-1/3 cups nonfat milk powder

Grated coconut or nut/seed meal

Mix first 7 ingredients together thoroughly. Refrigerate overnight. Form balls or other shapes and roll in grated coconut or nut/seed meal to coat the ball and keep it from sticking to anything.

ONO SWEETBALLS ☆

½ cup butter or margarine
½ cup honey
½ cup fresh milk (or coconut milk)
¾ - 1 lb. whey powder
2 cups chopped dates
2 cups carob chips
3 cups powdered milk
Fresh toasted coconut
½ cup walnuts (opt.)

Mix ingredients thoroughly. Form into balls or press onto cookie tray and cut into shapes. Yields about 60 pieces.

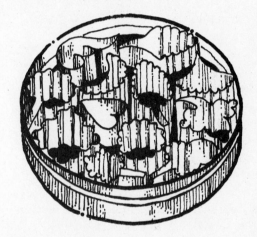

MOCHA MELTAWAYS ☆

½ cup butter or margarine
1 cup honey

¼ cup carob powder
2 Tbsp. Pero
2 Tbsp. malt syrup (opt.)
¼ tsp. allspice

1¾ - 2 cups milk powder (whole or buttermilk) or protein powder

Nuts or seeds, chopped fine

Cream honey and butter. Add next 4 ingredients and mix until well blended. Gradually add milk powder, stirring constantly until well blended. May have to mix with hands. Press evenly into a greased pan about ½" thick. Top with finely chopped nuts or seeds. Cover and chill. Cut into squares and serve.

NO-BAKE YOGURT CHEESECAKE ☆

Filling:
8 oz. cream cheese
3 Tbsp. honey
8 oz. yogurt

Blend filling ingredients in blender until smooth. Pour into a raw pie crust (see Basic Recipes Section, p. 32). Refrigerate and serve with berries or jam on top.

SWEDISH MUESLI ☐

2 large apples
2 bananas

¼ cup rolled oats
¼ cup lemon juice

2½ Tbsp. honey
1½ cups yogurt
1 Tbsp. raisins
¼ lb. chopped nuts or seeds

Peel, core and chop apples. Slice bananas. Combine next 2 ingredients and then add remaining ingredients and mix well. Let soak a few minutes. Serve for breakfast.

FRUIT KABOBS ☐

12 fresh strawberries
12 fresh pineapple chunks
12 bite-sized chunks of avocado
1 cup honeydew melon balls

½ cup fresh or frozen strawberries
½ cup low-fat yogurt
1 Tbsp. honey
Dash of cinnamon

Slice a honeydew melon in half. Scoop out one half to make about 1 cup of melon balls. Place fruit on skewers in order listed. Blend last 4 ingredients together in blender to use as a dip. Scoop out seeds from remaining half of honeydew melon and fill with dip when ready to serve.

ICE CREAM BOMBE ☆

2 compatible flavors of ice cream

Set a glass mixing bowl or salad bowl into the freezer and freeze until frosted. Remove from freezer and work quickly, as it is essential that the bowl remains cold. Oil the inside of the frozen bowl with a tasteless vegetable oil and set two 1" wide strips of wax paper in the bowl so the strips cross each other in the middle to form an "X" and all four ends of the wax paper extend a good 2" to 3" over the edge of the bowl. Now, put first layer of ice cream in bowl, covering whole bowl with a 2" to 3" layer of ice cream. To pack this first layer down, set a smaller bowl that's filled with ice cubes inside the first layer and push down gently and evenly. Set the whole thing in the freezer. Remove from the freezer a few hours later and remove ice cubes from the little bowl. Fill the little bowl about three-fourths of the way with hot water. Pour hot water out and lift small bowl out of first layer of ice cream (the hot water should have melted the first layer of ice cream just enough to make it easy to get the bowl out). Fill in the space with second ice cream flavor and freeze again. Right before serving, wrap a hot, damp towel around the outside of the mold bowl and invert the bowl. Let it sit like this about a minute and pull molded ice cream out with the wax paper that's sticking over edges of the bowl. Serve topped with carob sauce or your favorite fruit sauce.

FRUIT YOGURT FREEZE ☐

4 cups of your favorite fruit, cut up
1 cup yogurt
2 - 4 Tbsp. honey
1/8 tsp. vanilla
Dash cinnamon

Blend ingredients in blender and freeze. These make great popsicles in the summertime.

CURD DUMPLINGS IN A CASSEROLE ◯

Curds and whey from 1 qt. of milk
(see recipe this section, p. 462)

2 Tbsp. flaky nutritional yeast
2 Tbsp. fresh diced parsley
½ tsp. fresh diced thyme
½ tsp. Spike
½ cup grated cheese
½ cup cottage cheese
½ tsp. basil
½ tsp. oregano
1¼ cups bread crumbs
1¼ cups crumbled corn bread

1 cup zucchini, sliced in ½" rings
1 cup crookneck squash, sliced in ½" rings
¼ tsp. asafetida

3 sheets yuba, crumbled up
¾ cup diced celery
¼ cup diced bell pepper
Pinch cayenne
3 Tbsp. olive oil
½ tsp. Spike

2 cups chopped tomatoes
¼ cup flaky nutritional yeast
½ tsp. basil
½ tsp. coriander

Make curd and hang at least 4 hours. Save whey to use later in this recipe. Combine curd with next 10 ingredients and mix thoroughly. Form into dumplings 1½" to 2" in diameter and set aside. In a dry skillet, heat next 3 ingredients over medium flame until brown on both sides. Remove and put into an uncovered casserole dish. Sauté next 6 ingredients for 3 minutes, then pour them on top of zucchini and crookneck squash in the casserole dish. Saute next 4 ingredients and simmer until most of the liquid cooks out. Combine the tomatoes with the whey you've kept aside and bring to a boil. Pour ingredients into the casserole over other ingredients. Lay curd balls in casserole dish, being sure to submerge them under the sauce. Bake at 400° for 20 minutes.

YOGURT RICE CASSEROLE ◯

½ lb. rice
1 cup yogurt

¾ cup chopped nuts
¼ tsp. Spike

Sliced tomatoes
½ tsp. basil
1 Tbsp. soy sauce
Butter or margarine

Cook the rice and mix with yogurt. Place half of the mixture in an oiled casserole dish. Sprinkle with next 2 ingredients, leaving some aside. Top with sliced tomatoes and basil. Sprinkle with soy sauce and place pats of butter on tomatoes. Then put the rest of the yogurt-rice mixture on top and sprinkle with remaining nuts and Spike. Bake at 350° for 40 to 50 minutes.

CHEESE SOUFFLÉ

3 cups grated cheese
6 slices of airy, light whole-grain bread

2½ cups milk (dairy, soy or nut)
¼ cup whole wheat flour
1 tsp. baking powder
1 tsp. soy sauce
1 tsp. thyme
½ tsp. dry mustard powder
½ tsp. turmeric
¼ tsp. black pepper

It is important that the bread for this recipe is a light, well-risen bread, rather than the heavier, denser kind. Break bread into bite-sized pieces and line entire bottom of an oiled baking pan with a layer of bread pieces. Sprinkle with a cup of cheese. Add two more layers — bread, cheese, bread, cheese. Do not press or squash the bread down. Blend next 8 ingredients in a blender and pour over the bread and cheese layers. Let sit on the counter for 30 minutes . Bake at 350° for 1 hour in a pan of hot water (just set the pan with the soufflé in it in a larger baking pan that has a few inches of water in it, just so it won't dry out during baking). Remove from oven and let sit 10 to 15 minutes before serving.

CHICKPEA YOGURT SPREAD ○

1½ cups uncooked chickpeas (garbanzo)

2 Tbsp. butter or vegetable oil

2 cups yogurt
1 tsp. nutritional yeast
2 tsp. soy sauce
½ tsp. salt
¼ tsp. black pepper

Wash garbanzo beans. Soak 5 hours in 5 cups water. Rinse and drain. Add 5 cups of fresh water and bring to a boil. Cover and simmer until beans are tender and can be easily mashed. Drain. Mash well and toast in oil. Add remaining ingredients and mix well. Chopped celery and sweet pickles may also be added to enhance the flavor.

CURD BALLS WITH
TOMATO CHUTNEY

Make curd as described in Curds and Whey recipe (this section, p. 462). After it has hung 4 to 6 hours, divide into 2" round balls. Deep fry in oil until golden brown. Serve with Tomato Chutney (see Garden Vegetables Section, p. 263).

YOGURT COCONUT RICE ○

½ tsp. asafetida
3 Tbsp. butter or vegetable oil

4 cups cooked rice
1 tsp. ground ginger
½ tsp. ground cloves
½ tsp. ground coriander
½ tsp. cinnamon
2 cups plain yogurt
1½ cups flaked coconut
1 tsp. honey

Sauté first 2 ingredients together. Mix in remaining ingredients. Cover and simmer for 10 minutes.

POLYNESIAN BROWN RICE
WITH YOGURT ○

¼ tsp. asafetida
3 Tbsp. ghee or light oil

1 cup water
2 cups pineapple juice
1 cup brown rice
½ tsp. ground ginger
½ tsp. salt
Dash of black pepper

1 cup pineapple chunks
½ cup chopped walnuts
1 cup plain yogurt

Sauté first 2 ingredients together. Add next 6 ingredients and bring to a boil. Lower heat and cook 30 to 40 minutes or until rice is done. Stir in last 3 ingredients and leave on flame just long enough to heat. Serves 6.

CREAMY FONDUE ☆

4 cups grated Monterey Jack cheese
2/3 cup milk
1-1/3 cups cream cheese
2 tsp. honey
½ tsp. cardamom
2 Tbsp. flaky nutritional yeast
1/8 tsp. asafetida

Either combine ingredients in fondue pot or on top of double boiler. Let melt and mix well. Continue to mix until completely smooth. Serve in a chafing dish over medium flame. Dip cubes of French bread and lightly steamed chunks of vegetable in this with fondue forks. Makes a whole meal when served with a nice fresh salad.

MEXICAN FONDUE ☆

1 cup green chilies, diced
4 Tbsp. chopped olives
1 cup diced tomatoes (except seed & pulp)
½ cup flaky nutritional yeast

Add above 4 ingredients to Creamy Fondue recipe and prepare as directed above.

CHEESE CRACKERS ☆

2 cups butter or margarine
8 cups grated cheese
4 cups whole wheat flour

Combine ingredients. Roll out and cut into shapes. Bake at 350° for 10 minutes.

CHEESE-BRAN CRACKERS ☆

½ cup grated cheese
½ cup bran
½ cup whole wheat flour
2 Tbsp. sesame seeds
2 Tbsp. butter or margarine
¼ cup water

Mix all ingredients together well and chill dough in the refrigerator. Roll out like a pie crust between two floured sheets of wax paper. Cut into cracker shapes and bake at 350° for 10 to 15 minutes until golden. Cool and they become crisp.

ITALIAN BUTTERMILK SAUCE ☆

¼ tsp. asafetida
2 Tbsp. olive oil or other vegetable oil

2 Tbsp. whole wheat flour
2 Tbsp. tomato paste
1 tsp. basil

1 cup buttermilk

Toast first 2 ingredients together. Add next 3 ingredients and cook for a few minutes, until thickened. Then add the buttermilk. Heat only to desired serving temperature. Over-heating will cause curdling.

CABBAGE 'N YOGURT ○

3 Tbsp. ghee or light oil
2 tsp. cumin seed
½ tsp. cayenne
1 tsp. salt
2 tsp. turmeric

6 cups cabbage, chopped fine

½ cup yogurt

Heat ghee or light oil and add spices. Add cabbage and stir so it is well coated. Cook gently for 5 minutes. Add yogurt, mix well and serve.

VEGETABLE PUDDING ☆

Variety of colorful raw
vegetables for decoration
¼ cup ground walnuts

3 cups diced broccoli
3 cups diced cauliflower
2 cubes butter or margarine
1/3 cup diced celery
1/8 tsp. cayenne
1 tsp. asafetida
1 tsp. cardamom
½ tsp. nutmeg

3 Tbsp. milk
½ cup sour cream
½ cup cottage cheese
½ cup cream cheese
2 cups packed, grated Monterey Jack cheese

¼ cup diced walnuts
¼ cup diced cashews
¼ cup diced pecans
½ cup bread crumbs

Oil a casserole dish inside and lay wax paper inside flattened on all sides and bottom against the dish. Butter the inside surface of the wax paper. Cut 1/8" thin slices of different colored vegetables (such as carrots, yellow crookneck squash, zucchini, beets) lengthwise and widthwise to make strips and rounds of color. Arrange these in a colorful, decorative pattern on bottom and sides of buttered wax paper. Sprinkle ground nuts over vegetables. Refrigerate while doing next steps. Combine next 8 ingredients in a skillet and sauté covered for 20 minutes on medium heat or until vegetables are tender. Put ingredients (half the amount at a time) in the blender and blend until puréed. You'll need to continually stir ingredients so they'll all purée. Pour puréed vegetables back into frying pan. Combine next 5 ingredients in a bowl and add a little at a time to vegetable purée in skillet and cook 10 to 15 minutes over medium heat, stirring constantly. Remove from heat, add next 4 ingredients and mix well. Pour this mixture into the decorated, lined casserole. Put the casserole with ingredients in it inside a larger baking dish.

Fill the larger baking dish with water to reach halfway up the outside of casserole dish. Cover top surface of casserole with wax paper and bake at 375° for 1 hour and 15 minutes or until filling is firm to touch. Remove from oven and let set in water for 10 minutes. Remove from tray of water and pull off wax paper covering casserole. Put serving plate on top of casserole dish and turn upside down. Remove wax paper gently so design of vegetables stays intact on pudding. Serve hot.

BLENDER BROCCOLI YOGURT SOUP ○

1 Morga or other vegetable bouillon cube
12 oz. broccoli
2 cups water

2 cups water
½ tsp. sweet basil
½ tsp. salt
Dash of cayenne pepper
Black pepper to taste

¾ - 1 cup plain yogurt

Wash and chop broccoli. Cook in 2 cups water with bouillon cube until tender. Cool. Spoon into blender, add next 5 ingredients and blend until smooth. Add yogurt, blend for a second; chill. May also be served hot by blending all ingredients except yogurt. Pour into saucepan, bring to a boil, remove from heat and stir in yogurt.

CURDS & WHEY ○

1 quart milk
Juice of 3 lemons

Prepare curd by bringing milk to a boil. (Stir often to prevent bottom from burning.) Add strained lemon juice and lightly stir. Remove from heat and let sit a few minutes. Milk will curdle. Pour curds and whey through a colander lined with cheesecloth or muslin. Save whey. Let drain a few minutes and rinse. Use as is like cottage cheese, or hang in cheesecloth and use in other recipes.

CREAMY ENCHILADAS

1 dozen corn tortillas

Filling:
2 cups mashed, cooked beans
2 cups grated cheese
¼ tsp. asafetida
1 tsp. chili powder
1 Tbsp. soy sauce
2 Tbsp. nutritional yeast
4 tomatoes, diced
1 carrot, grated

Sauce:
2 cups milk
¼ cup arrowroot

1 cup grated cheese
¼ tsp. turmeric
1/8 tsp. cayenne

Dip corn tortillas one at a time into hot oil to soften. Lay one at a time into an oiled baking dish and fill each tortilla down the middle with filling (mix all 8 ingredients thoroughly) in a mounded strip a couple of inches wide. Fold two edges of the tortilla over the filling. Lay enchiladas side by side and fill casserole dish. Prepare sauce by mixing first 2 sauce ingredients together off the heat until arrowroot dissolves. Stir over heat until thickened. Add next 3 ingredients and stir until cheese melts. Pour this over the enchiladas, sprinkle with paprika and lay bell pepper rings on the sauce (opt.). Bake at 350° for 15 to 20 minutes.

BUTTERMILK VEGETABLE CURRY O

¼ cup vegetable oil or ghee

2 tsp. whole cumin seed
1 red chili pepper (seeded)
½ star anise flower, broken up
½ tsp. ground coriander
½ tsp. asafetida
1 tsp. turmeric

4 cups cubed potatoes
2 cups small cauliflower flowerettes
2 cups diced zucchini
6 Tbsp. water

1 cup buttermilk

Melt oil and add next 6 ingredients, cooking on low heat and stirring well until spices are toasted. Then add next 4 ingredients and mix well so the potatoes are coated. Cover with lid and cook for 20 minutes, stirring occasionally so vegetables won't stick. When potatoes are tender, turn off heat and add buttermilk. Serves 4 to 6.

SEÑORA CHAVEZ'S SPECIALTY

1 Tbsp. butter or margarine
1½ tsp. asafetida
1 tsp. cayenne
1 tsp. salt (opt.)

1 cup finely chopped celery

2 cups corn
3 cups tomatoes, cubed
2 cups zucchini, cubed
¼ cup water
1 lb. grated cheddar cheese

Melt butter and toast next 3 ingredients. Add celery and sauté until tender. Then layer in pan the next 3 ingredients in order given. Add water and put flame on medium-low. Cook covered about 15 minutes until zucchini is tender but still firm. Now add cheese. Cover and cook about 5 minutes more or until cheese has melted.

CAROB-MOCHA CHEESECAKE

Crust:
2-2/3 cups crushed graham crackers

1/3 cup butter or margarine
1/3 cup honey
3 Tbsp. water (if needed)

Put together as in crust for Carob Tofu "Mud" Pie (Tofu Section, p. 387). You can use the Tofu Mud Pie recipe if you want to cut down on cholesterol and saturated fat. But this is a "splurge" recipe that is full of cholesterol and saturated fat anyway. Pat with hands dipped in water (to prevent sticking) into a springform cheesecake pan. Pour in filling. After cooled, spring out of the springform pan and cut into tiny squares (2" x 2") and serve on top of delicate doilies for special effect.

Filling:
2 cups cream cheese, soft
3 Tbsp. butter or margarine
1 cup honey
2 Tbsp. egg replacer
2 tsp. Pero
1 tsp. vanilla
1/3 cup carob
2¾ cups sour cream

Preheat oven to 350° F. Whip all 8 ingredients together until smooth and fluffy. Use automatic or hand-powered egg beater for light and airy filling. Pour into graham cracker crust that's been patted into springform pan. Bake at 350° for 60 to 70 minutes. Remove from oven and let cool at room temperature. When cool, frost and refrigerate for a few hours to chill.

Icing:
1½ cups maple syrup
½ cup butter or margarine
2 tsp. Pero
1/3 cup carob
¼ cup milk powder

Mix all 5 ingredients together and top baked and cooled cheesecake. Refrigerate to chill.

FUDGY CAROB BROWNIES

½ cup butter or margarine
¾ cup honey
1 tsp. vanilla
4 oz. cream cheese

½ cup carob powder

1 cup milk (dairy, soy or other)

1½ cups whole wheat flour
1 heaping tsp. baking powder

Combine first 4 ingredients. Add carob and mix until carob is thoroughly blended. Add the milk and stir in gently but thoroughly. Add last 2 ingredients and mix well. Pour into an oiled cake pan and bake at 350° for 45 minutes. Cool and frost with carob frosting.

CAROB FROSTING

¼ cup butter or margarine
½ cup honey
½ tsp. vanilla
1 tsp. Pero in 1 tsp. hot water

½ cup water

½ cup carob powder
1½ cups nonfat, noninstant powdered milk

Combine first 4 ingredients. Add water and mix. Mix in last 2 ingredients.

LO-FAT CHEESECAKE ○

Crust:
Use Oilless or Graham Cracker Crust
(see Basic Recipes Section, pp. 32, 33)

Filling:
1 qt. yogurt cheese (see recipe, p. 453)
1 cup honey
1 Tbsp. lemon juice or ½ tsp. lemon extract
¼ cup whole wheat flour

Make crust. Mix next 4 ingredients together and pour into crust. Bake at 350° for 30 minutes. Allow to cool. Put on favorite fruit sauce or jam and refrigerate 8 hours.

ANOTHER LO-FAT FILLING ○

1 qt. curd (see recipe, p. 462)

3/8 cup honey
1 Tbsp. lemon juice or ½ tsp. lemon extract
¼ cup whole wheat flour

Hang curd for about 2 hours (still soft). Then knead until lumps are out and it is a smooth and creamy texture. Add next 3 ingredients. Mix well and follow the rest of the steps as given in Lo-fat Cheesecake recipe above.

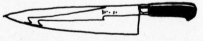

CUSTARD PIE ☆

¼ cup butter or margarine
2 cups milk
¼ cup arrowroot
½ cup honey
2 tsp. vanilla

Combine ingredients in a pot off of heat and mix until arrowroot dissolves. Put over heat and bring to a boil, stirring constantly to prevent lumping. Pour into a baked pie shell (see Basic Recipes Section, p. 33), cool and top with fruit or sprinkle with nutmeg. Or you can allow to cool and use in Danish Pastry (see recipe in Grain Section, p. 434) as a filling with fruit jellies.

EKADASI FUDGE ○

¼ cup raisins
1/3 cup sunflower seeds

1 banana, mashed
2 Tbsp. frozen orange juice concentrate
2 Tbsp. lemon juice
½ cup peanut butter
1 Tbsp. yogurt

1 cup non-instant powdered milk

Blend raisins and sunflower seeds in blender until ground. Put in bowl along with next 5 ingredients and mix together well. Put 1 cup of powdered milk into a sifter to remove all lumps. Add to other ingredients and mix well. Pour into a pie pan. Bake at 350° for 35 minutes. Chill at least 1 hour. Slice and serve.

GULAB JAMMONS

1/3 cup noninstant, nonfat milk powder
4 cups water

1 cup maple syrup or honey
1 cup water

Ghee or oil for frying

Heat ghee on a low temperature. Then combine maple syrup and water and place on the same low temperature as the ghee. Add water gradually to the milk powder to make a stiff dough. Use remaining water to mix successive batches of dough, using 1/3 cup milk powder. Each batch must be cooked before the next is mixed, otherwise the dough will dry out. Roll into ½" balls. Place all the balls into the heated ghee at once. Keep stirring to allow all sides of the balls to cook evenly. Continue cooking in this manner for 20 minutes. As the balls are cooking they will expand in size. Remove when dark brown and place in the heated maple syrup. Store in the sweet juice for three days at room temperature. Serve.

Note: It is important that the ghee and maple syrup mixture are the same temperature. This will keep the balls from collapsing.

ALMOND NECTAR DRINK ○

2 sticks agar-agar (1 cup flakes)
2-2/3 cups milk
¼ cup honey
1 tsp. almond extract

2 cups fruit juice
Honey to taste

Combine first 4 ingredients in a pot and let sit about 5 to 10 minutes to give agar-agar a chance to soften. Put over heat and bring to a boil, stirring occasionally to prevent sticking and burning. Boil gently until agar-agar is totally dissolved. Pour into cake pan or other flat container. Cool, then refrigerate. It should jell and be able to be cut into cubes. Cut cubes about ½" x ½". Float cubes in last 2 ingredients, which were previously blended together. Makes a refreshing dessert.

CAROB LOLLIPOPS ○

¾ cup honey
¼ cup butter or margarine
¼ cup carob
2 Tbsp. milk powder
1 Tbsp. Pero

½ tsp. vanilla

Combine first 5 ingredients and heat slowly over medium heat, stirring often until mixture reaches hard crack stage (300° on a candy thermometer, or when the mixture forms a hard ball when a drop is dripped into ice water). Take off burner and mix in vanilla. Pour in molds or on a buttered cookie sheet. Insert sticks and let cool.

CAROB COATING ○

½ cup oil
1 cup honey
2 tsp. vanilla
¼ cup lecithin
½ cup carob powder

½ cup water

1½ cups powdered milk

Blend ingredients in blender until smooth. Use as frosting or carob syrup, or heat on double boiler and use as coating for candies.

MILK NECTAR ○

½ gallon fresh nonfat milk

1/3 cup mochi sweet rice

1 cup maple syrup or honey

Bring milk to a boil in a one-gallon pot, stirring constantly to prevent sticking and burning. (An oversize pot will prevent milk from boiling over sides.) When the milk boils, pour it into another pot temporarily and scrub out first pot thoroughly. This step is important as it will allow the nectar to cook without any stirring or burning. Pour the milk back into the scrubbed out pot, place on a high flame and bring quickly to a boil again. Add the rice and mix thoroughly. Lower the heat to medium-high so the milk will still boil, cover the pot with the lid on halfway and continue cooking for 30 minutes. When the milk looks creamy and all the rice is completely cooked, then remove from the heat and add sweetener. Cool, then refrigerate. Serve cold. Stir before serving.

BHAVA SHAKTIS ☆

8 oz. cream cheese
2 sticks (1 cup) butter or margarine
2 cups whole wheat flour

Fruit filling

Soften butter and cream cheese at room temperature. Add flour and mix thoroughly into a ball of dough. Divide the dough into 4 equal parts and chill them in the refrigerator about 30 minutes. Flour the counter and, removing one ball of dough at a time from the refrigerator, roll a ball out until about 1/8'' thick (take care not to get dough stuck to counter). Can be rolled out in a square or round shape. Cut rolled dough into quarters. Place a generous scoop of a fruit filling (any given in book) or jam in the center of the dough. Bring flaps of dough to meet each other over the fruit filling and pinch all edges gently together to seal. Place this sealed edge down on an oiled cookie sheet. After the sheet is full, bake at 400° for 10 to 15 minutes until golden brown. Remove from the oven and allow to cool a bit. Ice with Milk Powder Frosting (see Basic Recipes Section, p. 35).

HONEY YOGURT COFFEECAKE ○

1 cup yogurt
1/3 cup honey
3 Tbsp. butter or margarine

1½ cups whole wheat flour
1 tsp. baking powder
½ tsp. baking soda
½ tsp. salt

Topping:
¼ cup butter or margarine
1/3 cup honey
4 Tbsp. whole wheat flour
¼ cup nuts

Preheat oven to 400° F. Cream first 3 ingredients together. Sift in dry ingredients and mix. Pour into cake pan that has been greased and floured. Spread on topping and bake at 400° for 30 minutes.

YOGURT & MALPOURA ☆

1 cup whole wheat pastry flour
½ cup honey
½ cup water or milk

Ghee or light oil for frying

3 cups yogurt, chilled
¼ - ½ cup honey
1 tsp. vanilla

1 cup sweetened strawberries or other berry

Combine honey and flour. Gradually add milk to make a fairly thick batter. Drop by tablespoons in one clean drop into hot (but not smoking hot) oil and fry until golden brown. Drain. Combine next 3 ingredients in a bowl and mix well. Toss in strawberries and malpouras. Stir well and let soak for 2 to 4 hours.

RASAGULLA ○

Curd from ½ gallon of milk
(see recipe for Curds & Whey, p. 462)

3 cups water
1 cup honey
2 - 3 drops rose water or ½ tsp. grated orange rind (opt.)

Hang curd for 4 to 5 hours. Take curd and knead as you would knead clay on smooth counter top until the curd is smooth and oily. Roll balls of curd about 1'' in diameter. Bring water and honey to a boil, then turn to simmer, stirring until honey dissolves. When honey is dissolved, remove about half of this sweet syrup and place in a bowl off the heat, leaving the other half in the pot to simmer over a low heat. Place as many curd balls in the cooking syrup to cover surface of the syrup, leaving space in between for curd balls to expand. Simmer balls for about 25 minutes, then remove them from the cooking syrup with a slotted spoon and place into the syrup in the bowl. Continue this process until all curd balls are used up, pour all syrup over cooked balls and refrigerate overnight.

(From U.S.D.A. Agriculture Handbook #8)
DESIRABLE PROTEIN SOURCES INCLUDED IN THIS BOOK
100 gm. edible portion

Food and description	Water (%)	Food Energy (calories)	Protein (gm.)	Fat (gm.)	Carbohydrate Total (gm.)	Fiber (gm.)	Ash (gm.)	Calcium (mg.)	Phosphorus (mg.)	Iron (mg.)	Sodium (mg.)	Potassium (mg.)	Vit. A (I.U.)	Thiamine (mg.)	Riboflavin (mg.)	Niacin (mg.)	Vit. C (mg.)
SOYBEANS																	
(Raw)	10.0	403	34.1	17.7	33.5	4.9	4.7	226	554	8.4	5	1,677	80	1.10	.31	2.2	–
(Cooked)	71.0	130	11.0	5.7	10.8	1.6	1.5	73	179	2.7	2	540	30	.21	.09	.6	0
Soybean Milk	92.4	33	3.4	1.5	2.2	0	.5	21	48	.8	–	–	40	.08	.03	.2	0
Okara *	84.5	65	3.5	1.9	6.9	2.3	.9	76	43	1.4	4	–	0	.05	.02	.3	0
Yuba *	8.7	432	52.3	24.1	11.9	0	3.0	270	590	11.0	80	–	20	.20	.08	2.0	0
Miso	53.0	171	10.5	4.6	23.5	2.3	8.4	68	309	1.7	2,950	334	40	.06	.10	.3	0
Tofu (soybean curd)	84.8	72	7.8	4.2	2.4	.1	.8	128	126	1.9	7	42	0	.06	.03	.1	0
LEGUMES																	
Garbanzo (dry, raw)	10.7	360	20.5	4.8	61.0	5.0	3.0	150	331	6.9	26	797	50	.31	.15	2.0	–
Lentils (cooked)	72.0	106	7.8	Trace	19.3	1.2	.9	25	119	2.1	–	249	20	.07	.06	.6	0
Limas (cooked)	64.1	138	8.2	.6	25.6	1.7	1.5	29	154	3.1	2	612	–	.13	.06	.7	–
Mung (dry, raw)	10.7	340	24.2	1.3	60.3	4.4	3.5	118	340	7.7	6	1,028	80	.38	.21	2.6	–
Pinto, Calico and Red Mexican (raw)	8.3	349	22.9	1.2	63.7	4.3	3.9	135	457	6.4	10	984	–	.84	.21	2.2	–
Red beans (cooked)	69.0	118	7.8	.5	21.4	1.5	1.3	38	140	2.4	3	340	Trace	.11	.06	.7	–
Split peas (cooked)	70.0	115	8.0	.3	20.8	.4	.9	11	89	1.7	13	296	40	.15	.09	.9	–
White beans (cooked)	69.0	118	7.8	.6	21.2	1.5	1.4	50	148	2.7	7	416	0	.14	.07	.7	0
NUTS & SEEDS																	
Almonds	4.7	598	18.6	54.2	19.5	2.6	3.0	234	504	4.7	4	773	0	.24	.92	3.5	Trace
Brazil nuts	4.6	654	14.3	66.9	10.9	3.1	3.3	186	693	3.4	1	715	Trace	.96	.12	1.6	–
Cashews	5.2	561	17.2	45.7	29.3	1.4	2.6	38	373	3.8	15	464	100	.43	.25	1.8	–
Filberts	5.8	634	12.6	62.4	16.7	3.0	2.5	209	337	3.4	2	704	–	.46	–	.9	Trace
Peanuts:																	
(Raw, with skins)	5.6	564	26.0	47.5	18.6	2.4	2.3	69	401	2.1	5	674	–	1.14	.13	17.2	0
(Roasted, with skins)	1.8	582	26.2	48.7	20.6	2.7	2.7	72	407	2.2	5	701	–	.32	.13	17.1	0
Pecans	3.4	687	9.2	71.2	14.6	2.3	1.6	73	289	2.4	Trace	603	130	.86	.13	.9	2
Pistachios	5.3	594	19.3	53.7	19.0	1.9	2.7	131	500	7.3	–	972	230	.67	–	1.4	0

Food and description	Water (%)	Food Energy (calories)	Protein (gm.)	Fat (gm.)	Carbohydrate Total (gm.)	Fiber (gm.)	Ash (gm.)	Calcium (mg.)	Phosphorus (mg.)	Iron (mg.)	Sodium (mg.)	Potassium (mg.)	Vit. A (I.U.)	Thiamine (mg.)	Riboflavin (mg.)	Niacin (mg.)	Vit. C (mg.)
NUTS AND SEEDS																	
Walnuts:																	
(Persian or English)	3.5	651	14.8	64.0	15.8	2.1	1.9	99	380	3.1	2	450	30	.33	.13	.9	2
Pumpkin seeds	4.4	553	29.0	46.7	15.0	1.9	4.9	51	1,144	11.2	–	–	70	.24	.19	2.4	–
Sesame seeds	5.4	563	18.6	49.1	21.6	6.3	5.3	1,160	616	10.5	60	725	30	.98	.24	5.4	0
Sunflower seeds	4.8	560	24.0	47.3	19.9	3.8	4.0	120	837	7.1	30	920	50	1.96	.23	5.4	–
DAIRY PRODUCTS																	
Cow's milk	87.4	65	3.5	3.5	4.9	0	.7	118	93	Trace	50	144	140	.03	.17	.1	1
Goat milk	87.5	67	3.2	4.0	4.6	0	.7	129	106	.1	34	180	(160)	.04	.11	.3	1
Cheese:																	
(Cheddar)	37.0	398	25.0	32.2	2.1	0	3.7	750	478	1.0	700	82	(1,310)	.03	.46	.1	(0)
(Cottage – creamed)	78.3	106	13.6	4.2	2.9	0	1.0	94	152	.3	229	85	(170)	.03	.25	.1	(0)
(Cottage – uncreamed)	79.0	86	17.0	.3	2.7	0	1.0	90	175	.4	290	72	(10)	.03	.28	(.1)	(0)
(Cream)	51.0	374	8.0	37.7	2.1	0	1.2	62	95	.2	250	74	(1,540)	(.02)	.24	.1	(0)
Yogurt (partially skim)	89.0	50	3.4	1.7	5.2	0	.7	120	94	Trace	51	143	70	.04	.18	.1	1
Buttermilk	90.5	36	3.6	.1	5.1	0	.7	121	95	Trace	130	140	Trace	.04	.18	.1	1
Butter	15.5	716	.6	81.0	.4	0	2.5	20	16	0	987	23	3,300	–	–	–	0
Ice cream (regular)	63.2	193	4.5	10.6	20.8	0	.9	146	115	.1	63	181	440	.04	.21	.1	1

* From Standard Tables of Food Composition

UNDESIRABLE PROTEIN SOURCES NOT INCLUDED IN THIS BOOK

100 gm. edible portion

Food and description	Water (%)	Food Energy (calories)	Protein (gm.)	Fat (gm.)	Carbohydrate Total (gm.)	Fiber (gm.)	Ash (gm.)	Calcium (mg.)	Phosphorus (mg.)	Iron (mg.)	Sodium (mg.)	Potassium (mg.)	Vit. A (I.U.)	Thiamine (mg.)	Riboflavin (mg.)	Niacin (mg.)	Vit. C (mg.)
BEEF																	
Total edible, trimmed to retain level, raw:																	
(Choice grade)	56.7	301	17.4	25.1	0	0	.8	10	161	2.6	65	355	50	.07	.15	4.2	–
(Good grade)	60.3	263	18.5	20.4	0	0	.8	11	171	2.8	65	355	40	.08	.16	4.4	–
(Standard grade)	63.9	225	19.4	15.8	0	0	.9	11	180	2.9	65	355	30	.08	.17	4.7	–

Food and description	Water (%)	Food Energy (calories)	Protein (gm.)	Fat (gm.)	Carbohydrate Total (gm.)	Fiber (gm.)	Ash (gm.)	Calcium (mg.)	Phosphorus (mg.)	Iron (mg.)	Sodium (mg.)	Potassium (mg.)	Vit. A (I.U.)	Thiamine (mg.)	Riboflavin (mg.)	Niacin (mg.)	Vit. C (mg.)
BEEF																	
Hamburger (ground beef):																	
(Lean, raw)	68.3	179	20.7	10.0	0	0	1.0	12	192	3.1	–	–	20	.09	.18	5.0	–
(Lean, cooked)	60.0	219	27.4	11.3	0	0	1.3	12	230	3.5	48	558	20	.09	.23	6.0	–
(Reg. ground, raw)	60.2	268	17.9	21.2	0	0	.7	10	156	2.7	–	236	40	.08	.16	4.3	–
(Reg. ground, cooked)	54.2	286	24.2	20.3	0	0	1.3	11	194	3.2	47	450	40	.09	.21	5.4	–
EGGS (Chicken)																	
(Fried)	67.7	216	13.8	17.2	.3	0	1.0	60	222	2.4	338	140	1,420	.10	.30	.1	0
(Hard-cooked)	73.7	163	12.9	11.5	.9	0	1.0	54	205	2.3	122	129	1,180	.09	.28	.1	0
FISH																	
Sticks	65.8	176	16.6	8.9	6.5	–	2.2	11	167	.4	–	–	0	.04	.07	1.6	–
Trout:																	
(Raw)	66.3	195	21.5	11.4	0	0	1.3	–	–	–	–	–	–	.08	.20	8.4	–
(Canned)	63.2	209	20.6	13.4	0	0	2.4	–	–	–	–	–	–	–	–	–	–
Tuna:																	
(Bluefin, raw)	70.5	145	25.2	4.1	0	0	1.3	–	–	1.3	–	–	–	–	–	–	–
(Yellowfin, raw)	71.5	133	24.7	3.0	0	0	1.4	–	–	–	37	–	–	–	–	–	–
(Canned in oil: Solids and liquid)	52.6	288	24.2	20.5	0	0	2.4	6	294	1.1	800	301	90	.04	.09	10.1	–
(Canned in water: Solids and liquid)	70.0	127	28.0	.8	0	0	1.2	16	190	1.6	41	279	–	–	.10	13.3	–
CHICKEN (without skin)																	
Light meat (cooked)	63.8	166	31.6	3.4	0	0	1.2	11	265	1.3	64	411	60	.04	.10	11.6	–
Dark meat (cooked)	64.4	176	28.0	6.3	0	0	1.2	13	229	1.7	86	321	150	.07	.23	5.6	–
HOT DOGS																	
(Cooked)	57.3	304	12.4	27.2	1.6	–	1.5	5	102	1.5	–	–	–	.15	.20	2.5	–

(Numbers in parentheses denote values imputed — usually from another form of the food or from a similar food. Zero in parentheses indicates that the amount of a constituent probably is none or is too small to measure. Dashes denote lack of reliable data for a constituent believed to be present in measurable amount. Calculated values, as those based on a recipe, are not in parentheses.)

MENUS

Menus

Contrary to the image that may be created by my being in the kitchen every time someone sees me cooking on the natural foods cooking show, I do not live in my kitchen, nor do I even spend a good deal of time there! Rather, in keeping with knowing that we eat to live and not live to eat, I have tried to get the business of feeding my family, friends and myself down to a science that allows me to get the most out of the kitchen and, simultaneously, to get out of the kitchen the most.

This is easily achieved with a little organizing or reorganizing of time. I would like to share a few hints with you on how this can be done and how you can go about incorporating the recipes in this book into your diet. The more experienced cooks can probably just skip over the few basic hints, but may be interested in using the suggested menus here as an introduction on how to harmoniously combine the tastes in recipes in this book that are new to them.

For the cook who is new to the world of natural foods, cooking can often be a bewildering and unfortunately disastrous experience! I know! . . . Having experienced entering the kitchen at the normal time to begin cooking dinner, and making my way out of the kitchen five hours later a complete wreck, with beans still the consistency of rocks, hungry children crying, and a highly irritated husband to deal with.

A few experiences like this could set everyone running off to the closest fast foods stand for dinner or pulling out the convenience foods stashed on the shelf. Among many people I know who have consciously made the effort to change their diet, this is a very common, yet unnecessary, experience.

To avoid such experiences, and to begin reorganizing food preparation time, there are a few mental attitudes about "natural foods taking **soooo** long to prepare" that need to be set aside. First of all, it takes just as long, or even longer, to cook a steak or heat up a frozen TV dinner as it does to prepare a properly planned natural foods meal. It takes no longer to slice a raw carrot than to open a can of sugar-syruped carrots or thaw out frozen ones (not to mention the loss in nutrition and extra use of energy in processing and transporting, which are discussed in more depth in the nutrition chapter of this book).

Of course, if you're working with unfamiliar ingredients and cooking methods, it will take more time in the beginning. As with all new things being learned, preparation and planning will take a little longer than they will when they become almost second nature.

Initially, it helps to organize cooking time by first organizing the kitchen. I'm not going to draw any map or chart here, as one pattern may make sense to one way of thinking and not to another. I've had friends come in the kitchen and help with cleanup. Usually when this happens it takes me days to locate everything, because the way they arrange and function in the kitchen are quite different from the way I do. The main thing is to arrange things so you know where everything is and don't have to waste too much time looking for utensils or ingredients.

To avoid having to search the whole kitchen and then run out to the store for a missing ingredient, I keep a shopping list posted in the kitchen where I write down ingredients that are almost running out. Actually, my shopping list is very basic (I hope the shopping list in the Basics Section is of some help to you) and I try to go shopping about twice a month. This is made possible by our simple menu plan.

For breakfast every day for years, our family has had pieces of fresh fruit and the Breakfast Drink (see Nuts and Seeds Section, p. 441). Shopping for breakfast consists of buying a few cases of fruit every few weeks and making sure our bulk jars of nuts, seeds, honey, carob, and raisins are stocked. For dinner, an average family meal consists of a fresh salad with lots of home-grown sprouts, a whole grain dish, and a legume or tofu dish. This may sound quite boring to you, but I think you'll find by trying the recipes in this book, and the suggested menus, that legumes and whole grains lend themselves to a whole spectrum of tastes and textures that are anything but boring.

Of course, planning and organizing your time doesn't necessitate weekly menu plans, but they may help in the beginning just to give you a feel for thinking a day ahead in meal planning. It's quite simple while making tonight's dinner to take a minute to think of what to make for dinner tomorrow night, and then soak the beans or take care of any other time-saving plan. Then the next day, beans and grains can be put on to boil during the course of the day as you work around the house, or if you're out all day, they can be put on as soon as you come home. That way they can be cooking as you shower, clean the house up a bit, etc., and make a salad and/or sauce to go with the main course. This is one great thing about most natural-food cooking. Boiling beans (when presoaked) may take 30 minutes to an hour, but you don't have to sit over them and stir them, etc. You can put them on boil and go about doing other things until they are done. So in reality, beans do not take **you** an hour to cook, although **they** do take an hour to cook.

Of course, boiling beans and cooking whole grains are not something you need to do every day. You can easily get into the pattern of cooking large quantities of grain and rice once or twice a week and using them to make amazing loaves, patties, stews, etc.

I hope this book will give you an idea of what a huge variety of delicious dishes can be made from healthy, natural ingredients with a little imagination. And, if you don't have an ingredient for a recipe, try substituting something else. These recipes and menus are not absolute rules, but are here to give you ideas and the courage to try experimenting and making new and exciting meals with whatever ingredients happen to be on hand. After all, that's how the recipes in this book came to be!

AN IDEA OF OUR FAMILY MENU

As I mentioned earlier, our day-to-day family meals are very simple and basic and have been the same for years.

We start every day out first with some spiritual "food" — by meditating and reading from scripture together. Then we have a breakfast consisting of pieces of fresh fruit and our "Breakfast Drink."

For the middle of the day, I pack each person a jar of water, herbal tea and/or juice. Our bodies are primarily made of liquid, so a lot of liquid is good for the body. I try to make sure each person gets between one and two quarts of liquid during the day. Then at mealtime I don't serve any liquids because they dilute the digestive juices and make it harder for the stomach to digest the food.

The second (and last) meal of the day is dinner, which I try to serve early (between four and five o'clock in the afternoon) so we can have time to digest and burn some of it off before bedtime. Our day-to-day dinners consist of a fresh vegetable and sprout salad with dressing, a whole-grain dish and a legume dish, and no dessert. That is not as boring as it sounds! You'll be surprised at how many thousands of different dishes can be prepared with these basic ingredients!

Following, I'll try to give you an idea of a typical week's menu in our household. The meals don't take long to prepare, yet they are nutritious, delicious (the children really don't miss dessert!) and satiating. I'm hoping this will give you an idea of how varied, yet simple and easy keeping yourself and loved ones in healthy foods actually is.

BREAKFAST

Breakfast is the same every day of the week. It consists of:
Breakfast Drink
Fruit of the season
(bought in cases to cut down on cost)

Planning and Preparation Time:
Seeds, nuts and raisins for the Breakfast Drink need to be soaked overnight. Measuring the ingredients and blending the drink in

the morning takes no more than 10 minutes. The fruit is a perfectly prepared package as it is, so all the preparation required is washing each piece well.

DINNER

Sunday:
Multiuse Avocado Curry
(use as soup or gravy for loaf)
Raw Vegetable Nut Loaf served on a bed of fresh salad greens and/or sprouts
Homemade Whole Wheat Buns

Planning and Preparation Time:
Make the Raw Vegetable Nut Loaf in the morning along with breakfast and refrigerate all day. About 30 to 45 minutes before dinner time, mix the dough for the Homemade Whole Wheat Buns and put them in to bake. While they're baking, blend the Multiuse Avocado Curry and make the bed of salad for the loaf to go on. Slice the loaf and top salad bed with it. By this time the buns should be done. Total dinner time work is about 45 minutes. Another good way to serve this menu is as a Raw Vegetable Nut Loaf sandwich and soup, or an open-faced Raw Vegetable Nut Loaf sandwich topped with gravy (use the Avocado Curry as the gravy). While preparing the dinner, put on a large pot of kidney or pinto beans to soak overnight.

Monday:
Chili
Brown rice
Fresh vegetable salad with Herb Dressing

Planning and Preparation Time:
Pour the soaking water off and add new water to beans that have been soaking since the night before. Put beans on to cook for about 1 hour. Boil the beans as you are doing other things around the house (this is assuming you're at home) or put them on as soon as you return home from work or play. At the same time, put a few days' worth of brown rice on to cook. While the beans and grains are cooking, prepare the chili sauce

for the beans, make the salad, and blend the Herb Dressing. When beans are done, add the proper amount to the simmering chili sauce and dinner is done in 1 to 1½ hours. Refrigerate leftover brown rice and beans for the days to come.

Tuesday:
Tofu Yum or Sweet-Sour Tofu
Fried Rice
Agar-agar Salad

Planning and Preparation Time:
Chop vegetable and start frying rice. If you're making Tofu Yum, reserve some vegetables for the batter. Make batter for Tofu Yum or start frying slices of tofu for Sweet-Sour Tofu. Soak agar-agar and start sweet-sour sauce in a pot as the Tofu Yum or tofu slices are browning. Stir sauce until thick, flip tofu to brown on both sides. Squeeze agar-agar out and make salad and dressing. (Be sure to remember to stir the rice as all other steps are being prepared.) This should all be able to be done within 35 minutes.

Wednesday:
Tostadas

Planning and Preparation Time:
Use leftover beans that were refrigerated and mash down to make refried beans. Follow all steps given in the Tostada recipe, using chapatis or corn tortillas which are either store-bought or frozen from another time. Preparation of four to five tostadas takes about 45 minutes. Soak a good quantity of garbanzos and soybeans (half and half together) to be prepared the next night.

Thursday:
Okara Roast (or Paté)
with Mock Turkey Gravy
Tomatoes Provencale
Summer Salad

Planning and Preparation Time:
Prepare roast or paté as described in the recipe. (If you don't have okara, the mixture of half garbanzo and half soybeans soaked the previous night will work.) Put the entree in the oven to bake. Immediately make the

summer salad and refrigerate it. Prepare the tomatoes for the Provencale by sautéing in a little butter in a skillet or wok. After the tomatoes are sautéd, add more butter to the skillet or wok and prepare the Mock Turkey Gravy. At the last minute, just before the roast comes out of the oven, put the tomatoes in to bake. The whole meal should take about 1 hour and 15 minutes to make. This includes putting the remaining soaked beans on to boil and possibly (while the oven is on) making biscuits for tomorrow.

Friday:
Scoops of Mock Tuna Salad
on a bed of fresh salad greens
Sesame Seed Dressing
Yeast Biscuits

Planning and Preparation Time:
If you prepared the biscuits the night before, you may want to warm them, although having them cold is more energy-efficient. If you decide to heat the biscuits, while they're heating, make the Mock Tuna with the beans cooked the night before. Blend the dressing and make the tossed fresh salad, being sure to check on whether the biscuits are warm. This meal is a quickie that shouldn't take more than a half hour.

Saturday:
"Bacon," Lettuce and Tomato
(BLT) Sandwich
Healthful (Comfrey) Smoothie

Planning and Preparation Time:
Make sandwiches using the Mock Bacon recipe and store-bought or homemade bread. If you make your own bread, add about 45 minutes to the preparation time. Blend the smoothie. This is also a quickie that should take about 20 minutes to make a line of sandwiches, as well as the smoothie.

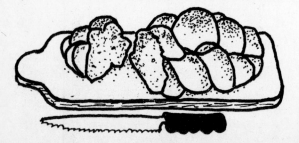

Of course, I know that not everyone eats like our family, nor will they even want to. So here are a few ideas for breakfast, lunch and dinner for both light and more substantial, satisfying meals that you can choose from according to your appetite. Perhaps you are ready to take the next step of trying to plan out how to budget your time in preparing the meals as I've described in "Planning and Preparation Time."

BREAKFAST
Hearty:
Scrambled Eggs Tofu
Mock Bacon
Toasted English Muffins
or
Whole Wheat Bread (Basic Bread Dough)
Pero/Coffee substitute

Light:
Raw Apple Pie
Breakfast Drink

LUNCH
Hearty:
Tofu Patty Sandwiches
or
Open-face Avocado Sandwich
with Crunchy Tofu Crisps
Potato Celery Soup
Gingerbread with scoop of plain yogurt
Herb tea

Light:
Gazpacho
Sweet Essene Bread

DINNER
Hearty:
Mexican Saimin
Tossed green salad with Tofu Dressing
Pot Pie
Carob Cake with Banana Ice Cream

Light:
Fresh salad with Sesame Seed Dressing
Nut Salad Patties
Bran Muffins

ALL-AMERICAN

Anyday American Meal
  Mock Sloppy Joe served over
  Homemade Whole Wheat Buns
  Root Slaw

All-American Dinner
  Hors d'oeuvres:
  Whole wheat sandwiches made from all or some of these fillings:
  Mock Tuna
  Scrambled Eggs Tofu
  Yogurt Cheese and Jam
  Cheese Mound
  Vegie-Nut Cheese Balls
  Legume Pate
  Nutty Herb Patties
  (Cut crusts from sandwiches, then slice sandwiches into small triangles.)

  Carrot Ice Cream Float

  Meal:
  Potato Celery Soup
  Garden Cornbread
  Tossed green salad with
  Thousand Isle Dressing
  Mock Southern Fried Chicken
  Green Potatoes with Brown Gravy
  Senora Chavez's Specialty
  Apple Pie

CHINESE

Anyday Chinese Meal
  Brown or Basmati Rice
  Ma's Stuffed Tofu
  Raw Chop Suey

Chinese Banquet
  Hors d'oeuvres:
  Crunchy Tofu Crisps
  Manapuas (small)
  Green Jao-Tze
  Chinese Dumplings in Dipping Sauce
  Hot herb tea

  Meal:
  Sizzling Rice Soup
  Brown or basmati rice

Mock Peking Duck
Nut Gems with Sweet-Sour Sauce
Vegetarian Chop Suey
Almond Nectar Drink

ITALIAN

Anyday Italian Meal
  Miso Spaghetti
  Fresh tossed salad with Herb Dressing

Italian Celebration
  Hors d'oeuvres:
  Quick Pizza
  Herb Cheese Rolls
  Marinated Stuffed Leaves
  Stuffed Summer Squash
  Healthy Soda

  Meal:
  Minestrone
  Tossed salad with Herb Dressing served with Avocado Molded Salad
  Lasagne
  Fruit Spumoni

EAST INDIAN

Anyday Indian Meal
  Dahl
  Toasted Grains and Vegetables
  Yogurt Cucumber Salad

Indian Feast
  Hors d'oeuvres:
  Poppers
  Vegetable Turnovers
  A variety of Vegetable Pakoras served with Tomato Chutney
  Orange Dahi

  Meal:
  Fresh tossed salad with
  Seeds 'n Things (hot salad dressing)
  Brown or basmati rice
  Buttermilk Vegetable Curry
  Split Pea Barats in Tomato Chutney
  Fig-Date Chutney
  Platter of sweet meats (Ginger-Date Sweet Balls, Gulab Jammons, Dreamy Burfi, Laddu, Down to Earth Coconut Candies)

JAPANESE

Any-day Japanese Meal
Favorite Rice Balls
Teriyaki Tofu
Agar-agar Salad

Japanese Festival
Hors d'oeuvres:
Traditional Nori Sushi
Sushi Variation #1, #2
Deep-fried or Baked Kombu
Raw Tofu with Dressings
Hot herb tea

Meal:
Soba
Brown or basmati rice
Mock Fillet of Fish in Nori
Tempuras
Nishime
Manju

MEXICAN

Any-day Mexican Meal
Tamale Pie
Ole Salad

Mexican Fiesta
Hors d'oeuvres:
Mexican Fondue

Meal:
Fiesta Salad
Spanish Rice with Peas
Chili Rellenos
Salsa Sauce
Papaya-Coconut Haupia

MID-EASTERN

Any-day Mid-Eastern Meal
Tabouli Salad
Marinated Stuffed Leaves

Mid-Eastern Bazaar
Curried Nut Soup
Falafel in Pita Bread with
Sesame Seed Dressing
Ratatouille
Rice Salad
Rose Petal Halvah

BREAKFAST OR BRUNCH PARTY

Fresh Apple Slices with Dips
Fancy French Toast with Honey
or Fresh Orange-Coconut Syrup
or
Quick 'n Easy Fancy Pancakes
Plum Chutney
Broiled Tofu
Nut Milk (served hot or cold)

SIMPLE LUNCHEON BUFFET

Coconut Chips
Cheese-Bran Crackers
Herb Cheese Rolls

Large tossed fresh vegetable and sprout salad
with a choice of the following toppings:
Mock Tuna
Stir-fried Taco (hot)
Thousand Isle Dressing
Yogurt Dressing
Eggless Mayonnaise

Relishable Cauliflower
Salsa Sauce
The Most Wonderful Apricot Cake
Malpouras
Mocha Meltaways
Herb tea

FESTIVE HOLIDAY DINNER

Hors d'oeuvres:
Yeast Popcorn and/or Popcorn Snack
Dill Dip, Miso Pate, Tangy Nut Dip
with thin slices of fresh vegetables as chips
Vegie-Nut Cheese Balls
Warm and Spicy Apple Drink
Meal:
Chilled Almond Yam Soup
Spinach Salad with
Sizzling Mock Bacon Dressing
Vegetable Strudel
Festive Mock Stuffed Turkey
Festive Holiday Stuffing
Zesty String Beans
Vegetable Roast
Spicy Blueberry Relish
Pear Dumplings with Pear Sauce

Conclusion

Although the diet and recipes presented in this book lead to a vegetarian diet, a vegetarian diet is not put forth as being the all in all, or glorified as being the goal in life, because it isn't. A vegetarian diet can help one move towards seeking the highest perfection and becomes a natural part of one's life once understanding of the goal in life is attained.

After all, even the purest vegetarian diet is primarily concerned with the body, which is temporary and bound to wither and die. Mahatma Ghandi put it quite well when he wrote about the vegetarian diet:

"It is for the building of the spirit and not of the body. Man is more than meat. It is the spirit in us for which we are concerned."

Spiritual understanding — that no one is the material body, but that each person is an eternal, individual spirit soul, or living entity, just inhabiting a particular body, and that the spirit soul's true position is as loving servant to the Supreme Soul (God) — is the ultimate goal of life. With this understanding comes the realization that there is a living entity present in all the different bodily forms: grass bodies, plant bodies, bug bodies, animal bodies, etc. In fact, it is the presence of the living entity, or spirit soul, within any particular bodily form that gives the body (which is just a lump of matter) life and value. This leads to a deep respect for all lives.

This brings to my mind a story which has stuck with me since I was little. As a prince, Lord Buddha was sheltered and raised in a palace surrounded by a beautiful pleasure garden because his father wanted him never to see suffering. Yet as a very young boy of five or six, in the midst of the pleasure garden, Lord Buddha was able to perceive suffering. He witnessed a butterfly being devoured by a frog, the frog by a snake, and the snake by a hawk. After observing this chain of events, he concluded that this world is a place of suffering because one living being has to cause pain and suffering to other living beings just to keep his body alive.

One living being lives off the body of other living beings. Of course, there are certain vegetarian foods (such as fallen fruits and leaves and ripe grains and legumes) that do not entail causing the plant pain. But even if a person eats in this way, he causes pain to other living beings as he goes about obtaining those foods. If he walks (on other living beings in bug bodies, grass bodies, plant bodies, etc.) or breathes (living beings in germ bodies that get breathed in are attacked by white blood cells once they enter the body) then there is killing and suffering going on.

We can't exist in this world without causing pain and suffering to others. This recognition that we keep our bodies alive by causing pain and suffering to others raises some important questions . . .

Will I just hardheartedly go stomping through the world figuring that's how it is, so "so what," or will I actually be concerned enough to try to cause the least amount of pain possible? If there is actual concern, it means we will try to keep these bodies alive by keeping the amount of pain we cause to others to a minimum by not causing any unnecessary killing. I simply point to the pictures here of healthy children whose bodies have been raised on a vegetarian diet from the moment of conception as living proof that eating meat is definitely unnecessary.

This leads to the question: If this body is kept alive on the suffering of others, then don't I have a responsibility to make my life worthwhile? Shouldn't my reason for maintaining this body be higher than living like a hippopotamus — eating to live rather than living to eat? Do I not have the responsibility to live my life for the highest purpose?

The hippopotamus is a vegetarian, but what does a hippopotamus do? He sleeps and we sleep. He mates and human beings mate. He defends and human beings defend. He eats (a vegetarian diet even!) and human beings eat (can choose to eat a vegetarian diet!). Eating a vegetarian diet without any higher pursuit or purpose in life is not any better than animal life. Thus vegetarianism in itself is not the highest perfection in life.

The highest perfection of human life is to realize that God does exist, that we are His eternal loving servants, and that our true enjoyment comes from doing His will. As it is said, "Man does not live on bread alone, but by every word that proceedeth from the mouth of God." Living by the words coming from God's mouth, or doing His will, is food for the soul.

Knowing what is God's will, what is pleasing or displeasing to Him, may seem so far away when we're in a position of not knowing God. But He doesn't leave us in the dark. He's always communicating with us, inviting us back to our home (which is oneness with Him through loving service), and speaking to us through His representatives and through scripture, letting us know what is pleasing to Him in every facet of our lives — including what we eat.

By a study of the scriptures of the world, we can learn what kind of diet is in harmony with the will of God and the laws of nature (which is part of His creation). I am humbly asking anyone who is interested in learning more and more what the will of God is in connection with eating to please read the following quotes, taken from various scriptures around the world, with an open mind and an open heart.

Unfortunately, sometimes people foolishly take the existence of scripture other than the one they are familiar with as a threat to their faith, security and/or team spirit. If we can only make our concern being able to develop our love for God and trying to learn more and more about Him so our love can grow (you can't love a stranger or a vague mystery!), then all such sectarian feelings will fall away. There is no envy between those who are trying to find out more about God and develop their love for Him. The very fact that different scripture exists in different parts of the planet can only strengthen one's faith, appreciation and love for God, because that fact alone is living testimony that God exists, that He loves all of His children and doesn't forget any of them, and speaks to all of them.

"Everything animate or inanimate that is within the universe is controlled and owned by the Lord. One should therefore accept only those things necessary for him-

self, which are set aside as his quota, and one must not accept other things, knowing well to Whom they belong."
— Sri Isopanishad, Mantra 1

In the Bible God gives us our quota:
"Behold, I have given you every herb-bearing seed which is upon the face of the earth and every tree in which is the fruit of a tree-yielding seed. To you it shall be for meat."
— Genesis 1:29

In the Mormon Doctrine and Covenants God says:
"Every herb in the season thereof, and every fruit in the season thereof; all these to be used with prudence and thanksgiving. Yea, flesh also of the beast and of the fowls of the air, I, the Lord, have ordained for the use of man with thanksgiving; nevertheless, they are to be used sparingly; and it is *pleasing unto me* that they should not be used, only in times of winter, or of cold, or of famine."
— Section 89; vs. 13 - 16

In connection with this we find that in the Bible after the flood, when there was nothing else, God gave Noah permission to eat flesh:
"Every moving thing that liveth shall be meat for you; even as the green herb have I given you all things. But flesh with the life thereof, which is the blood thereof, shall ye not eat. And surely your blood of your lives will I require."
— Genesis 9:3,4,5

"O son of Kunti, all that you do, all that you eat, all that you offer and give away, as well as all austerities that you may perform, should be done as an offering unto Me. If one offers me with love and devotion a leaf, a flower, fruit or water, I will accept it. The devotees of the Lord are released from all sins because they eat food which is offered first for sacrifice. Others, who prepare food for personal sense enjoyment, verily eat only sin . . ."
— Bhagavad-gita 3:13, 9:26, 9:37

People are independently striving so hard to solve the problems of health, economics and world hunger, when simply by living in harmony with the laws of God and nature, the problems summarized on the following page are automatically solved.

HEALTH: By nature human beings are provided with teeth and a digestive system which is designed to most effectively handle vegetarian foods. For example, our digestive tract is more similar to that of a horse than to that of a tiger. If we habitually put the kinds of foods in our digestive system that it is not meant to digest, the result will be disease. Recent research has linked meat-eating with cancer, heart and circulatory disease, digestive disorders and others.

There are other health hazards. Meat-eaters, being at the top of the "food chain," eat a higher proportion of pesticides and other food contaminants than vegetarians. A high percentage of the poisons present in this vegetation is retained and concentrated in the flesh of an animal. Flesh foods contain 40 times the amount of pesticide residues as root vegetables or grains, ten times as much as fruits, leafy vegetables and legumes, and even 2½ times as much as milk and other dairy products.

ECONOMICS: On this planet, which is like a tiny ball floating in space, we have a limited amount of resources. Raising animals for slaughter is an uneconomic use of these resources, as can be seen in the following figures:

In Hawaii, one acre of land can produce 100 pounds of beef protein every two years, or it can produce 3,213 pounds of protein from soybeans. This affects your pocketbook. For example, $11.25 will buy 4½ pounds of meat containing 355 grams of protein, or it will buy 25 pounds of soybeans containing 4,540 grams of protein—or nearly 12 times as much protein per penny. This uneconomic use of resources is also going on at the worldwide level.

WORLD HUNGER: Hunger is one result of an economic system based on satisfying people's wants rather than their needs. For example, to satisfy tongues addicted to the taste of flesh, we are raising beef cattle, which consume 12 to 20 pounds of protein in the form of grains and legumes to produce one pound of meat. One meat-eating person has the same effect on world food resources as five vegetarians who get their protein directly from grains and legumes.

"If the total protein available from these crops (grains and soybeans) were used directly by human beings, it could make up an estimated 90% of the world's protein deficiency." — The Book of Tofu, by Akiko Aioyagi and William Shurtleff

There are many other unhealthy things, such as sugar and tobacco, being grown on land which could be used to produce nourishing food for a hungry world

These and other problems plaguing the world today are nature's way of letting us know that we can no longer live ignoring

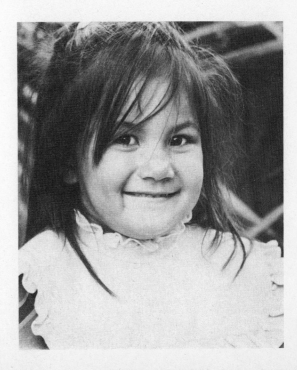

wisdom or metaphysical truths. Knowing this, E. F. Schumacher points out in his book, **Small Is Beautiful:**

". . . the philosophy of materialism is now being challenged by events. There has never been a time, in any society in any part of the world, without its sages and teachers to challenge materialism and plead for a different order of priorities. The languages have differed, the symbols have varied, yet the message has always been the same: 'Seek ye *first* the Kingdom of God, and all these things (the material things which you also need) shall be added unto you.' "

They shall be added, we are told, here on earth where we need them, not simply in an afterlife beyond our imagination. Today, however, this message reaches us not solely from the sages and saints, but from the actual course of physical events. It speaks to us in the language of terrorism, genocide, breakdown, pollution, exhaustion . . . It is apparent that there is not only a promise but also a threat in those astonishing words about the Kingdom of God — the threat that "unless you seek first the Kingdom, these other things, which you also need, will cease to be available to you."

In the richest countries on the planet, where material things are sought first, mis-taking the body as the self leads to thinking, "If I satisfy my body, I'll be happy." Thus trying to get satisfaction from external material goods and the single-minded pursuit of material goods and wealth becomes the goal in life. Ignorance of the existence of the soul apart from the body leads to misidentifying the body as the self and consuming more and more beyond what the body needs to keep healthy and alive. This is due to an inability to differentiate between the body's needs and greeds, and the needs of the soul. Trying to satisfy the eternal, infinite spiritual craving for happiness with temporary, finite material things has resulted in and will continue to result in unsatisfied individuals, social problems (which are found even in the richest countries and are evidence that the people aren't happy), an unbalanced environment, depletion of the earth's limited resources and fighting over them.

Thus the solution that gets to the root of so many problems we face is choosing to seek the highest perfection in life — love for God. Then we will be able to live in harmony with the laws of God and nature and learn to find happiness within ourselves. This inner spiritual satisfaction is what will enable us to live simply and self-sufficiently, taking only what we need.

Index

DESSERTS

The time has come to say goodbye. In Hawaii at times like this we say "aloha." Aloha is a word we use not only in parting, but also in greeting and to express love. It is appropriate in all these situations.

The word "aloha" is made up of three Hawaiian root words: a - lo - and ha. "A" means that which enables one to see. "Lo" means of the earth, and "ha" means the life air or life force. When I say "aloha" to you, I am saying "I can see the life force within your earthly form." And when you say "aloha" to me, you're saying, "I can see the life force in your earthly form." This aloha spirit is the gift Hawaii can give to the world.

Aloha,

Kathy Hoshijo

If you want to find out more about **The Self-Sufficiency Association**, or want more cookbooks, or want to send feedback, I would love to hear from you through:

KATHY'S KITCHEN
P.O. Box 1122 • Glendale, California 91209
2525 South King Street • Honolulu, Hawaii 96826